T0339851

ON THE CAUSES OF ECONOMIC GROWTH

ON THE CAUSES OF ECONOMIC GROWTH

THE LESSONS OF HISTORY

CARLOS SABILLON

Algora Publishing
New York

Library of Congress Cataloging-in-Publication Data —

Sabillon, Carlos, 1967-
    On the causes of economic growth : lessons of history / Carlos Sabillon.
        p. cm.
    Includes bibliographical references.
        ISBN 978-0-87586-588-1 (soft: alk. paper) — ISBN 978-0-87586-589-8 (hbk.: alk.
paper) — ISBN 978-0-87586-590-4 (ebook) 1. Economic development. 2. Economic
history. I. Title.
    HD82.S22 2008
    338.9—dc22
                                2007048166

Front Cover:
Crane with Top of Jinmao Building and Oriental Pear TV Tower
Image: © Keren Su/Corbis
Photographer: Keren Su
Date Photographed: October 25, 2006
Location Information: Shanghai, China

Printed in the United States

This book is dedicated to the few men and women who over the centuries have dedicated their lives to improving the lot of humanity by making scientific and technological progress. Over time, technology and science have been the only real and effective mechanism that has created wealth and delivered benefits to society.

TABLE OF CONTENTS

PREFACE · 1

INTRODUCTION · 3

  Manufacturing and Growth · 4

  Investment and Technology Creation · 5

  Theoretical Basis and Rival Ideas · 6

  Government Policy · 11

  Ideology and Public Policy · 12

  Wealth Creation and Wealth Distribution · 14

CHAPTER 1. FROM ANTIQUITY TO THE 15TH CENTURY · 15

  From the Beginning to the Neolithic Period · 15

  Economic Growth in Ancient Times · 16

  The First Millennium of the Christian Era—China · 20

  Europe — War and Growth in the Middle Ages · 23

  The British Isles · 25

  Germany · 27

  Japan · 30

  Levels of Education and Infrastructure · 35

CHAPTER 2. THE 16TH CENTURY · 37

  Misinterpretations of the Causes of Economic Growth · 37

  England · 39

  Germany · 45

  Russia · 49

  China and Japan · 50

CHAPTER 3. THE 17TH CENTURY   53

Support for Manufacturing in England   53

Germany   58

Russia   61

China   65

The United States of America   67

Japan   71

CHAPTER 4. THE 18TH CENTURY   75

Orthodox Interpretations of the Causes of Economic Growth in Britain   75

A Non-Orthodox Interpretation of the Causes of Growth   81

Continental Europe and Germany   85

Russia   87

China and Japan   91

Korea and Taiwan   94

The United States   97

CHAPTER 5. THE FIRST HALF OF THE 19TH CENTURY   103

Britain's Economic Development   103

The Elliptical Linkage Between Manufacturing and the Economy   108

Continental Europe and Germany   111

Russia in Stagnation   115

China   121

Japan   124

Korea and Taiwan   126

Hong Kong and Singapore   127

The United States   129

CHAPTER 6. THE SECOND HALF OF THE 19TH CENTURY IN THE UNITED STATES, GERMANY, AND RUSSIA   135

The United States   135

1850–69   *135*

1870–99   *139*

On Inflation, Capital, and Trade   142

Understanding Causality   144

Canada, Australia, and New Zealand   146

Germany   148

Unification, Trains, and Weapons   148

Correlation and Causality   151

Russia   157

The Crimean War and its Consequences   157

Railroads, Ideology, and Factories   161

CHAPTER 7. THE SECOND HALF OF THE 19TH CENTURY IN JAPAN, BRITAIN,

CHINA, AND THE NEWLY INDUSTRIALIZED COUNTRIES 167

Japan 167
Armament Build Up and Fast Economic Growth 167
Policy Errors and Support for Manufacturing 172
Great Britain 176
Economic Decline in Britain 176
Stimulation Efforts and Economic Misinterpretations 179
East Asia 185
Economic Stagnation in Manchu China 185
Korea and Taiwan 188
Singapore and Hong Kong 190

CHAPTER 8. THE FIRST HALF OF THE 20TH CENTURY IN EAST ASIA 195

Japan 195
War and Weapons 195
The Effects of Factory Promotion 200
China 206
Chaos and Weak Government 206
The Effects of Manufacturing 210
Taiwan and Korea 212
Singapore and Hong Kong 215

CHAPTER 9. THE FIRST HALF OF THE 20TH CENTURY IN GERMANY AND RUSSIA 219

Germany 219
1900–1919 219
The 1920s and the Depression 223
Misunderstanding Causality 229
World War II and Its Aftermath 231
Technology and Growth 234
Russia 236
1900–19 236
Soviet Policies and their Effects on Manufacturing 240
World War II and Reconstruction 244

CHAPTER 10. THE FIRST HALF OF THE 20TH CENTURY IN THE UNITED

STATES OF AMERICA AND GREAT BRITAIN 251

The United States of America 251
1900–29 251
The 1920s 255
The Great Depression 257
World War II and the 1940s 262
Technology and Factories 266
Productivity, Investment, and Savings 269
Great Britain 271
1900–19 271
The 1920s and the 1930s 275
The 1940s 280
Technology and Wealth Creation 283

CONCLUSION   289
  Guidelines for Growth   289

APPENDIX   293
  Methodology for Preparing the Charts   293

TABLES   295

REFERENCES   309

PREFACE

This book is intended to cater to the needs of policy makers. It therefore utilizes a language that is accessible to them as well as an abundance of historical examples to illustrate the fundamental tenets that are sustained. Since policy makers are mainly interested in concrete results, abstract notions and theoretical positions are reduced to the minimum. In order to reinforce its empirical approach and practical goals, the book presents clear policy recommendations for the attainment of fast and sustained economic growth.

This volume is nonetheless also intended for economists, social scientists, and people from the world of business who are interested in exploring new approaches and ideas and in attempting to find alternative solutions to the problems of poverty and unemployment.

The book aims to help readers understand the essence of the phenomenon of economic growth; in consequence, it offers a synthesis of world economic history. In its effort to present the big picture, only the most relevant passages of history are selected in order not to digress from the central thesis.

Several tables in the Appendix present the main macro-economic indicators of the countries analyzed, providing a clear historical overview.

INTRODUCTION

The following pages will analyze the period running from the birth of the first civilizations up to the mid-20th century and will attempt to extract from the empirical data an alternative to orthodox explanations of the causes of economic growth. The book will concentrate on the nations in Europe, East Asia, and North America that attained the fastest rates of growth and had the most influence on world affairs.

It will be argued that there is a missing factor, one which has been largely overlooked by economists and social scientists, that is fundamentally responsible for the generation of economic growth. It will be held that this factor is intimately linked to the manufacturing sector.

Manufacturing shall be understood as every economic activity that does not fall in the category of primary sector activities, construction, and services. The traditional division of economic sectors is not compatible with the purposes of this essay. Traditionally, the economy has been divided into three sectors and the secondary sector has been identified with industry. Orthodox definitions of industry include a mixture of several components. The most important is manufacturing, but it is accompanied by construction, mining, and in some cases even by transportation and telecommunications. Under the orthodox division of sectors, manufacturing does not have a place of its own because prevailing economic theories do not assign manufacturing a predominant role in the generation of economic growth.

For the purposes of this book, manufacturing will be classified separately, mining shall be included in the primary sector, construction will be placed in a separate category, and services will continue to remain independent. The term "manufacturing" will therefore not be utilized as synonymous to industry. The word "industry" will be avoided as much as possible. The term "factory," however, will be utilized as a synonym of manufacturing.

Throughout most of history, manufacturing took place mostly at the household level and in workshops. It was only in the 19th century that a few nations began to produce a large share of their manufacturing output in factories. The term "factory" will nonetheless be utilized to refer to all of manufacturing production, even when this type of production accounted for only a small share of total output. The differences between modern factory in-stallations and pre-modern handicraft production that orthodox studies present will not be discussed because they are irrelevant to the discussion at hand. What matters is the overall rate of production of this sector.

Positively defined, manufacturing shall be understood to be, by far, the most investment-intensive sector of the economy due to its almost unique capacity to create technology. The driving force for the creation of wealth lies in the capacity to create or reproduce technology, because technology is what actually improves living conditions.

The foundation underlying this thesis is the causal linkage between manufacturing and technology. This essay will attempt to demonstrate that manufacturing is practically the only sector with the capacity to coherently materialize man's attempts to overcome the limi-tations imposed by nature. The book will show that manufacturing is responsible for the creation of technology and, therefore, for economic growth.

Manufacturing and Growth

The past 5,000 years have supplied an abundance of evidence suggesting that the rate of manufacturing output correlates consistently with the fluctuations in the economy, in the West, East Asia, and Russia.

Many economists throughout history have pointed to industry's effects on growth, but their efforts have failed to present a consistent argument. In this essay, it will be held that manufacturing and not industry is the determinant sector for the generation of growth.

It must be emphasized that it is not the size of this sector as a share of GDP that matters, as so many economists have asserted, but the average rate by which it expands. At times, economic growth has been rapid while the manufacturing sector accounted for a small share of GDP, and on other occasions stagnation has prevailed with an equally small factory sector. Growth may be rapid in a nation that already possesses a large manufacturing sector and in other cases growth may be rapid where the manufacturing sector was in its infancy. No correlation can be drawn between any given size of the manufacturing sector and the pace of economic growth. However, in every case in which the economy expanded rapidly, it was accompanied by a rapid increase in manufacturing output.

Still more important for the purposes of this book is what made possible the growth of manufacturing (factories). History supplies a considerable amount of evidence showing that manufacturing production almost never expanded unless there was government sup-port for it.

The vast majority of this support has gone unnoticed, for it has been supplied indirectly by means of fiscal, financial, and non-financial incentives. When it did not go unobserved, such government support was very direct, including occasions when government construct-ed the production facilities, financed the whole operation, and oversaw daily operations. However, direct efforts in the form of state factories have been relatively few compared to indirect support aimed at private manufacturers.

The empirical data suggests that differing levels of subsidies for this sector cause pro-portionate rates of manufacturing output. Throughout the history of East Asia, Europe, and North America, weak factory-promotion efforts from the state went hand in hand with factory sluggish output and slow GDP growth. Strong support from policy makers coincided with high factory output and fast economic growth.

An effort must be made to avoid an overly simplistic understanding of the above. The issue is not whether there was government support for this sector, but the level at which such support was offered. At practically every stage in history, it is possible to uncover some form of subsidization for manufacturing; but what ultimately matters is the degree by which it was supplied. The evidence suggests that the level of support determines the rate of economic growth.

Investment and Technology Creation

History suggests that the manufacturing sector has rarely expanded without government support and has systematically stagnated in the absence of such support, for one reason. Manufacturing requires very large amounts of investment compared to other sectors. On top of that, primary sector activities, services, and construction require much shorter periods of time to recover an investment.

With these inherent characteristics, it is inevitable for private investors to instinctively shy away from the sector. Unless the government changes this natural state of affairs by giving abundant incentives for manufacturing production — thus guaranteeing a profitable venture — investment tends to remains non-existent.

The government therefore can play a determinant role in the generation of economic growth because the state is the only entity with the capacity to provide incentives of a significant scale. The evidence suggests that the private sector be induced to channel its resources into this sector only when the costs and risks of investment in factory production are reduced. Policy makers must constantly supply factory production with support in order for it to grow. Without support, it immediately stagnates.

Manufacturing is investment intensive apparently specifically because of its exceptional capacity to create technology. Manufacturing is the sole sector with the ability to generate technological breakthroughs. The evidence suggests a strong correlation between the output of manufacturing and the creation of technology. Throughout history, whenever governments increased their support to this sector and output rose faster, technological advances were commensurate. Over and over again, the two variables have fluctuated in unison, and there can be little doubt as to the direction of the causality. Government support for manufacturing is at the discretion of the people dictating policy; this is the component that can be directly and actively affected. Manufacturing growth, then, is the cause and technological advances the effect.

A very large share of investment in the sector, over all, has been aimed at the fabrication of armaments. Since the earliest of times, economic theorists and policy makers have viewed weaponry as a poorly allocated investment and a waste of resources. However, when war and similar events have forced much greater investment in the production of armaments, factory output overall has tended to go up and technology has also advanced more rapidly.

Periods of high armament output usually are periods when new technologies have appeared and overall wealth has been created — faster than in periods of less arms production. History has even seen periods of armament investment that correlated with accelerating economic growth that has extended for centuries.

Another important fact is that, throughout history, few inventions were actually founded upon a proper understanding of the scientific principles involved. Most discoveries are simply the result of trial and error efforts undertaken in formal or informal manufacturing establishments. The vast majority of inventors were people closely in touch with actual production, not theorists. Most technological advances, from the Paleolithic period to the mid-20th century, occurred when human beings set themselves to fabricate a device that could make life easier. As they invested resources in it and labored on it, they came upon a better way to achieve their goal. Out of the manufacturing effort sprang a new technology. That is how stone tools, metals, the wheel, the printing press, ships, trains, the tractor, many medicines and most other technologies made their appearance.

New technology has mostly come to life in the form of a manufactured good such as the plow, the chariot, paper, textiles, glass, the steam engine, the cotton gin, the telegraph, the telephone, the light bulb, the automobile, airplanes, spacecrafts, medical equipment, and pharmaceuticals. Since the advent of the first patent system in the world, in England in the 16th century, patents have almost always been directly tied to a manufactured good.

Analyzed over the long term, manufacturing has proven to be by far the most productivity-intensive sector. This phenomenon seems to fit well with what has been previously asserted concerning this sector's ability to create technological breakthroughs. Since technology is the fundamental variable determining productivity, it is inevitable that the sector that is most intimately linked to technology is also the one with the most productivity-enhancing characteristics. The evidence seems to indicate that the other sectors are only capable of passively dealing with technology. As technology recipients, these sectors inevitably end up showing inferior productivity performance.

This idea is further substantiated by the fact, that throughout history, overall rates of productivity have always been high when the factory promotion efforts of the state were strong. Total factor productivity, whether in Britain, Japan, Germany, the US, Russia, or China, regularly moved in tandem with the differing levels of support for the sector.

Theoretical Basis and Rival Ideas

Since the birth of the Industrial Revolution in the late 18th century, several economists have pondered over the role that industry plays in economic growth. Some began to ruminate over a possible link between the two, well before that date.

The first organized set of ideas on this topic came from the Mercantilist School, in the 16th and 17th century, followed in the 19th century by the Infant-Industry School. In the 20th century the Centrally Planned, the Keynesian and the Import-Substitution Schools developed some ideas on the matter as well. This book is concerned with how those theories translated into policies, not the theoretical aspects.

These currents of thought, in particular in their application, viewed our subject from a perspective very different from the one presented in this book. None of them focused on manufacturing. They centered on industry, which is a wider concept that includes manufacturing, mining and construction. Some did not even have industry as their main preoccupation. None of them thought that industry, and less still manufacturing, was the key to growth.

For the Mercantilist School, the key to growth was trade surpluses. They believed the wealth of a nation resulted from the accumulation of precious metals, which could only become possible with a positive trade balance. Since factory goods were the most exportable due to their longevity, Mercantilists thought the government should promote this sector.

However, since their main concern was increasing exports, they thought the state should promote any sector that could export goods, including agriculture, fishing, forestry and mining. The thesis presented in this book, on the other hand, believes these primary activities are incapable of generating technology advances and thus growth, and governments should not promote them.

Further, Mercantilists thought that trade protection (tariffs and quotas to discourage imports and encourage exports) was the most effective tool to promote manufacturing. The research that led to this book, however, reveals that trade protection does not help manufacturing and actually hampers it. There are other mechanisms that stimulate this sector.

Mercantilism was still in favor in many nations even in the post-World War II era. Nations in East Asia in particular followed this idea and, as they achieved satisfactory trade surpluses, they reduced support for manufacturing. That is not a policy measure endorsed by this book.

The Infant-Industry School thought that when a nation lacked a developed industrial base, this sector needed temporary state support to foster its growth. Once it had reached a level of development similar to that of the most advanced countries, they thought that continuing such support would have harmful effects on the economy. These economists believed in "the wisdom of the market" for allocating resources.

During the 19th and 20th centuries, many governments endorsed this view and began to reduce the level of support as soon as the national industry began to attain parity with the most advanced countries. That policy measure is not supported by the data presented in this.

Moreover, the Infant-Industry School emphasized trade protection as the main means to help industry. This author's research did not find data that could support such a view. On the contrary, the data amply suggests that protection hampers manufacturing productivity and lowers quality.

When the first socialist nation saw its birth in 1917 in Russia, the country was far behind the capitalist US and Western Europe in economic and manufacturing development. Its leaders adopted a centrally-planned economic program that gave investment priority to industry, particularly heavy industry. Trade blockades imposed by the West and continued threats of war gave the central planners added incentive to strive toward economic self sufficiency by producing domestically everything needed for a modern economy. The economic results were outstanding. Once they attained a relatively high level of self sufficiency as well as superpower military status, their allocations to industry fell.

China, following a variant of the centrally-planned model, especially after 1980, when the West removed the artificial barriers to open trade that held back the Soviet Union, Cuba, Zimbabwe and others, has managed to achieve an outstanding 10% growth rate, consistently outstripping every other system or country in the world.

The Keynesian School, an offshoot of the Liberal School, accorded the manufacturing sector even less importance. It only changed its view partially, in the wake of the Depression, as liberal policies proved incapable of solving the crisis.

Keynesians thought that significant state intervention could only be justified during periods of recession, and then investment priority should fall on infrastructure. As a secondary measure, the government might also invest in job training, education and industry. These economists did not even view industry as the second most important area of the economy to support.

From the birth of this trend in the early twentieth century up to the early twenty-first century, Keynesians have viewed manufacturing as having a marginal effect on growth and they continue to prioritize investment in infrastructure as the best counter-recessionary measure. Even when they did assign greater importance to manufacturing, they could only justify such support during periods of economic recession or stagnation. They did not view it as a long-term policy, which is what this book advocates.

The Import-Substitution School was derived in part from the Keynesian School. This school officially came into being in 1950 and in the following decades, Latin American countries became its greatest followers. Shocked by the collapse of international trade during the Depression of the 1930s, some economists focused on the effect of this collapse on developing countries. On the one hand, the high trade barriers erected by developed countries made it very difficult for developing countries to export primary goods, so they could not earn the foreign exchange needed to import capital goods. Economists thus advised poor countries to develop national industries that would substitute the imports and reduce their dependency on others. Further, since with the passage of time the trading terms for commodity exporters tend to decline, they argued that developing countries should strive to diversify their economies and develop a domestic industry.

These economists had a very similar position to that of the Infant-Industry School. They too called for trade protection as the main tool for the promotion of industry. This book, on the contrary, condemns trade protection because the presence of competition stimulates a sharper focus on quality and efficiency.

The originality of the Import-Substitution School resided in its recognition of the long-term tendency of primary goods to lose value relative to factory goods. However, their explanation of this phenomenon seems incoherent. They observed that industrial goods had a greater elasticity of demand, meaning that as incomes rise, demand for manufactured goods rises faster than for commodities. This may appear to be the case with food, but not necessarily with other goods. They also failed to explain why demand for manufactures was higher even when incomes stagnated or fell.

The Keynesian School, an offshoot of the Liberal School, accorded this sector even less importance. It only changed its view partially, in the wake of the Depression, as liberal policies proved incapable of solving the crisis.

Keynesians thought that significant state intervention could only be justified during periods of recession, and then investment priority should fall on infrastructure. As a secondary measure, the government might also invest in job training, education and industry. These economists did not even view industry as the second most important area of the economy to support.

From the birth of this trend in the early twentieth century up to the early twenty-first century, Keynesians have viewed manufacturing as having a marginal effect on growth and they continue to prioritize investment in infrastructure as the best counter-recessionary measure. Even when they did assign greater importance to manufacturing, they could only justify such support during periods of economic recession or stagnation. They did not view it as a long-term policy, which is what this book advocates.

The Import-Substitution School was derived in part from the Keynesian School. This school officially came into being in 1950 and in the following decades, Latin American countries became its greatest followers. Shocked by the collapse of international trade during the Depression of the 1930s, some economists focused on the effect of this collapse on developing countries. On the one hand, the high trade barriers erected by developed countries made it very difficult for developing countries to export primary goods, so they could not earn the foreign exchange needed to import capital goods. Economists thus advised poor countries to develop national industries that would substitute the imports and reduce their dependency on others. Further, since with the passage of time the trading terms for commodity exporters tend to decline, they argued that developing countries should strive to diversify their economies and develop a domestic industry.

These economists had a very similar position to that of the Infant-Industry School. They too called for trade protection as the main tool for the promotion of industry. This book, on the contrary, condemns trade protection because the presence of competition stimulates a sharper focus on quality and efficiency.

The originality of the Import-Substitution School resided in its recognition of the long-term tendency of primary goods to lose value relative to factory goods. However, their explanation of this phenomenon seems incoherent. They observed that industrial goods had a greater elasticity of demand, meaning that as incomes rise, demand for manufactured goods rises faster than for commodities. This may appear to be the case with food, but not necessarily with other goods. They also failed to explain why demand for manufactures was higher even when incomes stagnated or fell.

This book, on the other hand, presents a more consistent explanation as to why demand for factory goods is greater than for primary products. This book argues that factory goods embody a larger amount of technology than primary goods and are therefore worth more. Even when the incomes of a population do not rise, demand for factory goods continues to rise — in every field.

The Import-Substitution School only called for a temporary promotion of manufacturing. Once a nation succeeded in diversifying its economy so that industrial goods accounted for the majority of output and/or exports, the government no longer needed to support this sector.

This book, on the contrary, holds that the principle remains the same even if all of a nation's output and exports are industrial or even manufactured goods. For the economy to grow rapidly, factory output must always be increasing, and the rate of factory output is determined by the level of government subsidies.

These are not the only schools of thought that have touched on the importance of industry. Several other ideas have floated around and at times have become popular with policy makers. Britain's economic supremacy from the 16th to the 18th century as well as the rise to power of the U.S. and Germany in the 19th century were tightly linked to the rapid development of heavy industry (a combination of mining and heavy manufacturing). The situation in these countries led several economists to believe that the production of coal, machine tools, metals, ships, trains and other such goods was very important for the attainment of rapid growth. They thought these fields were important in spurring the development of all other areas of the economy.

In the 20th century, many leaders from socialist and capitalist countries alike bought into this idea and gave priority to heavy industry. The results were mixed. In some cases, the economy grew rapidly and in other instances it grew slowly. Besides, several economies have managed to attain fast economic growth over sustained periods without heavy industry. Some have even attained among the fastest rates of growth in the world while exclusively producing light manufactures.

The thesis presented in this book therefore holds that there is not necessarily a causal linkage between heavy industry and growth. It does not matter whether all of the production of a country is light or heavy. What matters most is the rate of overall factory output and that rate is determined by the amount of government aid.

Since at least the 16th century, a characteristic of the most developed nations was their superior technology. These countries produced the most technically-advanced goods and this in turn has convinced many economists that producing high-tech goods is particularly helpful for the attainment of rapid growth.

In the 20th century, numerous economists continued to uphold this idea and many governments gave priority to high-tech manufacturing. Some of these efforts correlated with rapid growth — but most did not.

By contrast, this book shows that low-tech manufacturing is as good at generating economic growth as high-tech manufacturing.

The idea of Industrial Policy is similar to the Infant Industry School in that the focus is on helping nascent fields of economic endeavor, principally through trade protection. However, contrary to the Infant Industry School, Industrial Policy maintains that government should supply constant support to industry even in fields that are well established.

This book agrees that support should be ongoing but further recommends that this support should be considerably greater than what the Industrial Policy concept recommends. France is the country that has most endorsed this concept of Industrial Policy, but Paris has never come close to implementing support on the scale this book proposes. In the last four decades, French governments have supplied a very low level of support to manufacturing. During that period the rate of economic growth was about 2%. This author suggests that with a decisive manufacturist policy a nation can easily attain a rate of 10% annual growth. In addition, while a rate of 2% over four decades allows unemployment and underemployment to go up systematically, with a rate of 10% even a high level of joblessness is rapidly eliminated.

These major schools of thought did not see manufacturing as the key to growth and, if anything, they saw manufacturing support as a temporary measure. All of them also endorsed manufacturing-stimulating measures that distorted the market forces that would otherwise govern trade. This book, on the contrary, focuses exclusively on the factory sector as the key to growth; it holds that support should be indefinite; and it repudiates trade protection.

These schools failed to link growth with technology. Most economists agree that these two variables are intimately linked, but they have not been able to pin down the variable or variables that cause technological growth. They cannot explain by which mechanism technology is created and neither can they decipher the mechanism that can accelerate its pace. This book establishes a direct link between manufacturing and technological advancement.

In summary, this book holds that when a government allocates 3% of GDP in subsidies to manufacturing, the rate of economic growth will be about 3%. If it allocates 10%, the economy will grow by about 10%. If a government wants to attain sustained economic growth of 10%, it must systematically allot 10% of the whole economy to this sector.

Exogenous Factors

History suggests that countless factors affect growth. Some of the economic ones are inflation, fiscal balance, infrastructural development, the size of government expenditure, and the type of economic system. Some of the non-economic variables are culture, natural resource availability, population density, war, natural catastrophes, religion and ethnicity.

However, up to the early twenty-first century, economists remained in the dark as to what causes economic growth. Its notorious moniker the *Dismal Science* remained as valid as a century earlier.

In the absence of a clear understanding of the causes of economic growth, variables such as inflation, fiscal balances, culture, and natural resources seem to play a role in growth. But history has recorded countless situations in which numerous adverse conditions were in place, and nations experienced rapid growth even so. Many nations at times had high inflation, large budget deficits, a non-entrepreneurial culture, inadequate infrastructure, an uneducated workforce and a lack of natural resources. Despite all that, whenever the government allocated ample resources to manufacturing the economy boomed.

At the same time, history has recorded numerous situations in which nations experienced highly favorable circumstances and stagnation prevailed even so. Notwithstanding the advantages of low inflation, balanced budgets, an entrepreneurial culture, top-level infrastructure, high educational standards and an abundance of natural resources, the economy stagnated whenever the government invested little in factories.

This phenomenon has occurred so regularly over the centuries and in so many regions of the world that it suggests this variable has a capacity to supersede even the worst situations.

Government Policy

The macro-economic policy implication that emanates from this historical analysis is that strong state support for manufacturing appears to be the fundamental tool that any government can use if it wishes to attain fast and sustained economic growth.

The benefits of decisive promotion of this sector are not limited to nations that are lagging behind the most advanced manufacturers. All nations, independent of their level of development, have a constant need to give their manufacturing sectors a strong dose of support. The moment the support stops, factory output tends to stagnate and along with it the rest of the economy.

Rapid production of factory goods in large quantities is not the exclusive domain of nations that are endowed with certain characteristics. This book intends to demonstrate that the least-developed nations, middle-income countries, and the most-developed economies can all attain faster and more sustained rates of factory output, for it is within the exclusive jurisdiction of each government to decide the level of support it offers this sector. From the perspective of manufacturism, economic growth is fundamentally an endogenous phenomenon.

An effort will as well be made to demonstrate that practically all countries can produce factory goods cost effectively and at high levels of quality. On this matter, what is relevant is the competitive pressure that falls on the manufacturing sector. In order to attain the highest levels of efficiency, competition must be increased; and on that matter mainstream economics has very clearly defined the policy mechanisms that deliver the best results.

The evidence suggests that a manufacturist policy is fully compatible with most of what mainstream economics proposes. However, people who have invested much time and energy in orthodox ideas area likely to misunderstand this thesis. The debate in the academic community and in policy-making circles revolved for so long around the subject of government intervention in the economy that, at first glance, a policy calling for large factory subsidies seems to mean calling for a very interventionist approach.

However, the history of numerous nations suggests that a strong factory promotion policy is fully compatible with one of limited government intervention in the economy. Minimal government expenditure (as a share of GDP) can easily coexist with very strong support of this sector. The cases of the US, Canada, and Argentina during the second half of the 19th century, as well as those of several other nations in the following fifty years, demonstrate the above. In these cases, private manufacturing was encouraged by a modest budget and that coincided with high rates of factory output and quick rates of economic growth.

Ideology and Public Policy

Practically all of the support that governments have supplied to manufacturing has been ideologically motivated. Governments have not generally promoted this sector because of a belief that manufacturing was the key to economic growth and technological development. Quite the contrary, it has most often been national security concerns that have driven policy makers to promote the sector.

War, however, was not the only factor. Governments have been driven to catch up in economic development with a rival or a neighbor by producing on their own soil the same manufactured goods the other possessed. Balance-of-payment concerns have induced many governments to promote manufacturing as they sought to substitute imports or to generate an increase in exports. Policy makers have also subsidized the factory sector in an effort to promote the development of high technology goods and create more employment. Policies of economic autarchy and policies attempting to promote the least developed regions of a country have also driven states to subsidize this sector, as have post-war reconstruction efforts.

In each of these cases, the state was not purposely zeroing on the manufacturing sector but ended up promoting it inadvertently. Precisely because manufacturing was not seen as the critical component, governments did not concentrate on it and the amount of support rarely reach high levels. Rarely, also, was it sustained for a long time.

Levels of support have varied from one government to another as well as from country to country. Even though overall support was very low until 1949, there have been some episodes in which the state promoted factory output decisively. The best examples are found in North America during the second half of the 19th century and in East Asia during the first half of the 20th century. That coincided with the fastest GDP growth rates in the world up to that date. North American and East Asian policy makers were driven to support manufacturing for ideological reasons, just as other countries had been, in previous instances. It is thus highly unlikely that the upper limits of support for the sector were reached. That means that even higher rates of GDP growth are probably possible and over more sustained periods, if factory promotion efforts are pushed to the limit.

The second half of the 20th century substantiates that idea. During this period, rates of economic growth were much higher than ever before (in several nations in East Asia and the Middle East). Higher levels of factory subsidies accompanied that rapid growth. The fact that ideological motivations continued to drive government policy in countries all over the world gives further credence to the idea that the limits of growth have not been reached.

It is worth mentioning that the ideological motivations that have driven governments to support manufacturing were major policy errors. Of all these motivations, war and national security concerns proved to be the worst reason for subsidizing the sector. Throughout history, most people had seen expenditures in armaments as an investment of resources that could have been much better utilized in other activities. The evidence suggests they were right, from the perspective that similar large investments in civilian manufacturing would have produced much greater benefits for society.

However, when governments did not feel that they needed to invest in the production of weapons, those resources were almost never channeled into civilian manufacturing. Had governments thought that manufacturing is the driving force in economic growth, they would surely have concentrated on promoting this sector directly and not merely as a by-product of inconsistent policies.

A clear understanding of the strong causal relationship between manufacturing support and economic growth should encourage governments to significantly reduce their weapon production programs and transfer those resources into civilian manufacturing.

There are other equally ill-advised ideological motivations that have driven nations to support this sector. Balance-of-payments concerns are the most noteworthy. The desire to achieve trade surpluses has driven many nations to grant subsidies, but once the trade deficits disappeared, the support vanished. Many governments have also raised trade barriers, which decreases the sector's capacity to raise productivity.

History suggests that policy makers need to constantly promote factories, and not just for a certain period of time — for the moment the support vanishes, the economy performs proportionately and unemployment starts to rise.

When governments have injected more resources into this sector because they sought to promote high technology goods, they were actually doing the right thing, for the data suggests manufacturing is fundamentally responsible for the generation of technology. However, technology-promotion efforts have mostly concentrated on the few manufacturing fields that at a certain moment in time were the most admired. As manufacturing (the entire sector and not just a few of its fields) is naturally endowed with the capacity to generate technology, it would seem that the best policy for accelerating the pace of technological development is one which offers across-the-board strong support to the whole sector.

The same holds true for job-creation policies. Most of these efforts have had practically nothing to do with manufacturing. Since the evidence suggests manufacturing is fundamentally responsible for economic growth and growth is the main factor determining job creation, it would seem that the best job-promotion policy is one that concentrates on promoting manufacturing.

In an effort to rapidly increase manufacturing, governments have frequently created state companies or nationalized privately-owned factories. But over and over again, public enterprises have proved to be less efficient to private sector enterprises in making rational use of resources. Overall they were more costly to operate and were less quality-conscious than private firms. Similarly, governments have also attempted to promote factories by securing profitable returns for producers through the creation of monopolies and cartels. Securing profits for manufacturers helps induce them to stay in manufacturing, but reducing internal competition removes incentives for efficiency and quality.

The evidence suggests that the only fully successful way to promote manufacturing is by means of fiscal, financial and non-financial incentives.

Wealth Creation and Wealth Distribution

Historically, there has been a correlation between manufacturing support and broader income distribution. On the one hand, the stimulation of manufacturing production has led to faster economic growth, which has reduced unemployment. Furthermore, manufacturing wages historically have been higher than those in agriculture, the services, and construction. The evidence suggests that this is related to the technology-intensive nature of this sector. Society is willing to pay higher prices for such goods and higher wages to the people who make them.

This means of broadening income distribution managed for almost two centuries to avoid opposition from the minority of society with the highest income. Traditional forms of redistribution, such as taxing the wealthy, have invariably aroused strong opposition from those at the top. In recent decades, as less and less of the economy of the developed countries is devoted to manufacturing, the gap between rich and poor is expanding at an unprecedented pace.

From the Beginning to the Neolithic Period

About 600,000 thousand years ago, the Earth underwent rapid climate change as the temperature fell significantly. In the millennia that followed, there were several periods in which the temperature rose again and then fell. The last Ice Age ended about 10,000 years ago.

The rapid climate changes forced humans to migrate to regions where conditions were more favorable for survival, and human populations became concentrated in particular places. As population density rose, the supply of natural resources in per capita terms decreased, and humans began to fight among each other for land. As fighting intensified to new levels, humans were driven to make greater efforts to defeat their competitors, which led them to create the first weapons. It was war that provided the stimulus for the fabrication effort.

The Paleolithic Period or Stone Age is when the first intentionally-crafted instruments were invented, and (of those that survived to be found by scientists) the first were made of stone. Archeological evidence across the world shows that the first stone tools were weapons. The appearance of the first tools signaled the advent of technology *per se*, because they significantly increased the capacity of their owners to, in this case, kill.

Despite such a negative aspect, new weapon technology also had positive ramifications because it could be used to satisfy civilian needs. Spears and cutting tools were soon used to increase the supply of food and they gave rise to the first clothes made from animal skin.

The advent of weapons technology thus provided positive outcomes that far outweighed the negative effects. More people avoided death from hunger and exposure than were killed by the weapons. As a result, population began to grow.

When the last ice age began to come to an end some 15,000 years ago, humans once again migrated to other regions. The Earth became progressively warmer, over several millennia. Large areas became dry, and people increasingly concentrated in regions with ample fresh water. By then, the world population had significantly increased, so that resources were even scarcer in per capita terms. That led to an intensification of war.

As warring intensified, more efforts were taken to assure survival. The tribes were forced to increase the share of resources allocated to the production of weapons. Archeological findings show a large increase in the production of weapons starting about 15,000 years ago in the northeast of Egypt and other nearby regions. That coincided with the invention of new technology with increased killing power but which also opened novel possibilities in civilian activities. Superior wood and stone weapons appeared and from these derived the first farm implements.

The first farming tools, simple tools of wood and stone, were of extremely limited application yet these tools produced a revolution because, for the first time, humans did not have to constantly follow the herds of animals that were the core of their diet. An exponential increase in the per capita food supply immediately translated into a lower incidence of famine.

This led to a significant rise in population, which paradoxically induced more warring and greater investments in armaments, which again created new technology, such as metallurgy. The first use of copper dates to the sixth millennium BC; it was the most important discovery of the time. Copper and other advances in weapon technology were soon incorporated into civilian tools, especially farm tools.

Economic Growth in Ancient Times

By about 3000 BC, humans living in the Nile Valley and at the mouth of the Euphrates and Tigris Rivers had made many technological innovations that brought major improvements in living conditions.

Tin and silver delivered a new world of possibilities. Bronze was perhaps the most significant of the new metals because of its hardness. Numerous utensils, tools, and devices were made from these metals. The wheel came into use, and so therefore the cart; chariots and sailing vessels were built.[1]

The historical and archaeological evidence shows that, from about 3000 BC to about 1000 BC, the Middle East had a much higher level of manufacturing output and the fastest rate of economic development in the world.[2]

Did manufacturing, technology, and economic growth all come at once out of mere happenstance? Nearly every one of the technological breakthroughs of the time sprang out of a manufacturing effort, indicating cause and effect. History suggests that it was war that drove the inhabitants of this region to invest more in technology.

Some 5,000 years ago, the Egyptians, Sumerians, Assyrians, Phoenicians, Hittites, Persians, and several other groups were jostling one another in a series of wars. By local standards, the rest of the world was relatively at peace. Scarcity of water in particular drove the Middle Easterners to fight more intensively than anywhere else.

As war became more intense, leaders were forced to allot a larger share of resources to manufacturing in order to make more, and better, weapons. Practically all of the major technological innovations of the time were directly linked to armaments. Metal smelting is

---

1 Clough, S. B.: *Grandeur de Décadence des Civilizations*, p. 30–34.
2 Ibid., p. 75, 110. *The Cambridge Economic History of Europe* Vol. II, p. 21, 28.

obvious. The wheel's most urgent application was to enhance troop mobility. The chariot was invented as a high-speed artillery machine and the sailing vessel was invented as a faster and more sea-worthy warship.[3]

The technologies that sprang out of the investments in military manufacturing made their way into civilian fields from agricultural implements to construction tools that made possible the first irrigation works and the first buildings. War ships were also adapted for commercial purposes and trade expanded considerably. They were also adapted for fishing and the food supply increased further.[4]

This phenomenon was repeated over and over around the world. Leaders made investments in armaments and, while they must have wished they could use the resources more productively, they ended up actually accelerating the pace of technological innovation and wealth creation.

Much suggests that if governments had invested such large resources in civilian manufacturing, they would have attained even better results. However, that almost never took place. Whenever the leaders felt that the military threat had decreased, they cut down on armament production and did not reallocate the resources into civilian manufacturing. Overall manufacturing output stagnated, technological progress slowed, and fewer new benefits came into society.

The evidence suggests the Middle East remained at the top of world development as long as support for manufacturing was the strongest in the world. When other regions started promoting manufacturing more enthusiastically (some 3,000 years ago), the Middle East started to lose its economic and technological lead.

Around the middle of the eighth century BC, Roman policy makers started to devise expansionist military plans, which demanded a considerable increase in armament production. They thus allocated a larger share of resources for the fabrication of weapons and related goods. Manufacturing output started to expand. Rome's drive to military conquest was sustained for centuries and manufacturing output in the Italian peninsula expanded faster than elsewhere. That coincided with a faster rate of technological innovation and wealth creation. Rome eventually surpassed all other nations of the world in overall development.[5]

The territories that Rome conquered experienced radical changes. Roman policy makers decided that each province should contribute to the enlargement and defense of the Empire. A larger share of each province's resources was thus allocated for the fabrication of weapons. The pace of manufacturing production went up, and there was an acceleration of economic growth in the provinces.[6]

Rome's promotion of this sector concentrated fundamentally on iron and armaments, although significant subsidies were also given to fields indirectly related to the military goals of the state. For iron and arms, Rome took the whole effort directly under its jurisdiction and created state factories. In most other manufacturing fields, the state played a less active role, but it offered significant incentives to private sector investors. Low taxation, guaranteed government purchases at prices that secured a profit, and land concessions were offered.

---

3 Fairbank, John: *China—A New History*, 1992, p. 31, 41.
4 Clough: p. 30, 35.
5 Davies, Norman: *Europe—A History*, p. 149–212.
6 Cleere, Henry & Crossley, David: *The Iron Industry of the Weald*, p. 66.

Eventually, Rome's policy makers reduced defense expenditures. Armament and related production stagnated and later declined. The economy did the same. The savings in defense expenditures were not allocated into civilian manufacturing but were spent in consumption and in non-manufacturing activities. In the third century AD, policy makers closed down numerous iron production centers and diminished incentives to numerous other manufacturing fields related to the war effort. History has recorded stagnation in this century. In the next two centuries, more resources were subtracted from manufacturing and the economy deteriorated further.[7]

On the opposite side of the world, similar events were taking place. In China, archaeological findings and historical records show a considerable increase in manufacturing production some 4,000 years ago. That coincided with a considerable spurt in economic and technological development.

As in the case of the Middle East and Rome, an exponential acceleration in the pace of manufacturing output coincided with the apparition of urban centers, and more developed agriculture, engineering, and architecture. There was also a more advanced legal system, a more organized financial system, and a considerably expanded sphere of commerce. The first Chinese dynasty (Hsia, 1800–1500 BC) came into being, together with a more developed form of government.[8]

The historical evidence suggests that, as in the Middle East and Rome, the acceleration in the pace of manufacturing production was fundamentally the result of a significant increase in the proportion of resources allocated to this sector. Metals were again at the core of this new phase of development. Bronze was the fastest growing manufacture of the time and most of it was used to make weapons. War was again the main factor pushing policy makers to allot resources to this sector.[9]

The northeast of China was the most densely population region, where there were more disputes over land. There was an intensification of warfare at about 1800 BC, in what today is northeast China, among the numerous mini-states that dotted the landscape. Governments of the time channeled larger investments into armament production, which translated into a faster overall pace of manufacturing output. The evidence shows that the majority of the metal and weapon production was carried out in government establishments.

At about 500 BC, a new phase of superior development began with iron and numerous other manufactures. War intensified as some 1,000 states fought against each other for almost three centuries. By the time the fighting ended, at about 221 BC, the whole northeast territory had fallen into the hands of a single ruler. These events drove governments to invest more abundantly in weapons and related goods, and the accelerated pace of manufacturing output coincided with a faster pace of technological development. Iron was the most noteworthy discovery of the time.[10]

Practically all iron smelters were government-owned and numerous other manufacturing fields were also in state hands. Since the advent of Chinese civilization some 4,000 years ago, heavy manufacturing was supported more enthusiastically than light manufacturing. In the civilizations of the Middle East and Rome, the same phenomenon was observed. Con-

7 Ibid., p. 62, 84, 85.
8 Gernet, Jacques: La Chine Ancienne, p. 15, 26, 31.
9 Eberhard, Wolfram: A History of China, p. 11.
10 Ibid., p. 47, 51.

sidering the strong linkage between heavy manufacturing and armaments, this may have been inevitable.[11]

The acceleration of manufacturing production in China was accompanied by impressive advances in agriculture. Although a smaller share of total resources was invested in agriculture, growth in this field accelerated as well. There was an increase in the per capita supply of food and the incidence of famines decreased. The population grew.[12]

These patterns held true in the civilizations of Egypt, Mesopotamia, and Rome. Larger investments in armaments coincided with a considerable improvement in agricultural production. New weapon technology, such as iron smelting, soon found its application in civilian fields, such as iron-tipped plows. All other primary sector activities also saw their birth and development as a result of manufactured goods. The evidence suggests that manufacturing is the sole sector with the capacity to create technology, and as such it is the only one capable of allowing the other sectors to progress.[13]

Japan went through a similar pattern, albeit somewhat later. In Japan, the Neolithic period with the fabrication of the first tools made of stone and wood,[14] began around 8000 BC, similar to China and other regions of the world. But the first use of metals in Japan began almost 3,000 years later than in the Middle East and about 2,000 years after it debuted in China. What caused the long delay?

Geography seems to have played a role. Japan is isolated, separated from the Korean Peninsula by 186 kilometers and from China by about 810 kilometers. Britain, by comparison, is only 32 kilometers away from France. This situation provided protective insularity against foreign aggression and therefore Japanese rulers were not pressured to allocate larger resources for the production of weapons. This insularity was so effective that it was only in the 13th century AD that the Japanese archipelago was for the first time confronted with a foreign invasion, as the Mongols attempted to conquer it.[15]

Historians and economists have tended to believe that this insularity hindered trade and therefore progress, but history is incapable of presenting a consistent correlation between trade and economic growth. In the Neolithic period, trade and more particularly foreign trade was non-existent in China, the Middle East, and all other regions of the world. Foreign trade therefore could not possibly have played a role in accelerating the passage to the age of metals.

The manufacturing thesis appears to hold true even for nations that were separated from other cultures and were less exposed to foreign aggression. Australia and New Zealand experienced no contact with any other culture for thousands of years. Thus the islanders had less incentive to invest in military manufacturing; and their economic performance was far below that of Japan. Oceania was still at the Neolithic stage of development when the British arrived in the 18th century AD.

A factor that was more important than foreign aggression was population density. Warfare was constant during the three millennia before the Christian era, but it was all small

---

11 Gernet: Ibid., p. 76, 77.

12 *The Cambridge History of China* Vol. I, p. 23, 24.

13 Chou, Chin-sheng: *An Economic History of China*, p. 14, 21.

14 Herail, Francine: *Histoire du Japon*, p. 11.

15 Tiedemann, Arthur (ed): *An Introduction to Japanese Civilization*, p. 4–6.

scale. Population density in Japan was much lower and that reduced the intensity of confrontation among the tribes of the archipelago.

In Australia and New Zealand population density was even lower, and there was a much larger supply of natural resources per person, which reduced the disputes over land, hunting sites, and water sources.

Japan emerged from the Neolithic period around 300 BC. Weaving technology was invented and cloth came into being. The potter's wheel was invented. The smelting of metal led to the production of a wide array of bronze and iron goods. The advent of this technology coincided with the intensification of war.

The areas in Japan that produced more armaments (the Tokyo area and in northern Kyushu) were also the most technologically developed. As war increased in scale around 300 BC, several princes allocated more funds for the making of war ships, which led to improvements in sea vessel technology. Ships became capable of travelling larger distances and Japanese vessels eventually reached the mainland. China and Korea were by then more developed and Japan began to import technology from the mainland. Japan did not have a Bronze Age; bronze and iron were introduced simultaneously from the continent. Weapons accounted for a large share of the imports and, once in Japan, policy makers allotted resources so that domestic producers could copy the technology. Subsidies were also supplied for the reproduction of imported farm tools, household utensils, and other factory goods.[16]

The increased investments in weapons and in civilian manufacturing coincided with an improvement of the economy and an increase in agricultural production.

The First Millennium of the Christian Era—China

For most of history, policy makers have thought that the climatic and geological conditions of a given territory were the most important variables determining agricultural performance. However, evidence suggests that manufacturing played a larger role. In China, the southern part of the country always had a kinder climate than the north, with a much longer growing season, less droughts and less floods.[17] However, it was in the northern part of the country where agriculture was born and prospered. More resources in that region had been devoted to manufacturing since the Neolithic period.

Up to the eighth century AD, southern China remained economically backward. Agricultural productivity in the north, where the smelting of metals and the invention of agricultural tools took place, was consistently higher. Up to the eighth century, the per capita output of manufactures remained higher in the north.[18]

For most of China's history, it was believed that agriculture was the only real productive activity and this sector was the only focus of developmental policy. However, famine and malnutrition were common, and whenever agricultural production expanded at a faster pace it coincided with the allocation of a larger share of the available resources to manufacturing.[19]

---

16 Ibid., p. 8–11.
17 *The Cambridge History of China* Vol. III, p. 23, 24.
18 *The Cambridge History of China* Vol. I, p. 560–562.
19 Ibid., p. 205.

War and in particular large-scale war frequently disrupted development plans, forcing the state to divert the resources of the nation to armament production. War demands almost always forced a cut in agricultural allocations. In spite of that, agriculture gave a better performance.

From the second century BC to the early third century AD, the Han emperors conquered the largest territory that had ever been brought under the rule of a single government in East Asia. They enlarged their domains in the northeast and subdued parts of the southeast of present-day China. To achieve that feat, the Hans increased the share of resources used for the fabrication of weapons and related goods. Once their conquering enthusiasm peaked, they continued to sustain a relatively high investment in armaments in order to maintain a well-equipped army. The increased per capita output of manufactured goods went hand in hand with an improvement of the economy. The per capita supply of food and of most other things rose.

By the late second century AD, Han rulers began to believe that their power was secure and they reduced investments in armaments. They did not transfer those resources to civilian manufacturing. The decreased support for manufacturing coincided with a deterioration of the economy. The food supply fell, rebellions broke out, and the government was unable to quell them. Finally, in 220, Han rule collapsed and their empire broke up into three kingdoms. Later, the territory that had been brought under Han rule (which was only approximately one-fourth of present-day China) was further divided into numerous kingdoms.[20]

The rulers during this Age of Division never undertook large conquering ventures. There was constant warfare, but mostly on a small scale. These rulers mostly allotted a much smaller share of the available resources for the fabrication of weapons and related goods than the Han had done. That was paralleled by a slower pace of economic and technological development.

During the period 220–580, the lower factory subsidization was reflected in a smaller per capita production of farming instruments and lower agricultural productivity, which coincided with a higher incidence of famines. In the Han period, the population had expanded; in the following period it contracted.

By the mid-sixth century, the rulers from the kingdom of Northern Wei set out to extend their domains. They vastly increased investment in weapons and shipbuilding, and equipped a large army and created a large navy. By 580 AD, they had brought under their rule most of what had been formerly under the control of the Han Dynasty. In that year, they founded the Sui Dynasty. The most outstanding Sui emperors were Wendi and Yangdi, who were determined conquerors. Yangdi attempted to conquer Korea but failed. The defeat led to rebellion among his troops. He was overthrown and the Sui Dynasty came to an end in 617. The next year, however, a new line of rulers who were even more interested in large scale conquering ventures took power.[21]

The Tang Dynasty (618-907) lasted much longer than the Sui. Tang rulers were determined to keep China united under their control. They also sought to expand the territory. The second Tang emperor launched conquering expeditions into Korea, the north of Vietnam, and parts of central Asia. Most of these military ventures were successful. Under Tang rule, the empire grew from about one fourth of present-day China to about one third of

20 Buckley, Patricia: *The Cambridge Illustrated History of China*, p. 80–86.
21 Fairbank, John & Goldman, Merle: *China —A New History*, p. 76.

today's China. These rulers significantly increased investment in armaments and related goods.[22]

The considerable increase in the resource allocation for the production of war-related goods was mirrored by a significant increase in the per capita output of manufactures and a considerable improvement of the economy. Technological innovation accelerated and agriculture grew faster. The larger food supply led to population growth. Domestic and foreign trade grew much faster. Construction also developed faster. Two large capitals were built and Chang'an became the largest city in the world, with about a million inhabitants. The Grand Canal was expanded under the Sui and again under the Tang, until the north and the south of the country were linked for the first time by means of an internal waterway.[23]

Heavy manufacturing was largely in state hands and most of light manufacturing was the result of the incentives the government offered to entrepreneurs. The evidence suggests that, even during the preceding centuries, in which factory subsidization was much lower and the rate of output of this sector fell, most of the factory output resulted from state subsidies.[24]

In China and in most of the rest of the world, government support of heavy manufacturing was almost always greater than for light manufacturing. War was the main driver. However, even when war was not in the offing, support for heavy manufacturing was almost always higher.

This is because more upfront investment is required than in light industry, and profits are harder to achieve. The private sector is reluctant to venture into it. Even in light manufacturing, spontaneous private sector investment in this domain has rarely taken place. Government support directly and indirectly was regularly required in order for investment to materialize.

Porcelain, for example, began to be produced in large amounts in China around the eighth century AD. Its development then — and for many centuries thereafter — was fundamentally the result of state intervention.[25]

The Song Dynasty (960–1279) was characterized by its large number of strong-willed and ambitious emperors. The Song rulers had large expansion plans and they poured resources into military manufacturing. They created numerous manufacturing establishments and increased the incentives to entrepreneurs. In heavy manufacturing, the support included state factories while in light manufacturing the government sought mostly to encourage private sector investment. Manufacturing increased sharply and most of the output was of armaments and related goods. By the late eleventh century, the north of China alone was annually producing more than twice as much iron as England produced during the mid-18th century.[26]

Technological innovation and the economy grew faster than ever before. Agriculture expanded, as well mining, fishing, forestry, and trade.

The Song rulers invested in shipbuilding and developed a strong navy. Chinese shipbuilding technology became the most advanced in the world. No other government was

---

22 Buckley: Ibid., p. 108–111.
23 Fairbank & Goldman: Ibid.
24 Denys Lombard: *La Chine Imperiale*, p. 1, 29, 60, 42.
25 Eberhard: Ibid., p. 197.
26 Fairbank: Ibid., p. 89.

promoting shipbuilding as strongly. Increased investment in warship manufacturing delivered superior technology that soon after became available for civilian uses. Better fishing vessels and superior transport vessels appeared, boosting the fish catch and other commercial activity.[27]

Trade expanded. The parallel between increased support for this sector and faster trade growth was not a new phenomenon. Stronger support systematically correlated with an increase of commercial activity. As with agriculture and all other non-military activities, the increase in trade appeared paradoxical, for it took place at a time when war had intensified.

Most economic historians have found it hard to explain this. But when manufacturing is seen as the generator of technology, and technology as the key to growth, the paradox is resolved.

History has experienced numerous episodes in which trade protection was endorsed and yet trade increased nevertheless. Conversely, this key explains as well why commerce has frequently stagnated or even declined, in spite of liberal trade policies, as it did under Mongol rule.

The Mongols conquered China in 1279 and remained in control until the year 1368. Mongol rule integrated China with the outside world more than ever, linking it with a vast empire that covered the majority of the Asian continent. It was a vast free trade zone. In spite of that, trade declined relative to the preceding period.[28]

As a conquered territory, the Mongols put a lid on the production of weapons in China as well as on most of heavy manufacturing, in order to diminish the possibilities of rebellion. They did the same in Russia and most of their other domains. The overall drop of manufacturing output coincided with a decrease in overall production. Fewer agricultural tools meant less food, and there was a proportional drop in all other economic activities. There was a noticeable decline in economic activity in China, Russia, and most other territories under Mongol rule.[29]

With less tradable goods, trade declined even though a vast free-trade zone had been created.

Europe — War and Growth in the Middle Ages

A similar phenomenon took place in Europe several centuries earlier. Trade under Roman control started to decline in the third century AD and continued on a downward trend until the fifth century, when it collapsed. Thereafter, it stagnated almost completely until the eighth century.

Rome had lost its expansionist drive in the early centuries of the Christian era, which led to a decrease in investment in armaments and related goods. Since the third century, the rate of factory output had declined considerably. This situation continued until the fifth century, when production collapsed, coinciding with the suspension of all subsidies to the sector as the government disintegrated. Until the eighth century, manufacturing output stagnated and support for this sector was below the level experienced during Roman times.[30] After the

27 Ibid., p. 93.
28 Lombard: Ibid., p. 98.
29 *The Cambridge Economic History of Europe* Vol. II, p. 583.
30 *The Cambridge Economic History of Europe* Vol. II, p. 223, 433.

fall of Rome, Europe was plunged into a continuous state of warfare — but almost exclusively on a small scale. This type of conflict requires mostly light weaponry (swords, bows, arrows) that require smaller investments than heavy weapons (catapults, warships). From the fifth to the eight century, there was a very low level of investment in armaments. Neither was there any noticeable effort to support civilian manufacturing. The end result was manufacturing stagnation. That coincided with a stagnant economy.

It was only in the ninth century that trade began to expand in Europe. The expansion was slow up to the 15th century. It has been frequently asserted that the feudal trade-blocking practices of the time were the main factor explaining poor state of trade during the Middle Ages. However, if that had been the main cause, then trade should have started to diminish only after the Empire fell and Europe broke up into feudal territories. The fact is that trade started to drop off well before the erection of trade barriers.

The only variable that systematically parallels the long-term fluctuations of trade is manufacturing. Feudalism was in place from the ninth to the 15th century, and trade blockages were common throughout that period. However, in the ninth century, when there was a considerable increase in government support for manufacturing, trade expanded at a much faster pace than in the four preceding centuries.[31]

The Carolingian Empire (originating in present-day France) was created in the late eighth century under expansionist Frankish rulers. They allotted a much larger share of resources to the armories. Several manufacturing fields, directly and indirectly related to weapons, also received considerably more support and there was an across-the-board rise in the output of manufactures.[32]

The ninth century expansionist efforts led to large-scale war which forced the parties to make much larger investments into armaments. Even though short lived, the Carolingian Empire extended over much of Western Europe. By the mid-ninth century, Charlemagne's empire was partitioned, but its parts did not fall back into an abundance of mini states. The Empire was divided into large territories similar to those of present day France, Germany, and Italy. Some time later, central authority also broke down in these territories but during the rest of the Middle Ages the governments of Europe ruled over much larger territories than those of the early Middle Ages. From the tenth to the 15th century, there were also numerous expansionist efforts among the states of Europe that led to war efforts that were much larger in scale than those of the preceding centuries.[33]

The trade barriers that existed in the first half of the Middle Ages were still in place during the second half, but now commercial activity expanded because the overall output of goods had increased.

Western Europe was not the only region that suggests a causal link between manufacturing and trade. In the territory now known as Russia commercial activity during the third to eighth century AD was even lower than that of Western Europe. At least, since it was never part of the Roman Empire, Russia did not suffer a drop in manufacturing when the empire declined. However, Russia's manufacturing sector had been far less developed in the first place. Russia had mostly avoided large scale war; this went hand in hand with a slower pace of growth.

---

31 Ibid., p. 434–440.
32 Holborn, Hajo: *A History of Modern Germany Vol. I*, p. 4.
33 Gaxotte, Pierre: *Histoire de l'Allemagne*, p. 38, 45, 61, 69.

Such a thesis can explain as well why, from the ninth to the twelfth century, Russia's commerce, economy, and technological growth accelerated abruptly. In the late ninth century, Prince Oleg unified western Russia. He made larger investments in weapons and overall manufacturing output rose. From then until the twelfth century, a continuation of expansionist efforts sustained and increased the investment in manufacturing. Then, during the 13th and 14th centuries, the Mongols conquered most of Russia and suppressed armament and related production. Trade fell and the economy did likewise.[34]

The British Isles

During the second half of the Middle Ages, the most active trading nations in Europe were England, Belgium, and Holland. These were also the nations that had the highest level of manufacturing development. The bulk of commerce took place in the cities and it was there where the factories were located.[35]

The case of England demonstrates how government support for manufacturing plays a key role in the economic development of a nation. By the late Middle Ages, England was the most advanced of the large nations of Europe and it retained its leading position for many more centuries. However, it had not always been that way. Up to the Roman conquest in the mid-first century AD, the British Isles had lagged behind continental Europe in economic development. The historical data also reveals there was less support for manufacturing in the British Isles, as well as less output of weapons (resulting from the lower level of warring activity). Wars were of a much lower intensity than in Southern Europe.[36]

When the Romans invaded in AD 43, they targeted the southeast of England, which was the most developed region of the Isles — over the preceding centuries the tribes of the southeast had experienced the most wars, as they constantly battled the tribes of northwest France. Their French adversaries tended to have superior weapons, and this forced the tribes of southeast England to invest more to match them. It was the Parisi who introduced iron in Britain in about 500 BC. The highest per capita production of manufactures in the Isles took place in the southeast of England.[37]

With the coming of the Romans, the production of weapons and related goods increased exponentially because the conquerors needed a domestic supply of these goods and created several factories in England. Overall manufacturing production rose significantly. There was an economic boom — but not in Scotland and Ireland.

Agriculture, mining, fishing, technology, urban centers, population and trade developed rapidly in England, and Scotland and Ireland were left behind. England's development, however, never surpassed that of the other Roman provinces during the first to fourth centuries, and this reflected Roman policy for armament production for all of its territorial domains. When Roman rule collapsed in the year 410 and support for manufacturing ended, the sector's output dropped considerably and this coincided with a marked deterioration of the English economy.[38]

---

34 Ibid., p. 10–23.
35 Murphy, Brian: *A History of the British Economy 1086–1740*, p. 33–50.
36 Clapham, John: *A Concise Economic History of Britain*, p. 11–15.
37 Ibid., p. 16.
38 Webster, Daniel: *The History of Ireland*, p. 11–18.

The economic downturn lasted until the eighth century, given the reduction of support for manufacturing in the British Isles and in the rest of Europe. Even the low-intensity wars of the period did not stimulate significant investment.

However, in the ninth century the first signs of economic revival took place — along with the first forms of large-scale war. Viking raids threatened to overtake the British Isles; numerous tribes merged to make common cause against the foreign aggressor. They channeled more resources into armaments and overall manufacturing output rose. Under pressure from the Vikings, by the mid-tenth century the West Saxon kings had unified practically all of England.

For the rest of the Middle Ages, war continued to grow in size as disputes with France intensified. This drove a concomitant increase in resources used for arms production, coincident with more rapid manufacturing production. That was paralleled with a progressive improvement of economic activity.[39]

The Hundred Years' War, from 1337 to 1453, between England and France, was unprecedented in scale. More resources from both nations were allocated for armament production.[40]

England and France increased per capita taxation. It was feared that the intensification of war and the rise in public debt would lead to economic ruin, but in fact economic activity and agriculture expanded. Once again, notwithstanding the war's impediments to trade, there was a noticeable increase in commercial activity.[41]

By the mid-14th century, the Bubonic Plague appeared and ravaged the population. In England, in the half century following 1348, the population dropped from about 4.8 million to just 2 million. Germany lost about a third of its population while France lost about two fifths. The epidemic waxed and waned, and vanished only in the 17th century in the British Isles and in the 18th century in continental Europe.[42]

Such a massive loss of work force should have created a large drop in production. There was also a large loss of life due to war. However, production did not contract. Quite the contrary, the economies of England and France systematically improved their performance.

The paradox is best explained by the surge in technological innovations which resulted from the higher level of manufacturing subsidies. Manufacturing is also the only logical explanation for England's taking the lead in Europe since the late Middle Ages.

There had been constant warfare between the southeast of England and the northwest of France for centuries. In 1066, the French Normans conquered the Saxons and became the rulers of England. They took seat in London while keeping their domains in France. In order to retain their French possessions, they had to invest more than France in warships and had to launch constant military expeditions to the mainland. From the start, France also had a larger population than England, and London had to develop superior war technology to compensate.[43]

This interpretation would be consistent with the fact that, at the start of the Hundred Years' War, English military technology was superior to that of France and by the end of the

39 Ibid., p. 21–23.
40 Trevelyan, G. M.: *A Shortened History of England*, p. 181.
41 Bolton, J. L.: *The Medieval English Economy 1150–1500*, p. 121, 208, 247, 59.
42 Murphy: Ibid., p. 61.
43 Ibid., p. 2, 3.

war, the gap had increased. The English held control of the seas during the Hundred Years' War, for they possessed superior naval technology. Since they invested more in the fabrication of ships, they inevitably ended up developing a more advanced ship technology.[44]

England and France, having engaged in the largest-scale wars in Europe during the Middle Ages, were also the countries that attained the fastest growth of manufacturing and economic development. English kings, however, invested more in weapons in per capita terms. And England enjoyed faster economic and technological development.

Germany

The history of Germany further supports this thesis. The territories that constitute present-day Germany dwelled in the Neolithic period for a much longer time than those in southern Europe. Up to the first century BC, living conditions were terribly primitive and agriculture was barely undertaken, while in the south of Europe a much more developed economy existed. Archaeological findings and historical accounts show that the per capita production of manufactured goods in the south was exponentially higher. That coincided with a much higher warring activity than in the north, which was less densely populated. There was constant battling among the Germans and Celts, but not on the scale of the wars of southern Europe. They therefore invested less in weaponry. They had less technological development, more primitive agriculture, and lower living conditions.[45]

When the Romans conquered parts of the south and west of Germany, at the end of the first century BC, they created numerous factories for the production of weapons, iron and related goods, and the economy of those regions immediately began to transform. The tribes living in the rest of Germany had no reason to allocate more resources for the production of weapons or any other manufactured good — and they remained at a Neolithic stage of development.

Germanic invasions in the fifth century AD were mostly responsible for the final destruction of the Roman Empire. The Germans had inferior weapons, but the Romans had decreased their production of armaments dramatically. After the collapse of the empire and up to the eighth century, warring progressively intensified in most of Germany, but these continued to be wars of a much lower scale than those Rome had undertaken. During the fifth to the eighth century, the center, the north and east of Germany experienced a higher per capita output of factory goods than formerly, paralleled by faster technological and economic development. For the south and the westernmost part, which had been under Roman rule, things took a different course. Although factory investment was higher than in the rest of Germany, it was lower than it had been during Roman times and that was accompanied by a deterioration of living conditions.[46]

In the late eighth century, Charlemagne (768-814) undertook the largest conquering effort since the fall of Rome and subdued most of present-day Germany. His victories were usually short-lived, as rebellion was constant, so he established garrisons to station his troops. To provide these troops with ready supplies of weapons and related factory goods, he created factories in German soil. In 825, his successor, Louis I, entrusted the region of

---

44 Trevelyan: Ibid., p. 183, 202.
45 Duroselle, Jean-Baptiste: *L'Europe—Histoire de ses peuples*, p. 37–50.
46 Ibid., p. 51–88.

Bavaria to one of his sons, Louis the German, who vastly increased funding for the production of weapons and related goods. He gradually extended his power over all of Carolingian Germany. In 843, with the Treaty of Verdun, his hold on the lands east of the Rhine was recognized. Some historians argue that the history of Germany begins at this moment.[47]

After the death of Louis the German in the 870s, his kingdom broke apart, but in 887 Arnulf of Carinthia partially restored it. In 911, Conrad I was elected king and most of what later became West Germany fell under his rule. Territories were nonetheless constantly breaking away. In the mid-tenth century, the Saxon king Otto I succeeded in acquiring so much territory that he laid the foundations of the Holy Roman Empire. Most of his successors, up to the end of Barbarossa's reign in 1250, managed to hold on to the territories. Rebellions were constant and a large army, well supplied with weapons, was maintained.[48]

The large increase in armament production in the ninth century coincided with greater technological development, a large increase in the per capita output of agricultural goods, a larger increase in the output of minerals and other primary goods, and an increase in trading activity. From the early tenth century until the mid-13th century, German kings ruled over the largest territory in Europe. This was achieved by investing more than most other European kingdoms in the production of weapons and related goods. Germany was the strongest and most stable power in Europe and one of the most economically developed. Food consumption rose, famines decreased, and population increased. The east was colonized. Universities were formed.[49]

Even during the period from the mid-tenth to the mid-13th century, the control of German emperors over their empire was relatively weak. There was no capital or centralized administration. Once they conquered parts of northern Italy, they became embroiled in Italian politics as well. There was also a growing dispute between the emperor and the Pope over the distribution of powers and this led to war with the Holy See. Since 1073, warfare with Rome was ongoing. The rivalry between the Welf and Hohenstaufen dynasties further undermined the empire. In 1273, a new dynasty took power. The Habsburgs ruled until 1806.[50]

It is argued that all of the above weakened the central government and local princes profited by consolidating their positions. All of this clearly did have a negative effect, but the fundamental reason for Germany to lag behind England and France technologically and economically after the 13th century seems to reside in the more passive stance taken toward manufacturing subsidies. Kings such as Otto I and Barbarossa were ambitious, but not like Charlemagne, and those who came after were even less active and expansionist. The prevailing idea of the times was that agriculture should be the focus for economic growth, and only as a side-effect of their foreign policy did the earlier rulers achieve the growth that comes from investing in manufacturing.

Most of the nobility was, as well, intent on maintaining the status quo. They sought to avoid all investments that could create more employment in the cities and produce a rural-urban migration that would deprive them of peasant-serfs to work the land.

In spite of that, there was a progressive increase in the subsidization of manufacturing. That was largely the result of external influences. Since the 14th century, England and France

---

47 Kitchen, Martin: *The Cambridge Illustrated History of Germany*, p. 9.
48 Barraclough, Geoffrey: *Mediaeval Germany Vol. I*, p. v–vii.
49 Kitchen: Ibid.
50 Rapp, Francis: *Les Origines Medievales de L'Allemagne*, p. 9, 10.

increased significantly the share of resources used for the making of weapons. Armament technology improved at a pace never seen before and there was a revolution in weaponry. Gunpowder and cannons came into use. The German princes immediately sent emissaries to acquire samples. They allotted funds so that their ironsmiths could reverse-engineer and replicate the new weapons. This effort required new investments. Pushing further in this direction was the intensification of war between the German states (which, while it remained much smaller in scale than in England and France, grew larger over time). The princes increasingly invested in weapons.[51]

Increased factory subsidization from the 13th to the 15th century coincided with an increasing per capita output of agriculture, mining, fishing, forestry, and handicrafts. Domestic and foreign trade also rose as well as technological development. Regional specialization and the division of labor became more accentuated, as well as productivity growth. Literacy improved and rural-urban migration accelerated. Cities developed like never before. Relative to England, France and the Low Countries, Germany began to lag, but relative to its previous history, it progressed.[52]

Population had been growing since the ninth century and it accelerated thereafter. However, in 1347, the Bubonic Plague ripped through Europe and during the first wave alone, which lasted about three years, about one fourth of the German population was swept to its grave. By 1470, the population was one third smaller than in 1340 (from 12 million down to 8 million). Villages were depopulated, cultivated land was abandoned, and agrarian incomes fell. In spite of that, during the 14th and 15th centuries the economy accelerated its pace.[53]

Investment in agriculture fell in the 14th and 15th centuries, and on top of that, the number of peasants working the land decreased considerably. Why then did farm output and the economy grow faster? Since war had intensified, a larger share of available resources was used to produce weapons and in consequence manufacturing output accelerated. New weapon technology was soon transferred to agricultural tools, which increased farm productivity significantly. Every acre was more productive, despite the reduction in the number of cultivators.

Such a thesis can also explain why cities continued to grow, notwithstanding the significant contraction of the population. Manufacturing is concentrated in the cities and throughout the Middle Ages manufacturing incomes were higher than those in agriculture. It was therefore inevitable that this sector was more attractive than farming.[54]

During the late Middle Ages, average wages increased steadily all across Europe, hand in hand with the larger investments in weapons throughout the continent due to the technological revolution. An arms race was under way. Salaries grew fastest in England, France, and the Low Countries — the places that invested more in weapons and other factory goods.[55]

The development of Germany's financial system also correlated with the levels of factory subsidization. Up to the eighth century, only very primitive money-lending operations were in existence. The growing per capita weapon production since the ninth century was mirrored by a growing per capita output of goods and services. As trading activity rose, barter

---

51 Ogilvie, Sheilagh (ed): *Germany — A New Social and Economic History* Vol. 2, p. 263–265.
52 Mathis, Franz: *Die Deutsche Wirtschaft in 16. Jahrhundert*, p. 4–6.
53 Scribner, Bob (ed): *Germany — A New Social and Economic History* Vol. I, p. 63–65.
54 Rapp: Ibid.
55 Cipolla, Carlo: *Before the Industrial Revolution*, p. 203.

was less satisfactory and the need for a common unit of exchange rose. The minting of coins increased. As the national wealth rose, capital became easier to accumulate and money-lending operations expanded proportionately. Eventually, moneylenders formalized their activities and established banks. The subsidization of manufacturing increased in the 15th century and banks reached their highest level of development in the Middle Ages.

The power of bankers also increased. Moneylenders and bankers had traditionally refused to lend to manufacturing, preferring activities that generated a quick return, such as trade, services, and to a lesser extent primary activities and construction. They also lent to governments, because returns were assured.[56]

War intensified in the 15th century but not all regions of Germany fought with the same intensity. The most intense wars were those between the central-south and the northeast. The central-south states invested most in weaponry and they happened to experience the fastest technological and economic growth. It was also there (Nuremberg and the surrounding regions) where banking and commerce flourished most. The main export goods of the central-south states were cannons, other weapons, and metals. For weapons, iron, machines, and other war-related goods, regional rulers mostly created state factories. For light manufactures, they supplied incentives to private producers.[57]

Manufacturing is also the factor most capable of explaining why technology fluctuated so erratically during the first 1,500 years of the Christian era in Germany and the rest of Europe. Technological development rose and fell in tandem with the factory subsidization policies of the Roman Empire and its successor states.

Japan

Japan entered a more advanced period of development in the early fourth century AD. New technology allowed for a considerable expansion of all economic sectors. The per capita availability of food increased. The improvement in living conditions coincided with an intensification of war, with a larger per capita output of weapons, and with a larger per capita output of factory goods. Archaeological findings in burial sites show a larger output of weapons since 300 AD as well as a larger production of tools, ornaments, and several other manufactures.[58]

At about that time, the Japanese princes from the province of Yamato (Kansai), which covered the present-day region of Tokyo and Osaka, undertook a large program of territorial expansion. They transferred resources from agriculture to manufacturing by raising taxes on farming and using the funds to finance numerous armories. Weapons per soldier increased considerably as swords, spears, daggers, bows, and arrows were produced in unprecedented amounts.

At the start of this large-scale conquering effort, the Yamato court controlled approximately one third of the main island of Honshu, by far the largest of the Japanese islands. By the mid-sixth century, the Yamato princes had conquered about three fourths of Honshu as well as two of the other large islands (Kyushu and Shikoku) and all of the southern smaller islands. Yamato princes also undertook conquering ventures beyond the archipelago. In the

---

56 Rovan, Joseph: *Histoire de l'Allemagne—Des origines a nos jours*, p. 139–190.
57 Ibid., p. 197–240.
58 Tiedemann: Ibid., p. 13.

fifth century, they went for Korea, which was the first attempt to subdue the peninsula. Prince Nintoku was the most successful conqueror and he secured the tip of Korea.[59]

Several Japanese princes also ventured in China and Korea as mercenaries and were rewarded by Chinese and Korean rulers with technology transfers. The mainland was considerably more advanced than the archipelago and it sent craftsmen as payment. These Chinese craftsmen were supplied with incentives in Japan such as land grants so that they would undertake manufacturing activities. A fairly large number of Chinese craftsmen migrated to Japan in the sixth century and they became very prominent in the Yamato court due to their superior knowledge. So large was their influence, that Chinese writing was adopted. Buddhism was also introduced in the sixth century as an import from Korea.[60]

The increased expenditures in military manufacturing in the fourth to sixth century, as well as the larger subsidies for civilian manufacturing, delivered faster factory output, and that coincided with an accelerated pace of technology. Armament production was the most heavily subsidized field and it was weapons technology that most progressed. Economic growth accelerated but it was still slow relative to that of the 20th century or even the 19th century. That was paralleled by an increase in support for manufacturing but still only a tiny fraction of the available resources. The immense majority of the archipelago's resources were utilized for agriculture, the other primary activities, services, and construction.

Construction absorbed a large share of resources. This period has been called the Era of the Large Tombs because princes took to constructing large mausoleums. Prince Nintoku's tomb was the largest. It was almost as bulky as Egypt's largest pyramid, but not as tall. Despite the increased warring, armories received a small share of resources compared to construction.[61]

The conquering drive began to decrease by the mid-sixth century and the Yamato rulers lost the tip of Korea around that time. More important was the cessation of territorial expansion within the archipelago. Economic decay accompanied the decreased production of armaments and civil war followed. The end of the civil war in 587 brought in a new line of rulers.

China had been fragmented for several centuries but under the Sui Dynasty (580–618), it became once again a unified political entity. The Sui Dynasty was short-lived but it was followed by the Tang Dynasty, which maintained the unity of the country and even expanded the borders. The unification of China provided the impetus and the model for similar efforts in Japan.[62]

The desire to unify the whole archipelago drove Prince Shotoku (574–622) to support military manufacturing. Taxes were raised for agriculture and commerce and lowered for manufacturing. The central government began also to collect taxes directly instead of letting local governments do it; central government revenue increased. The rulers created more state factories, in particular for the production of metals and armaments, and they also supplied more guaranteed government purchases at high prices to private craftsmen. Lower taxes for manufacturing also encouraged the private sector to shift resources to this sector. The unification drive was sustained up to the tenth century and by then military force

59 Mason, R. H. & Caiger, J. G.: *A History of Japan*, p. 28, 37.
60 Tiedemann: Ibid., p. 14.
61 Herail: Ibid.
62 Mason & Caiger: Ibid., p. 28.

had extended central government authority into northern Honshu and the southern tip of Hokkaido.[63]

The superior development and prosperity of Sui and Tang China inspired Japanese rulers to try to produce the goods that China had, in particular the most prestigious ones, those with the highest levels of technology. Japanese princes offered incentives such as large tracts of land to artisans from the mainland and they also sent Japanese to learn production methods in the continent. This last impelled them to increase investment in shipbuilding in order to increase contacts.

From the seventh to the tenth centuries, Japanese rulers allocated a larger share of the available resources to manufacturing, which was reflected in an increased per capita output of food, cloth, pottery, household utensils, and most other things. The improved living conditions led to an increase in population. Land under cultivation increased and farm productivity rose. Construction boomed. In 710, the first permanent capital was built, at Nara. Larger than its predecessors, it was modeled after the Chinese capital. In 794, Emperor Kammu built an even larger capital, called Heian. Heian became Kyoto and remained Japan's capital until 1868. Throughout the history of Japan, construction has made progress when support for manufacturing increased.[64]

Despite improvements, living conditions continued to be miserable. Famines were regular and malnutrition constant. Disease ravaged the population. In 735-37, a smallpox epidemic wiped out about one third of the population. That coincided with a per capita production of factory goods that continued to be extremely small.[65]

History suggests that the population's level of nutrition and health is proportional to the level of technological development. As subsidies rise, new farm technologies appear, increasing food productivity.

During this period, Japanese policy makers continued to view manufacturing as deserving little investment. Up to the seventh century, the capital was changed with every new emperor. Sometimes a new city was built and sometimes an existing one was refurbished, but those efforts diverted a large amount of resources to construction.[66]

On top of that, society was stratified and the system classified smiths, tanners, and others engaged in manufacturing as very low ranking. Government support for manufacturing had to be extremely weak. Worse still were the constant famines, which forced the government to view the promotion of agriculture as the only credible development policy. With land grants, tax exemptions, and subsidized farm inputs it constantly drove the private sector to allocate the bulk of its resources into agriculture. Despite the increased support for manufacturing during the seventh to tenth centuries, subsidies for agriculture remained substantially larger.[67]

By the late tenth century, the bulk of the archipelago was under the control of the central government and the rulers of the 11th and 12th centuries reduced funding for the armories. The Song Dynasty appeared in China in the mid-tenth century and flourished in the following two centuries. Japanese rulers could have invested in civilian manufacturing in

63 *The Cambridge Encyclopaedia of Japan*, p. 57.
64 Reischauer, Edwin & Craig, Albert: *Japan — Tradition and Transformation*, p. 12, 13.
65 Perez, Louis: *The History of Japan*, p. 25.
66 Kolb, Albert: Ostasien—*China, Japan, Korea*, p. 497–502.
67 Jansen, Marius (ed): *Warrior Rule in Japan*, p. ix.

order to reproduce the numerous Chinese civilian goods that Japan did not produce. However, they did not do so.

Governments tend to promote civilian manufacturing, too, whenever armament production is promoted. Larger armies need uniforms, so the government increases subsidies for textile production. Transportation technology is needed. Large-scale war brings nations in contact with the civilian manufactures of other nations. That often translates into efforts to produce similar civilian goods domestically.[68]

The lower overall support for manufacturing in Japan during the 11th and 12th centuries was paralleled by economic decay. As the economy deteriorated, the tax revenue declined. Many historians have claimed that the increasing privatization of land that started in the seventh century as the government granted land to stimulate the promotion of agriculture and manufacturing was responsible for the reduced tax revenue of the central government. They claim that by the eleventh century, so much land was in the hands of military regional rulers that it was more than that taxed by the central government. As a result, tax revenue to the central government decreased and they could no longer afford a large army. Regional military chiefs raised armies. Lower revenues also hindered the government from providing administration and judicial services, so the regional rulers began to establish their own governments. Central authority decreased. Civil war erupted in the 1180s as provincial military chieftains usurped power from the Kyoto aristocracy.

The evidence suggests that this was all an effect of the deteriorating economy and not the cause. If the policy of land privatization that started in the seventh century were to blame, the negative effects would have been seen earlier. Rather, in other regions of the world it is seen that tax revenue decreases whenever governments reduce support for manufacturing, independent of the land policy endorsed.

From the 13th until the 15th century, more than two hundred independent states appeared and the national system of taxes, justice, and common defense ceased to exist. The states were part of a loose coalition that was led by the Shogun, the prince controlling the largest kingdom in the archipelago.[69]

During the 13th to 15th centuries, the fragmentation of power led to constant warfare between the numerous states. There was no decisive attempt from any of the regional rulers to subdue the other states but war intensified relative to the preceding two centuries.[70]

Regional rulers increased investment in armaments. Each state produced considerably less weapons than the central government had produced up to the 12th century, but all of the states together did produce more than formerly. Per capita output of weapons rose. Armament production increased further because of the Mongol invasion of the 13th century. In 1274 and again in 1281 the Mongol emperor of China launched a large invasion. Despite their technologically superior weapons and larger armed force, the Mongols failed in their efforts. On both occasions, they were driven away by a typhoon, which the Japanese called "Kamikaze," or wind of the gods. These invasions, the first in the archipelago's history, inspired much larger investments in weapons over the next several decades.[71]

---

68 Herail: Ibid., p. 12.
69 Perez: Ibid., p. 26, 29.
70 Jansen: Ibid., p. ix–xii.
71 Perez: Ibid., p. 30, 31.

During the latter part of the 14th century, China's coast was plagued by Japanese pirate activity. The Ming dynasty demanded that the Shogun put an end to this. The threat of war and the incentives given by the Chinese drove the Shogun to increase significantly production of warships to suppress the pirates. By the early 15th century, piracy had been largely eliminated — and investment in manufacturing increased in Japan.[72]

As in the past, the increased investment in armaments in the 13th to 15th centuries was accompanied by increased support for civilian manufacturing. Since the states were constantly at risk of a blockade by enemy troops, they sought to produce everything domestically. Regional governments created their own factories and offered incentives to craftsmen so that they would undertake manufacturing activities that could cover the domestic demand. This had also taken place in the past but this time the efforts were larger because the intensification of war had meant tighter blockades.

The most common form of incentives was land concessions. Cloth production was seen by practically all the states as the most important civilian factory good and policy makers supplied weavers with the largest land concessions. That coincided with the civilian field that expanded the most and made the most technological progress.[73]

The greater support for manufacturing was followed by an improvement in living conditions. Agricultural productivity and output rose. More construction equipment allowed for improvements in irrigation and water control. More construction equipment allowed also for a larger building activity. Cities and port towns multiplied. Urban centers developed where manufacturing took place and their growth was proportionate to the size of the factory activity. Faster manufacturing growth coincided also with an increase in commerce. Domestic and foreign trade expanded more than ever before notwithstanding the intensification of warfare.[74]

Such a paradox can only be explained if it is assumed that manufacturing is the creator of technology. A faster output of this sector translated therefore into a faster growth of technology, which delivered a larger output of primary goods and handicrafts, thus increasing the supply of tradable goods. It also enlarged the supply of ships and carts, which facilitated transport while multiplying the number of construction implements, which made possible roads and ports. Kyoto was the largest producer of manufactures and it was also the main commercial center.[75]

As the production of goods rose, barter started to give way to commerce based on money. Barter disappeared first in urban centers, where factories were concentrated and the supply of goods was more abundant. Through history, the use of money has correlated very tightly with levels of manufacturing development. The higher the per capita output of factory goods, the sooner barter would disappear. The use of coins appeared in China, in other regions of Asia, and in Europe much earlier than in Japan. Right up until the 18th century, Japan had subsidized manufacturing less than many nations in Asia and Europe.[76]

Living conditions improved significantly from the 13th to the 15th century, but life was still miserable and brutal. Famines were regular and epidemics recurrent. In the 1420s, the

---

72 Sansom, George: *Histoire du Japon — Des Origines aux début du Japon moderne*, p. 545.
73 Yamamura, Kozo (ed): *The Cambridge History of Japan — Medieval Japan*, p. 346, 347, 394.
74 *The Cambridge Encyclopedia of Japan*, p. 60, 61.
75 Eisenstadt, S. N.: *Japanese Civilization — A Comparative View*, p. 174–176.
76 Yamamura: Ibid., p. 344, 345.

archipelago was ravaged by a famine and then by the black plague, which together took out about a third of the population. With little in the way of manufactured farm implements and so few fishing vessels, only a small amount of food could be extracted from the land and the sea. Food was scarce and malnutrition endemic. Water could not be purified and was always contaminated with disease-causing organisms. The extremely low per capita availability of factory goods again coincided with high levels of morbidity and mortality.[77]

Levels of Education and Infrastructure

Historical evidence also reveals a correlation between manufacturing and education, and between manufacturing and infrastructure. Progress on these two fronts has systematically correlated with the level of factory subsidization. Education in Europe during Roman times experienced a major leap forward. Then, during the first half of the Middle Ages, there was a retrenchment and only in the later part of that period was there a resurgence of manufacturing.

Massive infrastructure projects were developed during Roman times, and as soon as manufacturing production started to drop in the third century AD, roads, aqueducts and ports started to deteriorate. When the Empire fell in the fifth century, the infrastructure slipped into decay — until the ninth century, when progress was once again noticed. That went hand in hand with a significant resurgence in factory subsidies.[78]

In Russia, education and infrastructure did not fluctuate so erratically during the long period up to the 15th century, but it made very slow progress. This coincided with a slow but continuous increase in the state's efforts to promote factories. The only downturn that Russia experienced occurred from the mid-13th to the mid-15th century, when the Mongols took over and suppressed manufacturing.[79]

As in the case of Europe, China experienced numerous ups and downs on matters relating to education and infrastructure during the long period up to the 15th century, and all of them coincided with the fluctuations in manufacturing. During the Song Dynasty, the fastest development of education and infrastructure took place, coincidentally during the period when manufacturing was more strongly promoted.

History shows that in the long term, education, infrastructure, and everything else can only grow when technology is advancing; and the evidence suggests that manufacturing is responsible for the generation of technology. China experienced a major acceleration in the growth of this sector during 500 BC— AD 200, the very timeframe in which paper was invented. It goes without saying that a manufactured good such as paper can expand the possibilities for education exponentially. This was also the period in which iron came into use. This discovery ultimately delivered a large number of tools used for construction, considerably expanding the possibilities for infrastructure construction.

During the Song Dynasty (960–1279), when manufacturing expanded even faster than 500 BC—AD 200, education made more progress. Song China was the first society to print books, and it was also the first to produce quantities of steel. Paper, printing equipment,

77 Sansom: Ibid.
78 Davies: Ibid., p. 149–380.
79 Kirchner: Ibid., p. 2–34.

books, writing utensils, chairs, and desks expanded the horizons of education while metal bars, shovels, pickaxes, hammers, and nails did the same for infrastructure.[80]

Faster manufacturing growth also increased the wealth of society, allowing households to spend more on education. At the same time, government revenue rose, which allowed more funds to flow into public education and infrastructure.

---

80 Fairbank: Ibid., p. 89–93.

Misinterpretations of the Causes of Economic Growth

The 16th century marked a decisive change in world history. For the first time the world economy began to be integrated. More important still was the significant acceleration in the rates of economic growth. Europe, and more particularly Western Europe, had the fastest growth, and within Western Europe, England and Holland had the most flourishing economies. There have been numerous efforts to explain this situation. However, previous explanations have not been consistent with the facts.

The population in Western Europe grew faster during the 16th century than at any point in all its previous history. Many economists have seen population growth as a stimulant for economic activity. Adam Smith, among others, believed that population growth contributed significantly to economic performance by permitting specialization and therefore productivity improvements. He also thought that a rise in population inevitably forced up demand, which would lead to an increase in production.[81]

If population size, or growth rate, were a major element affecting the economy, then one would have expected a terrible downturn in economic performance during the 14th and 15th centuries when the population contracted. The fact is that most of Europe experienced faster rates of economic growth during these centuries than in the 12th and 13th centuries, when population was growing relatively quickly.

England, which attained the best economic performance in Europe during the later part of the Middle Ages and in the 16th century, is illustrative. During the 12th and 13th centuries, England experienced an average rate of population growth of about 0.2% annually, while during the 14th and 15th centuries population contracted by about 0.2%. Having population contracted so painfully during these last two centuries, one would have expected a contrac-

---

81 Davis, L.; Hughes, J. & McDougall, D.: *American Economic History*, p. 80.

tion of demand and therefore of production. That, however, was not the case. There was economic growth and it was even faster than in the preceding centuries.[82]

It has also been argued that the introduction of more developed methods of agriculture during the 16th century delivered better agricultural output, which increased peasant incomes. As a result, demand rose, forcing production upwards. But even though agriculture grew faster during this century than before, it grew more slowly than the economy as a whole. For agriculture to have propelled the rest of the economy, it would have to have grown faster than the economy and that was not the case.

The historical records up to the 20th century show that in practically all nations of the world, agricultural production systemically grew slower than GDP. In Britain, and in the vast majority of European nations, manufacturing regularly grew faster than agriculture and the economy. The figures suggest that the factory sector was the only one that could have propelled this growth.[83]

There are several other factors that conspire against the thesis that agriculture propelled the economy. In the preceding centuries, the only large-scale war had been the Hundred Years' War, but in the 16th century the continent was engulfed by conflicts of even larger scale. They absorbed a much larger share of the resources, reducing the share that flowed into agriculture, but in spite of that farming grew faster than before.

As less was invested in farming and more "wasted" on armaments, agriculture might have been expected to perform worse than in the past and the economy as a whole to have deteriorated. However, agricultural and the overall economy performed better than ever before, and the fact is that manufacturing received a larger share of overall resources. This sector grew at an unprecedented pace.

The argument that it was new methods of agriculture and the introduction of new crops from the Americas that delivered faster agricultural production also fails to add up.[84] The case of England is illustrative. The English colonized the American continent in the early 17th century. The establishment of colonies considerably increased the flow of new crops to England and during the first half of the century methods of agriculture were more advanced than during the 16th century. However, during the first half of the 17th century agricultural growth and the economy overall slowed down in England.[85] The performance was similar to or worse than that of the 16th century, for famines were somewhat more common.[86]

Spain had the best access to the new crops of the Americas during the 16th century; if agriculture were the driving force, then Spain should have attained the best agricultural and economic performance. And Spain's climate was better for agriculture than most of Europe. In spite of that, it was England that attained the best farm performance in Europe.

In the 16th century trade, too, increased. Many have seen this rapid rise of trade as the main factor propelling economic growth.[87] Western European countries had discovered a new continent and new trade routes to Asia, and these countries also experienced the fast-

---

82 Chambers, J. D.: *Population, Economy and Society in Pre-Industrial England*, p. 19, 10.
83 Floud, Roderick & McCloskey, Donald (ed); *The Economic History of Britain since 1700 Vol. I*, p. 47.
84 Gaxotte, Pierre: *Histoire de l'Allemagne*, p. 402.
85 Clarke, Peter & Slack, Paul: *English Towns in Transition 1500–1700*, p. 103
86 Parker, Geoffrey (ed): *The General Crisis of the Seventeenth Century*, 1978.
87 Jack, Sybil: *Trade and Industry in Tudor and Stuart England*, p. 122.

est development of trade at that time. Most economic historians have come to see the two as linked.

However, during the 15th century there was a noticeable rise in commercial activity in Europe even though America was still not in sight. In China, during that same century, trade also expanded much faster than before, although no new continent was discovered.[88]

Events that took place later demonstrate further inconsistencies with the trade–growth thesis. Commercial activity during the 19th century increased far more with respect to the preceding centuries than it did in the 16th century with respect to the Middle Ages, even though no new continent was discovered. Much suggests that the discovery of a new continent was not fundamental for the rise in trade and economic activity.

Much also suggests that trade was not pivotal for the economic upsurge in the 16th century. For most of the 20th century, Russia practiced a centrally planned system that severely curtailed commerce. Foreign trade fell abruptly. In spite of that, Russia grew exponentially faster than ever before, growing approximately twelve times faster than Western Europe did in the 16th century. The evidence shows that trade is an effect of growth and not the cause.

It is also argued that the economic growth in Western Europe during the 16th century was largely the result of the stunning inflows of precious metals from the Americas. Had that been true, Spain should have had the fastest growth. That, however, was not the case. England and Holland grew faster, by about 0.3%, annually while Spain averaged only 0.2%. (See tables in the appendix.)[89]

Also, the acceleration of economic growth during the 19th century in Europe was considerably more accentuated than that of the 16th century, even though there was no comparable inflow of precious metals.

England

While none of the orthodox explanations is consistent with the historical evidence, the manufacturing thesis is. Of all the centuries of the Middle Ages in Europe, the highest level of support for manufacturing came during the 15th century. In addition to the Hundred Years' War that increased military manufacturing in England and France, the scale of wars throughout Europe also grew. This meant a larger per capita output of military and civilian manufactures. The enhanced efforts to promote factories led to an acceleration of production, which increased the amount of tradable goods. That would explain why there was a significant rise in trade, even though America had not been yet discovered.[90]

This thesis can also explain why China experienced a large increase in trade during the 15th century even though no new continent was discovered, even though the country prac-

---

88 *The Cambridge History of China* Vol. VII, p. 232–236.
89 Ramsey, Peter: *The Price Revolution in Sixteen Century England*, p. 69–73; Sabillon, Carlos: *World Economic Historical Statistics*, p. 183–188; Madison, Angus: *The World Economy: Historical Statistics*; Madison, Angus: *The World Economy: A Millennial Perspective*; The figures mentioned above and several others in the following pages are derived from the compilation of data extracted from numerous sources. Although the data are drawn from the sources thought to be most authoritative, they should be construed only as indicating trends and characterizing major differences among economies rather than offering precise quantitative measures of those differences.
90 Holborn, Hajo: *A History of Modern Germany Vol. I*, p. 35, 51.

ticed a less liberal trade regime than during Mongol rule, and even though there was no new inflow of precious metals. The fall of the Mongols during the late 14th century brought to an end the policy of suppressing arms manufacture. The new Ming rulers increased allocations for weapons, ships, metals, textiles, and other manufacturing fields. A considerable increase in overall manufacturing output was accompanied by rapid growth in other sectors. With a larger amounts of goods, it was inevitable that trade expanded.[91]

This is, as well, consistent with the considerable acceleration in the pace of technological innovation in China. The Ming emperors invested more in ships than all other governments in the world and during the 15th century China possessed not only the largest fleet but also the most technologically advanced. Armaments and shipbuilding were the fields which saw the greatest technological development, and these were the two fields that received the most subsidies and attained the fastest rates of output. Many within the Ming government criticized those investments as a burden for the state. Since the large fleet was not even constructed for the sake of commercial purposes, but mostly as a symbol of the Emperor's power, many saw it as waste of resources.[92]

If resources were being wasted, the economy should have performed badly and technological innovation should have been at best stagnant. But there was a noticeable improvement on both fronts. This would be consistent with the thesis of this book, which asserts that manufacturing is the key to wealth creation. The evidence suggests that even when manufacturing expands principally because of increased production of un-consumable goods such as weapons and decorative ships, economic growth and technological innovation are still generated.

Manufacturing advances would also be the most coherent means for explaining why England attained the fastest rates of economic growth, of technological innovation, and of trade during the 16th century even though Spain accumulated the bulk of the precious metals from the Americas. Spain apparently had more funds available, but England invested more.

The English government allocated a larger share of the nation's resources to this sector than the other governments of Europe. Monarchs such as Henry VIII (1509–47) and Elizabeth I (1558–1603) were determined to make their country the supreme military and economic power of Europe. Since military power was intimately associated with armaments and economic power with the capacity to export abundantly; since the most exportable goods were manufactures, these motivations translated into increased support for manufacturing.

The rise of Spain and Portugal as maritime powers plus the desire to acquire territories and precious metals from the new continent placed England on a collision course with several nations who were pursuing the same goals. As wars grew in size and the number of combatant parties rose, governments were forced to make much larger military investments. Up to the 15th century, France was England's only significant adversary, but in the following century Spain, Holland, and Portugal were added. This was the first time in history when cannons were fitted onto ships; Henry VIII insisted on mounting the new artillery piece himself.[93]

---

91 Lombard, Denys: *La Chine Imperiale*, p. 109–114.
92 *The Cambridge History of China Vol. VII*, Ibid.
93 Trevelyan, G. M.: *A Shortened History of England*, p. 216.

The across-the-board increase in large-scale war in Europe during the 16th century coincided with an increase in manufacturing output, economic growth, technological innovation, and trade for practically all of the continent's countries. However, increases in factory output were more pronounced in the most war-driven countries. Western Europe was more involved in large-scale warfare than Eastern Europe, and concomitantly attained faster economic growth.

Within Western Europe, England took the lead in development and England was the country that most heavily subsidized the production of armaments and civilian manufactures. The case of England in the 16th century supports an idea also illustrated by the preceding century. The capacity to increase factory output lies almost exclusively within the power of each nation. A country does not need exogenous resources to increase manufacturing output. It can often be generated simply by the reallocation of existing resources.

A larger share of available resources can be directed to this sector through various means. Governments might restructure their budgetary allocations so that manufacturing receives a larger share. Governments regularly do this during times of war, as they cut expenditures in other domains and allot a larger portion for the production of armaments.

Governments can also increase taxes, or restructure the tax system to reduce taxation for manufacturing companies and people laboring in that sector while proportionately increasing taxation on other economic sectors. This technique, too, is commonly used in times of war and occasionally during peace times.

Throughout history, however, efforts to restructure budgets in order to favor manufacturing have been accompanied by a restructuring of taxes, by an increase in taxes, and by an increase in government borrowing. Regardless of how it took place, the fact remains that the decision to stimulate manufacturing production lay almost exclusively within the discretion of each government.

Aside from taxation and budgetary allocations, there are several other measures that governments have taken to channel resources into manufacturing. Foreign direct investment is one, and it, too, is only marginally affected by exogenous variables. The flow of foreign investment into manufacturing has depended fundamentally on the incentives that a government offered to foreigners.

Throughout Europe during the 16th century, there was a noticeable increase in taxation in per capita terms, an expansion of government borrowing, an increase in the share of budgetary allocations for armaments, and greater promotion of foreign investment in factories. Governments granted the large majority of subsidies to domestic capitalists and also created many state factories, but promoted foreign direct investment in an unprecedented way. These changes were more pronounced in England, where the drive for military and economic supremacy was arguably the strongest. Henry VIII went as far as to confiscate all the property of the monasteries to help finance his plans.[94]

Among the incentives offered by the English Crown to manufacturers were low taxation, grants, guaranteed purchases at prices that assured a profit, and free land for the factory. It also created the patent system. The patent system was conceived with the goal of protecting inventions and increasing inventors' profit. Since practically all inventions were directly linked to manufacturing, the patent system acted as a stimulant for factory investment.[95]

---

94 Clark, George: *The Wealth of England from 1496 to 1760*, p. 64, 65, 74.
95 Musson, A. E.: *The Growth of British Industry*, p. 29.

The Crown also offered monopoly rights, trade protection, and decrees forcing the population to consume certain manufactured goods. However, the evidence suggests that these three last measures did not help to increase output, because they reduced the competitive pressure on manufacturing and in that sense hampered productivity.

The incentives were not limited to war-related fields. The 16th century was the first time in European history when support for civilian manufacturing became noticeable, although at a much lower level than that offered to military manufacturing. England subsidized this domain more than her competitors did, and textiles enjoyed the most support. This was the fastest growing civilian manufacturing field.

It has been frequently argued that the growth of textiles was a windfall stemming from the religious exiles fleeing northwest Europe due to the Reformation. However, long before the beginning of the Reformation, skilled workers migrated to England as the Crown offered them incentives. Since the 14th century, some textile makers emigrated from present-day Holland and Belgium to England, a trend which increased during the 15th century. The Reformation, which began in 1517, did increase the number of manufacturing emigrants from northwest Europe to England; however, the fundamental reason for the large increase in foreign direct investment was that the English Crown offered considerably increased incentives.[96]

Even though textiles are civilian manufactures, military concerns were a major reason for the subsidies. Textiles were promoted to increase the supply of cloth for military uniforms and sails for battleships. The trade blockades and the embargoes that almost always accompanied war inspired the English government and most other European governments to try to substitute imports as much as possible by manufacturing domestically practically every needed good.

Policy makers also promoted civilian manufacturing out of balance-of-payments concerns. Governments in Europe and in most other regions of the world viewed balance-of-payments deficits, and more particularly trade deficits, very negatively. They therefore took measures to encourage domestic production to substitute imports and increase exports.

The English offered the most incentives to domestic and foreign producers. The economists of the time believed agriculture was the only real productive activity, but since the government was determined to increase exports, and factory goods were the ones most in demand, manufacturers ended up receiving significant subsidies. New industries related to silk, paper, jewelry, pewter, glazed earthenware, glass, and soap were the result of the large incentives offered to immigrant craftsmen from northwest Europe.[97]

The overall level of factory subsidization in England during the second half of the 16th century was higher than in the first half, and economic growth was faster as well. The very strong determination of Elizabeth I to attain military and economic supremacy drove the government to increase allocations to military and civilian manufacturing. Shipbuilding was particularly fostered to increase exploration and to confront the maritime powers of the time. That is why English exploration did not begin in earnest until the mid-16th century, when a route to China by way of Siberia was sought. This led to the opening of Russia for trade; and in 1580, Francis Drake became the first Englishman to circumnavigate the world.[98]

---

96 Clark: Ibid., p. 50.
97 Holderness, B. A.: *Pre-Industrial England*, p. 101.
98 Duroselle, Jean-Baptiste: *L'Europe—Histoire de ses peuples*, p. 189–215.

Elizabeth I even granted large mining concessions to German capitalists from Bavaria, who had the most advanced metal technology of the time. The mining concessions were complemented with a wide array of other incentives such as guaranteed government purchases at very profitable prices.[99]

Technology developed faster than ever before in the 16th century in Europe, albeit at different rates in the different regions of Europe. Progress was more accentuated in the Western part and especially in England. This coincided with the differing levels of factory subsidization between the Eastern and Western parts of the continent and between England and the other Western European nations.

England, which in the early 14th century was lagging technologically in numerous fields, had by the late 16th century fully caught up in practically all of them. For example, in textiles, England caught up with Holland, which had for centuries been at the lead in Europe. This went hand in hand with the fact that England provided the strongest support for textiles in Europe.

Reflecting this faster technical development, new employment possibilities associated with new technology appeared in England. The vast majority of these new jobs were directly associated with manufacturing. The birth of new fields such as silk, paper, glass and soap created numerous new jobs, but at the same time the introduction of new machinery in existing economic activities created technological unemployment. This was not the first time in history that new technology had eliminated jobs, but it was the first time that it became very noticeable. Gig-mills, a new mechanical device for cloth making, deprived old-fashioned hand workers of their livelihood, and in 1552 Parliament took the decision to prohibit them.[100]

The fastest creation and destruction of employment activities due to technology in Europe occurred in England, where the support of manufacturing was strongest.

The creation of the patent system also reflected the faster pace of technical development in England. Since this country experienced the most rapid rate of innovation during the 15th and 16th centuries, it was perhaps inevitable that it would be the first to establish a system for the protection of inventions.

The correlation between support and technology occurred everywhere. The fastest changes in technology throughout Europe took place in the manufacturing fields that received the most subsidies, such as metallurgy, armaments, and shipbuilding. The historical data also reveals that it was these domains which experienced the most progress in productivity.

Shipbuilding is highly illustrative. Having invested the most in battleships, England emerged from the Middle Ages with the most advanced shipbuilding technology in Europe. During the 16th century, even though Spain was in the greatest need of ships to supply and defend its large and far away possessions, England produced more ships. Notwithstanding Spain's larger supply of precious metals, England invested more in shipbuilding and enjoyed faster technological development.

When Spain set out to punish England in 1588 for assisting its rebellious Dutch possessions, its Invincible Armada of 130 ships was not only outnumbered by the English fleet of

---

99 Clark: Ibid., p. 51–53, 47.
100 Ibid., p. 50, 54.

200 but it was also technologically outclassed. English ships had canons that shot further, faster, and more precisely. They were also more maneuverable and more sea worthy.[101]

The evidence suggests that investment in factories is not dependent on having direct access to capital, but on having a government that is determined to attract investments in this sector.

The evidence also indicates that throughout Europe, productivity was systematically higher in manufacturing than in agriculture or any other sector. The vast majority of productivity improvements in agriculture and in all other non-manufacturing sectors were directly linked to manufacturing tools that facilitated the task.

Agriculture, which in those days was the largest sector of the economy, is emblematic. During the 16th century large tracts of land which had been lying unused were brought into cultivation through the use of new tools and devices for clearing, draining, leveling, and cutting. Marshes, fens, forests, and heath were drained and cleared. This phenomenon was most noticeable in England, the nation that fabricated those implements in larger numbers.[102]

There was also a significant rise in output per acre and this correlated with the invention of improved tools for plowing and harvesting. England produced more agricultural tools in Europe and it was also the nation with the fastest rates of farm output and productivity. In the 16th century, England had a surplus of corn for the first time in its history.[103]

The manufacturing thesis is also the best capable of explaining why England attained a superior agricultural development even though Spain had more access to the large amount of new crops from the Americas, had better climatic and geological conditions, and had more funds for investment. Since Spain gave less support to manufacturing, the output of agricultural implements was slower, and the rate of technological innovation in that field was also slower. The result was a smaller amount of farm implements, and of inferior technological level. Under those circumstances it was impossible for Spain to outperform or even match England agriculturally.

England had less access to the new crops from the Americas, but the most important factor was its ability to rapidly increase production of the crops it already possessed. One of the fundamental reasons for Europe's high mortality and morbidity rates of the time was malnutrition, which was the result of a diet limited to just a few comestibles and to an insufficient intake of those few comestibles. Vegetables and fruits, a relatively wide variety of which did grow in Europe, were barely cultivated during the Middle Ages. Grains were considered a production priority, but they were rarely produced in amounts that could satisfy the minimal needs of the population.

With the invention of many new agricultural tools in the 16th century, production capabilities rose significantly and for the first time in the continent's history legumes constituted a sizeable share of farm output. On top of that, grain harvests rose noticeably.[104]

Several economic historians have argued that the large-scale wars in 16th-century Europe did not take place in the British Isles, which might have helped the English to attain their superior agricultural and economic performance. However, if that were the reason, then Ireland and Scotland should have also performed well. But they both performed consider-

101 Holderness: Ibid., p. 11, 112, 99.
102 Clarkson, Leslie: *Death, Disease and Famine in Pre-Industrial England*, p. 23.
103 Ibid. p. 26, 217.
104 Bolton, J. B.: *The Medieval English Economy 1150–1500*, p. 32.

ably below the level of England and famine was more widespread in Ireland and Scotland than in England.[105]

Many historians have argued that the advent of capitalistic forms of agriculture accelerated farm output during the 16th century. The phenomenon of "enclosure," the private reclamation and fencing in of lands which had no official owner, brought more land under cultivation from the early 15th century to the early 19th century. There was indeed something of a correlation between enclosure and improved agricultural performance, but it was not very consistent. At its inception, enclosure coincided with an increase in agricultural output, and the consolidation of this phenomenon in the 16th century paralleled a stronger acceleration of farm output. However, during the 17th century, the enclosure movement was continuing in earnest yet agricultural results were inferior to those of the previous century.[106]

It is worth noting that, during the Middle Ages, private forms of tenure were predominant anyway; land was possessed privately and exploited privately. Enclosure seems to have been the result of economic growth and not the cause of it. As the economy grew faster and living conditions improved, the population expanded and demand for land rose, so people started to claim land that had previously been left uncultivated.

Trade expanded rapidly in Europe during the 16th century and the western part of the continent experienced the fastest growth. It is argued that the colonies of Western European nations facilitated trade. However, England and Holland expanded trade the most, although Spain and Portugal had more colonial possessions during that period.[107]

Like technology and agriculture, trade seems to be a by-product of manufacturing. Apparently, stronger support of manufacturing delivers more factory goods, more primary goods, and more means for carrying out trade. The new war ship technology delivered vessels that were larger and more seaworthy; and when that technology was transferred to civilian uses, it translated into ships that could transport more goods, at a faster speed, and along longer routes.

The even larger investments in metallurgy for arms delivered a new technology that significantly reduced the costs of metal production and made it cost effective to utilize metals in numerous other fields. The metal content of construction tools rose significantly. More and better infrastructure works were built. Advances in manufacturing output delivered increased wealth, and also made it possible to increase funding for infrastructure works. In the 16th century there was a considerable rise in public works throughout Europe. They were more abundant and of better quality in the western part of the continent, where support for this sector was stronger.[108]

Aside from agriculture, the other primary sector activities also grew rapidly in the 16th century. Factories were promoted more in Western Europe than in Eastern Europe, and the output of minerals, wood, and fishes expanded more rapidly in the West. England subsidized factories most, and the output of primary sector goods grew fastest there.[109]

---

105 Chambers: Ibid., p. 139.
106 Holderness: Ibid., p. 52, 53.
107 Jack: Ibid., p. 122.
108 Clark: Ibid., p. 45.
109 Ibid., p. 51–53.

Germany

In Germany, no significant effort was made to channel resources into civilian manufacturing. They had one of the lowest GDP rates in Western Europe.[110]

Large-scale war of the kind experienced by England, France, the Low Countries, and Spain during the 16th century was not undertaken in Germany, but war did intensify somewhat. From the 13th to the 15th century, Germany was militarily weaker than several nations in Europe, but mobilizing large troops over even small distances was so difficult that foreign powers remained out of its territory. In the 16th century, however, there was a revolution in transportation as far greater ships were designed and other new means of transport facilitated mobility.

In 1517, the German priest Martin Luther began a movement of protest against Rome, which soon evolved into a new Christian philosophy that contested the Catholic one. In a strongly religious era, this fuelled a bitter war between the two camps. Foreign powers were induced to invade German territory. Spain and France possessed larger armies than Germany had previously faced, and they fought with more technologically developed weapons. This forced German princes to allocate more resources to the arms industry.

War intensified among the maritime Atlantic nations of Europe in the 16th century, accompanied by an impressive development of weapons technology. German princes would have been driven to invest more in armaments because of this phenomenon, even if foreign troops had not invaded, because lagging too far behind in weapons technology was an invitation to would-be conquerors.[111]

The political configuration of the German states was a temptation to foreign monarchs in any case. By the early 16th century, the Atlantic monarchies of Europe had consolidated their power and unified large territories which previously had been fragmented. The Holy Roman Empire, on the other hand, was a vast territory including all of present-day Germany plus Switzerland, Holland, Alsace and Lorraine, parts of northern Italy, and much of Poland. The emperor was elected by the rulers of the states comprising the empire. There were about 2,500 regional authorities, most of which were tiny enclaves of no more than 400 square kilometers. Power rested largely in the hands of the electors and they could dictate policy to the emperor and even remove him from his post. The emperor had no imperial army, no budget, and no central administration — but he was far from toothless. Since the late 13th century, the Habsburgs had occupied the post of emperor. The personal state of the Habsburgs included Austria and several adjacent lands, which comprised more territory than that of any other state of the empire. The emperor also had the largest army.[112]

Habsburg rulers, however, as a lot, never undertook a large-scale campaign to unify the states. When the Habsburg emperor died in 1519, the Spanish and the French king each demanded that the title of emperor pass to them due to their blood linkages with the Habsburgs. For a number of reasons, the electors chose Charles I of Spain. He took the title of emperor of the Holy Roman Empire in 1520 under the name of Charles V.[113]

The iconoclastic thesis of Martin Luther led to a split in religious views and ushered in a tumultuous period. Charles I sought to reconvert those German states that had renounced

110 Holborn: Ibid., p. 29–37, 71–85.
111 Rovan, Joseph: *Histoire de l'Allemagne—Des origines a nos jours*, p. 249–337.
112 Gagliardo, John: *Germany under the Old Regime 1600–1790*, p. 1, 2, 14.
113 Rovan, Ibid., p. 260–262.

the Catholic faith. A large peasant revolt with Lutheran undertones marked the beginning of the Christian violence in 1524–25. The revolt was soon crushed, but not the Protestant movement. The king of France, much displeased with the decision of the electors, sided with the enemies of the Spanish king and increasingly supported the states that had embraced the protestant cause. The Protestant states joined forces and formed the Schmalkaldic League. War with the Catholic states followed. Charles I and his allies commanded larger armies but they came to a stalemate; both camps were exhausted. In 1555, a truce was achieved by the Peace of Augsburg, which recognized Lutheranism. Neither side was satisfied with that settlement and intermittent wars continued throughout the rest of the century.

The religious wars forced German princes to invest more in armaments and related goods, such as iron and the machinery that made the weapons. The recruitment of a larger number of soldiers created demand for a larger per capita output of uniforms and boots. Bigger subsidies were offered for textiles and footwear. Since the German states were at risk of being surrounded and cut off, subsidies were also increased for the production of most of the goods that were regularly imported, so that they could be self-sufficient. That mostly meant manufactures.[114]

To increase the supply of arms, iron, machines, and other heavy goods German governments mostly created state factories, while for civilian light goods they subsidized private producers. The most common subsidies were monetary grants, tax exemptions, monopoly rights, and land grants. Cheap labor was also provided. Textile production, for example, was frequently undertaken in state orphanages, in workhouses where beggars were kept, in penal institutions, and even in lunatic asylums. At times the state would create a factory, operate it for a while, and then sell it to capitalists at less than cost.

Increased factory subsidization in Germany during the 16th century was met by faster economic growth, probably about 0.2% per year. The accelerating production of factory goods was accompanied by accelerating development of the primary sector, trade, construction, and services. The division of labor, the use of money, the growth of finance, and productivity grew faster than ever before.[115]

Technological progress and social change in Germany accelerated in this century. History suggests that the most powerful agent of social change is technology. New technology creates wealth. Increased wealth enlarges the share of the population receiving education, and education radically changes peoples' attitudes. Since manufacturing was more heavily promoted during the 16th century and since this is the sector responsible for the creation of technology, faster social change was inevitable.[116]

Many argue that the spurt in technological and economic growth in Germany during the 16th century as well as in the rest of Western Europe came from the birth of capitalism. The fastest growing economy in Europe in this period was England; it grew by about 0.3% annually. But for most of the 20th century, Russia's economy was vastly more regulated than that of the England in the 16th century. Even so, it attained a rate of economic growth of about 2.4%. If capitalism were fundamental to growth, Russia's GDP rate should have been below that of England. (See tables in the appendix.)

---

114 Gagliardo: Ibid., p. 140, 141.
115 Ogilvie, Sheilagh (ed): *Germany—A New Social and Economic History Vol. 2*, p. 264.
116 Mathis, Franz: *Die Deutsche Wirtschaft im 16. Jahrhundert*, p. 2.

Neither was it because capitalism was just in its infancy. Western Europe continued to grow very slowly during the 17th and 18th centuries. If capitalism is the best economic system, it should have delivered rapid growth from the start. Western economists have vilified centrally-planned economies, but in every country where they were applied, they delivered faster GDP growth than capitalist Europe had seen up to the 18th century.

It is worth noting that in the 16th century, government expenditure as a share of GDP in Western Europe was about 2%. Government expenditure is the most important factor that can compete with market forces in directing the economy. During the 20th century, government expenditure as a share of GDP in Western Europe was about 25%; thus one could say that Europe was considerably more capitalistic or market-oriented in the 16th century than in the 20th century. In spite of that, economic growth was approximately eighteen times faster in the 20th century (3.6%). Orthodox arguments do not add up.

The evidence shows that capitalism had practically nothing to do with the spurt in economic growth of the 16th century. The evidence suggests that the considerable acceleration in the division of labor, the increased use of money, and the rise of banks were by-products of the faster economic growth. That in its turn had resulted from the increased subsidization of factories.

Such a thesis is consistent with the case of the Soviet Union (Russia) in the 20th century, when support for manufacturing was very strong and the rate of factory output was about 6.9% per year. Western European governments also gave this sector large subsidies in the 20th century. Factory output in Western Europe grew by about 4.4% annually while in the 16th century, when there was very little support for factories (the great majority of the state budget was used to subsidize agriculture, construction, and services[117]), it grew by just 0.3%.[118]

Even so, support in the 16th century was stronger than before; and that coincided with faster growth of agriculture in Germany. Land under cultivation increased as marshes were drained, meadows were made arable, and forests were cleared. That coincided with expanded production of farm tools and the development of technologically superior tools that made it easier to sow, harvest, cut and clear the land.[119]

Further substantiating the theory that manufacturing is causally related to the growth of primary sector activities is the fact that nearly every step forward in primary production has been the result of a manufactured good.

During the 16th century, England was the most productive in mineral output and was also the nation where the fabrication of shovels, pickaxes, bars, and other mining tools was undertaken on a larger scale. England as well produced wood at the fastest pace, and was the nation that fabricated axes, saws, and other related devices in the largest numbers. Ships, nets, and other fishing goods were also produced at the fastest pace and fish catches in England were larger than in the rest of Europe.

Manufacturing seems to have been responsible for the increased demand for primary sector goods. As the prime generator of wealth, increased manufacturing output gave the population more purchasing power. On the other hand, strong support for the sector ex-

117 Gagliardo: Ibid., p. 10–14.
118 Sabillon: Ibid., p. 109, 120; Madison, Angus: *The World Economy: Historical Statistics; Madison, Angus: The World Economy: A Millennial Perspective.*
119 Scribner, Bob (ed): *Germany — A New Social and Economic History Vol. 1*, p. 70, 71.

panded existing activities that utilized primary goods as inputs for production, and it also created completely new ones that also required primary goods to operate. Activities such as metal smelting, brewing, soap boiling and sugar refining were heavy consumers of firewood and coal.[120]

During the 16th century in Europe, service sector activities also grew. Eastern Europe showed the slowest rates of manufacturing output and this was the region where services developed the least. Within Western Europe, it was England, where factories were most enthusiastically promoted, that had the fastest growth of services

The causation of this phenomenon in financial services seems to have been as follows: the increased wealth that manufacturing created permitted a higher level of savings, and therefore an enlargement of financial assets. Although England was not the largest country in Europe, it had the largest and most developed banks. Spain extracted the most precious metals from the Americas but England's financial assets were greater. London became the financial capital of England and this city happened to be England's main factory producer.[121]

Of course, banking operations were only possible thanks to a number of factory goods such as coins, paper money, accounting books, and instruments for numerical measurements.

Educational services follow the pattern. During the 16th century in Europe, education progressed considerably but there were differences among the regions and the eastern part of the continent, the region with the slowest factory output, experienced the least progress. England produced the most paper, ink, printing presses, books, writing utensils, desks and seats, as well as more construction tools for building schools. At the same time, England was the country that recorded the highest school attendance levels. Without these education-related manufactures, educational services were not possible.[122]

Russia

Russia's economic activity picked up a bit in the 14th century, particularly in the northwest, Moscow and its surroundings. The Mongols never managed to conquer much of the northwest. The Muscovite rulers were committed to expelling the Mongols and they channeled larger investments into armaments. These investments were increased in the 15th century and more armaments were produced. Economic activity expanded. Along with these larger investments came an accelerated pace of technological development in military manufacturing. Much suggests that the introduction of superior forms of artillery led to the end of Mongol rule. As in other nations, technology first showed up in the creation of weapons and then it spread to civilian fields.[123]

Russia expanded considerably in the 16th century, particularly under Ivan the Terrible (1533–84). Ivan conquered the last Mongol possessions in the south. In the east, he subdued the Kazan Khanate, thus eliminating the last major obstacle to Russia's eastward expansion. In the west (in particular the Baltic states) and in the north, in Scandinavia, which were more developed and produced superior goods, his main goal was not land but plunder.[124]

---

120 Holderness: Ibid., p. 94, 95.
121 Musson: Ibid., p. 16.
122 Gaxotte: Ibid., p. 221, 222.
123 Kirchner, Walter: *A History of Russia*, p. 33–35.
124 Ibid., p. 45, 49.

To fulfill the larger military ambitions of the 16th century, Russia channeled a larger share of the nation's resources into military manufacturing. There was some increase in allocations for civilian manufacturing as well, but the bulk was for the fabrication of weapons. Nothing prevented the governments of Russia from giving as much support to civilian manufacturing as to the arms industry, but nothing gave them a clear incentive to do so. And as with Europe, China and other regions of the world, the private sector refused to commit its capital to the sector.[125] Investment in factories tended to materialize only when the government offered the necessary level of incentives that would guarantee a profitable venture. The higher the level of incentives, the more the private sector would commit its energies and resources to it.

Throughout the Middle Ages, large-scale war was more intensive in Europe and in particular in the Western part of the continent than in Russia, and more wealth was created there. Thus Russian entrepreneurs had less capital at their disposal. In the centuries that followed, Russian entrepreneurs continued to take the path of caution and conservatism and systematically lagged behind Western Europe. Many historians have concluded that there was something in the Russian culture that inhibited the private sector from investing as much as in Europe. A long-term analysis, however, reveals the inconsistency of the argument. Up to the mid-19th century, rates of investment in Russia lagged behind those of Europe, but during the late 19th century, investment there exceeded that of Western Europe. That just happened to be the first moment in Russia's history when support for manufacturing was higher than in Western Europe, and the first time when factory output grew faster.[126]

In Russia during the 16th century, the acceleration in the pace of manufacturing output coincided with faster overall economic growth, which is likely to have averaged about 0.1% annually. Agriculture, the other primary activities, and trade also grew faster. As in Europe, all this was paradoxical considering that war had become more encompassing and was therefore disrupting economic activity more than before. Seen from the perspective of manufacturing, however, this situation is easily explainable. (See tables in the appendix.)

Technological progress leapt forward during this century, even though most of the investment was in weaponry. Still, it was slower than in Europe and in particular Western Europe. This situation paralleled very closely Moscow's lower subsidization for the sector.[127]

China and Japan

The Chinese economy experienced a rebirth during the Ming Dynasty (1368-1644), and although growth was faster during the 16th century than during the Mongol period, it was noticeably slower than that of Western Europe. Up to the 15th century, China had maintained an economic and technological lead over Europe. However, Western Europe took the lead during the 16th century. China is likely to have grown by about 0.1% annually while Western Europe averaged about 0.2%.[128]

---

125 Kerblay, Basile: *Modern Soviet Society*, p. 172.
126 Guroff, Gregory & Carstensen, Fred (ed): *Entrepreneurship in Imperial Russia and the Soviet Union*, p. 57.
127 Ibid., p. 55, 56, 30; *Madison, Angus: The World Economy: A Millennial Perspective.*
128 Lombard: Ibid., p. 114; Sabillon: Ibid., p. 111; Madison, Angus: *The World Economy: Historical Statistics.*

The economic rebound during the Ming Dynasty has been explained by many economic historians as being a result of the modernization of agriculture. A larger food supply in the 15th century supposedly increased the size of the population, which created demand for more goods and services.[129]

That interpretation of events fails to explain why, during the 16th century, when further agricultural improvements were made, the economy failed to accelerate. It also cannot explain why China grew much slower than Western Europe, especially given that China wasted fewer resources in unproductive activities such as war. China allocated a greater share of total resources to agriculture, but Western Europe saw faster farm output.

Analyzed from the perspective of manufacturing, however, the developments in China become understandable. Ming rulers did not undertake any major military campaign of conquest, nor was there any aggression from abroad that would have forced much larger investments in armaments and related goods. While Western Europe experienced a massive rise in large-scale war, China did not, and therefore fewer resources were allocated to military manufacturing. As a result, factory output remained slower than in Western Europe.[130]

Up to the mid-14th century, the Mongols had suppressed manufacturing. Under the Mings of the 14th and 15th centuries, investment in armaments, iron, and other weapon-related goods increased. The Mings constantly led armies against the Mongols and progressively took away more land from them. As in the past, larger investments in armaments brought with them greater allocations of resources for civilian manufacturing. The larger investments in this sector coincided with faster economic growth.[131] During the course of the 16th century, the Mongol threat to China progressively diminished.

The Portuguese first arrived in China in the 16th century and in 1565 they were given permission to settle in Macao. Despite the gunboat diplomacy of the times, the Portuguese and other Europeans did not become a national security concern. In the 16th century, China seemed relatively secure, so Ming rulers invested less in the production of weapons and related goods. Reduced support for manufacturing was paralleled by a diminishing output and a slower economic pace.

Japan followed a similar course. During the 16th century, war intensified in the Japanese archipelago. In 1543 a Portuguese ship reached the islands and introduced firearms. The harquebus was technologically superior to any weapon the Japanese had seen and it made quite an impression. The daimyo of Tanegashima, where the Portuguese landed, immediately ordered his sword-smiths to make replicas. The superior power of firearms drove investments into production-replicating efforts. In just two decades, they succeeded in copying the technology and even improved it, in particular with the spring and trigger mechanisms. Many of the regional rulers or daimyos began to produce guns.[132]

With this superior weapon, many daimyos launched their armies on the path of conquest. Nobunaga (1539-82) allocated a larger share of his fief's resources for the production of firearms, ammunition, and warships. He equipped his ships with cannons, muskets, and iron plates. These were the first armored ships built in Japan. With such an arsenal he enlarged his domains and in 1573 took over Kyoto, becoming the ruler controlling the largest

129 Eberhard, Wolfram: *A History of China*, p. 256.
130 Eberhard: Ibid., p. 270–275.
131 *The Cambridge Encyclopedia of China*, 201.
132 *The Cambridge Encyclopedia of Japan*, p. 66.

territory. By the early 16th century there were about 250 states in the archipelago, which were almost independent from each other. Since the apparition of firearms, the trend began to more towards a unified central government.[133]

This was not the first time that military hardware played a decisive role in the battlefield. Through the history of Asia, the quantity and technological sophistication of weapons was usually determinant for success. Nobunaga not only had more weapons than his adversaries, but also had more advanced arms.

Nobunaga's successor Hideyoshi, who ruled from 1582–98, pushed the armament modernization program further, for he wanted to subdue the entire archipelago and to conquer Korea and parts of China. He also allocated more resources for the production of civilian factory goods that were directly or indirectly related with his military goals. With his vastly increased arsenal, he overpowered almost all of the nearby states and in 1592 launched an invasion over the mainland. He landed in Korea and succeeded in subduing the whole peninsula, but Chinese forces soon put his armies on the defensive and later the war came to a stalemate. When he died in 1598, his generals decided to withdraw from Korea.[134]

The intensification of war in the 16th century and the expanded production of weapons coincided with increases in per capita output of factory goods and faster economic growth. The economy seems to have grown by about 0.1% annually. (See tables in the appendix.)[135]

Agriculture grew faster as did mining, commerce, construction, and services. Mining witnessed impressive growth. Production of precious metals, in particular silver, was so fast that by the early 17th century Japan may have accounted for about one-third of world silver output. Construction also boomed and was by far the fastest in the later part of the century, when the level of support for manufacturing was the strongest.[136]

---

133 Whitney Hall, John (ed): *The Cambridge History of Japan—Early Modern Japan*, p. 54–58.
134 *The Cambridge Encyclopedia of Japan*, p. 61–63.
135 Sabillon: Ibid., p. 112; Madison, Angus: *The World Economy: Historical Statistics; Madison, Angus: The World Economy: A Millennial Perspective.*
136 Whitney Hall: Ibid., p. 59, 60, 70, 73, 96.

CHAPTER 3. THE 17TH CENTURY

Support for Manufacturing in England

During the 17th century, Western Europe attained the fastest rates of economic growth in the world. Western Europe was also the region where governments promoted manufacturing most enthusiastically. Among the large nations of this region, the strongest factory subsidization was undertaken in England and this was the fastest growing economy.

There were however strong differences in the performance of the English economy during the first and the second half of the century. There was a noticeable deceleration of GDP in the first half and during the second half the economy expanded.

During the years 1600–49, the monarchs of England reduced the budgetary allocations for manufacturing. The rule of James I (1603-1625) was characterized by conspicuous consumption, low investment in armaments, and disputes with Parliament that paralyzed government activity. The rule of Charles I (1625-1649) actually saw an increase in government inertia and stagnation of investment, as his reluctance to co-govern with Parliament inhibited the adoption of policies. The disputes and the economic crises that accompanied this political drama eventually led to civil war from 1642 to 1651. Unlike their predecessors, none of these monarchs was driven by the desire to expand the military and commercial power of England. Their lack of ambition translated into lower allocations for military and civilian manufacturing. [137]

The records suggest that during the first half of the 17th century, the rate of factory output dropped. All other economic sectors slowed as well and the pace of technological change slowed down. [138]

137 Clough, Shepard: *European Economic History—The Economic Development of Western Civilization*, p. 148–188.
138 Clarke, Peter & Slack, Paul: *English Towns in Transition 1500-1700*, p. 103.

Parliament sought to promote manufacturing, and rallied London, the east, and the southeast of the country, where factories were more concentrated, to the cause. The kings of this period saw manufacturing as a threat to their power because the new manufacturing businessmen were the ones who most contested their authority. They thus looked for support in the north of the country and in Wales, where agriculture was predominant. [139]

Since Parliament controlled the regions with the largest manufacturing base, it was able to produce more weapons — and in the civil war that ensued, Parliament and its faction won. The amount and technological sophistication of weapons is often what ultimately determines success in the battlefield. During the 16th and 17th century, the largest producer of armaments in Europe was England and this country won most wars, frequently against rivals who possessed larger populations. In a conventional confrontation of armies such as those of the 16th, the amount and technical sophistication of arms constantly proved to be the decisive factor.[140]

Having won the civil war, Parliament became the prime power of the country and the main arbiter of economic policy. It therefore began to enact legislation which, even though not directly intended for that purpose, ended up delivering more subsidies to manufacturing. Mercantilism was a doctrine very popular in those times and it sought to increase exports and maintain constant trade surpluses. This policy was inaugurated with Cromwell's Navigation Ordinance of 1651. This was reinforced by the passage of the Navigation Acts of 1660–63 and, some years later, by the Corn Laws that offered tariff protection to agriculture and manufacturing.[141]

There was as well a significant rise in fiscal, financial, and non-financial incentives in an effort to stimulate the production of arms, ships, armament-related goods, and civilian manufactures.

Several of these policies, however, had the negative effect of hampering competition. Trade protection in particular removes incentives for the constant improvement of the quality of goods and encourages a tolerance for elevated costs.[142]

The cause of manufacturing was hurt by frequent government efforts to prohibit or limit the utilization of labor-saving machines. The general population, those who stood to see their jobs eliminated, traditionally had been wary of technological innovations. New ideas in farming were generally met with suspicion by farmers. In the 16th and 17th century, when technical progress accelerated, protests against the new-fangled ideas were more frequent.[143]

Textiles, the fastest growing civilian manufacturing field and the one where the most technological progress was made in the 16th and 17th centuries, was the prime target of the anti-technology crusade. It was the field that most utilized new tools and machines, and it also encountered the most resistance to the adoption of new labor-saving devices. At times, the government prohibited the use of new tools altogether and at times it decreed a partial

139 Holderness, B. A.: *Pre-Industrial England*, p. 108.
140 Ibid., p. 4.
141 Ibid., p. 203–227.
142 Musson, A. E.: *The Growth of British Industry*, p. 74.
143 Clarkson, Leslie: *Death, Disease and Famine in Pre-Industrial England*, p. 26.

prohibition. Most of the time, most manufactured goods were not forbidden outright, but this policy nonetheless hampered development.[144]

Other regulations also hindered or were at best useless for the development of manufacturing. Among the most noteworthy were those that sought to coerce the population into consuming English manufactures. An act of 1571, for example, ordered the population to wear an English woolen cap and a law of Charles II in the late 17th century declared that every person dying on English soil had to be buried in an English-made woolen shroud. These efforts sought to stimulate demand but the evidence suggests that they were not effective.[145]

One of the worst productivity-damaging policies of the 16th and 17th centuries was the establishment of monopolies. The creation of monopolies did not occur exclusively in manufacturing but a large share of the sector was affected by this practice. In particular, during the first half of the 17th century, there was a noticeable rise in the granting of monopoly rights. The king's sources of revenue having been significantly cut by Parliament, the monarchs granted several monopolies to raise their income.[146]

Of the policies that did contribute to promote manufacturing, the Navigation Acts was probably the most innovative of the times. The Navigation Acts sought to keep foreigners out of the colonial trade by decreeing that all goods transported to and from English colonies had to be carried by English ships. It was fundamentally aimed at the Dutch, who by then had the supremacy in the carrying trade. This clash of interests soon led to war with the Netherlands in 1665 and again 1672.[147] By the mid-17th century, the Netherlands and England were the most economically developed nations in Europe. The Dutch had endorsed a similar policy and most experts and policy makers in England were convinced that rapid growth of international trade was determinant for prosperity. Spain and Portugal had enacted similar policies earlier, but they had not pushed the matter to its ultimate consequences.

Although the Navigation Acts did not directly target manufacturing (trade is not, in itself, determinant for the growth of this sector), they did cause more funds to be channeled into manufacturing because the expansion of trade required an expansion of the merchant fleet. Not only did the government decree tax incentives, grants, cheap financing, and subsidized raw materials for the fabrication of commercial ships, but it also undertook activities of industrial spying. Up to the first half of the 17th century, the Dutch possessed the most advanced technology for fabricating merchant ships. By the middle of the century, the English government ordered the capture of Dutch bulk freighters to dismantle and reverse-engineer on them in order to copy each part of the vessel. English investment in commercial shipbuilding during the second half of the 17th century was more enthusiastic than the one of the Netherlands. By the turn of the century, the shipyards of England were as efficient and technically advanced as the Dutch yards.[148]

The second half of the 17th century was also characterized by an intensification of large-scale war for England and by a significant rise in the fabrication of arms. During the first half of the century, England had lost military, economic, and political terrain to other European

---

144 Holderness: Ibid., p. 113.
145 Hill, C. P.: *British Economic and Social History*, p. 35.
146 Jack, Sybil: *Trade and Industry in Tudor and Stuart England*, p. 112.
147 Coleman, D. C.: *The Economy of England 1415–1750*, p. 185–187.
148 Holderness: Ibid., p. 100.

nations and during the second half, London tried to make up for the lost ground. During this period, the desire to be the supreme military and economic power in the continent took once again center stage and military and civilian manufacturing was promoted considerably more than at any other previous moment in the country's history.

This change in attitude coincided with an expansion of factory output, and agriculture, services, construction, mining, forestry, fishing, trade and technology grew faster than in the 16th century.[149]

During the second half of the 17th century there was also much deregulation and de-monopolization of the economy, which undoubtedly helped to increase productivity. However, the correlation between manufacturing and growth during the 17th century and the preceding history is so tight that it seems to be the main factor explaining the situation in that period. Over the long term, deregulation did not correlate consistently with growth, in England or in other nations of the world.[150]

As during all of the preceding centuries, the great majority of inventions during the 17th century were directly linked to manufacturing. The vast majority of inventors were men closely in touch with factory production and not theorists such as Newton or Descartes. Few inventions were founded upon a proper understanding of the scientific principles involved. The bulk of discoveries were simply the result of trial and error efforts undertaken in manufacturing establishments. In the preceding centuries, the same was observed. Since the Paleolithic Period, technology had tended to be created without the slightest understanding of the scientific principles involved. Human beings simply undertook fabrication efforts that aimed to satisfy some need and as they invested and labored on them, out of the manufacturing effort sprang a new technology. That is how stone tools, metals, the wheel, the printing press, and most other technologies were created.

It is as well worth noting that in England and the rest of Europe during the 17th, technology made the most progress in the fields that received the most subsidies, such as metallurgy, weapons, shipbuilding, and textiles.[151]

Of the nations in Europe, England was the most enthusiastic promoter of manufacturing and it was the country which experienced the fastest pace of technological change. A correlation is also found among the two halves of this century. During the first fifty years about 150 patents were registered while during the second half, when there was much stronger support, there were more than 250.[152]

The first scientific organization in the world appeared in the nation most recognized for manufacturing development. The Royal Society of Science saw its birth in England in 1662 and it established its offices in the city with the greatest factory output, London.[153]

All domains of the economy showed a strong correlation with the factory sector. Among the large nations of Europe, England subsidized this sector most energetically and the fastest growth of primary sector activities occurred in this country. Support in England was

---

149 Clarke & Slack: Ibid., p. 110.
150 Musson: Ibid., p. 29, 57.
151 Holderness: Ibid., p. 111.
152 Deane, Phyllis: *The First Industrial Revolution*, p. 135.
153 Musson: Ibid., p. 72.

much stronger during the second half of the century and the production of primary goods was also much faster during this period.[154]

As in the past, the expansion of agriculture was the result of productivity increases and of an enlargement of the land under cultivation. On both of these fronts, manufactured goods were the main agents delivering the expansion. Tillage was until the late 16th century concentrated upon the most moisture-retentive and fertile soils. With the advent of superior construction metal tools, in the 17th century, it became possible to build more sophisticated irrigation systems that converted previously unused land into arable land. At the same time, better plows and harvesters allowed for an increase in output per acre.[155]

Farm output rose faster than ever before in England in 1650–99, notwithstanding a rise in defense expenditures that subtracted resources from agriculture and notwithstanding low grain prices. The same goes for all other domains of the economy, which grew much faster in the second half.[156]

During the 17th century as well as in the preceding centuries, commerce required little fixed capital and had the fastest turnover. With those characteristics, trade was inevitably the most attractive business venture. Conversely shipbuilding, and more particularly the production of bulk freighters, was perhaps the most investment-intensive activity. It was also the one that took the longest to deliver a profit. With those characteristics, it was almost impossible to expect the private sector to undertake such a perilous venture.[157]

The case of England was not the exception but the rule. Elsewhere in Europe and the world, the same phenomenon held true. The large investments in shipbuilding in England during the second half of the 17th century were the result of government measures. The evidence suggests that without state subsidies, the private sector had not invested.

17th-century English businessmen also found public office more attractive than manufacturing. Successful businessmen were not averse to the profits of public office, which they sometimes purchased as an investment and exploited ruthlessly. This activity required few investments and provided a very fast return.[158]

Service sector activities during this century again mimicked the performance of manufacturing. Of the large states of Europe, England experienced the fastest development of services. In financial activities, England had no problem maintaining its leadership. English banks not only possessed the largest stock of capital, but they also utilized the most sophisticated banking methods. Holland was the only country in the continent to possess a slightly more developed financial system. Holland happened to be, together with England, the largest per capita producer of factory goods in Europe.[159]

The causation of this phenomenon seems to have been the following: the larger government allocations for manufacturing accelerated the pace of wealth creation, which increased savings. The financial assets of banks thus increased and banking transactions multiplied, which led to a faster development of the financial sector.

154 Clarkson: Ibid., p. 23–27.

155 Holderness: Ibid., p. 46.

156 Jones, E. L. (ed): *Agriculture and Economic Growth in England 1650–1815*, p. 159.

157 Grassby, Richard: *The Business Community of Seventeenth Century England*, p. 82.

158 Ibid., p. 229.

159 Floud, Roderick & McCloskey, Donald (ed): *The Economic History of Britain since 1700 Vol. I*, p. 151.

England also took the lead in developing social welfare. Social welfare is only possible when society has achieved a certain level of wealth that covers the minimum needs of a significant share of the population, leaving a surplus that allows for redistribution to the worst off. The first social welfare legislation of significance was enacted in 1600. The Poor Law provided a safety net of some sort for the people of lowest income. The state took further measures throughout the century to mitigate poverty, in particular during the second half (which was, by the way, when manufacturing expanded the fastest).[160]

Germany

The 17th century has come to be seen by many historians as a period of economic crisis in Europe. The first half was a period of economic slowdown, stagnation and even recession for most of the continent, although the second part saw more prosperous times. Even though the average GDP rate for the whole century was largely the same as in the 16th century, Europeans had come to nourish high expectations for the future. The spurt in economic activity during the 16th century had led many to believe that the economy would perform even better in the following years. When it did not, Europe became despondent.

Much suggests that the lack of continued rapid growth was due to a lack of stepped up factory subsidization. The majority of European monarchs in the 17th were not ambitious, driving men and wars did not grow in scale. Rates of factory output remained largely the same as in the preceding century.[161]

Of the large nations in Europe, France attained the second fastest rate of growth and the second fastest rate of manufacturing production. France engaged in more large-scale wars with its strong neighbor, England, than any other country, and was thus under more pressure than any other nation to invest significantly in manufacturing. However, given France's demographic superiority, French rulers concluded that they did not have to invest as much as the English did in armaments.

The mobilization of resources for war was more noticeable during the second half of the century. That was accompanied by faster economic growth. In 1665, the mercantilist comptroller-general of finance under Louis XIV, Jean Baptist Colbert, increased budgetary allocations for military and civilian manufacturing. Louis XIV was among the strongest rulers of the time and he had a powerful desire for territorial expansion. This required not only more weapons and ships, but also more civilian goods of all sorts. Then too, the English had aggressively developed their navy, and this enabled them to impose tighter trade blockades. France had to substitute imports more and more.[162]

Germany, still divided into some 2,400 mini states, continued to percolate in an environment of small-scale warfare which inhibited the nation from channeling resources into manufacturing. Even without political unity, each of the German states could have set policies in support of civilian manufacturing, but they had other things on their minds. Throughout history, governments have rarely undertaken to support civilian manufacturing unless there was ultimately a military reason, and Germany was no exception to the rule.[163]

---

160 Duroselle, Jean-Baptiste: *L'Europe—Histoire de ses peuples*, p. 217–226.
161 Parker, Geoffrey (ed): *The General Crisis of the Seventeenth Century.*
162 "The End Is Near", *Far Eastern Economic Review*, 23 February 1995, p. 49.
163 Bramsted, Ernest: *Germany*, p.76.

Germany fell into the worst war of its entire history, the Thirty Years War, from 1618 to 1648, a civil war pitching the Protestant northern states against the Catholic ones of the south. More than one third of the population lost their lives and the country was crippled. At the start of the conflict, there were about 20 million people and by the time it ended only about 13 million were left. (By comparison, 4% of the German population perished during the First World War and the 8% in the Second World War.)[164]

Although most Germans did not lose their lives on the battlefield but as a result of the epidemics and starvation that were exacerbated by the war, it was a tragedy of immense proportions. Still, it was a relatively low-intensity war, and required no major investments in manufacturing. The per capita investments in weapons were similar to those of the 16th century and investment in numerous civilian fields actually decreased.

From 1618 to 1630, the conflict was strictly a German internal affair but then foreign nations intervened. France and Sweden sided with the Protestants while Spain assisted the Catholics. The conflict grew in scale, but it was mostly the foreign powers that made the large investments in weapons and related goods. The arms used by Spanish, Swedish, and French troops were fabricated in Spain, Sweden, and France. The first half of the 17th century therefore witnessed a lower per capita output of factory goods and that coincided with a deteriorated economy. [165]

The Treaty of Westphalia in 1648 marked the end of the war and left Germany as fractured and divided as before. There was nonetheless a political reconfiguration and numerous states were consolidated into larger entities. The approximately 400 largest states of the pre-1618 period were regrouped into some 300 and the more than 2,000 mini states were reconfigured into some 1,500. The largest states emerged with increased sovereign powers and the smaller ones with less. The rest of the century witnessed numerous power struggles among the German princes, frequently in alliance with foreign powers, but the conflicts remained small in scale. In consequence, there was no compelling need to make major investments in armories. [166]

In the mid-17th century, however, London adopted a new trade policy. English policy makers became convinced that a favorable trade balance was fundamental for the well being of the country and endorsed a policy of export promotion. Since the most exportable goods were manufactures, more subsidies were supplied to this sector. As the most developed nation in Europe, England inspired admiration and its policies were followed by most other governments. German princes began to practice mercantilism, giving some importance to factory exports. More subsidies were supplied to civilian manufactures such as textiles. The greater overall subsidization of manufacturing in the second half of the 17th century went hand in hand with an increase in the per capita output of factory goods and a recovery of the German economy. [167]

The recovery, however, was less pronounced than in England, which was also emerging from a civil war. English policy makers were more motivated in promoting the sector. Germany was terribly depopulated after 1648 and most German states gave priority to repopulation efforts. Tax exemptions were given to people who settled on deserted farms and

164 Ibid., p. 84, 77.
165 Holborn, Hajo: *A History of Modern Germany*, p. 305–324.
166 Gaxotte, Pierre: *Histoire de l'Allemagne*, p. 337–371.
167 Gagliardo, John: *Germany under the Old Regime 1600–1790*, p. 125, 136, 151.

subsidies were provided for the purchase of wood, seeds, and farm animals. Since farming was considered the only real source of wealth, the feudal aristocracy wanted to have an abundance of peasants at its disposal. Manufacturing was definitely on the back burner.

Factory subsidization in Germany was pretty much the same in the 17th century as it had been in the preceding century, and the rate of economic growth followed suit. Manufacturing grew by about 0.3% annually and the economy by about 0.2%. Agriculture also expanded at a similar pace as in the 16th century, averaging about 0.1% per year. (See tables in the appendix.) [168]

During the 17th century, German goods were noticeably inferior in quality to those produced in France, the Low Countries, and England. Many experts at the time attributed the inferior quality to German culture. However, history suggests that the fundamental variable determining levels of quality is the technology implemented in the production process. Since the evidence also suggests that technology is generated by the manufacturing sector and Germany had one of the slowest rates of manufacturing in Western Europe, it was inevitable that it had an inferior technology and the quality of its goods was inferior.

Such a thesis is strongly substantiated by the events of the 19th century. During this period, German governments promoted manufacturing more than most other governments in Europe and by the end of that century the quality of German goods was already on a par with the best in the continent.

Many academics have argued that the slow growth of Germany in the 17th century was the result of the poor economic environment that prevailed in Europe. The constant warring and the high trade barriers supposedly limited export possibilities. The wars and the tariffs obviously hindered trade, but that cannot explain what took place. Exports as a share of GDP were insignificant, if not irrelevant. Thus, the reduction of exports in the first half of the century could only have affected the economy marginally. [169]

Also worth noting is that, throughout the history of Germany, Europe, and the rest of the world, exogenous variables have proved only to have a marginal effect on the economy. In the 19th century, world trade increased greatly and some nations, such as those in North America and Western Europe, grew rapidly. Others, however, were stagnant. India became strongly linked to the international economy and increased exports exponentially. However, its economy was almost stagnant. North America and Western Europe strongly promoted manufacturing while there was a lack of such subsidies in India.

The events that led to the Thirty Years War demonstrate the terrible dangers that accompany policies that do not give investment priority to manufacturing. Prices increased dramatically in 16th-century Europe. Inflation was more pronounced in Western Europe, in particular in Spain, due to the large inflow of precious metals from the Americas. Since policies in support of manufacturing were weak, the vast majority of the silver and gold was used for non-manufacturing activities and a large share was deployed for speculation. Financial speculation in the second half of the century in Spain led to mass bankruptcies.

In Germany, inflation and financial speculation also increased in the 16th century and continued into the next century. The speculation eventually led to bankruptcies, which in

---

168 Rovan, Joseph: *Histoire de l'Allemagne—Des origines a nos jours*, p. 327–366; Sabillon, Carlos: *World Economic Historical Statistics*, p. 182; Madison, Angus: *The World Economy: Historical Statistics*.
169 Gagliardo: Ibid., p. 126.

the 1610s pushed the economy into recession. Living conditions deteriorated, people became more desperate, and they began to look for scapegoats to blame for the rising poverty. They easily found many in those who practiced a different religion. A revolt in Bohemia in 1618 of the protestant aristocracy against the ruling Catholics marked the beginning of the Thirty Years War. [170]

In the centuries that followed, repeated cases of financial speculation were usually followed by economic downturns. In those times hardly any banking regulations existed and governments allowed bankers a free hand to do as they thought best. Their risk-averse and quick-return instincts continuously led bankers to refuse to make loans to manufacturing and to prefer such activities as commerce, real state, and services of a speculative nature.

Standards of living in Germany during this century continued to be much lower than in England, Holland, and France. Every aspect of the German economy continued to lag behind. Rates of production in agriculture, mining, construction and services were slower, as well as levels of productivity and technological development. Support for factories was smaller than in these three countries. [171]

Russia

In other countries of the region, a somewhat similar pattern of events was observed. The 17th century in Russia was characterized by a noticeable increase in large-scale war as the tsars repeatedly launched military campaigns against neighboring nations. During this century, there was scarcely a year in which Russia was not at war with Sweden, Poland, the Ottoman Empire or the Baltic states. This led the government to deploy a larger share of the nation's resources for the fabrication of weapons and related goods.[172]

Russia had first come into contact with the English in the 16th century. Since then, trade exchanges increased rapidly and English exports were the source of much admiration and envy among the Russians. The majority of those exports were manufactures. Since the import capacity of the country was very limited, the tsars sought to produce the goods domestically. They also sought to attract foreign investment, in particular in high technology domains.

In this century, military and civilian manufactures grew faster than ever before. The acceleration in the rate of factory output coincided with a proportionate acceleration in the pace of economic activity. This sector seems to have grown by about 0.3% annually and the economy by about 0.2%. [173]

History has also recorded a considerable increase of investment in Russia during this period and the chronicles suggest that the rise in investment was fundamentally the result of government intervention. The tsars gave greater incentives to foreign and domestic entrepreneurs. Although they were not particularly aimed at manufacturing, they affected this sector due to the armament and technology-related goals of the state.

---

170 Clough : Ibid., p. 195–214.
171 Bramsted: Ibid., p. 85.
172 Parker, W. H.: *A Historical Geography of Russia*, p. 99.
173 Blackwell, William: *The Beginnings of Russian Industrialization*, p. 11; Sabillon: Ibid., p. 120; Madison, Angus: *The World Economy: A Millennial Perspective*; Madison, Angus: *The World Economy: Historical Statistics*.

The tsars, however, proved very impatient with the speed of domestic and foreign investment. They thus decided to finance, build, and operate numerous manufacturing establishments in fields where the private sector would not venture. The ultimate source of capital for large establishments during this century was the state. Prior to the 17th century, there were no large manufacturing establishments in Russia. Practically all of the large factories that appeared in that period were owned by the state. The firms that were created produced iron, copper, other metals, weapons, tools, machines, textiles, glass, books, processed salt, and liquor. [174]

This was not the first time the government had intervened directly in manufacturing. In the preceding centuries, the state had also created numerous firms in arms and related fields. This was a considerably different approach to that of the English Crown. In England, private companies were responsible for the vast majority of manufacturing output.

In the period up to the 16th century, state-owned Russian enterprises performed poorly compared to private sector companies, and the same was true in the 17th century. Had the state companies been privatized and run by entrepreneurs, perhaps the quality of the goods would have improved. However, if the rulers had not made the original investments in those manufacturing enterprises, the evidence suggests capitalists would never have made any investments at all. Up to the 17th century, the private sector tended mostly to store and hoard gold, jewels, and other forms of wealth. There was hardly any private sector allocation of capital to manufacturing and the little that was invested came fundamentally as a result of the incentives the government offered.

The experience of other countries as well as that of Russia in later centuries suggests that the Russian private sector could have invested dramatically more than the tsars did. That, however, would have required the government to increase the level of subsidies offered. [175]

The evidence suggests that investment is fundamentally determined by the level of government support for the manufacturing sector, independent of whether that support is oriented toward the private sector or the public sector. When it is oriented toward the private sector, investment is maximized and productivity is higher. However, the main avenue for increasing investment is the government's decision to allocate a larger share of a nation's resources to this sector. That would explain why investment increased in Russia during the 17th century and why it lagged behind that of Western Europe and in particular England.

Russian history as well as that of other nations has systematically showed that the general population has a strong preference for consumption at the expense of investment. Even sectors with relatively low investment demands, such as agriculture, mining, forestry, fishing, construction, and services, were systematically incapable of inspiring much investment desire from the population. For manufacturing, which had by far the largest investment requirements, the interest was practically non-existent.

Even the government, which did not function according to the same principles as households and private enterprises, was generally slow to make large investments. In order to generate more revenue, governments do not need to work harder, nor do they need to worry much about profitable return on investment. Governments need only to set higher taxes and

174 Blackwell: Ibid., p. 12.
175 Kirchner, Walter: *A History of Russia*, p. 65, 66.

increase borrowing. However, when it came to manufacturing, they have usually done this only under the pressure of war.

Governments also have the capacity to reallocate the budget, so that they can allot a larger share to manufacturing without raising taxes or increasing public debt. However, again, most rulers have done this only under the pressure of war.

In the 17th century, the pace of technological progress in Russia accelerated. Although technical advancements were coming along faster, the pace was still slower than that of Western Europe, where factories received more support. [176]

The advisers of the time, whether in Russia or in Europe, could not tell what it was that drove progress. In 1651 a Frenchman, Jean de Gron, submitted to Tsar Aleksei Mikhailovich a plan for the economic development of Russia. The key point of his scheme was the establishment of numerous shipbuilding enterprises to create a large merchant fleet capable of expanding commerce. This was the year the Navigation Acts were passed into law. Like many people in England and in Western Europe, De Gron was convinced that increasing trade was pivotal for attaining economic growth.

The Tsar and his advisors, however, never took this advice from de Gron seriously and did not establish shipyards. It was felt that it would be too hard to raise the necessary capital. It was also said that even if the funds could be found, it would be wasted because high quality ships would never be built. By then, Western Europe was considerably ahead in shipbuilding technology. On the one hand, the Russian government recognized its inferiority and saw no hope of ever overcoming it, and on the other, Western European merchants actively discouraged the Tsar from attempting to launch a catch-up effort. It was actually argued that, independent of the efforts made, the fabrication of high performance ships would never become a reality because the Russians were not endowed with particular qualities that were indispensable for such an enterprise. [177]

De Gron thought that trade was the engine of growth and that large-scale production of ships would inevitably increase commerce and thus overall economic activity. However, he also thought that shipbuilding in itself would stimulate the expansion of a number of related fields and thus the performance of the economy.

The numerous critics and detractors of the Frenchman's development plan argued as well that the economy would not be stimulated because it would not affect the vast majority of the population, who were serfs, with a very low income. They claimed that demand would remain weak and the possibility of expanding it would be very limited.

A few decades later, in 1689, Peter the Great became Tsar. Nothing had changed in Russia's position with respect to shipbuilding and the purchasing power of the bulk of the population remained low, but his irrepressible desire to expand Russia's territory and to match Western Europe in technology drove him to override orthodox arguments. Peter's maritime ambitions were vast (militarily and commercially) and he did not hesitate to abundantly promote shipbuilding. He created numerous state yards and offered ample incentives to entrepreneurs. In no time, the fabrication of ships increased by a very large margin and sometime later, Russia saw the birth of its first navy and its first merchant fleet. During those years, the technological quality of Russia's ships rose very rapidly until they became

---

176 Guroff, Gregory & Carstensen, Fred (ed): *Entrepreneurship in Imperial Russia and the Soviet Union*, p. 56.
177 Ibid., p. 30–33.

competitive with those of Western Europe. During the late Petrine years, Russia even began to export ships to Western Europe.

This was not the only field that witnessed tremendous progress to the point of matching the levels of Western Europe. Several others that achieved a similar feat happen to be the fields that received the most subsidies (arms and armament-related goods). Contrary to what most of the pundits had asserted, economic growth accelerated considerably and so did demand, across the board. [178]

This was once again a clear example of how the development of new fields depended on practically nothing more than the desire of the government to encourage and subsidize those fields. The Petrine years also made it evident that a considerable rise in support for manufacturing would automatically increase economic activity and demand, independent of the disposable income of the population. It was also shown that, irrespective of the large investments that manufacturing requires, it is possible to raise the necessary capital to finance such investments.

In the 17th century and in particular during the years of Peter the Great, trade increased considerably. Foreign and domestic trade both rose, notwithstanding the intensification of warfare and the fact that an extraordinary share of resources was being wasted producing arms. Once again, only the manufacturing thesis can explain such a paradox. [179]

During this century, Russia noticeably improved its infrastructure, following a significant rise in the output of construction manufactures.[180]

The phenomenon seems to have unfolded as follows. Larger factory subsidies delivered faster growth of technology, which allowed for quicker production of building instruments and machines. At the same time, these goods embodied a higher level of technology, which allowed the construction of more and better roads, bridges and ports. The technology that originated in the armament factories spilled over to the other fields such as the factories producing construction equipment. The machines that created the new weapons were adapted for the production of shovels and pickaxes. The technology created to reduce the cost of metal production for arms was used to reduce costs for the metal parts of construction equipment.

In Russia during the 17th century, as well as earlier, practically the only development policy had been to foster agriculture. Famines in those times were so regular and malnutrition so endemic that governments saw the production of food as the fundamental goal of the state. However, during all of the preceding centuries, these policies had failed to liberate the nation from hunger and during the 17th century they failed again. The century actually opened with a terrible famine (1601–04), followed by several more in the ensuing decades.

Even so, the famines were less frequent and less widespread than in previous centuries, due to improved agricultural production. It may be hard to understand how farm output increased at a time when war was on the march. This same paradox was observed in Europe and in other regions of the world. A larger share of the economy was used to make weapons, and at the same time a larger share of the population was diverted away from farming and into the army. However, if it is assumed that manufacturing is the fundamental variable responsible for the generation of technology, the paradox is resolved.

---

178 Ibid., p. 36, 37.
179 Kellenbenz, Herman: *The Rise of the European Economy*, p. 159, 165.
180 Blackwell: Ibid., p. 13–15.

It seems that the larger investments that flowed into manufacturing accelerated the pace of technological development and the new technology soon found civilian uses. Some of these technologies improved farm implements, which enhanced agricultural productivity.

China

During the 17th century, China once again experienced slower economic growth than most countries of Western Europe and this coincided with a slower rate of manufacturing output. The Chinese government provided fewer subsidies to the sector than most governments of Western Europe.[181]

While most nations of Western Europe were engaged in ongoing large-scale wars, China had only to deal with peasant rebellions (one of which put an end to the Ming Dynasty), and pirate activity along the coast. But these events never managed to force the government into making large investments in weaponry because the intensity of the fighting was relatively low. The government very easily could have decreed massive investments into civilian manufacturing, but did not. There was little motivation to channel resources into military manufacturing and there was no spontaneous private sector investment into civilian manufacturing.[182]

During the first half century, the economy was largely stagnant and perhaps even contracted a little. Later, the economy grew fairly strongly.

The Ming Dynasty started to crumble in the beginning of the 17th century. The reigns of Wanli (1572-1620) and his successors were characterized by reduced investments in weapons and civilian craft production. With the Mongol threat gone and the Mings not interested in conquest, state expenditures in armaments and related goods fell significantly. The economy stalled. Per capita farm output decreased and famines spread, leading to peasant rebellions which progressively expanded in size until the dynasty was toppled in 1644.[183]

It is argued that China's defense of Korea against Japan in the 1590s exhausted China's fiscal resources, inhibiting investment in infrastructure and agriculture in the following decades. This supposedly caused economic decline. Such an interpretation, however, is not consistent with the evidence of the preceding centuries and millennia in which increased war expenditures programmatically coincided with an improvement of the economy. The fact is that Japan's invasion of the mainland was the first in more than a thousand years and Chinese forces easily managed to block their advance. The Japanese soon withdrew and this event only caused minor expenditures for the whole first half of the 17th.

The advent of the Manchu Dynasty in 1644 brought to the helm a line of more ambitious rulers. The first thing they did was to make larger investments in weapons to suppress the numerous rebellions throughout the country. Then, they built larger armories to fulfill their plans of territorial expansion.[184]

An energetic Manchu chief named Nurgaci and his son Hongtaiji consolidated power among the tribes of Manchuria in the early 17th century. They then launched a large-scale conquest effort over all of China and in 1644 they overthrew the last Ming emperor. After

181 Lombard, Denys: *La Chine Imperiale*, p. 112–115.
182 *The Cambridge History of China Vol. VII*, p. 490–496.
183 *The Cambridge Encyclopedia of China*, p. 202, 212.
184 Lombard: Ibid., p. 104–106.

the capital was taken, many Ming generals retreated to the provinces and continued to wage war against the Manchus. Rebellions in the southwest prevailed until the early 18th century. It was only in 1730 that the Manchus defeated all opposing forces.[185]

The Manchus had also other security threats. Since the 15th century, there had been increasing contact between China and Russia and increasing military clashes as well. The Manchus were determined not to let the Russians take away the land that they had acquired from the Ming. In 1685, the Chinese defeated the Russians at Albazin. Kangxi (1662-1722) wanted to extend the borders of his empire beyond the territory the Mings had ruled. In 1696, he led an army with artillery of Western design to meet the Mongols. The battle of Urga put an end to the nomadic domination of frontier wars in which cavalry charges had been invincible for two millennia. Large territories were acquired in the northwest. [186]

To subdue the Ming and the rebellions that followed as well as the Russians and conquer Mongol land, the Manchus needed larger arsenals. There were also the increasing contacts with Europeans in the 17th century which confronted the Manchus with the superior power of European armaments.

The first trade contact between England and China took place in 1637 when five English ships, having been refused permission to trade, shot their way into port and forced the authorities to accept them. The inferiority of Chinese weapons revealed by this show of force drove the Manchu rulers to allocate more resources to develop better guns.

The Manchu emperors were also interested in promoting civilian manufacturing. The new trade contacts with English merchants and other Europeans revealed the superior goods of the West. Most of these goods were manufactures, especially textiles. The emperors of 1650–99 decided to subsidize civilian manufacturing to a greater extent. [187]

The stronger factory support of the second half of the 17th century was accompanied by a larger per capita output of factory goods and faster economic growth. The per capita output of agriculture and the other primary activities, as well as commerce, construction, and services, increased substantially. Advances were made in science and technology. Population growth accelerated, as did urbanization. Education began to spread and so did social evolution.[188]

Barter increased during the first half of the century; in the second it decreased as money came into wider use. Throughout China's history, the use of money fluctuated in tandem with the amount of support given to manufacturing. The evidence suggests that the causation of the phenomenon was the following: when governments increased factory subsidies, the pace of output of goods and services accelerated. This created a more specialized economy and a larger base of trading activity that needed a common unit of exchange. Under Ming rule, taxes were collected in kind while under Manchu rule they were collected in silver. Despite the ups and downs of both dynasties, the Manchu Dynasty offered larger per capita factory subsidies and experienced faster GDP growth.

The land tax was the main source of government revenue during both dynasties. In the second half of the 17th century, agriculture was taxed more heavily but farm output grew

185 Nanquin, Susan & Rawski, Evelyn: *Chinese Society in the Eighteenth Century*, p. 4–6.
186 Huang, Ray: *China—A Macro History*, p. 187, 189.
187 Gray, Jack: *Rebellions and Revolutions*, p. 1.
188 Chang, Chun-shu & Chang, Hsueh-lun: *Crisis and Transformation in Seventeenth Century China*, p. 1.

faster. This was under a government that devoted a much larger share of revenues to subsidize manufacturing. Throughout history, Chinese governments believed that taxing agriculture lightly translated into greater farm output; there is not much evidence that that was the case. However, whenever farm taxes rose and larger resources were allocated to manufacturing, farm output grew faster.

It has been argued that the agricultural growth of the second half of the 17th century resulted from the introduction of new crops from the Americas such as maize, potatoes, and peanuts, which could be cultivated in marginal land such as steep hills and sandy soils; this supposedly increased the usable land and thus increased output. In reality, new crops from the Americas had been introduced since the 16th century but it was only in the mid-17th century, coincident with the increased production of better farm implements, that they were produced in any volume.

Others have argued that farm output increased because more agricultural land became available as a result of conquest. However, during Ming rule vast tracts of uncultivated fertile land were still available. In the first half of the 17th century, land that had been under cultivation was even abandoned. Only the manufacturing thesis can explain such a situation.[189]

Despite the improved farm output, famines continued to afflict China in the second half century. Hunger was endemic. The government offered tax exemptions and grants to farmers in the form of money or goods such as oxen, seeds, and tools. These were practically the only developmental efforts made by the government. Agricultural output grew at a very slow pace. Making agriculture an investment priority was evidently a failure, but policy makers were convinced that it was the only option.

The famines, however, were not distributed evenly throughout the century. They were considerably worse during the first half of the 17th century, when support for manufacturing was lower. In this period, the population was reportedly driven to acts of infanticide, slavery, and cannibalism. [190]

The United States of America

Across the Pacific Ocean, the situation was similar. The 17th century witnessed the birth of a nation that in a relatively small amount of time would not only become the largest economy in the world, but also the most developed.

In 1492 Columbus discovered the Americas. One year later, by means of the Treaty of Tordesillas, the Pope divided the new territory between Spain and Portugal. At first, England showed practically no interest in the new lands. The Spanish kings, on the other hand, undertook the most enthusiastic efforts of exploration. In 1519-21, Cortes conquered the Aztec Empire and in 1532-35 Pizarro overwhelmed the Inca Empire. In 1515, Spain began exploration of southern North America.

England and France feared they were missing out on an important opportunity, so they sent expeditions to explore the northern parts starting in 1525. These expeditions lasted until 1585. The English made a small effort to establish a settlement but it failed. In 1565 the Spaniards built a fort in Florida, which caused some alarm in London, but English monarchs

189 Nanquin & Rawski: Ibid., p. 22, 23.
190 *The Cambridge History of China Vol. VII*, p. 615–632.

continued to show little interest in America. From 1585 to 1598, London's foreign policy concentrated on colonizing Ireland. [191]

By the early 17th century, in what would later become the United States, there were only about one million Indians. Notwithstanding the vast and plentiful territory, famines and malnutrition were endemic and considerably more regular than in Europe, Russia or China. Life expectancy was also significantly lower and everyday life revolved almost exclusively around getting food. [192]

There was a complete lack of support for what we call manufacturing. The Indians were still at the Neolithic stage of development. Their tools were few, simple, and fabricated mostly from stone and wood. They could till only the most easily workable land and were almost completely dependent on natural resources. Most of the Indian population lived east of the Mississippi River, where rainfall, forests, and wild game were abundant.

The indigenous peoples of what later became known as Latin America had by then achieved a considerably higher level of development, which correlated with a higher per capita output of manufactures. Population density was higher and this engendered more disputes over land. The higher incidence of war forced the natives of the south to devote more resources to weapons and related manufactures, and they attained a higher level of technological development. [193]

By the early 17th century, London was not particularly interested in acquiring land in America, but it was not against private companies undertaking such a venture. The first permanent English colony in North America appeared in 1607 and was founded by the Virginia Company, which set up camp in what is now Jamestown, Virginia. At the outset of the colonizing venture, living conditions were terribly harsh. At a certain point, the settlement endured starvation. Other colonies had sprouted along the East Coast and they also endured famine.[194]

Despite having encouraged the foundation of settlements, London remained largely uninterested and the colonists were pretty much on their own. The first intervention from the Crown was actually to regulate exports and restrain the economic liberties of the colonies. In 1621, it forbade tobacco growers to export to anywhere but England. In 1624, when the Virginia Company went bankrupt, the Crown converted the settlement into a royal colony. Other private settlements that were established along the coast during the 17th century went bankrupt and the English government stepped in and converted them into colonies. Although London became the holder of these territories unintentionally, it eventually began to see some value in this expansion and progressively centralized its power over them. [195]

The food supply and living conditions improved noticeably as the 17th century moved along, but hunger and malnutrition continued to harass the colonists, notwithstanding the vastness of the territory and the abundance of natural resources. An analysis of the policies of this period goes a long way to explain why hunger was so widespread.

The English Crown had decreed a mercantilist system of production since the very beginning of the colonizing venture. In this system, the range of economic options was clearly

191 Yarnell, Allen (ed): *The American People—Creating a Nation and Society*, p. 1–29.
192 Chester, Wright: *Economic History of the United States*, p. 30.
193 Ibid., p. 31–33.
194 North, Douglas: *The Growth of the American Economy to 1860*, p. 33–49.
195 Yarnell: Ibid., p. 79.

defined. England concentrated on manufacturing and its overseas territories were to supply raw materials. The system had three aspects. The colonial market absorbed manufactures produced by the metropolis. It could not import manufactures from other nations and it could not engage in the production of practically any factory good that was produced by England. Before London took over the territories, private companies had the liberty to endorse whatever policies they saw fit, but all were convinced that the only way to make a profit was by exploiting raw materials. [196]

There was of course, practically speaking, no manufacturing production in the North American colonies during this period, and certainly no government subsidies for manufacturing. Practically the only form of manufacturing was that at the household level, which was used fundamentally for household consumption. Household production is the most primitive form of manufacturing.

The system in which an investor provides raw materials to artisans working in small workshops and later collects and sells the final product was largely absent. Workshop manufacturing is only possible when the overall level of production has reached a level much higher than that of the household. This type of production is nonetheless very primitive in comparison to the factory system, which only became widespread in the 19th century. [197]

Since the colonists did not produce many farm implements, they could not do much to increase the output per acre. Nor could they enlarge the amount of land under cultivation. The low production of manufactures also inhibited the colonies from exporting significantly. As a result, they could not earn the foreign exchange needed to import large amounts of farm implements. The land was vast and richly endowed with natural resources; but without manufactures, exploiting it was nearly impossible.

England had determined to make the colonies large producers of primary goods, but so long these policies remained in place, the colonies never became major producers. Only a few items like tobacco, cotton, sugar cane, and fish were exported in the 17th century (and not in large quantities). Production of primary goods was so low that it could not even meet the small domestic demand. [198]

Only in the 19th century did agriculture and the other primary activities grow rapidly. By then, government policies had stopped suppressing manufacturing and were on the contrary strongly promoting it.

Despite the growing intervention of London, its financial participation remained extremely slight. The Crown also sent few officials and troops to inspect and enforce its ordinances. So indifferent was the Crown and so weak the economic relationship that by the late 17th century the American colonies had less influence in London than any other part of the empire. Indian raids on the settlements were common but London did little to help. The colonists also received no imperial protection from French-inspired Indian attacks. Occasionally, the Crown sent armed contingents to fight the Indians, as in the 1670s, but most of the time it did not intervene. [199]

196 Adams, D. K.: *America in the 20th Century*, p. 2–9.
197 Faulkner, Harold: *Histoire Economique des Etas Unis d'Amérique Vol. I*, p. 81.
198 North: Ibid., p. 53.
199 Greene, Jack & Pole, J. R. (ed): *The Blackwell Encyclopedia of the American Revolution*, p. 11, 17, 18.

The colonists therefore took things in their own hands and colonial assemblies were largely responsible for deciding economic policy. They allocated a share of resources for the fabrication of weapons and related goods. The first successful iron furnace, which was built in Massachusetts in 1644, was financed by the local government.

Most colonists had left England because they wanted a better material life and more personal liberty. Once in America, they found their living conditions were much worse. They needed the types of factory goods available in England, so they undertook efforts to produce those goods. Since household production was insufficient, colonial assemblies offered incentives to people who would undertake production on a larger scale.

Up to 1650, the colonists traded freely with the Dutch and other Europeans. Then London passed the first of the Navigation Acts, in 1660 the second, and in 1696 the last one. These Acts required that only English or colonial ships conduct trade among England and its colonies. [200]

While these laws were not well enforced, they did restrict trade. This drove the colonists to allocate resources for shipbuilding, for otherwise they would have been excluded from foreign trade, which was seen as the most lucrative business. The rocky soils of New England were not very suitable for agriculture but they were endowed with vast hardwood forests, and this region soon became the main producer of sailing vessels. It also processed trees into pitch, tar, turpentine, and other related goods. Shipbuilding developed so fast that by 1660 England began purchasing ships made in Boston. [201]

Manufacturing in general and not just shipbuilding began since the early 17th century to grow faster in that region. Economists and historians have concluded that this region had a comparative advantage in manufactures, but the fact is that factory subsidies were more abundant in New England than anywhere else. The scarcity of good soil in that region forced the colonists to seek an alternative, but if the colonial assemblies of the southern colonies (which had ample fertile soil) had supplied a similar amount of subsidies for factory production, this sector would have grown just as fast. History suggests that geography, climate, and other such variables do not play much of a role in the rate of manufacturing output. The only variable that seems to matter is the level of government support for this sector and policy makers can freely decide the level they want.

During this century manufacturing grew faster in the Northeast, correlating with the territory with the highest per capita income. This geographic distribution of manufacturing continued until the 19th century and until then the fastest growing region was the Northeast.

Soon after the arrival of the first English settlers, African slaves were imported into the colonies. The first shipload of slaves arrived in Virginia in 1619, but it was only in the late 17th century that unskilled plantation labor began to be significantly replaced by African slaves. Most Africans were put to work in the large plantations of the Southeast. Those using slave labor thought it gave them an economic advantage, but if so, that region should have grown faster. That was not the case. Despite the harsher climate, in the Northeast economic growth during the 17th century was noticeably faster. [202]

---

200 Yarnell: Ibid.
201 Porter, Glenn (ed): *Encyclopedia of American Economic History Vol. 1*, p. 38, 39.
202 Krout, John: *The United States to 1877*, p. 13, 14.

Despite London's lack of interest in the colonies, it did gradually allocate more resources for manufacturing. The Crown would have preferred to keep the colonists captive to English producers, but other concerns such as national security led it to increase subsidies. The subsidies were nonetheless very small in comparison to those it supplied in England.

In the colonies, the local assemblies could have easily defied London's mercantilist laws and given more support to factories. However, they too were convinced that agriculture was the only sector that really deserved to be promoted.

Much suggests that before the Europeans arrived in North America, the economy was completely stagnant. In the 17th century, factory production accelerated greatly, but only along the northeast coast. Manufacturing for the whole territory that would later comprise the US probably grew by about 0.1% per year and the economy by about the same pace. Agriculture expanded at a slightly slower pace after remaining stagnant in the preceding centuries. (See tables in the appendix.) [203]

Japan

Ambitious Japanese rulers in the late 16th century succeeded in subduing the large majority of the independent states that had prevailed in the preceding centuries. In 1603, at the battle of Sekigahara, Ieyasu Tokugawa crushed his rivals and completed the unification of the archipelago. His rule lasted only until his death in 1616, but the dynasty he founded lasted until 1868.

Ieyasu's hold on power and that of his successors in the 17th century was tenuous. Numerous princes challenged their authority and there was a constant threat that the archipelago would again fragment into hundreds of independent states. [204]

Tokugawa rule over Japan was not the same as the control exercised by the typical ruling dynasty in China. Tokugawa rulers never managed to force the various states to relinquish their sovereignty. In the 17th century, they presided over a semi-centralized system of feudal rule consisting of more than two hundred fiefs subordinated to a single military government headquartered in Edo (later Tokyo). Heading the government was a military commander (Shogun) whose personal fief was by far the largest, accounting for about half of the island of Honshu or a fifth of the whole archipelago. The rest of Japan was only partially subjugated by the Shogun and his control over it was so tenuous that the central government could not directly levy taxes in it. [205]

The threat of insurrection and disintegration of central authority impelled the Shoguns of the 17th century to invest heavily in weapons production. They followed a policy of intimidation, building up vast arsenals relative to those of the daimyos, or regional rulers. In the 17th century, there were no internal or external wars but in order to consolidate power they diverted a large share of resources into the production of arms. As had occurred elsewhere, increased weapons production carried with it larger investments in civilian manufacturing because several fields were directly or indirectly associated with weapons.

203 Sabillon: Ibid., p. 147; Fogel, Robert William: *The Escape from Hunger and Premature Death, 1700–2100: Europe, America and the Third World*; Madison, Angus: *The World Economy: A Millennial Perspective*; Madison, Angus: *The World Economy: Historical Statistics*.
204 *The Cambridge Encyclopedia of Japan*, p. 61.
205 Bix, Herbert: *Peasant Protest in Japan 1590–1884*, p. xxv.

The rapid development of the future Tokyo during this century is an example of how military concerns can lead policy makers to invest more in civilian production. In the late 16th century, Edo was a small collection of fishing communities. Ieyasu Tokugawa head-quartered his government there. To succeed in ruling over the rest of Japan, he not only had to possess a large army but also an impressive capital that would project force. It also had to become a city that could self-supply in the event it was surrounded by enemy troops. Tokugawa therefore gave subsidies to all fields of civilian production, but gave preference to those in high technology, for they brought the most prestige.

Tokugawa and his successors (who continued this policy) subsidized agriculture and construction in particular. However, compared to the past, subsidies for manufacturing also went up substantially. By the end of the 17th century, Edo was the largest city in the world, with more than a million people.

Kyoto and Osaka were also under the direct control of the Shogun and were supplied with ample factory subsidies. They too grew quickly. By the 1690s, each had about 600,000 people — more than Paris. These two became the largest producers of silk and brocade textiles in the archipelago, as well as sake, seed oil, and other factory goods. [206]

In heavy fields like weapons, metals, and the machines that produced them, the government mostly created state factories, while in civilian fields it supplied subsidies to the private sector in the form of land concessions and tax exemptions. In those times, land was considered the most valuable asset. There were also grants in the form of money or inputs for production such as subsidized raw material and tools.

Through direct allocations and incentives, the government deployed a larger share of the archipelago's resources to boost manufacturing; this generated new levels of per capita output of factory goods and a higher rate of economic growth. In the 17th century, this sector apparently grew by about 0.3% annually and the economy by about 0.2%. [207]

Agriculture also grew faster than ever before and the much higher per capita availability of food reduced mortality. The population grew by about 0.2% annually and the number of Japanese almost doubled during the course of the century. By 1700, there were about 30 million. Rural–urban migration accelerated and commerce also grew much faster.

In the early 17th century, foreign trade grew rapidly and Japanese merchants extended their activities to regions never visited before, such as Southeast Asia. In the 1630s, however, the government adopted a policy of commercial seclusion and foreign trade largely came to an end. Even so, domestic trade for the rest of the century continued to grow. [208]

In 1549 a Portuguese Jesuit introduced Catholicism and sometime later Franciscan and Dominican missionaries arrived to spread their gospel. They converted many Japanese and began to interfere in politics. Some revolts even had Christian underpinnings, driving Shinto and Buddhist priests to become much opposed to the new religion. On the other hand, European traders also tended to interfere in domestic politics in order to obtain favorable trading concessions. Because of its connections with missionary activity and foreign political influence, Tokugawa shoguns regarded overseas trade as destabilizing. On top of that,

---

206 *The Cambridge Encyclopedia of Japan*, p. 69–71.
207 Smith, Thomas: *Native Sources of Japanese Industrialization 1750–1920*, p. 3; Sabillon: Ibid., p. 112; Madison, Angus: *The World Economy: Historical Statistics*; Madison, Angus: *The World Economy: A Millennial Perspective*.
208 Macpherson, W. J. (ed): *The Industrialization of Japan*, p. 21.

the ruling class had for centuries seen commerce as a parasitic endeavor and assumed that only farming created wealth. In 1614 all the missionaries were expelled and in 1639 an edict ended trade with Europe. Europeans were excluded, with the exception of the Dutch who were allowed a small trading post in a small island. [209]

Foreign trade and a liberal trade policy are seen by mainstream economics as fundamental variables for economic growth. The Japan of the 17th century, however, disproves such a view. For most of this century, Edo followed a policy of seclusion far more severe than the typical policy of trade protection. Still, the economy grew faster than ever before. The evidence suggests that the overall economic growth was spurred by the increased support for manufacturing. [210]

The belief that agriculture is the only true source of wealth is also incompatible with the facts. Given the constant famines, it is no wonder that people were obsessed with food production. The fact that the bulk of the population worked the land and that the farm tax was the main source of government revenue reinforced such a view. The economy apparently rested on rice. Policy makers believed that larger investments in agriculture and lower taxes for this sector translated into higher farm output. However, during the 17th century, agriculture was taxed more than before (it is estimated that about half of the harvest was taken as taxes). On top of that, a smaller share of government revenue was used to subsidize farming. Nevertheless, agricultural output accelerated and the per capita supply of food was higher. [211]

Land under cultivation increased and output per acre also rose. That coincided with a larger per capita production of farm tools such as plows and harvesters. The evidence suggests that it was manufacturing that generated the wealth, not agriculture *per se*.

Other events that also appear paradoxical can only be explained by the manufacturing thesis. The policies of the Tokugawa Shoguns during the 17th century were designed to reverse the growing contacts with the outside world of the preceding century. They wanted a stable (static) society with as little change as possible. However, there were major social and economic changes. Peasants migrated to the cities in unprecedented numbers, the population grew faster than before, and the division of labor was accentuated as numerous new occupations emerged. The use of money grew more than ever before, prices fluctuated, inflation appeared, and currency crises made their debut. Western ideas were propagated for the first time and traditions were not enforced so rigorously.[212]

China experienced the same phenomenon in the second half of the 17th century. An increase in support for manufacturing was accompanied by a loosening of traditions.

---

209 Susuki, Tessa: *A History of Japanese Economic Thought*, p. 9.
210 *The Cambridge Encyclopedia of Japan*, p. 63.
211 Bix: Ibid., p. 20.
212 Suzuki: Ibid., p. 7–11.

Chapter 4. The 18th Century

Orthodox Interpretations of the Causes of Economic Growth in Britain

The pace of history quickened in the 18th century. Economic growth accelerated sharply for the first time — still slow by today's standards, but fast enough to deliver noticeable changes in people's lives. The spurt in growth actually took place only at the very end of the century and only in Britain, but this acceleration would be soon experienced in numerous other countries.

By the standards of the late 19th century in North America and more still by those of East Asia during the late 20th century, Britain's growth rates during the late 18th century was feeble. (See tables at the end of the book.) However, the new economic dynamism was so radically different than anything previously experienced that the phenomenon ended up sparking a revolution.

Every single aspect of society experienced radical changes during those times and living conditions improved noticeably, but the causes of the changes were even more significant than the effects. Most economic historians have concluded that numerous factors were responsible for this revolution, including agricultural surpluses, sudden population growth, a rapid expansion of trade, the rapid growth of new territories under colonial rule, and abundant natural resources. Political stability, liberal economic policies, the drive of dissenters, the technological creativity of inventors, and the entrepreneurial energy of businessmen were also supposed to have contributed to the growth of the economy.[213]

Many have argued that agriculture was the main factor driving the economy, not just during the latter part of the century but throughout the whole period. The British economy had been expanding since the early 18th century at an unprecedented pace. Supporters of the agriculture argument claim that as this sector began to be modernized it delivered considerable productivity improvements, which increased farm output. This created surpluses,

---

213 Musson, A. E.: *The Growth of British Industry*, p. 75.

which delivered the capital necessary for much larger investments in other economic sectors. It has also been asserted that the higher agricultural incomes drove up demand for non-agricultural goods, thus boosting production in other sectors.[214]

It is held that the modernization of agriculture was the result of enclosure, the enlargement of farms, the adoption of new methods of agriculture, and the introduction of new crops. However, all of these variables were present during the 16th and 17th centuries and yet economic growth did not leap forward. The share of enclosed land increased from 45% of the total in 1500 to 71% in 1700, but by 1800 it had only risen to about 85%. Enclosure during the 18th century did not precede any faster than during the previous centuries and the spurt of economic growth in the later part of the century was not concomitant with an acceleration of enclosing activity.[215]

The size of farms did grow, but size, whether for agriculture or any other sector, is not a basic factor in the rate of output. New agricultural methods and new crops were introduced only slightly faster than during the previous centuries and there was no particular increase during the "spurt" years later in the century.

The four variables that were supposedly responsible for the modernization of agriculture did not increase in proportion with the increase in farm output, especially during the late 18th century. It is also worth noting that during the first half of the 17th century, more and more land was under enclosure, farm size continued to grow, new crops were introduced, and new methods of farm production continued to be adopted. But England's agriculture performed worse than during the previous half century.[216]

The argument stating that improved agricultural production delivered surpluses that allowed for more investment in the rest of the economy is also questionable. Agriculture in Britain for most of this century (1700–79) grew at an average annual rate of about 0.5%, and the population expanded at exactly the same pace. For surpluses to have occurred, agriculture would have had to grow faster than the population. Note also that in the decades preceding the spurt in growth (1760–79), agriculture did not even keep pace with population growth. It expanded by about 0.1% annually, while population grew by 0.5%. This represents a per capita agricultural deficit, not a surplus. It is also hard to see why the economy continued to grow at the same pace as before. The economy grew at practically the same pace in 1760–79 as it had in 1700–59. During the boom decades (1780–99) there was once again a deficit on the side of agriculture, for this domain expanded annually by about 0.8% while population grew by about 0.9%. (See tables at the end of the book.)[217]

If agriculture were the most important variable determining growth, or at least one of the most important, the economy should have slowed noticeably during the years 1760–79. However, the economy grew more than six times faster than agriculture. Even if the population had grown more slowly than agricultural output, with the almost stagnant rates of farming, it is impossible to see how agriculture could have propelled the rest of the economy.

---

214 Wrigley, E.: *Continuity, Chance and Change*, p. 35.
215 Floud, Roderick & McCloskey, Donald (ed): *The Economic History of Britain since 1700 Vol. I*, p. 98, 99.
216 Hill, C. P.: *British Economic and Social History*, p. 14, 12.
217 Floud, Roderick & McCloskey, Donald (ed): *The Economic History of Britain since 1700 Vol. II*, p. 2.

Farm output did accelerate considerably during the last two decades of the 18th century and many have argued that the acceleration pulled with it the rest of the economy. For agriculture to have pulled along the economy, we would expect it to have expanded at a much faster pace than the economy as a whole. That, however, was not the case. In 1780–99, agriculture averaged about 0.8% growth annually while the economy grew by about 1.4%. In 1700–79, evidence of a pulling effect was also absent. All this time agriculture grew slower than the rest of the economy. While farm output averaged about 0.5% growth annually, GDP expanded by about 0.7%.[218]

It has also been claimed that rising agricultural incomes were fundamentally responsible for the rise in demand for non-agricultural goods, but the evidence shows that during the 18th century, consumption of manufactures by farmers increased by about one third while manufacturing production increased more than three-fold. It was the urban economy and export markets what absorbed the bulk of factory goods.[219]

In the 18th century, Britain experienced by far its fastest rate of population growth up to that date. Population grew by about 0.6% annually while during the 17th century the rate had been just 0.2%. Many have concluded that the population boom was responsible for the acceleration of the economy. This idea seemed to be bolstered by the fact that the population expanded by about 1.4% in the 19th century, coinciding with even faster economic growth.

However, during the 20th century, the population averaged only a 0.5% increase, and the economy did not even show signs of weakness. During the 20th century, the British economy accelerated again and grew by about 3.0% annually, compared with 2.7% in the 19th century and 0.8% in the 18th century. During the 20th century the population grew more slowly than in the 18th century, but the economy grew four times faster than in the 18th. The evidence suggests there is no relationship of causality between population and growth.[220]

Many analysts have identified trade as the main, or one of the main, variables determining economic growth during the 18th century. Trade expanded dramatically during this period. It is argued that trade grew faster because of growing demand from abroad, in particular the North American colonies. Exports to North America did indeed increase, but the evidence indicates that the bulk of British production was consumed in Britain and not abroad. In this century, foreign trade accounted for about 20% of GDP. Since it represented a minor share of the economy, it is highly unlikely that trade could have acted as the driving force.[221]

If colonial trade had driven the acceleration of the economy, it is very hard to see why, during the war of American Independence (1775–83) and during the Napoleonic Wars (1793–1815) the British economy performed so well. In those years, trade with the US dried up or was severely hindered. If British exports to North America had been a very impor-

218 Floud & McCloskey (ed): Vol. I, 1994, p. 47.
219 Ibid., p. 119.
220 Chambers, J. D.: *Population, Economy and Society in Pre-Industrial England*, p. 10, 19; Sabillon, Carlos: *World Economic Historical Statistics*, p. 182; Fogel, Robert William: *The Escape from Hunger and Premature Death, 1700–2100: Europe, America and the Third World*; Madison, Angus: *The World Economy: Historical Statistics*.
221 Musson: Ibid., p. 61, 62.

tant factor, the British economy should at least have slowed down. The economy actually improved.[222]

During the boom in the last two decades of the 18th century, Britain no longer possessed the US as a colony and no longer possessed the exclusive right to trade with them. Then, in 1793, war with France significantly disrupted the Atlantic trade and trade with Europe, effectively stopping exports. Yet it was at this precise moment that the British economy surpassed all previous growth records. [223]

The evidence indicates that it was not trade with the colonies which spurred the expansion of the economy and neither was it trade in itself. Aside from the Napoleonic Wars, during the 18th century Britain engaged in three other wars with France and during each of those conflicts there were embargoes and blockades which significantly hampered trade. The economy, however, grew at an unprecedented rate. More important still is that in the years after the conflicts, there were recessions or economic slowdowns. The return to a situation in which trade was no longer obstructed should have brought economic prosperity, but the opposite occurred. [224]

It has also been said that trade liberalization was responsible for the rise in commercial activity, which propelled the economy. The evidence contradicts such a view. Most export duties were abolished in 1722 but that was largely counterbalanced by the erection of import barriers early in the century; this left the trade regime fundamentally unchanged. On average during the 18th century the trade regime remained significantly distorted and very similar to that of the 17th century. Had British commercial policy played a major role in determining the rate of trade and GDP growth, the performance of both should have remained basically unaltered. The fact is that both expanded much faster in the 18th century than in the preceding one hundred years. [225]

There are also claims that generous investment in infrastructure during the 18th century delivered a transport revolution that lowered costs and expanded the possibilities for trade. There was indeed a higher level of investment in roads, ports and canals, and investment increased even more during the later part of the century. However, it is also a fact that Britain had among the worst roads in Western Europe and its ports were regularly congested. [226]

If infrastructure played an important role in economic growth, it is hard to understand why other Western European nations that had a better infrastructure were not able to perform better. It seems more likely that the growth of roads and canals was one of the many effects of economic growth, and not the cause. [227]

Others have asserted that it was the exploitation of the colonies with their vast natural resources what provided the capital for more investment in Britain. The British Empire grew in size during this century and its colonies were as well exploited more intensively. However, the British economy soared during the late 18th century and investment did likewise, yet that was precisely when it lost its most productive colonial possession. Had the exploi-

222 Bogart, Ernest & Kemmerer, Donald: *Economic History of the American People*, p. 339, 341.
223 Floud & McCloskey (ed): *Vol. I*, p. 182, 188, 191.
224 Holderness, B. A.: *Pre-Industrial England*, p. 4, 5.
225 Coleman, D. C.: *The Economy of England 1415–1750*, p. 188.
226 Musson: Ibid., p. 70.
227 Deane, Phyllis: *The First Industrial Revolution*, p. 77, 79.

tation of colonies accounted for a noticeable share of the growth equation, Britain should have performed worse during the later part of that period. [228]

Britain triumphed in the War of Spanish Succession, and in 1713 Spain was forced to yield the monopoly of the African slave trade. African slaves had been introduced into British colonies since the 17th and since the early 18th their numbers grew. It has been argued that the exploitation of their labor financed Britain's higher rates of investment. Of all the colonies, slave labor was utilized most in the US. Britain lost this colony in 1776. If slave labor was largely responsible for the financing of investment, Britain should not have attained its best GDP rates at a time when it had lost its biggest contingent of slaves. It is as well worth noting that when Spain was exploiting the slave trade during the 16th and 17th centuries, its economic growth was regularly slower than that of England. Portugal was actually the first to trade Africans as slaves, in the 15th century, and continued using them in its colonies until the 19th century. Portugal, however, had one of the worst economic performances in Western Europe during all that time. From the historical evidence, it could be concluded that slavery hindered growth. [229]

Another argument puts the emphasis on natural resources. It is held that England was endowed with abundant natural resources which were essential for the development of the economy. But the two fastest growing fields in that century were textiles and iron. Cotton rapidly displaced wool as the main raw material for textile-making; and both cotton and iron ore (for the most part) had to be imported. [230]

Others have actually inverted the argument and stated that the lack of natural resources forced Britain to be highly inventive. That would fail to explain why, during the 19th century, the US managed to outperform Britain although it did enjoy an abundance of natural resources. The US not only grew much faster but also produced more inventions.

Political stability has also been posited as partially responsible for the improved economic performance. But Britain was as politically stable during the 16th century as during the 18th century, yet the economy did not perform as well. It is worth noticing that George III (1738–1820), who ruled during the late 18th century, experienced intermittent bouts of madness that caused political paralysis. However, the economy instead of deteriorating actually improved. \[231]

In 1702, 1757, 1769 and 1773 Parliament passed legislation liberalizing the economy. This has led many to conclude that liberalization significantly contributed to accelerate growth. Numerous regulations constraining business were phased out and monopolies were eliminated, which current economic thinking certainly considers positive steps, but if that had had a major effect on growth then the economy would not have slowed in the second half of the 19th century. During 1850–99, Britain renounced protectionism, adopted a free trade policy, and liberalized other areas of the economy. However, GDP grew slower than in 1800–49.[232]

During the 18th century, Britain had the fastest rate of technological development in the world and many claimed that British culture was responsible. The British were said to be

228 Floud & McCloskey (ed): *Vol. I*, p. 48, 183.
229 Krout, John: *The United States to 1877*, p. 32.
230 Floud & McCloskey (ed): *Vol. I*, p. 31.
231 Duroselle, Jean-Baptiste: *L'Europe—Histoire de ses peuples*, p. 245–260.
232 Musson: *Ibid.*, p. 73.

more inventive than the people of other nations. If that had been true, the pace of invention should have held steady over time. It did not. Innovations burst forth in the later part of the 18th century and in the last two decades more patents were registered than during the whole period 1500–1750.[233]

Britain was indeed the most inventive nation from the 16th to the 18th century, but during the 19th century (in particular the second half) it was outperformed by several nations. This suggests that the technological lead from the 16th to the 18th century was not the result of some trait determined by culture, genetics, climatic conditions or anything of the sort. This became even more evident in the 20th century, for Britain was once again outperformed technologically and economically by an even larger number of nations.

It has also been asserted that the British were more entrepreneurial than anybody else, and that this higher enthusiasm for business was largely responsible for their economic success in the 18th century. But in the next two centuries Britain was outperformed by several other nations, nations which in the 18th century were seen as lacking entrepreneurial drive. Since the late 19th century analysts actually began to argue that Britain had "lost" its entrepreneurial drive, even though earlier it had been posited that entrepreneurial drive was determined by culture, not short-term influences. If the ability to succeed in business has any effect on economic growth, then it is only a marginal one. [234]

It was also claimed that Protestantism had a stimulating effect on the economy, for it drove the population to work harder, to save more, and to invest more. If that had been true, the northern part of Germany should have been at the lead of development since the 16th century, for it was there that Protestantism was born. However, northern Germany lagged behind most of Western Europe from the 16th to the mid-19th century. Note also that from the 16th century onwards, Belgium and Holland showed almost the same rates of economic growth, even though Belgium remained Catholic and only Holland embraced Protestantism. More damning still for this argument is the case of Luxembourg. In 1800–1999, Catholic Luxembourg attained the fastest GDP figures in all of Europe. [235]

The vast majority of economic historians do not believe that any of these variables alone was responsible for the boom in the British economy. Although many believe that one or several were essential for growth, it is frequently asserted that it was the concomitant effect of all of them that delivered the improved performance. However, even that theory does not add up.

For example, conditions in Britain were much the same in the late 17th century as in the late 18th century: farming was modernized through the use of enclosure, the enlargement of farms, the use of new methods and new crops. The population grew, commerce expanded, and London promoted exports. It also had colonies, and it enjoyed the same stock of natural resources as it did a century later. It had political stability and it liberalized the economy. During the period 1650–99 it was also just as Protestant, as entrepreneurial, and as potentially inventive as it was a century later.

While some of these variables were less pronounced during the first period, others were more accentuated. On average, both periods were very similar. Yet only in 1750–99 did it experience a sharply faster rate of growth.

---

233 Deane: Ibid., p. 135, 136.
234 Ibid., p. 124.
235 Hobsbaum, E. J.: *Industry and Empire*, p. 23.

A Non-Orthodox Interpretation of the Causes of Growth

Unlike orthodox explanations, the manufacturing thesis adds up. The 18th century was a period in which large-scale war in Europe increased considerably. The size of the wars and the resources that they absorbed were much greater than those of previous times. Conflicts progressively grew in size and defense expenditures as a share of GDP kept expanding.

During this century, Britain poured more into the effort to acquire military and economic supremacy than any other country. It was Britain that most promoted the production of armaments and related civilian goods. That coincided with the highest rates of manufacturing and GDP growth in the world.

The enlargement of wars found its expression in several ways. There was an increase in the number of weapons per person. On average, each soldier carried more arms than in the past and on top of that, the number of men in the Armed Forces as a share of the total male population rose considerably. Britain engaged in five major wars during this century and weapons became progressively larger and more technologically sophisticated. [236]

This was largely the result of the internationalization of war, which brought into the fray a larger number of nations. The first war of the century, which took place from 1702–13, was fought among Britain, France, Spain and Holland. That of 1756–63 involved practically all of Western Europe and was fought in lands as far away as India, North America, and the Caribbean. The last war of the century started in 1793 and extended up to 1815, ensnarling nations from Western Europe, Eastern Europe, and Russia. [237]

To finance all this, the British government raised taxes. Government revenue increased four-fold during the years 1660–1740 and in the rest of the 18th century it rose even more. The budget expanded, especially in the area of defense expenditure (which was a very large item even in times of peace — during the peaceful years from 1729–38, defense as a share of government expenditure accounted for about 42%). [238]

The British government also borrowed considerably. During the 16th and 17th centuries, central government expenditure as a share of GDP was about 2%. During the 18th century, it rose to 3%. The much larger revenues of the state were partially utilized to supply more incentives to private manufacturers. Fiscal, financial, and non-financial incentives to manufacturing entrepreneurs as a share of company output were much higher than in the past. [239]

A great number of state factories were also created, although the bulk of output continued to come from private firms. During times of war, state factories proliferated; and war was frequent.

Unlike France, Britain was prepared to subordinate all of foreign policy to its economic ends. And unlike the Dutch, its aims were not dominated by commercial and financial interests but were increasingly shaped by manufacturers.

British policy in the 18th century was aggressive across the board. Its per capita production of iron was almost three times that of France and that output was consumed mostly by the army and the navy. The navy's tonnage increased almost five-fold. [240]

---

236 Coleman: Ibid., p. 189.
237 Dukes, Paul: *A History of Europe 1648–1948—The Arrival, The Rise, The Fall*, p. 69–212.
238 Coleman: Ibid., p. 195.
239 Jack, Sybil: *Trade and Industry in Tudor and Stuart England*, p. 47.
240 Hobsbawn: Ibid., p. 33, 34, 52.

Britain's military and economic ambitions were intrinsically linked with the desire to increase the size of its colonies. London believed that colonies were essential for the well-being of a nation because they provided cheap raw materials and secure export markets. Its biggest success in this period was the conquest of Canada. The government did not wage war and colonize for the benefit of manufacturers, but that was one consequence of its policies.[241]

During the 18th century, mercantilist policies of the mid-17th century remained in place. The government sought to maintain a favorable trade balance by promoting exports and substituting imports. Since the bulk of exports and imports were manufactures, the subsidies mostly favored this sector. During the 18th century, factory goods accounted for about 84% of British exports and textiles for about 75% of those manufactures.

In the 18th century, the scale of war, the desire to be the supreme economic power, and the fixation with trade surpluses only grew. That went hand in hand with a GDP rate that progressively accelerated. From 1700–59, manufacturing expanded on average by about 0.7% annually; from 1760–79 by about 1.3%; and from 1780–99 by 2.0%.[242]

Manufacturing could be responsible for the generation of growth only if this sector is intrinsically linked to the process of technology creation; and history indicates the existence of such a linkage. Throughout the 18th century, technology moved in tandem with manufacturing: the pace of innovation paralleled the sector's rate of output. Registered patents increased faster during the period 1700–59 than in the preceding century. They accelerated more during 1760–79 and grew still faster during 1780–99.

Most technological advances were embodied in factory goods. Practically all patents were directly linked to goods such as the steam engine, chlorine bleaching chemicals, synthetic soda, silk throwing machines, loom machines, combing machines, and improved equipment for metal-smelting, weapon-making, glass-making, pottery, and paper-production. It is also a fact that the majority of inventors were craftsmen. The famous Scotsman James Watt, who revolutionized the world with the first efficient steam engine, was a leading industrialist. The vast majority of inventions were made in manufacturing enterprises.[243]

Scientific societies were most widespread in Britain than anywhere else and Britain attained the fastest factory growth in the world. The number of scientists, technologists, and engineers also grew fastest in Britain. [244]

In the long term, technology is the fundamental variable determining productivity. Throughout history, fast technological growth has coincided with fast productivity growth. If manufacturing is the prime creator of technology, a correlation between levels of support for this sector and productivity should exist. The historical evidence confirms such an assumption.

In the years 1700–59, productivity growth in Britain averaged annually about 0.2%. Factory subsidies were increased in 1760–79 and productivity growth went up to about 0.4%. In 1780–99, support increased even more, factory output accelerated, and productivity grew by about 0.8% per year. [245]

---

241 Ibid., p. 33.
242 Ibid., p. 47, 13, 17.
243 Deane: Ibid., p. 135, 136; Needham, Joseph: *Clerks and Craftsmen in China and the West*, p. 163.
244 Musson: Ibid., p. 65, 73, 71.
245 Floud & McCloskey (ed): *Vol. II*, p. 8.

Manufacturing is the factor best capable of explaining why during the 18th century, technology, trade, agriculture, and the other sectors of the economy went up despite the intensification of war.

Manufacturing is also the only sector that could have propelled the economy, for it was the only one that grew faster than the economy at large. In this century, GDP averaged about 0.8% annually while agriculture averaged just 0.5%. Manufacturing, on the other hand, grew by about 1.1%. [246]

The manufacturing variable is also the only one capable of explaining why, during the period 1760–79, when agricultural production was stagnant as a result of numerous bad harvests, the economy continued to grow relatively strongly.

The development of agriculture and the other sectors, and the means by which this development took place, also reveal a strong link with manufacturing. The 18th century in Britain witnessed the invention of more agricultural tools than ever before. Farm devices were not only produced faster, but the technology of these tools developed at a faster speed. The first seed drill was produced in 1700; in 1730 the Rotherham triangular plow was patented. The first threshing machines appeared in the 1780s and throughout the whole period there were numerous improvements in hand-harvesting tools.

As in the past, larger investments in manufacturing, even if directed to the fabrication of weapons, created new technology that soon found its application in civilian uses. Iron was mostly produced for military use and production costs were significantly lowered in this period. As a result, iron became a cost-effective material for other products. The iron content of agricultural tools increased, making them stronger and more durable. The same improved machine tools that created new weapons also produced better plows, harvesters, and the like. During this century, Britain had the highest crop yields in Europe and it was also the largest producer of farm tools.[247]

Also during the 18th century, British trade increased faster than ever before. Exports as a share of GDP accounted for about 8% in 1700 and by 1800 they had grown to about 16%. That was a paradox considering the spread of war. To make matters worse, by the last quarter of the century Britain had even lost its exclusive trading rights with the United States.

Such a contradiction can only be explained by the manufacturing variable. The evidence suggests that the larger subsidies created new technology and thus new goods. As a result of the larger supply of goods, trading activity increased, even with all of the impediments that prevailed. An example of how innovation enhanced commerce is found in shipbuilding. As investments poured into the making of warships, the metal content of ships grew, making vessels more sea-worthy and larger. In 1787 the first warship made wholly of iron was launched. Some years later, the first commercial vessels made wholly of metal appeared and transport possibilities multiplied.

As with ships and agricultural tools, the metal content of other goods also went up and their performance improved. Construction tools were increasingly made of iron. This translated into better infrastructure works that improved the means to conduct trade. [248]

In matters of investment the 18th century was much like the preceding centuries. The private sector was focused on trade, and more particularly short-term trade, which had the

246 Floud & McCloskey (ed): *Vol. I*, p. 47, 45.
247 Deane: Ibid., p. 31, 39.
248 Hill: Ibid., p. 29, 30.

lowest investment requirements and the shortest turnover time. Without government in-centives, private banks refused to provide financing for long-term capital projects (most of which were in manufacturing). They mostly confined themselves to more liquid short-term credit. In this period commercial banks flourished, but they never showed interest in manufacturing.

The evidence suggests that entrepreneurs only showed interest in manufacturing when the state offered subsidies. Without the grants, the risks were simply too high. In the 18th century, factory subsidies were larger as a share of GDP and investment as a share of GDP was larger as well. The levels of investment fluctuated with the levels of subsidization. Sup-port was strongest in the late 18th century and it was then that Britain experienced the highest levels of investment. Investment as a share of GDP averaged about 4% from 1700–59. From 1760–79 it was about 6% and from 1780–99 it averaged about 9%. [249]

During the 18th century, there was much change in the political configuration of the British Isles. In 1707, Scotland was merged with England by the Act of Union, and the two territories together with Wales became known as Great Britain. Ireland, which had been conquered by England in the early 17th century, remained outside of the union. [250]

Before the union with England, Scotland had lagged behind its southern neighbor, and Ireland was similarly underdeveloped. Since the union, however, the factory promotion policies of England were transplanted to Scotland and were even expanded, as the Scots were determined to catch up. Ireland, which was treated as a colony, was ordered to apply policies promoting agriculture. Furthermore, Scotland's clergy enthusiastically supported material progress, whereas the religious view promoted in Ireland held that striving to boost development was tantamount to contesting the will of God. [251]

As soon as Scotland applied the new policies, the economy went into high gear. Ireland continued to limp along. Scotland's support of manufacturing, stronger than even England's, resulted in faster GDP growth than in England. Ireland's economy did not spurt, even in agriculture, while Scotland— despite having transferred resources from the primary sec-tor to manufacturing — experienced an agricultural revolution. Of the three, Scotland at-tained the fastest rates of factory output and the fastest rates of agriculture, trade, GDP, and technology.

Scotland endorsed numerous factory promotion policies, not least the fostering of for-eign direct investment, most of which came from England. Although English firms originally dominated high technology fields, they were eventually matched and even superseded by Scottish firms. That went hand in hand with Scotland's larger subsidies. Scottish factories rapidly caught up in methods of production. By the late 18th century, Scotland had devel-oped superior technology in fields such as cotton processing machines and steam engines. Ireland, on the other hand, continued to rely almost exclusively on English technology.

During the 18th century, population grew faster in Scotland than in England and many have suggested that that contributed to the acceleration of economic growth. However, Ire-

---

249 Musson: Ibid., p. 65, 67, 64, 69.
250 Cullen, L. & Smout, T. (ed): *Comparative Aspects of Scottish and Irish Economic and Social History 1600–1900*, p. 3.
251 L. Devine & D. Dickson (ed): *Ireland and Scotland 1600–1850*, p. 12, 20, 21, 15, 16.

land's population was growing even faster but its economy performed poorly. Where the population argument fails to explain, manufacturing succeeds very well. [252]

When Britain lost its most precious colonial possession (the US) in 1776, it redoubled its support for civilian manufacturing, thinking that without the raw materials from the US, producing textiles and other goods would become harder.

Most important still was the question of war. Britain had recently fought several wars with France and most policy makers had come to believe that a future conflict was inevitable. France's involvement in the American Revolution had reinforced this idea. Policy makers were convinced that the next war would be larger and harder to win. More was invested in military manufacturing from the 1780s onward, and when the war did break out in 1793, an even larger defense budget was approved. Factory output picked up speed in the 1780s and with more so in the 1790s. [253]

Continental Europe and Germany

During the 18th century, France provided the second largest subsidies to factories in Europe. Its geographic proximity brought her into constant conflict with Britain. This forced the French governments to try to match not just the arms of its adversary but also its civilian goods. However, France saw an advantage in possessing a larger population and a larger territory than Britain, and was not as convinced of the need to invest heavily in the military. The French were less driven by the idea of becoming the supreme military and economic power of the continent. Only during the reign of Louis XIV did France have a very ambitious ruler, but his reign ended in the early 18th. During the rest of that century, there was an absence of strong-willed monarchs and the main concern of the revolutionary leaders in the 1790s was not military and economic strength.

Although less driven then London, during the 18th century Paris supplied the second largest factory subsidies in Europe. That went hand in hand with the second fastest rate of manufacturing and the second fastest rate of economic growth. France was the first country in continental Europe to turn to the factory system. Britain pioneered the system in the mid-18th century and France followed suit a few decades later. The factory system, currently the most developed form of manufacturing, is only possible when this sector has attained a relatively high level of development. [254]

In Germany events followed a similar path, although much more slowly. Germany was still fragmented among some 1,800 states and its wars wee events compared to those of Britain and France. There were plenty of conflicts, but the vast majority were small and local, absorbing only a small amount of resources for weaponry and related goods. That went hand in hand with slower GDP figures. [255]

By Germany's own standards in comparison to the previous centuries, there was nevertheless a noticeable growth in the scale of war. Prussia was the largest of the German states and during this period several of its rulers launched major military campaigns. In particular Frederick William I (1713-40) and more still Frederick the Great (1740–86) boosted invest-

252 Ibid., p. 16, 19.
253 Floud & McCloskey (ed): *Vol. I*, p. 49, 96, 36.
254 Hill: Ibid., p. 23–27.
255 Mann, Golo: *The History of Germany since 1789*, p. 5–7.

ment in armament production. Frederick the Great presided over the fastest military expansion, and he seized Silesia and parts of Poland. [256]

France increasingly interfered in Germany during the 18th century and its superior weaponry pressured its neighbors into more military spending. Paris also supplied aid to the German states that were its allies and some of that money was used to promote manufacturing.

In the western and southern states, the scale of war also increased, although not as much as in Prussia. However, proximity to more developed nations such as France, Belgium, Switzerland and the Netherlands inspired these states to emulate the superior civilian manufactures that those countries produced. Government support for civilian manufacturing was thus higher than in the eastern states. [257]

In general, all the states by now were providing larger subsidies for civilian manufacturing in tune with the policy of mercantilism, which had become accepted throughout Europe. Colbert-style support for fields such as textiles, paper, refined sugar, glass, metals, porcelain, watches, carpets, tapestries, mirrors, hats, jewelry, processed tobacco, processed coffee, chocolate and toys, fostered the development of these industries. However, the German states were competing mostly among themselves, and not with France or Britain, which induced them to smaller promotion efforts. August the Strong of Saxony was the first to promote the fabrication of porcelain in the mid-18th century and soon after most other German princes did likewise. Porcelain, however, had been fabricated in some areas of Western Europe since the late Middle Ages. [258]

It was the investment-intensive and high-risk nature of manufacturing that inhibited the private sector from investing in it. The high start-up costs systematically scared off capitalists, even in fields where demand was strong. The first cotton spinning factories appeared in the 1780s, only after state governments provided considerable funds to buy the machinery from Britain. The state governments also financed the costs of smuggling the machines out of Britain because in those times, London prohibited their export. The private sector was even more reluctant to invest in heavy manufacturing. Iron and machine tool production was largely in state hands.

For civilian fields in light manufacturing, the governments provided tax exemptions, grants, land concessions, monopoly rights, and subsidized financing. State banks were founded in Prussia, Bavaria, Austria, and in several other German states. The governments ordered these banks to lend to manufacturing as private banks continued to abstain. Other subsidizing mechanisms consisted in forcing people to consume factory goods. Frederick the Great required Jews upon marriage to buy porcelain from the Berlin government factory. In the 18th century, most factories were in private hands but the vast majority of them owed their existence to government subsidies, just as in the preceding centuries. [259]

The large increase in support for manufacturing coincided with a noticeable acceleration in economic growth. During the 18th century, manufacturing in what we now call Germany seems to have expanded by about 0.6% annually. The economy grew by about 0.4%. This was twice as fast as in the preceding century but it was only about half as fast as Britain.

256 Pinson, Roppel : *Modern Germany*, p. 6.
257 Gaxotte, Pierre: *Histoire de l'Allemagne*, p. 403.
258 Clough, Shepard : *European Economic History—The Economic Development of Western Civilization*, p. 219–234.
259 Gagliardo, John: *Germany under the Old Regime 1600–1790*, p. 140–142, 147

The growth gap with its western neighbors increased, with effects that were immediately felt. In 1700, the German states were the largest producer of iron in the world but by 1790 Britain, France, and Russia had all surpassed them. [260]

Improved manufacturing output coincided with faster development of technology, and faster growth in agriculture and the other sectors. Productivity increased dramatically. Crop yields rose and most of the improvements in agriculture were directly associated with the new and more abundant tools, instruments, and devices that appeared. German farms were still far less productive than those in England, where farm implements were more advanced. [261]

In this century, Germany continued to endure trade deficits and it continued to be a net importer of capital. Its greatest trade imbalances were with Britain, France, the Low Countries, and Switzerland. These were also the main sources of investment capital, as had been the case in the previous centuries. However, a century later the situation had changed completely. By the late 19th century, Germany began to achieve trade surpluses with the rest of the world and it also became a net exporter of capital. This continued during the 20th century. [262]

This suggests that deficits in the trade and capital balance are not the result of culture or of some other immutable variable, as was thought in those times. Up to the 18th century, German governments subsidized the factory sector less than most of its main trading partners. However, since the 19th century they began to promote it more. Several countries in Europe, North America, and Asia have experienced the same pattern: so long as they supported manufacturing less than their main economic partners, they endured trade and capital account deficits, but when they offered more subsidies, the imbalances were overturned.

The evidence suggests that factory subsidies are the bottom line for determining trade balances. The causation of the phenomenon seems to be the following: ample subsidies deliver faster production growth and thus an abundance of exportable goods. Under those circumstances, trade surpluses are easy to attain and foreign exchange reserves grow rapidly. Then foreign loans are no longer needed because there is enough domestic capital to finance investment. As wealth accumulates, the country eventually may become a net creditor.

Russia

Russia shows some parallels. During the 18th century, Russia engaged in wars of a larger scale than ever before, and at the same time launched ambitious programs aimed at catching up with the most advanced nations in Europe.

Russia launched military campaigns in practically every direction, and confronted armies larger than their previous foes. The enemies also had more weapons per soldier which were more technologically sophisticated. Moscow was thus driven to match its adversaries, and channeled larger investments into the military. [263]

260 Ogilvie, Sheilagh (ed): *Germany—A New Social and Economic History Vol. 2*, p. 265; Sabillon: Ibid., p. 182; Madison, Angus: *The World Economy: Historical Statistics*; Fogel: Ibid.
261 Kitchen, Martin: *The Political Economy of Germany 1815–1914*, p. 26, 28; Gaxotte: Ibid., p. 389–402.
262 Gagliardo: Ibid., p. 150.
263 Dobb, Maurice: *Soviet Economic Development since 1917*, p. 55.

Trade increased considerably and the increased import of Western goods exposed more clearly the huge developmental gap with nations such as Britain and France. The desire to attain parity called for investment in civilian factory goods such as textiles, glass, porcelain, arts and crafts, metals, farm implements, ships, and machine tools, which accounted for the largest share of imports. [264]

Thus support for manufacturing as a whole was stepped up in the 18th century. This went hand in hand with faster economic growth, faster technological development, faster expansion of trade, and a swifter growth of productivity. Manufacturing appears to have grown by about 0.7% per year, the economy by about 0.5%, and agriculture by 0.3%. [265]

The tsars launched military campaigns against Turkey, the Ukraine, Poland, the Baltic states, and Sweden. Huge territories were conquered, of which the largest were the Ukraine, parts of Poland, and parts of the Ottoman Empire. The century opened up with the reign of Peter the Great, who was the most enthusiastic Russian conqueror of all times and the most anxious to catch up with the West. To finance his plans he raised taxes, borrowed in much larger amounts, confiscated Church assets, raised tariffs, and restructured the budget. [266]

Peter wanted more and better weapons, more and better civilian goods, a large navy, and a large merchant fleet. To promote these ends he supplied to the private sector free land for plant construction, tax exemptions, grants, and subsidized loans. He also guaranteed government purchases at prices that assured a profit, erected trade barriers, provided monopoly rights, and reduced labor costs by supplying business owners with prisoners of war, convicts, soldiers, and by institutionalizing serfdom in the factory. [267]

The private sector immediately began to increase its investments but did not increase them as fast as Peter wanted, so he decided to invest directly. At the start of his reign there were about 15 large manufacturing establishments in all of Russia and by the time the Tsar died in 1725, there were over 200 with a workforce of about 250 each. [268]

Before 1710, all large manufacturing establishments were state owned, but in that year Peter began a program of privatization for he was dissatisfied with the low productivity of state companies. By the end of his rule, about half had been turned over to entrepreneurs. Once they were privatized, costs were cut and quality improved.

It is worth noting that the privatization program encountered resistance from the private sector. Given the high maintenance costs of such large establishments, Russian capitalists were reluctant to take over the factories and the Tsar was obliged to provide incentives.

The reluctance of the private sector to invest in manufacturing varied in direct proportion to the level of investment required for each venture. Entrepreneurs were always less interested in heavy manufacturing than in light manufacturing. The government had to offer a strong dose of subsidies to get anyone to invest in textiles, glass, porcelain, and even liquor. When it came to iron, weapons and ships, still greater incentives were needed. Seeking to spark development in the Urals as well as to boost iron production, Peter decided to site a metallurgical complex near large coal and iron ore deposits found there. However, this

---

264 Kerblay, Basile: *Modern Soviet Society*, p. 171–173.
265 *The Cambridge Economic History of Europe Vol. VII*, p. 433, 448; Sabillon: Ibid., p. 120; Madison, Angus: *The World Economy: Historical Statistics; Madison, Angus: The World Economy: A Millennial Perspective*; Fogel: Ibid.
266 Kirchner, Walter: *A History of Russia*, p. 86–95.
267 Blackwell, William: *The Beginnings of Russian Industrialization*, p. 16–22.
268 Parker, W. H.: *A Historical Geography of Russia*, p. 114.

was frontier land hundreds of miles away from Moscow, meaning a vast increase in the costs and the risks associated with the project. No one wanted to put his money into such a scheme.[269]

Fiscal incentives include tax exemptions or tax reductions. Financial incentives include grants and subsidized loans. Non-financial incentives include free land for the factory and subsidized utilities. Through the history of Russia, Europe, and the rest of the world, these were the incentives that proved to have the best repercussions on the economy. It didn't matter if they were provided to foreign or domestic entrepreneurs. All that mattered was that they were supplied in large amounts. When foreigners possessed a superior technology as the domestic producers, it was more useful to provide the subsidies to the foreign companies. Peter the Great supplied ample subsidies to West European capitalists because that was the most effective way of acquiring the most advanced technology of the times.

Peter had a city built from scratch to serve as a manufacturing center. St. Petersburg was intended to concentrate on the production of high technology weapons, ships, and other goods. As a port with the closest links to the West, St. Petersburg had the best access to imported technology.

Peter sharply increased government expenditure, disregarding the advice of those who counseled that increasing public debt would wreck the economy. The military budget absorbed the bulk of the increase, sometimes accounting for three-fourths of government expenditure. The economic growth under Peter was unprecedented.[270]

Before and during Peter's reign, much of the Russian elite was opposed to industrialization. In those times the term "industrialization" was even less clearly defined than today and included fields from several sectors, but it was mostly identified with factory production. Most people thought that Russia did not have the natural capabilities to produce significant quantities of manufactured goods and that quality levels would never match those of Western Europe.[271]

Peter went ahead anyway, and expanded his arsenals, created a large navy, built a large merchant fleet, and produced other goods in large amounts. He succeeded in dramatically increasing Russian output, and made Russia competitive with Western Europe. By 1725, Russia led the world in the production of iron, beating even Britain by a large margin. By then, Russia was exporting a share of its iron production as well as ships and other manufactures to Western Europe.[272]

The rule of Peter the Great was a period of unprecedented support for manufacturing, and a period of unexampled economic growth.[273] Innovations appeared more frequently than in the rest of the century, and Western technology was imported faster. Schools and in particular technical schools were founded in larger numbers. Large infrastructure projects were undertaken. Roads, bridges, ports, and canals were built at a more rapid pace. Trade expanded and so did agriculture.[274]

---

269 Blackwell: Ibid., p. 18–26.
270 Kirchner: Ibid., p. 94, 95.
271 Nove, Alec: *Political Economy and Soviet Socialism*, p. 27–31.
272 Parker: Ibid., p. 117, 114, 129.
273 Kahan, Arcadius: *The Plow, the Hammer and the Knout*, p. 2, 3.
274 Blackwell: Ibid., p. 28–30.

After the death of Peter, the throne changed hands several times. No one could match his drive and determination, and there was a noticeable deceleration of the economy.[275]

He found a worthy successor in Catherine the Great (1762–96), during whose rule support for military and civilian manufacturing rose significantly. The budget was enlarged and more of it was used to promote factories. The government created numerous state companies and offered a higher dose of incentives to the private sector. This was reflected in an acceleration of economic growth.[276]

Catherine's enthusiasm for manufacturing, however, was not as forceful as that of Peter and during her reign economic growth was less pronounced than in the first quarter of the century. During Peter's reign, the number of large manufacturing establishments rose fifteen-fold, while during the rule of Catherine the increase was not even four fold.[277]

It is worth noting that internal tolls on domestic trade were abolished from 1726–62, and other liberalizing measures were undertaken, adding competitive pressure to the economy, but the economy did not improve and actually slowed down. This gives further credence to the idea that the bottom line for economic growth resides in the factory promotion efforts of the state and that influences such as liberalization play only a secondary role.[278]

During the reign of Catherine the Great further measures were taken to liberalize the economy. The most noteworthy was the law of 1767 which abolished Peter's system of monopolies on trade, manufacturing, and mining. Following the advice of Adam Smith, she dismantled this market distortion. The evidence suggests that Smith was right in seeking to increase competition, but the fact remains that during Catherine's rule the economy grew slower than during the Petrine years. Peter had supplied larger factory subsidies.[279]

During the 18th century, Russia endured numerous famines — but fewer than before, as agricultural production increased much faster and the diet improved. The increased per capita farm output was accompanied by increased production of farm implements.

More comestibles were also imported, as a result of increased exports — which was fundamentally the result of the growth of manufacturing. The share of manufactures in total exports rose considerably even though primary sector exports increased as well.[280]

The improvement in agricultural production was paradoxical in that farmers were more heavily taxed. The peasants regularly suffered the unrestrained depredations of Peter's army, which was sent out for six months of every year to collect taxes. As the taxes increased, so too did peasant resistance. Catherine the Great also taxed the peasantry very hard in order to support continual wars and a lavish court. At the same time, farm workers were being inducted into the military in larger numbers. Agricultural output should have deteriorated as investment of capital and labor was reduced. But it increased, instead.[281]

275 Kirchner: Ibid., p. 93–96, 108–113, 123.
276 Blackwell: Ibid., p. 20–26.
277 Parker: Ibid., p. 148, 164.
278 Kahan: Ibid., p. 1, 4.
279 Guroff, Gregory & Carstensen, Fred (ed): *Entrepreneurship in Imperial Russia and the Soviet Union*, p. 62.
280 Smith, R. & Christian, D.: *Bread and Salt*, p. 173, 189, 196.
281 Parker: Ibid., p. 136, 148.

China and Japan

During the 18th century, China doubled its territory. The Manchu emperors of this period — Kangxi (1662–1722), Yongzheng (1723–1735) and Quianlong (1736–1799) — were avid conquerors and they channeled a large share of resources to finance their armories. The significant rise in the rate of manufacturing output was paralleled by faster economic growth. [282]

The most enthusiastic conqueror was Quianlong and his reign oversaw the fastest economic growth of the century. Qianlong's greatest conquest took place in 1759 when he defeated the remnant Mongol armies, completing the occupation of Xinjiang. He was much hailed for his military victories but the reason why he was so dearly regarded was because the living conditions improved.

At its zenith in the late 18th century, the Manchu empire controlled all of present-day China plus Korea, coastal eastern Russia, Mongolia, Taiwan and parts of Burma, Vietnam, Bhutan and Nepal. [283]

In the 18th century, taxation as a share of the total economy reached new levels and government expenditure as a share of GDP also grew. The larger revenues were used to create state factories that produced weapons, metals, machinery, and other goods. They were also utilized to supply more grants to private manufacturers. The larger budget meant that a larger share of the economy went to finance factories but this was heightened by the larger share of government expenditure that was destined for the promotion of manufacturing. That coincided with faster agricultural growth, as well as with a faster development of domestic and foreign trade, services, and construction. The larger per capita food supply led to faster population growth. The division of labor accelerated and the use of money increased significantly. There was much minting of bronze coins in this century.

In the 18th century, manufacturing is likely to have grown by about 0.6% annually, the economy by about 0.4% and agriculture by about 0.3%. (See tables in the appendix.)

The economy expanded in spite of an increase in the proportion of resources diverted to weapons manufacture. Taxation on agriculture rose and peasants were recruited in larger numbers into the army. Still, farm output and farm productivity was up noticeably, in tandem with increased output of agricultural manufactures such as plows and harvesters. A larger production of ships allowed for more trade; this in its turn made possible the introduction of more crops from the Americas. More construction manufactures allowed for expanded development of roads, ports, and canals, which facilitated the spread of better rice varieties from the south. [284]

Expanding contacts with the West revealed more directly China's backwardness. China's governments took additional efforts to promote the production of goods, mostly civilian manufactures. Because the contacts with the West occurred along the coast, the coastal regions received the most grants and this was the region that attained the fastest economic growth during the 18th century.

---

282 Gray, Jack: *Rebellions and Revolutions*, p. 93, 2, 154.

283 Huang, Ray: *China—A Macro History*, p. 187–189.

284 Fairbank, John: *China—A New History*, p. 168, 169; Sabillon: Ibid., p. 111; Madison, Angus: *Chinese Economic Performance in the Long Run*; Madison, Angus: *The World Economy: A Millennial Perspective*.

Of course, even with the increased subsidies, the level of manufacturing promotion in China was lower than in Western Europe during the 18th century and rate of factory output was lower as well. That went hand in hand with slower economic growth than in the West, so that the developmental gap between the two continued to widen.

China's wars to that date had been against small armies using primitive weapons. The Manchus thus were under little pressure to upgrade their technology.

In Western Europe since the 16th century, wars had been of a much larger scale, forcing much larger investments. By the end of the 18th century in Britain, the most ambitious militarily, taxation in per capita terms was roughly seven times higher than in China and government expenditure as a share of GDP was roughly five times larger. [285]

Japan was also losing ground to the West, and to an even larger extent, for it had been growing more slowly than China for centuries. Manufacturing in Japan also grew more slowly than in China. [286]

The cause seems to have resided in the isolation of the archipelago prior to the 18th century. Japan's contacts with the rest of the world were minimal, and they had engaged in just a few short-lived skirmishes with foreign nations. Even within Japan, war was low intensity compared to China. The weapons industry and related goods received less support and delivered an overall lower per capita output of manufactured goods.

As in most other countries, support for civilian manufacturing was largely dependent on the support military manufacturing received. Not having confronted other nations' armies, Japan had not confronted their more advanced civilian goods either and policy makers had no reason to push the development of such goods.

In the 18th century, Japan's economy not only grew slower than China's, but it also grew slower than in the preceding century. The population contracted, urban centers declined, famine increased, and there were more peasant uprisings. Support for manufacturing decreased. [287]

By the early 18th century, the Tokugawa Shoguns had succeeded in keeping the archipelago unified for about a hundred years. The fragmentation of power that prevailed up to the 16th century and the fear of a return to that chaotic situation had forced them during the following century to increase investment in arms. Over time, no secessionist efforts were undertaken by the regional governments, so their fear began to decrease. By the early 18th century, Edo began to feel secure in its power and started to decrease allocations for military and civilian manufacturing. With no foreign threat in sight, the Shoguns decided to cut weapons expenditure. [288]

Here too it was believed that farming was the only real source of wealth creation. The central and the regional governments thought that the ideal society was one in which subsistence agriculture prevailed. The self-sufficient village community was idealized. In the 17th century, policy makers had increased support for manufacturing with reluctance, for they were certain that investments in weapons and related goods hampered the development of agriculture and the rest of the economy. As the national security concerns diminished in

---

285 Adshead, S. A.: *China in World History*, p. 245.
286 Morishima, Michio: *Why has Japan Succeeded?*, p. 20.
287 Smith, Thomas: *Native Sources of Japanese Industrialization 1750–1920*, p. 3.
288 Suzuki, Tessa: *A History of Japanese Economic Thought*, p. 8–10.

the 18th century, they immediately transferred resources back to agriculture,[289] which was soon followed by a progressive deterioration of the economy. As time went by, the rulers devoted fewer and fewer resources to manufacturing and the rate of manufacturing output diminished more and more. During the reign of Shogun Yoshimune (1726–46), signs of economic weakness appeared; they became more evident during the rule of his son Ieshige (1746–89). Neither one provided the necessary leadership, but government expenditure in manufacturing was higher during Yoshimune's rule, and there were fewer food riots and peasant uprisings. [290]

A series of natural catastrophes obliged the authorities to allocate even more resources for non-factory fields. An eruption of Mount Fuji in 1707 and Mount Asama in 1783 destroyed much of the infrastructure and housing stock. Earthquakes, tidal waves, and landslides were also more frequent than in the preceding century. Up to the 20th century, construction in Japan grew faster when manufacturing was strongly promoted. History suggests that the best reconstruction policy would have been one that gave investment priority to this sector.[291]

The typical relationship between the private sector and manufacturing was illustrated once again. As the Japanese state reduced subsidies to manufacturing, individuals with money looked the other way and put their capital into agriculture, services, and construction.

The regional rulers or daimyos were the wealthiest Japanese of the time and the samurai (professional soldiers) were among the wealthiest. They were the aristocracy of Japan. In the 18th century, the central government cut the pensions of the daimyos and samurai by about 35%. This forced many of them to go into business, which they had formerly considered an unworthy occupation. Given their high incomes, they were the best positioned for investing in manufacturing, but the majority went into services such as commerce, selling rank, and taking in lodgers. A large share engaged in farming and a few opted for construction. Only a tiny fraction channeled their capital into manufacturing. [292]

The largest manufacturing establishments of the time were owned by the state. The production of iron, copper, armaments, and ships was in government hands and even the output of textiles, sake, and wax was mostly done by state factories. In fields such as paper, mats, lanterns, furniture, metal articles, household utensils, and many other civilian domains production was almost exclusively in private hands. However, much of the output was bought by the central or regional governments at guaranteed prices that assured a profit. When governments reduced the guaranteed purchases, production tended to fall and when they increased them, output rose. [293]

The reduced subsidization in the 18th century was accompanied by a deceleration of this sector, which averaged about 0.2% per year. The economy followed suit and averaged about 0.1%. It is interesting to note that even the negligible level of manufacturing that took place in Japan in the 17th and 18th century, subsidies were required. Apparently, with

289 *The Cambridge Encyclopedia of Japan*, p. 70.
290 Takekoshi, Yosoburo: *The Economic Aspects of the History of the Civilization of Japan Vol. 3.*
291 *The Cambridge Encyclopedia of Japan*, p. 75.
292 Macpherson, W. J. (ed): *The Industrialization of Japan*, p. 41–43.
293 Allen, G. C.: *A Short Economic History of Modern Japan*, p. 17, 18.

no subsidies at all, manufacturing would come to a complete standstill, and the economy would stagnate completely.[294]

Seeking to increase revenues in the 18th century, the Japanese government established monopolies in manufacturing and commerce. This measure together with the creation of state enterprises proved to have negative effects on the economy as it reduced competition. The goal of increasing government revenue was not attained. In the 17th century, however, state revenue had risen and that coincided with increased factory subsidies.

In Europe and Russia, government revenue also fluctuated in synchrony with the levels of support for this sector. The large increase in the share of resources that European and Russian rulers allocated to manufacturing in the 18th century was accompanied by a large increase in public revenue. The evidence suggests that the best policy for increasing government revenue is by stimulating economic growth and that is best done by increasing support for manufacturing. [295]

The causation of this phenomenon seems to be as follows: larger factory subsidies deliver faster economic growth, which increase the amount of companies in a country. These companies thus start to pay corporate income taxes, sales taxes and others. At the same time, they employ a number of workers who immediately start to pay personal income taxes and the share of the population paying taxes grows. The tax base thus increases and it usually increases in larger amounts than the government money used to provide the subsidies.

Korea and Taiwan

The peninsula of Korea remained fragmented among several kingdoms up to the ninth century AD. By then, it was divided into three states (Koryo, Silla and Paekche). At the end of this century, the rulers from the kingdom of Koryo set out to subdue the other two, so they produced more weapons and raised larger armies. By 918, they had conquered their adversaries and established a dynasty that lasted until 1392. The name Korea comes from the Koryo Dynasty, for it was the first to unify the whole peninsula. The Choson Dynasty followed and it lasted until 1910. [296]

Up to the 16th century, internal and external war in Korea was less intense than in China. China's per capita output of weapons and related goods was higher and that coincided with a higher level of technological and economic development in China.

In the 17th century, China's influence in the peninsula became stronger. By 1644 the Manchus had not just conquered all of China but also the whole peninsula. The invasions of 1627 and 1637 established tributary relations over Korea, which lasted until 1910. The Manchus were determined conquerors and pursued a policy of territorial expansion until the late 18th century. They established large garrisons with their soldiers in all the major regions of China and their tributary states. To reduce the risk of rebellion, they promoted the production of weapons and related goods in those territories in order to have a ready supply of arms.

---

294 Sabillon: Ibid., p. 112; *Madison, Angus: The World Economy: A Millennial Perspective*; Madison, Angus: *The World Economy: Historical Statistics*; Madison, Angus: *Growth and Interaction in the World Economy*.

295 Allen, G. C.: Ibid., p. 14–19, 25–27.

296 Cumings, Bruce: *Korea's Place in the Sun—A Modern History*, p. 23–39, 76.

The first contacts with the West took place in the 17th century. In 1656 a Dutch shipwreck exposed the Koreans to the vastly superior military and civilian technology of Europe. Korean rulers were impressed and undertook some efforts to reproduce some of those factory goods. Thus, subsidization in the 17th century increased due to the contacts with the West and the dictates of the Manchus. That was reflected in faster economic growth. [297]

China's Manchu rulers became more expansionist oriented in the 18th century and demanded that every area under their control produce more goods that aided their military goals. Many of these goods were manufactures and Korean policy makers were driven to increase investment in this sector. Greater per capita production of factory goods was again paralleled by faster economic growth. That was accompanied by a larger per capita output of agricultural goods, minerals, fish, and wood. Trade increased faster as well as services, construction, infrastructure, technology, and productivity. [298]

Increased factory subsidization was also matched by an increased use of money. In China, Japan, and other regions of Asia, barter versus the use of a common unit of exchange fluctuated in unison with the level of manufacturing development. When this sector grew faster, the pace of technological development accelerated and all economic sectors did likewise. As the output of goods and services increased, the economy became more specialized and a common currency was needed in order to accommodate the more numerous economic transactions. [299]

Peace prevailed in Korea during the 18th century, in particular during the reign of Yongjo (1724–76) and Chongjo (1776–1800), but the demands from the Manchus obliged them to allot more resources for the production of arms and related goods. China's technological and economic superiority continued in the 18th century and the extended contacts with the peninsula exposed the Koreans to China's superior civilian goods. This inspired Korea's policy makers to production-replicating efforts. Growing contacts with Europeans delivered similar reactions. [300]

Korea's manufacturing and economic growth during the 18th century, faster than before, was nonetheless slower than that of China. Manufacturing in Korea seems to have averaged about 0.3% per year and the economy expanded by about 0.2%. (See tables in the appendix.)[301]

Even a small amount of manufacturing seems to require government support to get going. Up to the 17th century, practically all of heavy manufacturing and much of its light counterpart were in state hands because Koreans used their resources elsewhere. In the 18th century, the government privatized factories producing light goods such as textiles, as well as many of the ones producing heavy goods such as iron, other metals, and machines. And it gave them subsidies such as tax exemptions, monopoly rights, and guaranteed prices. Privatization improved efficiency, but it also showed that for private factories to function normally it was necessary to supply them regularly with subsidies. [302]

297 Chung, Chai-sik: *A Korean Confucian Encounter with the Modern World*, p. 1–5.
298 Eckert, Lee, Lew, Robinson, Wagner: *Korea—Old and New—A History*, p. 159–163.
299 Takekoshi: Ibid., p. 18–60, 143–150.
300 Cotterel, Arthur: *East Asia—From Chinese Predominance to the Rise of the Pacific Rim*, p. 127–129.
301 Sabillon: Ibid., p. 113; Madison, Angus: *The World Economy: Historical Statistics*.
302 Eckert, Lee, Lew, Robinson, Wagner: Ibid., p. 163.

Although factory subsidies rose, they were very low by today's standards. Given the perennial threat of hunger, common sense dictated that resources be directed to agriculture.

Confucian beliefs, which predominated in the peninsula, made things worse. The Confucian hierarchy placed craftsmen among the lowest ranking classes. People working in manufacturing were seen as having little or no value to society, while farmers were seen as the most productive. With such a view of the world, it was inevitable that only national security concerns would drive policy makers to supply some subsidies to manufacturing. The majority of government expenditure was given to agriculture and policies concentrated on encouraging the private sector to channel its resources into farming. [303]

The history of Taiwan is no different from that of its neighbors on this matter. Taiwan was known to the Chinese since the seventh century AD but settlement began only in the early 17th century, when recurrent famines in Fukien province encouraged mainlanders to migrate there. Before, it had been a base for Chinese and Japanese pirates and was inhabited by a very small aborigine population. The economy was based on subsistence agriculture, fishing and service activities. That was accompanied by stagnation and a level of development that was basically in the Neolithic period. [304]

The first signs of growth were seen in the 17th century, correlating with the first investments in manufacturing. China had by then a relatively developed factory sector and the migrants from Fukien carried to the island their tools and machines. As soon as they settled, they began to fabricate small amounts of goods, mostly for household consumption.

The Portuguese arrived in 1590, named it Ilha Formosa, and tried unsuccessfully to establish a settlement. The Dutch settled in the southwest in 1624 and the Spaniards in the north in 1626. The Dutch seized the Spanish-dominated north in 1646 but were expelled by a Chinese army in 1661. In 1683, the Manchus made it part of Fukien province. Due to the large migration, the population had by then risen to about 200,000.

The Europeans were not interested in manufacturing focusing almost exclusively in trading; however, because of a number of pressing circumstances, they were obliged to make a few investments in this sector. European trading operations in Asia tended to be directly or indirectly financed by their governments, which assured the flow of subsidies. Once the Manchus claimed sovereignty over the island, they began to supply some subsidies for manufacturing.

Government support for manufacturing in the 17th century (Chinese and European) was very weak and investment was insignificant in comparison to that in China. But even this anemic support was something new, and it led to an exponential increase in production. Agriculture, mining, fishing, and handicrafts rose faster than ever before. Technology, trade, construction and services did likewise. Relatively speaking, the economy boomed.

In the 18th century, the Manchus applied in Taiwan the same policies they implemented in all other regions under their control. They demanded that a larger share of available resources be utilized to produce goods that contributed to their military goals. The Taiwanese authorities complied, and this was paralleled by faster technological development and faster economic growth. The growth of agriculture and the other primary activities moved in tan-

303 Cumings: Ibid., p. 80.
304 Kolb, Albert: Ostasien—*China, Japan, Korea*, p. 434–444.

dem. Vast tracts of land were opened for cultivation, in particular for rice and sugarcane. Exports increased exponentially, mostly to China, Japan, and Southeast Asia. [305]

The United States

Across the Pacific, the same cause and effect relationship was observed. During the 18th century, the United States of America expanded its territory and its population grew from about 300,000 in 1700 to some 4.5 million. Mostly due to immigration, population grew at the breathtaking pace of about 5.5% annually.

During that same period, Britain had seen its population grow by about 0.6% per year. Since this was the fastest rate Britain had ever attained, it was argued that fast population growth was partially responsible for the economic acceleration of that period. Had population really played a major role in the acceleration of Britain, growth in the US should have been substantially faster. It wasn't even a little faster. Economic growth in the US was considerably slower than in Britain. [306]

The slow growth coincided with policies intended to hamper the development of manufacturing. During the first three quarters of the century, London continued its mercantilist policies and prohibited development of manufacturing. The colonists, on their side, although they had a considerable say in policy making, were not interested either in promoting this sector for a number of ideological reasons. They were nevertheless more motivated than in the past and did allocate more resources to it. The rate of factory output accelerated and so did GDP growth. [307]

Especially after 1713, when Spain yielded to British merchants the monopoly of the slave trade, the import of African slaves grew rapidly. However in the South, where most of the slaves were put to work, the economy expanded at the slowest pace. On this occasion as well as numerous others throughout history in which slave labor was utilized, there was an absence of fast or even a modest rate of economic growth. [308]

History shows that slavery contributed nothing to improve the performance of the American economy. The emphasis on agriculture in the South arguably diverted resources that could have gone into manufacturing and therefore retarded the development of this sector. Slavery thus retarded the attainment of better living conditions for the European population.

Since the early 17th century, when the English Crown began acquiring the bankrupt private settlements, it named a governor for each colony and sent officials from other administrative bodies, such as the Board of Trade and the Secretary of State, to regulate the functioning of the new territories. They were not, however, given much to work with and the colonists retained a strong role in deciding economic policy. Nonetheless, the Crown's political control increased during the course of the century.

In the early 18th century, wars were heating up in Europe, and Britain was the main participant. London's interest in the colonies decreased and policy initiatives from the gover-

---

305 Rubistein, Murray (ed): *Taiwan—A New History*, p. 135, 136.
306 North, Douglas: *The Growth of the American Economy to 1860*, p. 67– 69, 114.
307 Niemi, Albert: *U.S. Economic History*, p. 94.
308 Krout: Ibid., 32, 111.

nors did likewise. Colonial assemblies therefore increased their policy-making powers and decided to mimic the policies that London undertook in Britain.

London increased the level of subsidization for military and civilian manufacturing. The colonies thus decided to allocate more resources for the production of factory goods. Although Indian raids were a major threat, war was not the driving force so most of the increased subsidies went into civilian manufacturing. A growing number of British-made goods that arrived in the territories were in high demand due to their high technological content and the colonists undertook to replicate them. [309]

London's mercantilist policies hampered the development of manufacturing but not by much. In 1699 Parliament prohibited exports of garments from its American colonies due to protests from Irish textile producers. In 1732, English hat producers won the Hat Act, which prohibited the colonial export of hats. The Iron Acts of 1750 and 1757 prohibited the production of certain forms of iron. These laws were mostly aimed at restricting exports and not production, but lower exports tended to translate into lower production. However, due to the few British officials and troops in the colonies, these laws were only partially enforced and their effects were small.

Britain's enlarged allocations for ship production was copied by the colonies, leading to a large rise in output. From some 2,000 ships in 1700, the colonial fleet rose to about 3,000 by 1750. Piracy was a problem and to fight it the colonial assemblies allocated funds to produce armed ships to police the coast. Shipbuilding developed so fast that by 1775 about one third of British ships had been made in the colonies. [310]

Support increased to practically all manufacturing fields. Flour milling, rum distilling and the production of glass, paper, bricks, textiles, and hats grew the fastest. Iron received ample subsidies and by 1775 the Thirteen Colonies produced about one seventh of the world output. Land concessions were the most frequent form of incentive, although tax exemptions and grants were also supplied. [311]

France had been competing with England to acquire North American territories since the mid-16th century and in the 17th century French expeditions claimed vast territories. During the first half of the 18th century, the French enlarged and consolidated their possessions, which largely surrounded the Thirteen English colonies. This posed a threat, because the French had continued to encourage several Indian tribes to launch raids against the Thirteen Colonies. War between England and France had been almost continuous since the mid-17th century. The growing tension with the French drove London to tighten control over the colonies. The Seven Years' War (1756–63) was largely fought for the control of North America. The war increased British expenditures in the colonies by a large margin and also increased its political control. The Treasury took a new interest in colonial policy, focusing mostly on taxation.

Britain won the war and acquired most of the land the French had accumulated, including Canada and the territories west of the thirteen colonies. Although most of the weapons and related goods that were used in the war were made in Britain, a notable share was fabricated in the colonies. London paid for part of it and persuaded the colonists to pay for the rest.

---

309 Greene, Jack & Pole, J. R. (ed): *The Blackwell Encyclopedia of the American Revolution*, p. 12.
310 Vincent, Bernard (ed): *Histoire des Stas Unis*, p. 29.
311 Porter, Glen (ed): *Encyclopedia of American Economic History Vol. 1*, p. 39.

Despite the triumph, London was convinced that the French threat was not over. More resources were allocated for weapons in order to tighten defenses — and manufacturing output continued to rise.

Although the economy improved, this situation brought tension between the British and the colonists. After the war, London sought to extract more revenue from the colonies to offset the costs of administering and defending the enlarged North American territory. The Royal Navy was increasingly used for customs enforcement, causing friction with the colonial mercantile community. [312]

In 1765, London tried to raise revenue by enacting the Stamp Act. This was rejected by the colonies on the ground that English law stated that taxation without representation was illegal. By then, the colonists had practically no representation in the British parliament. Tensions continued to increase and in the early 1770s, the secessionist movement rapidly gained ground. War soon broke out and in 1776 the colonists declared independence. [313]

Support for manufacturing during the first three quarters of the 18th century was much stronger than in the 17th century, mostly because of the colonists but also because of Britain. The economy grew. However, the support given was still very small and the rate of output was too. By 1775, about 90% of the population earned their income from farming. Self-sufficient agriculture supplemented by hunting and fishing was the norm for most Americans.

Britain largely restricted the growth of manufacturing, but the colonists were also convinced that wealth could only be extracted from natural resources. The abundance of natural resources further misled them to believe that primary activities were the key to progress. [314]

However, in the last quarter of the century, when the US declared its independence and British restraints on manufacturing were phased out, everything changed. London imposed a trade blockade on the renegade territories. American policy makers feared economic ruin due to the strong dependence on imported British goods, so they supplied large subsidies to domestic producers to substitute the imports. On top of this, the revolutionaries were confronting the most powerful country in the world, which possessed the most potent navy. This forced the Americans to allocate a large share of resources to armories and shipyards.

The war lasted from 1775 to 1783 and its cost as a share of GDP was 63%. However, America's manufacturing base had been expanding and the economy was humming. The War ended with the Peace of Paris in 1783, when Britain officially recognized the United States as a sovereign nation. [315]

Once the war ended, the new government continued to promote manufacturing more than in colonial times. On the one hand, the new nation had numerous enemies. British and Spanish troops occupied neighboring territories and could launch an attack at any moment. Indian raids were also regular. Military production was expanded. On the other hand, Washington also sought to imitate the example of Britain, which by then was the most enthusiastic promoter of manufacturing in the world. [316]

These efforts received a major boost in 1789 when the first presidential election took place. The federalists won and George Washington became the first head of state. At that

312 Greene & Pole: Ibid., p. 9–11, 15.
313 Vincent: Ibid., p. 31
314 Porter: Ibid., p. 36.
315 Bogart, & Kemmerer: Ibid., p. 338–351, 356; "Unimaginable", *The Economist*, 22 February 2003, p. 71.
316 Adams, D.: America in the 20th Century, p. 21.

moment, the two groups that had dominated the Constituent Assembly were debating over policy. A group wanted a loose federation in which each colony would have powers similar to those of an independent country and the other wanted a strong central government.

Washington believed in a strong executive and was a man of much energy and determination. When he became president, the country had no navy, the army consisted of just 840 soldiers, and the national debt was very high. The Departments of War, Treasury, and State were the first he created. Alexander Hamilton became the first Secretary of the Treasury. Hamilton, another man of much energy and ambition, also was for a strong central government. [317]

Hamilton, the most influential economic policy maker of the time, wanted to rapidly create a manufacturing base by setting high trade barriers and bounty payments. His plan was only partially adopted and from 1789 to 1812 tariffs were raised to 10% on dutiable goods. During that period, larger land concessions, larger tax exemptions, and larger grants were supplied to manufacturers. The patent system was adopted in 1790. As a mechanism for the protection of technology, it increased the profit possibilities of manufacturers. [318]

The large increase in subsidies had immediate results and production of this sector rose. The first large-scale textile factory started operating in 1790. The trade barriers may have been an error, but the evidence suggests the grants as well as other forms of financial, non-financial, and fiscal assistance were not.

War between Britain and France broke out again in 1793 and lasted until 1815. The commercial blockades and embargoes generated by this war considerably interrupted the Atlantic trade. The American government therefore increased its import substitution efforts. Output accelerated further. The economy did likewise. The US took a neutral position in the war and wanted to profit by trading with both parties, but it did not possess enough ships to carry the merchandise. The American government thus increased subsidies for shipbuilding, which was followed by an exponential expansion of the merchant fleet. From 1789 to 1810, ship tonnage production increased seven fold. [319]

During the last quarter of the century, the large increase in support for manufacturing coincided with a leap in economic progress.

Support was increased throughout the century, and this was paralleled by faster technological development and faster economic growth. In this period, American policy makers sought to match the manufacturing development of Britain. They provided more support than most nations, and they enjoyed one of the fastest rates of economic growth in the world — at least in the Northeast, where industry was concentrated. In the rest of the US the economy was stagnant. As a result, the average for the whole nation was much lower than in Britain.

The factory rate for the whole territory is likely to have been of about 0.4% annually and the economy expanded by about 0.3% per year. Agriculture grew, averaging about 0.2%. Per capita wealth in the colonies thus, remained much lower than in Britain (about one third that of Britain). [320]

---

317 Jones, Maldwyn: *The Limits of Liberty—American History 1607–1980*, p. 76–79.
318 Niemi: Ibid., p. 99.
319 North: Ibid., p. 171–173.
320 Sabillon: Ibid., p. 147; Fogel: Ibid; Madison, Angus: *The World Economy—A Millennial Perspective*.

Everything grew faster during the 18th century (mining, fishing, forestry, domestic and foreign trade, housing, infrastructure, health services, and financial services). Education and literacy progressed considerably. The use of coins and paper money became commonplace. As in other regions of the world, a higher level of manufacturing development coincided with the termination of barter. [321]

Trade grew quickly but even so, the commercial balance continued to show a deficit. In the 17th century, trade deficits had also prevailed. Britain produced more tradable goods and exported at a faster pace. Since this was the US's main trading partner, the prevalence of deficits was inevitable. From the 16th to the 18th century, Britain provided the largest subsidies to manufacturing and enjoyed trade surpluses with the rest of the world. In the 19th century, Washington promoted manufacturing more enthusiastically than any other government in the world and the US achieved trade surpluses.

Other nations experienced the same phenomenon. When their rates of factory output were faster over sustained periods of time than those of their main trading partners, trade balances turned in their favor. The evidence suggests that stronger support for this sector than that supplied by other governments determines export surpluses.[322]

Many say that the faster economic growth of the 18th century in the US was largely the result of fast population growth. Many have argued that the increased population density allowed for further labor specialization and therefore higher productivity. If high population density were needed to stimulate growth, Canada and Australia should have remained in stagnation up to the late 20th century. Instead, they were among the fastest growing economies in those years. India and China were far more densely populated than the US, Canada, and Australia in 1800–1999, but they grew much slower. [323]

Still, the US economy, though growing, was not growing much by today's standards. Many economic historians have argued that growth was slow because of the small domestic market, which generated just a small level of demand. If local demand was what mattered most, think how fast India should have grown. In the 18th century and in the following two centuries India showed one of the slowest rates of economic growth in the world. [324]

In line with the manufacturing thesis, on the other hand, note that during the years 1800–1999, government subsidies for manufacturing were much larger in Canada and Australia than in India and China. That would explain why despite the extremely low population density of Canada and Australia, economic growth was much faster.

---

321 Engerman, Stanley & Gallman, Robert (ed): *The Cambridge Economic History of the United States Vol. 1*, p. 192, 206, 207.

322 Vincent: Ibid., p. 29, 30.

323 Greene & Pole: Ibid., p. 20; Sabillon: Ibid., p. 111–152.

324 Hoffman, Mccusker, Menard, Albert (ed): *The Economy of Early America—The Revolutionary Period 1763–1790*, p. 48

Chapter 5. The First Half of the 19th Century

Britain's Economic Development

In the first half of the 19th century, Britain again attained the fastest rates of economic growth in the world, and far faster than anything seen before. In the years 1750–99, GDP averaged about 0.9% annually and during 1800–49, the figure leaped to about 2.9%. (See tables at the end of the book.) [325]

Once again the manufacturing figures correlate with impressive precision with those of GDP. Having averaged approximately 1.6% annually during the first period, manufacturing jumped to about 3.6% during the second. During the years 1800–49, manufacturing was again the only sector that grew faster than the rest of the economy, and thus was the only one that could have delivered a pulling effect. Agriculture was up, as well, but it consistently lagged behind the rate of overall GDP and especially manufacturing, averaging 1.3%. [326]

As during all of the preceding history, the data suggests that the pace of factory output was fundamentally determined by government subsidies. The first fifteen years of the century were spent fighting the most armament-intensive war in Britain's history. On top of that, during the years 1812–14, London had to fight on two fronts, against Napoleon and his allies and against the US. The production of arms rose substantially and the government paid for all of them. Taxes rose, tariffs rose, and public sector borrowing went up.

The short-term pressures of the war forced the government to not only increase the level of public debt but also to run large budget deficits. During those times, it was strongly believed that state intervention in the economy should be kept to a bare minimum. It

325 Lee, C. H.: *The British Economy since 1700—A Macroeconomic Perspective*, p. 5; Sabillon, Carlos: *World Economic Historical Statistics*, p. 183; Madison, Angus: *Monitoring the World Economy 1820–1992*; Madison, Angus: *The World Economy: Historical Statistics*; Madison, Angus: *The World Economy: A Millennial Perspective.*

326 Floud, Roderick & McCloskey, Donald (ed): *The Economic History of Britain since 1700 Vol. I*, p. 47, 49, 121.

was thought that the government should constantly balance its revenue with its expenditures and if possible attain surpluses. Deficits and public debt were seen as hindrances to growth.[327]

Much suggests that those beliefs were well founded because throughout history, most state intervention was characterized by an inefficient allocation of resources, by a low return on investment, and by high levels of waste. However, most such state intervention was not intended to promote manufacturing. The belief that budget deficits and government debt had negative effects were also correct, for there is no logical reason for the state to spend beyond the limits that its revenue allows.

However, if budget deficits and government debt were in fact a serious hindrance to growth, the economy should have suffered. During the first fifteen years of the 19th century, Britain experienced the largest budget deficits and the largest national debt in all of its history up to that date. The national debt peaked at almost 200% as a share of GDP. Only in World War II did the borrowing reach a higher level. [328]

With so much debt, the economy should have performed terribly or it should at least have slowed down. It must be added that the money was being "wasted" in weapons and that the government was severely distorting market forces with new regulations. The fact, however, is that Britain experienced the fastest rates of growth up to that date.

The evidence suggests that state intervention, budget deficits, and government debt do have a negative effect on the economy, but their effect is marginal compared to the impact of factory subsidization, and since the support was much stronger than ever before, the economy expanded much faster.

The Congress of Vienna in 1815 sealed the end of the Napoleonic Wars. Almost as soon as the ink on the treaty dried, Britain moved to rapidly expand its empire. It took over large territories in Africa, Asia, and Oceania. This expansionist policy required a large fleet and the government offered generous subsidies to the producers of military and merchant ships.

Its triumph over France was the main factor encouraging London to expand its colonial possessions. However, the mercantilist dictum that colonies provided needed raw materials and serve as export markets was also a driving force. Mercantilism asserted that trade and more particularly exports were essential for economic growth. Since perishable agricultural goods were difficult to export, subsidies fell mostly on manufactures.

Another way in which mercantilism channeled resources into factories was by forcing other nations that were not under British colonial rule to consume British manufactures. Britain obliged numerous countries in Latin America, the Middle East, and East Asia to trade with her as a "most favored nation". By means of intimidation and diplomacy, it cajoled them to import finished goods from British manufacturers. This meant higher demand for British manufactures, which stimulated factory output. [329]

However, the number one factor driving factory production in the years after the Napoleonic Wars was investment in arms. France was defeated but not conquered and the possibility of another war with that country remained.

---

327 Tames, Richard: *Economy and Society in Nineteenth Century Britain*, p. 19.
328 "The Burdensome National Debt", *The Economist*, 10 February 1996, p. 70.
329 Cain, P. J.: *Economic Foundations of British Overseas Expansion 1815–1914*, p. 11, 34–39.

The first railway was opened in 1825. The Stockton–Darlington line covered just a short distance, and many influential Britons predicted that it would never outperform horse haulage and canals to become a major means of transport. [330]

They were soon proven wrong. By the 1830s, trains carried more passengers than any other means of transport and by the 1840s trains displaced canals as the main carriers of freight. The development of railroads also contributed to the growth of manufacturing, as it required more iron, steel, rails, locomotives, wagons, processed wood, and machine tools. British railways since the 1820s were built by private enterprises, but London gave considerable support. Legislation was passed guaranteeing the profitability of the venture. [331]

In order to stimulate business confidence, Parliament passed legislation creating joint-stock railway companies, the terms of whose authorization implied a qualified monopoly. By the 1840s, the railway amalgamation movement gathered strength and monopolies grew in size. This further stimulated the manufacture of iron, rails, locomotives and wagons, for it secured sales and profits. The government also supplied fiscal, financial, and non-financial incentives to the producers of railroad goods. [332]

Massive investments were required for the fabrication of railways. The steam-engine locomotive was at the core of this revolution and precisely because it embodied the latest technology, it was the most expensive part of the railroad. Producers received large subsidies.

In spite of the rising investments in railroad manufacturing during the first half of the 19th century, the bulk of the investments of this period were not in this field. Even during the 1840s railroads did not account for a large share of factory investment over all. The majority of capital went into arms, ships, machine tools, and textiles. However, railroad manufacturers did contribute to the increased rate of output of the sector and this coincided with a much higher overall level of investment. Investment as a share of GDP averaged about 12% while during the second half of the 18th century it had just been of 5%. [333]

This was not the first time in British history that investment had correlated with the level of support for manufacturing and neither was Britain the only nation where such a phenomenon took place. Over and over again, all other sectors proved to be less investment intensive. Investment in agriculture during this period was only a fraction of the total income of agriculture. In manufacturing, investment almost equaled the income. No wonder would-be investors preferred non-manufacturing activities and only when the government reduced the risks did factories see any private investment. [334]

In the first half of the 19th century, the British government increased factory subsidies and reduced the risks considerably. Investment went up, coincident with a proportionate rise in savings. Savings as a share of GDP averaged about 13% while during the years 1750–99 they had averaged about 5%. This was not the first time that savings had correlated with manufacturing in Britain. Savings had consistently followed the fluctuations of manufacturing. The evidence suggests savings are fundamentally determined by the speed by which

330 Chambers, J. D.: *The Workshop of the World*, p. 52.
331 Brown, Richard: *Society and Economy in Modern Britain 1700–1850*, p. 232, 238.
332 Taylor, Arthur: *Laissez Faire and State Intervention in Nineteenth Century Britain*, p. 41.
333 Floud & McCloskey (ed): Ibid., p. 52.
334 Chambers,: Ibid., p. 5, 16.

wealth is created. Therefore, as the government supplied larger factory subsidies, the economy grew faster and greater possibilities for saving appeared. [335]

The links with technology were also very clear during this period. The escalating pace of invention was reflected in a flurry of patent registrations, and technologies were also imported more quickly. [336]

Technological advances showed up in rapid changes to production methods, which frequently translated into the elimination of jobs. Workers and producers associated with the oldest technology opposed such changes and protested in numerous ways. The accelerating growth of factory output during the second half of the 18th century was accompanied by an increase of petitions demanding that Parliament restrict new technology. In the following fifty years, anti-technology petitions became more numerous. These were not the only forms of protests. There were also street marches and protests such as the Luddite riots of 1811–16. [337]

Practically all of those inventions that aroused the anger of the masses were embodied in manufactured goods. The Luddite rioters vented their frustrations against the labor-saving machines that had deprived many people of their traditional occupations and deprived them of a living. Threshing machines, which became widely used in the 1820s, were a prominent target of the agricultural riots of the 1830s.

Further evidence suggesting a causal link between factory support and technology is found in patents. Most patents registered in the years 1800–49 were directly tied to manufactured goods. [338]

The most heavily subsidized fields saw the most rapid technological change. Perhaps the most technical development had to do with iron production, while armaments, shipbuilding, machine tool, and textiles industries saw the second fastest technological development. Those were the fields most promoted by subsidies.

Many have claimed that textiles were the leading field during 1750–1850. In reality iron production was larger, had more diversifying effects on the rest of the economy, and experienced faster technical change. Although the investment requirements for iron were much higher than for textile making, more was invested in this field. Iron was the main raw material for arms and in consequence the government allocated more resources to it.

Textiles did grow very quickly and underwent rapid technological change, but textiles were less related to national security concerns. Military uniforms and sailcloth for battle ships are important, but not as necessary as iron. Textiles were also promoted for export reasons, and London did allocate abundant funds for this industry, but not like iron. [339]

The advent of so many labor-saving machines led many to conclude that unemployment was going to rise, and restrictions on machines were proposed. However, the supply of jobs increased faster than ever before and unemployment fell. Trains eliminated numerous canal workers' and coachmen's jobs but the production of rails, locomotives and wagons created more jobs, which also offered higher wages. The advent of trains also created many new jobs in railway line construction and in railway transport services. Other new fields also created

---

335 Taylor, Arthur (ed): *The Standard of Living in Britain in the Industrial Revolution*, p. 96.
336 Deane, Phyllis: *The First Industrial Revolution*, p. 135, 136.
337 Floud & McCloskey (ed): Ibid., p. 34.
338 Mathias, Peter: *The First Industrial Nation*, p. 313.
339 Deane: Ibid., p. 106.

more jobs than they eliminated. The fastest creation of jobs in Britain's history up to that date came along at a time when factory subsidies were at a new high. [340]

While rapid change does cause some dislocations, the apocalyptic visions of waves of unemployment proved to be false and on top of that the average wages rose. During the first half of the 19th century real incomes doubled. Living conditions improved sharply. Meat for the first time became part of the normal diet of the working class. [341]

Even income distribution made noticeable progress, so that income distribution was less unequal in 1850 than in 1800. This was not the first time in history that manufacturing gave signs of having redistributive powers, but it was the first time such a phenomenon became significantly noticeable. The causation of such event seems to have been as follows: as manufacturing jobs, which paid better, were filled by farm workers rendered redundant by the new machines, working class wages rose rapidly and increased as a share of GDP.

Since ancient times, wages were higher in manufacturing than in farming. That evidence suggests that on average, manufacturing wages were also systemically higher than in services and construction. This phenomenon was not just observed in Britain, but also in the rest of Europe. Since the earliest of times also, the prices of manufactures tended to appreciate against those of the primary sector. The evidence suggests that the terms of trade of agricultural goods, fish, minerals and wood have systemically deteriorated. It would seem that such a situation is due to the much larger capacity of manufactures to incorporate technology.

Since technology is the only thing that creates wealth and since the goods of this sector are the ones that embody the most technology, it is inevitable that they are the most attractive. As a result, society has always been willing to pay higher prices for them and higher wages to the people who make them. When manufacturing grows rapidly, a larger share of the population works in factories and in consequence a larger portion of the workforce earns the highest possible salaries. The share of total income that gets accrued to the working class thus rises.

That however was not the only way by which a spontaneous redistribution of income took place. The granting of larger factory subsidies led to faster economic growth, which reduced the level of unemployment. In all countries, the unemployed and underemployed have always had the lowest incomes and in the Britain of 1800–49 the situation was like that. When the economy grew much faster, the incomes of these people experienced a major boost because many of them got full-time jobs. This put them at an income level that was close to the national average.

By the 1820s in Britain, investment in manufacturing exceeded that for agriculture. This led to an unprecedented share of the population moving to the city, where they could earn wages that were much higher than in farming. The majority of urbanites who left other jobs to go into the factories also experienced a rise in income because most of them had been struggling in low-paying service jobs such as street vendors.[342]

A mass migration depopulated the countryside in a period of about two centuries. In 1800, in Western countries about 90% of the population lived in the countryside; by 2000, the figure had fallen to about 1%.[343]

---

340 Taylor (ed): Ibid., p. 99.
341 Ibid., p. 95, 100, 102, 112.
342 Floud & McCloskey (ed): Ibid., p. 45.
343 Chambers: Ibid., p. 9.

The first half of the 19th century witnessed an improvement of conditions for factory workers in Britain. Legislation was enacted and the relationship between capital and labor gradually became less strained. In 1802, the first law reducing the appallingly long work hours was enacted. (In the 17th and 18th centuries, factories employed such a small share of the workforce that the dreadful conditions did not attract much attention.) Still, working conditions were terribly abusive. Child bondage was common during this period with eighteen working hours per day and beatings to accelerate work. Working children were only fed once a day; they labored in poorly lit rooms, without sanitation, frequently flooded with rain, with a muddy floor; and they were kept jailed during off-work hours. By 1830, factories manned by adult workers had none of these disadvantages. It is also worth noticing that during 1800–49, the working conditions were worst in those enterprises with the fewest new machines.[344]

The Elliptical Linkage Between Manufacturing and the Economy

Although enormous resources were subtracted from agriculture during the first half of the 19th century, farm output nonetheless went up. Agriculture averaged about 0.5% growth annually in 1750–99, while the rate in 1800–49 more than doubled to about 1.3%.

Notwithstanding the substantial rural depopulation of that period, agriculture performed better than ever. It was precisely when resources were subtracted from agriculture in order to transfer them to the factories that agriculture grew at the fastest pace. Agricultural productivity reached higher levels than anywhere else in the world. The British by then were using more farm tools than anyone else.[345]

It has been argued that the capitalist agrarian institutions were responsible for raising the productivity, but the same capitalist institutions had been present for the preceding fifty years. Enclosure was actually slowing down in the early 19th century and by 1830 it had almost completely stopped. [346]

However, during this period London subsidized the manufacturing sector more forcefully than ever before and as a result Britain was putting out farm tools and machines at a much faster pace. At the same time, the technological content of these goods rose rapidly. New implements like threshing machines were capable of cultivating more land, faster, with less waste, and with fewer workers. That would explain why in spite of the rural depopulation, the large expenditures on weapons, and the reduction of resources from agriculture, farm output expanded so fast.

During the 1840s, synthetic fertilizers (a chemical product), were invented and they immediately revolutionized agriculture. Output per acre soared. Fertilizers are a typical technology that originated in military manufacturing and is later applied in civilian uses. Prior to the 1840s, the rapid advance of chemicals largely rested in the textile industry, which had been promoted mostly to secure army uniforms and sails for warships. The chemical industry also had important links with metals, which were abundantly promoted for the production of weapons, and some progress was related to the production of gun powder.

---

344 *The Long Debate on Poverty*, The Institute of Economic Affairs, p. 67, 69, 78.
345 Floud & McCloskey (ed): p. 47, 96.
346 Wrigley, E.: *Continuity, Chance and Change*, p. 34–36.

The development of fertilizers and a wide range of other chemical products was the result of government subsidies.[347]

While farms in England were booming in 1800–49, in Ireland they were failing, notwithstanding Ireland's 1801 accession to the Union. In that year, Ireland went from being a colony to being an integral part of Britain. Ireland was given the right to decide the basic lines of its economic policies but the men in Dublin persisted in their physiocratic beliefs and continued to concentrate their efforts on agriculture. Manufacturing in Ireland was scarcely promoted and the rate of output of this sector continued to grow very slowly. [348]

With very little investment in factories, it was impossible to produce farm implements and fertilizers in significant quantity. It was also impossible to generate the export revenue that would have permitted large-scale importation of foodstuffs. Malnutrition was endemic and during the 1840s a major famine struck Ireland, which largely depopulated the island.[349]

Many explanations have been posited for Britain's growth in the first half of the 19th century. Many analysts have argued that trade liberalization was fundamentally responsible, because it improved efficiency and because it fostered exports.

By the early 19th century, mercantilist ideas started giving way to free trade beliefs. These asserted that trade was not a zero sum game, but one in which all nations could profit. Given the fact that Britain had become self sufficient in food and had attained world supremacy in manufacturing, most policy makers came to believe that trade liberalization was worth a try. Foreign trade was liberalized and exports grew faster than ever. Although a correlation between liberalization and economic growth seems to be present, the details show it is incidental.

Agriculture protection measures began to fall only after 1815. Import barriers for manufacturing fell in the 1820s and the Navigation Acts were trimmed in that same decade. Trade protection was gradually phased out, but was not dropped entirely until the 1840s. Restrictions on machine exports were lifted in 1843, the Corn Laws were repealed in 1846, import barriers on manufactures were lifted a few years later, and the Navigation Acts were finally abolished in 1849. [350]

If it was trade liberalization that brought the improvement to the economy, then the first two decades of the 19th century should have been very slow, especially during the fifteen years of Napoleonic Wars, when trade was distorted most. The fact however is that economic growth was significant. Despite the liberalization that was undertaken later, Britain was still far from practicing a free trade regime. During the second half of the century, on the other hand, Britain did effectively practice free trade, but the GDP rate was slower. Had trade liberalization been responsible for the improved performance of 1800–49, then 1850–99 should have been even better. That was not the case.

Trade liberalization was a positive policy in that it fostered competition, but the evidence indicates that it had very little to do with the acceleration of the economy. The evidence also suggests that exports were not one of the fundamental agents propelling the

347 Pope, Rex (ed): *Atlas of British Social and Economic History since 1700*, p. 36.
348 Cullen, L. & Smout, T. (ed): *Comparative Aspects of Scottish and Irish Economic and Social History 1600–1900*, p. 3, 8, 11.
349 Brown: Ibid., p. 233–235.
350 Cain: Ibid., p. 11, 12, 17, 18.

economy. During most of this period, the rate of exports correlated with that of GDP, but not always; exports stagnated in 1839–46 and the economy nonetheless expanded rapidly. Lags were frequently observed between the fluctuations of exports and the business cycle. With manufacturing, however, the correlation was very tight. During the 1839–46 cycle, factory output grew rapidly as a result of accelerated output of railroad-related goods. Since those goods were consumed domestically, exports remained static. Exports did not grow, but wealth was nonetheless created. [351]

During the first half of the 19th century, Britain had the highest wages in the world and many came to believe that this was what delivered the fast GDP rates. Seeing that the rapid growth of technology was associated with labor-saving machines, many thought that high wages stimulated labor saving innovations. It was thought that high salaries forced producers to look for labor-substituting alternatives. However, had high wages been really behind the accelerated pace of GDP and technology, things should have been very different during the following fifty years. In the second half of the century, Britain continued to have the highest wages in the world but the economy slowed down. And several nations in North America, Western Europe, Oceania, and South America that had lower labor costs grew faster than Britain. [352]

The Napoleonic Wars were Britain's last major military conflict during the 19th. If defense expenditures had been a drag on the economy, as most intellectuals believe, Britain's economic performance should have improved during the second half of the 19th century when there were only two relatively small conflicts (the Crimean War, 1854–56, and the Boer War, 1899–1900). In the first half of the century there had been about fifteen years of war while in the second there were only three. However, in spite of the smaller defense expenditures, during 1850–99 the economy slowed down. [353]

Many ideas trying to explain this situation appeared. Some economists argued that the gold backing of the pound gave rise to the rapid growth of the first half of the 19th century. But the pound had been strongly backed by gold even during the 18th century. Since the early 1700s, the pound had been convertible into a fixed amount of gold and during the first 80% of the 18th century the GDP rate was slow in comparison to 1800–49. Note also that the gold standard was suspended in 1797 and completely restored only in 1821. During these years, however, economic growth was much faster. [354]

Many have pointed to the minimal government intervention in the economy and the low tax rate, relative to the 20th. These theorists have claimed that this was key to the rapid growth. However, during the 18th century Britain was probably the most highly taxed nation in the world and it nonetheless attained the fastest GDP. During the first half of the 19th century, overall levels of taxation rose further and Britain remained among the most highly taxed in the world. It nonetheless attained the best performance. It is also worth noting that the government intervened in the economy much more in 1800–49 than formerly. In spite of that, the economy experienced a considerably acceleration. [355]

351 Aldcroft, D. & Fearon, P. (ed): *British Fluctuations 1790–1939*, p. 25, 26, 31, 32.
352 Floud & McCloskey (ed): Ibid., p. 32.
353 Taylor (ed): Ibid., p. 106.
354 Tomlinson, Jim: *Problems of British Economic Policy 1870–1945*, p. 28.
355 Davis, Lance & Huttenback, Robert: *Mammon and the Pursuit of Empire*, p. 112.

Intervention has frequently delivered negative results, but the evidence suggests that there is one area where it delivers positive results. When the state intervenes to promote manufacturing, society benefits generally, even when the state levies taxes to do it.

The ideal of less government and less taxation goes hand in hand with the belief that balanced budgets and no government debt are positive for the economy. Many argue that all these combined will deliver fast economic growth. However, during the Napoleonic Wars, budget deficits and public debt reached stratospheric levels and the economy nonetheless moved ahead briskly. [356]

What this and numerous other episodes in history suggest is that support for manufacturing is the main ingredient in the formula for growth. That is why even while committing policy errors such as running up budget deficits and public debt, fast economic growth may still be achieved.

The British government maintained balanced or surplus budgets after the Napoleonic Wars in order to rapidly reduce the national debt. Overall government expenditure as a share of GDP fell and the national debt shrank; it was even eliminated some time later. The economy during 1816–49 remained strong and it actually grew faster than during the Napoleonic Wars.

During this period, nevertheless, the government maintained and even reinforced its system of support for manufacturing. The sector received more fiscal and non-financial incentives and financial incentives were maintained at about the same level. While intervening and spending less, the government concentrated more on manufacturing and as a result the sector's rate of output accelerated and the economy did likewise. [357]

Continental Europe and Germany

Of the large nations of Europe, France attained the second fastest rates of economic growth during the first half of the 19th century; it also provided the second strongest support for manufacturing. The Napoleonic Wars forced France to try to match its adversary's weapons in quality and quantity. After 1815, the animosity that remained and the possibility of a future war with Britain led to continued military production. The French government continued and enlarged its support for civilian manufacturing as well, in order to enhance self-sufficiency. Britain had the fastest rates of civilian production, but France wanted to narrow or close the gap.

The second highest rate of manufacturing output in Europe coincided with the second fastest development of primary activities, construction, services, and trade.

During the first half of the century, the economy in Germany also picked up speed, although not like in Britain or France. Factory subsidies rose noticeably. Manufacturing expanded by about 2.0% annually and the economy grew by about 1.5%, after having grown only about a third as fast in the previous fifty years. (See tables in the appendix.)[358]

In the early 19th century, Germany also went through the convolution of the Napoleonic Wars. Napoleon easily conquered one state after another. In 1806 he confronted Prussia, the

---

356 Tames: Ibid., p. 19.
357 Tomlinson: Ibid., p. 46.
358 Sabillon: Ibid., p. 182; Fogel, Robert William: *The Escape from Hunger and Premature Death, 1700–2100: Europe, America and the Third World*; Madison, Angus: *The World Economy: Historical Statistics*; Madison, Angus: *The World Economy: A Millennial Perspective.*

largest and best equipped of these states. The Prussian army was also easily defeated and this sent shock waves throughout the whole German territory. Even the aristocracy realized that drastic changes were needed. [359]

During the years in which Napoleon ruled the German states support for manufacturing dropped, output fell, and the overall economy performed similarly. There were, however, a few fields which grew rapidly as a result of Napoleon's continental blockade of British merchandise. Import-substitution efforts stimulated fields such as textiles, refined sugar, optic lenses, and precision implements.

It had been thought that the German states were only capable of producing agricultural goods, and possibly small amounts of manufactured goods of poor quality. During the Napoleonic Wars, however, the states managed to produce relatively large amounts of certain types of factory goods and even succeeded in making major technological breakthroughs. Up to that time, optic lenses and precision instruments were only produced in Britain due to their high technological content. Several German states succeeded in developing that technology.

Notwithstanding those bits of progress, overall manufacturing production dropped as Napoleon suppressed armament production and subsidies for civilian manufacturing remained minimal. Napoleon also implemented a trade regimen that was very unfavorable for the German states. While French and Italian goods had free access to the German market, German goods had to pay tariffs of up to 275% ad valorem in order to enter France or Italy.[360]

Important geopolitical changes took place in Germany during the wars as Napoleon fused numerous states in order to make larger ones that could act as a counterweight against Prussia and Austria. Many smaller states also fused on their own initiative. By the time Napoleon was finally defeated in 1814, the total had been reduced to some three dozen Germanys. When these three dozen states began to recover from the humiliation the French emperor had inflicted, they immediately started looking for ways to avoid a future defeat.

Their first conclusion was that they needed to overcome France's superiority in weapons. The flood of superior French civilian goods also showed that the states were lagging in civilian manufacturing. Once the Napoleonic continental system was ended, Germany was flooded with more advanced British goods and German producers experienced a severe drop in sales. This bolstered the argument of those who were calling for the states to step up manufacturing subsidies.[361]

The most vocal proponent of this idea was Frederick List (1789–1846). He believed that countries that were lagging in the production of factory goods needed to nourish their infant producers for a certain time with trade protection and subsidies. Once parity with the most manufacturized nations was reached, governments could suspend the assistance. List got to that idea by looking at the example of Britain, which had endorsed trade protection throughout the 18th as it attained superiority over the rest of Europe. The case of France, which had reached the highest levels of development while protecting its industries, also drove him to that conclusion.

---

359 Gaxotte, Pierre: *Histoire de l'Allemagne*, p. 452–457.
360 Ibid., p. 468, 469.
361 Bramsted, Ernest: *Germany*, p. 2, 92, 118.

The evidence suggests that List was also wrong in believing that manufacturing needed support only briefly and that once developed, it could sustain rapid growth without the help of the state. The history of Germany and other countries repeatedly demonstrated that the moment the support vanished, output stagnated or contracted. List missed noting that the investment-intensive nature of manufacturing makes it the least attractive for investors, so that only with constant subsidies is it possible to defy the natural state of affairs and attain a constant high rate of investment in this sector.[362]

List and others also sought to unify all the German states into a single country that could stand as an equal with France and Britain. To that end, List championed the elimination of tariffs among the German states. Prussian commercial unification occurred in 1819 and commercial unification among most of the states took place in 1835.

National unification also convinced List and many others that it would be important to promote the railroads, for they would integrate the German states politically and economically. They thought economic integration would create a wider market, which would give Germany more economic and political clout to confront the military powers of the continent.[363]

Classical economists on the other hand argued that Germany should content itself with producing agricultural goods, other primary goods, and a few manufactures like perfume and toys, which by then were among the few manufactures in which the Germans were internationally competitive. It was asserted that the historical characteristics of the states made them unsuitable to produce manufactured goods efficiently. However, national security concerns, the desire to match the most developed nations, and the desire to unify the states politically increased as the century wore on, and the arguments of classical economists were increasingly sidelined.[364]

Support for manufacturing was progressively increased, manufacturing output accelerated, and the rest of the economy moved in tandem. During 1816–49, growing numbers of state-owned factories were created and entrepreneurs received ever growing subsidies. As in the past, support was stronger in heavy manufacturing where the investment needs were largest, and where the products were more closely linked to the goals of the state. Private investors were not much inclined to risk their resources on weapons, iron, steel, shipbuilding, machine tools, and trains.

During the 1830s, the rate of manufacturing accelerated considerably as a result of the new railroads. The first railroad in Britain in 1825 had inspired the champions of political unification in Germany, and policy makers in the states began supplying subsidies to the producers of metals, rails, locomotives, wagons, and machine tools. They as well guaranteed a high rate of return to private railroad companies. Railroad construction began in 1830 and by 1838 the first railway began to carry freight and passengers in Bavaria. Support for military and civilian manufacturing was already on the rise, but with the coming of railroads, the subsidies increased. The sector had been growing faster since the end of the Napoleonic Wars, and in the 1830s it spiked upward as did GDP figures over all.[365]

362 Ibid., p. 118, 119.
363 Gaxotte: Ibid., p. 498, 499, 492.
364 Kitchen, Martin: *The Political Economy of Germany 1815–1914*, p. 45, 11, 26.
365 Ibid., p. 22, 27, 47.

In the 1840s, state governments offered still more generous subsidies for the developing railroads. Private sector investment rose rapidly, but still too slow to fulfill the goals of the governments. The states thus began to build their own railroads. State railroads meant guaranteed purchases to private manufacturers at prices that assured a profit. This also led to the creation of more state factories producing metals, rails, and locomotives.

The support for railroad expansion was so strong that by the end of the 1840s Germany had the second largest railroad network in Europe. Railroad-related manufacturing expanded at the second fastest pace in Europe and overall factory production also went up. GDP figures reached new highs.

The sector increased so fast that Germany's historical profile as a net importer of manufactures began to change. Germany began to self supply most of its needs and exports rose quickly. Until the 1830s, it had imported most of its textile machinery from France and Belgium, but by the 1840s Germany filled most of its own demand. Up to the 1830s, most of the iron used in Germany was imported, but by the 1840s German producers could supply most of the local demand. By then, most rails were made in German rolling mills.

In 1800-49, agricultural production also grew faster. Agricultural tools including plows, mowing machines, seed drills, and threshing machines were produced in larger numbers. Most of the machines were copied from those made in Britain and other countries, but some were completely new inventions. Independent of whether the technology was created domestically or imported, the fact is that those machines revolutionized agriculture. They not only increased the amount of land under cultivation, but also the output per acre. During this period in Prussia, the amount of land under cultivation doubled. The bulk of those farm implements came as the result of subsidies. [366]

During this half century, agriculture grew fastest in the 1840s, coincidental with the decade of the largest factory subsidies. However, notwithstanding the considerable enlargement of the food supply, famines continued to occur. The last one took place in 1848 and was compounded by a typhus epidemic, which together claimed thousands of lives. That in turn led to an uprising that forced significant changes in the social and political institutions of the states. By the way, the famine coincided with a steep contraction in manufacturing during the years 1847-48, which was accompanied by a steep recession. In spite of this, the incidence of famines dropped noticeably during the first half of the 19th century.

The evidence strongly suggests that the farm tools and agricultural machines were fundamentally responsible for the considerable rise in agricultural output. By the early 19th century, about one third of the land that was considered arable regularly lay fallow for lack of any means of cultivation. In those days, German farms were far behind Britain in terms of the per capita utilization of farm manufactures and the rate of output.

During the period 1800-49, mining in Germany also enjoyed a boom. The development was fastest during the 1840s, when the production of pickaxes, bars, shovels, and digging machines expanded most rapidly. The steam engine revolutionized mining in this decade as it was used to pump water out of deep mines, making deeper coal deposits accessible. The production of coal increased considerably.[367]

Infrastructure projects also expanded rapidly. The total miles of surfaced roads and navigable canals were increased sharply. Within the first half of the century, the fastest growth

---

366 Ibid., p. 50, 51, 52, 56, 61, 129.
367 Ibid., P. 80, 84, 15, 56, 32, 11.

of infrastructure occurred in the 1840s, the decade when the production of construction manufactures was fastest. In 1845, the largest canal of the era opened to traffic. Linking the Rhine, the Main, and the Danube, this became the most important waterway in Germany. Without dredgers, other digging machines and building equipment, the construction of canals would have been impossible. Technology was heavily concentrated in these goods and that is what allowed for such a radical transformation of nature.[368]

During the first half of the 19th century technology advanced in Germany faster than ever, especially in the 1840s. Anti-technology demonstrations were common as traditional occupations were destroyed. These demonstrations generally targeted the machines that had eliminated jobs or the factories that produced the machines. In the 1840s, the weavers of Silesia destroyed textile machines.

Russia in Stagnation

Russia's economic performance during the first half of the 19th century was dismal. Its rates of growth were far below those of Western Europe and they were even lower than its own record during the second half of the 18th century.

Most economic historians attribute the poor performance to several specific factors. Of all these factors, however, serfdom has been singled out as the most important. It has been argued that Russia's backwardness in relation to North Western Europe was principally the result of its rigid social system. Serfdom restrained the mobility of labor and this supposedly inhibited productivity improvements in all the sectors of the economy. [369]

Had that been true, it is hard to explain why the economy performed so much better during the 18th century. During the 18th century and in particular during the reign of Peter the Great, serfdom was more deeply entrenched than during 1800–49. Peter reinforced the system by institutionalizing it beyond agriculture (in the fields of mining and manufacturing), while in the first half of the next century serfdom was beginning to wane. By the 1820s, forced labor in manufacturing came to an end.[370]

GDP figures should have been lower during the 18th century, if widespread serfdom alone was such a significant factor. However, the evidence suggests that Russia's GDP in the years 1800–49 is likely to have grown on average by about 0.3% annually, while in the 18th century it averaged about 0.5%.[371]

It is also worth noting that on the eve of the abolition of serfdom in 1860, about 40% of Russia's population was free of any kind of serf status. That 40% represented a population of about 32 million, more than the whole population of France or Britain. If this argument held water then output in those sectors should have been higher than or at least similar to that of France or Britain. But in those years Russia produced considerably less than its western neighbors. Thus serfdom cannot be said to have constrained the amount of labor available at that time for manufacturing and mining in Russia.[372]

368 Gaxotte: Ibid., p. 500.
369 Parker, W. H.: *A Historical Geography of Russia*, p. 232, 243.
370 Nove, Alec: *Political Economy and Soviet Socialism*, p. 35.
371 Sabillon: Ibid., p.120; Madison, Angus: *The World Economy: Historical Statistics*; Madison, Angus: *The World Economy: A Millennial Perspective*; Fogel: Ibid
372 Supple, Barry (ed): *The Experience of Economic Growth*, p. 415.

It has also been argued that state intervention in the economy was larger in Russia than in Western Europe and such distortions had detrimental effects on production. There were indeed more trade distortions, more state companies, and more monopolies and cartels than in Western Europe, and there is no doubt that these policies hampered competition and thus efficiency. However, if that had been the major cause of the stagnation of the years 1800–49, the economic performance should have been worse during the 18th century because at that time, there were even more market distortions.

During the period 1920–90, competition-hindering practices were far greater than in the first half of the 19th century. Market forces were actually eliminated and in spite of that Russia experienced a dramatically faster rate of GDP growth than in 1800–49 — much faster than any other seventy-year period in Russian history. It is also important to mention that from 1920 to 1990, Russia endured a very rigid social structure that largely restrained the mobility of labor, not just in agriculture but in every other sector. That however did not inhibit Russia from attaining its best performance ever. It is evident that state intervention in and of itself was not cause of stagnation, either.[373]

Some have also argued that Russia's lack of natural resources was largely responsible for the stagnation of the first half of the 19th century. It is held that in order to access and utilize its resources, Russia had greater obstacles to overcome. The soil in most of the Northwest of the country was poor in comparison to that of Britain and France. There was fertile soil, but very far away from population centers. The climate was also harsher and population centers were very far away from the known deposits of iron ore and coal.

Of course the same geological, climatic, and geographic conditions were also present during the second half of the 19th century and in spite of that, GDP rates accelerated exponentially. During 1800–49, growth was about 0.3% annually and during the following fifty years it expanded by about 3.0%. (See tables in the appendix.) It cannot be argued that constant variables such as soil and climate deter economic growth in one period but not in the next period. Note also that Scandinavia, which has the same climatic and geological characteristics of Russia, attained much faster rates of growth during the first half of the 19th century.[374]

Others have actually inverted the argument and asserted that it was Russia's abundance of natural resources what hindered growth. It is claimed that the abundance of wood and the numerous water mills along the rivers of the Urals served as disincentives to the more rapid spread of steam and coal as sources of energy. If that was valid for the first half of the 19th century, then it should have also been valid for the following fifty years, and GDP rates shouldn't have differed by much. The fact is that they differed by a vast margin.

It was also argued that Russia's low wages relative to Western Europe prevented technological progress and organizational rationalization. The exact opposite argument was actually utilized in Britain during that same period. It was held that Britain's high wages stimulated investment in new labor-saving technology and thus delivered rapid growth. Low wages can hardly hinder growth in a given country while spurring growth in another. It is not either logically acceptable to argue that in one country low wages can hinder technology and economic growth, and that at the next moment the same low wages in the same

373 Ibid., p. 414.

374 Ibid., p. 416, 417; Sabillon: Ibid., p. 120; Madison, Angus: *The World Economy: Historical Statistics*; Fogel: Ibid.

country no longer produce those results. And yet Russia during the second half of the 19th century continued to have the lowest wages in Europe, but technology and the economy expanded much faster than during the preceding fifty years.[375]

It has also been stated that Russia's lack of an entrepreneurial class was largely responsible for the poor economic performance of the years 1800–49. However, there was hardly any more of an entrepreneurial class later that century, and the economy nonetheless performed far better. More to the point, from 1920 to 1990, the economy in the aggregate performed even better. A long-term analysis shows that the entrepreneurial factor was not the decisive variable affecting growth.

During 1800–1849, Russia had the least developed infrastructure in Europe. Many analysts have asserted that the weak transport and communication system were largely behind the poor economic performance. In the second half of the century Russia remained last in the class, but it did make significant progress in infrastructure development — and it outperformed Britain in terms of GDP growth rate. In that half century, Britain's infrastructure was one of the most advanced; but Britain's GDP growth was slower than Russia's. While Britain averaged about 2.4% growth annually, Russia managed 3.0%. The historical data suggests that Russia's backward infrastructure was not as important as the rate of infrastructure improvement in influencing the overall economic growth in the first half and in the latter half of 1800–99.[376]

During the 18th century, Russia sold a considerable amount of iron, ships, textiles, and several other goods to Britain. However, with the coming of the Napoleonic Wars, the British market disappeared. When the war ended, Britain had increased its production so much that it could self supply practically all of its needs. Russia was never able to export to Britain again in that half century. Many historians have claimed that the loss of the British market was a significant cause for the poor showing of this period. If so, the performance of the second half of the 19th century would have been similar to the first, because Russia was not able to export to Britain for the rest of the century. Yet in this second period Russia's growth was far more robust.

It is also worth noting that aside from the years of the Napoleonic Wars, other nations did succeed in exporting to Great Britain; France, Belgium, and Holland actually increased their trade to Britain during the first half of the century and so did newcomers such as the US and the German states.[377]

Some analysts have argued that the stagnation of this period and the systemic retardation with respect to Western Europe during the preceding centuries resulted from Russia's inability to have acquired colonies. In fact Russia conquered a great swath of territory from the mid-15th century right on through the 16th, 17th, 18th and first half of the 19th century. This was a territory that added up to as much as those acquired by Western European nations. The economy systematically performed poorly anyway. And during the years 1800–49, the economies of the German states and Switzerland grew much faster than Russia, even though they did not acquire colonies. So that was not the decisive factor.[378]

375 Brenner, Y.: *A Short History of Economic Progress*, p. 178.
376 Madison, Angus: *Economic Growth in Japan and the USSR*, p. 83; Sabillon: Ibid., p. 120, 183; Madison, Angus: *The World Economy: A Millennial Perspective*.
377 Blackwell, William: *The Beginnings of Russian Industrialization*, p. 58.
378 Blackwell, William: *The Industrialization of Russia*, p. 3.

It was as well held that Russia's vast territory, with a very low population density and a rudimentary communication system, amounted to a highly fractured market that made production and trade very difficult. But the United States, the German states, and the Swiss Cantons should have suffered as well, if that were a critical factor, for their confederate political configuration also created fragmented markets, and the US was extended over a large and scarcely populated territory with many isolated regions too. GDP figures in these three nations and in particular in the US were nonetheless vastly superior to Russia's from 1800 to 1849.[379]

While the orthodox interpretations suggest some contributing factors, they clearly do not add up to a full explanation for the discrepancy. The only factor that changes in tandem with the changes in results is support for manufacturing. During this period, Moscow's support for manufacturing fell and the growth rate of the sector sagged. Resources were shifted from the factories to other fields and the economy deteriorated.[380]

The motivations behind this situation were diverse. On the one hand, the French Revolution sent shock waves throughout Europe's monarchies. Many aristocrats were decapitated, imprisoned, exiled and dispossessed. Since it was the French bourgeoisie who had led the revolution, the Tsar and the Russian nobility concluded that it was in their best interest to suppress this social class and to snuff out anything that smelled of revolutionary spirit. Since the bourgeoisie was strongly linked to manufacturing, the suppression policy translated into a number of measures intended to hamper the growth of this sector. Grants, subsidized financing, tax benefits, free or subsidized land, and other incentives were significantly reduced.

The years 1800–49 in Europe were characterized by a rise in urban worker unrest aimed mainly at improving the living conditions of the proletariat. However, complaints frequently spilled over into demands for the abolition of the monarchy and the privileges of the aristocracy. The most vocal among the worker organizations were those that emanated from large factories. The tsars and their advisors were quick to notice that, and the government actively resisted the development of manufacturing for fear of the "scourge of the proletariat". The main developmental policy was increasing agricultural output (especially for export) in order not to disturb the privileged position of the aristocracy.[381]

Aside from those considerations, there were also a number of ideological factors that hampered the manufacturing sector. After the Napoleonic Wars, there was much debate over industrialization. Upper rank government officials were mostly inspired by the ideas of Adam Smith; they argued that Russia could not generate the vast amounts of capital needed for manufacturing and was better suited to remain a supplier of raw material and an importer of factory goods. There were also strong physiocratic tendencies among policy makers who saw agriculture as the key for growth. There were even romantic idealizations of rural life that asserted that, economically and morally, the Russian peasant was better off under serfdom than under the quasi-slavery of factory work.[382]

Alexander I, who assumed power after having conspired to assassinate his father, reigned from 1801–25. He was not passionate about military conquest nor did he have the

---

379 Parker: Ibid., p. 243.
380 Blackwell: *The Beginnings of Russian Industrialization*, p. 157, 174.
381 Brenner: Ibid., p. 176.
382 Blackwell: Ibid., p. 123.

ambition to match Western Europe's development. Increasingly led by mystical and pseudo-religious ideas, he neglected investment even more after the Napoleonic Wars. Nicholas I, who reigned from 1825–55, was no more interested in engaging in large-scale wars or in trying to catch up with Western Europe.[383]

Another factor was the absence of a major attack on Russia. Had Russia been seriously threatened, the leadership would have been probably galvanized to action. Because national security was not apparently at stake, Moscow saw no need for expanded output of arms and related goods.

During the first half of the 19th century, Russia was at war or engaged in military operations for about a third of the time, but these engagements never reached a high level of intensity. The largest war was that against Napoleon and it mostly consisted of intermittent short-term skirmishes. The war ended in 1807 and broke out again in 1812, but the French were mostly defeated by the cold weather. During this period, there were also small wars with Sweden, Turkey, Persia, Poland, and Hungary. Russia came out victorious in all of them, without the Russian army having to over stretch. These other adversaries had smaller armies and/or a lower level of armament technology as that of Russia. The defeat of the great Napoleon and victories over all of these nations convinced the government that the Russian Army was invincible, and confirmed their view that there was no need to increase military spending.[384]

The concomitant effect of these events persuaded the Russian government to limit its support for manufacturing and to merely maintain the existing level of factory output. In 1800–49, this sector expanded very slightly, averaging only 0.5% and the economy grew by about 0.3%.[385]

Even this terribly slow pace was only possible with the support of the government. The textile industry was the fastest growing civilian field and this was also the most subsidized field. Desperately in need of coarse woolen cloth for army uniforms during the Napoleonic Wars, the government promoted and protected the industry very enthusiastically. After the wars, this support declined considerably but nevertheless remained higher than for most other fields.[386]

Other civilian manufactures also witnessed some progress due to the pressures of war. With government help, the first beet sugar factory was founded in 1802 as the Napoleonic embargo on British goods created a scarcity of sugar. During the rest of 1800–49, beet sugar manufacturing developed relatively fast and there was also a continuation of subsidies.

Once arms production stagnated, there was practically no progress in heavy manufacturing. However, even the low level of production of the first four decades of the period would not have continued without support. A large share of the output of metals, arms, and machine tools came directly from state factories and the share coming from private producers was largely the result of government incentives. The largest steam engine producer was the state complex of Aleksandrovsk. In 1802, the first producer of agricultural machinery was founded — as a result of the lavish incentives offered by the government to a British

383 Kirchner, Walter: *A History of Russia*, p. 129, 139, 146, 133, 136, 131.
384 Blackwell: Ibid., p. 179, 184.
385 Nove, Alec: *An Economic History of the USSR*, p. 11; W. H. Parker: *A Historical Geography of Russia*, p. 243, 245; Sabillon: Ibid., p. 120.
386 Kirchner: Ibid., P. 141.

producer. Most of the industrial machinery produced was for the textile industry, and a very large share came from state factories. [387]

The 1840s showed the fastest rates of economic growth in this half century and this coincided with the strongest level of factory subsidization. The tsars came to recognize the need for railroads, even though they saw them as potentially aiding proletarian revolutionaries. By the mid-1830s, the government began to construct the first rail line from Moscow to St. Petersburg, thus bending on its policy of manufacturing suppression. This first rail line was fundamentally built for the rapid mobilization of troops in case of insurrection, although commercial considerations were also a motivation.

The government offered large subsidies to the producers of iron, rails, locomotives, wagons, and machine tools. The bulk of the goods necessary for the line were made in the 1840s. Factory output accelerated and the economy immediately began to grow faster. It was only in this decade that iron production surpassed 18th century peak levels.[388]

Many analysts have argued that Russia's faster growth in the 1840s resulted from Britain's repeal in the early part of this decade of laws that prohibited the export of machinery. It is true that with the introduction of the British steam power loom in the 1840s, textile output in Russia benefited considerably. Other British machines boosted other industries. However, the US, Germany, and the rest of Western Europe were also deprived of British machines during the decades prior to the 1840s, and they nonetheless attained much faster factory and GDP rates in 1800–39 than Russia in the 1840s. It is evident that the curtailment of British exports wasn't a major factor inhibiting growth in Russia.[389]

Technology remained largely stagnant during the first half of the 19th century, its progress noticeably slower than during the preceding fifty years. Within this period, however, the 1840s saw the greatest progress, coinciding with the decade when factories were most subsidized. During this half century, the retardation of Russia's technological development with respect to Western Europe became more evident and this coincided with a widening of the gap between the rate of manufacturing output in the West and that of Russia.[390]

Agriculture, mining, and the other primary activities were stagnant during this period and this went hand in hand with stagnation in the production and utilization of primary sector tools and machines. By the early 19th century, it was known that Russia had vast deposits of bituminous and anthracite coal as well as oil. However, the deposits languished in the ground simply because the machines needed to extract them were not available. The situation changed radically during the later part of the century, when manufacturing production expanded at a very quick pace. It was only then that the exploitation of minerals began in earnest.[391]

Moscow's only developmental policy was the promotion of agriculture and in spite of its efforts in this domain, farming performance was poor — even worse than in the preceding fifty years. During 1800–49, agricultural output slowed down to a rate of about 0.2% annually and the incidence of famines increased, giving rise to numerous peasant uprisings. Most peasant meals were just bread and water, only occasionally complemented with cabbage

---

387 Blackwell: Ibid., p. 38, 51, 53, 63, 65.
388 Ibid., p. 40, 56, 262, 274.
389 Dobb, Maurice: *Soviet Economic Development since 1917*, p. 57.
390 Blackwell: Ibid., p. 326.
391 Ibid., p. 62.

and potatoes. Since Russian agriculture utilized so few manufactured implements, it was impossible to raise the productivity per acre.[392]

All other sectors and domains of the Russian economy were also stagnant. Trade barely made any progress. Soon after the Congress of Vienna, high trade barriers were erected and they remained very high throughout the rest of this half century. From 1822 to 1850, the state imposed a 600% ad valorem tariff on pig iron.

Many have argued that the high levels of protection were fundamentally responsible for the stagnation of trade. However, if that had really been the case, commerce should have remained stagnant during the last decades of the century. Trade protection was high during the late 19th century but even so, trade accelerated dramatically. That correlated with an abundant subsidization of factories.

The government imposed the high trade barriers with the goal of assisting domestic producers who had experienced major losses after the Napoleonic Wars due to a flood of British imports. Had the trade barriers been of assistance to manufacturing, output would have increased. It did not. The tariffs not only failed to increase output, but they also hurt quality. This situation gives further credence to the belief that the key to increasing manufacturing lies with fiscal, financial and non-financial incentives, which were barely supplied during the years 1800–49.[393]

Grants were minuscule and private banks were not induced to lend to manufacturing. Left to do as they pleased, private banks concentrated mostly on financing commerce and on lending to the government. The state banks, in their turn, focused on lending to agriculture and much of the remaining went to finance commerce. In 1817 the State Commercial Bank was founded, and as its name indicates, it was only interested in financing trade. In 1824, however, it was ordered to lend a small share of its assets to manufacturing.

The development of financial institutions also stagnated during this half century. Banks stopped growing and the techniques and methods of operation made very few advances. With the creation of wealth stagnant, the overall level of savings could not grow and banks were therefore incapable of increasing assets. In Western Europe, bank assets grew very quickly and that coincided with an exponentially stronger level of factory subsidization.[394]

China

During the first half of the 19th century, China's Manchu rulers lost their conquering drive of the preceding century. Neither were they particularly interested in catching up with the West in producing civilian goods. The government allocated a smaller share of resources for the production of arms and civilian goods. This ultimately translated into a reduction in support for manufacturing and this coincided with an economic slowdown. Manufacturing averaged about 0.3% per year and the economy expanded by about 0.2%. (See tables at the end of the book.)[395]

392 Smith, R. & Christian, D.: *Bread and Salt*, p. 255; Kirchner: Ibid., p. 146, 147; Fogel: Ibid.; Madison, Angus: *The World Economy: Historical Statistics.*

393 Gatrell, Peter: *The Tsarist Economy 1850–1917*, p. 149.

394 Blackwell: Ibid., p. 88–90.

395 Howe, Christopher: *China's Economy*, p. 10–20; Sabillon: Ibid., p. 111; Madison, Angus: *Chinese Economic Performance in the Long Run*; Madison, Angus: *The World Economy: A Millennial Perspective.*

During 1800–49, China had a run of weak emperors. Jiaquing reigned from 1799 to 1820 and emperor Daoguang from 1821–50. Jiaquing was the son of the great Qianlong, but unlike his father, he had no interest in conquest or in large ventures. He and his advisors were convinced that investments in weapons and related goods were wasteful and subtracted wealth, so as soon as he took hold of power, he began to cut expenditures for the armories. Pirate activity along the coast had increased in the late 18th century and to discourage it, he reduced subsidies for shipbuilding to decrease shipping. A high seas fleet ceased to exist. Since 1800, the vaunted power of Manchu armies waned.[396]

There were several rebellions during this period with religious undertones. The largest was the White Lotus Rebellion (1796–1806). Another broke out in 1813, but both were crushed with relative ease with the existing arsenals and never represented a major national security concern that could have forced an increase in the allocations for military manufacturing.

During emperor Daoguang's rule, more government expenditures were transferred from the weapons budget to the non-manufacturing sectors. Even since the late 18th century, Qianlong had concluded that the natural limits to which China could territorially expand had been reached. Beyond those borders lived people with very different ethnicity and culture. His two successors took the same view, thus eliminating the justification for increasing armament production or even maintaining existing levels of output.[397]

The rapid growth of British imperialism and the quest for new export markets eventually led to a direct confrontation with China. When in 1839 Britain tried to force China to open up to trade and the Chinese opposed the sale of opium, war broke out. The First Opium War lasted from 1839 to 1842. Britain had far more advance weapons. While the typical Chinese warship had thirteen guns, British naval vessels had a hundred, which shot faster, further, and more precisely. Although Britain utilized only a tiny fraction of its navy and fought in the enemy's territory, it won. As the victor, Britain demanded the opening of five Treaty Ports. This was another example which suggested that technology is the bottom line for determining the outcome of wars. China had a huge demographic superiority and knew the battlefield better than anybody else. In spite of that, it lost.[398]

This was a terrible humiliation for China, terrible enough that the government should have been induced to make larger investments in armories and other factory fields. Unfortunately, the Emperor and his entourage were unable to rise to the occasion, and during the 1840s there was no significant increase in factory subsidies. Economic growth was terribly slow.[399]

The evidence suggests that reducing investment in armaments is a good idea, so long as those resources are transferred to civilian manufacturing. However, there was nothing within Beijing's view of the world that would encourage them to do that. Thus subsidization of factories was actually reduced in the first half of the 19th century, which dovetailed with a reduction in per capita output of factory goods and a noticeable economic deceleration. Every sector of the economy slowed down. Agricultural output fell and this led to a rise

---

396 Adshead, S. A.: *China in World History*, p. 246, 247.
397 The Cambridge Encyclopedia of China, p. 213–215.
398 Bergere, M., Bianco, L. & Domes, J.: *La Chine au XXe Siecle*, p. 39.
399 Gray, Jack: *Rebellions and Revolutions*, p. 2, 30.

in famines. During this period, Beijing's only developmental policy consisted in promoting agriculture and in spite of that, farming deteriorated.[400]

The lack of progress in manufacturing coincided with a lack of progress in technology. In this period, China's technological retardation with the West widened.[401]

China's population grew rapidly in the 18th century, averaging a rate of about 0.8% annually; it almost tripled in size. Many have argued that rapid population growth exhausted the available resources and caused economic decline in the 19th century. However, Britain in the 18th had a similar growth of population, which averaged about 0.6%, but Britain did not experience a similar deceleration in the 19th century. Even more damaging for this argument is the case of the US, where the population grew exponentially faster during the 18th and 19th centuries than in China, averaging more than 5.0%. At that astronomical rate, resources should have been rapidly depleted. The US nonetheless had the highest GDP figures in the world during the 19th century.[402]

The White Lotus Rebellion fiscally exhausted the government and from then on the budget was constantly in deficit. During the 18th century, the budget had been mostly balanced or in surplus. Since budget deficits have always been seen as causal agents for a poor economic performance, many have argued that the fiscal imbalances of the years 1800–49 were responsible for China's decline. History however does not substantiate such a claim, for a correlation between the two is impossible to find in China or elsewhere.

During the first half of the 19th century, the British were in control of India and maintained balanced budgets, but the economy performed worse than in China and averaged about 0.1% annually. Egypt was administered by Britain from the 1880s to the 1910s and fiscal rectitude was maintained the whole time. The Egyptian economy, however, grew at miserly pace. On the other hand, during the second half of the 20th century, South Korea experienced constant budget deficits and in spite of that it attained one of the highest rates of economic growth in the world, averaging about 7.1%. In the late 20th century, China ran constant budget deficits and attained extraordinary rates of economic growth.[403]

In the 18th century, China maintained a constant trade surplus with the rest of the world. In the early 19th century, due to the rapid growth of opium imports, the trade balance began to shift and starting in the 1820s it went into deficit. Many economic historians have argued that the shift in the trade balance was responsible for the deceleration of the economy. On this matter, history does not either present a consistent correlation that would indicate a causal linkage. During the years 1800–49, the US and Germany had constant trade deficits and in spite of that they attained much higher rates of economic growth. The American economy grew by about 2.7% annually and the German states by about 1.5%, while China grew by just 0.2%. Levels of support for manufacturing and rates of factory output did however correlate with the growth figures. In the US the expansion of factory output was about 3.3% per year, in the German states it was about 2.0%, and in China it was just 0.3%.[404]

400 Fairbank, John: *China—A New History*, p. 186–190.
401 Perkins, Dwight (ed): *China's Modern Economy in Historical Perspective*, p. 1–3.
402 Kolb, Albert: Ostasien—*China, Japan, Korea*, p. 151–217; Sabillon: Ibid., p. 111, 147, 183; Madison, Angus: *The World Economy: Historical Statistics*.
403 Sabillon: Ibid.
404 Kolb: Ibid.; Sabillon: Ibid., p. 111–182.

In 1684 the Manchus endorsed a free trade policy with the rest of the world. In 1757, however, they changed their mind and endorsed a very restrictive policy which limited foreign trade to the southern port of Canton. This policy was maintained until 1842. Many economic historians have argued that the slowdown of the first half of the 19th century was the result of the trade protection that prevailed in this period.

Here again, the evidence does not back such a claim. In the second half of the 19th century, trade protection progressively increased in several nations such as Germany and Russia, but there the economy instead of decelerating progressively gained in speed. Canada, Australia, and New Zealand had a free trade regime in the first half of the 19th century and the economy was largely stagnant. In the second half of the century, trade barriers rose considerably and the economy accelerated. Besides, China's trade restrictions were not seriously enforced. Before 1842, Europeans traded actively in Macao, Amoy, and several other posts along the coast.[405]

Japan

In Japan, there was no noticeable improvement in the economy during the first half of the 19th century. Rates of GDP continued to expand, but very slowly. This poor performance was paralleled by very low rates of subsidization for manufacturing. It seems this sector grew by about 0.3% per year and the economy by about 0.2%. (See tables at the end of the book.)[406]

During the period 1800–49, Japan did not engage in practically any form of military confrontation. No effort was made to increase the production of arms. Japan's policy of seclusion continued, restricting contact with the outside world. Given the very scant trading activity with more advanced nations, Japan was not confronted with the fact that other nations were producing superior goods. That would have almost surely driven them to at least some efforts to replicate those goods. Policies in this period tended to maintain the existing low level of support for military and civilian manufacturing.[407]

By the end of the 18th century, a growing number of warships, whalers, merchant vessels, and survey ships from Britain, Russia, France, and the US were appearing in Japanese waters. In 1804 a Russian envoy arrived in Nagasaki, requesting commercial relations. When his demands were refused, his men attacked the small island of Etorfu. In 1808 a British warship made an incursion in Nagasaki in an attempt to compile information about Japan and force some trade openings. In 1811 a Russian warship made a similar incursion. On these occasions, the Japanese were successful in repelling the foreigners with their small arsenals and they concluded that there was not a need to increase them.[408]

In the 1830s, a famine struck the archipelago, causing large peasant uprisings. The central government at Edo (later Tokyo) began to think that some changes were needed. Minor reforms were undertaken, but support for manufacturing was not increased. The outbreak of war in 1839 between Britain and China, and the defeat of the Chinese fleet, shocked Edo and convinced the Shogun that more policy changes were needed. This time, it was decided

---

405 Hao, Yen-ping: *The Commercial Revolution in Nineteenth Century China*, p. 15.
406 Allen, G. C.: *A Short Economic History of Modern Japan*, p. 20–27; Sabillon: Ibid., p. 112; Madison, Angus: *The World Economy: Historical Statistics*; Madison, Angus: *The World Economy: A Millennial Perspective*.
407 Levine, Salomon & Kawada, Hisashi: *Human Resources in Japanese Industrial Development*, p. 24–27.
408 Reischauer, Edwin: *Histoire du Japon et des Japonais Vol. I*, p. 127–134.

to allocate more funds for the enhancement of defense. Still, the recent events were seen as indicating only a small threat, so the armories only received slightly larger allocations. During the 1840s, the West stepped up pressure to open up to trade. The Americans were particularly insistent. In 1846 and 1849, the Americans tried unsuccessfully to open Japan using diplomacy backed by warships. These events forced Edo to invest more in armaments.[409]

Increased military preparedness was an important part of the Tempo administrative reforms in the early part of the 1840s. There was a small increase in the per capita output of weapons and other factory goods. That was accompanied by a very small improvement of the economy. On average during the years 1800–49, the share of budgetary resources used to subsidize manufacturing remained practically the same as in the 18th century and the pace of economic growth remained almost as slow.

The majority of the very small budget continued to be spent on subsidies for agriculture and other sectors such as construction, services, and fishing. A large share was also deployed for financing the undertakings of the court. By then, there were about 260 states that were only partially subordinated to Edo. To assure their allegiance, Edo demanded that the rulers (daimyos) of these states and their families spend alternate years in Edo at the Shogun's court. Hosting these people was a costly business.[410]

During this half century, the private sector continued to abstain from investing in factories. The start-up costs of producing metals, tools, machines or even textiles, footwear, and liquor were very high and the government provided almost no support. Japanese investors thus concluded that the risks were too high and the possibilities for profit too low and put their money elsewhere. Moneylenders and private banks behaved similarly. Banks constantly discriminated against manufacturing. Practically all of their lending was for the other sectors and the preferred fields were those that allowed for the quickest recuperation of loans, such as commerce.[411]

Despite the strong conservatism of Edo and the desire to inhibit all changes in society, there were nonetheless some changes in policy, albeit not with respect to manufacturing. In 1835, a program intended on spreading and upgrading education was initiated. Restrictions on geographical mobility were also relaxed, wages became more flexible, and in the 1840s foreign trade was liberalized a little. There was however no noticeable improvement in the economy. Several decades later, Japan started to achieve better GDP rates and Western experts argued that the acceleration was the result of the liberalizing reforms initiated in the 1830s.[412]

Logically, it is very hard to sustain that policies initiated at a certain moment in time fail to deliver positive results until several decades later. During the 19th and 20th century, many nations changed policies and saw an immediate acceleration of the economy. In many cases there wasn't a lag of even a few months from the moment the new policies were adopted to the uptick in the economy. It therefore becomes logical to conclude that those policies that did not deliver immediate improvements were simply not targeting correctly the variables that affect growth.

---

409 *The Cambridge Encyclopedia of Japan*, p. 76, 77.
410 Jansen, Marius & Rozman, Gilbert (ed): *Japan in Transition—From Tokugawa to Meiji*, p. 29.
411 Macpherson, W. J. (ed): *The Industrialization of Japan*, p. 123.
412 *The Cambridge History of Japan Vol. 5*, p. 571–600.

Korea and Taiwan

During the first half of the 19th century, the Korean economy was characterized by decay. That was paralleled by a synchronous reduction in the share of the peninsula's resources allocated to manufacturing.

During the 19th century, Korea remained under the indirect control of Beijing as a result of the Manchus' conquest of the peninsula in the mid-17th century. As a result, Beijing was largely responsible for policy making. Since the Manchus renounced conquest and considerably decreased the production of weapons and related factory goods in 1800–49, they demanded less of these goods from their vassal states such as Korea. Korean policy makers were more than happy to cut expenditures on this, for they considered it a waste of resources. The ruling elite was convinced that only farming created wealth and the Confucian quasi-caste system of social hierarchy asserted that people working in manufacturing were among the least worthy in society. As a result, resources that in the 18th century were allocated to manufacturing were transferred to other sectors (mostly to agriculture).[413]

In the period 1800–49, Korean rulers continued to practice a policy of seclusion similar to that of China and Japan. They were not interested in contacts with the outside world and believed that stability and the status quo were the best for the country. Common religious beliefs in the three nations led policy makers to idealize the self-sufficient village community that had prevailed for thousands of years. In Korea, however, the seclusion policy was implemented more tightly than in China and Japan. As a result, Korea experienced even less contact with the West and its superior technology. Foreign aggression was also absent, which would have probably forced larger investments in arms. Nor was there any attempt by Korean rulers to launch the peninsula on the path of conquest.[414]

The decreased allocation of resources for this sector during the 1800–49 years coincided with a deterioration of the economy. Despite increased subsidies for agriculture, this sector performed worse than in the 18th century and the per capita production of food decreased. Famines multiplied and peasant uprisings did likewise. All the other sectors experienced as well a slowdown. The evidence suggests that manufacturing grew by a mere 0.3% annually and the economy by about 0.2%.[415]

Technological innovation also decelerated. Technology was generated at a slower pace and imported at a slower rate. In the period 1800–49, the Korean aristocracy owned the large majority of the peninsula's capital. However, they systematically refused to invest in factories.

In this period, the financial position of the government deteriorated as tax revenue declined. Throughout the history of the peninsula and of other nations, a reduction in support for manufacturing tended to coincide with a lower revenue base. The causation of the phenomenon seems to have been the following: when governments allot a smaller share of national resources to this sector, the economy decelerates. This decreases the number and size of income-earning enterprises and corporate taxes fall. At the same time, unemployment rises and a smaller share of the population pays personal income taxes. The government thus collects fewer taxes.[416]

---

413 Cumings, Bruce: *Korea's Place in the Sun—A Modern History*, p. 54.
414 Chung, Chai-sik: *A Korean Confucian Encounter with the Modern World*, p. 1–6.
415 *A Handbook of Korea*, p. p. 82–84; Sabillon: Ibid., p. 113.
416 Cumings: Ibid., p. 55, 56.

Taiwan went through something similar as Korea. During the period 1800–49, Taiwan was also under the rule of Beijing but was more directly influenced by China than Korea. Beijing's decreased demand for weapons from its provinces translated also into lower subsidies for the few manufacturing establishments in Taiwan. During the First Opium War in the early 1840s, Britain attacked Taiwan. As in the rest of China, in its aftermath, the Manchu government made practically no effort to allocate more resources for the production of arms and related goods.[417]

There was mass migration from the mainland to the island from the mid-18th century to the first half of the 19th century. By 1811, about two thirds of Taiwan's population were mainlanders. This large migration brought with it people who were acquainted with a more developed form of manufacturing. Some of them brought the implements and machines used in China and undertook some factory production. This counterbalanced the decrease in support from Beijing. On average, the per capita output of manufactures seems to have remained the same as in the 18th century. That went hand in hand with an economy that expanded at about the same pace. Manufacturing in the years 1800–49 is likely to have grown by about 0.2% annually and the economy by about 0.1%.[418]

Hong Kong and Singapore

The history of Hong Kong presents similar parallels. Up to the 1830s, the approximately 1,000-square-kilometer space that later became known as Hong Kong was inhabited by a small community of fishermen and pirates. Only a small amount of farming activity was undertaken due to the absence of fertile soil, the lack of fresh water, and the mountainous structure. It was an economy totally dominated by primary activities and services. There was no manufacturing to speak of, and no economic growth in all that time.[419]

During the second half of the 18th century, China's exports of tea and silk to Britain rose considerably but little was imported from Britain. That translated into a bilateral trade deficit for Britain. In those times, mercantilist ideas prevailing in London claimed that trade surpluses were important for the well being of a nation. Britain had achieved a trade surplus with India (which by the early 19th century had been conquered by the English), and India produced opium. Due to its addictive effects, opium had the potential to rapidly overturn the trade balance with China. Since the mid-18th century, the British East India Company began to export opium to the south of China.[420]

Exports increased swiftly and opium consumption rose sharply, ravaging the population. To curtail this damaging trade, in 1757 the Chinese government restricted foreign trade to Canton. There was ample smuggling in the following decades, but the restrictions nonetheless hampered the activities of British merchants. In 1789, Beijing imposed more restrictions. British demands for trade liberalization and full diplomatic relations were rejected in 1793, in 1819, and in 1833. Despite the increased restrictions, demand rose and smuggling continued to be rampant. Imports of opium increased so fast that in the 1820s China began to experience a trade deficit, which worsened in the following decades. In 1838, emperor

417 Rubinstein, Murray (ed): *Taiwan—A New History*, p. 136, 137.
418 Kolb : Ibid., p. 434–444; Sabillon : Ibid., p. 114.
419 Kolb: Ibid., p. 444–450.
420 Hao: Ibid., p. 21

Daoguang prohibited all opium imports. The next year Chinese officials in the south seized a large amount of British opium and destroyed it. London retaliated by sending a naval force which subdued the Chinese.

In 1821, British merchants had started to use the harbor of Hong Kong to anchor opium vessels and as the war came to an end in 1842, the island of Hong Kong was ceded to the British by the Treaty of Nanking. A total of five ports were also opened to foreign trade.[421]

The British were only interested in trading and for the rest of the 1840s they made practically no investments in manufacturing. During the years 1800–49, therefore, investment in this sector was non-existent and the economy remained totally stagnant. The economy is likely to have averaged a rate of 0.0% annually. (See tables in the appendix.)[422]

Singapore's economic course was not much different from Hong Kong's. The island of Singapore was for centuries known as Temasek. Up to the 14th century it was an outpost of the Sumatran Empire, in the 15th century it became part of the Malacca Empire, in the 16th century the Portuguese established hegemony over the area, and in the 17th century the Dutch took control over the region. Up to the early 19th century, its only inhabitants were a few fishermen, pirates, and soldiers. It was an economy totally dominated by primary activities and services. The complete absence of manufacturing in all those centuries was accompanied by a complete stagnation of the economy.[423]

During the early 19th century, the Napoleonic Wars affected every part of the globe where Western European nations had colonies. The British took the Dutch Southeast Asian colonies under their control after the French occupied the Netherlands. Thomas Raffles established the first British government in those territories and ruled Java and Sumatra from 1811 to 1818.

The end of the Wars in 1814 compelled Britain to return to the Netherlands its Southeast Asian possessions. In 1818, Raffles was given the task of searching for a suitable transshipment place in the Straits of Malacca for the long voyage between India and China. In 1819, he chose the island of Temasek and renamed it Singapore. The British East India Company began immediately to establish warehouses to support its interest in trade. Raffles became the governor of the island and his efficient administration attracted numerous migrants.[424]

For some time after the arrival of the British, the Dutch threatened with war to take back Singapore. This threat led the British to make a few investments in manufacturing in order to reduce dependence on imports.

Singapore was not the only British territory in the region. A few small territories in the Malaysian Peninsula had been acquired since 1786. In 1826, Singapore and the surrounding Malaysian possessions were made the fourth presidency of British India, putting it at parity in importance with Bombay, Calcutta, and Madras. This higher status delivered a higher British presence, which meant more imports. The distance to Britain was so vast that importing goods from Europe entailed very high transport costs. As in the case of the three main British outposts in India, it was decided to produce a few factory goods domestically

421 Wang, Nora: *L'Asie Orientale du milieu du XIXe siècle à nos jours*, p. 50, 51.
422 Sabillon: Ibid., p. 112.
423 Harrison, Brian: *South-East Asia*, p. 9–150.
424 Purcell, Victor: *South and East Asia since 1800*, p. 29–31.

to reduce transport costs. Singapore was chosen as the manufacturing center for all the outposts in the Malaysian region.[425]

The provision of subsidies for manufacturing coincided with the end of economic stagnation. Those subsidies were nonetheless very small. Further dampening growth of this sector, Britain's mercantilist policies still categorized the colonies as simple providers of raw materials and as secure importers of British manufactures.

In consequence, the level for support for local manufacturing was very low, albeit stronger than in Hong Kong. The British arrived in Hong Kong in the 1840s, two decades after their appearance in Singapore. In Hong Kong the Chinese government vehemently opposed the establishment of factories, but in Singapore the British encountered no opposition.

In the first half of the 19th century, economic growth in Singapore was very slow, but it was much better than in Hong Kong. Factory output seems to have grown by about 0.7% annually and the economy by about 0.5%. (See tables at the end of the book.)[426]

The United States

The US experienced a dramatic increase in economic activity during the first half of the 19th century. Rates of GDP were among the highest of the world. After having grown by about 0.5% per year in the second half of the 18th century, the rate jumped to 2.7% in the years 1800–49.

This was actually one of those cases in which a significant change of policies was accompanied by a simultaneous and very pronounced acceleration of the economy. This new dynamism coincided with a considerable increase in the level of factory subsidies. After having grown by about 0.7% in 1750–99, manufacturing averaged about 3.3% in the following fifty years.[427]

The change of policies was the result of two factors. On the one hand, a new view of the world guided policy making and on the other, a number of events drove the government to promote this sector more.

This was the first half century in which the US was no longer forced to practice a policy of manufacturing suppression. During the colonial period, most Americans associated (at least in part) Britain's high wealth with the production of factory goods. Therefore, as soon as independence was attained, the new nation sought to imitate London by fostering this sector.

Britain's mercantilist policies had largely convinced the Americans of the existence of some form of linkage between manufacturing and wealth creation. As an ex-colony, the US was also driven to try to attain everything that its more developed ex-colonial master had achieved. And most of those achievements were directly associated with factory goods. The desire to imitate and match Britain existed since the very birth of the nation, but with the passage of time it became stronger.[428]

The US therefore largely copied and transplanted the whole package of factory promotion policies utilized by Britain, including trade protection. As in Germany, most American

---

425 Harrison: Ibid., p. 171–189.
426 Sabillon: Ibid., p. 158.
427 Ibid., p. 147; Fogel: Ibid.; Madison, Angus: *The World Economy: A Millennial Perspective*; Madison, Angus: *The World Economy: Historical Statistics*.
428 Harris, Seymour: *American Economic History*, p. 7–9.

---

policy makers thought that in the initial phase, industries needed trade protection. However, the case of Russia, which by 1800 had relatively well established industries, shows that whatever benefits high tariffs might provide, they do not encourage manufacturing growth. In the first half of the 19th century in Russia, tariffs were far higher than in the US or Germany, and manufacturing and the overall economy stagnated completely. That correlated with an absence of fiscal, financial, and non-financial incentives for manufacturing.

In comparison to 1750–99, during the first half of the 19th century Britain significantly increased investment in manufacturing. The Americans noticed this increase and felt compelled to do likewise. That would explain why, during the years 1800–49, the US attained a rate of factory output that was almost as fast as that of Britain.[429]

A number of other events also contributed significantly to the cause of manufacturing. This century debuted amidst the trade blockades and other disturbances of the Napoleonic Wars, which led Washington to increase the level of factory subsidies to encourage import substitution. The support rose even more in 1808 when Britain declared an embargo on the US for its opportunistic trade with the French. The threat of the embargo had long terrified the US government. Such an action was believed to be capable of crippling the economy due to its dependence on British imports. However, during the years of the embargo, the economy prospered and this coincided with a rise of subsidies for the production of substitutes.

War with Britain broke out in 1812 and lasted until 1814; support for armament production rose significantly as well as for civilian manufacturing. The US did not have to confront the whole British army because Britain deployed most of its forces against the French. However, Britain did have the most powerful navy in the world. To confront such an enemy, Washington allocated a considerable share of its resources to the armories and shipyards. The cost of the war was about 13% of GDP. Not all of this was deployed for the fabrication of weapons and other manufactures, but a large share flowed into factories.

The economy accelerated considerably, even though foreign trade almost ceased. To make matters worse, resources were wasted producing arms. In spite of that, the economy boomed. Viewed from an orthodox perspective, such events remain forever a paradox. Viewed from a manufacturist perspective, they add up.[430]

With the end of the war, the trade embargo was lifted and resources were no longer allocated wastefully. According to traditional understanding, under those circumstances the economy should have performed better but that was not the case. First there was a recession and then stagnation from 1815–20; there was also a contraction and stagnation of manufacturing.

With the end of hostilities in 1815, British imports flooded back in, and largely outsold American goods. The American government raised tariffs in 1816. Tariff and non-tariff barriers had been on the rise since 1789 and although a correlation between them and growth seems to have existed, a closer look reveals problems with that logic.[431] The increase in tariffs of 1816 did not deliver an acceleration of the economy, but the considerable drop in subsidies to military and civilian manufacturing did coincide with contraction and stagnation.

---

429 Faulkner, Harold: *Histoire Economique des Etas Unis d'Amérique Vol. IV*, p. 383–385.
430 Bogart, Ernest & Kemmerer, Donald: *Economic History of the American People*, p. 342; "Unimaginable", *The Economist*, 22 February 2003, 71.
431 Harris: Ibid., p. 29; North, Douglas: *The Growth of the American Economy to 1860*, p. 209.

In the following years, a correlation between trade protection and growth was also missing. Tariffs were raised to 43% of the value of imports in 1816, in 1824 they were put at 57%, and in 1828 they were raised still more. There was a noticeable acceleration of economic growth during the 1820s, but growth accelerated more during the 1830s and much more during the 1840s even through there was a drop in trade protection during these last two decades. In 1832 tariffs were lowered to 18% and remained at about that level until the beginning of the Civil War.[432]

Manufacturing is the only variable that manages to correlate consistently with the fluctuations of the economy throughout the period. As the tariff of 1816 failed to deliver the desired results, the government began some years later to raise the level of fiscal, financial, and non-financial incentives. On top of that, other measures were also adopted to favor the sector. In 1818, Congress restricted the coastal trade to American built ships, which was complemented with other subsidies to shipbuilders. This was the American version of the Navigation Acts.[433]

The 1820s saw the coming of the railroads and new factories that produced rails, locomotives, and wagons. Since the desire to imitate Britain was very strong, the American government quickly took numerous measures to promote the development of railroads. The first railroad in the US debuted in 1827, only two years after the first in Britain.

Aside from the desire to match England, the American government was also very interested in integrating its large and scarcely populated territory politically and economically. Since the Declaration of Independence, the original territory of the thirteen colonies had rapidly grown in size. In 1803 the Louisiana Purchase added a territory as large as the thirteen original colonies, in 1819 Washington obtained Florida from Spain, some years later it acquired the territory southeast of the Mississippi, and in 1845 it annexed Texas.[434]

The lack of transportation and communication segmented the US into numerous small and largely independent economic units. The government feared secession of the different regions and therefore invested abundantly to improve transportation and communication. It granted large incentives to private companies for road and canal construction. Aid consisted mostly of land grants but there were also tax and financial incentives. When the railroads appeared in the 1820s, the government began to offer larger incentives to railroad investors.[435] It gave large incentives to the builders of the rail line and to the manufacturers of all the components. With such enthusiastic support, the private sector reacted immediately and invested heavily. In a relative short period of time, railroads surpassed canals as the most important means of transport. By 1850, there were about 3,200 miles of canals while railroads had extended over almost 10,000 miles of track. The interest and support the government showered on railroads went up from decade to decade and this coincided with an acceleration of manufacturing production, which paralleled an acceleration of GDP.[436]

As time went along, there was an across-the-board increase in support to most factory fields. However, since the 1820s railroad-related manufacturing enjoyed the largest share of subsidies due to its tight links with the political priorities of the state.

432 Davis, L., Hughes, J. & McDougall, D.: *American Economic History*, p. 301–303, 293.
433 Adams, D.: *America in the 20th Century*, p. 21.
434 Krout, John: *The United States to 1877*, p. 114, 70, 187.
435 Davis, Hughes & McDougall: Ibid., p. 132, 277–279.
436 North: Ibid., p. 182.

During the course of the first half of the 19th century, Washington became increasingly determined to expand its territory in order to create a vast trans-continental nation. In 1846 it declared war on Mexico, because the Mexican government refused to sell a large share of its territory. The US had more and superior weapons and it easily won, annexing a great swath of land that reached the Pacific Coast. Once again, the outcome at the battlefield was determined by the amount and technological sophistication of the weapons utilized. This was the third war of the young nation and it was the easiest, given the weakness of the Mexican army. It cost only 3% of GDP. It nonetheless represented an occasion for pouring more resources into arms production, and indirectly it contributed to manufacturing by forcing Washington to redouble its integration efforts. Railroads were constructed all across the immense new terrain.[437]

The significant increase in subsidies for manufacturing coincided with a noticeable acceleration in the rate of output. The 1840s saw the first upsurge in factory output and the fastest growing fields were railroad-related goods and armaments. The factory system of production became thoroughly entrenched, displacing simpler forms of manufacturing. In the 1840s, the sector's rate of output coincided with unprecedented GDP rates. Manufacturing grew by about 4.7% annually and GDP by about 3.8%.[438]

In the course of the first half of the 19th century, government expenditure as a share of GDP progressively increased, allowing Washington to allocate a larger share of resources to manufacturing. On top of that, growing national security concerns led the government to use a growing share of the budget to subsidize this sector.

The gigantic territorial enlargement that the US achieved during the years 1800–49 expanded the land available for agriculture, and farming experienced a major upsurge. Many have argued that this propelled the economy forward. However, throughout the period agriculture systematically grew slower than GDP. The only sector that grew faster than the overall economy and which could therefore have acted as a propeller was manufacturing. By 1800, agriculture was by far the largest sector of the economy, but manufacturing grew so much faster in the following decades that by 1850 the output value of manufacturing had surpassed that of farming. During 1800–49, manufacturing grew by about 3.3% annually while agriculture expanded by only 1.8%.[439]

The evidence suggests that the accelerated growth of agriculture resulted from the rapid increase in the utilization of manufactured goods and not as a result of the increase in territory. The fact that output per acre rose significantly points strongly in this direction. Goods such as the iron plow that appeared in 1819, the reaper that debuted in 1834, the steel plow of 1839, and several other machines that made their advent during the 1840s, are what expanded the technological possibilities of farming. During this half century, the 1840s witnessed the largest factory subsidies and it was also the time of fastest agricultural growth.[440]

The strong linkages between manufacturing and technology expressed in numerous forms. During the course of this half century, the level of factory subsidization progressively increased and that correlated with an accelerating pace of technological development. The

---

437 Niemi, Albert: *U.S. Economic History*, p. 94–96; *Unimaginable*: Ibid.

438 Harris: Ibid., p. 29–38.

439 Sabillon: Ibid., p. 147; Madison, Angus: *The World Economy: Historical Statistics*; Madison, Angus: *The World Economy: A Millennial Perspective*; Fogel: Ibid.

440 Krout: Ibid., p. 11, 115.

1840s witnessed the highest rate of patent registration and the fastest importation of technology. Most patents were directly associated with manufactured goods such as textile machines, the telegraph, steam boats, ether, air-heating stoves, musical instruments, and above all armaments and railroad-related goods. [441]

It is also worth noting that the most strongly subsidized factory fields were also those that experienced the most technological change. Although the wars with Britain and Mexico were small, there was nonetheless a constant investment in arms, partly in order to supply the effort of "pacification" of the Indians, who were regularly battling with white settlers. Armament production received a relatively high level of support and experienced very rapid technological development. The use of interchangeable parts, which marked so profoundly the ulterior development of factory production, first arose in firearm manufacturing in the 1840s. Technological change was also heavily concentrated in railroad-related fields such as metallurgy, machine tools, steam power, and engineering goods. [442]

The US had relatively little access to British and European technology in those years, for these nations prohibited the export of machinery and experts (artisans, technicians, engineers). Although technology was jealously guarded, the US managed to be highly prolific in inventing and improving tools, utensils, instruments, contraptions, machines, and goods of all sorts. All this innovation was so quick paced, relatively speaking, that by the 1840s Britain began to import American technology. [443]

Through time, many have argued that backward nations cannot raise the capital needed for the vast investments that would permit rapid growth. Here was a case that clearly demonstrated the fallacy of that idea. The US not only managed to raise vast amounts of funds, but it also succeeded in raising amounts similar to those invested by Britain during those years. By raising taxes and borrowing from foreign and domestic sources, the government raised large amounts of capital. Not all of the increased revenues were utilized to promote manufacturing, but much of it was.

Most of the capital was raised domestically. The evidence suggests that the phenomenon occurred in the following manner: Bigger investments in manufacturing enhanced the technology base and therefore the wealth of the nation, increasing the pool of capital, which allowed for larger investments. As the share of GDP allocated to manufacturing rose, capital was created faster and more capital was available. It was a virtuous cycle. [444]

This was not the first time in history that such a phenomenon had taken place, nor was it the last. History suggests that the best capital-generation and investment-promoting policy is one that concentrates on subsidizing manufacturing.

Such an interpretation of events would explain why capital and investment were fundamentally concentrated in the Northeast of the US and why economic growth and technological development expanded much faster in this region.

During 1800–49, the bulk of the manufacturing investments were made in the Northeast. The weapons were mostly utilized to fight faraway foes such as the British, the Indians and the Mexicans, but the factories that produced the weapons were located in the Northeast. This region also produced practically all of the rails, wagons and locomotives. The South, in

---

441 Bogart & Kemmerer: Ibid., p. 356, 357.
442 Rosenberg, Nathan: *Technology and American Economic Growth*, p. 91, 12, 53, 59.
443 Knout: Ibid., p. 112, 114, 120
444 Harris: Ibid., p. 6, 39.

spite of exploiting slave labor, systematically experienced lower rates of GDP, of technological advancement, and of investment.

Further bolstering the manufacturing thesis is the case of New York. In this period, this city had the highest concentration of capital and it was also the main manufacturing center of the country.[445]

445 Krout: Ibid., p. 113.

CHAPTER 6. THE SECOND HALF OF THE 19TH CENTURY IN THE UNITED STATES, GERMANY, AND RUSSIA

The United States

1850–69

During the years 1850–99, there were major changes in the structure of the world economy. In this period more revolutionary changes took place than at any other previous moment in history. The transformations changed the living conditions of the world population more than the discovery of America had done. The world economy became more integrated, but more important still was the fact that economic growth in numerous nations accelerated to new levels and living conditions improved considerably.

Up to the mid-19th century, Britain had attained the highest rates of growth and the best that it had achieved was an annual rate of about 3% over a decade. During the second half of the 19th century, however, rates of up to 8% were attained. The nations that did the best were those which, up until then, had been seen by most analysts as inherently incapable of rapid growth. [446]

In all of these countries, the pronounced acceleration of economic growth coincided with a very large increase in the level of factory subsidies stemming from a change in ideological motivations. As in the past, governments did not supply subsidies to this sector because of any recognition of a direct causal link between manufacturing and growth. Rather it was because of national security concerns, goals of political integration, a need to catch up in development, and balance of payments problems.

These motivations found their strongest expression in the US and it was there where the largest promotion efforts were undertaken. It was also there where factory output and GDP

---

446 Kuznets, Simon: *Modern Economic Growth*, p. 64, 75, 252–256.

increased most. During 1850–99, factory output expanded by about 7.5% per year and economic growth was about 6.3% annually. (See tables in the appendix of the book.) This was the fastest rate of manufacturing in the world and the fastest rate of economic growth. [447]

During this period, the different American governments continued to be driven by the desire to catch up in economic development with Great Britain. However, the main reasons driving support had nothing to do with events taking place outside the US.

Even the subsidies used to catch up with other nations fell exclusively within the jurisdiction of the American government. The growth of manufacturing relied almost solely on the determination of Washington to see it grow, and exogenous variables affected it only marginally.

The Mexican–American war ended in 1847 and huge new territories were added to the United States. Together with other western territories that were added during the 1850s, this spurred the government to accelerate the building of railroads. As a young nation with a heterogeneous population and with territories separated by huge distances, with disparate needs and interests, the US had to struggle to forge a sense of unity and to stave off any move for secession. As the size of the country increased, this threat rose proportionately.

The government therefore embraced railroad construction more enthusiastically than any other country. Although trains were first produced in Britain, by 1850 the US had about 80% more track laid. The territorial expanse of the US was far larger but at that time the populations were about the same size. Meanwhile Russia was spread across a territory many times the size of the US and had a population larger than that of Britain and the US combined. However, by 1850 Russia had laid less than one tenth the mileage of rail lines as the United States. Moscow's policy makers were deliberately curbing the development of railroads and of manufacturing. [448]

Washington also felt pressured by the growing cultural diversification of the population. Up to the early 19th century, most of the population had originated in the British Isles, but in the decades that followed, continental Europeans and others began to arrive in large numbers. This added political volatility, giving more weight to the idea that the country could break apart. However, the strongest cultural divisions of the country were between the Northeast and the Southeast, and differences in economic interests helped drive the two regions apart. The political divide between the North and the South had existed since the early years of independence and ever since then, the gap grew wider. The national leadership had every reason to enlarge the incentives to the producers of railroad related-goods. [449]

The production of iron, steel, locomotives, wagons, machine tools, rails, and processed wood increased rapidly. These however were not the only fields that received more fiscal, financial, and non-financial incentives. In 1850, Congress granted subsidies to steamship builders. This effort sought to integrate the long coasts of the country and the interior (through navigable rivers and lakes). It as well sought to imitate Britain and to promote exports for balance of payments reasons. Ships were indispensable for trade with Europe. Another motivation was the fact that the most successful nations of the time had a self-

447 Kenwood, A. & Lougheed, A.: *The Growth of the International Economy 1820–1990*, p. 20, 128; Sabillon, Carlos: *World Economic Historical Statistics*, p. 147; Madison, Angus: *Monitoring the World Economy 1820–1992*; Fogel, Robert William: *The Escape from Hunger and Premature Death, 1700–2100: Europe, America and the Third World*.

448 Bagwell, Philip & Mingay, G.: *Britain and America 1850–1939*, p. 1, 40.

449 Davis, L., Hughes, J. & McDougall, D.: *American Economic History*, p. 284, 293.

produced commercial fleet. All the above drove Washington to the conclusion that the US needed also to produce a large amount of ships.[450]

As a result, the level of factory subsidization increased considerably during the 1850s. That correlated with a considerable acceleration of this sector and a proportionate spurt of the economy. Manufacturing averaged about 5.5% annually and GDP about 4.5%.[451]

Manufacturing and rail lines expanded rapidly and by 1860 the Northeast and the Southeast were rail linked. Other efforts to integrate the nation economically and politically included the expansion of the telegraph. Support was given to the producers of telegraph machines and wires and in 1861 San Francisco was linked with the East Coast.[452]

However by then the economic and political cleavages between the North and the South had grown to very high proportions and in 1861 the South attempted to secede. War broke out and lasted until 1865. By the time the conflict began, practically all of the production of railroad-related goods and other manufactures was done in the Northeast. The South had to supply most of its weapon needs with imports from Europe. The North on the other hand supplied practically all of its arms from its own factories. This was by far the most intense conflict the nation had experienced; it absorbed huge resources and had a cost of about 104% of GDP. By world standards of the time, it was a large-scale war. Although not all of the resources were used for the fabrication of weapons and other manufactures, a significant share was deployed for this purpose. While the North made massive investments in this domain, the South made significant purchases from Europe.[453]

There was a noticeable retrenchment of the railroad-promotion policy in order to finance the war, but it was not stopped; there was a fear that other regions might also think of seceding. The railway linking the Pacific to the East Coast was started in 1862.

The requirements of the war were so large that the funds stripped from railroads were not enough to fully finance the military. Washington decreed a very large increase in taxation and in borrowing, raised tariffs, and sold off assets (mostly land) as fast as it could. The national debt, which up to 1860 had remained at practically zero, rose in just a few years to account for about 40% of GDP.[454]

Before the war, the only source of revenue for the government was the tariff and land sales. Taxes were practically out of the picture. With the outbreak of the war, President Lincoln levied real estate taxes, excise taxes, sales taxes, and personal income taxes. The government also sold licenses. To enforce tax collection, he created the Internal Revenue Service. On trade matters, he raised tariffs from an average of about 20% to 47% of the value of imports. To organize the increased flow of funds into the government's coffers and channel them more adequately into the armories, he established nationally chartered banks and created a national currency (the greenback). In 1863 he also established the National Academy of Sciences — to seek new technology for the war. [455]

---

450 Bogart, Ernest & Kemmerer, Donald: *Economic History of the American People*, p. 466.

451 Hacker, Louis: *Major Documents in American Economic History Vol. I*, p. 71, 89; Madison, Angus: *The World Economy: Historical Statistics*.

452 Krout, John: *The United States to 1877*, p. 114, 137, 145.

453 Harris, Seymour: *American Economic History*, p. 216; "Unimaginable", *The Economist*, 22 February 2003, p. 71.

454 "The Burdensome National Debt", *The Economist*, 10 February 1996, p. 70.

455 "Was Lincoln the Father of Big Government?", *Fortune*, 9 December 1996, p. 23.

Government revenue increased as a result of the taxes and the tariffs, but it was still not enough to cover the huge investments in armaments that were required. The state therefore borrowed in large amounts and budget deficits became very large. Up to that date, the government had believed in the principle of small state intervention, balanced budgets, and low or no government debt. During 1861–65, government expenditure as a share of GDP soared, budget deficits ballooned, public debt rose to new highs, and trade barriers rose significantly. With all that distortion and "unhealthy" public finances, there should have been an economic catastrophe. However, the economy of the North prospered mightily. [456]

Since most of the distortion was undertaken to assist the production of weapons, a "wasteful" area, it is even harder to understand why economic growth was so strong. While orthodox interpretations do not add up, the manufacturist thesis does. The share of the nation's resources allocated to the manufacturing sector rose significantly and that was accompanied by a large acceleration of factory output. [457]

During these years, the Northern states attained the highest rates of manufacturing output up to that date and this coincided with unprecedented growth. The Confederate government did not take any significant measure to mobilize resources into manufacturing. Most of the weapons were bought from Europe and their small manufacturing base experienced a contraction as the embargo of the North cut the supply of machines and other implements that were necessary for production. The factory contraction coincided with a collapse of the economy. It is worth noting that in spite of the large budget deficits of the North, inflation remained relatively low, while in the South, hyperinflation accompanied the contraction of the economy. [458]

Technological development in the North was impressive. Patents proliferated and there were more major technical breakthroughs than in any similar span of time. Living conditions in the North improved noticeably, notwithstanding the apparent waste of resources.

The contraction of manufacturing in the South coincided with an absence of technological progress. There was actually technical regression as the goods that were the depositories of technology began to disappear. Living conditions declined.

It is also worth noting that practically all of the new technologies were directly linked to factory goods. Pointing further in the direction of this sector is the fact that the most subsidized factory fields were the ones which delivered the largest share of patents. The majority of the new patents were directly linked to weapons and other heavy manufacturing fields. [459]

Although originally intended for war purposes, the technological innovations almost immediately began to benefit the civilian economy of the North. Machine tool technology prospered and the same new machines that were capable of making superior weapons began to make more advanced agricultural implements, improved household utensils, and better textile machines. The massive investments in iron and steel, raw materials for weapons, enabled the creation of new technologies that considerably reduced the production costs of

456 Krout, John: *The United States to 1877*, p. 146, 142.
457 Faulkner, Harold: *Histoire Economique des Etas Unis d'Amérique Vol. IV*, p. 381.
458 Harris: Ibid., p. 46.
459 Bogart & Kemmerer: Ibid., p. 472.

these metals. As a result, the metal content of civilian goods rapidly increased. Metal naval ships were first pioneered in 1862, and some time later, metal commercial ships.[460]

The end of the Civil War in April 1865 meant the end of the large defense expenditures, which convinced most people that the economy would perform better than during the war. There was, however, a recession that lasted until 1867. This downturn coincided with a proportionate contraction in manufacturing resulting from the decrease in funding for the production of weapons. The drop in allocations for arms could had been easily compensated by an equivalent rise in allocations for civilian manufacturing, but conventional thinking said that the large government debt had to be eliminated as soon as possible.

However, the war had reinforced the fear of a geopolitical break up of the country and in 1867 the government concluded that it was better to run a large public debt than to risk a recidivist secessionist attempt from the South (or from some other region). In that year, Washington took the decision to renew the policy of expanding the railroads. This time, the goal was not just to link but to crisscross the nation with rail lines. The political class was convinced that the war would not have occurred if the country had been more thoroughly served by rail lines. Incentives for the production of metals, rails, locomotives and related goods were raised to higher levels than before the war. Manufacturing output immediately surged and the economy picked up again. [461]

The 1860s witnessed unprecedented factory subsidies and that coincided with unexampled economic growth. This sector averaged about 6.0% annually and the economy expanded by about 4.7%.

1870–99

The policy of binding the nation politically and economically by means of railroads was enthusiastically promoted through the early 20th century. Subsidies for the production of railroads goods continued at very high levels. During the pre-Civil War years the compounded aid of federal, state, and local governments accounted for about a fifth of the railroad capital, but during the postwar years governments supplied about half of the financing. In the last three decades of the 19th century, grants of public lands in excess of right of way requirements became much larger. Tax breaks were also offered to the companies that constructed the railways and the manufacturers that produced the railroad goods. [462]

The share of GDP allocated to manufacturing was larger and that correlated with faster economic growth. During the years 1870–99, manufacturing grew by about 8.7% per year and the economy by about 7.4% annually.

During this period, economic growth began to rapidly spread from the Northeast throughout the rest of the country. Much suggests that this was not a spontaneous development of events. It coincided with a new government policy intended on spreading factory production beyond its traditional location. This derived from the theory that future secessionist efforts would only be avoided if economic inequalities were eased. There was thus a need to promote in the rest of the country the same type of economy that prevailed in the Northeast. The government therefore began to actively subsidize factories beyond the

---

460 Rosenberg, Nathan: *Technology and American Economic History*, p. 100.

461 Harris: Ibid., p. 46, 47, 6.

462 Davis, Hughes & McDougall: Ibid., p. 140, 413; Madison, Angus: *The World Economy: Historical Statistics*; Madison, Angus: *Monitoring the World Economy 1820–1992*.

Northeast and for the first time the economy in the more remote regions also began to grow rapidly. [463]

It was not well understood how to promote factories efficiently and many errors were made. Even though Washington reduced trade barriers after the war, they nonetheless remained high during the rest of the 19th century, averaging about 32% of the value of imports. Numerous non-tariff barriers were also kept in place. Another error consisted in allowing the existence of monopolies and cartels. At first the government gave a green light and then it turned a blind eye to oligopoly practices as they permitted high profits and were seen as a stimulus to railroads and the geographic diffusion of factories. Cartels first appeared in railroads in the 1860s, spread rapidly to heavy manufacturing, and then became common in other fields. [464]

The establishment in 1887 of the Interstate Commerce Commission and the passage in 1890 of the Sherman Antitrust Act were efforts to foster competition, but it still took some time until anti-cartel legislation was seriously enforced. In spite of this, economic growth was impressive and productivity also grew at an impressive pace.

Some analysts have concluded that these practices are helpful in the early stages of development, but the evidence shows that in the presence of competition, the quality of goods is better. During the 20th century, numerous nations practiced central planning and many countries endorsed policies that significantly limited competition. In those cases, the quality of goods and services was low and it varied in proportion to the lack of market mechanisms. In the Soviet Union during the 1920s and 1930s, the quality of goods decreased precipitously even while the economy grew. The poor quality of products continued until the 1980s, the last decade of central planning. In India, since the late 1940s, the new independent government endorsed a different set of industrial policies and the quality of production fell significantly. Like the Soviet Union, India achieved a large increase in output, which coincided with a large increase in factory subsidies, but quality decreased. In Russia, quality rapidly improved since the 1990s, when the competition-hindering practices were eliminated and in India similar progresses were appreciated since the 1980s when the government began to dismantle the high tariffs, the monopolies, and the state firms. In Singapore, high quality products appeared since the mid 19th century, coinciding with an absence of anti-competitive policies. The same took place in Hong Kong since the early 20th century. These two economies were at a nascent stage of development and that was not an obstacle for a fast manufacturing and economic growth. History suggests that trade barriers do not hamper the growth of production but it hampers quality. History disproves the liberal thesis that free trade is the engine of growth, but gives credence to the claim that productivity benefits from competition.

The rapid growth in the US during the late 19th century despite the cartels and trade barriers showed that liberalization was not the key for growth. However, it did suggest that factory subsidies were at the core of wealth creation. At no similar amount of time during the 20th century was economic growth as fast as during the late 19th century. That was paralleled by fewer factory subsidies during the 20th century.

Government expenditure as a share of GDP grew considerably during the late 19th century and there was also a marked increase of state intervention in practically all aspects of

463 Krout, John: *The United States since 1865*, p. 27.
464 Davis, Hughes & McDougall: Ibid., p. 133, 301, 147.

the economy. A policy of small government expenditure, low taxation, and few regulations on business is commonly posited as essential for growth. If that were true, the 18th century should have been characterized by impressive economic figures. That was not the case. And in the 17th century, when government expenditure as a share of the total economy was even more insignificant and regulations on business were even fewer, the economy performed even worse.

The historical evidence suggests that when the increase in taxation and state expenditure go to support manufacturing, the results are highly positive. That does not mean that overall government expenditure must increase to supply manufacturing with more resources. Logic suggests that first there should be a transfer of budgetary resources from other expense areas. Government revenue that is used to subsidize primary activities, construction, and services can be used to promote factory production instead. To a certain extent, that is what took place in the late 19th century in the United States.[465]

That was a period that saw the invention of a multitude of new products, an unprecedented burgeoning of creativity which correlated with the fastest manufacturing output up to that date. The majority of patents were directly linked to factory goods such as the telephone, the electric bulb, the gasoline engine, the typesetting machine, medicines, serums, machines tools, railroad-related goods, and weapons.[466]

Technological change was more heavily concentrated in metallurgy, machines tools, steam power, engineering goods, and trains. Those heavy manufacturing fields happened to be the most subsidized fields. Railroad-related factory production was the most heavily subsidized, but all fields that seemed to contribute to the political and economic integration of the country were also promoted. In 1876, Alexander Bell patented the telephone and the government immediately endorsed its production. A similar approach had been taken with the discovery of the telegraph in 1837, but this time the political goals were stronger.[467]

It is also worth noting that during the last decades of the 19th century more and more scientists and technologists emerged. For the first time, they multiplied faster than the workforce. The number of inventors grew even though there was no particular policy to promote them; and their rapid multiplication coincided with the development of a technology that owed little to scientific knowledge. The machine-based technology of the late 19th century was mostly the result of crude empiricism, of trial and error, of learning by doing.

As was the case throughout history, the creation of technology did not depend upon the mastery of complex bodies of knowledge and a clear understanding of the causality of any given phenomenon. The inventors were not laboratory scientists in white coats, but men tinkering in factories and workshops. It was in these establishments where the bulk of discoveries were made.[468]

The evidence suggests that the phenomenon of innovation occurred in the following manner: as support for manufacturing increased, factories multiplied and more people became involved in the effort to make new types of goods. Those efforts led people to generate technology breakthroughs. As more people became involved in such efforts, it was inevitable that more inventors and inventions came along.

465 Ibid., p. 147, 346, 347, 132, 134.
466 Bogart & Kemmerer: Ibid., p. 472.
467 "Computers Can Do a Great Job", *Time*, 13 November 1995, p. 22.
468 Rosenberg: Ibid., p. 41, 53, 118.

The rapid creation of technology during this period was highly associated with labor saving machines and with new goods that eliminated numerous occupations in all sectors of the economy. However, notwithstanding the rapid destruction of jobs and the population explosion, unemployment remained at manageable levels. The new technology ended up creating more jobs than it destroyed and the higher level of technology embedded in the new machines also delivered better working conditions and higher wages.

During these decades, the pro-business policy of the government was largely unreceptive to labor demands but in spite of that, working conditions improved and wages went up faster than ever before. Seen from the perspective of manufacturing, that apparent paradox becomes understandable for it is technology that most improves living conditions. The evidence suggests that workers benefit more from a decisive factory promotion policy than from socially righteous regulations.

During the whole 19th century, manufacturing was the sector that experienced the highest growth of productivity. This was further evidence suggesting that manufacturing is the prime generator of technology.[469]

On Inflation, Capital, and Trade

Prices dropped in the 1870s. Prices in the US fell by about 25% despite the doubling of the money supply and the very rapid economic growth. Low inflation and high economic growth were also observed during the 1880s and 1890s. In the late 19th century, there was no inflation at all. By the late 20th century, American economists commonly argued that high economic growth rates inevitably led to high inflation, and by high economic growth rates they meant an annual rate of more than 3%. By high inflation, they also meant more than 3% per year. However, during the late 19th century economic growth averaged more than 7% per year, without inflation.[470]

This reveals that there are other variables that can control inflation, aside from the traditional measures such as fiscal rectitude, sound monetary policy, and high levels of competition. Much suggests that high expenditures in manufacturing also contribute to curb inflation.

Such a phenomenon would seem to take form in the following way: since manufacturing is the prime generator of technology and technology is the bottom line for productivity improvements, strong promotion of factories automatically delivers rapid productivity growth. This last significantly curbs inflation. The fact that competition in the late 19th century was hampered by trade barriers and cartels further reinforces the thesis that a strong factory promotion policy has strong inflation-thwarting effects.

By the late 20th century, it became common for economists to assert that price stability was best achieved by putting monetary policy in the hands of an independent central bank, free of political influence. However, during the late 19th century, when the US attained its lowest rates of inflation together with the fastest GDP figures in all of its history, the country was without an independent central bank. There was no central bank at all. Central banking had been terminated in 1836 and did not reappear until 1914, with the creation of

---

469 Kolko, Gabriel: *Main Currents in Modern American History*, p. 72.
470 Harris: Ibid., p. 81, 6.

the Federal Reserve System. During all of that time, central bank operations were directly undertaken by the Treasury, which was highly exposed to political interference.[471]

There is strong empirical evidence suggesting that the creation of a central bank with full independence is a positive policy undertaking. However, the fact that the economy did so well in the late 19th century without such a bank in place shows that there are other variables that can control inflation. The manufacturing variable seems to be one of them.

By the late 20th century, it also became common to argue that central bank independence contributed to the acceleration of the economy. That could be true, but its absence was no hindrance to growth during the late 19th century. The very rapid growth of those years suggests that the benefits of central bank independence are only marginal.

The US continued to be a net capital importer during the second half of the 19th century, borrowing from Europe and attracting foreign direct investment. Most of the borrowed money was utilized for the promotion of railroads and at times foreign funds accounted for a very large share of railroad investment capital, but the vast majority of the funds were raised in the United States. Domestically raised capital accounted for more than three fourths of the investment in manufacturing and this was the sector that absorbed the largest share of investment. [472]

The events of this period demonstrate once again that it is possible for a nation to raise vast amounts of investment capital out of its own resources even if its level of development is low. These events also show that the bottom line for raising large amounts of capital lie in the decision of the government to endorse a factory promotion policy.

During 1850–99, there were parallels again between manufacturing and the other sectors of the economy. Increased subsidies for this sector were accompanied by more rapid growth in farming, fishing, services, trade, and construction. The government took away more resources from the other sectors in order to transfer them to the factories and even so, the other sectors grew faster.

Domestic and foreign trade grew very rapidly. It is worth noting that without the rapid growth in the production of the trains and ships, it would have been impossible to swiftly increase cargo transport. The speed by which each area of transportation developed correlated with the level of subsidies for each industry. Train producers received by far the largest subsidies and internal trade grew faster than foreign trade. Ship producers were not associated with the priorities of the state.

Although internal trade grew faster, foreign trade did grow rapidly. Europe was America's main trading partner. In spite of the high trade barriers of the US, American imports increased faster than ever before and in spite of rising trade barriers in continental Europe, American exports grew quickly.[473]

According to orthodox economic theory, trans-Atlantic trade should have decreased, but it did not. This contradictory situation becomes understandable only when the problem is approached from the perspective of manufacturing. The evidence suggests that the strong manufacturing support in the US and in continental Europe translated into more and better goods. The sharp rise in the supply newer, better goods was accompanied by a rise in demand for those goods. Trade was bound to increase notwithstanding the high trade bar-

471 Hacker: Ibid., p. 54.
472 Kolko: Ibid., p. 2, 3.
473 Ibid., p. 37.

riers. Without the barriers, trade presumably would have increased even more. However, an increase in production is key to increasing trade, and that seems to occur only when governments allocate more resources to manufacturing.

The causation of the phenomenon seems to be as follows: greater manufacturing subsidies enabled the development of new technology, including the generation, distribution and application of electricity. Although trade barriers affected the price of light bulbs and electric generators, the benefits provided by these new goods was so large that even elevated prices did not deter people from acquiring it. Countless new industries including entertainment services, transport services and educational services expanded as a result of the electricity-generating goods.

Similarly, breakthroughs in healthcare technology were so valuable that even artificially high prices did not deter consumers. Before 1867, as a result of infections contracted during operations, more people were killed than cured at the hands of surgeons. Antisepsis, which the British surgeon Joseph Lister discovered, offered incalculable benefits. There are many examples in history where technology has created its own demand.[474] Health services expanded hand in hand with the fastest increase in invention and production of medicines, serums, and medical instruments in history. Without pharmaceuticals, medical instruments, and numerous other factory goods, most of the health advances of the period would never have materialized.

Understanding Causality

Agricultural production and productivity as well made significant improvements and they were directly linked to the rapidly rising utilization of threshing machines, reaping machines, tractors, and chemical manure. Mechanization of agriculture started around the mid-19th century but since the Civil War its pace accelerated considerably. That was paralleled by the acceleration of factory output. The invention of the tractor in 1892 was the outcome of a trial-and-error manufacturing effort. It was an Iowa blacksmith who fabricated the first farm vehicle powered by a gasoline engine.[475]

It is argued that the labor shortages of the Civil War stimulated mechanization. However, the rate of mechanization did not slow down in the following decades, when the country was at peace and when immigrants arrived in large numbers to look for work. During 1870–99, there were no artificial war-induced labor shortages, but industry and other activities were becoming mechanized faster than at any previous period. However, the rates of rationalization and mechanization varied in direct proportion to the level of government support for the sector. Factory subsidization became progressively stronger during the course of the 19th century, with a significant rise since the Civil War.

It is also argued that improvements in agricultural production during the second half of the 19th century were the main reason for the economic boom. Supposedly, it generated surplus capital allowing more investment in the other sectors and it liberated labor to be re-deployed in other economic activities. That thesis does not add up with the historical data. During that period, manufacturing was the fastest growing sector and thus that which

---

474 Rosenberg: Ibid., p. 16.
475 Adams, D.: *America in the 20th Century*, p. 22.

generated capital fastest. It was therefore the one most likely to have had the capacity to finance investment in the rest of the economy.

It is also a fact that there was plenty of labor to go around. The birth rate was very high and so was immigration. Many people were indeed relieved of their farming jobs and forced to look for other employment, but even if that had not been the case, the other sectors would have still found workers because of the rapid population growth. There was also a considerable pool of unemployed and a much larger pool of under-employed labor.[476]

Now, if agriculture had caused the spurt in the economy, it should have been the fastest growing sector. Farm output during the years 1850–99 grew almost twice as fast as in the preceding fifty years, but only half as fast as the economy. If agriculture had pulled the economy along, it would have had to be growing faster than GDP. The only sector that grew faster than the economy was manufacturing, and it grew more than twice as fast as agriculture. Manufacturing averaged about 7.5% per year, GDP about 6.3%, and agriculture about 3.0%.[477]

Many have asserted that it was the great wealth of natural resources that made possible the rapid growth. However, during the preceding fifty years the natural resources were actually more abundant in per capita terms because the overall population was much smaller. The economy nonetheless grew considerably slower. This argument is even harder to sustain when the situation of the 18th century is analyzed. In that period, the per capita supply of natural resources was significantly larger because the size of the population was a tiny fraction of the 1850–99 population. In spite of that, the economy was almost stagnant.

In the years 1850–99, there was also a much higher output of the other primary domains, which coincided with elevated production of primary sector implements and machines. In 1850, petroleum's contribution to the energy supply of the US was zero but with the rapid development of excavation equipment, digging tools, and drilling machines, by 1900 the figure had jumped to 5%. The same occurred with numerous other minerals, with fish catches, and with the felling of trees. It was the machines what made the exploitation of the natural resources possible. Without the factory goods, the resources could be abundant but they could not get exploited. [478]

Others have argued that it was the entrepreneurial spirit of the population what made the economic growth possible. It is said that individuals of great energy and vision such as Andrew Carnegie, John Rockefeller, George Westinghouse, and J.P. Morgan were largely responsible for the great economic performance. The cultural origin of this strong business drive resided, according to this argument, in the Calvinist philosophy of the country which persuaded the population to work hard, study hard, and save money.

If entrepreneurial drive had played a major stimulating role, then it is hard to understand why such a culturally determined variable did not deliver similar results earlier. GDP figures were considerably different during the first and the second half of the 19th century. In the first half the economy grew by about 2.7% per year while in the second it averaged about 6.3%. If the prevailing culture encouraged work and parsimonious conduct in 1850–99, surely it should have done the same thing in the preceding 50 years.[479]

476 Harris: Ibid., p. 187, 4.
477 Faulkner: Ibid., p. 381; Sabillon: Ibid., p. 147.
478 Davis, Hughes & McDougall: Ibid., p. 67, 61, 102.
479 Bogart & Kemmerer: Ibid., p. 474.

Associated with this idea was the argument concerning education. By 1850, the United States had the world's highest share of population enrolled in school and in the following fifty years it actually enlarged its educational lead. Many have asserted that this highly educated population was largely responsible for the rapid growth. If having the best-educated workforce had been fundamental for attaining the fastest rates of growth in the world, its superior GDP rates should have been sustained during the first half of the 20th century. In 1900–49, the US continued to have the highest educational levels in the world. In spite of that, Japan grew faster — the US grew by about 3.5% annually and Japan by 4.5%. That coincided with a stronger factory promotion policy in Japan and faster rates of factory output (4.2% for the US and 6.3% for Japan).[480]

The US population was expanding rapidly during the second half of the 19th century, averaging a rate of about 4% annually. Many historians have asserted that this rate contributed significantly to growth as it fostered specialization and pushed demand upwards. The data suggests otherwise, because population grew significantly slower than GDP. In order for increased demand to have been a major factor, the population should have grown at the same pace or faster. On the other hand, population growth also slowed down by the end of the century and the economy instead of decelerating actually gained speed.[481]

On top of that, the population grew even faster (about 6%) during the first half while the economy did not grow rapidly. Why would rapid population growth during the years 1850–99 cause rapid economic growth and an even faster rate of population during 1800–49 cause slower GDP growth? It is obviously not that simple. And during the second half of the 19th century, Australia's population was growing even faster than that of the US, yet Australia attained a slower rate of GDP growth. Factory promotion policies in Australia were less aggressive than in the US and they had lower rates of manufacturing output. Furthermore, in the 18th century the US population grew faster than in the period 1850–99, while the economy stagnated. That correlated with little factory subsidization in those days.[482]

Many have therefore argued that it was the concomitant effect of all of the factors previously mentioned which delivered the growth of the years 1850–99. However, even taken all together these factors do not correlate with the economic data. During the first half of the 19th century America enjoyed rapid population growth, heavy immigration from Europe, abundant natural resources, the same entrepreneurial drive, the same commitment to education, and the same Protestant culture as in the second half of the century. GDP figures nonetheless were considerably less inspiring.

Canada, Australia, and New Zealand

During 1850–99, the second fastest growing economy in the world was that of Canada. That was paralleled by the second most aggressive factory promotion policies in the world and the second best rate of factory output.

The government's motivations to decree such generous subsidies were very similar to those of the US. In 1848, Britain granted self-government to Canada and from this moment on the Canadian government's priority was integrating politically and economically the vast

---

480 Rosenberg: Ibid., p. 35, 9; Sabillon: Ibid., p. 112, 147.
481 Krout: *The United States since 1865*, p. 25.
482 Kenwood & Lougheed: Ibid., p. 20.

territory under its jurisdiction. Canada's territory was not only larger than that of the US, but also considerably less populated. On top of that, one of its largest and most populous provinces (Quebec) had nourished separatist desires since the 18th century.[483]

As in the US, the government of Canada saw railroads as the best means to integrate the country. It thus offered large subsidies to the producers of railroad-related goods. During this period, Canada and the US had the largest budgets in the world for railroads (as a share of GDP). Since Canada never underwent a real separatist effort and less still a civil war, the country endured a smaller pressure to manufacture and support for this sector was less strong than in the United States.

As in the US, support for this sector was not limited to railroad-related goods. The government also subsidized the factories that processed the vast natural resources the country possessed. Canada's comparative advantage was seen as residing in its large agricultural, mineral, forest, and fishing resources. The British had repeatedly maintained that Canada was not capable of manufacturing any kind of goods; that is why the first Canadian governments proceeded conservatively, limiting their manufacturing efforts to the processing of natural resources.

During the years 1850–99, government expenditure for manufacturing as a share of GDP was slightly below that of the United States. Other forms of incentives were also at levels similar to its neighbor's. This slightly lower subsidization coincided with slightly slower rates of factory output, which averaged about 6% annually. GDP grew by about 5%. [484]

Economic growth in Canada had been very slow during the first half of the 19th century. This coincided with Britain's mercantilist policies that deliberately sought to hinder the development of manufacturing. Canada possessed gigantic natural resources but primary sector production grew slowly in that period.

A similar phenomenon occurred in Australia and New Zealand. During the years 1800–49, support for manufacturing was very weak and primary sector output grew very slowly. However, when in the middle of the century Britain granted self-government, the factory-repressive mercantilist policies came to an end. The new governments of both nations gave priority status to the processing of their vast natural resources and to railroads, and that was accompanied by an impressive acceleration of the economy.

With their vast and thinly populated territories, they shared the same view of the world as Washington and Ottawa. They too had large railroad budgets and they too were among the most enthusiastic promoters of factory production. However, because separatist tendencies were less of a threat than in North America, they were under less pressure and were therefore less driven to invest in manufacturing. Thus they succeeded in significantly accelerating the rate of factory output and GDP, but not as high as in North America. During 1850–99, manufacturing production in Australia and New Zealand was among the highest in the world and GDP rates were also among the highest. [485]

483 Cornell, Hamelin, Ouellet, Trudel: *Canada—Unite et diversite*, p. 254–355.

484 Davis, Lance & Huttenback, Robert: *Mammon and the Pursuit of Empire*, p. 95; Sabillon: Ibid., p. 147; Madison, Angus: *The World Economy: Historical Statistics*; Madison, Angus: *The World Economy: A Millennial Perspective*.

485 Davis, Lance & Huttenback, Robert: Ibid., p. 105; Madison, Angus: *Monitoring the World Economy 1820–1992*.

Germany

Unification, Trains, and Weapons

During the second half of the 19th century, German policy makers were among the most decisive factory subsidizers in Europe and the country enjoyed one of the highest rates of economic growth in the continent. Factory output rates surpassed those of Britain — even though, up until the mid-century, most Europeans believed that Germany would never manage to produce factory goods in large amounts. By the end of the century Germany even produced goods of higher quality and technology than Britain.[486]

As with other countries the motivations were ideological, but a particular confluence of events generated more pressure on Germany. The fear of military aggression from abroad and the desire to politically unify the German states as a nation were major influences. Another was the desire to expand the territorial frontiers of the country. To a lesser extent, there were also balance-of-payments concerns and the desire to catch up with the most advanced nations in Europe.

By 1850, Germany was still composed of some three dozen fully independent states, unified only commercially. It was felt that a unified nation would be stronger, and railroads were seen by most state governments as the best means to achieve that goal. This led to more subsidies for railroad-related manufacturing.[487]

There were several wars that continuously grew in scale, forcing larger investments in the production of arms, and growing subsidies for the production of trains and military equipment, plus an across-the-board policy to catch up with the most developed nations in Europe. This last translated into more subsidies for civilian manufacturing. Additionally, the desire to achieve a favorable trade balance pushed German governments to promote exports and substitute imports, which were mostly factory goods.

Subsidies for this sector were larger than ever before in 1850–99, and the economy grew faster than ever before. Manufacturing averaged about 4.8% annually and the economy grew by about 3.9% per year.[488]

The first decade of this period (the 1850s) witnessed an increase in grants, in subsidized financing, in tax benefits, and in land concessions to the producers of metals, rails, locomotives, arms, and numerous civilian wares. There was also an increase in the creation and expansion of state-owned factories. Several banks, created fundamentally to finance manufacturing, appeared during this period. Some were state owned and others were private. The government offered private banks a large number of incentives to induce them to lend a large share of their assets to manufacturing.

In Prussia, which was leading the drive for unification, the state-owned Prussian Bank was founded in the 1830s. It subsidized private sector production in numerous fields and it also financed and owned iron, armament, and textile factories. During the 1850s, the government supplied more funds to the bank and thus its loans rose.[489]

486 Berghahn, V.: *Modern Germany*, p. 1, 2.
487 Gaxotte, Pierre: *Histoire de l'Allemagne*, p. 500–509.
488 Bettelheim, Charles: L'Economie Allemande sous le Nazisme Vol. I, p. 14, 15; Sabillon: Ibid., p. 182; Madison, Angus: *The World Economy: Historical Statistics*; Fogel: Ibid.
489 Kitchen, Martin: *The Political Economy of Germany 1815–1914*, p. 87–89.

During the 1850s, the fastest growing field was railroad manufacturing and state govern-ments financed about 70% of the investment that flowed into that field. The share of financ-ing that came from the state in the previous decade had been lower and during the 1830s it was lower still. These differing levels of subsidization coincided with proportionate rates of train production and of manufacturing in general. The economy continuously accelerated.

Many people had initially dismissed trains as interesting toys; but by the 1850s, most of those in the aristocracy, the military, and the bourgeoisie who had opposed the development of the railroads had turned into devoted supporters. This — plus the faster expansion of the railroad industry in the US since the 1820s — makes it evident that railroad goods and manufacturing in general could have developed earlier, had the authorities pushed it. The high factory subsidies of the 1850s were accompanied by a growth of this sector of about 3.0% annually and the economy averaged about 2.5%.

By the 1850s, the belief that Germany would never manage to produce manufactures in large amounts was supplanted by the belief that diverting too much investment from agriculture to manufacturing would translate into a reduced food supply. Instead, the food supply increased faster than ever before. As an expanding share from overall investment flowed into the factories during the following decades, the per capita food supply became larger and larger.[490]

Common sense might suggest that only large investments in agriculture could gener-ate higher food output. But in reality, as a larger share of the nation's resources flowed into factories, the technology base expanded, and with a larger technology base, the spillover of innovations was bound to contribute to more efficient production of food as well. Greater investments in metals led to technology breakthroughs that reduced the costs of producing metals. Metal began to be a viable material for all sorts of equipment beyond weapons and trains. It could now be used to make machines that processed food and to make cans that could preserve food.

Prussia's Chancellor Bismarck was determined to unify the states. The 1860s witnessed a continuation of rapid railroad construction as well as an increase in the production of arms. Prussia went to war against Denmark in 1864 and won, adding to its territory the northern state of Schleswig–Holstein.[491] Prussia went to war against Austria in 1866 and proceeded to annex several smaller states.[492]

Bismarck was also convinced that in order to persuade the rest of the German states to relinquish their sovereignty, a major war with France was needed. Napoleon had humiliated them and the defeat was still fresh in the mind of Germans. Bismarck increased his invest-ment in arms even more. This, plus the continuation of large subsidies for train-making in the other states delivered unprecedented factory growth and economic growth. Manufac-turing output averaged about 3.7% and the economy expanded by about 3.0% per year.[493]

Factory output went up, and hand in hand with it came an accelerated pace of tech-nological change. Patents were registered at a faster rate and technology was imported at a quicker pace. The 1860s saw for example the advent of new chemicals, pharmaceuticals, electrical equipment, plus cement, and mechanical instruments. Steel became affordable

490 Ibid., p. 133, 97–99, 93; Fogel: Ibid.
491 Gaxotte: Ibid., p. 515.
492 Ibid., p. 513, 518.
493 Bramsted, Ernest: *Germany*, p. 2, 141–149.

and for the first time in German history, the output of steel exceeded that of iron. Just about every single invention found its expression in manufactured goods. As in other countries, the fields that received the most support, like armaments and trains, were the ones that experienced the fastest technical progress.[494]

In 1870, Bismarck's wish was fulfilled and war with France broke out. All the German states rallied behind Prussia and made common cause. Resources were mobilized for the production of arms and the Deutsche Bank was founded with the assistance of the government to increase funding for the armories. Most other banks were also induced by the states to do likewise. Armament production and overall manufacturing were up and the economy flourished.[495]

The banks also prospered. This was not the first time that banks had been pressured by the government to channel their funds into manufacturing and it would not be the last. Throughout the 19th century and in particular the years 1850–99, German governments increasingly induced banks to lend to manufacturing. By means of incentives and regulation, private banks were forced to lend a growing share of their assets to the sector. The bankers disliked the interference, but the increased pressure coincided with faster GDP growth and larger profits for the banks.

Left to do as they please, banks finance only low-risk and quick-return activities such as commerce, other service activities, and real state. Under those circumstances, manufacturing cannot find financing, and cannot expand.

Prussia invested more in arms than France did in the decades prior to the year 1870 and it also invested more during the war. During the war, the French were still using bronze cannons while the Germans had steel, which shot faster, further, and with greater precision. The war was short lived.

As the victor, Germany demanded the annexation of large French territories (Alsace and Lorraine) and large war reparations in cash and in kind. Having defeated Europe's second strongest military power, Bismarck convinced the German states that unification could provide them with the means to become one of the top powers of the continent. The states agreed to the proposal and in 1871 Germany as a unified nation was born.[496]

Bismarck led the new government and he prioritized the consolidation, overcoming the last minute hesitations of numerous states who feared relinquishing their sovereignty. Berlin decreed more funds for the development of railroads in furtherance of this goal.

The government was also convinced that a future war with France was inevitable, for Paris would never accept the loss of its two northern provinces. More was thus allotted for the fabrication of weapons. During the years following the war, half of the large war reparations that France paid to Germany were spent on weapons and related heavy industry. During the 1870s, the Armed Forces consumed about 70% of the government budget.

Once they were unified, the Germans' desire to catch up developmentally with the most advanced nations in Europe also became stronger and this translated into more subsidies for the production of civilian factory goods. The desire to run trade surpluses also contributed to the large allocations for factories.[497]

---

494 Bettelheim: Ibid., p. 15; Kitchen: Ibid., p. 123–126.
495 Bramsted: Ibid., p. 121.
496 Gaxotte: Ibid., p. 521–525.
497 Kitchen: Ibid., p. 132, 147.

Factory production during the 1870s averaged about 4.4% and the economy expanded by about 3.6% per year.

During the last two decades of the 19th century, the fear of a major war with France and the threat of conflict with other powers rose as Paris and other governments poured more money into their military budgets. An arms race was underway. Defense expenditure rose to about 75% of the budget and government expenditure augmented considerably. Taxes and public borrowing increased significantly. Britain's expansion of its already large navy, and a widespread belief that the island owed its wealth to its colonial possessions, persuaded the German government to heavily incentivize shipbuilding. Berlin was determined to develop a large military and commercial fleet.[498]

During the 1880s, Berlin started supplying ship producers with very large subsidies such as grants, cheap financing, and low taxes. Sea vessel production, which up until the 1870s had been very small, began to grow at a fast pace. Shipbuilding accelerated even more during the 1890s because in 1888 a new Emperor took over the throne and William II was obsessed with building a navy that could match that of Britain.

This together with increased armament production, the continuation of ample support for railroad-related goods, and a relatively strong subsidization of civilian manufacturing delivered an acceleration of factory output. That coincided with an acceleration of economic growth. During the last two decades of the 19th century factory output averaged about 6.4% annually and GDP about 5.3%.[499]

Correlation and Causality

The progressive acceleration of factory production during the second half of the 19th century coincided with a progressive acceleration in the pace of technology advances. Patent registrations were up and technology imports also accelerated. Technology can be created or it can be reproduced. Creating it is more time consuming and capital intensive but even reproducing others' inventions requires vast amounts of capital. These advances of the late 19th century were enabled by massive government support.

Independent of whether the technology was imported or created domestically, it was systematically incorporated in factory goods such as machines, equipment, contraptions, instruments, weapons, ships, chemicals, and pharmaceuticals. Even though much was imported, a growing number of technologies were significantly improved by indigenous efforts. There were also a growing number of discoveries that were strictly the result of German inventiveness. Germany, which through centuries had been accused of lacking scientific capability, was by the late 19th century the most innovative nation in Europe. That coincided with the most decisive promotion of manufacturing among the large nations of Europe. In 1885, Karl Benz built the first gasoline automobile in the world and in the 1890s aspirin, one of the most sought-after pain relievers of the 20th century, was invented in the laboratories of Bayer. The symbiosis between manufacturing and technology was particularly clear in such factory goods as optical instruments, electrical devices, and synthetic fibers that were at the forefront of innovation. The inventors made their discoveries as they labored in factories and not in universities.[500]

---

498 Ibid., p. 184, 253.
499 Bettelheim: Ibid.; Madison, Angus: *The World Economy: Historical Statistics.*
500 Gaxotte: Ibid, p. 564.

Productivity grew rapidly during the second half of the 19th century as a result of the many technological advances. However, there is strong reason to believe that productivity could have grown even faster had certain policy errors not been committed. First the state governments and then the federal authorities created a large number of state enterprises in practically all fields of the economy. Most were factories but there were also banks, mining companies, and firms in several others fields. During the 1870s, Bismarck even nationalized railroads. Levels of efficiency in these enterprises were systematically below those of the private sector. Had these enterprises been privatized, the evidence suggests they would have attained a better performance.[501]

By the mid-19th century, Germany's trade regime was quite liberal but manufacturers were increasingly demanding the erection of trade barriers. In the 1860s, heavy good producers and textile makers became even more vociferous in their demands, but the agrarians dominated politics and were convinced that free trade was bad for manufacturing, so only a small dose of protection was approved. However, by the mid-1870s industrial interests gained the upper hand in government and trade barriers were raised. During the rest of the 19th century, tariffs and non-tariff barriers were raised still more. In 1850–99, monopolies and cartels were also on the rise.[502]

The evidence suggests the considerable increase in state companies, trade barriers, and cartels during this half century was a policy error. However, that situation coincided with an accelerating economy, which substantiates the manufacturing thesis. Only under this premise can such an apparent paradox be explained. If private sector production, free trade, and competition were pivotal for growth, the economy should have progressively deteriorated. If we add to that the growing government expenditure, regulation, and expenditure in weapons, there is more reason to have expected a deterioration of the economy. However, the economy actually improved more and more.

Government expenditure as a share of the GDP rose from about 4% in 1850 to about 11% by 1900 — a drop in the bucket, compared to today. By the late 20th century, the compounded expenditure of federal, state, and local government was about 48% of GDP.[503]

It is worth noting that in spite of the very small government expenditure of the late 19th century, economic growth reached sustained rates of 5% annually. By the late 20th century, on the other hand, GDP growth was only 2% notwithstanding a government expenditure that was almost five times larger. This and examples from other countries show that large government expenditure is no guarantee for growth. The historical evidence, however, cannot substantiate the claim that a small budget assists growth either. In the 18th century and before, government expenditure in Germany was very small, accounting for about 1% of GDP. The economy languished in almost complete stagnation.

All of these episodes suggest that the most important focus for government expenditure should be the subsidization of manufacturing. The evidence suggests that when such expenditure is too small, as it was during the 18th century, then even if the whole budget is used to promote factories the economy will still be unable to grow rapidly. When the government budget has reached a size of about 10% of GDP, as was the case in the late 19th century, if most of it is used to promote factories, the economy will grow rapidly. By the late 20th

---

501 Kitchen: Ibid., p. 101, 253.
502 Bramsted: Ibid., p. 119, 149, 124.
503 "Fiscal Consolidation in Germany", *The Economist*, 29 June 1996, p. 70.

century, a far smaller share of Germany's resources was allocated to manufacturing than one hundred years earlier. The budget had been vastly increased but the bulk of the expanded budget was spent on social welfare, infrastructure projects, and other things that had nothing to do with factory production.

Also substantiating the thesis of manufacturing as the driving force is the fact that in 1850–99, the numerous fluctuations of the business cycle systematically coincided with the differing levels of support for this sector. Whenever the government dropped its promotion efforts — because a major rail line had been completed, a war had come to an end, or a change of government had momentarily paralyzed policy — recession or slower growth was experienced.[504]

Foreign trade grew rapidly during this half century notwithstanding the rapid rise of protectionism. Tariff and non-tariff barriers were in place but German imports grew anyway. Exports grew even faster despite the rise in trade barriers in most European countries and in most other nations that traded with Germany. If trade barriers were the main variable determining flows of trade, as orthodox arguments claim, then Germany's trade flow should have contracted during the years 1850–99. But that is not what happened, and the only variable that succeeds in deciphering this paradox is manufacturing.

During this period, factory goods not only grew faster than before but the technological content of these goods was much higher than formerly. Trains and ships for example, were not just more numerous, but they were also faster, safer and more comfortable. Medicines and medical instruments were not just more abundant, but they also cured more diseases. As a result, demand for these goods was much higher. That would explain why foreign trade rose despite the high trade barriers. Higher prices could not stop people from acquiring these goods because the benefits they provided were far superior to anything seen before. Also worth noting is that despite the rise in prices resulting from tariffs and cartels, the rapid growth of technology counterbalanced by reducing costs of production and the final price paid by the consumer was sometimes lower than formerly.

Most people associate new technology with totally new products, but new technology has mostly appeared in the form of reduced costs of production or small improvements to existing goods. Reduced costs allow a larger share of the population to consume a good.

Manufacturing also increased the possibilities for commerce in numerous other ways. In 1876, a German invented the compression refrigerator. This immediately revolutionized trade as the possibility of preserving foodstuffs and other perishable goods allowed them to be transported.

During the second half of the 19th century, commercial activity grew more in Germany than in Britain, notwithstanding Britain's free trade policy. Britain was then offering far less support for the sector and had far lower rates of factory output to show. While manufacturing in Germany averaged about 4.8% annual growth, in Britain it grew by just 2.8%. As a result, Britain had fewer goods to trade.[505]

All other sectors and fields of the German economy followed the expansion of trade. Agriculture grew much faster notwithstanding the smaller share of overall investment that it received. The fabrication of farm machinery multiplied and the production of fertilizer boomed. The first chemical fertilizer plant was built in 1855. Much suggests that it was

504 Kitchen: Ibid., p. 97.
505 Ibid., p. 203, 61; Sabillon: Ibid., p. 182, 183; Madison, Angus: *Monitoring the World Economy 1820–1992.*

these technology-intensive goods what allowed for agriculture to grow by about 2.3% per year, which was approximately three times faster than in the preceding fifty years.

Many have argued that the accelerated pace of agricultural production in Germany was the main factor responsible for the better GDP figures of the period 1850–99. That is very unlikely considering that farming systematically grew at a slower pace, averaging only 2.3% while GDP expanded by 3.9%. Only manufacturing could have delivered a pulling effect on the economy for this was the only sector that grew faster (4.8%). It is also worth noting that agricultural productivity systematically remained below that of manufacturing, as it had for the preceding fifty years. It is hard to argue that a sector with weak productivity performance and a slow rate of output was the one that propelled the economy forward.[506]

The same story may be seen in the rest of Europe, North America, Russia, and Japan during the second half of the 19th century. In all of these nations, agricultural production and productivity were up, but in all of them, manufacturing was growing even faster.

The acceleration of farm output in all of these nations occurred when the state increased its factory promotion efforts. So impressive was the growth of agriculture that for the first time in history the world experienced a crisis of grain overproduction in the 1870s. Agriculture grew rapidly only in these countries, which were the only nations that provided ample subsidies to factories. In most of Asia, Africa, and Latin America food continued to be scarce.[507]

The rapid factory output in Germany during 1850–99 went hand in hand with a rapid growth of savings and capital. After having been a capital-poor nation, all of sudden Germany became a capital-rich nation. Since the 1880s, it became a net exporter of capital and soon after one of the largest lenders and investors in the rest of the world.[508]

There were new breakthroughs in nutrition, housing, health, and education. Life expectancy rose and infant mortality dropped. So much wealth was created that there was even enough to finance the first state sponsored social welfare system in the world. The 1880s witnessed the advent of unemployment benefits, pensions, and health care for the working class.

Nations have different cultures and culture is hard to define, but it does affect policies. Germany was in the 1880s less developed than the US, which clearly indicates that wealth alone does not explain why Germany was the first to develop a welfare system. However, it is evident that without a large creation of wealth, a welfare system cannot come into being. During the 20th century, Western nations were the most developed and these were the first to set a welfare system. Japan established a welfare system after World War II, after it had already benefited from a century of rapid economic growth. By the 1990s, Singapore had the most advanced welfare system in Southeast Asia and it happened to be the country with by far the highest per capita income in that region during the 20th century.

Labor conditions in Germany also improved during the second half of the 19th century. Child labor was limited, maternity leave was offered, working hours were reduced, protection against accidents at the workplace was decreed, and minimum wages were established. By 1850, the average number of working hours per week was about 93, but by 1900 it had dropped to 62. Labor conditions improved more in the cities, where factories were con-

---

506 Kitchen: Ibid., p. 156, 254; Berghahn: Ibid., p. 4, 5.
507 Bairoch, Paul: *Economics and World History*, p. 11, 151, 53.
508 Bettelheim: Ibid., p. 14.

centrated. Unionization and labor activism rose rapidly, but as living conditions improved, workers never became radical in their demands.[509] Some analysts have claimed that the welfare system was put in place to avoid worker radicalization and that its birth owes more to labor militancy than to the creation of wealth. However, wealth is clearly a precondition.

Faster manufacturing output in the second half of the 19th century included output of more printing presses, books, ink, pencils, blackboards and desks. Germany was one of the first countries to develop a system of compulsory primary and middle school education. Middle school was introduced in 1872. Education advanced hand in hand with the unprecedented rate of factory output.

Health care also made progress, mostly as a direct result of innovations in pharmaceuticals and medical instruments. Better nutrition followed from the improved agricultural manufactures and from the fact that more food was available, from the factories, in processed form. Better sanitation also helped, but this too was made possible by the increased output of factory goods. The incidence of cholera, typhus, diphtheria, and scarlet fever rapidly decreased as water began to be treated with chemicals and as sewage works began to be constructed. Without the new steel construction equipment as well as the cement that appeared during that period, these infrastructure works would never have been possible.[510]

Germany had an unprecedented population explosion in the late 1800s; its populace was growing faster than most other countries of Europe. Since this coincided with the fastest GDP rates up to that date and with one of the fastest rates in all of Europe, many see this as one of the main causes of economic growth. The problem with this argument is that the economy grew at the same speed a century later, even without significant population growth. During the period 1850–99, the population expanded by about 1.7% annually and GDP grew by about 3.9%. In 1950–99, the population grew by just 0.5%, yet GDP was up 3.8%.[511]

It is difficult to argue that during a certain period of time population growth had a strong effect on economic growth and in other periods it did not. It must as well be pointed out that the GDP figures were rising much faster than the population figures; if population growth were pulling the economy along, the population should have grown faster.

Also, the second half of the 19th century was a period of large-scale emigration from Germany to the American continent. The large flows of Europeans to the US have been credited with contributing to the economic growth of the United States. The skills of these emigrants supposedly had a positive effect on the American economy. But it is not seen that Germany suffered any equal and opposite decline as it lost skilled laborers. The evidence suggests that if population or emigration has an effect on growth, then the effect is complex, varies with other factors, and is not directly linear.[512]

Others have argued that Germany's growth was aided by the drive of its entrepreneurs. Men like the self-made steel king Friedrich Krupp were supposed to have (with their vision and energy) contributed significantly to the acceleration of economic growth. Many analysts also argue that there was something about the German culture that made people

---

509 Kitchen: Ibid., p. 176, 177; Berghahn: Ibid., p. 7, 9, 276.
510 Ibid., p. 13, 14, 16; Gaxotte: Ibid., p. 564, 565, 544.
511 Berghahn: Ibid., p. 3, 253; *World Development Report 1981, 1991 & 2001*–Basic Indicators, The World Bank; Madison, Angus: *The World Economy: A Millennial Perspective.*
512 Bramsted: Ibid., 121

work harder. If that were true, then why was growth so slow during the 18th century, when the same culture was present? During the 18th century, GDP figures were only one tenth the rate of 1850–99.

Why would a nation produce numerous energetic entrepreneurs only at certain moments in history? Most likely because the fundamental variable responsible for growth and therefore for the rapid development of business has nothing to do with culture. Krupp was illustrative. During that period, steel and weapons were the most generously subsidized fields of manufacturing and he was the largest producer of steel and the biggest supplier of cannons to the army. His son F. Krupp II also became one of the most admired businessmen; he became the main supplier of battleships for the navy. Had it not been for the large subsidies the government offered, there would have been no opportunity for these men to prove themselves as world class entrepreneurs. The output of steel, weapons, and ships would not have grown so fast, and these men would not have become so wealthy. During the 18th century there were numerous hard driven, workaholic, and visionary businessmen, but during this period government support for manufacturing was very low.

In 1848 and 1849 major gold deposits were discovered in California and Australia; many have argued that the larger supply of gold stimulated economic growth as it facilitated international payments. There was indeed a noticeable acceleration of growth in numerous regions of the world, but the gold could not have played a major role in Germany; no gold was discovered there. Rather, Britain possessed Australia as a colony and because Britain was the most important financial center of the world, it processed a large share of the gold through its banks. In spite of this, Britain's GDP rates were much slower than Germany's during the second half of the 19th century.[513]

By the late 19th century, many economists and policy makers believed that Britain largely owed its wealth to its colonial possessions. As Britain, France, and other European nations scrambled for Africa's territory, Germany was also lured by the imperialist drive. It began to seek to conquer territories in the 1880s and acquired Southwest Africa (Namibia), Cameron, Togo, most of the future Tanzania, and part of the island of New Guinea. In 1884 all of these lands became protectorates. The economy accelerated during the 1880s and 1890s, and it was thought that the colonies had played a contributory role.[514]

Had colonies played a positive role, Britain should have had the best GDP rates. Not only did it have the largest colonial possessions in the world, but during the years 1850–99 it acquired more African territory than anybody else. Britain actually performed worse than any other large nation in Europe (in particular during the 1880s and 1890s). Even Russia grew faster, in spite of its lack of colonies. Switzerland and Luxembourg, which never acquired colonies or expanded their territory, also grew much faster than Britain. The factory thesis again holds well against this data because manufacturing subsidies were greater in Germany, Russia, Switzerland, and Luxembourg and they enjoyed faster rates of factory output than Britain.

---

513 Ibid., p. 123.
514 Kitchen: Ibid., p. 180, 186, 12.

Russia

The Crimean War and its Consequences

During the second half of the 19th century, Russia's economy accelerated relative to the preceding fifty years and GDP growth averaged about 3.0% annually, exceeding that of Britain and other European countries that had systematically outperformed Russia. Britain averaged only 2.4%. (See tables at the end of the book.) Never before had Russia experienced anything like it. In 1800–49, GDP growth had been only a tenth as fast.

During this period, there were a number of shattering events that forced the Russian government to decree a radical change of policies that inadvertently translated into a gigantic increase in factory subsidies. This correlated with a strong acceleration in the rate of factory output. The superior GDP rates with respect to Britain and several other European countries coincided as well with superior rates of manufacturing output. This sector averaged about 4.0% annually, while in Britain the figure was just 2.8%.[515]

During this half century, national security concerns were at the core of the radical change in policies. However, balance of payments worries, an ambition to catch up with the West's development, and a need for geopolitical integration also played a role. At no moment during this period was the government convinced that the promotion of factories had a direct and positive effect on the economy. However, because of a confluence of pressing circumstances, Moscow increased significantly the level of subsidization. This support nonetheless was not as strong as in the US, Canada, Australia, Germany, and several other countries; and the rates of factory output and GDP growth were commensurately lower than in those countries.[516]

During the first half of the 19th century, the Russian government had been deliberately hindering the development of manufacturing. Although some support was given in order to create the first railroad linking Moscow and St. Petersburg, the overall level of subsidies was still very low. In 1852, that rail line was completed and the government felt that the country did not need any more rail lines. The apparent military successes of the preceding decades had also convinced the government that only small defense expenditures were needed.[517]

In 1854, however, war broke out in the Crimea pitting Russia against an alliance of the Ottoman Empire, France, and Britain. Since there was no railroad to the Crimea, soldiers had to march from Moscow to the front: a major logistical problem. Relative to Britain and France, Russia's firearms were obsolete and there was a shortage of ammunition from the beginning to the end of the war. The French had about five times more steam-powered war vessels than the Russians, and Britain had six times more. On top of that, the Russian forces had insufficient supplies of food, uniforms, and medicine.[518]

By 1856 the war was over and Russia had suffered a major defeat. It was particularly humiliating because the war was fought in Russia's territory, where it was supposed to have an advantage. The country was shocked and the government resolved to take immediate action to avoid a repetition. The need for more and better weapons, as well as more railroads

---

515 Nove, Alec: *An Economic History of the USSR*, p. 12, 13, 11; Sabillon: Ibid., p 120, 183; Fogel: Ibid.; Madison, Angus: *The World Economy: Historical Statistics*.
516 Kahan, Arcadius: *Russian Economic History*, p. 13.
517 *The Fontana Economic History of Europe—The Emergence of Industrial Societies*, p. 488.
518 Blackwell, William: *The Beginnings of Russian Industrialization*, p. 185.

to transport troops, was now clear. Moscow therefore allocated a much larger share of the country's resources to the factories that produced railroad and military goods.[519]

The war shocked the government into action but strong beliefs against manufacturing were deeply entrenched. The growth of a middle class and of an urban working class would threaten the power of the tsar and the nobility. On top of that, there were deep physiocratic beliefs and budgetary restraints. These fears were so strong that despite the recent defeat the leadership could stomach only a modest increase in subsidies for the rest of the 1850s. In this decade there was a significant increase in the rate of manufacturing output, but it was still very little relatively to numerous Western European nations. Manufacturing averaged about 0.8% annually and the economy expanded by about 0.6%.[520]

The mixed feelings about manufacturing continued for many more years, but they progressively tilted in favor of supporting the sector. In 1861, modernizers in the government gained more power. One of their first measures consisted in putting an end to serfdom. The serfs were emancipated in that year and by 1866 two other pieces of legislation had phased out most aspects of feudalism. No longer could serfs be flogged, sold, bartered for dogs, lost at cards, or be killed by their masters. They were given freedom, allotted some land in the first agrarian reform in Russian history, and were allowed to change their occupation and move freely throughout the country.[521]

By then, serfdom was seen throughout Europe as the main hindrance for the rapid development of the economy because it supposedly inhibited the flow of labor and capital into more productive fields. It was also argued that it hampered population growth (and therefore demand), because it limited the use of money and because it acted as an impediment to trade. The correlation between feudalism and growth actually had been weak in Europe, but there were nonetheless some minor parallels that seemed to suggest causality. The Russian government of the 1860s was convinced of such a linkage.[522]

Together with the termination of serfdom came a liberalization of foreign trade, which up until then had been highly protected. Tariffs and non-tariffs barriers were reduced to a low level. The decrees of 1861 also prescribed a very large increase in the supply of fiscal, financial, and non-financial incentives to the producers of trains, weapons, and other factory goods. Grants, subsidized financing, low taxation, government purchases with high prices, and land grants were supplied in much larger amounts than before. More state factories were also created. The incentives were the highest for railroad goods, less high for arms, and less still for goods indirectly associated with those fields. Support for civilian manufactures was somewhat higher than before, as the government developed a stronger desire to catch up with the West, and it sought to earn more foreign exchange in order to pay for the increased imports of machinery.[523]

The very large increase in the share of the country's resources allocated to manufacturing coincided with a very large acceleration in the rate of GDP. For the first time in Russian history, the country attained rates which were comparable to those that the best performers

---

519 Kirchner, Walter: *A History of Russia*, p. 149–160.
520 *The Cambridge Economic History of Europe Vol. VII*, p. 268; Madison, Angus: *Monitoring the World Economy 1820–1992*.
521 Madison, Angus: *Economic Growth in Japan and the USSR*, p. 84, 85.
522 Brenner, Y.: *A Short History of Economic Progress*, p. 178, 179.
523 Dobb, Maurice: *Soviet Economic Development since 1917*, p. 45, 57.

in the West had attained since the late 18th century. During the 1860s, manufacturing output averaged about 2.8% annually and GDP expanded by about 2.0%.[524]

During the rest of the 19th century, economic growth progressively accelerated, as did the level of factory subsidies. A series of events moved the government in that direction.

The decisive triumph of Germany over France in 1871 sent shock waves to Moscow. If France had recently humiliated Russia in its own backyard with only a fraction of its forces and Germany had crushed the entire French army in French territory, then the potential for Germany to inflict a defeat on Russia was very high. And Germany was closer to Russia than France was; Moscow saw that larger defense expenditures were needed.

The gigantic progress that Germany had achieved in such a small amount of time was also a slap in the face to those in Russian government circles who argued that Russia was predisposed to remain forever a producer of just primary goods. If Germany had moved from an agrarian economy to one capable of producing impressive manufactures, than Russia must be able to do so as well.

As a result, more fiscal, financial, and non-financial incentives were offered to the private sector and more state factories were created. Manufacturing output accelerated and during the 1870s averaged about 3.2% per year. The economy expanded by about 2.5%.[525]

However, the vacillations of the Russian government lingered on. Russia got another incentive at the Congress of Berlin in 1878, where European and world geopolitics were decided without the consent of Moscow. It became clear that having a voice in such matters depended on having the military and economic power to back it up. Moscow decided to raise government expenditure again as a share of GDP and at the same time it allocated a larger share of the budget for the production of railroad goods, arms, and numerous civilian goods. The stronger subsidization in the 1880s coincided with an acceleration in the rate factory output. This sector averaged about 5.0% per year and GDP grew by about 3.9%.[526]

Since the 1860s, the government had created state banks that focused on factory production and it also began to aid entrepreneurs to set up private banks that largely catered to the needs of this sector. As time went on, the state created more of these public and private banks. Not all of the bank loans were used to finance factories, but a significant share was deployed for this purpose. During the 1880s, this policy was pushed further as the banks were instructed to lend a larger share of their assets to the sector, and on more favorable terms. The cost of capital was reduced by setting interest rates below those dictated by the market and by giving periods of maturity that extended beyond those normally decreed by commercial banks.

The policy of attracting foreign direct investment had started in the 16th century but it was only pushed in earnest since the 1860s. Since the tsars were interested in the latest railroad and military technology, they attracted investment mostly in manufacturing, and they offered more subsidies. This translated into high inflows of foreign capital. Incentives to foreign investors rose over time and by the 1880s foreign capital as a share of total new investment in manufacturing was about 41%. In the late 19th century, Russia was attracting more foreign direct investment in manufacturing than many of its European rivals, no doubt

524 Gatrell, Peter: *The Tsarist Economy 1850–1917*, p. 41; Madison, Angus: *The World Economy: Historical Statistics*.

525 *The Cambridge Economic History of Europe Vol. VII*, p. 414, 465; Fogel: Ibid.

526 Madison, Angus: *Economic Growth in Japan and the USSR*, p. 92, 90, 91.

because of the government incentives which were among the most generous on the continent. Foreign borrowing to finance factories also increased considerably from the 1860s onward.[527]

In spite of the humiliation at the Congress of Berlin, which impelled the Russian government to accelerate the pace of production of trains and weapons, the long-held fears about manufacturing continued to linger in the heads of most policy makers. Shocks on the international scene forced them to overcome their reticence.[528]

Since the early 1870s, the Transport Ministry had attempted to construct a railroad which would traverse the whole of Siberia and reach the Pacific coast, but the Finance Ministry had blocked the effort for fear of seeing the state indebtedness increase. Since the mood among policy makers with respect to manufacturing was not enthusiastic, the majority sided with the Finance Ministry. During the 1880s the efforts to build a Trans-Siberian railway were once again blocked. However, since the mid-19th century, Japan had embarked on a large scale armament policy and by the latter part of the century it was showing increasing imperialist tendencies. In the 1880s, Japan began to make territorial claims in Northeast Asia and its naval fleet expanded rapidly. On top of that, by then the inhabitants of Siberia were beginning to demand independence. [529] Under the threat that Japan could grab Russia's Pacific territories and that Siberia would secede, the government finally approved the construction of the Trans-Siberian Railroad. The arguments of the Finance Ministry and the traditional foes of manufacturing were sidelined. The investments for this rail line were justified on the grounds that they would facilitate the defense of Russia's Asian territories and would significantly contribute to the political and economic integration of Siberia.

Construction of the Trans-Siberian Railroad began in 1891 and it was finished only in 1916, but the vast majority of the work was done during the 1890s. To complete this gigantic venture, which was to become the largest rail line in the world, the government created and operated many iron, steel, locomotive, and machine tool enterprises. To finance these factories, it raised taxes and borrowed more from the West. It also offered more incentives to domestic and foreign entrepreneurs. [530]

Russian and foreign producers received more fiscal, financial, and non-financial incentives. During the 1890s foreign investment poured in. The share of foreign capital of total new investment in manufacturing rose to 43%. In spite of the heavy involvement of foreign firms, it was Russian companies that accounted for the bulk of output. However, independent of whether the output came from foreign companies, Russian private firms or Russian state enterprises, the bottom line is that government subsidies were responsible for practically all of factory output.

In countries such as Britain and the US, government support was mostly supplied indirectly, but in Russia it was very direct. By 1900, 70% of railroads were in government hands and the state had been directly responsible for the production of a similar share of the manufactured goods that made those railroads possible. [531]

---

527 Gatrell: Ibid., p. 228.
528 Supple, Barry (ed): *The Experience of Economic Growth*, p. 434.
529 Westwood, J.: *Endurance and Endeavor*, p. 137.
530 Blackwell, William: *The Industrialization of Russia*, p. 46–50.
531 Brenner: Ibid., p. 181, 182.

During the 1890s, increased support for manufacturing was once again paralleled by a faster rate of factory output and quicker GDP growth (manufacturing averaged about 8.0% annually and GDP about 6.1%). Output grew so fast that it even exceeded the rates attained by Germany and practically all other European nations. This coincided with a higher level of factory subsidization than elsewhere in Europe. [532]

Railroads, Ideology, and Factories

Modern factory production began in light manufacturing during the 1830s, in fields such as cotton spinning and beet sugar. These happened to be the most subsidized fields of the time. During the second half of the 19th century and in particular the last decades, mechanical methods of production advanced most in heavy manufacturing. It was in iron, steel, locomotives, machines tools, and arms were machinery and mechanical motive power were most used. And these were the most subsidized fields. [533]

Technological development during the second half of the 19th century increased at a breathtaking pace in comparison to the preceding fifty years and this coincided with an exponential increase in the share of resources allocated to manufacturing. During the course of this period, there was a progressive acceleration of technological development and this was paralleled by growing subsidies for the sector. On all aspects, the correlation is very tight.

Throughout history, technological development has been acquired in two ways: by importing goods that embody technology, and by creating new technologies domestically. Frequently, both locally produced and foreign technological advances have come on line simultaneously but when nations find themselves at a lower stage of development than others, they have tended to expedite the acquisition of technological advances by importing them.

By the time the Crimean War ended, Russia was lagging badly behind Western Europe and for the next few decades it imported most of its technology needs. By the 1860s, however, it started to achieve rates of factory output better than several nations in Western Europe and by the end of the 19th century its manufacturing base was growing fastest. The faster growth of these last decades coincided with faster technical development than most nations in Europe and as a result Russia began to catch up. Domestic inventions began to proliferate. The number of Russian scientists and technologists increased. [534]

In its efforts to promote trains, weapons, and civilian goods the government committed several policy errors. A relative liberal trade policy had been decreed in the 1860s but as time went on, tariffs were progressively raised and in 1891 they were put at even higher levels. By the turn of the century, average ad valorem tariffs were at about 131%. There were also high non-tariffs barriers.[535]

Since the 1870s oligopolies and monopolies proliferated. The government thought that captive markets would provide higher profits and more investments would flow into the desired fields. Much suggests that the goal of assuring high profits for factory producers was a positive one, but with tariffs and cartels there is a decrease in competition, and that hurts quality. History suggests that a much better alternative would have been an increase in fiscal, financial, and non-financial incentives such as grants, tax exemptions and subsi-

---

532 Supple (ed): Ibid., p. 428.
533 *The Cambridge Economic History of Europe Vol. VII*, p. 308.
534 Supple (ed): Ibid., p. 433.
535 Madison: *Economic Growth in Japan and the USSR*, p. 91.

dized financing. These last distort market forces but if they are given to private producers (domestic or foreign), there is no decrease in competition.

The policy of increasing the number of state enterprises and of expanding the production capacity of the existing ones was also an error. For centuries, state companies systematically delivered levels of efficiency inferior to private companies and that was certainly true in the second half of the 19th century in Russia. [536]

These policy errors nonetheless are very revealing of the true nature of growth. Orthodox economic theory states that a liberal trade policy, strong internal competition, and private sector production are indispensable for fast GDP growth. During the second half of the 19th century, Russia was largely missing on these three aspects but it nonetheless attained its fastest rates of growth up to that date. Worse still is that as time went on, trade protection rose, cartels became more numerous, and the share of state companies in total production grew larger. However, GDP figures instead of decelerating gained in speed. [537]

Russia grew by about 6% while Germany grew by about 5% during the 1890s; yet Germany's average tariff was only approximately one fourth as high as that of Russia. Cartels were also less widespread and state enterprises were less numerous. However, Germany offered less support to factories and had a lower rate of factory output (6% against 8% in Russia). Britain, which was practicing a wholehearted liberal trade policy, which had relatively few cartels, and which had practically no state companies, performed relatively poorly, in line with London's relatively low subsidization of factories. Factory output in the 1890s averaged only approximately 2.4% annually and the economy expanded by about 2.0%.

As the second half of the 19th century progressed, Russia's state debt and government expenditure as a share of GDP rose. Resources were increasingly allocated to nonproductive uses such as weapons (and trains which could not be justified on commercial terms). These facts make it even harder to understand why GDP figures progressively accelerated. The paradox nonetheless is easily resolved when it is accepted that manufacturing is fundamentally responsible for the generation of technology and thus for economic growth. [538]

Ever since the end of the Crimean War, Moscow had hoped that the private sector would assist it to develop railroads and to increase armaments. However, investors systematically avoided those choices. Domestic and foreign entrepreneurs showed interest only after the government raised the level of incentives considerably and even then, they never satisfied the expectations of the government. That is why the state resorted to the creation of its own enterprises. [539]

The attitude of private banks also reflected the capital-intensive nature of this sector. The risk-averse attitude of commercial banks led them to abstain from lending to manufacturing, for this sector required much larger amounts of capital per unit of output than the other sectors. On top of that, it also took much longer to recuperate the investment. Commercial banks were unwilling to lend even to light manufacturers, who required lower investments than heavy producers and whose return on investment came sooner. Manu-

536 Blackwell: Ibid., p. 35–37.
537 Nove, Alec: *Political Economy and Soviet Socialism*, p. 35.
538 *The Cambridge Economic History of Europe Vol. VII*, p. 271–274.
539 Kahan: Ibid., p. 19.

facturers were supplied with loans only when the government subjected private banks to a carrot and stick policy of regulation and incentives. [540]

During the second half of the 19th century, agricultural production in Russia increased much faster than ever before and one theory held that it was due to the expansion of agriculture into the rich black soil lands of the south and southeast of the country. Up to the mid-19th century, farm output had at best grown by about 0.3% annually over a single decade, but during the second part of this century rates reached almost the 3.0% mark. Since the 16th century, the tsars had been continuously conquering new territories and the new lands constantly delivered new agricultural frontiers. However, farm output up to the mid-19th century had never increased that fast. It is therefore highly unlikely that the continued colonization of new lands was responsible for the growth. Agricultural productivity was also unprecedented in 1850–99, and that cannot be explained by the colonization of new agricultural lands. Had the territories in the south and the southeast not been available for exploitation, output would have nevertheless increased as a result of the higher output per acre. [541]

It is evident that some other factor accounted for the better farm output and manufacturing is the one that best explains the whole situation. Not only was the whole fifty-year period characterized by record-size subsidies for this sector, but the level of support increased as the decades went by. This coincided with an accelerating pace of farm productivity.

It is interesting to note that during this period, resources were taken away from agriculture through higher taxation and decreased budgetary allocations. In spite of that, this domain grew. The other primary activities also grew faster as resources were transferred to the factories.

The exploitation of minerals increased dramatically during the second half of the 19th century, in parallel with a dramatic increase in the production and utilization of mining equipment and machines. Coal, iron ore, and several other minerals were extracted in large amounts even though for centuries it had been argued that Russia had poor deposits of these minerals. [542]

By the late 19th century, in spite of the rapid development of mining, Russia had a much lower per capita output of minerals than Northwestern Europe and North America. This coincided with an inferior overall level of manufacturing development. Mining equipment and machines in the West were more abundant and possessed a higher level of technology. They thus could extract more from the ground. [543]

During the years 1850–99, trade increased, paralleling increased output of factory goods. Subsidies for this sector were larger in the late 19th century and commercial activity grew faster then. Again, the correlation is very tight. [544]

The manufacturing variable is the only one that can explain why, as trade barriers increased, exports and imports rose. The evidence suggests that the causation of the phenomenon is as follows: more subsidies for the sector delivered more factory goods and primary goods, therefore increasing the quantity of tradable goods. More support meant also more

---

540 Gatrell: Ibid., p. 210.
541 Smith, R. & Christian, D.: *Bread and Salt*, p. 255.
542 Supple (ed): Ibid., p. 419–422.
543 Blackwell: Ibid., p. 50.
544 Kahan: Ibid., p. 66, 169–171.

means for conducting trade: trains and ships, as well as more and better ports, roads, and canals. This infrastructure development went hand in hand with increased production of construction equipment.

Education also improved, correlating with an unprecedented production of printing machines, paper, ink, books, and numerous other learning utensils. Literacy increased by leaps and bounds, but by the turn of the century it was still considerably below the levels of the West. In 1900, about 72% of the population in Russia older than ten was illiterate while in France, Britain, and Germany the figure was 23%. That paralleled Russia's much lower per capita output of factory goods. [545]

Throughout history, most economists and policy makers have tended to believe that education plays an important role in economic growth. History, however, suggests that improvements in education were the result and not the cause of economic growth. Growth seems to have been the result of manufacturing. This sector not only delivered the goods that allowed education to expand, but also the wealth that financed the construction of more educational establishments.

That would explain why Russia during the 1890s, in spite of having a population considerably less educated than that of Western Europe, attained faster rates of economic growth. Britain, which at the time was probably the most educated nation in Europe, had a GDP rate of only about 2% per year while Russia, one of the least educated, reached 6%. That correlated with Moscow's much larger factory subsidies. [546]

The dynamism of the Russian economy during the second half of the 19th century instigated a large discussion over the causes of such a phenomenon. Many argued that the spurt was the result of the large increase in the population. It is true that during this period Russia's population grew faster than ever before and that its growth progressively accelerated. However, a closer analysis of the situation reveals a lack of parallelism.

During 1850–99, population in Russia grew faster than in Germany, but Germany attained much better GDP figures. Population growth in Russia averaged about 2.2% and GDP about 3.0% while in Germany the respective figures were 1.7% and 3.9%. It should have been Russia that had the faster growth. And for population to have a pulling effect on the economy, it would have had to grow at the same pace or faster than the economy. That was not the case, in Russia and in several other countries. As with most other variables, the growth of population seems to have been the result of the improved living conditions that fast economic growth delivered, and not the cause. [547]

Many also argued that the elimination of feudalism allowed for a more efficient utilization of resources, allowing more labor and capital flows from agriculture to the other sectors. Had feudal institutions been a terrible hindrance for growth, it would be hard to understand why Britain, which eliminated feudalism in the mid-17th century, attained GDP rates that did not exceed the 1% mark over a decade until the late 18th century. Russia, on the other hand, where remnants of feudalism lingered on until 1917, managed to attain rates of up to 6% in the 1890s. [548]

---

545 Gatrell: Ibid., p. 32–34, 50.
546 Westwood: Ibid., p. 174.
547 Kahan: Ibid., p. 65, 66, 2, 3; Sabillon: Ibid.,p. 120, 182.
548 Gatrell: Ibid., p. 42, 141, 165, 231.

Others asserted that the elimination of serfdom and the agricultural reforms delivered a large acceleration in the rate of farming, which propelled the rest of the economy. Had agriculture been the driving force, farm rates should have been faster than GDP. That was never the case. The only sector that systematically grew faster than GDP was manufacturing. During 1850–99, manufacturing in Russia expanded on average by about 4.0% annually, GDP by about 3.0%, and agriculture by only 1.6%. [549]

During the second half of the 19th century, foreign trade and in particular exports rose rapidly. The parallels with the performance of the economy led many to conclude that exports were the engine (or at least an important factor) of growth. The correlation existed in general terms but it was not very consistent. At times it broke down, as for example during the 1880s when exports dropped. During these years, about three fourths of Russia's exports were agricultural goods and a steep fall in world grain prices delivered a drop in the value of Russia's exports. Notwithstanding the drop, the economy not only avoided a contraction or even stagnation, but it actually experienced a noticeable acceleration. Had exports been significantly responsible for growth, the economy should have shown some signs of weakness. That was not so. This situation did however coincide with a considerable increase in the subsidization of manufacturing. During this decade, most of the fabricated goods were related to trains and weapons, for domestic consumption. That would explain why the decline in exports did not have a negative impact on the economy. [550]

Others argued that the large inflows of foreign direct investment were largely responsible for the acceleration of growth. Since foreign technology was often superior and foreign firms also brought superior managerial expertise, many came to see this as the key to growth. By 1900, about 28% of the capital of private companies in Russia was foreign owned. Since flows of foreign direct investment had continuously expanded since the 1860s, this seemed to correlate with the accelerating GDP figures. However, during the years 1900–13 flows of foreign investment continued to grow rapidly and by 1913, 33% of the output of private companies was in foreign hands. This time, however, the economy experienced no acceleration. There was growth but it was considerably slower than in the 1890s. That coincided with a decrease in factory subsides and a deceleration of manufacturing. [551]

Living conditions improved dramatically during 1850–99 and probably more progress was made on this front than during all of the preceding history of the country. Infant mortality dropped significantly, life expectancy rose, and nutrition improved, as did housing, education, and working conditions.

In the mid-19th century, the average length of the working day in Russia was about fourteen hours, seven days a week. There were no work restrictions for children and women, no compensation in case of accidents, hygienic conditions were catastrophic, lighting was terribly deficient, and wages were miserable. During the second half of the 19th century, however, all of this began rapidly to improve. Wages rose faster than ever before and in the later part of the century they rose the fastest, coinciding with the years of larger factory subsidies.

Working conditions improved and the first law on this matter was enacted in 1882, limiting the industrial employment of women and children. In 1885, an eight-hour maximum

549 *The Fontana Economic History of Europe*, p. 489, 492.
550 *The Cambridge Economic History of Europe Vol. VII*, p. 266.
551 Nove: Ibid., p. 18.

workday for children between the ages of 12–15 was approved and in 1896 another law limited the working day for adult workers to eleven hours, with Sunday free. Throughout the whole period, working conditions were much better in manufacturing than in agriculture. It is also worth noting that the factories with the most advanced technology had the highest wages, the shortest workweek, and offered the best treatment to workers. In these establishments, working conditions were also better than in construction and services.[552]

In 1891 a major famine claimed about 400,000 lives. Many blamed the famine on the government's large investments in the Trans-Siberian Railroad. Since the end of the Crimean War, when allocations for manufacturing began to increase rapidly, there was a constant fear that a reduction in the share of the nation's resources allotted to agriculture would translate into a lower supply of food. However, as the years moved along, the supply of food in per capita terms continuously increased. It actually increased much faster than ever before. By the late 19th century, for the first time in Russia's history, meat and dairy products began to be consumed by the masses.

The government increasingly sought to export grain to finance the large investments in manufacturing and that is why the food shortage was blamed on the factory policy. In reality, the evidence suggests it was the other way around. It was the factory policy that systematically increased the food supply as it boosted productivity by making farm machinery, fertilizers, and processed food available.

Many have argued that the peasantry was sacrificed for manufacturing, but the living conditions for the peasants improved. The famine of 1891 was not the only one during this period, but 1850–99 witnessed far fewer famines than any preceding fifty-year period. [553]

---

552 Westwood: Ibid., p. 180, 283.
553 Smith & Christian: Ibid., p. 262, 288.

Chapter 7. The Second Half of the 19th Century in Japan, Britain, China, and the Newly Industrialized Countries

Japan

Armament Build Up and Fast Economic Growth

During the second half of the 19th century, Japan experienced a gigantic acceleration in its rates of economic growth. In the US and Germany, GDP figures were much faster. However, the figures that Japan attained relative to its previous performance represented a much larger improvement than that of these Western nations.

More important was the fact that Japan's growth was paralleled by an abrupt change of macro-economic policies. Even though not explicitly intended for that purpose, the change in policies ended up increasing the share of resources allocated to manufacturing. A series of military-political events forced the government to adopt a policy of strong support for the sector and there was an impressive acceleration in the rate of manufacturing, which averaged about 3.0% annually, while during the preceding fifty years the figure had been about 0.3%. GDP grew likewise and averaged about 2.4% after having grown by just 0.2%. (See tables at the end of the book.[554]

During this half-century, Japan and Singapore were the only nations in Asia that attained fast GDP figures and they were the only ones that strongly promoted this sector.

By the mid-19th century, Japanese policy makers were adhering strictly to the policy of seclusion and could see no need for allocating more resources to manufacturing. Suddenly, the West intruded forcefully into the archipelago and everything changed. In 1854, an American military-commercial expedition arrived to Japan and demanded that the country open

---

[554] Allen, G. C.: *A Short Economic History of Modern Japan*, p. 245; Sabillon, Carlos: *World Economic Historical Statistics*, p. 112; Madison, Angus: *The World Economy: A Millennial Perspective*; Madison, Angus: *Monitoring the World Economy 1820–1992*.

up to trade. The gigantic military superiority of American gunships obliged the authorities to accept the demands of the foreigners. Japanese rulers saw that something radical had to be done in order to avoid future humiliations. It became evident that their capacity to resist future aggressions relied fundamentally in their ability to possess weapons that were at least as powerful as those of the West.

The Tokugawa government therefore took measures to promote the production of weapons and related goods. It abolished restrictions on the fabrication of ocean going ships, it borrowed from the West, it borrowed domestically, and it raised taxes. The state purchased warships from the West, which were dismantled in order to reproduce every part of them in the newly created dockyards. The government also bought Western machinery and equipment, and created ironworks and numerous other plants along Western lines. As a result, manufacturing output experienced a considerable acceleration and the economy shadowed. [555]

Japan only reluctantly opened to foreign trade in 1854, allowing minimal commercial activity, and in 1858 the West demanded greater access. The next year three more ports were opened to trade. Once again, the Japanese were forced to accept conditions which they did not want. This convinced the government that its armament policy needed to be accelerated.

In the 1850s, the share of the nation's resources allocated to manufacturing increased exponentially but it was still a small share relative to the West. This sector spurted, but averaged only some 1.2% annually and the economy did likewise, expanding by about 0.9%.[556]

In 1863–64 the government tried to renege on its commercial agreements and Western gunships bombarded two ports. This further defeat made Japanese rulers ever more determined to increase armament output. Taxation, foreign borrowing, and domestic borrowing increased noticeably. The government bought more machines from the West, it created more state factories, and it offered more incentives to would-be private manufacturers. The government also sent missions to Western Europe and North America to inquire over how best to organize a modern society and produce modern weapons.

Western powers imposed from the start a free trade regime on Japan. As more ports were opened, more Western goods entered the country, which easily outsold domestic products. The state was forced to grant subsidies to numerous civilian fields that were ravaged by foreign goods. Since most of the Western goods were factory goods, civilian manufacturing received that support. The subsidies were offered to guarantee a domestic supply of those goods so that in case of war the country could be self sufficient. However, the country was also in need of earning foreign exchange to repay the foreign loans and increase its import capacity of machinery and equipment. Since it was resource poor, the only option for increasing exports was with factory goods.

In the 1860s thus, there was a considerable increase in support for military and civilian manufacturing and there was a pronounced acceleration in the rate of factory output and GDP. There was nonetheless much vacillation among policy makers, for it was the nobility who governed and its interests were tightly linked to the land and not to the urban economy where factories concentrate. They viewed manufacturing with suspicion and as something which could undermine their hold on power. Their strong desires to become militarily mus-

555 Allen: Ibid., p. 21, 26.
556 Sabillon: Ibid.; Madison, Angus: Monitoring the World Economy 1820–1992.

cular were tempered by the fear of losing control of the government. The end result was a significant rise in subsidies, but which was still below those of the West. Manufacturing expanded by about 1.7% annually and GDP by about 1.4%. [557]

The speed by which weapons were produced was insufficient for the country's national goals and many were unsatisfied with the rulers. The Boshin War of 1867–68 put an end to the Shogunate as progressive elements overthrew the house of Tokugawa and installed a new government. The new Meiji policy makers, who installed an emperor, were determined to transform the country into a military superpower. They wanted parity with the West and were prepared to do everything to achieve that goal. They raised taxes sharply and borrowed more both domestically and abroad. The state imported far more Western machines and distributed them throughout the country so that local governments would create state factories within their jurisdictions. State factories sprang up in many locations.

There was also a very large increase in the incentives offered to the private sector. The prime incentive consisted in supplying entrepreneurs with foreign machinery at subsidized prices as well as free samples of Western goods so that they could disassemble them and copy every part. There was as well some financial assistance. Lower taxes were also offered in the early 1870s.[558]

As in other countries, the desire to mobilize troops rapidly drove the government to promote railroads and the first debuted in the early 1870s. The state financed in full the whole venture and built most of the rails and locomotives in its factories. During this decade and in the following ones, railroads were not promoted as enthusiastically as in numerous Western nations. As an archipelago with a politically unified territory, railroads were never seen as a national security priority. For almost a century after the arrival of Commodore Perry and his gunboat commercial demands, priority was given to the fabrication of weapons and ships. These were the fastest growing fields.

The Meiji government took over the armories of the old regime and enlarged them considerably. Iron was subsidized as much as weapons because it was fundamental for the fabrication of arms. Civilian fields in direct linkage to the military were also given priority. The state for example created textile, garment, and footwear factories and also supplied lavish incentives to entrepreneurs in these fields to secure a ready supply of uniforms and boots for its troops. The fabrication of commercial sea vessels was also abundantly promoted for the strategic need of having a merchant navy to back its military counterpart. In 1874 the government bought advanced commercial ships from the West and transferred them to a private company (Mitsubishi), which after having reverse engineered them began to fabricate replicas under strong financial assistance from the state.

Larger foreign loans were taken during the 1870s and the foreign debt increased. The government sought to save foreign exchange by trying to substitute imports as much as possible and by trying to increase exports. Since the majority of imports were manufactures and since Japan was resource poor, it was this sector that received the bulk of subsidies. Numerous state factories were founded in fields such as chemicals, cement, paper, sugar, tiles, and even liquor. Subsidies to entrepreneurs increased and practically all of the large

557 Morishima, Michio: *Why Has Japan Succeeded?*, p. 53–58, 88; Sabillon: Ibid.; Madison, Angus: *The World Economy: Historical Statistics.*
558 Allen: Ibid., p. 28.

private firms that were created in that decade owed their existence to state assistance. Even the existing ones owned their rapid enlargement to subsidies. [559]

Although the central and local governments created an abundance of state companies during the 1870s, the majority of production was done in private enterprises. Independent of the type of firm that created a good, the bottom line is that the bulk of factory output was the direct result of government support. The share of the nation's resources allocated to manufacturing was much larger than ever before and this coincided with unprecedented GDP growth. Rates however did not increase significantly with respect to the 1860s because policy makers continued to harbor beliefs which hindered them from increasing support.

The inquiring missions that were sent to the West returned with the ideas of the West. The Japanese became persuaded that the elimination of feudalism was fundamental for the modernization of Japan. In 1869, therefore, feudalism was abolished and the nobility was dispossessed of most of its privileges. The nobility, which was much dissatisfied with its loss of power in 1868, found even more reason to be displeased with this measure. This event inspired it even more to see manufacturing as its enemy and it therefore increased its efforts to derail the government's plans to support this sector. It conspired and it even attempted to overthrow the government in the rebellions of 1874 and 1877. The rebellions failed, but they distracted the Meiji policy makers from increasing manufacturing output.

Aside from the tempering effects of the opposition, there was also much vacillation and hesitation among the Meiji rulers about the level of support that the sector should receive. There were for example strong physiocratic ideas, which envisioned a worsening of the food supply if too many resources were subtracted from agriculture. There were also large fears about getting too highly in debt with foreign countries.

The cumulative effect of these fears kept the government from adopting a more enthusiastic factory promotion policy. Support was therefore increased but not by much, and this was reflected in proportionate growth figures. During the 1870s manufacturing averaged about 2.5% and GDP about 2.0%. [560]

The suppression of the 1877 rebellion marked the end of the attempts of the landed aristocracy to hamper the modernization goals of the state. At the same time, the fears of a reduced food supply began to wane by the late 1870s, as food production had been growing much faster than ever before. Japan's rulers couldn't understand why food production rose as farming received a decreasing share of investment, but the fact is that the results were positive. As a result, the government did not feel it had to limit its subsidies to manufacturing.

During the 1870s (as during the preceding two decades) the US attained the fastest economic growth in the world, which was accompanied by a rise in American military power. The US had humiliated Japan in the preceding decades and Japanese rulers were quick to notice the rise of American might and see in it the potential for future aggression. This confluence of events drove the government to increase the level of support in the 1880s.

Taxation rose once again as well as domestic and foreign borrowing. There was also a large rise in fiscal, financial, and non-financial incentives to private manufacturers but this time there was not a large increase in the creation of state factories. Some state companies were founded in key heavy fields, but the government largely renounced to its policy of direct investment in the sector. In the preceding decades, the performance of most state

---

559 Ibid., p. 32–34.
560 Ibid., p. 31, 36.

enterprises had been inferior to that of private firms and several had been financial failures. There was thus much privatization since 1880. Most of the privatized factories were sold at below market prices and as soon as this happened, their performance improved. [561]

To compensate for the renunciation of direct investments, the government created banks that concentrated on lending to manufacturing. Since the early 1880s, numerous private banks were created which owed about one third of their initial capital to the state and which were thereafter supplied with subsidized capital by the Central Bank. The Central Bank was established in 1882 for precisely that purpose. The prime mission of the Central Bank was to supply abundant long term financing for the production of arms and related goods. Since the historic natural inclination of private banks had been to channel the bulk of their resources into rapid turnover activities such as commerce, the government sought to counterbalance this situation by means of regulation and by naming the presidents of the banks. The Finance Ministry named the president of these banks. [562]

The banks were modeled after the example of those in France and Germany. In these nations, policy makers had arrived at the conclusion that the only way to channel a large share of private banking assets into investment-intensive activities was with a policy of incentives and government pressure.

During the 1880s, Japan followed the example of several European nations and began to allow practices that reduced competition in order to permit higher profits for the private sector. Cartels started to appear and even national monopolies were created. In the course of the following years, cartels became more numerous. The advent of cartels was not limited to manufacturing, but most of them were in this sector. Export subsidies also rose in this decade due to strong balance of payments concerns. [563]

There was also greater promotion of railroads. Contrary to the preceding decade, most of the railroads were built by entrepreneurs but the state supplied large fiscal, financial, and non-financial incentives to the producers of rails and locomotives.

During the 1880s, there was a significant increase in support for practically all fields of manufacturing. That coincided with a faster rate of factory output that averaged about 3.6% annually. GDP accelerated and expanded by about 3.0%. [564]

During the 1890s, there was a further decrease in the power of the landed nobility and therefore a reduction in their capacity to oppose modernization. The new urbanite magnates of manufacturing and banking gained in economic and political importance, and they increasingly influenced policy.

There was also a further rise in the food supply and a consequent decrease in the fear of hunger. American economic and military power continued to increase, accompanied by the growing gunboat diplomacy of Europeans in Asia. Simultaneously, Japan began to develop its own imperialist desires. The concomitant effect of those factors drove the Japanese government in the 1890s to allocate a still larger share of the archipelago's resources to manufacturing.

Taxes were raised once again and public borrowing expanded more. Government expending as a share of GDP rose to new levels and most of the increased revenue was allotted

---

561 Levine, Salomon & Kawada, Hisashi: *Human Resources in Japanese Industrial Development*, p. 29, 30.
562 *The Cambridge History of Japan Vol. 5*, p. 609–614.
563 Allen: Ibid., p. 46, 48, 52, 53.
564 *The Cambridge History of Japan Vol. 6*, p. 394, 391.

to manufacturing. Taxes on factory production were lowered some more and financial and non-financial incentives to this sector were raised. State companies were founded during this decade but only in small numbers, while privatization continued to move forward. Shipbuilding was particularly promoted, mostly for the navy but also for commercial purposes.

During the 1890s, Japan began to follow the imperialist example of the West and in 1894–95 it engaged in war with China. During the conflict, warship production increased very rapidly. By then, Japan had acquired a large arsenal of modern weapons. That was paralleled by an easy and decisive triumph over China, which forced Beijing to cede Taiwan, the Pescadores and the Liaodong peninsula. The victory over China convinced the government that its possibilities for future conquest resided fundamentally on the development of a strong navy and a large commercial fleet. That is why immediately after the conclusion of the war more subsidies were decreed for shipbuilding.

The Shipbuilding Encouragement Act of 1896 raised considerably the amount of grants to the producers of ships. Weapons, railroad goods, and civilian manufactures were also promoted more than before. During the 1890s, manufacturing production grew at a record pace, averaging about 6.0%. GDP figures shadowed and averaged about 4.7% annually.[565]

The war of 1894–95 proved once again that the decisive variable in determining the outcome of wars is the amount and technological content of the weapons utilized. Japan not only had many more warships than China, but they were larger, faster, more maneuverable, and had more guns; and each of those guns shot faster, further and more accurately.

Policy Errors and Support for Manufacturing

The rising promotion of manufacturing during 1850–99 coincided with an ascending rate of economic growth. However, not even during the 1890s, when the subsidies were at their highest level, was the government supplying as much support as other nations and GDP rates were commensurately lower. As the coming decades would demonstrate, stronger support was possible and when that occurred faster economic growth took place. On top of that, during the fifty-year period, the government also committed a number of other policy errors that hampered economic performance.

During the second half of the 19th century, the government founded and operated a large amount of enterprises that were less efficient than their private sector counterparts. There was some correction of that error since 1880 as many were privatized, but far into the 20th century and the state still continued to create and operate companies.

Monopolies and other forms of competition hindering practices were abolished in 1868, but soon after, the government began to tolerate and even promote a growing amount of cartels. This policy was intended on luring investment by allowing more profit possibilities, but the evidence suggests that such a goal would have been better attained by increasing fiscal, financial, and non-financial incentives.

Cartels hampered internal competition and in consequence productivity. However, notwithstanding their negative effects, they correlated with accelerating GDP figures. The historical evidence suggests that their effects were only marginal and the only thing that can explain such a phenomenon were the rising levels of subsidies for factories.

565 Allen: Ibid., p. 80–82; Madison, Angus: *Monitoring the World Economy 1820–1992*; Sabillon: Ibid.

During the course of the second half of the 19th century, the government progressively increased the supply of export subsidies. This trade distortion was unnecessary, for the historical evidence suggests that fast export growth is fundamentally dependent on fast manufacturing growth. Export subsidies do not increase production and just shift a share of existing output towards the foreign market. A larger supply of incentives for production is what would have delivered an even larger increase in exports.[566]

Of an even greater importance on trade matters is the fact that during practically the entire half century, Japan practiced an import regime free of barriers. The West went to Japan looking for new markets and it imposed on the archipelago a tariff-free regime. During those years, the vast majority of nations in Europe, North America, and Oceania practiced trade protection because they were convinced that it was necessary for the promotion of manufacturing. The case of Japan, however, clearly demonstrated that factory output was not dependent upon import barriers. Tariffs were implemented only in 1911. However, during the first decade of the 20th century economic growth accelerated even more.

During 1850–99, Japan's economic growth was slower than in the majority of the future Western nations. However, during the years 1890–1910, Japan's GDP figures were faster than in the West, notwithstanding its free trade regime. Factory subsidies were smaller than the West in 1850–89 (as a share of GDP), but were larger in the following two decades. During both of these periods, rates of factory output shadowed the differing levels of support.[567]

Japan demonstrated that rapid GDP growth was possible while practicing free trade and Western nations demonstrated that it was also possible while practicing protectionism. The common denominator in both was factory subsidies.

Up to the mid-19th century, Japan had been lagging technologically, not just with Europe but also with Russia and China. Up until then, it had been argued that the Japanese culture did not foster invention. However, during the second half of the 19th century, technology developed at an unprecedented pace; it soon surpassed China. Most of the technology Japan consumed was imported but a noticeable share was created domestically.

It is worth noting that during 1850–99 in practically all corners of the world the development of technology reflected the level of subsidies that each field received. In Japan, technological change occurred fastest in weapons and shipbuilding, which were the fields most heavily promoted. In North America, railroad goods experienced the fastest technical progress and this field received the largest budgetary allocations. In France, Germany, and Russia land weapons and railroad goods were the most subsidized fields and these were the areas that experienced more invention. In Britain, the most promoted field was shipbuilding, which was the industry that experienced the most technical upgrading. In this half century, Argentina grew much faster than most European countries and technology was imported at a very fast pace. There were nonetheless a few domestic innovations and they concentrated in processed foods, which was the area that received the bulk of subsidies.

Rapid technological changes during this period occurred only in the nations that offered strong support for manufacturing. Subsidies for this sector were extremely low in Africa, Asia, and Latin America and these regions experienced very little technological progress. Of these regions, the one that offered the largest subsidies was Latin America and this was also the area that experienced the most technical change.

---

566 Allen: Ibid., p. 37, 48, 128–130.
567 Bairoch, Paul: *Economics and World History*, p. 38–54.

The evidence suggests that manufacturing is predisposed to be the most capital-hungry sector because it is the fundamental generator of technology. That is the reason why in Japan and in other nations it was harder to persuade the private sector into making investments in heavy manufacturing than in light manufacturing, for this domain is the most investment intensive of the two. Heavy manufacturing attempts to achieve goals that are harder to accomplish and in consequence it needs even more specialized technology. To develop this superior technology, it needs more resources (like capital equipment and trained technicians).[568]

The strong link between manufacturing and technology was also seen in other fields of the economy. Mining expanded rapidly, notwithstanding Japan's poor mineral deposits. Production of excavating equipment and drilling machines reached new levels. Prior to the 1860s, it had been argued that Japan had not developed heavy manufacturing because it had poor deposits of coal and iron ore. However, as soon as the government decreed a strong support for the sector, heavy manufacturing and mining began to grow. The case of Japan suggests that the development of mining is more dependent on the level of manufacturing subsidies, than on the mineral base of a nation.[569]

The same phenomenon was observed with the other primary sector activities and with the other economic sectors. The development of forestry, fishing, construction, and services paralleled the development of the tools, machines, and equipment that were utilized in these activities.

In educational services, it was the increased production of paper, printing machines, books, pencils, and blackboards what was responsible for the large progress. Educational services made more progress during this half-century than in all of Japan's preceding history and this went hand in hand with unprecedented factory subsidies. About 10% of the school-age population attended primary school in 1850 but by 1900 the figure had risen to about 93%. During this period, Japan founded its first university (Tokyo University, 1877). The government's efforts to promote weapons, ships, and trains also led to the restructuring of the educational system, which gave emphasis to fields such as mathematics, engineering, and natural sciences. [570]

Most economists see Japan's unprecedented growth in the years 1850–99 as stemming from the combined influence of the elimination of feudalism, fast agricultural growth, fast population growth, fast trade growth, and the improvements in infrastructure and education. Similar arguments were utilized to explain the acceleration of economic growth in Western countries, and there too they failed to match the facts.[571]

Fast agricultural, population, and trade growth as well as a rapid development of infrastructure and education seem more to have been effects of growth than its cause. Agriculture and population grew at a slower pace than GDP, and were therefore incapable of propelling the economy. The only factor that could have acted as an engine was manufacturing, for it constantly expanded faster than GDP. Average annual factory growth in 1850–99 was about 3.0%, the economy expanded by 2.4%, and agriculture averaged just 1.3%. Population grew even slower, averaging only 0.8%

568 Allen: Ibid., p. 79.
569 Ibid., p. 38, 63, 79, 80.
570 Morishima: Ibid., p. 135, 97, 104.
571 Levine & Kawada: Ibid., p. 28, 29.

It is also argued that there was a considerable acceleration of agricultural production in the decades preceding the 1880s that created the surplus capital which made possible the spurt of GDP since the 1880s. It is true that agriculture grew faster in these decades, but during all of those years its rate was inferior to that of GDP and much slower than that of manufacturing. The acceleration in the rate of farm output since the 1850s coincided with the large increase in support for manufacturing and from thereafter the accelerating pace of agriculture continued to correlate with the rising factory promotion efforts of the state.[572]

Trade couldn't have been the decisive factor in growth either. Trade did, as a matter of fact, grow faster than GDP during this period but a more encompassing analysis over time reveals a number of inconsistencies. The trade–growth correlation broke down during the 1930s. During this decade, international commerce collapsed and Japan experienced also a noticeable reversal of its trade figures. The economy, however, accelerated and attained a growth rate of 5.4%. If commerce really played a decisive role in economic growth, then the GDP figures should have been negative, stagnant, or at least slow. The factory thesis, on the other hand, has no problem addressing this situation. During the 1930s, Tokyo abundantly subsidized this sector to produce arms. Manufacturing averaged a rate of 8.5% annually, which was mostly consumed domestically.[573]

The state of the infrastructure and the level of education also fail to account for these disparities. Japan made great progress on both counts during the second half of the 19th century, but, as with trade, the correlation breaks down in the long term. Despite the progress achieved, by 1900 Japan was still considerably lagging in education and infrastructure with respect to Western Europe. However, during the 1890s Japan's economy grew much faster than that of several Western nations. It grew more than twice as fast as Britain.

A century later the situation had radically changed. By the late 20th century, Japan had leapfrogged everybody else in education and was at parity in infrastructure with the most advanced nations of the world. By the 1990s, its workforce was far better educated than that of a hundred years earlier and its infrastructure was second to none. In spite of that, GDP growth averaged only 1.5% annually while in the 1890s it had grown more than three times faster. More to the point is that, in the 1990s, Tokyo dramatically increased investment in infrastructure but the economy grew slower than that of most Western nations.

It is also argued that as a latecomer, Japan was able to take advantage of the existing and accumulated stock of world technology, and thus enjoyed accelerated economic growth. That was certainly true, to some extent, but that does not explain why so many nations in Asia, Latin America, and Africa, which were also lagging technologically, were not capable of doing the same. Those nations invested far less in factory subsidization, in some cases out of ideological belief that such investments were "expensive and wasteful".[574]

None of these variables, independently or as a group, can add up consistently with the facts. Only the manufacturing thesis can explain why, notwithstanding the growing regulation, the enlargement of government expenditure, and the growing taxation, an economy was capable of avoiding a downturn in this half century. Only this thesis can explain why, despite the growing public sector debt, the growing number of cartels, and the growing

572 Nafziger, Wayne: *Learning from the Japanese*, p. 91, 7.
573 Allen: Ibid., p. 216, 138–142.
574 *The Cambridge History of Japan Vol. 5*, p. 617.

share of GDP allocated to weapons, the economy was capable of growing progressively faster.

The example of Japan during the second half of the 19th century gave further credence to the idea that economic growth is fundamentally an endogenous phenomenon. The decision to raise the level of support for manufacturing lay exclusively within the jurisdiction of the Japanese government. Even the supply of foreign capital was only barely affected by the events and decisions that took place in foreign countries. The government borrowed considerably during this period but most of the loans were raised domestically. By the end of the 19th century, about four fifths of the loans had been raised in Japan. Not to mention that if Japan had wanted to borrow more from the West, it could have easily done it. The small foreign share of borrowing was mostly the result of a self-imposed policy, as the government sought to minimize its dependence from the outside world.[575]

Great Britain

Economic Decline in Britain

Economic growth slowed in Britain during the second half of the 19th century. After having attained an average annual rate of about 2.9% during the period 1800–49, the figure dropped to just 2.4% in the following fifty years.

Several nations that had for long lagged behind Britain and were seen as incapable of ever growing as fast, all of sudden began to attain faster GDP rates. As a result, Britain's economic world supremacy began to vanish. [576]

This inversion of growth rates paralleled a noticeable drop in the level of support that London supplied to manufacturing and a very large increase in the subsidies the governments of other nations gave to this sector. During the years 1850–99, factory output in Britain expanded at an average annual rate of just 2.8%, while during the preceding fifty years it had grown by about 3.6%. [577]

Misled by a number of events that took place during this half century, the British government concluded that there wasn't a need to invest as much in factories as formerly. As a result, it decreased the allocations for this sector. During this period, Britain did not engage in any large-scale war. There was only the Crimean War from 1854–56, which was just a medium sized conflict that gave no indication that future wars with Russia were in the coming. On top of that, it was an easy win for Britain. [578]

On the other hand, Britain's historic archenemy increasingly became friendlier and even fought on the side of Britain against the Russians during the Crimean War. By the mid-19th century, France was no longer seen by London as a nation with whom war was inevitable. Spain, which had also been a regular foe from the 16th to the 18th century, ceased to be one after the Napoleonic Wars. There was thus, no longer a need to invest as much in weapons as formerly. As time went on, relations with France improved even more and the fear of a

575 Allen: Ibid., p. 48.
576 Bagwell, Philip & Mingay, G.: *Britain and America 1850–1939*, p. 6; Sabillon: Ibid., p. 183; Madison, Angus: *The World Economy: A Millennial Perspective*.
577 Floud, Roderick & McCloskey, Donald (ed): *The Economic History of Britain since 1700 Vol. 1*, p. 49.
578 Mathias, Peter: *The First Industrial Nation*, p. 207.

large-scale war receded still more. The Franco–Prussian war of 1870–71, made it evident that France was no longer the second military power in Europe and German unification pointed further in that direction. However, Germany had never engaged in war with Britain and it was too far away to be felt as a major threat.

Given this confluence of events, the government allocated fewer funds and resources for the production of arms and related goods, and this coincided with a lower rate of factory output. The drop in military manufacturing could have been easily compensated and even overcompensated by a large increase in subsidies for civilian manufacturing, but the fact is that such a transfer of resources did not take place.

Rails and locomotives were the main source of factory production in North America, Russia, and several countries in Europe, but in Britain they were only modestly promoted. While in these countries political and economic integration of their large territories was their main priority, in Britain this was not a matter of concern. Not only was Britain a relatively small and densely populated country, but during this period it was never at risk that any of its regions would break away.

A comparison with the US is illustrative. During 1850–99, the US was the nation which more enthusiastically endorsed train production and as a result the output of rails and locomotives increased more than nine fold. In Britain, they didn't even increase two fold. The desire to have an efficient means for troop mobilization had led several nations to promote trains decisively, but as an island, ships were more important for the mobilization of troops and London therefore felt in little need of trains.

It is argued that as a result of the high costs of land, British railroads were the most expensive to construct in the world. That however does not change the fact that government incentives for the production of trains were much lower than in the countries previously mentioned. History supplies many examples of nations with high costs of production that had no problem fabricating goods very quickly. These situations always coincided with a strong factory promotion policy. [579]

Had other fields of civilian manufacturing been abundantly promoted, overall factory output could have still surpassed the rates of the first half of the century and even those of the US. However, there was nothing in the economic ideas that prevailed in those times, which stated that strong support for manufacturing "per se" was useful for the economy. The end result was a lower promotion effort

The 2.8% rate of factory output of this period was nonetheless one of the fastest in the world. No nation in Africa, Latin America, and Asia with the exception of South Africa, Japan, Singapore, and Argentina matched or surpassed such a pace. Even many nations in Europe attained slower rates. Even though Britain no longer subsidized this sector with the same enthusiasm, it nonetheless continued to support it more than most nations of the world. In places like Africa, Asia, and Latin America support was almost non-existent and in many nations of Europe, it was lower than in Britain. During this period, British per capita investment in arms was one of the highest in the world. In 1850–99, defense absorbed about 4% of GDP. [580]

Even though large-scale war largely disappeared, the risk of war was far from having been eliminated and a large supply of weapons was still needed. On top of that, Britain's vast

---

579 Bagwell & Mingay: Ibid., p. 1, 40, 27–29.
580 Davis, Lance & Huttenback, Robert: *Mammon and the Pursuit of Empire*, p. 129, 113, 105, 92.

territorial dominions throughout the world demanded constant surveillance and a gigantic navy was the only means to do that. Warships were fabricated in very large numbers and commercial vessels to back the requirements of the navy were also promoted. During this half century, the output of ship tonnage increased faster than anywhere else and by 1900 Britain was still the largest producer of ships in the world. The large expenses that were required to defend the colonies were criticized by many in Parliament and many clamored for making the colonies pay for a share of those expenditures. However, given the fear that pressure on that front could lead to desires for independence, Britain continued to cover colonial defense requirements in its entirety. [581]

Fiscal, financial, and non-financial incentives for the manufacturing of railroad goods were low when compared to those of the US, Canada, Germany and a few other countries, but they were much higher than in practically all other nations of the world. Even though import barriers had been dismantled, the government continued to believe that exports were essential for economic growth. It therefore supplied subsidies to exporters and they fell mostly on manufacturing because by then practically all of Britain's exports were factory goods. [582]

Support for manufacturing within the British Isles was not homogeneous and the different levels of subsidization were shadowed by the differing rates of economic growth. During 1850–99, Ireland, where the political class continued to concentrate on the promotion of agriculture, continued to attain the slowest GDP growth figures. Scotland on the other hand, continued to follow a similar policy as England and granted a relative abundant dose of subsidies to manufacturers. By 1900, Scotland had the same number of people as Ireland but produced about four times more factory goods. It also produced twice as many agricultural goods even though it allocated a much smaller share of its total resources to farming. During this fifty-year period, Scotland's GDP figures were also considerably better than Ireland's.[583]

During these years, England and Scotland no longer believed in physiocratic ideas. By then, they were convinced sympathizers of manufacturing but they were even stronger believers in non-interventionism. Prime Minister Robert Peel in the mid-19th century thought that such a goal was best achieved by letting market forces operate freely. Their own history and that of several other nations had already demonstrated that budget deficits and debt were not a major hindrance for faster economic growth. However, British policy makers believed that small government, balanced budgets, and no public sector debt were determinant for growth. Factory and GDP figures did not increase.[584]

On the other hand, they were also wrong in believing that small government, balanced budgets, and low debt were incompatible with an increase in support for manufacturing. The case of the US was proof that they were compatible.

During the late 19th century, US central government expenditure as a share of GDP was as low as in Britain (about 5%), but Washington subsidized factories far more enthusiastically. In spite of that, public sector debt was low and budget surpluses were the norm. The

581 Pope, Rex (ed): *Atlas of British Social and Economic History since 1700*, p. 51.
582 Taylor, Arthur: *Laissez-Faire and State Intervention in Nineteenth Century Britain*, p. 41.
583 Cullen, L. & Smout, T. (ed): *Comparative Aspects of Scottish and Irish Economic and Social History 1600–1900*, p. 3, 14.
584 Cain, P. J.: *Economic Foundations of British Overseas Expansion 1815–1914*, p. 19.

British government was spending as much as the American government, but a large share was flowing into non-manufacturing activities such as housing, education, health, agriculture, and mining. It was also used to pay for a growing bureaucracy that was needed to enforce the rising legislation on labor regulations, industrial pollution, food adulteration, etc. The US government on the other hand, was concentrating its resources fundamentally on financing the production of trains.[585]

Many argued that London was right in its decision to invest the money in those non-manufacturing activities because there was a strong need to improve the people's living conditions. However, during this period it was the American populace that experienced the fastest amelioration of living conditions. By 1900 the US had the longest life expectancy in the world, the highest per capita consumption of food, the highest educational levels, and the best housing. That resulted from having attained the fastest GDP rates in the world during the preceding fifty years, which coincided with the fastest rates of factory output.

The evidence suggests that Britain could have grown much faster had it concentrated the same 5% of government expenditure on manufacturing. It didn't, and GDP growth was only 2%, while the US averaged about 6%. The expenditure of regional and local governments in both countries increased overall expenditure to almost a tenth of GDP. In both countries, the authorities at the regional and local level allocated resources to manufacturing, but the American authorities allotted much more. The evidence suggests that even the US could have attained faster growth for a noticeable share of the budget was not used for manufacturing.

Stimulation Efforts and Economic Misinterpretations

The discovery of gold in Australia (1848) and in California (1849) convinced many intellectuals that Britain would be among the main beneficiaries. Since it had the most developed financial system, it was thought that Britain would be better capable of processing the growing international payments that would be made with the precious metal. Reality, however, did not develop as predicted. Even nations that had no contact with the gold like Germany, Russia, and Argentina ended up attaining faster GDP figures during the following fifty years. This situation coincided with a more decisive support for manufacturing in these three countries.

Many in Britain thought that the continental wars of the 1860s and that of 1870–71, plus the large railroad demands from the US and from its colonies (in particular Canada, Australia, and New Zealand), would boost demand for British goods and uplift the economy. It was thought that since the economies of Germany, the US, Canada, Australia, and New Zealand boomed and they had strong linkages with Britain, there would be positive spillover effects. The linkages were indeed there, but the boost never took place. What's more, as time went on and these five economies improved their rates of growth, that of Britain slowly deteriorated more and more. While during the 1850s GDP averaged about 2.8% annually, by the 1890s it was of only 2.0%. That coincided with factory subsidies in these nations that progressively increased, while in Britain they progressively decreased. [586]

The second half of the 19th century, witnessed the establishment of the Bank of England as the main arbiter of monetary policy. As time moved along, there was also an improvement

---

585 Kuznets, Simon: *Modern Economic Growth*, p. 236, 237.
586 Tames, Richard: *Economy and Society in Nineteenth Century Britain*, p. 22, 23, 25.

in the Bank's techniques of operation. However, it was only in the 1880s that this bank was fully recognized as a Central Bank. For long, financial crises had been regular and frequently they were accompanied by recessions. It was thought that by establishing a central monetary authority that would regulate financial activities, crises and recessions would be largely avoided and the performance of the economy would improve. It was also believed that interest rates were fundamental for determining the availability of credit and therefore of investment. Since the Central Bank was given the power to influence interest rates, it was thought that it would have a positive effect on investment and therefore on economic growth.

Much was achieved with the establishment of the Central Bank for financial crises were considerably reduced. However, the economy instead of improving actually deteriorated. It is as well worth noting, that the assumptions about the effect that interest rates have on investment, also proved to be false. During the late 19th century, economic activity was not particularly responsive to the variation in rates of interest. [587]

Interest rates were for example low during this period but there was no investment boom. There were other moments in history in which interest rates were high and investment was nonetheless high. The evidence suggests that what is fundamentally responsible for investment is the level of factory subsidization and subsidies for this sector were indeed relatively low in Britain in the late 19th century.

Investment as a share of GDP fell from about 11% during the first half of the century to 9% during the second half. In the US on the other hand, it grew from about 9% to 20%. This situation paralleled a modest drop in the level of factory subsidies in Britain in 1850–99 and a very large increase in the factory promotion efforts of Washington in that same period. It is worth noting that during the second half of the century, the US had no Central Bank and it nonetheless attained the fastest GDP rates in the world. [588]

Commercial banks during this period accounted for only a small share of the financing that private manufacturing received and since the 1880s they were even less explicitly involved in the long term financing of British factories. The largest share of their funds was used to finance government-backed projects such as railroads in North America, Oceania, and Latin America. Since London backed relatively few manufacturing projects in British soil, the banks concluded that the risks of lending to domestic producers were too high. [589]

As the economy slowed, London took a number of measures to stimulate the economy and the most relevant consisted in the creation of public works programs. The government had long since undertaken infrastructure works, but this was the first time that it was done for the purpose of stimulating the economy and creating employment. This was also the first time that large allocations were made for that purpose. The first budget for public works was decreed in 1886 and in the following years there were similar efforts, but the economy never showed signs of responding positively. The 1880s and 1890s actually witnessed the worst GDP figures of the 19th century.

This was one of the first times in history in which investments in infrastructure proved not to have growth-generating capacities and in the 20th century hundreds of similar situations throughout the world made the above more evident. However, economists and policy

---

587 Aldcroft, D. & Fearon, P. (ed): *British Fluctuations 1790–1939*, p. 44, 49–51, 55.
588 Lee, C. H.: *The British Economy since 1700 — A Macroeconomic Perspective*, p. 28.
589 Elbaum, Bernard & Lazonick, William (ed): *The Decline of the British Economy*, p. 3.

makers kept on believing that large allocations for roads, ports, and airports were highly useful.

By then, unemployment was not high but underemployment was endemic and many in government circles thought that laziness was the cause, so penal measures were enacted against the able-bodied who were seen as unwilling to work. That also failed to improve GDP figures or to reduce underemployment.

With the progressive deceleration of the economy, many policy makers came to the conclusion that the conquest of more territories would stimulate the economy. It was thought it would supply export markets and cheap raw materials. Britain, therefore, once again launched itself on the path of conquest and considerably expanded its colonial possessions during the late 19th century. Most of the new territories were in Africa. However, in spite of the vast territories acquired and their abundance of natural resources, the economy continued to decelerate. [590]

Nothing seemed to work and fear among the political class was on the rise because several other countries were rapidly growing to be militarily and economically stronger. On top of that, GDP rates were so slow, that there was a rise of economic problems. Underemployment progressively rose during this period and income distribution became more uneven. [591]

Many argued that this situation was the result of the erection of trade barriers by most of Britain's trading partners. It is true that most nations in continental Europe, the US and even Canada, Australia, and New Zealand significantly raised trade barriers during this period. However, it is also true that all of those nations were enduring the protectionism of all the others. The US was also blocked from exporting to continental Europe, to Canada, to Australia, etc. US exports nonetheless, grew about twice as fast as in Britain in the late 19th century and GDP grew about three times faster. Germany was also getting blocked by most of its neighbors, by Russia, by the US, and by others, but it nevertheless managed to increase its exports and its GDP figures twice as fast as Britain. These countries only had a small advantage over Britain, but their GDP and export figures were far superior. It is highly unlikely, therefore, that trade barriers were the cause or a main cause of Britain's weak performance. [592]

It is also worth noting that Japan and Argentina practiced a free trade system during the second half of the 19th century and were therefore in exactly the same situation of Britain. However, instead of experiencing a deceleration they went through an impressive acceleration, not just in its GDP figures but also in exports. During 1850–99, economic growth in Britain averaged about 2.4% annually, but in Argentina it was of 4.3%. [593]

The evidence strongly suggests that the protectionism of its trading partners was not the cause of Britain's problems. There was a growing amount of people calling for protection during the late 19th century but fortunately, the British government stood firm by its beliefs. The evidence suggests that had it raised tariffs, the economy would have surely not experienced the slightest improvement, but competition would have inevitably been hampered and along with it cost efficiency and quality. [594]

590 Tomlinson, Jim: *Problems of British Economic Policy 1870–1945*, p. 18, 19, 22, 52.
591 Wrigley, E.: *Continuity, Chance and Change*, p. 69.
592 Bagwell & Mingay: Ibid., p. 249, 257.
593 Sabillon: Ibid., p. 123, 183.
594 Cain: Ibid., p. 43, 44, 48.

Britain began to export capital in large amounts in the mid-19th century and by the turn of the century it reached enormous proportions. Most were loans to North America, Oceania, and Latin America and by the late 19th century they accounted for about 30% of GDP. Since at the same time the economy was losing speed, many concluded that it was the cause or a main cause of it. It was argued that the outflow of money hampered investment in Britain. The historical records, however, do not chronicle any scarcity of funds for domestic investment during the second half of the 19th century. In spite of the large outflow of capital, there was still a large amount of it which remained in Britain and which could have financed much larger domestic investments. However, nobody was interested in borrowing that capital, neither the private sector nor the government.[595]

Examples from other countries also demonstrate the inconsistency of this argument. In the 1930s, the US was the nation with the largest amount of surplus capital in the world and it did not export any of it. In spite of that, growth was terribly slow. During World War II on the other hand, the US exported its wealth and actually gave it for free to its military allies. In spite of that, investment was high and economic growth was spectacular.

While Britain lent its capital with commercial interest rates in the years 1850–99 and recovered it in full, the US gave it away for free during 1940–45 because of national security concerns. If exporting large amounts of capital had a negative effect on growth, the US should have attained a poor performance during World War II. That was not the case.

It is as well asserted that since the 1870s, world agricultural markets were saturated and the price of farm commodities fell. This supposedly limited the export possibilities of Britain's main trading partners and thus their capacity to import British goods, affecting negatively the British economy. Agricultural markets were indeed glutted since the 1870s, but the truth of the matter is that the import capacity of continental Europe and North America actually rose. What's more, it rose much faster than ever before. In consequence, it couldn't have been because of saturated agricultural markets that Britain was hindered from exporting more and from growing faster. [596]

During the second half of the 19th century, Britain's rate of investment in technical education was slower than during the first half, and this correlated with a slower pace of technological development and of productivity. Many argued that the lower investments in technical education were responsible for the deceleration of innovation, productivity, and economic growth.

By the late 19th century, Japan had a labor force that was considerably less technically educated than that of Britain. In spite of that, GDP, productivity, and technology rose much faster than in Britain. How could a nation that had a much lower share of literate people, of technicians, of engineers, and of scientists be capable of attaining a much better performance? It is evident that there is no causality between levels of education and growth. The evidence suggests that education is an effect of growth and not the cause. [597]

By the late 19th century, Britain's labor movement was more organized than in other Western nations and management had lost much decision-making power. Labor costs were also among the highest in the world, if not the highest. It was therefore asserted that managers had a lower motivation to invest in new technologies and as a result investment fell. If

---

595 Tomlinson: Ibid., p. 33.
596 Tames: Ibid., p. 25.
597 Chambers, J. D.: *The Workshop of the World*, p. 40.

having lower labor costs and having a less unionized workforce was important for increasing investment, than countries such as those in Africa, Latin America, and Asia should have attained very high levels of investment. That was not the case. The bulk of these nations attained much lower rates of investment than Britain and they also experienced much slower GDP rates. Britain's poor performance was evidently not the result of its high wages and high levels of unionization.

By the mid-19th century, Britain was the most developed nation in the world, and as such it had the highest per capita levels of consumption. Many economists argued that the British had reached a level in which their needs were largely satisfied and in consequence demand could not grow fast. Under such circumstances, production had to grow slowly.

During the years 1850–99, economic growth in the US was so fast, that by 1900 income per head was already higher than in Britain. If demand in Britain during this period could not grow fast because it was already satisfied, than by the early 20th century demand and production in the US should have completely stagnated, because by then levels of per capita consumption were higher than in Britain. However, during the first decade of the 20th century consumer demand in the US rose very rapidly and GDP averaged about 5% annually. This was more than twice as fast as Britain during the preceding decades. [598]

None of these arguments managed to add up consistently with the facts and the policy efforts that emanated from them failed to reverse the poor performance of the economy. The thesis of manufacturing, however, manages to intertwine very coherently with the data. During the years 1900–09, the American government abundantly subsidized the sector and factory output averaged about 6% annually.

Seen from the perspective that manufacturing is the prime generator of technology, it becomes understandable why demand grew so rapidly even though by then Americans had the highest per capita consumption in the world. It is technology what improves living conditions and people have an unlimited desire to improve their lives. As a result, strong support for manufacturing translates into the creation of a large amount of goods (with improved or new technology), which make life easier. Goods like trains, automobiles, electric instruments, household utensils, and medicines (which were among the fastest growing ones in those years). Demand therefore has to be strong, not just because of the strong desirability of the new goods, but also because of the rapid creation of wealth resulting from the fast factory output. This last delivers low unemployment and rapidly rising wages, which supply a growing purchasing power to the population.

The much lower levels of support for factory production in Britain relative to the US and Germany coincided with a much slower rate of technological development. The decreased support relative to the first half of the 19th century matched Britain's slowing rate of innovation.

Productivity went through a similar situation. The average annual rate of productivity in 1850–99 was slower than in the preceding fifty years and it was much lower than in the US and Germany during that same period. [599]

Since many Western countries attained a rate of innovation that was much faster than Britain, by the turn of the century Britain had lost its leading position in numerous fields. Britain nonetheless retained supremacy in shipbuilding and this was the most subsidized

598 Elbaum & Lazonick (ed): Ibid., p. 6, 7.
599 Aldcroft, Derek & Richardson, Harry: *The British Economy 1870–1939*, p. 4, 129.

field. By 1900 British shipbuilding technology was still the most advanced in the world. As an island nation ruling a vast empire, they decided to invest abundantly in the production of warships and commercial ships throughout the period. By the turn of the century, Britain was still the largest producer of ships in the world.

The development of ship technology was so fast, that it delivered a revolution. For millennia, wood and sails had been the main characteristics of ships, but during the years 1850–99 all that changed. It was supplanted by superior materials and more advanced forms of propulsion. In 1862, the shipping tonnage made of iron was for the first time larger than that made of wood and by the turn of the century the bulk of output was of metal. During the 1870s, steam powered ships began to be produced in larger numbers than sailing vessels and by the turn of the century large sail vessels were no longer produced. [600]

Chemical fertilizers, which were not subsidized as much as ships, lost their lead by the late 19th century, while automobile technology was from the start behind that of several developed countries. Support was lower than in Germany, the US, and France and automobile production began later than in these three countries. It was only in 1895 that car production began, while in Germany it had started a decade earlier.

As in the past, all technological progress was directly linked to manufactured goods. Perhaps the most revolutionary discovery of the time was electricity. Although not as tangible as most factory goods, electricity belongs to this sector as well as the machines and devices that make it possible. The generators, the light bulbs, the lamps, the wires, and the wall connections are also factory goods. Electricity debuted in the 1870s and it immediately transformed and improved the lives of the British. Demand grew at an exponential pace. [601]

The development of every sector and domain of the economy correlated with the levels of support that manufacturing received. During the years 1850–99, agriculture, mining, construction, trade, and services experienced a slower pace of development than during the preceding fifty years. It was nonetheless the second fastest in all of British history and in consequence there was much progress on all fronts.

There was for example a rapid mechanization of agriculture. By 1850, less than 1% of grain acreage was cut by reaping machines but by 1870 the figure had jumped to 45%. Since the 1850s, steam threshing equipment and the utilization of binder machines spread rapidly and while very little chemical fertilizer was used in 1850, by the turn of the century its usage was widespread. The rate of agricultural output was not as fast as during the first half of the 19th century but it was nonetheless the second fastest in British history. By 1900 the country was still one of the largest producers and consumers of foodstuffs in the world. It had lost its top position but it was still among the top. [602]

As during practically all of the preceding history, farm output (1.1%) grew at a slower pace than the economy (2.4%) and slower still than manufacturing (2.8%), making it impossible that it could have acted as a propeller of economic growth. [603]

The progress in mining was also directly linked to factory goods. Coal is illustrative. The rapid exploitation of coal deposits during the first half of the 19th century had led to the exhaustion of existing deposits and by the 1860s many predicted an energy crisis in the near

600 Pope (ed): Ibid., p. 46, 49, 51.
601 Ibid., p. 36, 55.
602 McCloskey, Donald (ed): *Essays on a Mature Economy—Britain after 1870*, p. 215–217, 148.
603 Mathias: Ibid., p. 309–313; Sabillon: Ibid., p. 183.

future. However, steam-powered excavating machines were invented in the 1870s. These devices could dig deeper and discovered coal deposits which were even larger than those currently being exploited.[604]

Services were no different than primary sector activities. Medical services illustrate the progress in this sector that resulted from the utilization of manufactured goods. Wide-scale vaccination, which was first carried out during 1850–99, brought morbidity and mortality down rapidly. The vaccines, the syringes, the needles, and the alcohol carried a high content of technology. Medical services went through a revolution during these decades as doctors began to practice surgery for the first time. Surgery was only possible due the advent of pharmaceutical breakthroughs in anesthesia and antisepsis.[605]

Service sector productivity was considerably lower than that of manufacturing in this period. The historical data also suggests that during the preceding periods, productivity in services was much lower than in manufacturing. A similar phenomenon occurred in agriculture, the other primary activities, and construction. Such a phenomenon can be explained if it is assumed that manufacturing is fundamentally responsible for the creation of technology. Since technology is the main propeller of productivity, it is inevitable that the other sectors, which are just passive recipients of technology, had a lower productivity performance. [606]

Although living conditions did not improve as fast as during the first half of the 19th century, they did rise rapidly. Working conditions and wages improved rapidly. All that coincided with the second greatest factory subsidization in the country's history.[607]

East Asia

Economic Stagnation in Manchu China

China's economic performance during the second half of the 19th century was even worse than during the preceding fifty years. The economy decelerated to the point of total stagnation. After having grown by about 0.2% in 1800–49, GDP averaged about 0.0% annually in the following fifty years. (See tables in the appendix.)

Living conditions deteriorated significantly, famines became more regular and violence became encompassing. This catastrophic situation was accompanied by an almost complete absence of government intervention in favor of manufacturing and by a totally stagnant rate of factory output. After having expanded by about 0.3%, this sector averaged 0.0% in 1850–99. While Japan, which had for centuries lagged behind China, spurted out of stagnation and grew as fast as the West, China performed worse than in the past and its retardation with the West widened. [608]

There was an abundance of reasons why China should have reacted like Japan and adopted a decisive factory promotion policy. However, the people who governed China had such a strong ideological conviction against this sector, that nothing was capable of making them change their mind. The military humiliation that Japan endured in the mid-1850s at

---

604 Chambers: Ibid., p. 44.
605 Deane, Phyllis: *The First Industrial Revolution*, p. 30.
606 Kirby, M. W.: *The Decline of British Economic Power since 1870*, p. 4.
607 Breach, R. & Hartwell, R. (ed): *The British Economy and Society 1870-1970*, p. 82–86.
608 King, Frank: *Money and Monetary Policy in China*, p. 10, 19; Sabillon: Ibid., p. 111; Madison, Angus: *Chinese Economic Performance in the Long Run*.

the hands of the US was nothing in comparison to the one China endured in the early 1840s by the British. While Japan did not lose any land, China did. That loss of territory should have been enough to convince Beijing to launch a large armament program, but the vast majority of policy makers were convinced that such an effort would modernize and change China. They were particularly fearful that modernization would disturb Confucian values and alter Chinese culture. More still, they were afraid that such changes would corrode their power.

In the years 1856–60, Britain and France led jointly a military expedition and easily defeated the Chinese forces, extracting more territorial concessions. This further loss of face should have convinced the Chinese government that it had to change its policies. However, the conservatives in the Imperial court continued to block all efforts to increase rapidly the production of weapons, trains, and related goods.

In a country as large as China, a rapid development of railroads was seen by the few modernists in the court as the second most important means to confront the threat from the West, but unfortunately they did not succeed in moving policy in that direction.

In 1883–85, French troops once more invaded China and imposed their will. Beijing had to again endure powerless this ignominious situation for its weapons could not match those of the invaders. By then, the example of Japan had made it very evident that endorsing a policy of support for manufacturing was very effective for putting an end to the abuses of the West. However, the Empress Dowager Cixi and her clique of advisors were convinced that they would lose power if they would do that. The Tokugawa rulers of Japan had significantly increased armament output immediately after American naval ships forced them to submit in 1854. Some fourteen years later, they were forcefully dethroned. China's rulers actually saw the case of Japan as the example that should not be followed. [609]

In 1894–95, however, Japan inflicted a terrible military defeat on China and grabbed the island of Taiwan. Over the years European nations had increasingly sliced pieces of Chinese territory, but the loss of Taiwan represented by far the largest territory. Worse still was that the one who had wrested that land was a country that had for centuries lived under the shadow of China and was considered by Beijing as inferior. The defeat by Japan was the worst possible humiliation and in spite of that, the fear of losing power was stronger than that of loosing pieces of territory. Once again, no significant change in policy was undertaken and Peking only approved a very small increase in subsidies for manufacturing. [610]

During the years 1850–99 period, therefore, investment in the sector was only barely perceptible. The government constructed a few small armories and dockyards in the 1860s, but in the next decade it changed strategy and stopped making direct investments. It began to supply a few incentives to the private sector but they were so small, that entrepreneurs barely committed their capital to this sector. From 1870–1900, only about a dozen large enterprises were formed and the majority weren't even in manufacturing. The Chinese rulers were so fearful of this sector that they even opposed the installation of factories in the territories which foreign powers had wrested from China. Foreigners did not obtain from China the legal right to establish manufacturing firms until 1895 with the Treaty of Shimonoseki, as the all-encompassing victory that Japan attained forced Beijing to bend on this matter. [611]

609 Ibid., p. 188.
610 Rostow, Walt: *The World Economy*, p. 523
611 Hou, Chi Ming: *Foreign Investment and Economic Development in China 1840–1937*, p. 130, 13, 79.

In 1850–99, the bulk of government expenditure went into sustaining the lavishness of the court, into agriculture, and into a few other non-manufacturing domains. No laws in support of manufacturing were passed and the level of incentives relative to the preceding fifty years fell a little. Manufacturing output stagnated completely and by 1900 the production of this sector was practically identical as in 1850. This coincided with a complete stagnation of the economy. [612]

All other sectors and domains of the economy shadowed the performance of manufacturing. Agriculture, which was practically the only domain that received support from the state, did worse than during the years 1800–49 and saw no growth. In consequence, the per capita supply of food decreased and the incidence of famines rose. The worst famine was that of 1876–79, which affected four provinces and claimed about eleven million lives. Even when famines were not present, the deterioration of an already precarious situation drove the population to despair and rebellions multiplied. There were four major rebellions during the second half of the 19th century. The worst was the Taiping rebellion of 1850–64, which was responsible for about twenty million deaths. [613]

Production of other primary sector activities such as mining, forestry, and fishing also stagnated and trade performed similarly. Domestic and foreign trade barely experienced any progress. If the production of factory goods remained static, primary goods could not increase and if primary goods and manufactures did not expand, it was extremely hard for trade to rise.

During this period, terms of trade constantly deteriorated. This seems to have also been inevitable considering that most of China's main trading partners experienced much faster rates of manufacturing output. In consequence, they had a larger amount of tradable goods. They therefore exported more to China than what they imported from her. More important still was that China's goods contained considerably less technology than those from other nations and were thus considerably less valuable. Their prices constantly lost value relative to the prices from foreign goods. It was similar to Britain, which also experienced a deterioration of its terms of trade, as many of its main trading partners attained faster rates of factory production. [614]

Many argued that China's terrible performance during this half century was the result of its unskilled labor force and the unwillingness of the population to work hard. The historical data does not substantiate this idea. [615]

The Chinese were as unskilled after 1895 as they were before, but after that year GDP figures accelerated considerably. By 1949, the skills of the population had only barely improved, but during the 1950s growth was strong. If the skill level of a population were a decisive factor in the performance of the economy, then GDP figures should not have varied so abruptly.

The argument asserting that the Chinese lacked working energy is also incompatible with the historical evidence. During 1850–99, the average workweek was almost one hundred hours. By the late 20th century, on the other hand, the workweek was only half as long. However, in the 1990s China attained one of the fastest rates of economic growth in

612 Eberhard, Wolfram: *A History of China*, p. 98–100.
613 King: Ibid., p. 4, 5.
614 Hou: Ibid., p. 197.
615 Rawski, Thomas: *Economic Growth in Pre-War China*, p. 33–42.

the world. Such events correlated with proportionate levels of support for the sector and proportionate rates of factory output.

A similar argument was the one that Max Weber formulated in the late 19th century. The German sociologist, who searched for the cultural roots of Western capitalism in the Protestant ethic, stated that Confucianism was largely responsible for the economic backwardness of China because it opposed the pursuit of profit. If Confucianism would hinder profit-making efforts, it becomes hard to understand why in 1950–99 the Taiwanese and Hong Kongese were so good at making profits. It is also impossible to understand why China, during 1980–99, made such large profits. By the late 20th century, these three Chinese societies had still strong Confucian traditions; however, that showed no signs of hindering the attainment of fast economic growth.

If Confucianism impeded growth during the second half of the 19th century, then it should have also acted as a hindrance one hundred years later. Interestingly enough, by the late 20th century it many Western analysts were asserting that the Confucian culture was largely responsible for the impressive performance of China and East Asia. Such accommodations are logically unacceptable. [616]

Korea and Taiwan

Korea went through a similar ordeal to China's, for ideology prevailed in Seoul during the second half of the 19th century. As a result, similar irrational policies were endorsed.

During this period, a series of military threats from abroad forced policy makers to increase support for manufacturing. They however only augmented it by a very small amount because they were convinced that such subsidies would disturb the social stability that had prevailed for millennia and in their view that was the worst that could occur to the peninsula. Only under duress and the threat of conquest, did they acquiesce to some changes.[617]

During this period, Korea was indirectly ruled by China, which also wanted as little economic and social change as possible. Had a Korean king endorsed strong promotion of armament production, it is very likely that Chinese troops would have stepped in. Seoul might have been able to endorse strong subsidies for civilian manufacturing, but no such initiative was forthcoming. [618]

Since the late 18th century, a growing number of Western and Russian ships navigated along the Korean coast in search of trading and fishing opportunities. Seoul had a policy of total seclusion and repelled all foreign contacts.

By the mid-19th century, nonetheless, things started to change. The British victory over China in 1842 was a shock to Korea. If a small naval force could subdue the strongest military power of Asia, then it was evident that Korea was even more precarious. Foreign pressure continued to increase and in 1854 American warships forcefully opened Japan to trade. Korean policy makers concluded that it was necessary to increase investment in weapons, but only small allocations were made. In 1860, a combined force of British and French troops defeated China for the second time. Seoul further increased allocations for armaments, but again by only a small amount. A few years later, an American merchant ship forcefully tried

---

616 "New Fashion for Old Wisdom", *The Economist*, 21 January 1995, p. 67.
617 Chung, Chai-sik: *A Korean Confucian Encounter with the Modern World*, p. 1–8.
618 Cotterel, Arthur: *East Asia—From Chinese Predominance to the Rise of the Pacific Rim*, p. 131.

to make an incursion and was sunk by the Koreans. In 1866, French warships trying to break open the peninsula were repulsed.[619]

Impressed by the overthrow of the Tokugawa regime in Japan in 1868, the Korean court immediately took notice of the Meiji reformers' weapon and factory promotion policy. Seoul endorsed similar policies, but at a lower level.. In 1871, an American flotilla sent to retaliate for the sinking of the American merchant ship a decade earlier was beaten back by the Koreas.

In the meantime, Japan had gained military strength. Since the 1850s, Tokyo had repeatedly failed to establish diplomatic relations with Korea; in 1876 it sent a large fleet to press the matter. Confronted with such a superior naval force, the Koreans capitulated and signed the first international treaty granting to the Japanese extraterritorial legal rights and opening Korean ports to them. Western powers immediately sent naval forces to demand similar advantages and also extracted trade treaties.[620]

This caused further changes in policy. A modernization program was initiated which included larger allocations for weapons and related factory goods. King Konjong however only increased subsidies by a small amount. After a military mutiny in Seoul in 1882, protesting the rights granted to the Japanese, Tokyo intervened a second time. China sent troops at the request of its vassal and Japan retreated.[621]

The ruling class was increasingly divided and a minority became very disappointed with the slowness of the reforms. In 1884 the reformers seized power in a coup but a Manchu contingent overthrew them three days later. The mutiny and the coup nonetheless forced King Konjong to accelerate the modernization program and that translated into more subsidies for manufacturing.

As in the past, however, the increases were very small. The large majority of the budget continued to be deployed in the non-manufacturing sectors. Aside from the large share used to promote agriculture, much was used to pay war reparations to foreigners and for administrative reorganization.

To pay for the modernization program, farm taxes rose and a revolt ensued in 1894. Since the government was unable to suppress the Tonghak revolt, Seoul called in Chinese troops. Tokyo used the opportunity to send troops to Korea even though Seoul had not requested them. Chinese troops quelled the revolt but fighting with Japanese troops erupted. A full-blown war followed and by 1895 China capitulated. In the Treaty of Shimonoseki of that year, Japan established its hegemony over Korea and China relinquished most of its rights over the peninsula.[622]

During 1850–99, the significant rise in support for manufacturing coincided with a considerable acceleration of the sector and of the economy. Manufacturing is likely to have grown by about 0.9% per year and the economy by about 0.6%.[623]

During 1850–99, Beijing ruled Taiwan and China practiced a policy of manufacturing suppression. Factory stagnation prevailed in China and in Taiwan the situation was similar. Taiwan nonetheless became the center of China's national security concerns and at the very

619 *A Handbook of Korea*, p. 83–86.
620 Cumings, Bruce: *Korea's Place in the Sun—A Modern History*, p. 86.
621 Cotterel: Ibid., p. 130, 131.
622 *A Handbook of Korea*, p. 86–91.
623 Sabillon: Ibid., p. 113.

end of the 19th century it became a Japanese possession. Beijing felt forced to supply some subsidies for manufacturing, and once Tokyo took control of the island, it began to supply more.[624]

During the first Opium War, Britain attacked Taiwan. With the end of the second Opium War in 1860, Britain and France forced China to open several other ports to foreign trade. Two of these ports were located in Taiwan. Since then, Beijing became increasingly fearful that foreign forces would invade the island, so it sent capable officials to build the island's defenses. In 1869, British warships bombarded one of the island's ports and months later, American forces invaded the island for a punitive expedition against a tribe that had harmed US interests. In 1874, on the grounds that it sought to protect Japanese fishermen, Tokyo sent a punitive expedition against Taiwan and in 1884–85 French naval forces blockaded the island and assaulted several ports in retaliation of China's defense of Vietnam.

Beijing reacted by separating Taiwan from Fukien province and gave the island provincial status. It also promoted migration from the mainland, constructed a railroad, established steamship services, telegraphic links, and enhanced defenses with Western military hardware.[625]

In the Sino–Japanese war of 1894–95, Tokyo forced Beijing to cede Taiwan to Japan. The domestic population of the island used the opportunity to declare independence, but soon after, Japanese troops landed in mass and suppressed the independence movement.

All of these events had some effect on manufacturing. Beijing increasingly enhanced the defenses of the island in the course of the years 1850–94, but the bulk of the weapons were fabricated in Britain or in China. There was nonetheless a small increase in the investments made for the production of arms and related factory goods. Once the Japanese took hold of the island, they proceeded to convert it into a major producer of agricultural goods that complemented the needs of Japan. Investment from the archipelago arrived in large amounts deployed mostly for the development of primary activities and infrastructure. A number of factors nonetheless, inspired the Japanese to set up some factories, which delivered a faster growth of the sector.[626]

During 1850–99, the level of support for manufacturing in Taiwan rose somewhat and that was paralleled by a small improvement of the economy. Manufacturing is likely to have expanded by about 0.4% per year and the economy by about 0.3%. Growth in all fields accelerated. Per capita agricultural output rose and exports of tea, camphor, and sugar cane flourished. The extraction of minerals, fish, and the exploitation of forests also increased.[627]

Singapore and Hong Kong

In other regions of East Asia where economic growth was experienced, a similar development of events took place.

In 1819, Singapore became a British colony. High transport costs to this far flung outpost forced British policy makers to decree some support for manufacturing. British authorities promoted the production of the goods that had the highest transport costs. However, since Britain's mercantilist policies viewed colonies as just providers of raw materials and as se-

---

624 Rubinstein, Murray (ed): *Taiwan—A New History*, p. 163–200.
625 Ibid., p. 165–167.
626 Ibid., p. 202–208.
627 Ibid., p. 165; Sabillon: Ibid., p. 114.

cure importers of British factory goods, the desire to produce manufactures in the island was not large. In consequence, subsidies for the sector were very low and so was the rate of economic growth.[628]

Over time, factories received increasing state aid. There were several reasons for such a change. Among them was the reduction of Britain's mercantilist view of the world, the acquisition of nearby colonies, monopolistic goals, and the fear of Japanese competition.

By 1850, Britain had significantly dismantled its mercantilist system; it was no longer convinced that it was important for the well being of the nation. Thus one of the original reasons for suppressing manufacturing in the colonies was gone. London ordered the colonial authorities in Singapore to supply more incentives for the production of those manufactures with high transport costs.

In the 1840s, large tin deposits were discovered in the Malay Peninsula. Britain began supplying subsidies for the processing of the mineral in Singapore, which had the best port in the region. A decisive increase in support for the sector came after Britain gained control over much of Malaysia in the 1870s and progressively began to extract much larger amounts of tin and other raw materials. That share of the processed and manufactured goods derived from these materials intended for use in Asia then began to be produced locally. Capitalists received larger fiscal, financial, and non-financial incentives and the authorities even granted monopolies. Large numbers of Chinese workers were imported to the new factories.

Malaysia was one of the few territories in the world with large tin ore deposits. To achieve a monopoly, London sought that as little raw material as possible would leave its colonies unprocessed. High export duties were imposed on tin ore and at times ore exports were banned. However, what contributed most to the processing of the mineral were the tax exemptions, the land concessions for the factories, and the grants. This attracted considerable direct investment from Europe (in particular Britain) and the production of smelted tin rose rapidly. The share of the mineral processed in the island rose. By 1900, Singapore had the world's largest and most technologically advanced tin smelting factory. This field received the largest subsidies and this was the fastest growing manufacturing field.[629]

Because Singapore had been chosen as the chief port of call in the region, it also became the main manufacturing center of the region. For export and import reasons it became strategically important to place the factories as close to the port. Most of the Malaysian tin was processed in Singapore. Other primary goods from the region experienced a similar development. Pineapples were at the core of fruit production in Malaysia and support was supplied for food processing. By the early 20th century, Singapore was the second largest producer in the world of canned pineapples (after Hawaii). Malaysia became also a large producer of raw wood and Singapore progressively processed more and more of that wood.

Another way in which Malaysia contributed to the development of manufacturing in Singapore was by increasing the market for factory goods that, because of their high transport costs, were allowed by the British to be produced in the colonies. Originally, Singapore undertook this task just for its domestic market and other small adjacent territories under British rule. However, with the coming of the large Malay states, the island was also given the task to manufacture for the Malay market.

---

628 Huff, W. G.: *The Economic Growth of Singapore*, p. 7.
629 Ibid., p. 8, 14, 22, 60, 61.

More subsidies were thus supplied to foreign companies so that they would produce high weight-to-cost goods. During the late 19th century, there was much investment in bricks, tiles, cement, and a wide range of metal products. Eventually, even goods with low transport costs such as textiles received subsidies to fend off the rising Japanese competition. Due to its nearness, Japan's transport costs were lower than Britain and it also had lower labor costs. Singapore had much lower labor costs than Japan and its transport costs were practically non-existent for its own market and for that of Malaysia.[630]

The factory promotion efforts of the colonial authorities increased considerably during the second half of the 19th century and this coincided with a significant acceleration in the rate of economic growth. Manufacturing spurted and grew by about 2.8% annually while the economy did it by about 2.3%.[631]

It is worth noting that when the British took over the island in the early 19th century, it was practically deserted and the colonizers never sought to develop agriculture or any other primary activity. At first, it was intended exclusively as a resting port for the long voyage between India and China, and later on, as the main port of call for the Southeast Asian region. Even though there was never a transfer of resources from agriculture to the other sectors, manufacturing experienced a relative fast development. Together with Japan it attained the fastest manufacturing growth during the second half of the 19th century in the whole of Asia.

Orthodox arguments have asserted that a large agricultural sector that eventually generates surpluses can stimulate the initial development of manufacturing. The case of Singapore shows that that is not the only path to manufacturing. Singapore also suggests that import barriers are not necessarily required to enable a nation to establish a manufacturing base.

The British decreed a free trade policy in 1819 which was maintained throughout the whole period of colonial rule. The absence of tariffs (and non-tariff barriers) did not impede the development of manufacturing. While the growth of factory output during the 19th century did not attain rates such as those in Western nations (which did raise trade barriers), the evidence suggests that this was due to a lower supply of fiscal, financial, and non-financial incentives than in Western nations, and not because of free trade.[632]

During the first half of the 20th century, Singapore continued to practice free trade and in spite of the lack of protection, manufacturing expanded at a much faster pace. This coincided with a significant increase in factory subsidies. On this occasion, GDP rates were similar or faster than most Western nations even though these nations continued to protect their markets. In 1950–99 Singapore gained independence but it continued to endorse free trade, while the West and Japan had significant trade barriers. Its manufacturing sector accelerated considerably and grew much faster than all Western nations. That was accompanied by much larger factory subsidies. The economy also grew much faster than all others, including Japan, which was the most protectionist developed nation in this period.

In Hong Kong, events developed along similar lines. In 1843, Beijing ceded to Britain the island of Hong Kong after its defeat in the First Opium War. In 1860, after the Second Opium War, China ceded the Kowloon Peninsula. Finally, by the Convention of 1898, the

---

630 Ibid., p. 203, 213, 214.
631 Sabillon: Ibid., p. 158.
632 *Trade Policy Review—Singapore Vol. I*, p. 1–11.

New Territories and 235 islands were leased to Britain for 99 years. All the above amounted to about one thousand square kilometers, constituting what we now call Hong Kong.

British mercantilism was against promoting manufacturing in the colonies. Nevertheless, to exploit the reality of China and its ceded possessions, teeming with people too poor to be much use as consumers but perfectly useful as potential laborers, and so far away from England that trading was costly, required a different model.[633]

However, Beijing strongly opposed factory production in the territories it ceded to foreign nations and Britain was only capable of establishing a few production establishments. Beijing granted to foreigners an unlimited right to invest in manufacturing only in 1895. Immediately thereafter, investment multiplied. The British colonial government, therefore, supplied only a small dose of factory subsidies in 1850–99. Subsidies nonetheless rose dramatically relative to the preceding fifty years and that coincided with an exponential acceleration of manufacturing and GDP. Factory output and GDP, however, grew much slower than in Singapore where the British did not encounter opposition towards investing in this sector. During 1850–99, manufacturing in Hong Kong is likely to have expanded by about 1.0% per year and the economy by about 0.8% annually.[634]

Manufacturing and GPD growth in Hong Kong were pretty slow up to the late 19th century. However, the acceleration occurred without the slightest transfer of resources from agriculture or other primary activities to manufacturing. Before the 1840s, the territory was inhabited by only a small fishing population and by pirates, who exclusively incurred in a few primary and service activities. The British had primarily sought to create a port with the necessary infrastructure for the sale of their wares. In spite of this, manufacturing started to grow much faster than ever before without any shift of resources from the primary sector.[635]

The rise in factory production also occurred notwithstanding the free trade policy which the British applied on all of its colonies. The ideal of sovereignty being moot in Hong Kong as it was in Singapore, the territory demonstrated that the birth and growth of a manufacturing base were perfectly possible, even in the absence of trade protection to infant producers.

---

633 Hopkins, Keith (ed): *Hong Kong—The Industrial Colony*, p. 23.
634 Sabillon: Ibid., p. 112.
635 Hopkins: Ibid., p. 145.

CHAPTER 8. THE FIRST HALF OF THE 20TH CENTURY IN EAST ASIA

Japan

War and Weapons

The first half of the 20th century marked the beginning of a new era. This was the first time since the 16th century when a nation which was not situated in the Western Hemisphere or which did not possess a Western culture, attained the fastest rates of economic growth in the world. For long, most intellectuals in the West and in the rest of the world had been convinced that Western culture was determinant or important for a positive economic performance. All of a sudden, such an idea was no longer tenable.

In the years 1900–49, Japan attained the fastest GDP figures in the world and not only did it outperform everybody else, but it also did it by a considerable margin. While Japan grew by about 4.5% annually, Germany averaged 3.6%, and the US grew by just 3.5%. (See tables at the end of the book.)

More important still about Japan's much improved performance was that it occurred while factory subsidization rose considerably. The US had been the fastest grower in the second half of the 19th century and the significant deceleration of its rate of growth coincided as well with a significant reduction in the factory promotion efforts of the state. In Germany, a similar correlation was observed. In the three, the level of support for the sector paralleled proportionate rates of manufacturing output. In Japan, factory production averaged about 6.3% per year, in Germany 4.7%, and in the US 4.2%. [636]

During this fifty years period, the Japanese government became strongly interested in large-scale military conquest and to materialize its goals, it decreed a massive armament program. Tokyo also decreed ample support for the numerous fields that were directly and

---

636 Allen, G. C.: *A Short Economic History of Modern Japan*, p. 245; Sabillon, Carlos: *World Economic Historical Statistics*, p. 112, 147, 183; Madison, Angus: *The World Economy: Historical Statistics*.

indirectly linked with weapons, of which the vast majority were factory goods. Japan as well sought to economically conquer most of Asia, driving the government to grant abundant incentives to the producers of export goods. Since the most exportable goods were manufactures, the incentives mostly assisted this sector. [637]

During this half century, the level of subsidization for the sector was not homogeneous. Driven by fluctuating ideological motivations, at times subsidies were abundant and in other occasions they were scarce. Here again, the correlation was very tight, for factory rates and GDP figures paralleled the differing levels of subsidization.

The pace of technological development and rates of productivity moved also in full synchrony with the differing levels of subsidization. These increased at a much faster pace than ever before, coinciding with the unprecedented factory promotion efforts. Worth also noticing is that practically all other sectors and domains of the economy shadowed the performance of manufacturing. They grew at a much faster pace than ever before although resources were subtracted from them in order to transfer them to manufacturing.

Events seem to have taken place in the following manner. After having easily defeated China in 1895, which had historically been the strongest nation in East Asia, Japan concluded that it could go ahead and acquire broader territories and influence in the region. As a cluster of islands, its best method for attaining its military goals was through a large navy. Almost as soon as China surrendered, the government decreed more subsidies for shipbuilding. Japan was interested in the territories that were located in the north of China and to the north of China, and these last belonged to Russia. Even the territories in northern China were under Russian influence. Aware that Russia's military capabilities were far superior to those of China, Tokyo allotted greater resources for the production of weapons. In 1904, war with Russia broke out and although the stock of Russian weapons and their technology was similar to that of Japan, Moscow endured a crushing defeat. The war was mostly fought at sea and on this particular element, Japan had superior warship technology and a larger number of vessels. Russia had superior land weapons, but they were only barely used and most of its forces were concentrated west of the Urals. Again the evidence suggests that the decisive factor at the battlefield is the quantitative and qualitative level of the armaments used. [638]

During the war (1904–05), Tokyo made massive investments in armaments and shipbuilding. With the end of the conflict, defense expenditures dropped but they soon rose again, as the triumph over Russia expanded the desire for further military inroads into East Asia. With larger territories under its control, Japan had more secured markets for its exports so it enlarged the subsidies to the producers of civilian manufactures such as textiles, metals, commercial ships, and machine tools.

During the first decade of the 20th century, there was a noticeable increase in the subsidization of military and civilian manufacturing and this sector accelerated to a rate of about 7.0% annually. The economy did likewise and expanded by about 5.2%. [639]

Japan's increased desire for conquest became evident in 1910, when it launched a major invasion of the whole Korean peninsula. This was the largest territory that it had attempted to subdue and the vastness of the country and its large population, drove the government to invest more in arms and related goods. Government expenditure rose once again. Japan's

637 Morishima, Michio: *Why Has Japan Succeeded?*, p. 96, 97, 128.
638 *The Cambridge History of Japan Vol. 6*, p. 433–435, 387.
639 Vie, Michel: *Le Japon Contemporain*, p. 55–57, 91.

superior weapon technology delivered a resounding defeat over Korean forces and the peninsula was thoroughly conquered. Once again, the amount and technological sophistication of weapons played the decisive role at the battlefield.

During the second decade of the 20th century, military expenditure as a share of GDP rose to about 9% and this was by far the largest segment of the budget. Tokyo used about a third of the budget to make weapons, while a smaller share was used to finance the production of related goods such as metals, petrochemicals, machine tools, uniforms, boots, canned food, medicines, and transport ships. Another share was utilized to assist the financing of export goods, which were in their vast majority factory goods. [640]

During this decade, export promotion efforts increased as a result of its newly acquired colony of Korea. Japan also forced other nations in the region to lower trade barriers for Japanese goods and World War I decreased significantly European exports to Asia and permitted Japan to increase its share of the region's imports. The government thus supplied to civilian manufactures more fiscal, financial, and non-financial incentives. The increased subsidies coincided with an unprecedented growth of exports.

Overall support for manufacturing during the 1910s rose more than ever before and this coincided with a faster pace of factory output and a faster rate of GDP. Manufacturing averaged about 8.4% and GDP about 6.3% annually. [641]

With Japan's relatively large colonial possessions and its dominant position in East Asia in the 1920s, Japanese policy makers felt satisfied. No further attempts of conquest were made. During this decade, defense expenditure decreased and support for weapons-related goods diminished. The policy of promoting exports also experienced a reversal as the government concluded that Japanese producers had already attained a noticeable level of maturity and were no longer in need of much assistance. A major earthquake in 1923 also subtracted resources as it shifted funds from manufacturing towards reconstruction efforts.

As the military goals became smaller, the government thought necessary to increase its budgetary allocations for agriculture. Physiocratic ideas were still strong and in the previous decades, the transfer of resources to manufacturing had been done reluctantly and only under the duress of the large national security concerns. In the 1920s, therefore, Tokyo retransferred resources to farming and to other primary activities. Meanwhile the rate of factory output went down, which averaged about 3.1%. The economy also slowed down to about 2.4%.[642]

Authoritarianism had been rapidly on the wane since the late 19th century, and during the early 1920s universal male suffrage was implemented. A recession struck in the early 1920s and during the following years the democratically-elected rulers were not able to reactivate the economy to the high figures of the preceding decades. The military became restless and in 1926 they overthrew the government on the argument that it was economically incompetent. The economy, however, did not improve and in 1929 it fell into recession.

By 1931, the military had become frustrated with the failure of the numerous reactivation efforts and decided to launch the country on the road of conquest again. They argued that new territories would provide raw materials and export markets which would propel the economy out of the depression.

640 Morishima: Ibid., p. 126–136.
641 Allen: Ibid., p. 82, 94, 97, 112, 128; Madison, Angus: *Monitoring the World Economy 1820–1992.*
642 Vie: Ibid., p. 104.

Tokyo thus set its sight on Manchuria, China's northeastern territory. The Manchurian campaign was initiated in 1931 and it was accompanied by a huge increase in budgetary expenditures for the production of weapons and related goods. The conquest of Manchuria represented the largest effort of this sort that Japan had ever undertaken. This Chinese territory was not only larger than Korea and Taiwan combined, but it was also many times the size of Japan. The level of support for military manufacturing and related fields was therefore much higher than ever before. Overall factory output immediately picked up and the economy did likewise. The recession ended at the precise moment when factories began to receive large subsidies. Despite possessing a much smaller population, Japan easily wrested the large territory from China. Once again, the amount and technological sophistication of weapons proved decisive at the battlefield. [643]

By 1936, the Japanese military adopted a plan to conquer the rest of China. They demanded larger defense investments but the finance minister argued that such spending was financially unsound and would wreck the economy. He was murdered and the military immediately received their larger budget. Taxes went up steeply, government borrowing rose considerably, and defense expenditure increased to account for about 48% of government expenditure (in 1937). Strong support for military manufacturing increased further during the rest of the 1930s as the conquest of China continued. [644]

The 1930s witnessed new levels of support for military manufacturing and related fields and this coincided with an unprecedented output of these goods. Large subsidies were granted to the producers of weapons, metals, ships, automobiles, chemicals, machine tools, airplanes, and electrical goods. There was however a small decrease in support for civilian manufacturing because numerous fields were not associated with the military campaigns. The policy of promoting exports was nonetheless pursued, although not as enthusiastically as in the past. The end result was a very rapid growth of the sector. During this decade, average factory output was about 8.5% annually and GDP expanded by about 5.4%. [645]

The invasion of China started in 1937 and by the start of the next decade the large allocations for arms continued as big parts of China remained unconquered. Pushing further in the direction of larger defense expenditures was Japan's desire to subdue other nations of Asia. The military came to conclude that the US was preventing Japan from conquering the rest of Asia and so it resolved to attack and destroy the American Pacific Fleet. In order to confront such a strong adversary, Tokyo invested more in weapons. In late 1941, Japan launched an attack on Hawaii. [646]

In the early 1940s, huge defense expenditures coincided with an impressive growth of factory output, which was paralleled by impressive economic growth.

By then, however, the US was the most manufacturized nation in the world and as such it possessed the most advanced technology in the world. Most of the technology the US possessed was in civilian fields but just as history had repeatedly witnessed an easy transfer of technology from military to civilian uses, it was also easy to transfer it from civilian to military. In no time, the US started producing technologically advanced weapons that rivaled those of Japan and by the end of the war it had even surpassed the archipelago on

643 Levine, Salomon & Kawada, Hisashi: *Human Resources in Japanese Industrial Development*, p. 33.
644 Allen: Ibid., p. 100–106, 136–139, 142.
645 *The Cambridge History of Japan Vol. 6*, p. 471, 436, 458, 580, 581.
646 Morishima: Ibid., p. 95, 128.

this front. On top of that, the US was a much larger economy and could produce more arms. As a result, the Americans soon began to take the upper hand in the war and implemented an increasingly effective blockade that deprived Japan of certain essential imports, like oil. Manufacturing production began to slow down in 1943 and the economy did likewise. With the initiation of large-scale Allied aerial bombardments in 1944, which largely targeted weapons production facilities, the output of the sector contracted until the end of the war in mid-1945. GDP plummeted.[647]

By the time the war ended in August 1945, Japan had lost about 3 million people and about two fifths of its national wealth. Manufacturing contracted to about half its peak level in 1942. They were not permitted to produce any kind of weapons and the American occupying forces prohibited the production of most heavy manufactured goods due, at least ostensibly, to their strong linkage with arms. By curtailing heavy manufacturing, the Americans sought to keep Japan dependent and prevent them from embarking on the path of conquest in the future.[648]

From the end of the war until 1947, the provisional government was not capable of providing practically any form of support to the producers of heavy manufactured goods. The American occupying force, however, did not oppose the government's efforts to stimulate the production of light manufacturing so long it was strictly of a civilian nature. A system of incentives for this domain was rapidly organized. During these years, savings were negligible, resources scare, and the US was not interested in financing Japan's reconstruction. In spite of that, the government managed to allocate a large share of the available resources to light manufacturing.[649]

Practically all of the production came from private companies, but the evidence suggests that without the attractive package of fiscal, financial, and non-financial incentives, Japanese capitalists had not reactivated production. Military factories were wholly transformed to civilian production. Machine gun firms began to produce sewing machines and rangefinder plants started to produce cameras. This wasn't the first time that such a phenomenon had occurred, but this was the first time that it had occurred in Asia on such a scale. [650]

The scarcity of capital resulting from the war was compounded by the financial obligations that the victors imposed. Japan had to pay war reparations and it was only in 1949 that most of them were liquidated. Resources were so scarce, that during 1945–47, food shortages and malnutrition were widespread. On top of that, it was very hard to export because the bulk of the country's mercantile marine had been destroyed. With all of these hindrances, it is hard to see how the economy could have performed well. The fact, however, is that the economy immediately revived and that correlated with a relative strong subsidization of factories. Factory output from the end of the war up to 1947 averaged about 6% annually and GDP was about 4%. [651]

This was a clear example of the endogenous nature of growth. It was proof that the growth of manufacturing was fundamentally dependent on the commitment of the government to see it grow. The bottom line consisted simply in reallocating the existing resources

647 Vie: Ibid., p. 112; Bremond, J., Chalaye, C. & Loeb, M.: *l'Economie du Japon*, p. 12.
648 *The Cambridge History of Japan Vol. 6*, p. 492; Le Japon d'Aujourd'hui, p. 37.
649 Tsuru, Shigeto: *Japan's Capitalism*, p. 38.
650 Allen: Ibid., p. 172; Morishima: Ibid., p. 163.
651 *The Cambridge History of Japan Vol. 6*, p. 492–494, 474.

so that this sector would receive a large share. This situation suggested that if a large share of the available resources were allotted to this sector, economic growth was assured, even under the worse circumstances.

By the end of 1947, the rapid expansion of the Soviet Union and the loss of Western control of economies worldwide, in Korea, in Indochina and all of Eastern and Central Europe, created a new national security concern for the United States. When Soviet tanks invaded Czechoslovakia in February of 1948, the US changed tack and decided to assist both Germany and Japan in their recovery efforts in order to develop strong allies. Since early that year, the American government allowed Tokyo to promote all fields of heavy manufacturing with the sole exception of weapons.[652]

On top of that, Washington immediately decreed a relatively large package of financial assistance, which was known as the Dodge Plan. This capital was mainly intended for promoting the recovery of manufacturing, because by then, this was the largest sector, and because factory goods were largely associated with exports and the country was desperately in need of foreign exchange. The Japanese government agreed. With backing from Washington, Tokyo was also capable of borrowing large sums of money from international financial organizations and from Western commercial banks (mostly American). This money was invested mainly in manufacturing. [653]

During 1948–49, the Japanese government greatly increased the incentives it offered to private sector producers and factory output immediately spurted, averaging about 19% annually. The economy followed suit and averaged about 16% per year.

However, the compounded average of this decade of violent fluctuations was not as positive as most of the preceding decades. During the 1940s, factory output was about 4.5% per year and GDP expanded by about 3.0%.[654]

The Effects of Factory Promotion

Technology made more progress during the first half of the 20th century than ever before, paralleling the unprecedented factory promotion efforts of Tokyo. The fluctuating levels of support for the sector coincided also with the fluctuating rates of technological development. On top of that, technology constantly found its materialization on factory goods and patents were systematically linked to this sort of goods. All this suggests a relationship of causality.

During the first decade of the 20th century, technical progress was faster than during the preceding decade and factory subsidization witnessed a noticeable rise. During 1910–19, technology imports and the registration of patents occurred at an accelerating rate and the share of the archipelago's resources allocated to manufacturing increased. In the 1920s, support decreased considerably; this was accompanied by a significant slowdown in the rate of innovation. During this decade, foreign direct investment rose in high technology fields. Ford and General Motors established automobile assembly plants. In spite of that, technological development was considerably slower than during the preceding decades.

During the 1930s, on the other hand, the exact opposite took place as the West put a large number of restrictions on its exports to Japan in retaliation for the invasion of Man-

---

652 "The American Shogun", *Newsweek*, 26 May 1997, p. 23.
653 "Bretton Woods Revisited", *The Economist*, 9 July 1994, p. 74.
654 Sabillon: Ibid., p. 112; Madison, Angus: *The World Economy: Historical Statistics.*

churia and the rest of China. Japan's technology imports were largely curtailed but techno-logical development took place rapidly, coinciding with Tokyo's strong factory promotion efforts. Progress was so fast that by the end of the 1930s Japan had technologically caught up with the most advanced nations in fields such as ships, armaments, metals, machines tools, chemicals, and airplanes. Innovation concentrated almost exclusively in heavy manufactur-ing fields, which were the most subsidized fields. There was a very rapid growth of labor saving machines. [655]

During the 1940s, technology fluctuated wildly. In the early years of this decade, it made very large progress to the point of taking the world lead in certain fields like warships and fighter planes. This ran parallel to the vast allocations for arms. Around the middle of the decade, technology stagnated and then contracted, coalescing with a contraction of factory output. And by the end of the decade, technological development was very fast, coinciding once again with a very strong promotion of manufacturing. [656]

From 1900 to 1949, technological development took place mostly in heavy manufactur-ing, coinciding with the domain that most received subsidies. The only moment in which the development of technology was no longer linked to weapons, was during the late 1940s, when support concentrated exclusively on civilian manufacturing.

Productivity as well correlated with the differing levels of factory subsidization. Dur-ing the first two decades of the century, productivity grew faster than during the previous decades, notwithstanding the rising numbers of cartels in those years. During 1910-19, tariff barriers were implemented for the first time and in spite of this productivity hindering mea-sure, productivity rose very fast. In the 1920s, the rate of productivity decelerated noticeably paralleling a decreased subsidization of factories.

During the 1930s, cartels proliferated, trade barriers rose, and the West imposed an embargo on Japan. In spite of that, productivity grew much faster than in the 1920s. That coincided with a large increase in the share of the nation's resources allocated to factories. In the early 1940s, there were even more competition-hindering practices but productivity grew faster. By the middle of the decade, it had pretty much stagnated and by the end of the decade it once again rose very fast. This all coincided with a strong subsidization of facto-ries in the early and later part of that decade, and with a factory-hindering situation in the intermediate years.

It is also worth noting that in 1900-49, this sector attained the fastest rates of produc-tivity. It grew faster than agriculture or any other primary activity as well as faster than con-struction and services. This period witnessed unprecedented rates of productivity, which correlated with the strongest subsidization of factories up to that date. [657]

Much suggests that during the first half of the 20th century, the Japanese government committed many policy errors that inhibited productivity growth and a better economic performance. One of them was the growing number of cartels, which were only reduced after 1945. Cartels mostly flourished in heavy manufacturing because the investment re-quirements of this field were larger and the government thought that this approach would reduce production costs.

655 Allen: Ibid., p. 123, 139, 150.
656 "Japan's Aerospace Giants are Flying Low", *Newsweek*, 5 December 1994, p. 31.
657 Allen: Ibid., p. 150.

History suggests that a better way to increase investment lay in raising the level of fiscal, financial, and non-financial incentives. In the second half of the 20th century, cartels were less numerous than during the first half and rates of investment and economic growth were much faster. That coincided with more fiscal, financial, and non-financial incentives.

However, the large number of cartels of the period 1900–49 is actually a strong piece of evidence in favor of the manufacturing thesis. During this period, cartels were more abundant than during the preceding fifty years and in spite of that the rate of investment and economic growth was almost twice as fast as during the 1850–99 period. Factory output grew about double as fast (6.3% against 3.0%). That would also explain why the US, which was less tolerant of cartels, attained slower rates of economic growth. In this period, Washington promoted factories less enthusiastically than Japan. [658]

Other policy errors consisted in the erection of trade barriers. In 1911, Japan raised tariffs from zero to about 20% of the value of imports. From then on, there were brief periods of reduction, although in general, tariffs and non-tariff barriers kept on rising for the rest of this half century period. By blocking imports, policy makers thought that they would assist domestic capitalists in their investment efforts. The clearest evidence that this policy was incapable of increasing investment and growth was the poor performance of the 1920s. During this decade, trade barriers were much higher than during the 1900s, but the rate of investment and GDP was much lower. In the tariff-free 1900–09 years, the Japanese economy grew by 5.2% annually while in the tariff-high 1920s it grew by just 2.4%.

Much suggests that trade barriers were harmful to the economy, but the high trade barriers of the 1930s and the accompanying fast rates of growth suggest that they were not a major obstacle for growth. The fact that trade was considerably more hindered during the period 1900–49, than during the preceding fifty years and GDP figures were nonetheless twice as fast, substantiates this idea further. [659]

Another policy error consisted in allocating many resources for the production of weapons. For centuries, most economists and policy makers in all nations of the world have disapproved of investments in arms because the general population could not consume those goods. However, if producing arms had been a major hindrance for growth, it becomes impossible to explain the events of the years 1900–49 and the events of the preceding fifty years. The second half of the 19th century witnessed a gigantic increase in the share of Japan's resources used to produce armaments. However, GDP figures went up sharply. During the following fifty years, the share of overall resources invested in weapons almost doubled, but economic growth almost doubled in speed. During 1800–49, less than 1% of GDP was spent on defense. In 1850–99, it was 6% and from 1900–49 the share rose to 12%. The respective GDP figures were 0.2%, 2.4%, and 4.5%.

If investment in weapons would be harmful for the economy, then it should have been the first half of the 19th century the period with the fastest economic growth and the years 1900–49, the period with the worst performance. That was not so. Economic growth was approximately twenty-two times faster during 1900–49 than a century earlier.

History suggests that a better economic performance had been attained if the resources that went into the armories had been invested in civilian factories. Had they gone into any other sector, much suggests the economic performance had been considerably inferior.

---

658 Ibid., p. 130, 152.
659 Ibid., p. 128, 129

This last is precisely what took place during the first half of the 19th century and the preceding centuries. During these periods, the share of the country's resources invested in arms was insignificant and policy makers allocated practically all of the remaining resources to primary activities, services, and construction. Civilian manufacturing received practically nothing and the economy remained almost perennially in stagnation. In the decades following the end of World War II, Japan attained much faster GDP rates than during any previous period and it did it while investing practically nothing in weapons but massively in civilian manufacturing. [660]

Much suggests that during the first half of the 20th century, Japanese policy makers committed other errors. Even though they had largely renounced the policy of making direct investments, there were still a few enterprises that were created and managed by the state, and several others that were not privatized. As time went on, privatization moved forward and the share of GDP resulting from state companies progressively shrunk. However, by 1949 and there were still many state firms. [661]

In this period, the economy was also more regulated than ever before and the vast majority of these regulations seem to have been harmful to the economy (in particular during the 1930s and 1940s). The government decreed a large amount of controls on wages and prices. Some of these controls were made to channel more resources into the production of weapons and related fields and others were done to control inflation. The history of Japan and of numerous other countries suggests that the first goal would have been better achieved by raising the level of fiscal, financial, and non-financial incentives. The second goal, by establishing an independent Central Bank whose priority had been the maintenance of low inflation. [662]

The 1930s and the 1940s were also periods in which state borrowing increased considerably and public sector debt rose to high levels. This was also a measure that was not in the best interest of the economy for history shows that healthy public finances are conducive to a better economic performance. However, the fact is that budget deficits did not preclude fast economic growth.

The evidence suggests that unhealthy public finances and controls on wages and prices are not a significant obstacle for growth. An economy is better managed without these distortions, but if they are present, their effect is only marginally negative. So long the state supplies ample support to manufacturing, rapid growth is assured.

The 1950s and 1960s corroborate the thesis that these distortions were totally unnecessary. During these decades, the budget was largely balanced, government debt was considerably lower, and controls on prices and wages were far below the preceding two decades. GDP rates were not only faster than in 1930–49, but also faster than in all of Japan's history. The period 1950–69 was as well characterized by the most decisive factory promotion efforts in all of the archipelago's history. Economic growth in 1950–69 was of 10% per year while in the 1930–49 it was of just 4%. [663]

660 Tanaka, Heizo: *Contemporary Japanese Economy and Economy Policy*, p. 5; Madison, Angus: *The World Economy: A Millennial Perspective.*
661 Allen: Ibid., p. 127, 136.
662 Levine & Kawada: Ibid., p. 34.
663 "More of the Same", *Far Eastern Economic Review*, 5 October 1995, p. 88.

During the first half of the 20th century, the government continued to worry about a food shortage due to the decreasing share of overall investment that was allocated to agriculture. However, reality ended up moving in exactly the opposite direction. As the share that agriculture received fell and the share of manufacturing rose, the per capita supply of food progressively increased. It was not just that more and better tractors delivered a faster rate of farm output, but food-processing factories also diminished waste. Production of canned food rose rapidly.

Fishing, mining, and forestry made as well unprecedented progress during this period, coinciding with the highest levels of factory subsidization up to that date. There was an unprecedented production of fishing vessels, mining machinery, and forestry equipment. [664]

Trade also grew faster than ever before. The rapid expansion of manufacturing delivered more factory goods and more primary goods that enlarged the availability of tradable goods. A stronger support of the sector also made possible more ships, trains, and motor trucks that vastly increased the possibilities for transporting goods. Motor vehicles debuted during this half century and made a significant contribution to the expansion of domestic trade. More and superior construction tools and machines also made possible more and superior works of infrastructure.

Services and construction experienced a faster pace of development than formerly and this also paralleled an unprecedented production of service-related and construction-related manufactures. Without these factory goods, service and construction activities were not feasible.

The unprecedented economic growth of Japan during 1900–49 and the fact that it grew faster than all other nations in the world, drove many economists and policy makers to speculate about the causes of such a phenomenon.

It was argued that investments in education and infrastructure had made possible the faster economic growth. There was indeed much investment in these fields, but if education and infrastructure were causally responsible for growth, then a long-term cross-country correlation should exist. During that same period, the US had a better-educated workforce and a superior infrastructure, but it nonetheless attained slower GDP figures. If we add to that the fact that the US regulated its economy less, and that it spent significantly less on weapons, then accepted economic wisdom cannot explain why its performance was lower than Japan's. [665]

By the 1990s, Japan had made major progress on both counts. By then, it possessed the best-educated workforce among developed countries and had one of the best infrastructure systems in the world. However, it attained low rates of economic growth. On top of that, the government made large investments in infrastructure and education in an effort to stimulate the economy out an almost stagnant situation, but the GDP figures refused to show an improvement, averaging just 1.5% per year. A similar situation took place during the 1920s. In order to reactivate the economy, the government invested abundantly in harbors, highways, bridges, housing, and schools. Not only did growth remained slow, but in 1929 the economy plunged into the worst recession in Japan's history. [666]

---

664 Allen: Ibid., p. 116, 118.
665 *The Cambridge History of Japan Vol. 6*, p. 402–410, 461, 465, 490.
666 "Japan", *Businessweek International*, 29 August 1994, p. 23.

Some asserted that Japan's superior performance in 1900–49, resided not so much on the large expenditures in education, but on them having been concentrated on engineering and natural sciences, which had more direct linkages to production. This was indeed a particularity of Japan relative to the West, but the parallelism again breaks down in the long term. By the 1990s, the country had a workforce which had continued to be fundamentally educated on matters of engineering and natural sciences, but that did not save the country from enduring a very slow rate of economic growth. [667]

Another hypothesis stated that Confucian values, which preached discipline and hard work, were largely responsible for the rapid growth. This couldn't have either been a major causal factor because the Confucian values had also been present during practically all of the preceding history, and up to the mid-19th century they delivered absolutely no growth. It is also hard to explain why the same Confucian values delivered a rate of growth during the second half of the 19th century which was only approximately half as fast as that of 1900–49. The above is even harder to understand when it is taken in consideration that Confucianism was less strictly followed during the first half of the 20th century than before.

Others claimed that population growth was largely responsible for the acceleration of the GDP figures. Population did as a matter of fact grow much faster than ever before. While during the period 1850–99, it grew by about 0.8% annually, in the following fifty years the rate was of 1.3%. The correlation however ends there, because the traditional argument of population is that it increases demand and under those circumstances, one would expect a rate that was faster or similar than GDP. GDP, however, grew three times faster (about 4.5%). It is also worth noting that during the second half of the 20th century, the rate of population slowed down to a rate of just 0.9% and in spite of that, the economy accelerated considerably. [668]

Many economists and policy makers saw trade and more particularly exports as fundamentally responsible for the acceleration of economic growth. Trade indeed grew much faster than ever before in the years 1900–49 and it also grew at a rate that was similar to that of GDP. Although there was an apparent correlation, at moments the parallelism was not maintained. During the 1930s, trade grew considerably slower than GDP, indicating that it was not the prime cause. It is also worth noting that during 1937–41, trade contracted while the economy experienced a noticeable acceleration. The level of factory subsidization and the rate of factory output nonetheless, correlated at all times with the GDP figures.

Japan's exports up to the mid-20th century, were largely limited to textiles and a few other goods like ships, iron, and machine tools. These happened to be the most heavily subsidized civilian fields. During the second half of the 20th century, Japan's exports diversified dramatically to include practically all fields of civilian manufacturing and this coincided with an across the board support for all civilian fields. The evidence suggests that exports were the result of the support the state supplied to manufacturing and were therefore not the cause of growth. [669]

By 1900, the share of agriculture in the economy had shrunken considerably and during the following fifty years it contracted much more. It became therefore increasingly hard to

---

667 Morishima: Ibid., p. 135, 52.

668 Tabb, William: *The Postwar Japanese System*, p. 139–141; Sabillon: Ibid., p. 112; Madison, Angus: *The World Economy: Historical Statistics*.

669 Vie: Ibid., p. 29.

argue that this domain was the propeller of growth. However, during this period farming grew faster than ever before and some still found that this domain could have been responsible for the acceleration of the economy. Farm output expanded by about 1.7% annually, but such a rate was only approximately one third as fast as that of GDP. For agriculture to have delivered a pulling effect on the rest of the economy, logic demands that it should have grown at a faster pace than GDP. That was not the case. [670]

Another blow to the farm argument is the situation of the 1920s. Tokyo significantly enlarged farm subsidies to agriculture during this decade, in an effort to reactivate the economy. This was actually the domain that received the most support and in spite of that, the economy refused to come out of a quasi stagnation. During the depression (1929–31), farm relief increased still more but the economy experienced negative figures.[671]

Living conditions of the Japanese improved in an unprecedented way during the years 1900–49. Life expectancy, working conditions, health, education, nutrition, housing, liberty, the rule of law, and the emancipation of women all progressed. A rapid creation of wealth moved the society beyond survival concerns.[672]

China

Chaos and Weak Government

During the first half of the 20th century, China's economy accelerated, but it was starting from a very low rate. There was little subsidization of factories and very slow rates of manufacturing output. During 1900–49, manufacturing expanded by about 0.6% annually and GDP by about 0.5%. (See tables at the end of the book.)[673]

During this period China had a number of short-lived governments, none of which gave significant support to factories. At times, central government even disappeared and subsidies for the sector did likewise. Several foreign governments with interests in China did offer some support. Japan was particularly responsible for the relatively rapid growth of manufacturing in Manchuria and Western nations spurred the growth of factories along the coast.[674]

The humiliation that China endured at the hands of Japan in the war of 1894–95 delivered some changes, in particular on matters referring to manufacturing. It finally convinced the Chinese government to invest at least somewhat in armories. It also forced Beijing to allow the establishment of factories in the numerous treaty ports and land concessions which foreign nations had wrested from China. By the early 20th century, as many as 37 treaty ports such as Hong Kong, Shanghai, Tsingtao, and Tientsin were in the hands of foreign nations. There were also about half a dozen foreign leased areas that were considerably larger than the treaty ports.[675]

---

670 Bremond, Chalaye & Loeb: Ibid., p. 12.

671 Allen: Ibid., p. 100, 128, 156.

672 "The Economics of Aging", *The Economist*, 27 January 1996, p. 13.

673 Sabillon: Ibid., p. 111; *Madison, Angus: Chinese Economic Performance in the Long Run*; Madison, Angus: *The World Economy: Historical Statistics*.

674 Howe, Christopher: *China's Economy*.

675 Fairbank; John: *China—A New History*, p. 202.

The foreign nations that possessed these concessions supplied a number of incentives to the private sector manufactures of their respective countries so that they would invest in those territories. Some state factories were also created. Their main economic goal was to sell to the Chinese market. During those years, the majority of the foreign factories produced textiles because this was the good in the highest demand.

In the first three decades, as more of these territorial concessions were granted and more subsidies were provided, there was an accelerating rate of manufacturing output and an accelerating rate of GDP. This trend was reversed in the 1940s.[676]

Support from the Chinese government fluctuated. During the first decade of the 20th century, subsidies for the production of weapons and railroad goods increased. It was actually only after 1895 that railroads began to be built. Many of the trains that were put in circulation were fabricated in China. Most of the railroads built in those years were the work of foreigners in their concessions and some of the goods that made them possible were fabricated within the concessions.

During 1900–09, manufacturing averaged about 0.4% annually and GDP about 0.3%.[677] China continued to be governed by the Manchus and they adhered to the belief that a rapid development of manufacturing would contribute to their downfall. They thus only reluctantly acquiesced to a small increase in the level of support. Many in the Manchu Court argued that the backwardness of China was the result of the decay of traditional Chinese culture, and that modernization would bring further decay.[678]

In 1900, famine, social unrest, and political controversy culminated in the Boxer Rebellion, which claimed the lives of numerous foreigners. Western powers sent troops and the rebellion was rapidly crushed. Again, it became evident that the quantity and technical sophistication of armaments determined the outcome in the battlefield.

Beijing was forced to pay reparations to the victors. Many have argued that these reparations on top of those paid to Japan as a result of the war of 1895 inhibited larger investments in manufacturing. From 1896 to 1911, China repaid a sum that was three times larger than the total foreign and Chinese capital invested in factories. However, if paying large war reparations inhibited investments in manufacturing, Germany should have been unable to invest in that sector during the post-World War I and post-World War II years. On both occasions Germany's reparations were much larger than China's as a share of GDP. Germany, however, attained levels of investment in manufacturing, which were exponentially higher than those of China. GDP figures were also exponentially faster.[679]

The indemnities of the Boxer war continued to be paid until the 1940s, but most of the victorious states placed the money at China's disposal for educational purposes. On top of that, they largely diminished over time. However, at no moment during 1900–49 did China attained high levels of investment or state support manufacturing.[680]

There were no state banks to channel funds to manufacturing and there was no policy to induce private banks to lend a significant share of their assets to manufacturing. Finan-

676 Rostow, Walt: *The World Economy*, p. 522.
677 Rawski, Thomas: *Economic Growth in Pre-War China*, p. 208; Sabillon: Ibid.; Madison, Angus: *The World Economy: Historical Statistics*.
678 Harding, Harry: *China's Second Revolution*, p. 21.
679 Cowan, C. D. (ed): *The Economic Development of China and Japan*, p. 101.
680 Eberhard, Wolfram: *A History of China*, p. 311.

cial and non-financial incentives were barely noticeable and taxation on manufacturing was very high once central, provincial, and local taxes were added. There were several "buy Chinese" campaigns and boycotts against foreign goods, but they were ineffective in stimulating domestic factory production.[681]

The Manchus were overthrown in 1911. The first elected government in China's history took office in 1912. During the short life of this government, factory subsidies for trains, weapons, and civilian manufactures rose a little. By 1916, however, the first presidential government came to an end and central government dissolved. Localized wars proliferated in the provinces. Support for manufacturing plummeted to almost nothing. In 1927, Chiang Kai-shek consolidated power over all of China but in the early 1930s the central government broke down again and was not re-established until 1949.[682]

Beijing's decreased support for the sector since 1916 was worsened by World War I, which led to a drop in Western investment. This loss subsidies would have easily translated into a large contraction of manufacturing had it not been for the Japanese. The Japanese began to invest in northeast China in 1895 and with their triumph over Russia in 1905 they took over Russia's zones of influence and began to invest even more. The decrease of Western production in the treaty ports during World War I was seen by Tokyo as a window of opportunity to supplant Western products. Tokyo supplied more incentives to Japanese entrepreneurs, who installed factories in the northeast coastal regions during the 1910s. This prevented the stagnation or contraction of factory output nationwide.[683]

From the start, Japan had a much larger interest in promoting factory production in China than Western nations. The West was mainly interested in indirect exports, while Japan was aiming to take over large territories. Tokyo was also more interested than the West in increasing its sales in China.

Beijing's subsidization varied throughout the 1910s, but on average it was similar as in the preceding decade. Foreign governments increased their subsidies slightly, so that there was a small overall rise in support. Average annual manufacturing output during the 1910s was about 0.7% and GDP expanded by about 0.5%.[684]

During the first decade of the 20th century, the fastest growing region of China was the coast, the area receiving the largest factory subsidies. In the 1910s, however, the fastest growing region was Manchuria, the area where incentives for manufacturing were more abundant.[685]

During most of the 1920s, China was plagued by small-scale and localized wars which did not justify large investments in weapons. When central government was re-established in 1927, modernists hoped that Beijing would allocate significant resources for weapons, trains, and other manufacturing fields, but it did not do so. Chiang Kai-shek and the Nationalist leadership thought that it was better to invest in the service side of the military apparatus, such as recruiting and training more soldiers. They allotted funds for armaments, but bought them from foreign nations. There was nonetheless some investment in weapons and trains, but nothing that could be slightly comparable to the level of subsidization in

---

681 Hou, Chi-ming: *Foreign Investment and Economic Development in China 1840–1937*, p. 133, 149, 150.
682 Bergere, M. Bianco, L. & Domes, J.: *La Chine au XXe Siecle*, p. 1.
683 Rostow: Ibid., p. 522–524.
684 Rawski: Ibid., p. 70–72; Sabillon: Ibid.
685 Gray, Jack: *Rebellions and Revolutions*, p. 154, 166, 167, 2.

Japan. Only approximately 5% of the few foreign loans that China took during this and the preceding decades were for the promotion of manufacturing.[686]

While the level of domestic support for manufacturing remained unchanged, support from foreign governments rose significantly. Western foreign investment rose just by a little in the Treaty ports, but Japanese investment rose by a large margin. After the conquest of the Korean Peninsula, Japan's military developed a large interest in the neighboring territory of Manchuria. This territory was already under Japanese influence. Tokyo made large investments in light manufacturing fields in an effort to economically colonize this region. The Japanese also allocated more funds for the fabrication of metals, rails, and locomotives in order to have more transport possibilities.

In the 1920s, foreign direct investment was much higher than formerly but still only a small share, approximately 15%, financed factory production — an increase, but still far short of the support given in Western countries. Overall, manufacturing grew by about 1.2% annually and GDP by about 0.9%.[687]

During this decade, Manchuria again experienced the fastest rates of economic growth. The rest of the coastal region attained the second fastest GDP rates while the interior continued to be the economic laggard. This matched the pattern of factory subsidization. Manchuria, which had systematically lingered behind other regions of China up to the late 19th century, was by the late 1920s at the lead. By then, its GDP per capita was about 15% higher than the rest of China. By then, its per capita output of manufactures was also higher than the national average.[688]

During this half century, the fastest rates of growth were experienced in the 1930s, the decade with the largest factory subsidies. The decade started with a noticeable increase in the production of armaments and railroad goods by the Kuomintang (KMT) government in Beijing. However, as the decade progressed, such production diminished as several zones fell into communist hands. Western foreign direct investment did not increase during the 1930s, as a result of the Depression in the West, and there were even some outflows of foreign capital. Japanese investment, however, increased dramatically. In 1931, Tokyo launched a large-scale invasion of Manchuria and began to invest unprecedented sums in that territory, reaching investment levels similar to the ones in Japan.[689]

The bulk of investment was in heavy manufacturing fields such as iron, steel, rails, locomotives, weapons, chemicals, and machine tools. While in Japan shipbuilding received the largest subsidies, in Manchuria the priority was given to railroad goods. By 1936, about 40% of railways in China were in Manchuria.

Not satisfied with its conquest of Manchuria, Tokyo decided in 1937 to subdue the rest of China. The Japanese possessed more arms and more technologically advanced arms. Despite the vast numerical superiority of Chinese forces, the Japanese easily defeated them. Armaments seemed to be the deciding factor at the battlefield.

The conquest of the rest of China led Tokyo to decree even more support for manufacturing in Manchuria and a little in the rest of China. Overall this meant a significant rise in support for the country as a whole during the 1930s. That was paralleled by a very large rise

686 Rawski: Ibid., p. 9, 245.
687 Howe: Ibid., p. xxii; Madison, Angus: *The World Economy: Historical Statistics.*
688 Rostow: Ibid., p. 525.
689 Perkins, Dwight (ed): *China's Modern Economy in Historical Perspective*, p. 204–213.

in the rate of factory output and GDP. Manufacturing averaged about 2.9% and GDP about 2.1% [690]

Manchuria again had the strongest support and was the fastest growing region. In the rest of China, subsidies only barely increased and manufacturing output and GDP went up in parallel. By 1939, the development gap between Manchuria and the rest of China had considerably widened and the per capita product of this region was about two thirds higher than the national average.

In 1940, a pro-Japanese government was established in Nanking while the Nationalists and the Communists retreated to the interior. Japan continued to strongly promote manufacturing during the early 1940s, in Manchuria, but soon after, things changed. After a series of defeats on the battlefield and with the economic embargo of the Allies, it became impossible to fabricate much in Japan, much less abroad. Production in Manchuria was paralyzed well before the end of the war.

Factory output began to contract since 1943. At the very end of the war, the Soviets invaded Manchuria and removed much of the machinery and equipment from the mostly abandoned and paralyzed Japanese factories and took them to the Soviet Union. This delivered a further blow to factory production.

In the rest of the country the situation was even worse. In the zones the Nationalists and Communists controlled, there was no enthusiastic support for manufacturing during the first half of this decade and output remained almost completely stagnant. After the Japanese withdrew from China in 1945, the Allies handed power to the Nationalists.

Vast resources were wasted through corruption. To make matters worse, inflation skyrocketed. On top of that, the Japanese occupation considerably disturbed production in the Treaty Ports that it overran. Had the Japanese not invaded, factory output would have nonetheless contracted in the Western concessions because World War II forced the West to concentrate its resources in Europe. It is also worth noting that in 1943 port treaty concessions were abolished and with the exception of Hong Kong and Macao, foreign investment in all the others largely vanished.[691]

During the 1940s, the steep drop of support in Manchuria, the maintenance of very low levels of subsidies in the rest of China, and the noticeable drop in support in the Treaty Ports, coincided with negative factory figures. China experienced during this decade, the worst recession in its history. Manufacturing contracted by about -2.3% annually and GDP by about -1.4%.[692]

The Effects of Manufacturing

By 1949, China was one of the least developed countries in Asia and it was also considerably behind Western countries. This ran in parallel with Beijing's century long weaker promotion of manufacturing relative to most of Asia. It also coincided with centuries of smaller factory subsidies than those supplied in the West. By then, only about 1% of China's workforce labored in factories, while in Western countries the share was about one third.[693]

---

690 Rawski: Ibid., p. 209, 272, 280, 175; Madison, Angus: *Chinese Economic Performance in the Long Run.*
691 Bergere, Bianco & Domes: Ibid., p. II, III.
692 Perkins (ed): Ibid., p. 132, 27; Madison, Angus: *The World Economy: Historical Statistics.*
693 Howe: Ibid., p. xxii, xxi.

During 1900–49, the development of technology was very slow. During this period, China imported all of the technology it used. In the first four decades of the 20th century, the pace of technological imports progressively accelerated and this coincided with a progressive increase in the level of factory subsidization.

Manufacturing contracted in the 1940s, the only decade in which a technological reversal was seen. Less medicine and fewer books meant poorer health and less education, fewer trains and ships meant less scope to transport goods, and less farm implements meant lower agricultural productivity. As the level of technology fell, so, inevitably, did living conditions.

Technology advanced fastest in Manchuria and second fastest along the coast, in tandem with the level of manufacturing support and the rate of factory production.[694]

China did not create technology during the first half of the 20th century and the small technological development that took place was all the result of imports. However, importing technology can be done slowly, rapidly or at intermediate speeds and China imported it at a very slow pace.

History suggests that a nation can attempt to make large investments in agriculture, education, construction, and other similar activities by borrowing abundantly and raising taxes. However, if it fails to invest in manufacturing, it is soon incapable of making large investments because technology and wealth will have not expanded and it becomes therefore impossible to secure more loans or to tax more. Since only manufacturing seems capable of creating wealth, it is only when resources are abundantly allocated to this sector it that enough wealth is created to allow for even larger investments.

During this period, the rate of agriculture, mining, fishing, and forestry remained constantly low; farm implements, mining equipment, fishing gear, and forestry machines were in short supply. Farm output grew fastest in the 1930s, when the strongest factory subsidization and the fastest production of agricultural implements were seen. The other primary activities also experienced their fastest growth during this decade.[695]

In the 1940s, war, anarchy and weak government reduced support for manufacturing, and there was a large contraction of agriculture. By 1949, farm output was about two thirds lower than during the peak levels of the 1930s. Services, construction, and trade also trailed.

Manchuria, the region where primary goods, services, construction, and trade had grown fastest, and where that factory subsidies fell the most, suffered the most dramatic downturn in the 1940s.[696]

Seeking to explain the vast gap in economic performance between China and Japan, some experts have speculated that there were particular cultural traits of Chinese society that inhibited the production of factory goods. However, despite its lackluster performance in the intervening centuries, up to the 15th century China had been the world leader in this matter. Up to the 15th century, China had probably the highest per capita output of manufactures in the world and up to the 18th century, it had a higher per capita output than Japan. More recent history further proves the fallacy of this idea. First under the rule of Mao and then under Deng, China attained rates of factory output that were far superior

694 Fairbank: Ibid., p. 331–333.
695 Gray: Ibid., p. 162–164.
696 Eberhard: Ibid., p. 345.

to those of the past. They were also faster than Japan and numerous nations that up to 1949 had performed better than China. By the end of the 20th century, China even attained one of the fastest rates of factory output in the world and became the third largest producer of manufactured goods in the world. It is evident that culture did not play a major role on this matter.[697]

By 1949, China was the most populous country in the world, with about 600 million people. Some experts have theorized that this vast population somehow impeded fast economic growth. However, China is still by far the largest nation in the world and it now has one of the fastest rates of growth in the world.[698]

Others have argued that state intervention, monopolistic restrictions and innumerable regulations, curbed the economy. During 1900–49, however, central government expenditure as a share of GDP averaged just 2%, only about one fifth as much as in Japan. There were numerous monopolies, competition-hindering practices, and regulations, but there were more in Japan. Yet Japan achieved the fastest rates of growth in the world. And the region in China with the most state intervention, competition-hindering practices, and regulations was Manchuria, that same region that had the fastest growth. Market forces had even less influence in China in the second half of the 20th century; even so, the economy grew exponentially faster than in the first half of the century.[699]

Still others have asserted that low incomes and a small urban population meant little demand for non-agricultural goods and services and a very small labor force available to work in those higher value-added sectors. Of course, Japan and the Western countries had also begun from that state. However, they all managed to come out of stagnation and in all of these countries that moment coincided with the initiation of a strong factory promotion policy.

In 1950, China implemented a strong manufacturing promotion policy and finally spurted out of stagnation. Had low incomes and a high rural share of the population been an obstacle for growth, the economy should have remained stagnant. By 1949 incomes had actually fallen and the rural share of the population had risen relative to the 1930s. The depression of the 1940s drove millions of Chinese back to the land as employment and wages fell in the cities. The economy, however, grew rapidly during the 1950s.

The meager growth of 1900–49 delivered little progress. Living conditions only barely improved.

Taiwan and Korea

Japan took Taiwan from China in 1895, originally intending to use it as a source of raw materials and as a secure export market. At first, Japan fostered primary sector production and built the necessary infrastructure. Rice and sugar cane were at the center of the developmental plans of the first fifteen years as well as the construction of harbors and roads. Investment in manufacturing was minimal. Even so, this was practically the first time the

---

697 "A Lighter Shade of Red", *Far Eastern Economic Review*, 28 April 1994, p. 79; Perkins (ed): Ibid., p. 12.
698 Eberhard: Ibid., p. 284–286.
699 Rawski: Ibid., p. 2, 15, 23.

sector was promoted in the island and this was also the first time that manufacturing experienced much growth.[700]

That was paralleled by a considerable acceleration in the rate of economic growth. During the 1900s, manufacturing averaged about 1.0% annually and the economy grew by 0.7%.

By 1910, with the invasion of Korea, Japan began to change its attitude towards its colonies. The original policy of only investing the bare minimum in manufacturing and not allowing the growth of domestic factories so that they would not compete against those in Japan, began to give way to a different approach.[701]

The rising military ambitions and the easiness with which Japan conquered Taiwan and Korea made Japanese policy makers think that these two territories could become an integral part of Japan. Tokyo therefore began to transplant the policies applied in Japan and increased the level of factory subsidization in Taiwan. There were larger direct government investments and more incentives to private producers. In Japan, labor costs had rapidly risen since the late 19th century and manufacturers demanded that they be given a chance to exploit the much cheaper workforce of Taiwan. Given this situation, Tokyo saw investment in this sector as compatible with the interests of the metropolis. During the 1910s, foreign direct investment in manufacturing increased by a large amount. Manufacturing accelerated and averaged about 2.6% annually. GDP did likewise and expanded by about 1.8%.[702]

During the 1920s, the desire to further integrate the island drove Tokyo to transplant more of the policies practiced in Japan to Taiwan, and this translated into a rise in the level of subsidies for manufacturing. There was more investment and it mostly flowed into textiles, copper smelting, oil refining, and shipbuilding. Tokyo also made some direct investments in fields such as electricity generation and rail production. The overall output of manufacturing rose noticeably and averaged about 3.3%, while GDP grew by about 2.3%.

In the 1930s, Tokyo's aggressive military campaign of conquest over China led Japanese policy makers to use Taiwan as a supplier of weapons-related goods. There was also a continuation of the policy of utilizing the island as a means to reduce costs of labor-intensive manufacturing and of fostering economic integration with Japan. Increasing further the level of support was the situation in Japan. In this decade, Tokyo promoted factories in the archipelago more enthusiastically than in the 1920s and the same was done in Taiwan. This increased level of support went hand in hand with faster factory output averaging about 4.4% annually. GDP followed along, averaging about 3.4%.

Japan continued to significantly subsidize the sector in Taiwan up to the early 1940s and there was also fast economic growth. Soon after, Japan was blockaded and attacked by the Allies, forcing a decrease in production in the archipelago and in its colonies. Japan held Taiwan until 1945 and by then, factory output had contracted by a large amount. With the defeat of Japan, the Allies devolved Taiwan to China but the political chaos prevailing in the mainland and Beijing's absence of manufacturing promotion policies, ended by delivering a regressive effect on the island. During the rest of the 1940s, factory production in Taiwan experienced a significant fall. For the whole decade, the sector contracted by about -1.8% per year and the economy shrank by about -1.0%.[703]

---

700 "Into the World", *Time*, 19 June 1995, p. 45.

701 *The Cambridge History of Japan Vol. 6*, p. 255–258.

702 Wade, Robert: *Governing the Market*, p. 74.

703 Harberger, Arnold (ed): *World Economic Growth*, p. 302–304.

Despite the depression of the 1940s, the first half of the 20th century witnessed by far the best economic performance in all of Taiwan's history up to that date. That correlated with unprecedented support for the sector. During 1900–49, manufacturing grew, averaging about 1.9% per year, and the economy expanded by about 1.4%. By the late 1940s and in spite of the contraction, Taiwan was with Manchuria the most developed region of China. These were also the areas with the highest concentration of factories.[704]

For centuries, the only developmental policy that Chinese and Taiwanese policy makers endorsed was the promotion of agriculture and other primary activities. However, up to the late 19th century, farming, fishing, mining, and forestry remained stagnant. During the first half of the 20th century on the other hand, the policies of the island did not exclusively concentrate on promoting primary production. This was the first time when resources were subtracted from the primary sector in significant amounts to increase the share for manufacturing, and this was the first time that agriculture and the other primary activities attained some descent growth. Farm output grew by about 1.0% while in the previous fifty years the figure was about 0.2%.

During this half century, living conditions in Taiwan improved more than ever before, correlating with unprecedented manufacturing subsidies.

Korea also developed quickly during 1900–49. Until the 19th century, economic growth had been almost stagnant. That ran in parallel to manufacturing suppression policies. In 1900–09, these policies were still largely in place and this sector is likely to have grown by about 0.9% annually and the economy by about 0.7%.

In 1910, Japan invaded the peninsula and although originally intended to be just a supplier of raw material, Tokyo soon after began to use it also as a manufacturing base. During the years of Japanese domination, which extended up to 1945, the promotion efforts of Tokyo concentrated fundamentally on agriculture and Korea eventually become Japan's main rice supplier. However, since the first years, there was a large amount of investment that flowed into factories by direct and indirect means and which increased over time.

Relative to the past, there was a vast amount of investment in heavy and light manufacturing. In fields like metals, shipbuilding, railroad goods, weapons, and chemicals Tokyo's intervention was more direct as many of these factories were in state hands. In light manufacturing, the colonial authorities were less interventionist and opted for providing considerable fiscal, financial, and non-financial incentives to Japanese entrepreneurs.

Support for manufacturing increased noticeably in the more than three decades of Japanese occupation and the economy took off. While up to the early 20th century manufacturing and GDP had remained almost stagnant, from 1910 to 1940 factory output averaged about 2.9% annually and GDP about 2.2%.[705]

During this half century period, the 1930s witnessed the strongest support of the sector, coalescing with the fastest economic growth. The 1940s witnessed the weakest support, and this was accompanied by the slowest GDP figures. In this decade, factory output and GDP stagnated. This coincided with years of support and years of an absence of it, which largely neutralized each other.

The motivations pushing Tokyo to promote manufacturing in Korea were the same as in Taiwan and Manchuria. They included economic integration with the archipelago, a source

704 Wade: Ibid., p. 74; Sabillon: Ibid., p. 114.
705 *The Cambridge History of Japan Vol.* 6, p. 256–258.

of cheap labor, and a nearby base for armament production for its armies in Korea and in China.

During the first half of the 20th century, technology expanded in the peninsula. In Taiwan, technology was also developing faster. In both cases, the fastest growth of technology occurred during the 1930s, correlating with the moment of larger factory subsidies.

As with Taiwan, this was the first period in the peninsula's history in which macroeconomic policies had not exclusively concentrated on promoting agriculture and other primary activities. That correlated with the first time when agriculture, mining, forestry, and fishing grew at a pace which was not sclerotic.

During 1900–49, manufacturing in Korea grew by about 2.0% per year, GDP by about 1.5%, and agriculture by about 1.1%. In the preceding fifty years, the respective figures were less than half as fast. There was an unprecedented proliferation of farm machines, mining implements, fishing boats, and forestry equipment. The evidence suggests that these factory goods allowed for the spurt of primary production. [706]

Singapore and Hong Kong

During the first half of the 20th century in Singapore, the share of resources allocated to manufacturing increased considerably and that was accompanied by faster economic growth. Several factors were behind that situation. On the one hand, London's mercantilist vision of the world decreased; on the other hand, the output of Malaysian primary goods rose notably. At the same time, Japanese exports to Southeast Asia were increasing, and in response Britain had to step up its export promotion efforts.

Because London was less against the development of manufacturing in its colonies there were more subsidies for the manufacturing fields that were previously promoted as well as significant incentives for new fields such as processed oil and rubber. There was much support for the processing of rubber because Malaysia became a major world producer of rubber trees. During the inter-war period, Singapore even became the world's main center for re-milling rubber. Malaysia also became a major producer of oil. Incentives were thus supplied to oil refineries so that they would establish operations in the island. Tin processing factories also received larger subsidies than formerly.

The rapidly rising Japanese competition in numerous other fields persuaded the authorities to provide more generous to factory producers. Since the Japanese were particularly strong in heavy manufacturing, even these fields received much support. Automobile production and shipbuilding became considerable subsidies during these years. Driven by an attractive package of incentives, in 1926 the Ford Motor Company established an automobile assembly plant in Singapore. Most of the increased factory output was the result of foreign direct investment although domestic entrepreneurs also had access to the subsidies. [707]

The considerable increase in state factory promotion efforts in 1900–49 coincided with a considerable acceleration in the rate of factory output, which averaged about 4.4% annually. The economy expanded by about 3.5%.

---

706 Sabillon: Ibid., p. 113.
707 Huff, W. G.: *The Economic Growth of Singapore*, p. 14, 22, 31, 33, 208, 214.

This was a faster rate than that of several Western countries. That correlated with Singapore's more attractive fiscal, financial, and non-financial incentives than those of Western nations.[708]

Hong Kong went through a similar experience during the first half of the 20th century. Factory output grew faster than in the preceding fifty years and it also grew as fast as in the West.

With the elimination of China's restrictions on factory production in 1895, Britain was able to subsidize this sector as much as it wanted. The colonial government offered more incentives and production began to grow faster. By then, Japan was already a strong exporter and the prime target of its exports was China. In the decades that followed, Japan increased even more its exports and not only did it have much lower transport costs than Britain, but also lower labor costs. To confront this competition, Britain felt forced to significantly increase subsidies to the producers of the goods that Japan exported. Textiles received the largest subsidies, and were Japan's main export. The producers of ships received also many incentives because this was another of Japan's main exports. This was shadowed by an exponential increase in the production of textiles, ships, and several other goods.

A series of events also ended up by having a significant effect on manufacturing production. World War I cut significantly the flow of imports from the West and the colonial government gave large subsidies to those who would produce domestically those goods. There was also the Japanese invasion of China in 1937 that drove many Cantonese factories to migrate to Hong Kong. However, in December 1941 the Japanese took over the colony and during their occupation, factory production came to a halt. That coincided with an economic contraction.

The end of World War II in 1945 and the chaos that reigned in China due to the civil war led to a huge wave of emigration to the colony. By 1945, the population of Hong Kong was about 600,000, but by 1949 twice as many (about 1.3 million refugees) had migrated to the colony. The bulk of them arrived in 1948–49. A few of these refugees were manufacturers, who took with them their machinery and equipment. However, the vast majority barely had a few personal belongings.

To employ this vast mass of people that threatened the stability of the territory, the colonial government hugely increased the subsidies to the producers of labor-intensive factory goods. Government expenditure increased significantly, but the colonial authorizes mostly shifted resources from infrastructure and other fields towards the factories in domains such as textiles and apparel. Up until then the majority of the small budget had been used to finance infrastructure. Manufacturing immediately began to grow at a phenomenal pace and the economy did likewise. In 1948–49, factory output grew by about 28% annually and the economy by about 23%.[709]

The first half of the 20th century was therefore characterized by a very large increase in the factory promotion efforts of the colonial authorities. That was paralleled by a large acceleration in the rate of factory output and of the economy. Manufacturing averaged about 4.0% annually and GDP about 3.3%. (See tables at the end of the book.)[710]

---

708 Ibid., p. 31, 275.
709 Hopkins, Keith (ed): *Hong Kong—The Industrial Colony*, p. 1, 7, 25, 247.
710 Sabillon: Ibid., p. 158, 112.

The strong acceleration again took place without any noticeable shift of resources from agriculture to manufacturing. Even though the overall wealth of the colony was extremely low by the late 19th century and the primary sector was practically non-existent, the abundant incentives succeeded in attracting an abundance of capital from the rest of the world. It also succeeded in transferring resources from services, which by then was by far the largest sector of the economy, to the factories.

Agriculture dominated the economy in the vast majority of nations that attained fast manufacturing output since the 19th century. Because of its large size, it seemed as if it was determinant for the development of the other sectors. A careful analysis of the historical evidence suggests that such a causality relationship never took place.

The case of Hong Kong and Singapore suggest that the initial development of manufacturing is not dependent on a large primary sector that generates first a surplus. During the first half of the 20th century, these two British colonies attained rates of factory output that were faster or similar than those of Western countries notwithstanding their minuscule primary sectors.

The case of Hong Kong and Singapore shows that manufacturing and economic growth are perfectly possible while practicing free trade; there is no causal link.

Hong Kong and Singapore suggest that foreign ownership does not have negative effects. Since the birth of these two British enclaves, foreign companies accounted for the majority of output. Many locals and foreign analysts condemned such a situation arguing that it led to political and economic dependence. The political dependence was inevitable so long they were colonies, but in 1959 Singapore gained independence. Since the preceding economic results had been positive, the independent governments did not repudiate the existing situation and continued to abundantly promote foreign investment. By the 2000s, about 60% of Singaporean enterprises were in foreign hands and the inhabitants had better living conditions than 99% of the countries of the world. The island also had higher per capita incomes than 90% of Western nations and Singapore had the lowest level of crime in the world. It was also the cleanest country in the world.

The case of Hong Kong is similar but not quite because Britain only relinquished the territory in 1997, but did not grant independence. Instead, it handed it over to China. Despite the perennial foreign majority ownership of production, by the 2000s it was wealthier than Japan and practically all European countries.

The evidence suggests that foreign ownership does not conspire against progress.

CHAPTER 9. THE FIRST HALF OF THE 20TH CENTURY IN GERMANY AND RUSSIA

Germany

1900–1919

German performance during the first half of the 20th century was similar to the previous fifty years. The GDP continued to expand on average by about 3.6% annually. The level of manufacturing subsidization remained about the same and factory output rates averaged about 4.7%.[711]

Technology and productivity continued to grow at a pace similar to the previous half century. Further suggesting a causal link, the many fluctuations of technology and productivity during this period moved in tandem with the varying levels of factory subsidization. When support was strong, GDP grew fast. When it was weak, its pace was slow.

The German unification effected in 1871 was still being consolidated at the turn of the century. Some separatist demands were still heard, and the effort to strengthen ties by building railroads was therefore continued. However, the pressure was easing and support for this field in the 1900s was not as strong as formerly.

The export-promotion and import-substitution policies continued, driven by national security concerns.[712] There was still a belief that a major war was inevitable. All the European powers invested abundantly in the fabrication of weapons, and the Germans were no laggards in this. Since 1896, the imperialist drive, in particular over Africa, had increased and the armies of European colonizers were on several occasions very close to outright confron-

---

711 Sabillon, Carlos: *World Economic Historical Statistics*, p. 182; Fogel, Robert William: *The Escape from Hunger and Premature Death, 1700–2100: Europe, America and the Third World*; Madison, Angus: *Monitoring the World Economy 1820–1992.*

712 Gaxotte, Pierre: *Histoire de l'Allemagne*, p. 564–579.

---

tation because of territorial disputes. The weapons intended to fight wars in Europe were also used to suppress rebellion in the conquered territories. In 1904, the German army liquidated about 80,000 Africans from the Guerrero tribe in what would later become Namibia. To further Germany's goal of acquiring large overseas territories, the government invested heavily in shipbuilding.

Tensions were rising. In 1907, a Triple Alliance between Britain, France, and Russia threatened Germany, and in 1908 Austria took over Bosnia–Herzegovina.[713]

During the first decade of the 20th century, in response to the arms race, imperialism, geopolitical unification, and balance of payment concerns, the German government significantly subsidized manufacturing. Although armament and ship production grew faster than in the preceding decade and the promotion of exports witnessed a slight increase, train subsidies fell. Train production had been the largest factory field in the previous decades. The end result was a rate of factory output that, although relatively strong, was nonetheless slower than the one of the preceding decade. GDP moved in tandem. During the 1900s, manufacturing averaged about 4.5% and GDP about 3.8% annually.[714]

By then, many policy makers had come to believe that manufacturing was very important for the economy, but most also thought that state support for manufacturing would have negative political effects that could threaten their interests. Up to the end of World War I, Germany was governed by the aristocracy, the bourgeoisie, and the military. Workers had practically no say in policy making. However, demands from manufacturing workers had been rapidly on the rise since the mid-19th century. The aristocracy feared that the working class wanted to eliminate its political and economic privileges. The bourgeoisie feared that the rising demands of workers would reduce its profits and perhaps even lead to financial ruin. The military was concerned that social conflict would drive the nation towards a civil war, leaving the country weak and exposed to an attack from a foreign power. The aristocracy, the bourgeoisie, and the military decided to keep a lid on the problem by limiting the development of this sector.[715]

The 1910s was an odd and convoluted decade. During the first years, several factors drove Berlin to support manufacturing while other factors impeded them from supplying much more. Tensions in the continent, such as the war of 1912 in the Balkans, reminded Germany and the other powers in Europe that a large-scale war could erupt at any moment and suggested that large investments in weapons were needed. On the other hand, the fear of a rise in labor demands put a brake on manufacturing investments. This coincided with a similar rate of factory output and GDP in 1910–12 as during the preceding decade.[716]

In 1913, factory production contracted, with textiles, electrical goods, and chemicals the most affected. The economy contracted. Unemployment more than doubled and many feared that the recession would be a prolonged one. Many German businessmen argued that the recession could be overcome if Germany annexed parts of Belgium and France, thus securing a supply of cheap raw materials. The recession exacerbated the belief in Germany that war was inevitable, and in June of 1914 the heir to the throne of Austria was assassi-

---

713 Kitchen, Martin: *The Political Economy of Germany 1815–1914*, p. 222–251.
714 Berghahn, V.: *Modern Germany*, p. 33.
715 Ibid., p. 30, 39.
716 Gaxotte: Ibid., p. 564, p. 580–584.

nated in Sarajevo. Austria declared war on Serbia and this led to a chain reaction of troop mobilization and war declarations by Russia, France, Germany, and Britain.[717]

Germany could have invested far more in weapons during the preceding decades but their victory over France in 1871 had been so complete that they were lulled into a sense of security.

Almost as soon as the war of 1870–71 ended, German generals elaborated detailed plans for a future conflict with France, which presented Germany as the winner. However, the battle of the Marne in September of 1914 put an end to Germany's advance into France. From then until the end of hostilities, the situation was largely static and never moved more than a few kilometers.[718]

Germany had to fight on several fronts, against the Russians in the East, against the French in the West, against the British at sea, and eventually against the Americans, but it is also true that it had allies who shared part of the fighting burden. It is also true that Russia rapidly collapsed. The US entered the war only at the very end.

From the start, Germany concentrated the bulk of its forces in the western front against France — and from the start, it found itself confronted by a similar amount of weapons employing a similar level of technology. France had almost as many tanks and other artillery pieces as Germany, as well as mines, flame throwers, poison gas, fighter planes, barbed wire, and munitions. It would seem as if, under those circumstances, it did not matter how shrewd and inventive were the German plans for the war. The situation remained static.

At sea, where again both sides were similarly equipped, the situation remained also static. At the start of the war, Germany had about the same level of warship technology as Britain, but Britain had a larger number of vessels and together with those of France they successfully blockaded Germany. On the other hand, Germany had a completely new weapon which surprised everybody and gave her a certain advantage at sea. The submarine revolutionized sea warfare. However, although it permitted the destruction of a large amount of the Allied Navy and merchant fleet, it never managed to break the maritime blockade and it eventually drove the Americans to enter the war.[719]

The outbreak of hostilities immediately drove much larger investments in weapons and related factory goods. Government expenditure and incentives for numerous civilian factory fields were reduced, but the increased investments in arms and related goods were so large that overall manufacturing production increased considerably. The economy immediately spurted out of recession. The war did not go well for Germany from the start, so Berlin allocated a growing share of the country's resources for armament production, culminating in mid-1916 when a total mobilization of the nation's resources was ordained.[720]

Regulations progressively increased and eventually the economy became almost centrally planned. The very strong support for armament production coincided with a very rapid growth of this sector. This in its turn was mirrored by fast economic growth that accelerated still more in 1916. The economy grew so fast that unemployment, which stood at about 5% in 1913, fell to about 1% the following year; and underemployment, which was very high among the young, women, and the old, rapidly diminished. Labor shortages were felt from

717 Kitchen: Ibid., p. 264–278.
718 Bramsted, Ernest: *Germany*, p. 165.
719 Ibid., p. 166, 123.
720 Berghahn: Ibid., p. 47–50, 266, 68.

the first year of the war and growing numbers of housewives, retirees, and youngsters were recruited into the factories. The economy grew so fast that the domestic pool of under-employed was eventually exhausted and foreign workers were imported. Thousands of Belgian and Polish workers were drafted into the factories. This was the first time in the country's history that unemployment and even underemployment was eliminated.

Germany sent large armies to the battlefields and lost about 2.4 million men to the war. However, that is not enough to the complete elimination of unemployment. The huge increase in production of those years reveals that there was much more than job substitution. Hundreds of factories were created from scratch and the existing ones increased output by a large margin. The submarine was the most relevant example of the newly created enterprises. By 1913, Germany had a couple of prototype submarines but by 1916 the number had risen to 160. Thousands labored in the newly created submarine yards.[721]

With the Americans' entry into the war in 1917, the commercial blockade tightened considerably more by embargoing also neutral countries. Many essential raw materials and other imports were cut off. Even by 1916, Germany was feeling exhausted, as Berlin's peace offer of that year revealed. Food began to be scarce by 1917 and factory production was significantly disrupted as a result of the embargo. Manufacturing output began to slow down and so did the economy. By early 1918, Germany was even more obstructed in its manufacturing efforts. The reduced capacity to produce weapons forced her, months later, to surrender. Factory output began to contract since early in that year and with the end of the war most factories ground to a halt.

Most of the war was not fought on German soil and its factories were not bombarded. However, surrender meant that the Allies would decide Germany's future and they immediately prohibited all armament and related production. The Allies did not devolve economic sovereignty until the signing of the Versailles Treaty. As a result, the German authorities could not initiate promotion efforts even for civilian manufacturing, and that translated into a very large reduction of support for manufacturing. Factory output contracted sharply in 1918 and 1919, and there was a painful economic contraction. The government tried to stimulate demand by paying unemployment benefits to millions; this only generated high inflation. The economy remained depressed.[722]

During 1910–19, the violent fluctuations in support for the sector coincided with the abrupt ups and downs of factory output and GDP. Manufacturing averaged about 1.9% annually and GDP about 1.2%.

The war was very destructive for France and Belgium. Most of it was fought in their territories, and the Germans dismantled thousands of French and Belgian factories and took their parts to Germany. In the aftermath of the war, these two countries were the most vocal in demanding large war reparations. They not only wanted to recuperate what they had lost, but also desired to keep Germany economically weak, thinking that that would minimize the risks of future aggression.[723]

Germany lost about 10% of its territory, all of its colonies, about nine tenths of its merchant fleet, and what remained of its navy, and it was obliged to make large payments in

721 Gaxotte: Ibid., p. 589, p. 593–597, 617, 618.
722 Ibid., p. 610–612, 616, 619.
723 Munting, Roger & Holderness, B.: *Crisis, Recovery and War*, p. 124; Madison, Angus: *The World Economy: Historical Statistics*.

kind in the following years. Even the French agreed that the reparations were excessive, but that was part of their plan for keeping the enemy weak. Neither the US nor anybody else was interested in financing economic recovery. Germany endured political chaos in the years that followed, almost bordering on civil war. In 1919, several small regional wars took place and in 1920 there was a coup and a leftist insurrection.[724]

The 1920s and the Depression

Under those circumstances it is extremely hard to see how Germany could have reactivated its economy. However, as soon as the government regained policy-making powers in early 1920, it began to supply as much support as it could to manufacturing. With the few resources available, it channeled a considerable amount of funds into the factories and production immediately spurted. From 1920–22, support for manufacturing was strong notwithstanding the low level of savings, the small amount of foreign financing, and the large war reparations to be paid. This coincided with fast GDP growth.[725]

It was understood that the steep cost of war reparations would delay recovery. Therefore, in 1923 the new capital of Weimar began to delay payments; in retaliation France and Belgium sent troops to occupy the coal and metal producing Ruhr region. German workers refused to work for the foreigners, so they were removed from their posts and replaced by French and Belgian workers, who immediately began to produce goods that were in their vast majority taken to France and Belgium.[726]

It was as if the Ruhr no longer belonged to Germany; that meant a contraction of factory output. Worse still were the effects on the rest of German manufacturing, which was largely dependent on coal and metals. Most of the factories came to a halt during 1923, and the sector contracted. So did the overall GDP. Unemployment skyrocketed and instead of channeling resources into manufacturing in order to create goods that could act as substitutes for coal and metals, the government increased the allocations for unemployment benefits. Continuing to pay salaries, they hoped to keep demand and thus production at about the same level as in 1922, but the result was hyperinflation. Prices increased by the hour and the Central Bank could not print paper money fast enough to meet demand. Trains were actually needed to transport the daily quotas of currency.[727]

Many have argued that the hyperinflation caused the depression. The hyperinflation contributed to the dire economic situation but much suggests that it was not the cause of it. Some countries have endured hyperinflation and have nonetheless attained economic growth. During the 1980s, Brazil averaged a yearly rate of inflation of 328% while GDP averaged about 3% per year. During the 1990s, inflation in Brazil averaged about 726% annually, but GDP still averaged about 3%. This coincided with a very lax monetary and fiscal policy, but also with modest levels of factory subsidization. Brazil's rates of factory output averaged about 3%.[728]

---

724 Berghahn: Ibid., p. 67–69.

725 Bettelheim, Charles: *l'Economie Allemande sous le Nazisme Vol. I*, p. 15–18, 20, 23, 24.

726 Gaxotte: Ibid., p. 621–625.

727 Munting, & Holderness: Ibid., p. 126.

728 *Rapport sur le développement dans le Monde 1991*, Banque Mondiale, p. 227, 229; "Latin American and Asian Inflation", *The Economist*, 8 April 1995, p. 128.

In Germany, however, support for manufacturing collapsed in 1923. If there had been very strong support, perhaps the country could have avoided the depression and even the hyperinflation. Inflation probably would have risen, but not by much. During 1914–17, the money supply grew very rapidly and budget deficits were also large. In spite of that, prices remained relatively stable. In those years, the new emission of money was mostly utilized to finance a larger output of arms and related goods. Factory output grew rapidly, the economy did likewise, and inflation averaged only some 10% annually.[729]

The depression and its sequel of poverty and hunger drove many Germans to desperation. The year 1923 was full of coup attempts, of which the most noteworthy was that of the Nazis in Bavaria.

Realizing that political chaos could bring extremists to power and lead Germany in the wrong direction again, the Allies considerably relaxed the burdens of the reparations and even assisted in recovery efforts. The Americans came out with a package of financial assistance, the Dawes Plan of 1924, which allowed for large sums of American capital to flow into Germany in the form of loans. Most of these loans were taken by central, state, and local governments and a large share of them was used to subsidize manufacturers. Factories also received fiscal and non-financial incentives. These new subsidies coincided with a very rapid growth of investment in manufacturing which lasted until the end of the decade. The incentives also attracted a considerable amount of foreign direct investment, mostly from the United States. Economic performance was strong.[730]

The currency stabilized in 1924 and inflation dropped to single digits. For the rest of the decade, prices remained low. However, the events of the following years demonstrate that no causal linkage existed between low inflation and growth. During 1930–32, Germany experienced a steep deflation of prices. However, the economy experienced a terrible depression. If low inflation was the cause or at least a pre-condition for rapid growth, the early 1930s should have experienced rapid growth. That was not the case.[731]

For most of history, up to the 18th century, there was little or no inflation, yet economic stagnation was almost complete. There is much evidence that nations are much better off if they maintain low levels of inflation, but it is not a precondition for fast economic growth.

Even though factory output and GDP fluctuated considerably during the 1920s, on average the results were very positive. Manufacturing output was about 5.0% and GDP grew by about 4.4%. The imports of capital during 1924–29 were mostly channeled into social programs and infrastructure, not manufacturing (and some was lost to corruption). During 1920–23, most of the available resources were also not allocated to manufacturing.

During the 1920s, the government sought only to reactivate the manufacturing base, not to give it a boost; to rebuild the merchant fleet; and to re-establish the country's European lead in chemicals, metals, machine tools, electrical goods, optical instruments, and precision devices. There was no plan to overtake the US or to manufacture at a breathtaking pace.[732]

In October of 1929, the New York Stock Exchange crashed as a result of financial speculation. To cover their losses, US banks demanded an immediate repayment of their loans to Europe. In per capita terms, Germany had borrowed most, then Austria, then France, and

---

729 Berghahn: Ibid., p. 48, 72.

730 Ibid., p. 80, 100.

731 Bramsted: Ibid., p. 174–176.

732 Munting & Holderness: Ibid., p. 128; Madison, Angus: *Monitoring the World Economy 1820–1992.*

the least Britain. This largely reflected their economic situation in the aftermath of World War I. German governments and banks were obliged to repay immediately, and suddenly found themselves unable to supply working capital to manufacturing.

The evidence suggests capital was abundant, but nobody thought it essential to give financing priority to manufacturing. A significant reduction of support for the sector. This coincided with a sharp contraction of factory output and a painful contraction of the economy. From 1929 to 1932, manufacturing contracted by about 45% and GDP by about 40%.

In other European countries a similar situation took place. American banks recalled debts and no special measure to re-channel resources into manufacturing occurred. This coincided with a contraction of manufacturing and GDP.[733]

The governments of these countries and in particular Germany believed that a policy of deflation was the best way of combating economic collapse. They thought that budgets had to be balanced. If state revenue declined, state expenditure had to be cut. In 1930, the government drastically reduced social security benefits and public servant salaries. The evidence suggests that reducing allocations for these service activities was positive, but the government also reduced funds for all other areas. Lower expenditure translated into lower fiscal, financial, and nonfinancial incentives for factories. GDP contracted. Government spending was cut further, but in 1931 and 1932 the economy continued to contract. As factory subsidies fell, the output of this sector did likewise and the economy declined. That meant higher unemployment and more bankruptcies, which translated into less personal tax revenue and less corporate tax revenue for the government.[734]

The disinflationary policies of Germany and most other nations in Europe consisted also in raising interest rates. However, that could not deliver recovery. Devaluation of the currency was undertaken by most governments as well. Only Weimar, obsessed by the hyperinflation of 1923, did not devalue in 1931. However, neither the countries that devalued nor the ones that held tight saw any improvement in their economies.

In the US, Keynesian theories on the influence of demand were endorsed since 1933 and the results were mediocre at best. Washington dropped interest rates, even into negative territory. State expenditure increased significantly and concentrated on the domains that Keynesian policies most recommend (infrastructure above all but also education, construction, and job training). In spite of those measures, the American economy, which had contracted as much as that of Germany, remained dormant and by the end of the 1930s unemployment was still at 17%.

It is argued that during the 1920s, Germany's labor costs in general but more particularly in manufacturing, increased faster than in most developed countries and therefore dragged down the competitiveness of exports. According to many analysts, this was a major factor causing the depression. Although the argument sounds rational, the events of the second half of the 20th century invalidate such a claim. During the 1950s, wages in Germany increased faster than in practically all other Western nations, but during the following decade no depression took place. Quite on the contrary, in this decade Germany experienced its fastest GDP rates ever. During the 1960s, wages and in particular those in manufacturing increased again faster than in the vast majority of developed nations and in the 1970s the country again avoided depression. By the 1990s, labor costs had continued to rise and by

733 Bettelheim: Ibid., p. 21, 26–29.
734 Berghahn: Ibid., p. 115, 116.

then Germany had the highest factory wages among large developed nations, and still no depression had taken place.

Now, labor costs in Japan during the 1950s increased almost as fast as in Germany and during the following decade instead of enduring a depression, the archipelago went on to attain even faster GDP rates. They were actually the fastest in all of its history. Japan's growth during the 1960s was the quickest among developed countries while simultaneously experiencing an even faster rise in wages than in the preceding decade. In spite of that, in the 1970s rapid growth was again attained.

By 1989, Luxembourg had by far the highest per capita incomes in the world (about double as high as Germany) and wages followed suit, the highest in the world. In spite of that, in the 1990s the economy grew by 5% annually, which was much faster than the large majority of countries in the world despite their much lower labor costs. The evidence suggests an absence of a causality linkage between labor costs and economic growth.[735]

In 1928, the world had a crisis of agricultural overproduction and prices fell. Many have asserted that the contraction of farm prices brought down the rest of the economy. But agricultural overproduction crises had existed since the 1870s and they were never accompanied by a depression. During the late 19th century, agriculture accounted for a much larger share of GDP than in the early 1930s and in spite of that, it did not pull down the economy with it when it suffered an overproduction crisis. More to the point is that world agricultural markets continued to be saturated during the second half of the 20th century. In spite of that, the world economy grew much faster than ever before.[736]

It is also argued that increased trade barriers during the late 1920s raised costs and decreased export competitiveness, contributing significantly to the depression. But during most of Germany's history of rapid economic growth, trade protection was in place. During the late 19th century, trade barriers increased considerably and the economy progressively accelerated. During World War I, trade was distorted more than ever before and the economy boomed. During the Nazi 1930s, trade barriers raised more than during the late 1920s but the economy surged spectacularly. Trade protection can hurt, but history suggests that it is not a major factor affecting growth.

Many analysts have asserted as well that the main factor responsible for the depression was the orgy of borrowing in the US and Germany during the 1920s, which created a mountain of debt. In the 1950s, borrowing levels in the Federal Republic of Germany were higher than in the 1920s. In spite of that, the economy grew rapidly during the 1960s (5% annually). Japan also borrowed heavily during the 1950s and actually more than Germany in per capita terms. Nevertheless, in the following decade it attained GDP rates faster than those of Germany (11% per year). South Korea as well borrowed massively during the 1960s and in the following decade it borrowed even more. That was accompanied by very fast GDP figures during the 1970s (10%).

A long-term cross-country analysis suggests that borrowing heavily is by no means conducive to a poor economic performance. High levels of debt can even be conducive to rapid growth — so long as the funds are invested in manufacturing. That is exactly what took place in the three countries mentioned.[737]

---

735 Munting & Holderness: Ibid., p. 135, 131, 134.
736 Berghahn: Ibid., p. 108, 113, 120.
737 Gaxotte: Ibid., p. 637.

History suggests that when governments do not decree clear policies in support of manufacturing, capital flows shift towards the other sectors in search of faster returns. A decrease, for example, in support for arms and railroad goods in 1873 coincided with a big increase in financial speculation, which immediately led to the collapse of the stock exchanges of Vienna and Berlin. This was paralleled by a contraction of factory production and of GDP. However, soon after the government was again supplying large subsidies for the production of weapons and trains, and guiding banks into lending to these fields, they were rewarded with strong economic growth.[738]

In Germany's 1928 elections, while unemployment was at about 6%, the Nazis garnered only 2% of the parliamentary seats. As the economy contracted, unemployment rose precipitously and by 1932 it reached the staggering figure of 30%. With almost one third of the working-age population on the dole, the Nazis won 37% and became the largest political party. The inability of the traditional political parties to solve the crisis drove the middle class towards the National Socialists. The historical data strongly suggests that if economic policy had promoted factories, the economy would have performed better and the piercing dissatisfaction of the populace would not have driven them to radical ideologies. History suggests that radical views decrease in proportion to the speed by which a population improves its material wealth. While conditions are improving, violent ideologies do not take hold.[739]

The Nazis and Manufacturing

In 1932, about 900,000 Germans (who did not receive unemployment benefits) died of hunger and exposure. People were desperate and the only ones who claimed to have a solution were the Nazis. Adolph Hitler was sworn as Chancellor in January 30, 1933.

Foreign trade was restrained by regulations and import quotas and a large share of trade was done by barter.[740] Berlin annulled the relative independence that the Central Bank had enjoyed in the aftermath of the 1923 inflation crisis and the priority function of keeping prices low was sidelined. Although inflation did not again become excessive, it nonetheless increased at a much faster pace than in the previous years; to dampen it more, price controls were put in place. Worse still, many exchange rates were fixed instead of being allowed to float.[741]

The government set controls on capital, labor, and prices. They created many state enterprises and the government became the largest buyer. Government expenditure as a share of GDP rose significantly. From 1932 to 1938, it increased from 17% to 33%. Taxation rose sharply and public sector borrowing increased even more, bringing large budget deficits and very large public sector debt. In the view of most observers, probably the worst error consisted in allocating too many resources for the production of weapons.[742]

With so many policy errors, most economists of the time thought the economy would deteriorate even further. According to orthodox views, economic ruin was sure to follow.

---

738 Kitchen: Ibid., p. 136, 140–142.
739 Gaxotte: Ibid., p. 636, 654–661.
740 Munting & Holderness: Ibid., p. 139–143.
741 Gaxotte: Ibid., p. 679–681.
742 Bettelheim: Ibid., p. 38.

However, the economy began to grow rapidly and during the years 1933–39 Germany experienced unprecedented economic growth. GDP averaged about 12% annually and un-employment was eliminated. By the end of the decade over-employment appeared, as large numbers of women, retirees, the very young, and foreigners joined the workforce.[743]

They inadvertently assisted manufacturing. To defeat the armies of Europe, Hitler need-ed a major technological and numerical lead in weapons. The nation channeled vast resourc-es into armories. Knowing that the outbreak of war would immediately bring trade block-ades and commercial embargoes, they also sought to substitute imports as much as possible. Huge subsidies flowed into civilian production. No seven-year period in Germany's history had experienced such a strong level of factory subsidization and factory output grew at an unprecedented rate, about 16% per year, 1933–39. [744]

Resources were poured into factories. Even though savings were very low, they man-aged to increase taxes considerably. Foreign borrowing was out of the question, because most foreign lenders were short of funds and because there was a desire to avoid economic dependency, they managed to mobilize a very large amount of capital.

The budget was also restructured, transferring resources from unemployment benefits, housing, education, and health to defense. The majority of government revenue was utilized to supply grants and interest-free long-term loans to manufacturers. The government also created state companies in fields like iron, steel, and weapons, although most of the funds flowed into private companies. The Nazis even privatized numerous enterprises.[745]

The government also guaranteed the purchase not just of armaments and armament-related goods but also of a large amount of civilian goods at prices that assured large profit margins. Grants were supplied in particular to the producers of weapons, iron, steel, syn-thetic rubber, synthetic oil, and machine tools. To priority fields like these, the state also supplied raw materials, land for the factory, equipment at below-market prices, and foreign exchange. That was precisely the reason for establishing so many fixed exchange rates at below-market levels. Tax exemptions were also offered.[746]

This demonstrates that even if the level of savings or the wealth of a country is very low, if the government decrees an energetic factory promotion policy, technology and therefore wealth immediately begin to grow. As these effects took hold in Germany, the pool of sav-ings expanded, which allowed for a still larger level of investment.

Many have argued that Germany's fast economic growth since 1933 was mostly the result of the large investments in infrastructure, of which the construction of the motor-way network was the most relevant. Better infrastructure facilitated economic activity and trade. Investing in infrastructure is the quintessential public spending stimulation measure of Keynesianism. However, was abundantly tried in the US during the 1930s and it did not work. In France, there were also efforts of this nature and the economy remained flat. Keynesianism was discussed and rejected by the Nazis even before their arrival to power.

Only in 1933 did expenditures in public works overtake arms expenditures; this was actually the least dynamic year during the period of 1933 to 1939. However, defense expen-ditures were significant even in that year, rising from 0.9% of GDP in 1932 to 3.2%. To that

---

743 Bettelheim, Charles: L'Economie Allemande sous le Nazisme Vol. II, p. 9–127.

744 Ibid., p. 84.

745 Gaxotte: Ibid., p. 678.

746 Bettelheim: l'Economie Allemande sous le Nazisme Vol. II, p. 82, 37, 78–81.

has to be added the big expenditures for armament-related fields such as iron, steel, machine tools, and shipbuilding, plus the funds that flowed into numerous factory fields for autarchy-seeking goals. Once all of this is taken in consideration, it becomes clear that even in 1933, manufacturing received the largest share of government revenue.

Generous fiscal and nonfinancial incentives promoted the production of a vast array of goods and mobilized vast private sector resources towards this sector. Private banks were encouraged to lend a much larger share of their assets on easy terms to the producers of the goods that they favored, which in their vast majority were manufactures.

The share of state expenditure destined for infrastructure shrunk significantly during the 1930s while that destined for arms and related factory goods rose by a large margin. That was paralleled by an accelerating economy. By 1938, military expenditures as a share of GDP accounted for 28%. This was the largest share that Germany or any other nation not at war had ever spent on weapons. As in all other countries, it was not all spent on armaments; a large share was used to finance military services, but more was spent on weapons than ever before. A noticeable share of the rest of the budget, which by then had reached a historic high of 33% of GDP, was used to financially support manufacturing fields related to the militaristic goals.[747]

In 1936, the Armed Forces felt that they were sufficiently armed to confront and even defeat any major European power. Hitler, however, wanted more. He promulgated a fouryear plan of large-scale armament production and allocated a much larger share of the nation's resources for this purpose.

Most economists told Hitler that it was no longer possible to emit new bonds, increase public sector debt, run larger budget deficits, and enlarge the production of goods that could not be consumed. They said that his plan would cause economic ruin. Hitler fired the economists, including the reputed Dr. Schacht (who was head of the Central Bank and had stabilized inflation in 1924), and supplanted him with Goering. Goering decreed a large increase in state borrowing, which was almost exclusively utilized to finance armament production. Budget deficits grew larger, public debt increased dramatically, monetary policy was handled more loosely, and weapon production surged.[748]

The economy grew.

Misunderstanding Causality

By 1929, about 33% of working-age women were employed in nonhousehold jobs. By 1939 women accounted for about 37% of all workers, especially in the factories.[749]

Rural–urban migration increased very rapidly. During 1933–39, about 1.5 million peasants abandoned the land and moved to the cities — despite an official policy to encourage people to move "back to the land." Urban jobs offered far higher wages than those of agriculture.[750]

The myth that mechanization creates unemployment (the more it was used, the more jobs would be eliminated) also failed. That myth was popular even in the US, where many

---

747 Bairoch, Paul: *Economics and World History*, p. 13
748 Gaxotte: Ibid., p. 687, 696.
749 Berghahn: Ibid., p. 148, 140–43.
750 Bettelheim: *l'Economie Allemande sous le Nazisme Vol. II*, p. 37.

argued that the high unemployment of the Depression years was partially due to increased utilization of machinery.[751]

During 1933–39, the per capita usage of machinery and equipment increased extremely rapidly. Rationalization actually rose faster than ever before, coinciding with an unprecedented subsidization of manufacturing. German agriculture became largely mechanized, too. In 1932, about 26,000 tractors worked the land, but by 1941 the number had risen to 125,000, most of them produced in Germany.[752]

Oil and high technology goods had to be imported, so they had to promote exports in order to earn foreign exchange. In an effort to maintain export competitiveness and curtail inflation, they imposed wage controls. Wages rose rapidly anyway.

It was not the imposition of dictatorship that gave them this dramatic economic growth. Germany grew rapidly again during the postwar years, as a democracy. From 1948 to 1954, GDP expanded faster than in the years 1933–39.[753]

It was not higher inflation that gave them this dramatic economic growth. Inflation in Germany during the postWorld War II years was low, although economic growth was very fast. During the 1950s, GDP averaged about 8% annually while inflation only grew by 2%. Cross-country comparisons show that rapid growth is possible with low inflation. During the 1960s, Hong Kong and Taiwan attained a GDP rate of about 10% annually with an inflation rate of just 2%, and Singapore grew by 9% per year while inflation averaged only 1%.[754]

On the other hand, during the 1970s, in Germany and in practically all developed countries, inflation increased considerably and the economy instead of growing faster decelerated.[755]

Numerous countries experienced severe economic traumas during the 1930s. However, some attained rapid growth and the differing performances all coincided with the differing levels of support for manufacturing. Japan was a large factory subsidizer and it attained the fastest rates of manufacturing and GDP (about 8.5% and 5.4% respectively).

Britain increased its defense budget since 1933 and this coincided with the end of the depression. Still, Britain had much slower factory output during 1933–39 than Germany, and had slower economic growth. Even though the economic contraction in Britain during the early 1930s was less severe than in Germany, the average GDP growth rate for the whole decade was lower. Manufacturing subsidies were lower than in Germany and output during the 1930s in Britain was about 4.2% annually and GDP averaged about 3.5%.[756]

For those who argued that totalitarian government was largely responsible for the fast economic growth of Germany, Italy is a contrary example. There was nothing in the Italian fascists' view of the world that saw large investments in manufacturing as important. They attained only a modest rate of factory output (3.0%) and a modest rate of GDP (2.4%).[757]

In 1930, the US spent about 0.9% on defense and by 1938 the share had only barely risen to 1.8%. The large subsidies that were offered for train production had largely come to an

751 "Technology and Unemployment", *The Economist*, 11 February 1995, p. 21.
752 Roustang, Guy: *Développement Economique de l'Allemagne Orientale*, p. 52.
753 Berghahn: Ibid., p. 138, 139.
754 Hardach, Karl: *Wirtschafts Geschichte Deutschlands in 20 Jahrhundert*, p. 192.
755 "Inflation", *The Economist*, 22 March 1997, p. 142.
756 Munting & Holderness: Ibid., p. 227, 228.
757 Ibid., p. 238; Sabillon: Ibid., p. 185.

end in the early 20th century. Factory output was low and so was GDP (about 0.8% and 0.6% respectively).[758]

In the Soviet Union, on the other hand, economic growth was strong during the 1930s, notwithstanding the government's endorsement of a centrally-controlled system that hampered efficiency. Despite wholesale destruction of agricultural assets by peasants rebelling against collectivization, the economy thrived. Factory promotion efforts and a much larger production of armaments gave a manufacturing output averaging about 17% annually and real GDP (adjusted to capitalist standards) of about 6% per year.[759]

World War II and Its Aftermath

World War II began in September of 1939 as the Nazis launched a major invasion of Eastern Europe. Berlin stepped up investments in arms and related goods even more. In mid-1941, a massive invasion of Russia began and still more resources were allocated for the production of weapons. In that same year the US entered the war.

Factory production was disrupted by the blockade of the British navy. Increasing scarcity of basic raw materials and other imports began to slow down production. The bombardments also became more intense. By 1943, factory production was no longer capable of growing. In 1944, manufacturing contracted significantly. From the first half of 1945 until surrender, factory production contracted much more.[760]

Economic growth was still strong in 1940; it rapidly decelerated as the country was hemmed in, and there was a steep economic contraction until the end of the war. Upon the capitulation of Germany in June of 1945, the country was partitioned into a Western part controlled by the United States, Britain, and France and a smaller Eastern part controlled by the Soviet Union.

The Americans and their Allies decided that Germany should not be allowed to produce weapons or any other good that could be linked to weapons, such as heavy manufacturing.[761] When the war ended, the economy had contracted by more than a third from its peak level in the early 1940s. About 55% of housing was destroyed or severely damaged, about 4.3 million Germans were dead, and many more were wounded or physically incapacitated. Savings were practically nonexistent, and none of the victorious nations was inclined to supply any form of recovery assistance, including the US, which had accumulated the majority of world gold reserves and whose economic situation was outstanding.[762]

The Soviet Union had lost 25 million of its citizens to the war and had endured an almost complete destruction of the western part of the country. The Soviets dismantled a very large share of the remaining manufacturing base of East Germany and took the machines to the Soviet Union. The Allies also dismantled about 12% of the existing machinery and equipment.[763]

West German economic policy makers had therefore very limited room for maneuver during 1946–47 and those of the East even less. The scant sovereignty that was allowed them

758 Hughes, Jonathan: *American Economic History*, p. 436–450.
759 Clarke, Roger & Matko, Dubravko: *Soviet Economic Facts 1917–81*, p. 7–12.
760 Roustang: Ibid., p. 14–17.
761 Bramsted: Ibid., p. 9.
762 Berghahn: Ibid., p. 156–180; "Memories of War", *The Economist*, 6 May 1995, p. 19, 20.
763 Krisch, Henry: *The German Democratic Republic*, p. 90–92.

in the West was utilized to try to reactivate factory production, which had been Germany's main economic sector. Notwithstanding the absence of foreign financing and the scarcity of savings, widespread hunger and even starvation, resources were channeled into civilian manufacturing. The sector immediately began to grow and the economy did likewise.[764]

Investment in agriculture and construction were considered more important, however. The problem of food and housing was compounded in the West by the mass expulsions of Germans from Eastern Europe. The Germans had sought to colonize several countries in the region and sent millions of Germans to settle there. When the war ended, they were expelled together with people of German ancestry who had lived there for centuries. About 12 million Germans had to flee from Eastern Europe and about 2 million died during the migration from exposure, hunger, typhus, and aggressions.[765]

However, what most inhibited a whole-scale reactivation of the sector were the restrictions imposed by the victors on heavy manufacturing. Even fields like automobile production were blacklisted.

Since most of the manufacturing had been heavy, only a small share of it could be brought back into production. Turning a factory that produced heavy goods into one that produced light goods was not easy. Manufacturing in West Germany began to grow modestly in 1946–47 at about 4% per year and the economy expanded slightly more slowly. The Soviets felt pressured to allow for some recovery in East Germany and the authorities began also to supply modest support for manufacturing. That coincided with a proportionate rate of factory output and GDP.[766]

Tensions between the Soviets and their capitalist war allies rapidly escalated after the end of the war.

Germany was not the only country in Western Europe with slow economic growth — at a time when only rapid growth could have begun to alleviate the suffering of the population. Hunger and broad-scale unemployment prevailed in most countries. In Italy, there was even starvation. But Washington thought that it had already invested enough in the region and felt that Europeans should solve their own problems. By 1947, the White House, which emphasized foreign policy, thought that Europe needed some financial assistance for recovery, but Congress was unwilling to approve even small amounts of funds.[767]

Then, in February of 1948, the Soviets invaded Czechoslovakia. Congress swiftly approved a gigantic aid program for Western Europe. Only two months after the Soviet invasion, the first aid cargoes began arriving in Europe. The five-year aid program accounted for just 3% of the GDP of the seventeen recipient countries. It was, however, a significant step up from no investment capital at all. It was also large relative to the aid programs of later decades. The whole American aid budget of the 1990s for the entire world (inflation adjusted) was only a sixth as large.

The Marshall Plan sought to accelerate economic recovery, and at that moment, the main characteristic of the economic malaise in Western Europe was the paralysis of the large manufacturing sector (which the US had just destroyed). The US therefore decided that the aid should be mostly utilized for bringing the factories back into production. The

---

764 *GDR and Eastern Europe*, p. 5–7.
765 "Taking Revenge", *Newsweek*, 8 May 1995, p. 18, 19.
766 Roustang: Ibid., p. 20–36, 41.
767 "The Man and the Plan", *Newsweek*, 26 May 1997, p. 12–15.

majority of the aid was directed to the supply of machinery, equipment, and spare parts for the factories. Another share went in the form of raw materials for this sector and only a small share consisted of food, clothing, and medicines. A significant portion was allocated to infrastructure.[768]

Washington also took measures so that the newly created international organizations such as the World Bank (International Bank for Reconstruction and Development) and the IMF (International Monetary Fund), would lend to Western Europe on favorable terms. The government gave American commercial banks incentives and pressured them so that they would lend to Europe.

For Germany, the Soviet invasion of Czechoslovakia translated into much more than a large foreign aid program. The Allies and in particular the US changed their position with respect to Germany. The Americans lifted restrictions on heavy manufacturing and West Germany was allowed to fabricate anything except weapons. The new policy makers in Bonn immediately decreed a huge increase in support for manufacturing and factory output began to grow at an impressive pace. During 1948–49, this sector's rate of output was about 27% annually and the economy grew by 23% each year.

Many analysts have argued that the rapid growth in these years was purely the result of the reactivation of the installed capacity and the American aid. However, if growing rapidly after a war would be easy, Germany, Italy and Japan should have grown fast since 1946, but the spurt in growth occurred only until 1948. If Marshall Aid would have been responsible for the rapid growth since 1948, Britain should have attained the fastest growth in Europe because it received the largest amount of that aid (as a share of GDP). However, Britain attained the slowest rates in all of Western Europe during the late 1940s, 1950s, 1960s. That coincided with the country that least promoted manufacturing in the continent. Spain received the smallest amount of aid because it did not suffer bombardments and in the postwar it was still ruled by Franco, a fascist ally of Hitler and Mussolini. However, Spain in the 1950–69 years grew by about 7% per year while Britain grew by just 3%. Note that Britain had much to reconstruct. The correlation only exists with manufacturing because Franco promoted this sector abundantly and attained factory rates of 9% while Britain only got 3%.

Stalin had opposed the Marshall Plan, which Washington had also offered to Eastern Europe; but once it was underway, the Soviets felt pressured to offer similar support on its side, concluding that a strong Eastern Germany would be important in maintaining a bulwark against the spread of capitalism. The Soviets thus allowed the authorities in Eastern Germany to reactivate heavy manufacturing (minus weapons) and offered a package of financial assistance. Support was abundant and factory output immediately began to grow rapidly. The economy did likewise.

The same held true throughout Europe. The desire to speed up reconstruction, plus American and Soviet aid, and rivalry between the two systems led the majority of governments to endorse strong policies in support of manufacturing. In practically all of these countries, rapid growth of factory output went hand in hand with rapid economic growth overall. In Italy, Rome granted large subsidies and the average rates of factory output and GDP growth during 1946–49 were almost identical to those of Germany. Contrary to the fascist years, the new Italian policy makers were determined to strongly promote this sec-

---

768 "A Lifeline for Europe", *Newsweek*, 26 May 1997, p. 18.

tor. Exceptions nonetheless existed. In Britain, support was modest and factory output and GDP grew at a much slower pace.[769]

In the convoluted and war-torn 1940s, Germany allocated a smaller percentage of resources to manufacturing than in the preceding decade. That coincided with a deceleration in the rate of this sector, which averaged about 5.1% growth annually. The economy also decelerated, expanding only by about 3.5%.[770]

Technology and Growth

In Germany during the first half of the 20th century, the pace of technological development systematically paralleled the level of factory subsidization. It grew relatively fast during the 1900s, coinciding with strong support. During World War I, the pace accelerated considerably and then during 1918–19 technology contracted. The years of war were characterized by a very strong promotion of factories and in the two following years support fell. During the 1920s, technical progress was on average fast coalescing with a relatively large dose of subsidies for this sector.

Rationalization and productivity, which are intimately linked with technology, paralleled the fluctuations of manufacturing. During 1900–13, productivity grew rapidly, which coincided with a rapid increase in the production of machinery and equipment. During World War I, productivity and rationalization grew even faster and so did machines and arms. In the 1920s productivity grew rapidly, although slower than during World War I.[771]

In the early 1930s, technical progress came to a halt and actually contracted as the goods harboring technology diminished in numbers. That paralleled public policies that subtracted support to the sector. From 1933 to 1939 Berlin granted large factory subsidies, which shadowed a very large creation of technology. Productivity and rationalization grew at an impressive pace, even though the West imposed an embargo on Germany and it was hard to import high-tech goods. Many of the best scientists fled the country, but in spite of that inventions multiplied rapidly.

There was still much innovation up to the end of World War II, but the overall pace of technology grew slower than during the preceding years and eventually it contracted. This coincided with a slower pace of manufacturing growth in 1940–43 and with a large contraction of the sector in the following two years. Then from 1946–47, some technological development took place accompanied by a modest level of subsidies for the sector. During the following two years, technology grew at a breathtaking pace and factories enjoyed a huge dose of subsidies. Although it was practically all imported, technical progress grew by leaps and bounds.

As in preceding periods, the most subsidized manufacturing fields were the ones that experienced the fastest technological development. During 1900–13, arms, trains, ships, iron and steel received the largest incentives and these fields experienced the fastest growth of patents. During World War I, inventions were almost exclusively circumscribed to arms and related goods, like submarines, fighter airplanes, and the machines that built them.

---

769 Bramsted: Ibid., p. 9–12, 239.
770 Munting & Holderness: Ibid., p. 247; Sabillon: Ibid., p. 182; Madison, Angus: *The World Economy: Historical Statistics*.
771 Munting & Holderness: Ibid., p. 128–132.

In the 1920s, technology and innovation were no longer linked with armaments or even with railroad goods. Government policies exclusively concentrated on promoting civilian factory production. Support for trains was also very low. The state granted large subsidies for commercial ships, automobiles, civilian airplanes, chemicals, optic instruments and electrical goods. These happened to be the fields that experienced the fastest technological development.

From 1933 to 1945, technology once again became almost exclusively linked to weapons, as the government focused on producing arms. The rate of invention was outstanding and the jet engine, the rocket, and synthetic fuel stood out as some of the most impressive discoveries. Then, from 1946–49 the development of technology had absolutely nothing to do with weapons. Subsidies were concentrated in civilian fields.[772]

In the period 1900–49, manufacturing attained the fastest productivity growth. Yet investment in this sector as a share of GDP was a little bit larger than the share of factory output from GDP. For every dollar invested, the country obtained a little less than a dollar of output. The German government gave manufacturing one of the strongest levels of support in the world during the first half of the 20th century and they were rewarded with by one of the fastest rates of technological development in the world. In the second half of the 20th century, many countries grew even faster. In all cases, that coincided with an even stronger subsidization of factories. Taiwan grew by about 8.4% annually, Hong Kong by about 8.7%, Qatar by 9.1%, Nauru by 9.6%, and the United Arab Emirates by about 10.0%. Factory rates correlated proportionately in every one of these countries.

Overall government expenditure during the period 1850–99 averaged about 10% and during the following fifty years it was about 22%. Economic growth, however, was almost identical in both periods and this coincided with almost identical levels of support for manufacturing. Most of the increased government expenditure went into social welfare, health, education, social housing, and infrastructure, which belong to the service and construction sectors.

It is only natural that governments sought to improve the living conditions of the masses. However, the surest way to achieve that is by attaining fast GDP rates, and history suggests that the way to do that is by channeling resources into manufacturing.

The economic results of 1900–49 have been interpreted variously. Many economists point to the strong growth of exports. Exports indeed grew slightly faster than GDP. However, during World War I, the economy grew fast even though foreign trade and exports contracted. From 1933–41, GDP grew very fast while exports only barely expanded. While foreign trade and exports did not fluctuate in unison with the economy, levels of factory subsidization and rates of manufacturing did.[773]

Others attribute the rapid growth to the enterprising and inventive spirit of the Germans. It is beyond any doubt that the Germans possessed those qualities but prior to the mid-19th century those same qualities failed to deliver rapid growth. The same could be said of the late 20th century. A culturally-determined asset such as hard work should be constant over the long term. However, during 1980–99 the German economy grew slowly. There is no correlation.

772 Ibid., p. 237–239.
773 Hardach: Ibid., p. 259–261.

Another variable that could no longer be utilized to try to explain growth was population. During the period 1850–99, it had been argued that fast population growth had contributed to generate fast economic growth. In those years, population expanded by about 1.7% annually. However, during the first half of the 20th century, population grew by just 0.3%. Even in the second half of the 19th century, GDP grew twice as fast as the rate of population. It could not have pulled along the economy. During the first half of the 20th century, GDP grew about twelve times faster than population.

During the first half of the 20th century, living conditions improved considerably in Germany. Life expectancy went from about 44 years in 1900 to about 65 in 1949 and infant mortality dropped from about 170 per 1,000 live births to about 50. Working conditions improved, and the average number of hours worked per year dropped significantly. The work week in sectors like construction, mining, and manufacturing went from about 64 to 50. Much suggests that all of this progress was due to the promotion of factories.[774]

Russia

1900–19

In the first half of the 20th century, Russia went through three major wars, a civil war, two peasant rebellions, an unstable monarchy, and a dictatorship. In spite of all this, Russia managed to attain relatively rapid economic growth.

During most of this period, Russia's economic system was centrally planned and prices were not set according to "market" influence. This makes it very hard to measure the GDP in terms that compare to those of capitalist economies. Various attempts to compare the Soviet economy with capitalist economies have produced statistical indexes that recalculated the official data. But even when one takes the most extreme and highly improbable recastings of the official Soviet data, arbitrarily reducing the numbers by as much as half (as shown in the Appendix), the rates of growth of the last three decades still show signs of great dynamism. Even under this most conservative estimate, economic growth during the period 1900–49 averaged about 3.1% annually, which was slightly faster than the preceding fifty years and much faster than anything prior to the mid-19th century. (See tables at the end of the book.)

These unprecedented GDP rates were achieved precisely during the period that saw the strongest support for manufacturing in the country's history, and the fastest rates of factory output. The sector grew by about 9.0% annually.[775]

In the early years of the 20th century, the tsarist government allocated considerable resources for the production of railroads and related goods. Moscow also allotted funds for the production of weapons, believing in the inevitability of a future large-scale war. Balance-of-payments motivations as well persuaded policy makers to supply subsidies for export and import substitution purposes.

By 1904, the Pacific Coast had been rail linked to Moscow. The Trans-Siberian Railroad was the largest of these efforts and most of it had been completed by the turn of the century.

---

774 Berghahn: Ibid., p. 276, 27.
775 Clarke & Matko: ibid., p. 7–12; Sabillon: ibid., p. 120; Madison, Angus: *Monitoring the World Economy 1820–1992.*

Some railroad construction was still under way until 1914, but the main lines had already been built. Subsidies for train production were reduced. Output of these and related goods slowed. Average manufacturing growth during the first decade of the 20th century fell to about 3.0% per year and GDP averaged about 2.2%.[776]

With the brief exception of the late 19th century, throughout history Russia had promoted this sector less than Western European countries. By the early 20th century the per capita output of manufactures was much lower. Per capita output of even iron, which was one of the goods Russia produced in largest amounts, lagged considerably behind the West. This was paralleled by much lower living conditions.[777] In spite of possessing a much smaller population, Britain by then produced about twice as many tons of iron as Russia.

The economic and technological retardation was more than enough reason to have induced the Russian government into supplying a higher dose of incentives to the producers of factory goods. There were also several shocking events that should have pushed Moscow further in this direction. However, because of circumstances that exerted pressure in the opposite direction, the increased support never materialized.

By the turn of the century, it was clear that a major war was nearing and that more investment in weapons was needed. War with Japan broke out in 1904 and the Russians were easily defeated. Even though many attributed the defeat to bad tactics and incompetence from the Russian generals, it became clear that the Japanese had a larger and more developed navy.[778]

About half of the fertile land in Russia had been allotted to the peasants as a result of the land reform which followed the emancipation of the serfs in the 1860s. Still, a large share of the peasantry remained landless and those who possessed land had a number of restrictions attached to it. Many thought that this incomplete land reform was hampering farm production and thus economic growth. Long-held physiocratic beliefs about the priority of agriculture in growth were still endorsed in Moscow. On top of that, many asserted the poverty of the peasants was largely the result of the large investments in manufacturing during the preceding decades, which had deprived them of resources.[779]

This view kept the Tsar and his advisors in a dilemma. The Pacific had been rail linked but it was clear that a single rail line was insufficient for rapid troop mobilization or for an adequate political and economic integration of Siberia and the East Coast. However, more rail lines could not be politically justified because that would subtract more funds for agriculture, which would impoverish the peasants further, possibly leading to rebellion. The same reasoning was applied for weapons. When the Japanese crushed the Russian forces in the 1904–05 war, it became evident that more weapons were needed. However, just as the war ended and the government was preparing to invest more in this field, a major peasant revolt erupted which put the dilemma once again on the table.

The government concluded that the loss of its zones of influence in China and the loss of a few small territories in the East Coast were less of a threat to the stability of the monarchy than a large scale peasant rebellion. The peasants were placated and other matters were put on hold. In 1906, Moscow initiated a new phase of agrarian reform that supplied more land

776 Dobb, Maurice: *Soviet Economic Development since 1917*, p. 34–37, 58–66.
777 *The Cambridge Economic History of Europe Vol. VII*, p. 271, 415.
778 Westwood, J.: *Endurance and Endeavor*, p. 141, 143.
779 Supple, Barry (ed): *The Experience of Economic Growth*, p. 429.

to the peasants and liberated them from most of the restrictions of the commune system. The Peasant Bank was created to finance a land distribution program and to increase funding for farm production.[780]

Another belief conspiring against the manufacturing sector was the notion, still current at that time, that Russia could not become a competitive exporter of manufactured goods like Germany, Britain, and France. As a result, civilian factory production was not strongly promoted. By the early 20th century, Russia was the world's largest exporter of grains. It supplied nearly two fifths of Western Europe's imports and foodstuffs accounted for the large majority of its overall exports. Most believed Russia was predisposed to be competitive only in agriculture and other primary products. Manufacturing exports were insignificant and by 1911 they accounted for only 2% of total exports.[781] (About a century earlier, Germany had been in exactly the same situation, yet later on it even managed to outperform Britain on exports. Such a radical transformation apparently resulted from the change in policies which allocated a much larger share of Germany's resources to manufacturing, for that was the only thing that changed.)

During 1910–13, manufacturing was only modestly promoted. This was shadowed by modest rates of factory output and GDP. In 1914, Russia declared war on the Austro–Hungarian Empire and Germany. By then, the vast majority of Russia's imports came from the West and in particular from Germany. The war cut imports and this translated into the disappearance of goods that were essential for factory production such as machinery, equipment, and spare parts. The government could have mobilized the whole economy for war and produced all the goods that it could no longer import. However, the ambivalent Tsar could not commit strongly to a manufacturing policy.[782]

The Tsar and many of his advisors thought that Germany would not be able to withstand the combined forces of France and Britain and would at best allocate a small amount of its forces to fight Russia. Moscow also concluded that since Russia possessed far more soldiers, it would compensate for the inferior amount and quality of its weapons. Nicholas II saw no reason to make large investments in the production of arms and related goods. Armament production was increased, but not by much, and not enough to compensate for the sector-wide dislocation from the reduction of essential imports. Overall manufacturing output began to contract in 1914. The economy did likewise.

Moscow soon discovered that its calculations were wrong. Germany not only took the offensive against France and Britain, but it also inflicted heavy losses to the Russian army and conquered much of its western territories. Russia lost its Polish and Baltic domains, the most highly manufacturized parts of the empire. The loss of the factory goods produced in those territories, used as inputs for manufacturing production in the rest of Russia, contributed still more to dislocate production.

The defeat of the large Russian army by just a small German force proved once again that the determining factor in winning wars resides in manufacturing. The amount and sophistication of the weapons usually determines the outcome of battles, because superior technology can compensate for other disadvantages, including number of men on the ground.[783]

---

780 Madison, Angus: *Economic Growth in Japan and the USSR*, p. 87, 88.
781 Parker, W. H.: *A Historical Geography of Russia*, p. 299–305.
782 Blackwell, William: *The Industrialization of Russia*, p. 56.
783 Dobb: Ibid., p. 69–72.

Moscow sent millions of ill-equipped soldiers to the front; they were no match for the German artillery. Russia's weapon producers were incapable of supplying the country's war needs, at most meeting one third of the demand. The Russian forces were also lacking munitions, uniforms, medicines, canned food, and boots. The initial military defeats and territorial losses were not enough to convince the Tsar to mobilize all resources for the production of weapons and related goods. He continued to vacillate, hoping that Western powers would soon defeat Germany. In the meantime manufacturing contracted further.

As the economy deteriorated, unemployment rose and real wages declined. This led to a growing number of strikes, which paralyzed factory production even more. By 1916, even war priority fields like iron and steel were about 20% below the output level of 1913.

Only a few cities and factories were shelled or bombed, but by 1917 this situation continued and manufacturing output contracted further. As the economy deteriorated more, the political scene in Moscow became chaotic and amidst the anarchy that reigned, the Bolsheviks took over power in October of that year, in an anticlimactic and bloodless coup.

The Bolsheviks' first policy move was to overturn capitalism by liquidating private property. They endorsed a large-scale program of nationalization and an encompassing land reform program. They threw out the financial obligations of the tsarist government and repudiated the foreign debt. The new rulers nationalized foreign property and assets as well, without compensation.[784]

These acts enraged Westerners who were the creditors and the owners of the nationalized assets, and they retaliated by cutting all lending to Russia. In early 1918, Lenin negotiated a peace treaty with the Germans that drove the Western Allies to cut off all trade with Russia. When World War I ended, most of the vast territories that Moscow had ceded to Germany devolved to Russia. However, the West maintained its trade embargo and its financial blockade in retaliation for the repudiation of the debt and the nationalization of foreign assets. The Bolsheviks constantly made calls for an international proletarian revolution, and the West began to see Moscow as an enemy. As a result, as soon as World War I ended, the West began to lend support to the opposition.[785]

The inability to import machinery, equipment, and materials essential for the production of factory goods continued therefore to cause a contraction on the sector. Civil war prevailed until early 1921 and the opposition White armies sought to sabotage production, which hampered the economy even more. Amid a myriad of detrimental factors, Moscow was slow to provide support specifically for the manufacturing sector. They thought that since peasants accounted for the majority of the population and agriculture accounted for the majority of the economy, in this crisis the best developmental policy was to channel abundant resources into farming. Their efforts were accompanied by recession.

By 1919, manufacturing output was far below that of a decade earlier and the economy had contracted proportionately. The large reduction of support delivered an average factory rate of about -3.5% annually during the 1910s and GDP shrank by about 2.6% per year.[786]

---

784 Blackwell: Ibid., p. 42, 57–59, 64–67.

785 Madison: *Economic Growth in Japan and the USSR*, p. 93–96.

786 Nove, Alec: *An Economic History of the USSR*, p. 46–63; Madison, Angus: *The World Economy: Historical Statistics*.

Soviet Policies and their Effects on Manufacturing

Farm output and the economy continued to decline and the only thing that increased was inflation. There was hyperinflation during these years. The year 1920 was the last full year of civil war and of policies that concentrated on agriculture. This was also the last year of factory contraction and of economic decline.[787]

In 1921, a recovery plan named the New Economic Program (NEP) commenced. For a number of reasons, it included measures for factory promotion. Although practically nobody viewed factory production as essential for recovery, it began to be seen as politically useful. On the one hand, World War I had made it clear that without an abundance of weapons with a high technological content, defeat was almost guaranteed. Reinforcing this idea was the support the West lent to the White armies. It became clear that capitalist countries would be a constant threat in the future and that only with large arsenals could they defend their new system. Expenditures for the production of arms were therefore considerably increased.

The commercial and financial blockade of the West meant that the newly-named Soviet Union needed to substitute all the goods that it had been importing. Since the bulk of those goods were manufactures, more investment was allotted to this sector. Moscow decreed strong support for civilian and military manufacturing since 1921, and the economy began to grow rapidly.[788]

At that moment, the country had no gold reserves. Foreign loans were also unobtainable, foreign direct investment was out of the picture, imports were blockaded, World War I and the civil war had dislocated the economy, and a large-scale famine was ravaging the population. In spite of that, the economy began to grow rapidly. This points towards the endogenous nature of economic growth. Positive results can often be attained by just reallocating existing resources in the direction of factories. Foreign resources may be quite unnecessary.

The circumstances were terribly unfavorable and at that moment policy makers also initiated a system of large-scale state intervention, which totally distorted market forces. By 1920, manufacturing had been completely nationalized. With so many factors that today's theorists consider deleterious, a worsening of the economy should have occurred. But growth was very strong.

These events suggest that manufacturing is endowed with such potent growth-generating capacities that fast economic growth is still possible even under the worst of circumstances — so long as the state allocates a large share of the available resources to this sector.

During these years there was much debate among the Party leadership over whether agricultural production should take precedence over manufacturing or vice versa. As the 1920s moved along, those in favor of factories progressively gained the upper hand. In late 1925, the fourteenth Party Congress decided that manufacturing needed to grow much faster for only this sector could guarantee the political and economic independence of the Soviet Union. Priority was given to heavy manufacturing and in particular to machine tools, which were seen as the base for the further growth of this sector.[789]

787 Blackwell: Ibid., p. 78, 54.
788 Dobb: Ibid., p. 99–161.
789 Ibid., p. 172–234.

Stalin favored increasing support for the sector and once he consolidated power within the Party in 1928, he began to push further in that direction. Even though he had no elaborate blueprint and knew very little of economics, in 1929 he began a massive program in support of factory production giving also birth to the first fiveyear plan. He focused on large-scale projects and gigantic production plans. Support for the sector progressively rose during the 1920s, coinciding with an accelerating pace of economic growth.[790]

Factory production during this decade grew extremely fast averaging about 21% per year. The Soviet official figures state the economy grew by about 16% per year but most Western analysts believe that the official figures must be considerably discounted in order to make them compatible with those of market economies. Since most Soviet production was of poor quality, the real level of production was therefore lower. Most specialists believe the official figures need to be reduced by about one half. Under those terms, during the 1920s real GDP growth averaged about 8%.[791]

A rate of 8% was a very impressive figure. Nothing but the strong factory promotion efforts of Moscow can explain it.

The NEP, a hybrid of capitalism and war communism, lasted until 1928. About half of the economy was in private hands. Many have thus argued that it was the dynamism of the private sector what made such growth possible. On the other hand, although much of the economy remained privately owned, the share of the state grew to new levels. During the 1920s there was also an unprecedented degree of state intervention in all aspects of the economy. In spite of that, the economy grew faster than ever before. The Soviet Union even attained a faster GDP growth rate than any capitalist country in the world. For a country committing so many policy "errors," such a performance was impossible — according to orthodox economic thinking.[792]

During the 1920s, the vast majority of private enterprises were in agriculture. Many Western economists argued that since agriculture employed the majority of the population and accounted for a large share of GDP, the growth of this domain had propelled the rest of the economy. However, agriculture grew slower than the overall economy, so that it could hardly have delivered a pulling effect on the rest of the economy.[793]

Manufacturing is the only sector that could have pulled along the rest of the economy. During the 1920s, it expanded by about 21% while agriculture grew by just 6%. Aside from that, during all of those years, manufacturing attained the fastest productivity rates of any sector.[794]

It is also argued that attaining rapid growth was easy because reactivating the paralyzed production capacity was not a demanding task. Enterprises had only been barely damaged by the wars, and bringing them back into production was indeed relatively easy. However, by 1926 the economy had fully recovered to the best pre-war levels, and then it kept growing. Had the rapid growth been the result of a pure reactivation of the firms created during capitalist times, then the economy should have stagnated or done even worse in the follow-

---

790 Blackwell: Ibid., p. 92, 134.

791 Clarke & Matko: Ibid., p. 6–15.

792 Westwood: Ibid., p. 379.

793 Durchess, Gerard: *L'Economie de l'URSS*, p. 11, 12.

794 *The Cambridge Economic History of Europe Vol. VII*, p. 270.

ing years. That did not occur. GDP actually accelerated, coinciding with increased support for manufacturing.

Foreign trade during the 1920s was almost nonexistent, far below the rate of 1900–13. Many commentators, up to the end of tsarist rule, had argued that a major factor propelling economic growth was foreign trade and more particularly exports. Russia had become since the late 19th century a large exporter. The years 1920s suggested that exports couldn't have been responsible for the growth of those years, because during this decade, the Soviet Union made practically no exports. In spite of that, the country attained an even faster GDP rate than in the late 19th century.[795]

Many within the Party leadership and in particular Stalin had never sympathized much with the NEP and its partial acceptance of capitalism. When they gained control of policy making, they dumped the NEP and began to eliminate what was of left of private property. They initiated a massive collectivization program of agriculture intended on creating gigantic state-owned farms. The peasantry in protest destroyed farm buildings, agricultural equipment, and livestock. The early 1930s were traumatic and production contracted. However, the collectivization program was accompanied by very strong support for manufacturing. Factory production grew at a double-digit pace and the economy also expanded very fast.[796]

Food production dropped so much that millions starved to death, but the economy nonetheless grew rapidly. This further proves there is no causal link between agriculture and growth, and supports the manufacturing thesis. This sector grew so fast that by 1932 there were twice as many factory workers as in 1929.

By the late 1920s, recovery had already been achieved, so the Party leadership began to pursue more ambitious goals. In 1934, because of the military threats posed by Germany, Stalin allocated more resources than originally planned for the production of arms. Although investment in arms slackened a little after the Nazi–Soviet pact of 1936, by 1938 they were again on the rise.

Factory promotion was strong in the 1930s. The sector grew on average by about 17% annually and the economy by about 14%. The rate of real wealth creation was about 6%.[797]

Notwithstanding the very large waste of resources, 6% is still rapid growth. According to today's theories, a country which had practically no foreign trade, no private property, and ignored market forces, should have suffered from abysmal economic performance. Yet it attained the fastest GDP rate in the world. During the 1930s, not even Japan or Germany managed to grow as fast. Most capitalist countries had much lower GDP growth rates. The US, for example, averaged less than 1% during this decade.[798]

Western economists made numerous efforts to explain this phenomenon. Many argued that the rapid growth was the result of the considerable imports of machinery and equipment from the US, Britain, and other developed countries. The USSR imported considerable quantities of capital goods, and invited in foreign consultants to help run the machines. The imported machines, however, represented only a small share of the producer goods that

795 Madison: *Economic Growth in Japan and the USSR*, p. 101–103.
796 Dobb: Ibid., p. 237–241.
797 Blackwell: Ibid., p. 86–88, 134–145; Fogel: Ibid.
798 Kasar, Michel: *Soviet Economics*, p. 190–195.

were put into operation. The imports were only large when compared to their total absence in the 1920s.

The Soviet Union did not have sufficient foreign exchange for vast imports and they were not interested in establishing large commercial linkages with the West. The West, in its turn, was wary about transferring technology to a regime that was calling for the destruction of capitalism, that had still not paid its debt, and that had not provided compensation for the nationalized foreign assets. The West knew that machine tool technology could be easily transferred from civilian to military uses, and therefore did not sell to the Soviets the machines with the latest technology.[799]

As a share of GDP, Japan imported far more machinery and equipment from the West during the late 19th century — but it did not grow as fast as the Soviet Union during the 1930s. Japan even had the supposed advantage of a market economy. Even if the Soviets had imported vast amounts of machinery and the West had transferred its best technology, orthodox economic theory cannot account for the rapid growth as long as the Soviet Union was operating a centrally planned system. Under such a system, according to mainstream economics, not even the best machinery in the world can deliver such positive results.

The literacy rate has also been cited as a factor. In 1929, universal education began and a largely illiterate population was transformed. By 1939, all the population younger under the age of fifty could read and write. The share that completed secondary and university studies also increased by leaps and bounds. Many Western analysts have argued that the massive investments in education were largely responsible for the rapid growth.[800] However, education and economic growth have failed to show a strong causal link in other instances. In the US during the 1930s, expenditures for education rose significantly, but that did not succeed in reactivating the American economy. In any case, the US population in those years had a much higher level of education than that of the Soviet Union. It was the rate of increase that was greater in the Soviet Union. Now, according to orthodox arguments, the more educated a population is, the faster growth should be. If that were true, the Soviet Union should have attained much faster GDP figures during the 1980s than during the 1930s because by then its population was much better educated. However, the 1980s witnessed the slowest rates of growth in Soviet history.

Many have argued that the authoritarian government contributed to rapid growth, since Stalin's dictatorship could force people to work hard. Fear supposedly made the system work. But if despotic rule and fear were a determinant variable, the country should have begun to attain rapid growth since the times of Ivan the Terrible, in the 16th century, if not much earlier. However, during all those centuries, the economy remained practically stagnant. Russian history has its share of despotic rulers. Discipline in the Stalinist system of production was far less barbaric and more democratic than the punishments meted out under serfdom. In historical perspective, it was actually at the time when repression had most decreased that the country attained its fastest rates of growth.[801]

Although forced labor was certainly used during these times, it only affected a small share of the population. At its peak, in the 1930s, about 9 million men and women worked under these conditions, that is, about 7% of the workforce. Under serfdom, up to the 1860s,

799 Campbell, Robert: *Soviet Economic Power*, p. 113–129.
800 Madison: *Economic Growth in Japan and the USSR*, p. 100–102.
801 "Russia's Emerging Market", *The Economist*, 8 April 1995, p. 3.

the majority of the population worked under conditions approaching that of slavery. Economic growth was almost stagnant under serfdom.[802]

That accelerated growth could hardly be attributed to the reactivation of production capacity that had been created during tsarist times. In the 1930s the majority of output came from newly-built enterprises. Even the production from enterprises that had been created during an earlier capitalist era cannot be explained under the basic assumptions of mainstream economics. Thos assumptions hold that enterprises operating under a centrally-planned system perform badly, independent of the economic system that gave them birth.

By contrast, in the US, despite its claim to be a highly efficient capitalist system, growth was not even 1% per year in the 1930s. According to mainstream economics, the Soviet Union should have experienced a terrible depression. The fact is that it had the fastest growth in the world in that period.

The manufacturing thesis seems to be the only one capable of deciphering this apparent paradox. The ideological motivations of the Party leadership were strong and the government aggressively promoted the manufacturing sector. This was reflected in the fastest rates of growth in factory output in the world. By 1938, the Soviet Union had become the largest producer of tractors and railway locomotives in the world, as well as one of the largest producers of weapons.[803]

World War II and Reconstruction

Stalin began to prepare against a future threat soon after Hitler became Chancellor. Defense expenditures were at about 3% of GDP in 1932, but by 1937 they had risen to about 8%. In 1939, World War II broke loose. By 1940, defense accounted for about 15% of national income.[804]

And indeed, in June of 1941, Hitler launched an attack against the Soviet Union. German troops took the Russian army by surprise and advanced rapidly up to the outskirts of Moscow and Leningrad — despite the numerical superiority of the Russian army and the fact that the battles were fought on the Soviets' home territory. There is much to suggest that the main reason for the Soviet defeat resided in their technologically inferior weapons and in their relatively small armaments inventory.[805]

During World War I, the French had also been taken by surprise but they soon stopped the German advance. Coincidentally, they had had a slightly higher per capita investment in weaponry in the preceding decades. During World War II, on the other hand, the French were not taken by surprise but they soon surrendered; it happens that they had made much less investment in weapons during the 1930s. It is true that their commitment to fight was much lower than in World War I. However, it is also a fact that they possessed fewer weapons than Germany, and Paris concluded that its human and material losses would be too high if it fought back.

Although the Soviets had significantly increased their investments in weapons, by 1940 defense as a share of GDP was just 15%, while in Germany it was almost half of GDP. Germany had a large advantage in weapons — and this was enough to overcome the disadvantages

802 Blackwell: p. 11–114.
803 Dobb: Ibid., p. 280.
804 Kasar: Ibid., p. 203.
805 Brenner, Y.: *A Short History of Economic Progress*, p. 226.

of fighting on two fronts and of confronting much larger armies. Once again, it is evident that the decisive factor for military victory resided in the arsenals a nation possessed, for these goods were the depositories of technology.

Up until the day of the attack, Stalin had hoped to avoid a war, which he saw as a diversion from the developmental goals he was pursuing. However, once it became clear that there was no way of avoiding it, Stalin ordered a total mobilization for war. Machinery and equipment was transferred wholesale deep into the eastern part of the country, as well as scientists, engineers, and workers. By 1942, defense spending accounted for 55% of GDP and the bulk of those resources went into weapons and related factory goods. This was perhaps the highest share reached anywhere in the world, at any moment in history.[806]

Weapon production surged, and with their new arsenals the Soviets were no longer helpless. In 1942, they managed to stop the advance of the Germans. About 3,500 large-scale factory complexes were created and by 1943 weapons production outstripped that of Germany. With all of these armaments, the Soviets began to take the offensive and the Germans were forced to retreat. Once again, military manufacturing proved to be the decisive factor on the battlefield.

More important for our study was the way the Soviet economy responded in these years. Through all of the preceding centuries, the region west of the Urals had attained the fastest rates of economic growth. During the World War II years, however, it was the eastern part which attained the fastest growth. Impressive double-digit GDP rates were achieved and this coincided with an even faster rate of factory output. It had long been argued that western Russians were more enterprising and were better workers, but the fact is that throughout history, allocations for manufacturing had flowed mostly to the west. In the World War II years, the government for the first time granted larger allocations to the east — and all of a sudden, the economy of the east grew much faster.[807]

The economy in the western part of the country contracted dramatically from 1941 to 1943, coinciding with a widespread destruction of factories. Apart from the devastation resulting from the bombardments, the Soviets practiced a scorched-earth policy (as they retreated), seeking to destroy everything that could be useful to the occupying enemy. The Soviets destroyed the production installations, mostly factories. When the Red Army took the offensive and began to expel the Germans two years later, these also endorsed a scorched-earth policy. Ukraine and Byelorussia were the most devastated. In 1943, the gross output of manufacturing in the Ukraine was just 1% of the 1940 level. However, as soon as the Germans were expelled, Stalin allotted vast resources for manufacturing in the western provinces and the economy there immediately began to grow.

By the end of the war in 1945, the economy in the eastern part of the country had expanded greatly, even though the vast majority of production had been dedicated to weapons. Although growth in the western part had been fast since 1943, the obliteration had been so thorough that by the end of the war the economy in this region was still far below the 1940 level. It is estimated that the devastation in the Soviet Union accounted for half of all the destruction in Europe. About 25 million Soviet citizens died and another 25 million were

---

806 Nove: Ibid., p. 273, 274, 285.
807 Dobb: Ibid., p. 290–302.

rendered homeless. The Soviet Union endured more destruction and loss of life than any other country.[808]

The fourth five-year plan began in 1946 and it was designed to restore the economy to its prewar level, although Stalin and most in the Party thought that it would take much longer. The strong ideological motivations of the past in support of manufacturing were still there, plus the one dealing with reconstruction. Since the destruction of the war had largely targeted factories, the reconstruction effort prioritized this sector. Factory reconstruction was reflected in impressive economic growth. The growth of manufacturing was so fast that by 1948 factory output had already surpassed pre-war levels.

The war vastly convinced the Soviet leadership to allot massive resources to this sector. It was thought that if investment in arms had been much larger prior to 1941, the material and human losses would have been much lower. Stalin was also convinced that further struggles with capitalist countries were in the offing. Acts such as the CIA's assistance to the armed nationalists in the Ukraine after the war and the shipping by British intelligence of anti-Soviet emigrants back to the Baltic republics lent credence to such fears. Large investments for the production of arms were thus decreed immediately after the conflict ended and the Armed Forces' hardware was fully modernized with German technology.[809]

The Soviet Union in the late 1940s was a totally managed economy which spent abundantly on weapons. In spite of that, it grew very quickly. This baffled Western analysts. Many argued that growth resulted from the large war reparations that were taken from Germany, Manchuria, Finland, Romania, and Hungary. Many also claimed that it was the result of the nation's patriotic enthusiasm for reconstruction work.

If war reparations had been responsible for the rapid growth during 1946–49, the economy should have performed badly during the 1950s when the reparations had tapered off. However, economic growth continued to be strong.

Also, by 1950 production already exceeded the pre-war production level and economic growth was still rapid in the 1960s. This belies the idea that it was a fever for reconstruction that drove the population to work. Nothing else remains to explain the performance of the Soviet economy during these years except the manufacturing variable. Average manufacturing output grew by about 18% annually during the last four years of the 1940s, and during the 1950s it was 12%.

The 1940s was therefore a decade of strong fluctuations, with years of steep contractions and years of impressive growth. On average, manufacturing grew by about 7.1% per year and GDP expanded by about 5.0%. It wasn't market forces that drove the economy during this decade, and armaments were produced in unprecedented amounts. Even if we take the official statistics with a grain of salt, the objective evidence suggests that real growth was about 2.2%[810]

Most economists agree that technological growth is the key to economic growth, but they have systematically been unable to locate the key to it. They cannot explain by which mechanism technology is created and neither can they decipher the mechanism that can accelerate its pace of development. The thesis of manufacturing, however, manages to pin technology very directly to investment in this sector. During the first half of the 20th cen-

808 Westwood: Ibid., p. 366–368.

809 Keep, John: *Last of the Empires*, p. 22.

810 Clarke & Matko: Ibid., p. 10–12; Madison, Angus: *The World Economy: Historical Statistics.*

tury, the fluctuations of factory output were systematically paralleled by the fluctuations of technology advances.[811]

During 1900–13, there was a moderate level of support for the sector and technology (imported and domestically created) grew at a modest pace. From 1914 to 1920, a much smaller share of the nation's resources became allocated to this sector and all of a sudden, technical progress came to a halt. The technological possibilities of the country actually contracted as the production that embodied technology decreased. Then during the 1920s, even though it became impossible to import technology, progress on this front surged and that coincided with a strong promotion of the sector. In the following decade support remained very strong, in the Soviet Union, factory output grew very fast, and technical innovation expanded rapidly, notwithstanding the difficulty importing technology and the political repression of the most educated social tiers.

The 1940s witnessed rapid technological development and this ran in parallel with strong support for manufacturing. Innovations proliferated, perhaps most notably in the harnessing of atomic energy. To the consternation of the West, which preferred to believe in Soviet technical incompetence, Moscow detonated its first atomic device in 1949.

Innovation in particular fields also moved in tandem with the government's particular allotment of resources. During 1900–13, the technology showing the most progress was that related to the railroads, which were the field the tsarist regime subsidized most. In 1914–20, only weapons technology progressed — and this was practically the only factory field which received support. During the 1920s, on the other hand, civilian fields experienced fast progress, for government incentive efforts were concentrated fundamentally on promoting civilian manufacturing.

In the 1930s, civilian manufactures like machine tools, agricultural machinery, metals, and railroad goods saw the most rapid technological development. Those were the fields that received the largest budgetary allocations. Armament technology also advanced fast — much faster than during the preceding decade, coinciding with a very large increase in defense expenditures. In the 1940s, the vast majority of technical progress was concentrated in weapons and during this decade defense expenditures accounted for about two thirds of the budget. Gigantic investments began to be made for the production of an atomic bomb almost as soon as the Americans dropped atomic devices over Hiroshima and Nagasaki. In just a few years the Soviets had mastered the technology.[812]

The generation of technology is something that by its own nature requires vast amounts of resources. It would be therefore logical to expect that, if manufacturing has an intrinsic and unique capacity to generate technology, policies intended to giving strong support to this sector would correlate with periods of high investment. That is precisely what the history of Russia shows. During 1900–13, investment as a share of GDP was about 9%, coinciding with modest levels of subsidization for the sector. In 1914–20, investment fell to nonexistent levels. There was actually capital flight, correlating with regressive policies on manufacturing.[813]

During the 1920s, Moscow promoted the sector very strongly and investment immediately rose to high levels, averaging about 26% of GDP. During the 1930s, Moscow's decisive

811 "The Search for the Sources of Growth", *The Journal of Economic History*, June 1993, p. 217.
812 Westwood: Ibid., p. 381.
813 Gatrell, Peter: *The Tsarist Economy 1850–1917*, p. 229.

factory promotion policy continued and investment averaged about 28%. In the 1940s, again, a large share of the nation's resources was allocated to this sector.[814]

Agriculture fluctuated in unison with manufacturing. During the first two decades of the 20th century, support for manufacturing was extremely low (regressive, on average), and agriculture contracted. During the following three decades, factory output grew at a very fast pace and agriculture did likewise. The rate of agricultural production during 1900–19 was about –0.5% annually and during 1920–49 it averaged about 3.7%.[815]

Production of farm factory goods in 1920–49, such as tractors, harvesters, and fertilizers grew at an exponential pace relative to 1900–19. Such data suggests that manufacturing was the fundamental variable determining agricultural growth. The events that took place in the early 1930s substantiate such a thesis. Agriculture in these years contracted considerably because of the large destruction of farm manufactures. In the following years, farm output recovered rapidly and this coincided with extraordinary production of agricultural machinery and related goods.

The last Russian famine of the 20th century took place during the 1940s. It was mostly confined to the southwestern part of the country (the Ukraine, Byelorussia, and Moldova). These happened to be the provinces most ravaged by the war, where farm machinery and the factories that produced them were most thoroughly destroyed.[816]

The other primary sector activities were also helpless without axes, saws, mining equipment, and fishing vessels because these technology-laden factory goods were by now necessary to maintain productivity. Up to the mid-19th century, it had been asserted that Russia lacked many important minerals; but when, in the following decades, the state began to energetically promote factories, large deposits of coal and iron ore were discovered. Up to the second decade of the 20th century, most believed the country was poorly endowed with non-ferrous metal ores, but once they initiated a very strong factory promotion policy in the 1920s, discoveries of these minerals multiplied. The years 1920–49 witnessed an unprecedented burst of production of mining machinery and equipment, paralleled by an unprecedented rate of mineral output.[817]

During the first two decades of the 20th century, construction largely stagnated and this correlated with stagnation in the output of factory goods (and more particularly of construction-related manufactures). During the following three decades, on the other hand, construction grew very rapidly and that coincided with the allocation of a large share of the country's resources to manufacturing.

Services developed rapidly. The evidence suggests that like the other sectors, services are also dependent on factory goods for their development. Without buses, trams, trains, trucks, ships and airplanes, transport services are practically impossible and during the 1920–49 period the production of these goods surged. Without telegraphs and telephones, telecommunications services are also impossible. In these years, there was a large output of these goods and these services significantly multiplied.

During the first half of the 20th century, the different governments of Russia promoted factories more aggressively than in any previous period. Living conditions improved dra-

---

814 Madison: *Economic Growth in Japan and the USSR*, p. 100.
815 Dobb: Ibid., p. 39, 277, 288.
816 Keep: Ibid., p. 16.
817 Supple (ed): Ibid., p. 423, 424.

matically. Mortality dropped faster than ever before, food consumption rose at a faster pace, housing improved, educational levels rose beyond expectations, working conditions became noticeably less brutal, and the situation of women improved significantly.[818]

The evidence suggests Russia could have obtained many more benefits from the same level of support had market forces not been distorted (in particular during Soviet times). In an economy where market forces are largely undisturbed, more economic growth is extracted for every unit of factory output. Factory output grew by about 9% and the economy expanded in real terms by about 3% per year. Much suggests that in a highly competitive economy, the same 9% delivered as much as 8%.[819]

During the second half of the 20th century, Singapore attained a rate of factory output of more than 9% per year and the economy grew by about 8% overall. The government of Singapore was one of the most enthusiastic promoters of manufacturing in the world — and it was also among the most market-oriented.

The evidence suggests the nationalization of private assets, the creation of state factories, trade barriers, cartels, and most regulations are unnecessary. It seems that the promotion of factories needs only abundant tax, financial, and non-financial incentives.

818 Westwood: Ibid., p. 174–180, 315.
819 Sabillon: Ibid., p. 120, 158; Madison, Angus: *The World Economy: A Millennial Perspective.*

The United States of America

1900–29

The economy slowed considerably during the first half of the 20th century in the US, compared to the impressive figures of 1850–99, dropping from an average rate of about 6.3% annually to just 3.5%. That was still one of the fastest rates of growth in the world, but the Americans of the time could not be consoled with the knowledge that very few countries grew faster. Life for a large share of the population was still very hard and only with a faster GDP rate could they have significantly improved their living conditions.

A lucky confluence of events had allowed for a very rapid growth during the period 1850–99. Much suggests that the uptick resulted inadvertently from the strong promotion of manufacturing in the first period. The slower GDP figures of the second period coincided with a proportionate decrease in support for the sector. Manufacturing averaged about 7.5% annually during the second half of the 19th century, and in the following fifty years the figure dropped to 4.2%.[820]

The first decade of the 20th century was the first period in which the level of factory subsidization dropped. By the turn of the century, just about every state had a railroad that connected it with the rest of the country. Numerous states were already crisscrossed by trains, and since the end of the Civil War, there had been no call for secession from any region of the country. The goal of unifying the country economically and politically — so that secession would become unthinkable — had to a great extent been achieved. The government there-

---

820 Sabillon, Carlos: *World Economic Historical Statistics*, Ibid., p. 147; Madison, Angus: *The World Economy: Historical Statistics; Madison, Angus: Monitoring the World Economy 1820–1992.*

---

fore began to reduce subsidies to the producers of railroad goods. Fiscal, financial, and non-financial incentives for the making of rails, locomotives, iron, steel, and machine tools fell.

Subsidies for other fields were increased, but not by enough to compensate. Shipbuilding received the greatest subsidies.

The Spanish–American War of 1898 was the first test of the new navy. Although the it was far from rivaling that of the Britain, it had many more warships than Spain and its vessels possessed more powerful cannons and machine guns. The war in Cuba was over in just a few months with a decisive victory for the US. Once again, the quantity and technological content of arms proved to be the bottom line for success at the battlefield.

The peace treaty provided the outright cession to the US of the Spanish possessions of Puerto Rico, Guam, and the Philippines plus a protectorate over Cuba. By 1913 Santo Domingo, Haiti, Nicaragua, and the Panama Canal Zone had also become protectorates. Theodore Roosevelt's administration and his "big stick" policy was the epitome of the 1900s era of territorial expansion.[821]

A decrease in support during the 1900s coincided with economic deceleration. Washington's promotion efforts were nonetheless still very strong by world standards and the US enjoyed a relatively high rate of factory output and economic growth. This sector averaged a growth of about 5.8% annually and GDP expanded by about 5.2%.[822]

The automobile debuted in Germany in 1885. Production in the US began soon after but up to the early 20th century, the government supplied few subsidies to this field and production was very slow. By 1910, however, the government decided that automobiles, like trains, could help in the political and economic unification of the country. The government therefore transferred a large share of the subsidies it gave to train makers to automobile producers. [823]

The subsidization of automobiles during the 1910s coincided with a considerable acceleration in the rate of car production. Aside from fiscal, financial, and non-financial incentives the government also sought to promote these goods by developing an extensive system of roads. Roads had been few and of bad quality until the early 20th century, which had largely limited automobile utilization to the cities. By 1910, surfaced roads covered only about half as many miles as railroads. Since then, federal, state, and local governments began to abundantly invest in roads. The reduced funds for the promotion of railroads were used to promote automobiles and to build roads. Factories thus received a smaller share of resources because roads are a construction activity. [824]

The support that most other fields of manufacturing received during the years 1910–13 years remained largely unchanged and the increase that automobiles became was far from compensating the reduction that train producers experienced.

Electrification had begun in the last two decades of the 19th century. It was a revolutionary mode of lighting and impressed by its numerous advantages, the government started to supply a considerable amount of incentives to the producers of electricity and to the producers of the machines that generated electricity.[825]

821 Fite, Gilbert & Reese, Jim: *An Economic History of the United States*, p. 513, 470–473.
822 "More than Meets the Eye", *The Economist*, 26 December 1992, p. 87.
823 Harris, Seymour: *American Economic History*, p. 68–70, 32.
824 Davis, L., Hughes, J. & McDougall, D.: *American Economic History*, p. 290–292.
825 Davis, Lance, Easterlin, Richard & Parker, William (ed): *American Economic Growth*, p. 272–274.

However, there was no particular national security concern or any other kind of strong political motivation behind this field. Although the support given to this new field coincided with a fast pace of electricity generation, it was also not strong enough to procure for the maintenance of a factory rate similar to that of the 1900s. The lower factory subsidies of 1910–13, coincided with a lower rate of GDP. [826]

World War I began in 1914 and all of a sudden there was a rush of European investors trying to convert their American securities into cash. This caused the value of stocks to drop and the New York Stock Exchange (NYSE) crashed. The authorities closed the stock exchange until mid-1915. With the devaluation of stocks, American banks found themselves with depreciated assets and demanded repayment in full of commercial loans to recover some of their assets. This left much of manufacturing short of working capital, which forced the sector to reduce production. The reduction in factory output in 1914 coincided with a contraction of GDP.

The next year demand from the combating countries in Europe rose strongly as they clamored for munitions and many civilian factory goods. There was also a significant drop of imports from Europe that forced domestic substitution. That was shadowed by fast factory output that coincided with the end of the recession. The years 1915–16 were characterized by a very rapid growth. [827]

Although the US wanted to stay out of the conflict, a number of events pressed Washington in the opposite direction and in April of 1917 it entered the war on the side of the Allies. Resources were considerably mobilized for the war. Taxes were significantly raised and government borrowing rose by a large margin. The cost of the war as a share of GDP accounted for about 24%. The US never became a main combatant in the conflict but the confrontation was of such large dimensions, that even a moderate participation in it required large investments. However, most of the mobilization for the war consisted in transferring resources from civilian to military manufacturing and the overall rate of factory output only modestly increased in 1917. Warship production grew rapidly as well as most other types of weapons and munitions, but most civilian fields witnessed a contraction. [828]

Even the investments that flowed into armaments were not huge, made evident by the fact that much of the war material utilized by American troops had been produced in France or Britain. The moderate rate of manufacturing during 1917 shadowed a proportionate GDP rate. By the beginning of 1918, it became clear that the Central Powers would soon capitulate, so government support for arms and related goods decreased considerably. This drop in subsidies was not transferred to civilian producers which went hand in hand with a sharp drop in factory production and a steep economic contraction. The next year the Allies dwelled in indecisiveness about what to do with the defeated Central Powers and that indecisiveness reflected in domestic policy. In 1919, only a share of the prewar support for the sector was restored and that coincided with a slight drop in manufacturing and GDP. [829]

In the 1910s, as a result of the decreased subsidization of trains and the convolution of World War I, the level of support for manufacturing fell considerably. That paralleled a rate

826 Kenwood, A. & Lougheed, A.: *The Growth of the International Economy 1820–1990*, p. 128, 20.
827 Fite & Reese: Ibid., p. 509–528.
828 Adams, D.: *America in the 20th Century*, p. 35–41; "Unimaginable", *The Economist*, 22 February 2003, p. 71.
829 Harris: Ibid., p. 69, 221–225.

of factory output about half as fast as in the 1900s. Manufacturing averaged about 3.7% annually and the American economy grew by about 3.0%.

The Wilson administration that dominated this decade thought the country no longer needed more railroads. There was nothing else in the beliefs of the time that committed Washington to supply large subsidies to the sector. On top of that, the government was also persuaded of the need for more social welfare expenditures. A large share of the resources subtracted from manufacturing was allocated to social services.

A government's main goal is usually the rapid improvement of the living conditions of the populace. History suggests that the only means to achieve that goal is with fast economic growth. The policies of the Wilson administration, however, served to slow the economy and thus slowed improvements in living conditions.

Asides from a slower creation of wealth, such policies did not ameliorate income distribution and the goal of creating a more equitable society failed. The history of the US and of numerous other countries, suggests that the fastest improvements in income distribution occurs when the economy grows rapidly. That was for example what happened during the late 19th century. Rapid growth seems to have innate redistributive powers. [830]

Not to mention that at that moment, the fundamental problem of the US was not the reduction of income disparities, but the creation of wealth. Even by 1919 and about half of the population still lived below or at subsistence levels. Even a socialist redistribution of wealth would have not improved by much the living conditions of the masses. Wealth was still so low, that even the rich died young. [831]

Technology during those years dwelled at such low levels, that life expectancy was just fifty and epidemics frequently erased significant portions of the population. In 1918, an influenza epidemic put a premature end to about half a million Americans. Rich and poor succumbed to the disease simply because the technology did not exist to combat it. World War I caused the death of some 75,000 Americans, but in comparison to the influenza epidemic, it looked like a minor wound in the life of the nation. [832]

In comparison to several European countries, the US had minor losses during World War I. The total loss of human life of all the warring nations was about ten million. However, in just one year, the 1918 influenza epidemic claimed worldwide more than double the amount of lives of the four years of war. More than twenty million people succumbed to this highly contagious airborne transmitted disease, simply because the technology to control it did not exist. Wealth has historically been associated with paper bills, precious metals, land or other assets of the sort. Real wealth, however, has fundamentally to do with technology. The richest man in the world without the technology to treat a bacterial infection is condemned to death, but a penniless man with access to antibiotics will live longer. [833]

What the American population of 1918 needed was technology and not social welfare, and the history of the world suggests that technology manages only to materialize when there is manufacturing growth. History also suggests the growth of this sector is determined by the level of subsidies it receives. Had the government used the budgetary allocations it assigned to social welfare, agriculture, construction, and services to promote manufacturing, it is highly probable that the influenza epidemic would have been thwarted.

830 Adams: Ibid., p. 27.
831 Kolko, Gabriel: *Main Currents in Modern American History*, p. 102–104.
832 "Can We Stay Young?", *Time*, 9 December 1996, p. 66.
833 Boulding, Kenneth: *The Structure of a Modern Economy*, p. 14.

Several years later, the technology to control influenza came into being precisely under these circumstances. During the Second World War, Washington made extensive investments in manufacturing because it was prepared to do anything to win the war. Since American and Allied troops suffered numerous losses to influenza, the government decided to make very large investments in pharmaceuticals to find a cure for this disease. Soon after, the first vaccines came into use. As in the past, the speed by which technology was created depended fundamentally on the level of subsidization that manufacturing received. [834]

The 1920s

During 1918–19, the government tried to fight the recession by lobbying the business community to lower prices to stimulate demand, but businessmen were unreceptive to such pleads. However, when in 1920 the government began to spend a lot on shipbuilding, chemicals, metals, airplanes, automobiles, and electricity as well as to supply numerous loans to Europe so that they would buy American machinery and equipment, the economy boomed.

In 1921 a new government took office and decided to discontinue the loan program for Europe, which delivered an abrupt drop in purchases of American factory goods. Government expenditure in support of manufacturing also decreased and all of a sudden a deep recession materialized. The new Republican government subtracted support because it thought that reducing the large government debt that had resulted from the war was essential for growth. However, soon after it changed track and during the rest of the decade it supplied a large amount of subsidies to factory producers, which was shadowed by fast economic growth. [835]

The motivations driving the governments of the 1920s to supply support to the sector were numerous. The impetus of a geopolitical and economic integration of the vast American territory was still partially alive and the automobile was seen as the best mechanism to achieve this goal. The automobile and its impressive flexibility relative to railroads had actually given a new lease of life to this old motivation that had seen its birth about a century earlier. Because this was the main motivation, car making received the largest subsidies. In this decade, this was the fastest growing factory field.

Even though by the end of World War I the US was the most manufacturized country in the world, it was not the leader in all fields. By the end of this conflict several European nations produced more sophisticated aircraft, chemicals, ships, and submarines. Even though airplanes had seen their birth in the US with the Wright Brothers maiden flight in 1904, by 1918 Germany and Britain had the most advanced technology. [836]

That coincided with the huge investments that Germany and Britain made in fighter planes during the war while Washington made minuscule allocations. Before entering the war, airplanes in the US were something of a curiosity. As soon as it entered the conflict, a crash program was put into action and investment rose by a large amount. However, relative to what the main combatants allotted, it was still a small amount and factories produced only a few planes by the time of the armistice. By then, it became evident to the Americans that they were significantly lagging in this important field. The Americans thus demanded

---

834 "The Good Doctor", *Time*, 3 July 1995, p. 55.
835 Fite & Reese: Ibid., p. 529–531.
836 "Blue Skies–Red Ink–Black Future", *The Economist*, 6 May 1995, p. 65.

as part of the war reparations, patents of German aircraft as well as the machines that built them and whole planes (that were dismantled in order to copy its parts).

During the 1920s, defense expenditures were far below the war years but Washington allotted considerable funds for airplane construction. Although the government could not politically justify large defense expenditures in any field of arms, it significantly subsidized airplane making on the ground that the Post Office needed them for better mail delivery.

A similar development of events occurred with chemicals. Although chemical production had started well before the outbreak of the war, growth during the 1920s accelerated exponentially. The Germans were far ahead in this field and victory allowed the Americans to capture patents and all of the necessary hardware that was required for its production. The lead of the Germans coincided with the strong subsidization of Berlin, during and before the war, mostly for the sake of developing chemical weapons.

Washington's desire to achieve parity with the most developed countries was the justification for the large incentives supplied to this field. Even though the deadly power of chemical weapons convinced the American government of important national security reasons for promoting them, it was the civilian side of chemicals which attracted the most attention. By then, plastics was one of the most innovative goods which impressed most policy makers. [837]

The production of automobiles, chemicals, airplanes, and most other factory fields needed abundant machinery and equipment. The government thus also supplied ample subsidies to these fields.

For automobiles, machinery, chemicals, tractors, airplanes, and electricity support was relatively constant throughout the decade and this coincided with relatively constant rates of output of these fields. In shipbuilding, however, the incentives were only large at the very beginning of the decade and at the very end. Grants, subsidized loans, and tax reductions were largely absent during the in-between years and this coincided with rapid ship output only during the first and the last years of the 1920s. Aside from fiscal and financial incentives, shipbuilders also received guaranteed government purchases at prices that assured a profit. Under the Jones Act of 1920, the government bought ships at high prices and then resold them for a fraction of the price it had paid. By 1921, the state owned about 40% of the ship tonnage of the merchant marine and many of these vessels were resold for as little as 10% of the original price. [838]

Although it seemed as if the procurement of subsidies to manufacturers deteriorated the financial position of the state, the end result was exactly the opposite because public debt fell. This was not the first time that such a phenomenon had taken place. Throughout history, strong support for manufacturing tended to coincide with balanced budgets or even with surpluses.

The causality of the phenomenon seems to have occurred in the following manner: Fast factory output delivered a rapid creation of wealth, which increased considerably the total number of firms and individuals that paid taxes. That ultimately delivered larger tax revenues. The new revenues usually exceeded the amounts that were supplied as subsidies to the factories.

---

837 Davis, Easterlin & Parker (ed): Ibid., p. 451–464.
838 Fite & Reese: Ibid., p. 549.

During the 1920s the government was completely satisfied with the development of railroads and gave practically no support to the producers of trains. This was shadowed by a contraction of output in this field and the development of railroads came to a halt. In spite of the large decrease in subsidies for trains, the overall level of factory subsidization rose. This ran in parallel with a faster rate of factory output that averaged about 4.7% annually. GDP also expanded faster growing by about 4.0%.

The strong pro-business stance of both political parties, but more particularly of the Republicans, who governed during the vast majority of the decade, also contributed to raise the factory promotion efforts of the state. The Republicans were not directly targeting this sector but by then the country had a large manufacturing base and the manufacturers were the most effective lobbying group. They thus took most of the subsidies.

However, since the Republicans believed that facilitating business was fundamental for growth, they also endorsed policies that hindered efficiency. Enterprises demanded tariff protection and these were raised in 1921. The next year they were raised again and remained at that level during the rest of the decade. On top of that, antitrust laws were suspended for all practical purposes. The effort to reduce cartels and trade barriers that had started by the turn of the century was reversed.

The evidence suggests that cartels and tariffs reduce efficiency, but such a situation ended by substantiating further the manufacturing thesis. It would seem as if only the relatively strong support for this sector can consistently explain why in spite of these two productivity-hindering practices, was it possible for the economy to accelerate its pace. [839]

The government was somewhat limited in the financial incentives it could supply to the sector because of its desire to lower taxes and to shrink the national debt. So Washington opted for reducing social welfare services and subsidies for agriculture, and transferring part of them to manufacturing. The business community in agriculture was relatively weak in comparison to the well-organized Association of Manufacturers and could not hinder the government from taking this measure. [840]

Much suggests that the state could have easily channeled many more resources into manufacturing while simultaneously reducing public expenditure and the national debt, had it made more pronounced cuts in social welfare, agriculture, construction, and services.

Agriculture was largely depressed during this decade and this situation went actually a step further to substantiate the manufacturing thesis. The argument which claimed that agriculture acted as a propeller on the economy was never a very consistent one, even when this domain grew at a relatively fast pace. During the 1920s, however, farming grew at a very slow pace. [841]

The Great Depression

Even though the pro-business approach of the government in this decade contributed to supply support to manufacturing, it also ended up by creating the means that would later on subtract support from the sector. Banks practically did as they pleased because financial regulations hardly existed. American banks were no different than those in other countries. When the government exerted no pressure on them to lend to manufacturing, they chan-

839 Ibid., P. 520–541.
840 Adams: Ibid., p. 33, 50, 51.
841 "More than Meets the Eye", p. 87.

neled the bulk of their assets into quick return activities like commerce, services, construction, and financial speculation. There was speculation on a grand scale during these years, in particular in the stock exchange, where large fortunes could be made in as little as a few hours, and in October of 1929 the New York Stock Exchange crashed.

Stock prices fell abruptly and banks found themselves with sharply depreciated assets. To cover their losses, they demanded immediate repayment of their loans. The majority of the existing loans were made to finance trade and in particular short-term trade, which meant that many financed the commercial activities of manufacturing companies. Loans for the creation of a factory were rare but banks made many for the short-term operations of manufacturers. When these loans were no longer available, producers did not have the funds to buy inputs and a large drop in factory output followed. That coincided with a proportionate drop in GDP in 1930.

The Hoover administration thought the best policy to follow was to do nothing, convinced of the self-healing capacities of the economy. Thousands of companies went bankrupt. The economic contraction meant that many banks were unable to recover their loans. That in its turn caused banks to lend even less to manufacturing, which meant an even larger contraction of factory output in 1931 and another large decline of the economy. As unemployment reached new levels, the government dumped the do-nothing policy and began to increase public expenditure in infrastructure works such as highways, ports, dams, and government buildings.[842]

Since 1931, the government provided funds to help distressed banks and in 1932 it supplied more funds for the financing of banks, insurance companies, and railroad-service firms. However, these measures not only failed to reactivate the economy but they even failed to prevent the depression from worsening. In 1932, GDP again contracted.

The last three years of the Hoover administration were characterized by policies that subtracted support to manufacturing as the government transferred resources from this sector to the others. Budgetary allocations used to subsidize factories were used to assist banks and finance infrastructure.

Aside from the smaller share allocated to this sector, there was also the fall in government revenue, which worsened the situation. As the economy contracted, companies went bankrupt by the thousands and unemployment rapidly rose, reducing corporate taxes and personal taxes. Government revenue thus shrunk. That translated into lower funds available for the financing of manufacturing. The evidence suggests the shrunken state revenue was still more than enough to have supplied manufacturing with abundant subsidies, had it all been allocated to it. However, nobody even considered such a possibility.

When in 1931–32 the government increased expenditure to reactivate the economy, practically all of it was allocated to non-factory activities because nobody in Washington believed that factory growth was the key to economic growth. Just about every policy maker believed that infrastructure was more important. The bulk thought that stabilizing banks was more important. During 1930–32, more than five thousand banks failed and the political class concluded that subsidies for this field were fundamental for recovery.

The frenzied speculation at the stock exchange had given birth to the crisis and the buying of stocks had been largely aided by low interest rates. The Federal Reserve Bank

---

842 Adams: Ibid., p. 87.

thus countered with a very tight monetary policy and significantly raised interest rates in 1930. [843]

Not that a low interest rate policy would have done much for the sector, but the abrupt reaction of the Fed to raise interest rates, was illustrative of a political class which was light years away from understanding what resided at the core of economic growth.

Another of the measures taken, which also illustrated this lack of knowledge, was the erection of still higher trade barriers than the ones of the 1920s. In 1930, the government approved the Smoot–Hawley Act and raised tariffs by a large margin. It was actually intended on assisting manufacturing and agriculture, but history had repeatedly suggested that trade protection does not aid manufacturing. The years that followed corroborated that. From 1929 to 1932, manufacturing contracted by about 41% and GDP by about 35%. [844]

By 1932, unemployment had reached the stratospheric figure of 24% and there was nothing in the events of that year which suggested that a recovery would soon occur. By then, the population had become convinced that the Republicans would not solve the crisis so it gave a major victory to the Democrats. In early 1933, Franklin D. Roosevelt was sworn into the presidency. Although Roosevelt had ample political power when he assumed office to initiate new and even radical economic programs, he and his advisors had no economic program in any meaningful and operational sense of the term. [845]

This administration knew as little about the causes of economic growth as the preceding one. That is why despite the numerous public policy experiments that it undertook, its results were not much better.

No major group in the economy had been hit harder by the Depression than farmers, so almost as soon as the new government took office, it decreed an extensive price support system for agriculture. Since the early 1930s were characterized by deflation, the new administration believed that raising domestic prices would contribute to overcome the crisis and it sought to do so by partly manipulating the dollar. That is why at the London Economic Conference Roosevelt rejected currency stabilization with the currencies of Europe. The US also stopped converting currency into gold and the dollar was devalued. [846]

Washington also pursued the goal of increasing prices by having the Fed practice a very loose monetary policy. During 1933–39, the Fed lowered the discount rate so much, that interest rates even became negative. While real interest rates had averaged about 9% during 1930–32, the figure was about -1% in the rest of the decade. On trade policy, the government also decided to reverse direction and in 1934 trade barriers fell. Considerable measures to restructure the financial system were as well decreed and in 1933 the Glass–Steagal Act created a new federal corporation to guarantee bank deposits in order to restore confidence among savers in the banks. [847]

Another reversal of policy was the creation of numerous regulatory bodies intended to limit many business practices, which the Democrats deemed responsible for the crisis. Of these practices, the fixing of prices by cartels was the most repudiated. The government also passed legislation to separate commercial and investment banking. Up until then, most

843 Fite & Reese: Ibid., p. 575–590.
844 Ibid., p. 592–611.
845 Chandler, Lester: *America's Greatest Depression*, p. 132–134.
846 Adams: Ibid., p. 76–97, 240.
847 Boulding: Ibid., p. 177, 70.

banks had done both activities and it was thought that if by October 1929 they had been separated, commercial banks would have not cut funding to business because their stock market losses would have been small. Another new policy consisted of legalizing unions and sanctioning minimum wage legislation. Washington thought that higher wages would increase demand and therefore stimulate production. [848]

Perhaps the most noteworthy of the measures taken by the Roosevelt administrations in the 1930s was the high degree of public expenditure. It was the first government in the history of the country to increase spending a lot and at the same time use it for public works. By 1929, total government expenditure (federal, state & local) as a share of GDP was about 8% and by 1936 it had doubled to 16%. The largest share of this increase was used for infrastructure. A myriad of federal agencies used their capital to construct highways, dams, public buildings, recreation areas, ports, airports, land conservation works, water conservation works, and public housing. Even writers, actors, and musicians gained from federal projects and only a small share was utilized to promote factory production. [849]

By early 1939, the government had invested abundantly in infrastructure, construction, agriculture, education, banking, and other services. It had also restructured the financial system, promoted labor unions, established minimum wage, devalued the currency, dumped the gold standard, decreed negative interest rates, lowered trade barriers, and eliminated cartels. In spite of all that, unemployment was still at 19%. There had been some economic growth, but at such a slow pace, that the unemployment figures had only barely diminished. During the Roosevelt administrations, the government for the first time argued that budget deficits and a large public debt were not necessarily negative so long the funds were invested in "growth generating" activities like infrastructure, agriculture, education, and job training. The budget deficits and public debt were greater than any time since the Civil War, but economic growth was weak. [850]

Many during the 1930s criticized the Hoover administration for not having fiscally stimulated the economy as much as the following government, but the fact is that the performance of the economy during 1933–39 was mediocre. The persistence of the crisis compelled politicians to abandon one recovery plan after another. Corporatism, state planning, trust busting, and Keynesianism came and went and came again and the crisis still proved incurable. It's very intractability suggests that something more fundamental and immune to all the experimental innovations of public policy was awry at the core of the country's economy.

Many began to argue that the persistence of the slump was due to price distortions resulting from the increased state intervention and the enhanced power of labor unions. This argument obviously forgot that during 1930–32, state intervention was much lower and labor unions accounted for a smaller share of the workforce. In spite of that, the economy performed many times worse than in the rest of the 1930s. It is also worth noting that from 1933 to 1939, Britain attained faster GDP figures than the US even though it had a larger share of the labor force belonging to unions and government intervention in the economy was also larger.

848 Davis, Hughes & McDougall: Ibid., p. 135–145.
849 Hughes, Jonathan: *American Economic History*, p. 490–495.
850 "The Burdensome National Debt", *The Economist*, 10 February 1996, p. 70.

Others began to argue that modern capitalist economies inevitably reach a stage of slow growth as they mature. If that had been true, then GDP figures should have slowed down even more during the following decades because by then, the economy had reached a still higher level of maturity. The fact, however, is that the economy expanded exponentially faster during the 1940s and continued to grow fast during the following decades. By the 1990s, the US was far wealthier than in the 1930s and in spite of that, the economy grew about five times faster.

The same argument had been heard during the late 19th century in Britain, as growth progressively decelerated and the numerous efforts of the government to reverse the tide failed. In Britain also, that analysis proved false because from the 1910s to the 1990s, the GDP rate was faster than during the late 19th century, even though by then, the country had a much higher level of development. [851]

Many explained the situation in the US by arguing that the rapid growth of labor saving equipment during the 1920s was responsible for the slow growth and the high unemployment of the 1930s. During the late 19th century, however, new machines eliminated jobs at a faster pace than in the 1920s. In spite of that, economic growth was very fast and unemployment low. The years 1940–69 also suggested that a rapid growth of labor saving machines did not lead to stagnation or high unemployment. The inconsistency of this argument becomes even more evident when the case of several East Asian nations is analyzed. During the second half of the 20th century, these countries utilized labor saving equipment at an unprecedented pace in world history and that actually coincided with the fastest rates of economic growth in history and the lowest levels of unemployment.[852]

While no logical explanation of the slow growth of 1933–39 has gained currency, the thesis of manufacturing succeeds very well. The vast majority of the efforts Washington undertook during these years had nothing to do with manufacturing. It supported manufacturing only marginally (albeit considerably more than the preceding Republican government), and that coincided with a modest growth of factory output and modest GDP rates. Neither Roosevelt nor anybody in his government believed this sector to be essential for growth. Even by the late 1930s and most policy makers were still persuaded that this sector would recover spontaneously. [853]

Electricity generation was the only manufacturing field enthusiastically promoted, but even in this field and the funds were mostly utilized for the promotion of non-factory activities. The generation of electricity is a manufacturing undertaking, but there are different ways of producing it, and some are more manufacturing-intensive than others. Probably the least manufacturing intensive is by means of hydropower; dams require tremendous investment for their construction. The vast majority of the electricity projects of the 1930s were hydropower dams. Dam projects were also used to irrigation, water conservation, and flood control. This situation illustrates clearly the way in which resources were diverted from manufacturing. The Tennessee Valley Authority stood out as the most illustrative of these projects. [854]

851 Fraser, J. & Gerstle, G.: *The Rise and Fall of the New Deal Order*, p. 33.
852 Bogart, Ernest & Kemmerer, Donald: *Economic History of the American People*, p. 632.
853 Kolko: Ibid., p. 146.
854 Davis, Hughes & McDougall: Ibid., p. 141.

In 1931, Japan invaded Manchuria and six years later it invaded the rest of China. Although Washington condemned the aggression, it took no concrete countermeasures. At that moment, the Philippines were under American control and seemed as a possible future target of Japanese imperialism, but American policy makers decided to play down the matter.

By 1938 Germany had already annexed Austria and a part of Czechoslovakia. Some European countries had increased their defense expenditures significantly. Washington, however left its defense budget largely unchanged, accounting only for a diminutive part of GDP.

It was only in September of the next year, when all-out war broke out in Europe, that this changed. The Roosevelt administration increased investment in weapons and in related factory goods. The government thought that getting involved in the war would divert resources needed to fight the high unemployment and would leave the country economically worse off. Everybody, including the Republicans, the labor unions, and big business thought that defense expenditures were heavy drains on the national treasury and that they hampered consumption.[855] In comparison to the expenditures that Britain, Germany, and Russia made, those of the US were insignificant. However, the relatively large defense budget of 1939 translated into a noticeable increase in the overall rate of factory output. This coincided with a considerable acceleration of the economy.

During the 1930s, Washington's factory promotion efforts had been very weak and that coincided with a very slow rate of economic growth. Factory output averaged about 0.8% annually and GDP expanded by about 0.6%.

World War II and the 1940s

The rapid capitulation of France, the massive scale of the combat between Germany and Britain, and the fascist rhetoric rapidly convinced American policy makers that the potential for getting directly involved in the war was high. In consequence, in 1940 Washington approved much larger defense expenditures. Large subsidies were supplied to the producers of munitions, metals, machine tools, canned food, medicines, spare parts, military uniforms, and boots due to the strong war needs coming from Britain. The government thought that Britain needed to be assisted immediately and that it couldn't wait until the private sector would decide to make large investments, so it supplied abundant incentives. The strong promotion of military and civilian manufacturing in 1940 delivered a very rapid growth of factory output, shadowed by a fast GDP rate. [856]

The frantic pace by which Britain bought American goods exhausted the monetary reserves of the United Kingdom. By December of 1940, London had run out of cash. If Britain couldn't continue to buy US weapons, a triumph of the Germans seemed eminent. Washington became convinced that if Britain fell, the Germans would take over all of its colonies in Africa and Asia, and eventually they would move into Latin America. Pressed by these threatening national security concerns, the government decided to produce huge amounts of weapons and the thousands of other goods that Britain needed, transfer them at no cost to Britain, and wait for some form of compensation after the war. Expenditures for arms for 1941 went up and support for the production of related factory goods also expanded by a large margin.

---

855 Munting, Roger & Holderness, B.: *Crisis, Recovery and War*, p. 227.
856 Hughes: Ibid., p. 472–480.

As the war began and the government called for stepped-up production of weapons, everybody predicted a worsening of the economy. As the exact opposite occurred, many argued that the improved economy resulted from the large sales made to Britain in 1939–40. However, when in the next year Washington decided to invest even more in weapons and give them for free to Britain, practically everyone began to predict total economic ruin. As in the past, these predictions proved wrong. The economy accelerated even more growing at a double-digit pace and this was paralleled by an even faster rate of factory output. [857]

In December of 1941, the Japanese launched a surprise attack against the naval installations in Hawaii and the US entered the war, having from the start to fight on two fronts. The Japanese and the Germans were well armed and on top of that they possessed the most advanced weapon technology in the world.

A gigantic production of weapons was therefore required and for 1942 Washington made much larger defense expenditures. The US not only had to supply its troops but to a large extent, also those of Britain and other countries which were fighting the Axis Powers. The even larger allocations in 1942 for the production of military and civilian manufactures delivered an even faster growth of factory output, which coincided with a faster economic growth.

In the first year of war, the Americans underestimated their enemies and made little progress against them. That is why for 1943, a still larger share of the nation's resources was allocated to the armories. That was shadowed by a faster rate of GDP.[858]

By 1943, defense accounted for about 45% of GDP, of which the majority was used to produce arms and other manufactures. This was by far the largest share of the American economy that had ever been used to produce goods that could not be consumed. The government deployed almost the whole budget for defense. It is also worth noting that a very large share of the most skilled workforce, was recruited into the Armed Forces.[859]

On top of that, prices, capital, and labor were distorted. Regulations of all sorts multiplied and numerous state companies were created. In those years, government-owned factories accounted for about one fourth of the manufacturing output. The state also became the largest buyer as Washington bought a very large share of the output of the private sector. At no other moment in American history had government intervention been so decisive.

Worsening this situation was that budget deficits and the national debt reached new levels. The large New Deal deficits of the 1930s were midgets in comparison to the ones of World War II. As a result, the national debt rose to stratospheric levels. Not even the debt resulting from the Civil War or World War I came slightly close. The national debt of the Civil War peaked at about 40% of GDP and that of World War I was lower. That of World War II, however, peaked at about 130%. Total government expenditure also rose to new levels reaching about 50% of GDP in 1943.[860]

To that it has to be added that foreign trade was badly distorted and hindered; that education, job training, agriculture and infrastructure were neglected; that monetary policy was handled irresponsibly; and that competition-hindering practices flourished. If liberal economic theory would be valid, the performance of the economy should have been terrible.

---

857 Adams: Ibid., p. 103–116.
858 Ibid., p. 105–106.
859 Davis, Hughes & McDougall: Ibid., p. 138, 441.
860 Boulding: Ibid., p. 44, 70, 71.

A combination of so many negative things should have delivered a catastrophe of such large proportions that the depression of the early 1930s would have looked like years of prosperity. The fact nonetheless is that during 1940–43, GDP grew by 15% per year. Never before had the US reached such growth figures and never before had the factory promotion efforts of the state been as strong. Factory output averaged about 19% annually.

Everybody was convinced that the large military expenditures would depress civilian incomes, but the fact is that real incomes rose rapidly. Everybody was certain that the numerous market distortions would cause financial ruin, but the fact is that the economy flourished and business blossomed. Everybody was persuaded that unemployment would worsen, but the fact is that by 1943 the high double-digit figures of the late 1930s had already reached zero. By then, even large-scale over-employment had appeared. Women and retirees entered the workforce in droves, exceeding by much their peek share participation of the late 1920s.[861]

Many argued that unemployment fell because so many Americans were at war. There was indeed a massive recruitment into the Armed Forces of able-bodied men, but that can't explain satisfactorily what took place. By 1944, the Armed Forces had absorbed about 18% of the workforce while during the mid-1930s the figure had been of less than 1%. That was indeed a large increase. Unemployment however started to shrink since 1939 and rapidly shrunk further in the next two years, at a time when the US was still not at war and recruitment had only barely increased. The fact that the workforce increased from about 46 million in 1939 to 53 million in 1943, is the ultimate prove of the large creation of jobs. The evidence suggests that the elimination of unemployment was not the result of job substitution.[862]

The high unemployment rates of the late 1930s were actually worse than what the official figures showed. During those years, many of those who found jobs were forced to work reduced hours and in activities below their skill level. During World War II on the other hand, over-time was the norm and under-qualified workers labored in activities that were above their skill levels because all the skilled workers had already been hired. The average workweek increased from about 38 hours in 1938 to about 48 hours in 1943.[863]

The events of 1940–43 are impossible to explain in the light of orthodox ideas. Only the manufacturing thesis seems capable of making sense out of a confluence of events that seemed to have conspired massively against a positive economic performance.

As the war started in Europe and the government made larger allocations for military and civilian manufacturing, Washington felt in the need to cut social welfare and unemployment benefits. Everybody concluded that unemployment would rise because of the waste resulting from the production of weapons. It was also thought that the unemployed would be worst off because of the cut in benefits. Practically all saw an increase in poverty as inevitable. As the national security concerns increased more and more, resources were increasingly transferred from social welfare programs to manufacturing, up to the point when the welfare programs received practically nothing.

However, the opposite happened. As more resources flowed into the factories, unemployment and underemployment declined, real incomes rose, and over-employment appeared. Poverty witnessed actually the fastest decline in the history of the US

---

861 Adams: Ibid., p. 106.
862 Harris: Ibid., p. 227; Boulding: Ibid., p. 20, 177.
863 Niemi, Albert: *U.S. Economic History*, p. 282.

The years 1940–43 suggested that the most effective way of combating unemployment and poverty is by promoting manufacturing as much as possible. It seems to be that even when the resources of a nation are almost exclusively utilized to make weapons, the economic and social benefits are still much larger than when they are invested in nonmanufacturing civilian activities. Much nonetheless suggests that if those same resources are allocated to civilian manufacturing, the economic and social benefits are even larger.

By 1943, however, nobody in government circles believed that investing in this sector was the key for economic growth and if the war had not occurred, strong support for the sector had never taken place. That is precisely what started happening in 1944. By the end of 1943, the Allies had taken the offensive on all fronts (in Western Europe, in Eastern Europe, in Africa, in the Middle East, in the Pacific, and in Asia). Since victory seemed eminent, Washington decided that it was no longer necessary to invest as much in the war effort and defense expenditures as a share of GDP fell. Allocations for war-related factory goods were also cut. Nobody in Washington thought in transferring the reduced military expenditures to civilian manufacturing. That translated into a pronounced deceleration in the rate of factory output and a proportionate slow down of the economy (in 1944).[864]

By late 1944, victory seemed even more imminent and a still lower defense budget was approved for the coming months. When in June of 1945 and in August of that same year the Germans and the Japanese capitulated, investment in armaments and in related factory goods fell broadly. Once again, nobody thought in utilizing those resources for the promotion of civilian manufacturing. Everybody thought the resources that were no longer wasted in armaments would translate into a peace dividend for the civilian economy. In 1945, defense as a share of GDP averaged about half the level of 1943. However, the abundant benefits did not materialize and it was the exact opposite what took place. There was a large drop in factory output shadowed by a large contraction in GDP.

The impressive economic results during most of the war and the tight collaboration between business, the government, and the military that took place in those years, led most policy makers to the conclusion that such a situation was an important ingredient for fast economic growth. So when the war ended, better channels of communication between these three were developed. The increased cooperation among these three in the months after the war was nonetheless incapable of avoiding the depression. Many thus argued that the transition to a peace economy had to be traumatic. To cope with the rising unemployment, the Truman administration enacted the Employment Act of 1946, which embodied the quintessence of Keynesian planning for a peacetime society by providing ample unemployment compensation. On top of that, the government considerably enlarged the social welfare budget.[865]

Real interest rates had been negative during the war and many concluded that the maintenance of a loose monetary policy would contribute to the continuation of fast economic growth. Real interest rates thus, became even more negative. The economy, however, failed to respond to these policies and in 1946 GDP once again contracted. This correlated with a defense budget, which dropped from about 23% of GDP in the last year of the war to just 6% in the next.

---

864 Hughes: Ibid., p. 476.
865 Kolko: Ibid., p. 311, 324.

Once again, there was no transfer of defense expenditures to non-war-related manufacturing. That paralleled a double-digit contraction of factory output, which was accompanied by a proportionate double-digit contraction of GDP. As during the two preceding years, the peace dividend remained elusive.

When in 1947, the government out of desperation, decided to give support to manufacturing, all of a sudden this sector and the economy expanded relatively fast. However, not the Democrats or the Republicans believed that supplying abundant subsidies to this sector on a constant basis was essential or even important for rapid growth. Therefore, support soon started to decline and by 1949 it was again at very low levels. This coincided with a deceleration of GDP that in 1949 reached total stagnation.[866]

Economists were right in condemning the bulk of the measures taken by the government during World War II. The evidence suggests that tight regulation was unnecessary, as well as a loose monetary policy. The acceptance and even encouragement of cartels; the creation of state companies; the controls on capital, wages and prices; the maintenance of budget deficits; the large public sector debt; and the expenditures on weapons all appear to have been errors. However, it seems economists and policy makers misinterpreted the events of those years as they concluded that support for manufacturing was a policy not worth applying during peace time.[867]

The large supply of subsidies during the war took numerous forms. The Defense Plant Corporation built and equipped numerous production facilities and made them available to private contractors on very favorable terms. The government also supplied abundant fiscal, financial, and non-financial incentives to existing private producers. Companies could transfer all or a large portion of their research and development costs to the state. These incentives could have been maintained after the war by transferring them to civilian manufacturing, but nobody in Washington believed that such a policy would bring positive results. Had the government proceeded in such a way, it is highly likely that the impressive growth of 1940–43 would have been maintained indefinitely.

Hong Kong and Singapore did precisely that during the second half of the 20th century. The governments of these two economies supplied a vast amount of subsidies to private civilian manufacturing. They built and equipped numerous production facilities and made them available to private contractors on very favorable terms. They also supplied an abundance of fiscal, financial, and other non-financial incentives to domestic and foreign producers. That coincided with impressive rates of factory output and outstanding rates of GDP.[868]

In spite of the missed opportunities, during the 1940s Washington's factory promotion efforts were exponentially stronger than those of the preceding decade, coalescing with an exponentially faster rate of factory output. This sector averaged about 6.0%. The economy accelerated proportionately and expanded by about 4.8%.[869]

---

866 Adams: Ibid., p. 160–162; "Reelection by Numbers", *The Economist*, 27 May 1995, p. 49.
867 Hughes: Ibid., p. 482.
868 Kolko: Ibid., p. 312; Hopkins, Keith (ed): Hong Kong — *The Industrial Colony*, p. 1–147.
869 "More than Meets the Eye", *The Economist*, 26 December 1992, p. 87; Sabillon: Ibid.

Technology and Factories

The first half of the 20th century witnessed such a tight correlation between manufacturing and technology, that the possibility of a parallelism resulting from serendipity is very unlikely.

During the years 1900–49, the rate of factory output ran systematically in parallel to the rate of technology. When support for the sector was strong, technology made its apparition at a fast pace and when it was weak, technical progress moved at a slow pace.

The first decade of the 20th century witnessed rapid technological development and this correlated with a strong support for the sector. During 1910–19, the level of subsidies and the rate of factory output decreased considerably and this was shadowed by a significant deceleration in the rate of technical progress. In the 1920s, technology became imported, created, and consumed at a faster pace. That went hand in hand with a simultaneous increase in the incentives offered to manufacturers. During the 1930s, technology only barely advanced and this ran in parallel to the supply of few subsidies. And in the 1940s (in particular the early part of this decade), there was an explosion of innovation, which correlated with the allocation to the factory sector of a huge share of the nation's resources.[870]

Further evidence substantiating this thesis is the fact that the manufacturing fields that experienced the most technological development were those that received the most support. During the 1900s, railroad technology made the most progress and the largest subsidies went to the producers of trains. In the 1910s, automobile makers became the most incentives and this field innovated faster. Fields that enhanced their technology rapidly during the 1920s were automobiles, chemicals, airplanes, electricity-generating machines, and radios. These fields received the largest grants. During the 1930s, the only factory field that witnessed some technological progress was electricity and this was the only one which became large allocations. The 1940s on the other hand saw a very rapid development of technology, which concentrated almost exclusively on arms and related goods. It was the producers of these factory goods who received the bulk of the abundant government allocations.[871]

The rate of technological development during the first half of the 20th century was slower than the one attained during the preceding fifty years. That coincided with the stronger factory subsidization of the years 1850–99. Of the technology the US utilized during the second half of the 19th century, a very large share was imported from Europe. During the years 1900–49, however, the imported share was considerably smaller. Despite the increased inventiveness of Americans, the overall rate of progress slowed down.

Nationalism has driven numerous countries throughout history to attempt to develop as much technology as possible, on the belief that such an effort improves the performance of the economy. The evidence, however, suggests that such reasoning is defective. History suggests that the bottom line for the well being of a nation resides in the attainment of the fastest possible growth of technology, even if all of the technology is imported. Since the evidence also suggests that the rate of technology depends fundamentally on the level of factory subsidization, it follows that the best technology-promotion policy is one that concentrates on abundantly promoting this sector.

---

870 Fite & Reese: Ibid., p. 529.
871 Rosenberg, Nathan: *Technology and American Economic Growth*, p. 107, 14, 15.

History suggests as well that the intensity by which manufacturing is promoted deter-mines the speed by which a nation catches up technologically with the most advanced. Once it has caught up, it will be automatically driven to create the majority of its technology. That is exactly what happened with the US during the second half of the 19th century. It has been frequently argued that once a nation catches up, progress on this front must inevitably slow down for it is much easier to copy technology than to create it. The considerable slow down of the US during the first half of the 20th century, seemed to give credence to such an idea. Nonetheless the 1940s, and in particular the early years of that decade, seemed to indicate that an extremely fast pace of innovation was possible even when a nation had already at-tained a highly developed status.

So fast was the technological development of this decade and in particular the war years that there was not enough time to think of how the numerous inventions could be utilized in civilian fields. The Pentagon financed in full the research and development that delivered the first computer. It also provided other subsidies for its production such as guaranteeing its purchase at high prices. Computers were created to decipher enemy codes. Since the machines were originally construed for military purposes, even by 1949 and the top man-agement of IBM could still not see how that technology would ever be utilized for civilian purposes. In that year, the head of the company recommended that IBM quit the production of computers because he could not see how there would ever be civilian demand for it. He thought world demand would be satisfied with just a few dozen of them.

The invention of the radar is another illustrative example. The technology that resulted from this enemy detection machine was endowed with the capacity to move molecules at a very fast speed. Faster moving molecules had the capacity to heat food very rapidly. Howev-er, it was only in the mid-1950s that someone came up with the idea of microwave ovens.[872]

Antibiotics and vaccines against influenza were also discovered during World War II. Bacterial infections and influenza epidemics had ravaged the American population for cen-turies and during the bulk of that time there was practically no government support for pharmaceuticals. During the war, however, thousands of American and Allied troops died from these diseases and under such a strong national security pressure, the government al-located large funds to promote this field.

Alexander Fleming had discovered penicillin in 1928, but the British government de-cided it could not justify financing its development. Penicillin thus remained a chemical formula in the hands of the private sector, which likewise was not prepared to risk the vast developmental costs that were needed. Suddenly, with the outbreak of World War II, there was a dramatic need to make penicillin widely available. Britain was under heavy bombard-ment, so London sent two doctors with the formula to Washington to enlist American help. The Roosevelt administration immediately allotted substantial funds for its development and by the next year a method of mass production had already been developed.

However, as soon as investment funds were made available, the impossible became real-ity and in 1943 penicillin began to pour forth to meet the need for antibiotics.[873]

The discovery of atomic energy is another example of how the bottom line for creating new technology resides in channeling large resources into manufacturing. The idea of gen-erating atomic energy existed only in hypothetical models up to the early 1940s and most

---

872 "The Shock of the Not Quite New", *The Economist*, 18 June 1994, p. 85.
873 "On Penicillin and Partnerships", *The Economist*, 10 June 1995, p. 26.

physicists doubted it could ever be harnessed. The Manhattan Project changed all that in just a few years. This was the Pentagon's most technology-intensive and capital-intensive project.

The manufacturing-technology thesis is further substantiated by the fact that technology systematically found its materialization in manufactured goods. Practically all inventions came into being in the form of factory goods such as airplanes, automobiles, radios, plastics, pharmaceuticals, computers — or atomic bombs. The patents registered during 1900–49 were practically all directly tied to factory goods.

Productivity, Investment, and Savings

Because technology is fundamentally responsible for productivity, it is inevitable that if manufacturing is the generator of technology, then this sector should attain the fastest productivity rates. The empirical data indicates that. During the first half of the 20th century, manufacturing productivity had by far the fastest rates among all economic sectors. It is also worth noting that relative to the period 1850–99, productivity expanded at a slower pace, coalescing with the stronger factory promotion efforts of the second half of the 19th century. [874]

Productivity also tended to fluctuate in unison with the differing levels of factory subsidization. The fastest productivity rates were attained during the 1900s, the 1920s and the 1940s, coinciding with the decades of strongest support. The lowest rates (1910s and 1930s) were those in the periods when fewer subsidies were granted.[875]

Levels of investment fluctuated considerably during this fifty-year period but they moved in tandem with the differing levels of support for the sector. The 1900s, the 1920s, and the 1940s saw the highest rates of investment and the largest subsidies were handed out in these decades. Investment as a share of GDP was higher during 1850–99 than during the following fifty years, correlating with stronger support in the first period. While investment as a share of GDP averaged about 20% during the period 1850–99, during the following fifty years the figure dropped to about 12%.[876]

Savings seems to be a reflection of levels of wealth and the rate by which wealth is created seems to be the fundamental variable determining levels of savings. If manufacturing is the main factor responsible for the creation of wealth, then levels of savings should parallel levels of subsidies for this sector. The empirical evidence shows a parallelism. Levels of savings were highest during the 1900s, the 1920s, and the 1940s. During the 1930s, savings as a share of GDP fell dramatically and that ran in parallel to a pronounced fall in the factory promotion efforts of the state. Then, during the 1940s they rose rapidly, coinciding with Washington's decisive promotion of the sector. [877]

History suggests that the best policy for the promotion of savings and investment is a very decisive support of manufacturing.

During the first half of the 20th century, corporate profits as a share of national income fluctuated considerably. They attained the highest levels during the 1900s, the 1920s, and the 1940s. The 1930s experienced the lowest levels, coalescing with the weakest subsidiza-

---

874 Bogart & Kemmerer: *Economic History of the American People*, p. 635–637.
875 Krugman, Paul: *The Age of Diminished Expectations*, p. 12.
876 Davis, Hughes & McDougall: Ibid., p. 160, 157–159.
877 Kolko: Ibid., p. 317.

tion of factories. In this decade, corporate profits averaged only approximately 3% while in the 1940s they rose to about 14%, paralleling Washington's vast increase in allocations for manufacturing. [878]

A similar development of events took place during the second half of the 19th century. The largest profit margins were experienced during the last decades of this period. That went hand in hand with higher subsidies from Washington in 1880–99.

The causation of the phenomenon seems to be the following: larger factory subsidies deliver faster economic growth which improves the business environment and allows companies to increase sales. Larger sales decrease the risk of losses and bankruptcies, thus assuring larger profits.

The evidence suggests that the business interests of primary sector producers, construction firms, and service enterprises are better served when macro-economic policies are oriented towards the promotion of factories.

The first half of the 20th century witnessed a pronounced economic deceleration from the preceding half century and it also experienced wild economic fluctuations. There have been numerous efforts to explain these events, but all of them have been unable to add up consistently with the facts.

Factors such as agriculture and population never managed to add up during the preceding periods, but there were at least some aspects of these arguments that seemed strong. During the first half of the 20th century, however, the situation for agriculture and population changed so much, that it was no longer possible to even consider these variables as growth factors. By 1900, agriculture accounted for about 17% of GDP and by 1949 it had dropped to just 7%. [879]

With such a small share, it was no longer possible to argue that there had been a big transfer of surplus resources from a large agricultural sector to the rest of the economy. On top of that, agriculture once again grew at a much slower pace than the economy, eliminating therefore the possibility that it could have acted as a propeller. While agriculture averaged about 1.6% annually (1900–49), GDP averaged about 3.5%. Manufacturing on the other hand averaged about 4.2% and as the fastest growing sector, it was again the only one with the capacity for having acted as the engine of growth. [880]

The rate of population growth dropped during the first half of the 20th century. While during the period 1850–99 the rate had been about 4.2% per year, in the following fifty years it dropped to just 1.4%. Many had tried to explain the rising GDP figures of the second half of the 19th century, with the argument that the rapid demographic enlargement had created additional demand. Even then was that argument weak because population grew about 30% slower than the economy, making it unlikely that it could have had a pulling effect. However, during the first half of the 20th century, the gap between population and GDP grew wider as population grew less than half as fast as GDP. It became therefore still less possible that population could have had a demand-pulling effect on the economy. [881]

---

878 Boulding: Ibid., p. 207–209.
879 Clough: Ibid., p. 6.
880 Davis, Hughes & McDougall: Ibid., p. 416; Sabillon: Ibid.; Madison, Angus: *The World Economy: Historical Statistics.*
881 Burns, Arthur: *Production Trends in the United States since 1870*, p. 262–264.

Even though the rate by which living conditions improved was not as fast as during the second half of the 19th century, the first half of the 20th century witnessed a rapid improvement in the quality of life. Mortality and morbidity dropped considerably, housing improved noticeably, education made large strides, and working conditions improved significantly.

All of this progress coincided with a relatively strong factory subsidization. The persistent correlation suggests a causal linkage between this sector and human progress.

Great Britain

1900–19

During the first half of the 20th century, Great Britain attained a faster rate of economic growth than in the preceding fifty years (3.3% annually). That correlated with a stronger government support for manufacturing and a faster rate of factory output (4.0%). (See tables in the appendix.)[882]

Britain's GDP rates, however, continued to lag behind several other countries such as Japan, Germany, and the US. There is much to suggest that the situation was not accidental. The evidence suggests that the governments of these countries supplied greater incentives to factories than London did, for the ideological motivations which drove London to promote the sector were weaker than in these other countries. Even though Britain lagged during this period behind Japan and many Western nations, it nonetheless grew much faster than most other countries in the world. This coincided with a weaker subsidization of factories in Latin America, Asia, and Africa.

During the first decade of the 20th century, all of Europe was under the specter of an eminent war and London was convinced that Britain would participate in it. However, France and Germany were at the center of this apocalyptic vision because they had fought a war in 1870–71 and the outcome of that conflict had delivered much resentment. London therefore thought that its participation would be limited and that it did not need to invest abundantly in weapons and related goods. [883]

There was also a scramble for African and Asian colonies among European nations, which demanded some investment in weapons and above all in shipbuilding. Britain was indeed the largest holder of colonies but its conquering efforts had started centuries earlier and by the 1900s they had largely come to an end because by then the bulk of Africa and Asia had been subdued. As a result, government support for the production of naval and commercial sea vessels decreased and ship production decelerated.

As a nation that had practically no problems with the political unity of its territories, policy makers were not under pressure to promote railroads. More still was that by then, there was a relative high density of railways. In consequence, the producers of rails and locomotives received few incentives and the output of this field only barely increased.

Since the motivation of the government to produce weapons, ships and trains was low, other fields in direct contact with these such as iron, steel, and machine tools also received few subsidies. Even with the slow growth of all of these fields, which up until then had accounted for the majority of manufacturing output, other fields could have grown so rap-

---

882 Sabillon: Ibid., p. 183; *Madison, Angus: Monitoring the World Economy 1820–1992.*
883 Ashworth, William: *An Economic History of England 1870–1939*, p. 264–266.

idly that the overall output of the sector would have been fast. However, nothing in the ideas of the time claimed that manufacturing was the key to prosperity and less still that government support was decisive for the expansion of this sector. During the 1900s, policy makers regularly ignored the increasing calls that were made for more state support for the sector.[884]

Part of the business community lobbied hard for more incentives to manufacturing, presenting the case of Germany and the US as examples to follow. A few intellectuals and policy makers also put forward arguments in favor of support, but the vast majority of the political class and the intellectual elite, was convinced that support harmed the economy. Several means of promotion undertaken by the governments of the US and Germany such as trade protection, cartels, and state firms had indeed negative effects on the economy. However, fiscal, financial, and non-financial incentives were highly positive. Unfortunately, nobody could differentiate among the numerous forms of assistance and all were condemned. The end result was an overall low level of subsidies. During the 1900s, factory output averaged about 2.5% annually and GDP about 2.0%.[885]

The US and Germany attained a GDP rate about twice as fast and many analysts argued that the fundamental factor explaining these large differences was a scarcity of capital. It was affirmed that Britain's huge lending during the late 19th and early 20th century had deprived the nation of funds. Although Britain exported an abundance of capital, the fact is that in the decades before World War I large reserves of capital remained in Britain that could have been utilized to increase investment significantly. It wasn't funds what was missing, but a desire on the part of the business community to make large investments. [886]

That same phenomenon had been observed throughout the whole of British history. Without government support, the private sector would not invest in manufacturing because the risks were too high. Whenever investment in this sector was low, overall investment was also low and the economy performed similarly.

By then, Germany had become the most admired nation in Europe. A large share of the British business community became convinced that a prime reason behind the slower growth was the absence of a developed welfare system, such as the one in Germany that would deliver a more satisfied workforce. By then, labor–capital disputes in Britain were regular and days lost to strikes were numerous. It was thought that efficiency would improve if labor demands became satisfied because strikes would disappear or at least diminish. [887]

Throughout history, a higher satisfaction of labor demands always reduced the number of strikes and the degree of labor unrest. However, a correlation with the economy is absent. In the 1990s, Britain lost fewer working days (measured in per capita terms) since records began in 1891. By then, measures to please labor and real incomes had largely increased relative to the 1900s. However, during the 1990s economic growth averaged only 2.3% annually. Even though workers were exponentially more satisfied than in the 1900s, GDP figures were almost identical.

The same could be said of Germany, which by then had an even more harmonious record of capital–labor relations. During the 1990s, economic growth in Germany averaged only

884 Elbaum, Bernard & Lazonick, William (ed): *The Decline of the British Economy*, p. 10–12.
885 Aldcroft, Derek & Richardson, Harry: *The British Economy 1870–1939*, p. 105, 4.
886 Elbaum & Lazonick (ed): Ibid., p. 3, 4.
887 Thane, Pat & Sutcliffe, Anthony (ed): *Essays in Social History*, p. 283.

1.6% even though by then strikes were much lower than in the early 20th century. In the 1900s, however, GDP averaged about 3.8%. The historical data reveals an absence of a correlation and therefore suggests that Britain's slow growth in the early 20th century was not because of an underdeveloped welfare system. [888]

Others actually argued the opposite and stated that the rise of social welfare programs since the late 19th century harmed the economy as it subtracted resources for investment. Resources allocated for social welfare were indeed resources that could no longer be invested, but if no such allocations had been made, it is highly unlikely that they would have been invested. As Germany demonstrated, much larger investments could be made while spending much more than Britain in social welfare. The evidence suggests that London's main problem was that it saw no logic in strongly subsidizing factories which resulted in low investment. Had no funds been allocated to social welfare, those funds would have just languished in bank accounts, under mattresses or they had been consumed.

Others asserted that Britain's slow growth was the result of its commitment to free trade. Germany, the US, and several of Britain's main trading partners practiced protection in the 1900s and it was this situation what anchored this position. However, a long term correlation between protectionism and growth cannot be established. During that same decade, Japan practiced free trade and it nonetheless grew by more than 5% per year. The bulk of Western countries during the post-World War II decades reduced trade barriers considerably. Tariffs were set at a similar level as those of Britain but Britain's rates of growth continued to lag behind most of these nations. [889]

During the first decade of the 20th century, Britain lagged technologically behind several nations in fields like electrical goods, scientific instruments, road vehicles, and chemicals. Many argued the British had a cultural bias towards technology-static fields and that such a bias was hampering a better economic performance. The evidence in support of a cultural inclination to produce certain things and not others, in Britain and in other countries of the world, had long proven to be weak. Many times throughout history it was asserted that a given country would never be able to produce this or that good or even whole categories of goods because of cultural impediments. The number of times those assumptions proved false was almost as large as the number of times that they were made.

From the 16th century to the mid-19th century, Britain maintained technological leadership over the rest of the world and during that time many actually asserted that the British were culturally predisposed to be more inventive than everybody else. The 16th to mid-19th century period, coincided with the time in which London subsidized manufacturing more decisively than any other government in the world. From then onwards, however, several other governments began to promote factories more enthusiastically and that coincided with a faster technological growth in those countries. It is most likely not as a result of serendipity that up to 1914, Britain retained technological leadership in fields such as shipbuilding, naval weapons, textile machinery, and heavy machine tools. These happened to be the most subsidized fields and they were also more subsidized than in other countries. [890]

Policies remained largely unchanged during 1910–13 as the same weak political motivations in support of the sector continued to prevail. That coincided with a slow rate of

888 "The British Disease", *The Economist*, 3 April 1993, p. 35.
889 Gamble, Andrew: *Britain in Decline*, p. 62–89.
890 Kirby, M. W.: *The Decline of British Economic Power since 1870*, p. 3, 9.

economic growth. Tensions in Europe, however, rapidly increased and in 1914 war broke loose. Britain declared war on Germany and her allies in August of that year. The Franco–Prussian War of 1870–71 had delivered a revolution in armaments and the cost of weapons had exploded. By the early 20th century, most policy makers and intellectuals, in particular in Britain, thought that a major war would be economically ruinous.[891]

To finance the large output of the more expensive arms that this war required, London raised taxes significantly and borrowed abundantly. As a result state expenditure, budget deficits, and public sector debt rose dramatically. These financial imbalances were what most economists and policy makers feared, for most thought that they were terribly harmful for the economy. On top of that, state intervention in practically every aspect of the economy rose. Numerous enterprises were nationalized, goods were requisitioned, wages were set, prices were fixed, and the government created numerous enterprises.[892]

Worse still was that the government made these distortions to produce goods that could not be consumed and that were going to be destroyed. Everybody predicted a recession. But economic growth accelerated considerably after the initiation of hostilities and, as more and more resources were diverted to weapons production, GDP grew even faster. Unemployment, which for years had been at double digits, was eliminated in a few years.[893]

It is also worth noting that during World War I, foreign trade was disrupted and British exports dropped considerably. It had long been argued that exports were one of the main engines of growth. But during 1914–17, the economy accelerated impressively despite the steep drop in exports. Meanwhile, there was a massive promotion of factories.

Civilian manufacturing experienced a noticeable contraction as thousands of factories were ordered to discontinue their normal activities and produce weapons. However, overall production increased by a large amount.[894]

By early 1918, the outcome of the war seemed already sealed. With the entrance of the Americans in the war some months earlier, London became even more convinced that allocations for weapons and related goods needed to be cut. Since nobody believed this sector to be responsible for the creation of wealth, the resources utilized for the war were not transferred to civilian manufacturing. As soon as support was taken away, manufacturing began to decelerate and then it contracted. During the last year of the war, the economy experienced a contraction.

Well before the end of the war the government laid grandiose schemes for a better post-war economy and conditions were favorable for a boom. There was a scarcity of civilian goods and export markets waited to be recovered. There was also a backlog of worn out machinery that needed to be replaced. Machinery and equipment in Britain was much older than in Germany and the United States. However, in 1919 the economy once again contracted and that coincided with the absence of factory subsidies as well as with negative factory figures.

In that year, the politicians concentrated on sorting out war reparations and dictating the political future of Germany. Less initiative was taken on economic matters. Since war resources were not transferred to civilian manufacturing, the situation amounted to a reduc-

---

891 Pollard, Sidney: *The Development of the British Economy*, p. 13–16.
892 Ashworth: Ibid., p. 273–284.
893 Breach, R. & Hartwell, R. (ed): *British Economy and Society 1870–1970*, p. 86.
894 Aldcroft, Derek: *The British Economy Vol. 1*, p. 2.

tion of support. The boom that everybody had predicted failed to arrive. There was an orgy of financial speculation as many tried to capitalize on the scarcity of goods.[895]

The second decade of the 20th century was therefore a period in which years of rapid growth were followed by years of contraction. Relative to the preceding decade nonetheless, the 1910s witnessed a pronounced acceleration of the economy. That coincided with a considerable increase in the factory promotion efforts of London. Manufacturing averaged about 4.2% per year and GDP expanded by about 3.5%.

The 1920s and the 1930s

The experience of the war convinced many British policy makers that an increase in support for the sector would probably deliver better economic results. Germany and France both had promoted factories more than Britain and their increased rates of factory output had been even faster.

Nobody understood this phenomenon, but the linkages were too strong to go completely unnoticed. The political class agreed to promote the sector with a few more incentives. Military triumph also brought Britain a large amount of reparations and they included German patents in fields were Britain was lagging, such as land-based weapons, chemicals, automobiles, electrical goods, submarines, and scientific instruments. British forces took back home not just the patents but also the machines that built them and whole samples of the goods. For reasons of national security, export promotion, and national pride, London was driven to supply significant subsidies to would-be investors in these fields.[896]

During the 1920s, factory subsidies rose relative to the pre-war years, but were still far below the World War I years. The sector received subsidies so that export markets could be recovered, but this sort of motivation had existed for centuries. The only new motivations were the lessons of the war and the desire to develop new fields. These, however, were not strong enough to impel radical changes. A concern for national security had always been the most potent force pushing policy makers and this concern drove the British. As these concerns diminished, the level of subsidization fell. The end result was a rate of factory output that increased faster than that it had in the 1900s, but more slowly than in the 1910s. Manufacturing growth during the 1920s averaged about 2.9% and GDP about 2.5%.[897]

The strong economic performance thought inevitable in the post war years never materialized. It is worth noting that during the war, Britain did not get invaded and naval and aerial bombardments were negligible. Its largest loss was the sinking of 40% of its merchant fleet. However, instead of investing to rebuild it, London opted for grabbing a large share of Germany's commercial fleet. That was part of the war reparations. British policy makers thought they were making major savings, which would translate into higher levels of wealth for the population. The fact is that during the 1920s, economic growth was slow and unemployment high.[898]

Germany on the other hand, had to rebuild its entire merchant fleet because the Allies took away 90% of it. It also had to rebuild the vast amount of machinery and equipment the Allies carried away. In spite of that, it became much faster growth. That coincided with a

---

895 Ibid., p. 2–8.
896 Elbaum & Lazonick (ed): Ibid., p. 11–13.
897 Aldcroft & Richardson: Ibid., p. 4.
898 Ashworth: Ibid., p. 286.

much stronger subsidization of factories and a rate of factory output that was almost twice as fast. That was shadowed by an economic growth in Germany that was almost twice as fast. While in the 1920s Britain endured an average unemployment rate of about 12%, Germany had to put up with only 6%.

As a promotional measure, London allowed manufacturers to negotiate common pricing policies and to amalgamate, but financial incentives were relatively few in comparison to the ones Weimar supplied. Grants and subsidized loans were scarce and fiscal incentives were also less attractive than in Germany.

Even though Britain was better positioned for the attainment of fast export growth, it was Germany which made the most gains in foreign markets. While Germany had to pay very large war reparations during the 1920s and had a number of restrictions imposed by the Allies, Britain was the recipient of the reparations and had full liberty. Germany had lost its colonies and therefore its assured export markets, while Britain had the largest colonial possessions in the world. In spite of all that, Germany became a much faster growth of exports and that coincided with a much higher level of factory subsidization. Britain actually lost export market share, in particular in fields such as iron, steel and shipbuilding, while Germany gained export share in these and several other fields.[899]

This was not a new phenomenon. Britain had begun to lose export markets since the mid-19th century, coinciding with the moment when several governments in North America, Western Europe, and East Asia began a more decisive factory promotion policy. During the late 19th century, while London slightly reduced its promotion efforts, several of these countries largely increased their support, and this was paralleled by a rapid loss of market share. Since the 1890s, American, German, and Japanese goods began to displace British goods even in its colonial possessions. [900]

It was argued that high labor costs were fundamentally responsible for the diminished export competitiveness, which also led to a slower economic growth than its main trading partners. The problem with that argument is that by the 1920s German and American labor costs were higher than those of Britain.

It was also asserted that an overvalued exchange rate was to blame for the poor export performance. This argument came into being since 1925 when the gold standard was restored at its pre-war parity. However, during the first half of this decade the economy did not either perform well and exports did not rose fast, even though then the exchange rate was much lower relative to the currencies of its main trading partners. [901]

There was no correlation between labor costs and exports or between the exchange rate and exports. None of these variables could have been the cause or an important cause of the weak export performance of Britain. The evidence suggests that they couldn't have been responsible for the weak GDP figures, either.

Britain began to experience trade deficits since the 1870s. Many argued that they were the result of the trade barriers that were erected by its main commercial partners. However, the deficits remained throughout the 20th century even though during the 1930s London also practiced protectionism and during the second half of the century its main trading partners endorsed a liberal trade policy. This coincided with the fact that throughout the 20th

899 Breach & Hartwell (ed): Ibid., p. 142.
900 Kirby: Ibid., p. 17, 141.
901 Aldcroft: Ibid., p. 11–13.

century, most of its main trading partners promoted factories more decisively. From the 16th century to the mid-19th century, London promoted manufacturing more enthusiastically than any other country in the world and this was paralleled by constant trade surpluses. As the largest producer of manufactures, it had more goods suitable for trading.[902]

A similar phenomenon occurred with the countries that by the 1920s were forcing British goods to retreat from world markets. The US for example experienced trade deficits from the 17th century up to the mid-19th century, coinciding with the period in which its main trading partners supplied more subsidies to manufacturing. From the 1880s until the mid-20th century, however, and even though Washington was not particularly interested in promoting exports, the US experienced trade surpluses. During these decades support for the sector was higher than in most of its trading partners. Germany also experienced a similar phenomenon. For centuries up to the late 19th century, it endured trade deficits. During all that time, the factory promotion efforts of German policy makers were lower than those in most European countries. From the 1890s onwards, surpluses appeared, coalescing with the start of larger factory subsidies than its partners.[903]

Many also claimed that the trade deficits were partially responsible for the poor economic performance of Britain. The cross-country data, however, does not agree. Numerous nations have attained fast GDP figures over sustained periods of time while enduring constant trade deficits. That was the case of the US from the 1840s to the 1870s, Germany from the 1860s to the 1880s, Japan from the 1880s to the early 20th century, and Argentina from the 1860s to the 1890s. The rapid growth in all of these countries correlated with a strong support of the sector and fast factory output. Since in these and the following decades factory subsidies were larger than in most of their competitors, the trade deficits eventually ended.

The evidence suggests that prolonged trade deficits are the effect of a slow economic growth, or more particularly, of a slower economic growth than that of a country's main trading partners. That was the situation of Britain since the late 19th century.

The Labor Party in Britain was created in 1906 out of a union of socialist societies and trade unions. Although at first it won only a few seats in Parliament, by 1918 it had become the second largest political organization in Britain. It remained out of government during the 1920s, but its large presence in Parliament led to the enactment of more social welfare legislation. Many argued that increased welfare expenditures significantly contributed to the inferior performance relative to several competitors.

In those years, per capita welfare expenditures in the US were indeed lower than in Britain, but in Germany they were higher. Germany nonetheless attained a much faster GDP rate. Welfare expenditures were resources that evidently did not get invested, but as the case of Germany suggested, they were not the fundamental reason why Britain attained a slow rate of growth.[904]

The stock market crash in October 1929 and the ensuing depression in the US reverted in Britain in several ways. The collapse of production in the US carried with it a collapse in Britain's capacity to export to America as this country experienced a huge reduction in its ability to import. To make matters worse, the US erected very high trade barriers in 1930.

902 Lee, C. H.: *The British Economy since 1700 — A Macroeconomic Perspective*, p. 219.
903 Niemi: Ibid., p. 18.
904 Gamble: Ibid., p. 89.

Most of Europe experienced also a steep contraction in its capacity to import and British exports were no longer able to find buyers. Exports fell dramatically.

On the other hand, during the 1920s Britain had borrowed considerably from the US. As the stock crash devalued the financial assets of American banks, these demanded an immediate repayment of the loans in order to prop up their balance sheets. British banks also recalled their loans and all of a sudden British factories encountered a liquidity problem due to insufficient financing for their regular operations. They were thus forced to cut production. Had Britain not borrowed from the US and had financing not been reduced, factory production would have still contracted because manufactures accounted for practically all exports and export markets had shrunk. The liquidity problem made the situation worse. It must be noted that the capital British banks provided to manufacturers was not for the creation of factories, but for short-term trade operations and as this was cut, producers could not buy their inputs.

However, the second part of the 1930s and the World War II years suggested that Britain did not need foreign financing or foreign markets in order to attain fast economic growth. Much suggests that if London had decreed a decisive factory promotion policy since late 1929, not a single year of contraction had been endured and rapid growth would have been experienced since 1930. That is precisely what Japan did since 1931 and since that year it attained rapid growth. That is also what Britain did later in the decade and the economy responded similarly.

During the early 1930s, however, London continued to belief in the same unscientific ideas of the preceding decades. Even though the numerous ideas that determined macroeconomic policy were not coherently structured, they ultimately translated into policies that supplied only a small dose of subsidies to manufacturing.[905]

The abrupt reduction of private financing for the sector could have been easily counterbalanced by a significant rise of financial incentives from the state. However, London decided that the best policy to follow was to do nothing, hoping that the economy would recover on its own. The contraction carried with it numerous bankruptcies, which reduced the income of domestic banks, driving them to become even more unwilling to make loans. The bankruptcies also led to a reduction of corporate and personal taxes, which led to lower government revenue. That translated into lower grants for manufacturers, which delivered a further contraction of factory output. The government or the banks were not directly targeting manufacturing, but this sector nonetheless suffered a severe cut in financing as funding fell in a across the board manner.

As the depression continued the next year, the government started to renounce to the idea that a recovery would occur spontaneously and several measures began to be taken. In 1931, the gold standard was dumped and the currency devalued. Since the mid-1920s, it had been argued that the overvalued exchange rate was hurting exports. However, in that year exports and the economy continued to contract and in 1932 there was more of the same.[906]

Since 1930, spending for public works rose, which were increased still more in the next two years. However, this measure also failed to have positive effects. As the crisis worsened, London reconsidered several of its most cherished policies and in 1932 it raised trade barriers, putting an end to the era of free trade. A further plunge in GDP was experienced. From

---

905 Aldcroft: Ibid., p. 44–46.
906 Gamble: Ibid., p. 101.

1929 to 1932, GDP contracted by about 6%. Of the large Western nations that participated in World War I, Britain contracted the least and it also experienced the least decline in factory output.[907]

Manufacturing saw a fall of about 11% during those years while exports dropped by about 38%. The broad drop in exports suggested an absence of a causality linkage between exports and growth because the contraction in GDP was not proportionate. The policies that subtracted support and the factory figures on the other hand, were consistent and proportionate with the whole situation. By 1932 unemployment reached 23%.[908]

Measure after measure failed to deliver positive results and it seemed as if nothing could redress the crisis. Then, in January of 1933, Hitler was sworn in as Germany's Chancellor. His aggressive rhetoric implied the possibility of a future war, and his enlarged defense budget also sent threatening signals throughout Europe.

Under the pressure of this national security threat, British policy makers decreed much larger expenditures for the production of arms and related goods. Everybody predicted a worsening of the crisis as resources were diverted from civilian uses to "unproductive domains," but the result was exactly the opposite. The much larger defense allocations in 1933 increased factory output and there was an immediate change in the direction of the economy. The recession suddenly came to an end.[909]

At first, the armament budget was not large but since the Germans kept increasing their investments in weapons, London felt forced to do the same. This delivered a rate of factory output that accelerated with every year that went by and this coincided with accelerating GDP figures.

The potential of a future large-scale war, which would thoroughly disturb foreign trade, also impelled London to increase its support for the production of civilian factory goods that were normally imported. That translated into a wide-scale effort of import substitution.

As with the expenditures for weapons, those supplied to the producers of weapon-related goods and other civilian goods were considerably smaller than those of Berlin, for up to the last minute, London hoped to avoid a war. Britain did not match the investment efforts of the Nazis. During 1933–39, military expenditures as a share of GDP averaged about 9% while those of Germany averaged about 15%. That coincided with much faster rates of factory output and GDP in Germany.

Foreign trade remained terribly depressed during these years and foreign loans remained also out of the picture, but the economy succeeded in recovering, bringing an unemployment rate of about 23% in 1932 down to 9% in 1939. The more the government spent on weapons and the more markets were distorted to substitute imports, the more everybody predicted an imminent catastrophe. The economy, however, strengthened with every year that went by. Manufacturers received grants, subsidized loans, loan guarantees, and tax exemptions. They also became subsidized factory premises, subsidized utility rates, and guaranteed state purchases at prices that assured a profit.[910]

Aside from weapons, the fields that received the most support were metals, ships, airplanes, electric trains, motor vehicles, chemicals, and electricity. These happened to be the

---

907 Breach & Hartwell (ed): Ibid., p. 145.
908 Bagwell, Philip & Mingay, G.: *Britain and America 1850–1939*, p. 249, 257.
909 Aldcroft: Ibid., 47–56.
910 Ibid., p. 110–127.

fastest growing fields. Production of arms increased so fast, that Britain even caught up in certain weapons with Germany. By the start of the war, production of aircraft was even at par with Germany. It would seem as if this quantitative similarity is responsible for the Royal Air Force's ability to hold its position in aerial warfare since the onset of the conflict. However, on land Britain was forced to retreat. That coincided with a much lower production of land weapons relative to Germany. Once again, the evidence suggests that weapons played the determinant factor deciding the outcome of battles for these goods were the depositories of technology.[911]

Even though the economy was terribly depressed by 1932 and despite the absence of foreign funds, Britain managed to fully reactivate its economy by mobilizing its existing resources into the factories. Resources were simply transferred from construction, services, and primary activities onto manufacturing. Most economists and policy makers of the time were largely convinced that transferring resources from one sector to another was a zero sum game, in which the increase in output of one sector would be negated by a proportionate decrease in the other. That was indeed the case when for example resources were transferred from agriculture to construction or to services or vice versa. Since nobody understood or even suspected the possibility of a causality linkage between manufacturing and technology, it was also thought that a zero sum effect took place with this sector.

When it came to military manufacturing, it was even thought that allocating resources to this domain delivered a reduction of wealth for society. Had they thought of the possibility that this sector creates technology, it wouldn't have surprised them that by 1939, at a time when one quarter of the economy was used for defense, Britain attained the fastest GDP rates of the decade.

It is therefore logical to presume that Britain could have attained double-digit economic growth since 1930 had it allocated as many resources to the sector as it did in 1939. Wealth would have surely been created at an even faster pace had it done this by allotting the resources to civilian manufacturing. However, what took place during 1930–32 was that resources were transferred from manufacturing to the other sectors and that, coincided with a reduction of wealth. Interesting to notice is that even by 1939 and the majority of resources were allocated to non-manufacturing activities such as highway construction, housing, other building activities, agriculture, mining, and numerous service activities.[912]

During the 1930s, factory promotion efforts did increase significantly relative to the 1920s and this coincided with a significant acceleration in the rate of factory output and GDP. This sector grew on average by about 4.2% annually and GDP shadowed, expanding by about 3.5%.

Exports, on the other hand, contracted on average by about -4% each year.

The 1940s

In September of 1939, the Germans invaded Poland, and Britain declared war on Germany. Poland's Armed Forces as well as those of several other nations were rapidly crushed, but Britain did not collapse. This coincided with a vast quantitative and technological superiority of German weapons relative to practically all countries in continental Europe, but not with respect to Britain. France had invested very little in armaments during the 1930s

---

911 Breach & Hartwell (ed): Ibid., p. 143.
912 Aldcroft: Ibid., p. 165, 122–127.

because it feared provoking Germany and concentrated on diplomacy. When the conflict started, its arsenals were not just much smaller than those of Germany, but also technologically inferior.

Germany's land weapons were far superior to those of Britain and on that front the British army could not confront the enemy. However, at sea and in the skies British forces were capable of holding the line. That ran parallel to the quantity and quality of Britain's military assets. Britain had a similar amount of warships and fighter planes as the enemy while the level of technology of these weapons was about the same for both camps. The evidence suggests this hardware similarity is mainly responsible for explaining why the war at sea and in the air stalemated. Once again, weapons seem to have been the decisive factor at the battlefield due to their high embodiment of technology.

With all of her allies defeated, Britain had to confront the Germans and their colossal arsenals practically alone. London mobilized completely for war. It shifted resources wholesale to the production of still more weapons. From 1940 to 1943, more than half of GDP was utilized to cover the defense expenditures and the majority of it was used to produce weapons and other factory goods. These were by far the largest defense expenditures in the entire history of the country and the production of arms grew at an unprecedented pace. Even though civilian production declined, the overall support that was supplied to manufacturing was far above anything previously undertaken. This coincided with unprecedented rates of economic growth.[913]

Everybody predicted economic ruin due to the huge amount of resources that were used to produce inconsumable goods, but the end result was exactly the opposite. By 1942, unemployment had been completely eliminated and over-employment began to appear. Women, retirees, and the very young entered the workforce in droves and by 1943 Britain had the largest share in the world of women in the workforce. Interesting to notice is that prior to the war, most believed that women did not possess the ability to work in heavy manufacturing or in other technology-intensive fields. However, British housewives proved competent in making high-tech arms. The same phenomenon was observed in Germany, the US, and other nations.

By early 1944, the outcome of the war seemed decided and London concluded that defense spending needed to be cut. This translated into smaller allocations for the production of weapons and related goods. Manufacturing output all of a sudden stopped growing at a double digit pace and in 1944 it expanded at a slow pace. This was paralleled by a proportionate deceleration of GDP.

There was still war during the first half of 1945, but by then its outcome seemed even clearer, so London decreed even smaller allocations for defense. Once the conflict ended, investment in armaments and related fields fell broadly. Since the war expenditures were not transferred to civilian manufacturing, this translated into a very large reduction of resources for the sector, which coincided with a massive contraction of the economy.[914]

During World War II, Britain endured for the first time in its history a direct attack on its territory. There was much aerial bombardment which caused considerable physical damage of urban areas. Factories were particularly targeted by the Nazi Air Force and German submarines were very effective in torpedoing British ships. The enemy destroyed about one

913 Aldcroft: Ibid., p. 170.
914 Ibid., p. 166–170, 190.

eighth of housing and one third of shipping tonnage was sunk. Britain had much to recon-struct and on top of that it had no longer to waste its resources in weapons.

Most economists and policy makers predicted fast economic growth, but in the second half of 1945 there was a dramatic contraction and in 1946 there was another steep recession. Although there was some economic recovery during the rest of the decade, the forecasted rapid growth never arrived.

The Labor's Party first victory took place immediately after the end of the war in 1945 and the new government decided that what the country needed was social welfare pro-grams. The social welfare share of the budget grew to new levels. Had the Conservatives continued to rule, the country's welfare expenditures might not have increased as much, but they would have risen for the Conservatives too were convinced that such a policy was good for the country. Just about everybody agreed that a larger system of unemployment benefit, the creation of a national health service, and other social schemes would mollify the public after the sufferings of the war. Most also thought that such schemes would be positive for the economy.[915]

Nobody among the political class believed that support for manufacturing was the de-cisive factor for improving the living conditions of the masses. Much suggests that if no increase in welfare expenditures had been decreed or even a cut in them had taken place, the government would have still not utilized those saved resources for the promotion of civilian manufacturing.

It is worth noting that when the US began to disburse its Marshall Aid to Europe in 1948, Britain became the largest amount. However, during 1948–60, Britain attained the slowest GDP figures among the seventeen countries that received this aid. This coincided with Britain's weaker subsidization of factories relative to the other countries in Western Europe. Germany, which received less per capita Marshall Aid, but which gave the most enthusiastic support to this sector, attained the fastest GDP rates in the continent.[916]

The recently installed Labor government had nonetheless some new ideas about manu-facturing. However, they had nothing to do with allocating more resources to it. In their socialistic view of the world, creating a less unequal society was top priority. They thus decided to nationalize large enterprises. Labor was not particularly targeting manufactur-ing, but many of the companies it took over were in this sector. Labor was mostly targeting big firms. From 1945–51, large producers of iron, steel, trains, telecommunications equip-ment, and electricity were nationalized. Non-manufacturing enterprises in fields like coal, rail transport, dockyards services, airlines, inland waterways, road transport, and the Bank of England were also taken over.[917]

Nationalization had crept into the Labor Party's constitution since 1918 even though its theoretical underpinnings were extremely weak. Once under their control, the Labor government could have allotted far more resources to these factories. However, it decided not to because increasing the output of this sector was not the goal. It is also worth noting that once the nationalized enterprises began to be managed by the state, they became less responsive to market signals and efficiency suffered. The quality of their goods fell.

---

915 Gamble: Ibid., p. 102.
916 Munting & Holderness: Ibid., p. 248.
917 Millward, R. & Singleton, J. (ed): *The Political Economy of Nationalization in Britain 1920–1950*, p. 2–4.

The significant destruction of housing during the war convinced Labor and the Conservatives that a generous house-building program was required. Had the Conservatives been in power, the program had been more market oriented, but the same large resources would have been allotted to this field. The whole political class believed that channeling abundant investments in housing was the best mechanism to satisfy the urgent accommodation needs of the British. It was however Germany, which best satisfied the even larger housing needs of the post-war years. Germany had an exponentially larger share of its buildings destroyed, but it invested less in this domain (as a share of GDP) than Britain. However, houses were built at a faster pace than in Britain. That coincided with the allocation of a larger share of Germany's resources to manufacturing.[918]

History suggests that wealth needs first to be created so that the construction of housing takes place and wealth seems to only be created when resources get allocated to manufacturing. Therefore, by allocating the largest possible share of a nation's resources to this sector is how houses get built at the fastest pace. That would consistently explain what took place in Europe after the war.

It wasn't as if London abstained from providing subsidies to this sector, but in comparison to the ones Bonn supplied, they were small. The Distribution of Industry Act of 1945 procured funds for the construction of factories in depressed areas. The war experience of how resources could be allocated to under-employed areas shaped these policies. The evidence suggests that this sort of support was responsible for the manufacturing growth that took place in the late 1940s. However, the subsidies were only a fraction of the ones approved during the early 1940s. That was paralleled by slow growth.[919]

In spite of it all, in the 1940s support for the sector was much higher than in the preceding decade and that coincided with a much faster rate of factory output and a much faster growth of the economy. Manufacturing averaged about 6.3% annually and GDP about 5.0%. This decade witnessed the strongest subsidization of factories in the whole of British history and this ran parallel with an unprecedented rate of economic growth. At no moment during the second half of the 20th century did London allocate as large a share of the nation's resources to this sector and never again did the economy grow as fast.

Technology and Wealth Creation

The bottom line for the creation of wealth lies in the creation or reproduction of technology, because technology is the only means for actively controlling and altering objects of the physical environment in the interest of some human need.

Since the evidence suggests that manufacturing determines technology, an increase in support for this sector should correlate with an acceleration of the pace of technological development. Such a correlation was observed in Britain during the first half of the 20th century because the government allotted a larger share of national income to the factories than in the preceding fifty years and that correlated with a faster rate of technical progress. While manufacturing in Britain grew by about 2.8% annually in 1850–99, in the following half century it expanded by about 4.0%.

The short-term fluctuations of technology moved also in unison with proportionate levels of subsidization for this sector. During the first decade of the century, technology grew

---

918 More, Charles: *The Industrial Age*, p. 260–263.
919 Ibid., p. 262.

slowly and this coincided with few factory subsidies. By then, Germany took the lead in Europe in inventiveness and it was argued that the British had lost their innovative drive and that the Germans were prone to invention. The fact is that by then, Berlin was the most enthusiastic promoter of factories among the large nations in Europe

During the 1910s, the British became all of a sudden more inventive and that coincided with a rate of factory output that was almost twice as fast as in the preceding decade. The bulk of technological growth occurred during World War I and it was precisely during these years when factories were most promoted.

In the 1920s, technological progress decelerated a little and there was a simultaneous small drop in the factory promotion efforts of London. In the early 1930s, manufacturing contracted and innovation vanished. During the rest of the decade, there were ample subsidies for the sector and that ran tandem to a rapid growth of technology. Then, during World War II, technological innovations came fast and furious and major inventions appeared one after another (ranging from radar to magnetron valves, nylon, DDT, and other insecticides). This coincided with an unprecedented promotion of factories. During the second half of the 1940s, however, the defense budget was cut and technical progress ground to a halt.[920]

Note also that during this fifty-year period, technological progress was more accentuated in the manufacturing fields that received the largest subsidies. During the first decade of the century, shipbuilding received more subsidies than any other field and it was the most innovative area of the economy. During the 1910s, arms underwent more technological change than any other field, correlating with the domain that received the bulk of budgetary allocations. In the 1920s chemicals, automobiles, electricity, and electrical goods received the largest subsidies and these were also the ones which experienced the fastest technological growth. During the 1930s, the promotion efforts of London concentrated on armaments but also on shipbuilding, airplanes, and electric trains. Technology made the most progress in armaments but there were as well many advances in these other fields. Then, in the 1940s innovation occurred almost exclusively in arms and this again happened to be the domain that became the bulk of government allocations.

The events in other countries present a similar correlation. Technological progress during the years 1900–49 was slower in Britain than in several developed countries. Japan attained the fastest pace of technical progress in the world and this happened to be the world's most decisive factory subsidizer.

Research and development (R&D) presents also a correlation with manufacturing. British R&D expenditures as a share of GDP were smaller than in several developed countries, coalescing with a more decisive support for manufacturing in many of these countries. British technology producers relied heavily on government funding to finance their R&D expenditures. However, in countries like Japan, Germany and the US, the share of state funds in the overall R&D expenditures of the private sector was higher. [921]

Precisely because R&D expenditures are so large, governments have sought to stimulate the innovation process by absorbing part of the costs. The more governments have absorbed R&D costs, the faster has been the growth of technology. During the first half of the 1930s, London paid for only a very small share of the R&D costs of the private sector and state laboratories were supplied with only a few funds. Innovation was almost stagnant. Then, in

920 Aldcroft: Ibid., p. 190
921 Elbaum & Lazonick (ed): Ibid., p. 189, 190.

the second half of this decade the government paid for a much larger share of private sector R&D expenditures and channeled much larger funds into state laboratories. All of a sudden, innovation materialized at a relatively fast speed. In the first half of the 1940s, London paid for a still larger share of R&D expenditures. Innovation boomed and technological development in general increased at a breathtaking pace. Then, during the second half of the 1940s, government financing for private and public R&D dropped massively and inventions became rare.

It is also worth noting that the bulk of the R&D funds that London granted to the private sector and to state laboratories, was to create the technology that would make a manufacture good possible. Goods such as more precise weapons, more powerful arms, larger and more seaworthy vessels, faster and more air-worthy air planes, faster and less polluting trains, chemicals with insect-destroying capacities, and pharmaceuticals with disease-preventing abilities. Only a very small fraction of the funds was used for purely theoretical science. The bulk of the funds went into the laboratories of private and state manufacturing companies. The private sector R&D was even more focused on this sector because all of it flowed into factories.

In Britain from 1900–49 the private sector paid for a large share of its R&D costs. However, the confluence of events of this and the preceding periods suggests that if the government had not absorbed part of the costs, the private sector would have spent considerably less. The private sector has always known that the creation of new technology tends to generate vast profits. So long no other enterprise possesses that technology, a monopoly is automatically created and under those circumstances, it can demand the price that it wants on its goods. However, because the generation of technology is so hard to materialize, the whole process of innovation is predisposed to absorb a gigantic amount of resources. These vast investments instinctively drive the private sector to shy away from this effort and to look for alternatives, which demand lower investments. The creation of technology is also very time consuming and the private sector seeks always to attain profits in the shortest amount of time.

The historical data suggests a correlation between manufacturing and productivity. During the 1900s, support for manufacturing was weak and then it increased noticeably in the following decade, coinciding with a slow rate of productivity in the first decade and a significant acceleration in the second. Then, in the 1920s productivity decelerated a little and so did the level of subsidization and the rate of factory output. In the 1930s, it grew at a faster pace and the factory promotion efforts of the state were stronger. And in the 1940s, state allocations for this sector were still larger, factory production expanded faster, and productivity grew more. [922]

During the first half of the 20th century, productivity in Britain grew slower than in countries such as Japan, Germany, and the US. That was paralleled by larger factory subsidies in these three countries. It is also worth noting that in Britain and in those countries, productivity in manufacturing was faster than in all the other sectors of the economy. The evidence suggests that the other sectors are mere recipients of technology. As a result, they are inevitably predisposed to have lower productivity rates. [923]

---

922 Ibid., p. 189.
923 Aldcroft & Richardson: Ibid., p. 129.

During this half century in Britain, the most subsidized factory fields were also the most competitive ones. In this period, shipbuilding received more grants than any other field. It also attained the fastest rates of output, the fastest technological growth, and the fastest rates of productivity. By the late 1940s, shipbuilding was the most competitive British export.[924]

Even though economic growth in Britain during the years 1900–49 accelerated noticeably with respect to the previous half century, it was nonetheless slower than several of its main competitors. Since by the turn of the century, the level of development of these nations had already caught up with that of Britain, in the following fifty years Britain fell behind. This situation was very painful for a country that had for so many centuries been at the top. To make matters worse, the absence of fast economic growth delivered a high rate of unemployment. This led to soul-searching and much mental effort was undertaken to explain this phenomenon.

Many argued that the adherence to gold and in particular at a high exchange rate, damaged export competitiveness. However, on numerous occasions the gold standard was suspended but the economy did not react well. From 1918–24 and from 1931–35, the gold standard was debarred and the currency devalued, but the economy nonetheless performed poorly. In other occasions, as during World War I and World War II, when the gold standard was also suspended, the economy grew rapidly. There was simply no correlation. It was evident that this variable at best played a minuscule role in growth. Manufacturing, however, correlated the whole time.[925]

During the first half of the 20th century, the share of agriculture in GDP shrunk a lot. It thus became extremely hard to present this domain as the one that had propelled the economy. However, there were some who still believed that it played a role in growth. The statistical data begged to disagree. As in the past, agriculture again grew at a much slower pace than GDP, making it practically impossible that it could have pulled the economy. In this half century, farming grew by about 1.8% annually, while GDP did it by 3.3%. Manufacturing however expanded faster, averaging about 4.0%.[926]

The way in which agriculture made progress, strongly suggested that its development depended on manufacturing. The fastest growth of farm output and the fastest improvements in farm productivity took place during the years when the largest incentives were given to factories. During the 1940s, Britain experienced the fastest growth of agricultural production and productivity, and it was then when the fastest production of farm factory goods took place. Just during the World War II years, the utilization of tractors quadrupled. New machines such as the milking machine and the combine harvester appeared during this decade. The evidence suggests these goods were fundamentally responsible for the large improvements of productivity of those years because they completed tasks faster and better.[927]

Population was another variable that could no longer be considered as a causal agent. In the 18th and 19th century, population had been presented as having played an important

924 Aldcroft: Ibid., p. 174, 173.
925 Tomlinson, Jim: *Problems of British Economic Policy 1870–1945*, p. 32, 55.
926 Sabillon: Ibid., p. 183; Madison, Angus: *Monitoring the World Economy 1820–1992*; Madison, Angus: *The World Economy: Historical Statistics*.
927 More: Ibid., p. 331, 332.

role in growth. Even then was this variable unable to correlate, but at least some elements of it seemed to add up. However, in the years 1900–49, even those elements disappeared.

Population growth declined significantly during this fifty-year period relative to the previous half century. If population was an important growth factor, the first half of the 20th century should have experienced a noticeable deceleration of the economy. The economy, however, went the other way and accelerated significantly. Population growth averaged about 0.7% annually after having expanded by 1.2% in 1850–99, but GDP went from 2.4% in the second half of the 19th century to 3.3% in 1900–49.[928]

During the period 1900–49, living conditions in Britain improved faster than in the previous fifty years. Even though not as much progress was attained as in several other countries like Japan, Germany and the US, Britain nonetheless did much better than most nations of the world. This all moved in tandem with a more decisive support for manufacturing relative to 1850–99. It also coincided with a weaker subsidization than in Japan, Germany and the US, and with a stronger promotion of factories relative to the immense majority of the other nations of the world.[929]

---

928 Sabillon: Ibid.
929 Rose, Michael: *The Relief of Poverty 1834–1914.*

CONCLUSION

Notwithstanding the individual traits of the economic history of various nations, there are aspects which are common to all of them and which have a direct connection to the phenomenon of economic growth.

Out of the vast mass of information that history has made available it is possible to extract the variables that are fundamentally responsible for fueling growth. By identifying the factors which were systematically present during periods of growth and absent during periods of stagnation, it is possible to distil the causal determinants of wealth creation. The variables that intervene in the growth process are numerous, but there is one that seems to be of paramount importance. When that variable is missing, growth is practically impossible and when it is present, the historical record shows that almost nothing can prevent it. There have been times when all the factors considered to fuel growth were missing except that one, and still rapid economic growth was achieved; this strongly suggests that the bottom line for the creation of wealth resides with this one factor.

Needless to say, this factor needs several others to maximize its potential. Alone, it can deliver growth, but without certain other conditions, inefficiency and waste appear to be inevitable.

The determinant factor for growth is the level of government support for the manufacturing sector.

Guidelines for Growth

The events that made up human history up to the mid-20th century in East Asia, Western Europe, the US, and Russia all point to the conclusion that economic growth is an endogenous phenomenon that can be manipulated by government policy.

The history of these nations suggests that growth is intimately linked to the manufacturing sector because of the almost unique capacity of this sector to create and reproduce technology. The generation of technology is the most resource-demanding of efforts, so that this sector is predisposed to be extremely investment intensive. Private sector investors tend to prefer less risky endeavors which can flourish with much lower investments and offer a much faster return on investment. History suggests that the invisible hand of the market alone will not deliver significant investment in manufacturing and technology will not be generated. Under those circumstances, wealth is not created and economic stagnation prevails.

The state has the only hand big enough to induce the private sector to go into manufacturing, by offering incentives that offset high production costs and reduce the risk of venturing into this sector. The more the state underwrites these efforts, the more attractive the sector becomes for capitalists and entrepreneurs. That is why the state plays a determinant role in the generation of growth.

The fundamental factor determining manufacturing growth is the level of government support for the manufacturing sector. And the growth rate of the manufacturing sector is the key factor for determining the rate of overall economic growth. What matters is not the size of this sector as a share of GDP, but the average annual rate of growth.

However, the degree to which market forces are free to operate within an economy affects how much growth will be extracted from every unit of manufacturing output. Competition is the second most important variable affecting growth: the higher the level of competition, the more efficiently wealth is extracted per unit of factory output.

Thus, when economic growth is the only, or the highest, goal, governments must promote the growth of the manufacturing sector as much as possible while simultaneously liberalizing the economy as much as possible.

The empirical evidence suggests that the most effective way to promote manufacturing is by means of fiscal, financial and non-financial incentives. Other efforts such as the establishment of state-run factories, trade protection, cartels, and regulations of numerous sorts may bring benefits in terms of keeping manufacturing in local hands, or mitigating unemployment, but these are not the strongest ways to deliver economic growth and they can lead to poor quality and high production costs.

In order to attain the fastest possible rates of growth, fiscal, financial and non-financial incentives must be provided simultaneously and at the highest possible level.

An Income Redistribution Policy

History suggests that while the manufacturing sector is expanding, wealth is spread among a wider population. Wealth is created faster and the workers as well as the investor class experience a rise in income. In this scenario, even while in the aggregate the wealthy take a smaller percentage of the economy, their incomes are rising, so they permit the trend to continue. Under this policy, the rich are not taxed more heavily nor are their assets expropriated, and they do not feel that their position in society is undermined.

The way by which this phenomenon takes place is intricate and it is determined by two factors. On the one hand, a factory-stimulation policy reduces unemployment and boosts the incomes of workers. On average, manufacturing wages are those in many of the service sectors. That has been a constant throughout history, in all continents. Therefore, a strong pro-manufacturing policy increases the share of the population employed in manufacturing, and the share of national income accrued to the working class inevitably rises. Governments that are particularly interested in improving income distribution therefore have an additional reason for endorsing a manufacturing policy.

The largely stagnant GDP figures of the 1980s in the Soviet Union and East European countries (about 1.0% annually) coincided with reduced support of manufacturing. But the US in the 1930s performed even worse and Japan, Germany and France in the 1990s were hardly better. Economic stagnation can be a sign that the basic tenets of a system are feeble, but that also applies to capitalist countries, which grew relatively slowly throughout most of their history.

In the last decades of the 20th century, policies of liberalization and privatization were applied almost worldwide. Many governments cut their social welfare budgets. Economic growth did not improve and in many countries it worsened. The resources saved were not transferred to factories and GDP rates remained low.

Are laissez-faire policies and free markets the answer? No. History suggests that when markets are left to operate freely, they do not allocate resources to manufacturing. The very nature of capitalism conspires against manufacturing as well as against the average worker, because when markets are left to run their natural course, they allot practically all of the available resources to services, construction and primary activities. Wage income goes down and technological inventiveness is unable to enter the manufacturing stream to boost the overall economy. Growth grinds to a halt.

APPENDIX

Methodology for Preparing the Charts

The data used to prepare the historical charts came from numerous sources. For the period running from the 16th century to the mid-20th century, it was extracted from economic, history and economic history books as cited in the individual chapters. For the second half of the 20th century, most of the data came from the publications of the World Bank, the Organization for Economic Cooperation and Development, the International Monetary Fund, the World Trade Organization, the United Nations' specialized agencies, research institutes and country statistical publications. Books and journals also supplied a considerable amount of data for this last period.

Although international standards of coverage, definition, and classification apply to most statistics reported by international agencies, governments and other sources, there are inevitably differences in timeliness and reliability arising from differences in these sources' capabilities and the resources devoted to basic data collection and compilation. For some topics, competing sources of data were reviewed to ensure that the most reliable data available are presented. In some instances, where available data are deemed too weak to provide reliable measures of levels and trends or do not adequately adhere to international standards, the data are not shown. Because data quality and inter-country comparisons are often problematic, readers are encouraged to consult the notes at the bottom of several charts.

Even though some territories such as Hong Kong are not politically independent countries, they are presented in a way similar to sovereign countries because authorities report separate economic statistics and because of their relevance for the main goal of this book. This book's priority is presenting information on economic growth, and economies such as Hong Kong attained an impressive rate of growth in the 20th century.

The charts concentrate fundamentally on showing the long-, medium- and short-term trends of the main economic indicators. The variables that are of most interest are gross domestic product, manufacturing, and agriculture. Data on population, inflation, unemployment, exports, services, construction and life expectancy is also compiled, although in a less consistent way over different time periods. Charts are structured chronologically, one for each economy. Each nation's chart was constructed by compiling data extracted from numerous statistical sources. Then it was assembled together in an organized and coherent way.

The charts are an effort to display the factors that have been most frequently presented as determinant for the attainment of prosperity. Most figures are presented on an average annual-rate basis in order to facilitate comparisons. One variable is presented as a proportion of the total workforce, which also allows for easy comparisons among nations of different size and over different periods of time.

The variable that is not measured on an average annual-rate basis is unemployment. Unemployment is measured as a share of the total workforce.

Gross domestic product is gross value added, at purchaser prices, by all resident producers in the economy plus any taxes and minus any subsidies not included in the value of the products. Agriculture includes also forestry and fishing. Manufacturing is used similar to the traditional definition of industry but does not include mining and construction. Manufacturing here refers to all production that takes place in a factory. Services are all intangible activities that do not fall into agriculture, manufacturing or construction. Exports represent the value of all goods provided to the rest of the world. Population includes all residents, regardless of legal status or citizenship, living in a country. Inflation is the increase in prices.

For Russia, China, and the Democratic Republic of Germany, it was necessary to do more than merely compiling and organizing chronologically-consistent statistics. Their official figures were not generated on the same basis used by Westernized nations and do not lend themselves to comparison with them. The official figures are therefore presented side by side with figures recalculated to take into account, as previously discussed, the lowest, most unlikely estimates. Official figures [presented in brackets] are those provided by governments, international organizations and most books — which tend to reproduce the figures provided by governments. Only the GDP figures were reconstructed. Rates of output of manufacturing, agriculture and of all the other variables were left as the official figures presented them.

Despite efforts made to standardize the data, full compatibility cannot be assured and care must be taken in interpreting the indicators. Many factors affect data availability, comparability and reliability. Statistical systems in the least developed countries were still weak even in the 1990s. The further back in time, the less reliable is the information. Cross-national and inter-temporal comparisons involve complex technical and conceptual problems that cannot be resolved unequivocally. For these reasons, although the data are drawn from the sources thought to be most authoritative, they should be construed only as indicating trends and characterizing major differences among economies rather than offering precise quantitative measures of those differences.

The growth rates presented in this book are compiled from official sources. The compiled data had to be reorganized because it comprised periods that did not lend themselves to comparison. Even the World Bank does not provide information for every decade in an organized form. Instead of supplying a figure for the 1960s, they provide figures that cover the period 1960–70. As for books of economic history, they usually provide periods such as 1947–58, 1918–38 or 1870–1914. Economic historians looking at the big picture tend to present figures that are not very useful for cross-national comparisons. Angus Maddison, in *L'Economie Chinoise — Une Perspective Historique,* for example, provides useful figures for the 18th century in China, India, Japan, the US and Europe, but the time span is 1700–1820. Thus the mathematical work in this book consisted in adding, subtracting, stitching the pieces together, and taking averages.

TABLES

The figures are presented on an average annual percentage basis with the exception of unemployment, which is measured as a proportion of the total workforce.

Man – Manufacturing

Agri – Agriculture

Serv – Service sector

Pop – Population

Inf – Inflation

Ex – Exports

Unem – Unemployment

TABLE 1. GREAT BRITAIN

	Man	GDP	Agri	Serv	Pop	Inf	Ex	Unem
16th Century	0.4	0.3	0.2		0.2	1.7		
17th Century	0.4	0.3	0.2		0.2	0.4		
18th Century	1.1	0.8	0.5		0.6	0.9		
19th Century	3.2	2.7	1.2		1.4	0.1		
20th Century	3.5	3.0	0.8	3.4	0.5	4.0		7.5
1700–59	0.7	0.7	0.6		0.4			
1760–79	1.3	0.6	0.1		0.5			
1780–99	2.0	1.4	0.8		0.9			
1800–49	3.6	2.9	1.3		1.6	0.2		
1850–99	2.8	2.4	1.1		1.2	0.0		
1900–49	4.0	3.3	1.8	3.6	0.7	1.8		8.6
1950–99	2.9	2.7	-0.3	3.1	0.3	6.3	4.7	6.5
1800s	2.7	2.3	0.7		1.2	0.4		
1810s	3.4	2.7	1.2		1.5	0.3		
1820s	3.9	3.4	1.6		1.7	0.2		
1830s	4.0	3.3	1.7		1.8	0.1		
1840s	3.8	3.0	1.4		1.7	0.0		
1850s	3.0	2.8	1.3		1.4	0.0		
1860s	3.0	2.6	1.2		1.3	0.0		
1870s	2.9	2.5	1.0	2.2	1.2	0.0		
1880s	2.7	2.2	0.9	2.1	1.1	0.0		
1890s	2.4	2.0	0.9	1.9	1.0	0.0		
1900s	2.5	2.0	0.6	2.4	1.0	0.0		6.8
1910s	4.2	3.5	1.1	3.1	0.6	0.1		5.2
1920s	2.9	2.5	0.9	3.5	0.9	1.9		12.1
1930s	4.2	3.5	1.2	3.8	0.8	2.1	-4.0	15.4
1940s	6.3	5.0	5.0	5.0	0.4	5.0		3.6
1950s	3.4	3.0	2.7	3.0	0.5	3.0	5.1	4.7
1960s	3.5	3.1	2.4	2.7	0.4	4.1	4.8	5.1
1970s	2.3	2.3	1.0	2.4	0.3	14.2	8.2	6.7
1980s	3.0	2.6	-7.2	4.8	0.3	6.1	3.0	8.3
1990s	2.5	2.3	0.4	2.5	0.2	3.9	2.2	7.4

The figures for the sixteenth century were taken from *The World Economy Historical Statistics* (Angus Maddison); *The World Economy: A Millennium Perspective* (Angus Maddison); *A Concise Economic History of Europe* (John Clapham); *The Cambridge Economic History of Europe* Vol. III; *A History of the British Economy* (Brian Murphy); *The Wealth of England from 1496 to 1760* (George Clarke); *The Price Revolution in Sixteenth Century England* (Peter Ramsey); *Trade and Industry in Tudor and Stuart England* (Sybil Jack); *Pre-Industrial England* (B. A. Holderness).

The figures for the seventeenth century were taken from *Population, Economy and Society* (J. D. Chambers); *The General Crisis of the Seventeenth Century* (Geoffrey Parker); *English Towns in Transition 1500–1700* (Peter Clark & Paul Slack); *The Business Community of Seventeenth Century England* (Richard Grassby); *The World Economy Historical Statistics* (Angus Maddison); *The World Economy: A Millennium Perspective* (Angus Maddison); *A Concise Economic History of Europe* (John Clapham); *The Cambridge Economic History of Europe* Vol. IV; *A History of the British Economy* (Brian Murphy).

The figures for the eighteenth century were taken from *The Economic History of Britain Since 1700* Vol. I & II (Roderick Floud & Donald McCloskey); *The Growth of British Industry* (A. E. Musson); *British Economic and Social History* (C. P. Hill); *The Economy of England 1415–1750* (D. C. Coleman); *Agriculture and Economic Growth in England 1650–1815* (E. L. Jones); *Industry and Empire* (E. J. Hobsbawm); *The First Industrial Revolution* (Phyllis Deane); *Ireland and Scotland 1600–1850* (T. Devin & D. Dickson); *The World Economy Historical Statistics* (Angus Maddison); *The World Economy: A Millennium Perspective* (Angus Maddison); *A Concise Economic History of Europe* (John Clapham); *The Cambridge Economic History of Europe* Vol. V; *A History of the British Economy* (Brian Murphy); *The Escape from Hunger and Premature Death 1700–2100 Europe, America and the Third World* (Robert Fogel).

The figures for the first half of the nineteenth century were taken from *The Economic History of Britain Since 1700* Vol. II (Roderick Floud & Donald McCloskey); *Comparative Aspects of Scottish and Irish Economic and Social History 1600–1900* (L. Cullen & T. Smout); *The Workshop of the World* (J. D. Chambers); *Landowners, Capitalists and Entrepreneurs* (F. Thompson); *Atlas of British Social and Economic History since 1700* (Rex Pope); *The World Economy Historical Statistics* (Angus Maddison); *The World Economy: A Millennium Perspective* (Angus Maddison); *A Concise Economic History of Europe* (John Clapham); *The Escape from Hunger and Premature Death 1700–2100 Europe, America and the Third World* (Robert Fogel); *Society and Economy in Modern Britain 1700–1850* (Richard Brown); *Laissez Faire and State Intervention in Nineteenth Century Britain* (Richard Tames); *Economy and Society in Nineteenth Century Britain* (Richard Tames).

The figures for the second half of the nineteenth century were taken from *Economic Foundations for British Overseas Expansion 1815–1914* (P. J. Cain); *Essays on a Mature Economy: Britain After 1840* (Donald McCloskey); *The Decline of British Economic Power since 1870* (M. W. Dirby); *British Fluctuations 1790–1939* (D. Aldcroft & P. Pearson); *Society and Economy in Modern Britain 1700–1850* (Richard Brown); *Laissez Faire and State Intervention in Nineteenth Century Britain* (Richard Tames); *Economy and Society in Nineteenth Century Britain* (Richard Tames); *Continuity, Chance and Change* (E. Wrigley); *Britain and America 1850–1939* (Philip Bagwell & G. Mingay); *The Relief of Poverty 1834–1914* (Michael Rose); *The British Economy since 1700 — A Macroeconomic Perspective* (C. H. Lee); *The First Industrial Nation* (Peter Mathias); *The Standard of Living in Britain in the Industrial Revolution* (Arthur Taylor0; *Monitoring the World Economy, 1820–1992* (Angus Maddison).

The figures for the first half of the twentieth century were taken from *Problems of British Economic Policy 1870–1945* (Jim Tomlinson); *The British Economy 1870–1939* (Derek Aldcroft & Harry Richardson); *An Economic History of England 1870–1939* (William Ashworth); *Britain in Decline* (Andrew Gamble); *Mammon and the Pursuit of Empire* (Lance Davis & Robert Huttenback); *The Decline of the British Economy* (Bernard Elbaum & William Lazonick); *The Political Economy of Nationalization in Britain 1920–1950* (R. Millward & J. Singleton); *Monitoring the World Economy, 1820–1992* (Angus Maddison); *Modern Economic Growth* (Simon Kuznets); *Economics and World History* (Paul Bairoch).

The figures for the second half of the twentieth century were taken from *World Development Report 1981, 1991 & 2001* (The World Bank); *British Economy and Society 1870–1970* (R. Breach & R. Hartwell); *The British Disease* (G. Allen); *The British Economy* Vol. I (Derek Aldcroft); *Plenty and Want* (John Burnett); *British Economic Performance 1945–1975* (B. Alford); *The Economy in Question* (J. Allen & D. Massey); *The Development of the British Economy* (Sidney Pollard); *The Industrial Age* (Charles Moore); *Monitoring the World Economy, 1820–1992* (Angus Maddison).

TABLE 2. THE UNITED STATES OF AMERICA

	Man	GDP	Agri	Serv	Pop	Inf	Ex	Unem
16th Century	0.0	0.0	0.0		0.0	0.0		
17th Century	0.1	0.1	0.1			0.0		
18th Century	0.4	0.3	0.2		5.5	0.0		
19th Century	5.4	4.5	2.4		5.1	0.0		
20th Century	4.2	3.5	1.7	3.9	1.3	2.5		6.5
1800-49	3.3	2.7	1.8		5.9	0.0		
1850-99	7.5	6.3	3.0		4.2	0.0		
1900-49	4.2	3.5	1.6	4.1	1.4	1.2		7.6
1950-99	4.1	3.4	1.7	3.7	1.2	3.8	5.7	5.3
1800s	2.3	1.8	1.4			0.1		
1810s	2.0	1.6	1.6			0.1		
1820s	3.7	3.0	1.6			0.0		
1830s	4.2	3.5	2.0			0.0		
1840s	4.7	3.8	2.2			0.0		
1850s	5.5	4.5	2.3			0.0		
1860s	6.0	4.7	2.0			0.7		
1870s	8.0	6.9	3.5	6.6		-0.9		
1880s	9.4	7.8	4.0	8.0		0.0		
1890s	8.6	7.5	3.0	7.7		0.0		
1900s	5.8	5.2	3.0	5.5		0.4		4.0
1910s	3.7	3.0	1.6	4.0		1.3		5.2
1920s	4.7	4.0	0.8	4.9		1.1		5.1
1930s	0.8	0.6	0.1	1.2		0.4		18.0
1940s	6.0	4.8	2.5	5.0		3.0		6.1
1950s	5.3	4.3	3.0	5.2	1.8	2.3	6.4	4.3
1960s	5.5	4.4	0.3	4.3	1.3	2.8	6.1	4.0
1970s	3.4	3.0	0.9	3.4	1.0	6.9	6.9	6.3
1980s	2.9	2.5	3.2	3.3	1.0	4.0	3.4	6.5
1990s	3.2	2.9	1.1	2.1	1.0	3.0	5.8	5.6

The figures for the sixteenth century were taken from *The World Economy Historical Statistics* (Angus Maddison); *The World Economy: A Millennium Perspective* (Angus Maddison); *The United States to 1877* (John Krout); *American Economic Growth* (Lance Davis, Richard Easterlin & William Parker); *An Economic History of the United States* (Gilbert Fite & Jim Reese); *American Economic History* (Jonathan Hughes); *American Economic History* (L. Davis, J. Hughes & D. McDougall); *The Growth of the American Economy to 1860* (Douglas North); *Histoire Economique des Etas Unis* Vol. I (Harold Faulkner).

The figures for the seventeenth century were taken from *Economic History of the American People* (Ernest Bogart & Donald Kemmerer); *The World Economy Historical Statistics* (Angus Maddison); *The World Economy A Millennium Perspective* (Angus Maddison); *The United States to 1877* (John Krout); *American Economic History* (L. Davis, J. Hughes & D. McDougall); *The Growth of the American Economy to 1860* (Douglas North); *Histoire Economique des Etas Unis* Vol. I (Harold Faulkner); *U.S. Economic History* (Albert Niemi); *Economic History of the United States* (Chester Wright).

The figures for the eighteenth century were taken from *American Economic History* (Jonathan Hughes); *The Escape from Hunger and Premature Death 1700–2100 Europe, America and the Third World* (Robert Fogel); *The World Economy Historical Statistics* (Angus Maddison); *The World Economy A Millennium Perspective* (Angus Maddison); *The United States to 1877* (John Krout); *American Economic History* (L. Davis, J. Hughes

& D. McDougall); *The Growth of the American Economy to 1860* (Douglas North); *Histoire Economique des Etas Unis* Vol. I (Harold Faulkner); *U.S. Economic History* (Albert Niemi); *Economic History of the United States* (Chester Wright); *Economic History of the American People* (Ernest Bogart & Donald Kemmerer).

The figures for the first half of the nineteenth century were taken from *Technology and American Economic Growth* (Nathan Rosenberg); *Major Documents in American Economic History* Vol. I (Louis Hacker); *American Economic Growth* (Lance Davis, Richard Easterlin & William Parker); *An Economic History of the United States* (Gilbert Fite & Jim Reese); *American Economic History* (Jonathan Hughes); *The World Economy Historical Statistics* (Angus Maddison); *The World Economy A Millennium Perspective* (Angus Maddison); *The Escape from Hunger and Premature Death 1700–2100 Europe, America and the Third World* (Robert Fogel).

The figures for the second half of the nineteenth century were taken from *The United States since 1865* (John Krout); *Histoire Economique des Etas Unis* (Shepard Clough); *Main Currents in Modern American History* (Gabriel Kolko); *American Economic History* (Seymour Harris); *Technology and American Economic Growth* (Nathan Rosenberg); *Production Trends in the United States since 1870* (Arthur Burns); *The World Economy* (Walt Rostow); *Modern Economic Growth* (Simon Kuznets); *Economics and World History* (Paul Bairoch); *The Escape from Hunger and Premature Death 1700–2100 Europe, America and the Third World* (Robert Fogel); *Monitoring the World Economy 1820–1992* (Angus Maddison).

The figures for the first half of the twentieth century were taken from *America in the 20th Century* (D. Adams); *The Structure of a Modern Economy* (Kenneth Boulding); *America's Greatest Depression* (Lester Chandler); *Technology and American Economic Growth* (Nathan Rosenberg); *The Rise and Fall of the New Deal Order* (J. Fraser & G. Gerstle); *American Economic Growth* (Lance Davis, Richard Easterlin & William Parker); *An Economic History of the United States* (Gilbert Fite & Jim Reese); *American Economic History* (Jonathan Hughes); *The Growth of the International Economy 1820–1990* (A. Kenwood & A. Louheed); *The Escape from Hunger and Premature Death 1700–2100 Europe, America and the Third World* (Robert Fogel); *Monitoring the World Economy 1820–1992* (Angus Maddison); "More than Meets the Eye," *The Economist*, Dec. 26, 1992.

The figures for the second of the twentieth century were taken from *World Development Report 1981, 1991 & 2001* (The World Bank); *The Age of Diminished Expectations* (Paul Krugman); *American Economic History* (Jonathan Hughes); *The Escape from Hunger and Premature Death, 1700–2100: Europe, America and the Third World* (Robert Fogel); *Monitoring the World Economy, 1820–1992* (Angus Maddison); "More than Meets the Eye," *The Economist*, Dec. 26, 1992.

TABLE 3. GERMANY

	Man	GDP	Agri	Serv	Pop	Inf	Ex	Unem
16th Century	0.3	0.2	0.1		0.2			
17th Century	0.3	0.2	0.1		-0.1			
18th Century	0.6	0.4	0.3		0.2			
19th Century	3.4	2.7	1.6		1.2			
20th Century	4.6	3.7	2.0	4.3	0.4			
1800-49	2.0	1.5	0.8		0.7			
1850-99	4.8	3.9	2.3		1.7			
1900-49	4.7	3.6	1.9	4.6	0.3			
1950-99	4.5	3.8	2.1	4.0	0.5	3.1	7.5	5.6 (Western Germany)
1800-39	1.8	1.4	0.7					
1840s	2.6	2.0	1.2					
1850s	3.0	2.5	1.6					
1860s	3.7	3.0	2.0					
1870s	4.4	3.6	2.0					
1880s	6.6	5.4	3.0	6.6				

1890s	6.2	5.1	2.8	6.0				
1900s	4.5	3.8	2.2	4.4				
1910s	1.9	1.2	0.3	2.2				
1920s	5.2	4.4	2.7	5.0				
1930s	6.8	5.0	2.4	6.9				
1940s	5.1	3.5	2.3	4.7				
1950s	9.3	8.0	4.0	9.4	1.2	2.2	15.0	8.1 (Western Germany)
1960s	5.7	4.6	1.7	4.2	0.9	2.7	10.1	1.2 (Western Germany)
1970s	3.2	2.6	1.5	1.7	0.1	5.3	6.0	3.0 (Western Germany)
1980s	2.4	2.0	1.6	2.9	0.0	2.7	4.4	6.1 (Western Germany)
1990s	2.0	1.6	1.2	1.8	0.4	2.8	2.2	9.6 (Western Germany)

GERMAN DEMOCRATIC REPUBLIC (EAST GERMANY)

	Man	GDP	Agri	Unem
1950s	12.2	5.1 (10)	3.6	
1960s	5.1	2.0 (4)	2.0	
1970s	6.3	2.4 (5)	2.1	
1980s	3.9	1.7 (3)	1.8	
1990s	1.4	2.0		17.0

The figures for the sixteenth century were taken from *The World Economy Historical Statistics* (Angus Maddison); *The World Economy A Millennium Perspective* (Angus Maddison); *The Cambridge Economic History of Europe* Vol. III; *Histoire de l'Allemagne* (Pierre Gaxotte); *Histoire de l'Allemagne* (Joseph Rovan).

The figures for the seventeenth century were taken from *A History of Modern Germany* Vol. I (Hajo Holborn); *Germany* (Ernest Bramsted); *The World Economy Historical Statistics* (Angus Maddison); *The World Economy A Millennium Perspective* (Angus Maddison); *The Cambridge Economic History of Europe* Vol. III & IV; *Germany and the Old Regime 1600-1790* (John Gagliardo); *The World Economy* (Walt Rostow).

The figures for the eighteenth century were taken from *The Cambridge Economic History of Europe* Vol. IV & V; *Histoire de la Allemagne* (Pierre Gaxotte); *The World Economy Historical Statistics* (Angus Maddison); *The World Economy A Millennium Perspective* (Angus Maddison); *Economics of World History* (Paul Bairoch); *Germany and the Old Regime 1600-1790* (John Gagliardo); *Modern Germany* (Roppel Pinson); *The Escape from Hunger and Premature Death 1700-2100 Europe, America and the Third World* (Robert Fogel).

The figures for the first half of the nineteenth century were taken from *European Economic History: The Economic Development of Western Civilization* (Shepard Clough); *The World Economy Historical Statistics* (Angus Maddison); *The World Economy A Millennium Perspective* (Angus Maddison); *The Cambridge Economic History of Europe* Vol. V & VI; *Histoire de l'Allemagne* (Pierre Gaxotte); *Economics of World History* (Paul Bairoch); *Germany and the Old Regime 1600-1790* (John Gagliardo); *The Escape from Hunger and Premature Death, 1700-2100: Europe, America and the Third World* (Robert Fogel).

The figures for the second half of the nineteenth century were taken from *The Political Economy of Germany 1815-1914* (Martin Kitchen); *L'Economie Allemande sous le Nazisme* Vol. I (Charles Bettelheim); *The History of Germany since 1789* (Golo Mann); *Germany* (*A New Social and Economic History* Vol. 2 (Sheilagh Ogilvie); *Monitoring the World Economy 1820-1992* (Angus Maddison); *Modern Economic Growth* (Simon Kuznets); *The Growth of the International Economy 1820-1990* (A. Kenwood & A. Lougheed); *The World Economy* (Walt Rostow).

The figures for the first half of the twentieth century were taken from *Modern Germany* (V. Berghahn); *Crisis, Recovery and War* (Roger Munting & B. Holderness); *The Political Economy of Germany 1815-1914* (Martin Kitchen); *L'Economie Allemande sous le Nazisme* Vol. I & Vol. II (Charles Bettelheim); *Wirtschafts Geschichte Deutschlands im 20 Jahrhundert* (Karl Hardach); *Modern Economic Growth* (Simon Kuznets); *The*

Growth of the International Economy 1820–1990 (A. Kenwood & A. Lougheed); *The World Economy* (Walt Rostow); *The World Economy Historical Statistics* (Angus Maddison); *Monitoring The World Economy 1820–1992* (Angus Maddison); *The Escape from Hunger and Premature Death, 1700–2100: Europe, America and the Third World* (Robert Fogel).

The figures for the second half of the twentieth century for Western Germany were taken from the *World Development Report 1981, 1991 & 2001* (The World Bank); *Wirtschafts Geschichte Deutschlands im 20 Jahrhundert* (Karl Hardach); *Deutsche Bundesbank Annual Report 1991–1999*; *The Federal Republic of Germany 1991* (International Monetary Fund); *Germany OECD Economic Surveys* (OECD); *German Unification* (International Monetary Fund 1990); *German Unification in European Perspective* (Wolfgang Heisenberg).

For Eastern Germany, the figures for the second half of the twentieth century were taken from the *World Development Report 1981*; *Developpement Economique de L'Allemagne Orientale* (Guy Roustang); *The German Democratic Republic* (Henry Krisch); *German Unification* (International Monetary Fund 1990); *German Unification in European Perspective* (Wolfgang Heisenberg).

Two sets of GDP figures are shown for Eastern Germany for the period 1950–89. The official figures are shown in parentheses, side by side with the most extreme and highly improbable recastings of the official data by Western analysts who arbitrarily reduce the numbers by half.

TABLE 4. RUSSIA

	Man	GDP	Agri	Serv	Pop	Inf	Ex
16th Century	0.2	0.1	0.1		0.1		
17th Century	0.3	0.2	0.1		0.2		
18th Century	0.7	0.5	0.3		1.1		
19th Century	2.3	1.7	0.9		1.2		
20th Century	6.9	2.4 (4.9)	1.9		0.9		
1800-49	0.5	0.3	0.2		0.2		
1850-99	4.0	3.0	1.6		2.2		
1900-49	9.0	3.1 (6.4)	2.0		0.8		
1950-99	4.7	1.7 (3.4)	1.6	3.3	1.0		
1800-39	0.3	0.2	0.2				
1840s	0.5	0.4	0.3				
1850s	0.8	0.6	0.4				
1860s	2.8	2.0	1.2				
1870s	3.2	2.5	1.7				
1880s	5.0	3.9	2.0				
1890s	8.0	6.1	2.8				
1900s	3.0	2.2	2.0				
1910s	-3.5	-2.6	-3.0				
1920s	21.1	8.0 (16)	5.9				
1930s	17.2	5.8 (14)	0.1				
1940s	7.1	2.2 (5)	5.1				
1950s	12.2	4.1 (9)	4.8	4.6			
1960s	9.1	3.0 (7)	2.9	5.7			
1970s	6.2	2.3 (4)	2.0	4.0			
1980s	4.3	1.4 (2)	1.1	3.8	0.6		
1990s	-9.0	-3.0 (-6)	-2.6	-1.8	-0.1	413.8	

The figures for the sixteenth century were taken from *The Rise of the European Economy* (Herman Kellenbenz); *The World Economy Historical Statistics* (Angus Maddison); *The World Economy A Millennium Perspective* (Angus Maddison); *The Cambridge Economic History of Europe* Vol. III; *A History of Russia* (Walter Kirchner); *A Historical Geography of Russia* (W. H. Parker).

The figures for the seventeenth century were taken from *Entrepreneurship in Imperial Russia and the Soviet Union* (Gregory Guroff & Fred Carstensen); *Bread and Salt* (R. Smith & D. Christian); *The World Economy Historical Statistics* (Angus Maddison); *The World Economy A Millennium Perspective* (Angus Maddison); *The Cambridge Economic History of Europe* Vol. III & IV; *A History of Russia* (Walter Kirchner); *A Historical Geography of Russia* (W. H. Parker); *The Rise of the European Economy* (Herman Kellenbenz).

The figures for the eighteenth century were taken from *The Beginning of Russian Industrialization* (William Blackwell); *The Plow, the Hammer and the Knout* (Kahan Arcadius); *Political Economy and Soviet Socialism* (Alec Nove); *The World Economy Historical Statistics* (Angus Maddison); *The World Economy A Millennium Perspective* (Angus Maddison); *The Cambridge Economic History of Europe* Vol. IV & V; *The Escape from Hunger and Premature Death 1700–2100 Europe, America and the Third World* (Robert Fogel); *The Experience of Economic Growth* (Barry Supple); *A History of Russia* (Walter Kirchner); *A Historical Geography of Russia* (W. H. Parker); *The Rise of the European Economy* (Herman Kellenbenz).

The figures for the first half of the nineteenth century were taken from *The World Economy Historical Statistics* (Angus Maddison); *The World Economy A Millennium Perspective* (Angus Maddison); *The Cambridge Economic History of Europe* Vol. V & VI; *Economics of World History* (Paul Bairoch); *The Escape from Hunger and Premature Death 1700–2100 Europe, America and the Third World* (Robert Fogel); *The Experience of Economic Growth* (Barry Supple); *The Rise of the European Economy* (Herman Kellenbenz); *The Beginning of Russian Industrialization* (William Blackwell); *The Fontana Economic History of Europe: The Emergence of Industrial Societies*; *Bread and Salt* (R. Smith & D. Christian); *Economic Growth in Japan and the USSR* (Angus Maddison).

The figures for the second half of the nineteenth century were taken from *Soviet Economic Facts 1917–70* (Roger Clarke); *An Economic History of the USSR* (Alec Nove); *A Historical Geography of Russia* (W. H. Parker); *Russian Economic History* (Kahan Arcadius); *The Tsarist Economy 1850–1917* (Peter Gatrell); *Political Economy and Soviet Socialism* (Alec Nove); *The Cambridge Economic History of Europe* Vol. VII; *The Fontana Economic History of Europe (The Emergence of Industrial Societies)*; *The Experience of Economic Growth* (Barry Supple); *Economic Growth in Japan and the USSR* (Angus Maddison); *A Short History of Economic Progress* (Y. Brenner); *The Industrialization of Russia* (William Blackwell); Endurance and Endeavour (J. Westwood); *Monitoring the World Economy 1820–1992* (Angus Maddison).

The figures for the first half of the twentieth century were taken from *Soviet Economic Facts 1917–70* (Roger Clarke); *Soviet Economic Facts 1917–81* (Roger Clarke & Dubravko Matko); *Soviet Economic Development Since 1917* (Maurice Dobb); *An Economic History of the USSR* (Alec Nove); *L'Economie de l'URSS* (Pierre George); *Soviet Economics* (Michael Kasar); *Russian Economic History* (Kahan Arcadius); *Soviet Economic Power* (Robert Campbell); *The Tsarist Economy 1850–1917* (Peter Gatrell); *Modern Soviet Society* (Basile Kerblay); *Political Economy and Soviet Socialism* (Alec Nove); *The Cambridge Economic History of Europe* Vol. VIII; *The Fontana Economic History of Europe (The Emergence of Industrial Societies)*; *The Fontana Economic History of Europe (Contemporary Societies)*; *The Experience of Economic Growth* (Barry Supple); *Economic Growth in Japan and the USSR* (Angus Maddison); *A Short History of Economic Progress* (Y. Brenner); *The Industrialization of Russia* (William Blackwell); Endurance and Endeavour (J. Westwood); *Monitoring the World Economy 1820–1992* (Angus Maddison).

The figures for the second half of the twentieth century were taken from *World Development Report 1981, 1991 & 2001* (The World Bank); *Soviet Economic Facts 1917–70* (Roger Clarke); *Soviet Economic Facts 1917–81* (Roger Clarke & Dubravko Matko); *Gorbachev's Struggle for Economic Reform* (Anders Aslund); *Economic Reforms in the European Centrally Planned Economies (Economic Commission for Europe)*; *The Soviet Economic Decline* (W. Easterly & S. Fischer); *Structural Factors in the Economic Reforms of China, Eastern Europe and the Former Soviet Union* (Economic Policy April 1994); *Rethinking the Soviet Experience* (Stephen Cohen); *The Soviet Colossus* (Michael Kort); *Endurance and Endeavour* (J. Westwood); *Last of the Empires* (John Keep).

Two sets of GDP figures are shown for the period 1950–89. Again, the official figures are shown in parentheses, side by side with the most conservative recastings of the official data by Western analysts who arbitrarily reduce the numbers by half, or even more. Western analysts have declared that the inefficiencies in the USSR were higher than in the GDR, and they reduce their figures to suit that theory.

The figures up to the 1990s refer to the territory comprising the Soviet Union; thereafter, the figures refer to Russia alone.

TABLE 5. JAPAN

	Man	GDP	Agri	Serv	Pop	Inf	Ex	Unem
16th Century	0.2	0.1	0.1		0.1			
17th Century	0.3	0.2	0.2		0.2			
18th Century	0.2	0.1	0.1		0.0			
19th Century	1.7	1.3	0.7		0.5			
20th Century	7.0	5.4	1.8	6.1	1.1			
1800-49	0.3	0.2	0.1		0.2			
1850-99	3.0	2.4	1.3		0.8			
1900-49	6.3	4.5	1.7	5.7	1.3			
1950-99	7.6	6.2	1.9	6.6	0.9	3.7	10.3	2.3
1850s	1.2	0.9	0.6					
1860s	1.7	1.4	0.8					
1870s	2.5	2.0	1.1					
1880s	3.6	3.0	1.7					
1890s	6.0	4.7	2.1					
1900s	7.0	5.2	2.6	6.6				
1910s	8.4	6.3	2.9	8.2				
1920s	3.1	2.4	1.8	3.0				
1930s	8.5	5.4	2.5	8.0				
1940s	4.5	3.0	-1.7	2.6				
1950s	11.1	9.1	3.8	10.0	1.3	3.1	14.2	3.6
1960s	13.4	11.3	4.0	11.7	1.0	4.9	17.0	0.9
1970s	6.2	5.2	1.1	4.9	1.1	8.2	9.1	1.7
1980s	5.3	4.0	0.4	3.9	0.6	1.3	7.4	2.2
1990s	1.9	1.5	0.3	2.3	0.5	1.2	3.8	3.1

The figures for the sixteenth century were taken from *The Cambridge History of Japan (Early Modern Japan* (John Whitney); *The World Economy Historical Statistics* (Angus Maddison); *The World Economy A Millennium Perspective* (Angus Maddison); *The Cambridge Encyclopedia of Japan*.

The figures for the seventeenth century were taken from *Peasant Protest in Japan 1590–1884* (Herbert Bix); *The Cambridge History of Japan – Early Modern Japan* (John Whitney); *The Cambridge Encyclopedia of Japan*; *The Economic Aspects of the History of the Civilization of Japan* Vol. 3 (Yosoburo Takekoshi); *The World Economy: Historical Statistics* (Angus Maddison); *The World Economy: A Millennium Perspective* (Angus Maddison).

The figures for the eighteenth century were taken from *Native Sources of Japanese Industrialization* (Thomas Smith); *A History of Japanese Economic Thought* (Tessa Suzuki); *The Economic Aspects of the History of the Civilization of Japan* Vol. 3 (Yosoburo Takekoshi); *The World Economy Historical Statistics* (Angus Maddison); *The World Economy A Millennium Perspective* (Angus Maddison); *The Escape from Hunger and Premature Death 1700–2100 Europe, America and the Third World* (Robert Fogel).

The figures for the first half of the nineteenth century were taken from *The Industrialization of Japan* (W. J. Macpherson); *A Short Economic History of Modern Japan* (G. C. Allen); *The World Economy Historical Statistics* (Angus Maddison); *The World Economy: A Millennium Perspective* (Angus Maddison); *The Cambridge History of Japan* Vol. 5; *The Escape from Hunger and Premature Death 1700–2100 Europe, America and the Third World* (Robert Fogel).

The figures for the second half of the nineteenth century were taken from *The Industrialization of Japan* (W. J. Macpherson); *Why Japan Succeeded* (Michio Morishima); *Growth and Interaction in the World Economy* (Angus Maddison); *Histoire du Japon et des Japonais* Vol. I (Edwin Reischauer); *Japan in Transition from Tokugawa to Meiji* (Marius Jansen & Gilbert Rozman); *Economics and World History* (Paul Bairoch); *L'Economie du Japon* (J. Bremond, C. Chalaye & M. Loeb); *Monitoring The World Economy 1820–1992* (Angus Maddison).

The figures for the first half of the twentieth century were taken from *Human Resources in Japanese Industrial Development* (Salomon Levine & Hisashi Kawada); *The Cambridge History of Japan* Vol. 6; *Monitoring the World Economy 1820–1992* (Angus Maddison); *The World Economy* (Walt Rostow); *The Growth of the International Economy 1820–1990* (A. Kenwood & A. Lougheed); *Modern Economic Growth* (Simon Kuznets); *Soleils* (Tibor Mende); *L'Economie du Japon* (J. Bremond, C. Chalaye & M. Loeb); *Monitoring the World Economy 1820–1992* (Angus Maddison).

The figures for the second half of the twentieth century were taken from the *World Development Report 1981, 1991 & 2001* (The World Bank); *The Post War Japanese System* (William Tabb); *Learning from the Japanese* (Wayne Nafziger); *Japan's Capitalism* (Shigeto Tsuru); *Contemporary Japanese Economy and Economic Policy* (Heizo Takenaka); *Structural Adjustment in Japan 1970–82* (R. Dore); *Le Japon d'Aujourd'hui* (Ministere des Affaires Etrangeres); *Le Japon Contemporain* (Michel Vie); *Trade Policy Review Japan 1992* Vol. I & II (GATT).

TABLE 6. CHINA

	Man	GDP	Agri	Serv	Pop	Inf	Ex
16th Century	0.2	0.1	0.1		0.1		
17th Century	0.2	0.1	0.1		0.1		
18th Century	0.6	0.4	0.3		0.8		
19th Century	0.2	0.1	0.1		0.3		
20th Century	7.4	2.7	2.2		1.0		
1800-49	0.3	0.2	0.2		0.6		
1850-99	0.0	0.0	0.0		0.0		
1900-49	0.6	0.5	0.4		0.3		
1950-99	14.2	4.9 (9)	4.0	10.1	1.7		9.1
1900s	0.4	0.3	0.2		0.2		
1910s	0.7	0.5	0.3		0.3		
1920s	1.2	0.9	0.6		0.4		
1930s	2.9	2.1	1.4		0.6		
1940s	-2.3	-1.4	-0.5		0.0		
1950s	17.0	4.6 (13)	5.0	12.0	2.3		7.9
1960s	10.1	2.2 (5)	1.5	7.1	1.9		3.1
1970s	10.8	3.0 (6)	3.2	8.7	1.9		7.0
1980s	16.2	7.1 (10)	6.3	13.5	1.4	5.8	12.2
1990s	17.0	7.7 (11)	4.2	9.2	1.2	7.0	16.1

The figures for the sixteenth century were taken from *A History of China* (Wolfram Eberhard); *Chinese Economic Performance in the Long Run* (Angus Maddison); *The World Economy Historical Statistics* (Angus Maddison); *The World Economy A Millennium Perspective* (Angus Maddison); *The Cambridge Encyclopedia of China*; *La Chine Imperiale* (Denys Lombard); *The Cambridge History of China* Vol. V–VII; *Une Prehistoire—La Chine des Printemps et des Automnes* (Alain Reynaud); *La Chine Ancienne* (Jacques Gernet;

The figures for the seventeenth century were taken from *Chinese Economic Performance in the Long Run* (Angus Maddison); *China A Macro History* (Ray Huang); *Rebellions and Revolutions* (Jack Gray); *Crisis and Transformation in Seventeenth Century China* (Chun-shu Chang & Hsueh-lun Chang); *The Cambridge History of China* Vol. VII; *China Among Equal* (Morris Rosabi); *A History of China* (Wolfram Eberhard); *The World Economy Historical Statistics* (Angus Maddison); *The World Economy: A Millennium Perspective* (Angus Maddison).

The figures for the eighteenth century were taken from *Chinese Society in the Eighteenth Century* (Susan Nanquin & Evelyn Rawski); *China A New History* (John Fairbank); *Chinese Economic Performance in the Long Run* (Angus Maddison); *China in World History* (S. A. Adshead); *The World Economy Historical Statistics* (Angus Maddison); *The World Economy A Millennium Perspective* (Angus Maddison); *Bureaucratie et Famine en Chine au 18e Siecle* (Pierre Will); *A History of China* (Wolfram Eberhard); *The Escape from Hunger and Premature Death 1700–2100 Europe, America and the Third World* (Robert Fogel).

The figures for the first half of the nineteenth century were taken from *China's Economy* (Christopher Howe); *Chinese Economic Performance in the Long Run* (Angus Maddison); *China in World History* (S. A. Adshead); *China's Modern Economy in Historical Perspective* (Dwight Perkins); *An Economic History of China* (Chin-sheng Chou); *The World Economy* (Walt Rostow); *The Escape from Hunger and Premature Death 1700–2100 Europe, America and the Third World* (Robert Fogel).

The figures for the second half of the nineteenth century were taken from *Ostasien—China, Japan, Korea* (Albert Kolb); *China's Modern Economy in Historical Perspective* (Dwight Perkins); *The Commercial Revolution in Nineteenth Century China* (Yen-ping Hao); *Money and Monetary Policy in China* (Frank King); *Foreign Investment and Economic Development in China 1840–1937* (Chi-ming Hou); *A History of China* (Wolfram Eberhard); *China's Economy* (Christopher Howe); *A History of China* (Wolfram Eberhard).

The figures for the first half of the twentieth century were taken from *La Chine au XXe Siecle* (M. Bergere, L. Bianco & J. Domes); *Money and Monetary Policy in China* (Frank King); *Chinese Economic Performance in the Long Run* (Angus Maddison); *Foreign Investment and Economic Development in China 1840–1937* (Chi-ming Hou); *A History of China* (Wolfram Eberhard); *Economic Growth in Pre War China* (Thomas Rawski); *The Economic Development of China and Japan* (C. D. Cowan); *East Asia—From Chinese Predominance to the Rise of the Pacific Rim* (Arthur Cotterel).

The figures for the second half of the twentieth century were taken from the *World Development Report 1981, 1991 & 2001* (The World Bank); *China's Second Revolution* (Harry Harding); *Economic Growth and Employment in China* (Thomas Rawski); *China in the Nineties* (D. Goodman & G. Segal); *China's New Development Strategy* (J. Gray & G. White); *China Briefing 1987* (J. Major & A. Kane); *China at the Threshold of a Market Economy* (International Monetary Fund).

As with Eastern Germany and Russia, the official GDP figures for the period 1950–99 are shown in parentheses, side by side with numbers generated by Western analysts who posit that planned economies must be inefficient. Since the 1990s, the Chinese government has increasingly allowed market forces to shape the economy. The difference between the two sets of figures is reduced to reflect that change.

TABLE 7. KOREA (SOUTH KOREA)

	Man	GDP	Agri	Serv	Pop	Inf	Ex	Unem
18th Century	0.3	0.2	0.1		0.1			
19th Century	0.6	0.4	0.3		0.3			
20th Century	6.5	4.3	2.0		1.2			
1800-49	0.3	0.2	0.1		0.2			
1850-99	0.9	0.6	0.4		0.4			
1900-49	2.0	1.5	1.1		0.9			
1950-99	11.0	7.1	2.9	7.7	1.5	16.3		
1900s	0.9	0.7	0.3		0.4			
1910s	2.1	1.6	1.3		1.0			
1920s	2.6	2.0	1.7		1.4			
1930s	4.0	3.1	2.5		1.8			
1940s	0.2	0.1	0.3		0.0			
1950s	1.1	0.7	0.5	1.3	0.7	36.3		
1960s	15.0	8.4	4.2	10.8	2.5	15.1	34.1	
1970s	17.8	10.3	4.8	11.6	1.9	18.2	25.7	
1980s	13.6	9.7	3.3	9.2	1.2	5.0	14.2	
1990s	7.5	6.4	1.5	5.8	1.0	7.0	7.0	3.1

The figures for the eighteenth century were taken from *Korea's Place in the Sun: A Modern History* (Bruce Cumings); *A Korean Confucian Encounter with the Modern World* (Chai-sik Chung); *Korea Old and New: A History* (Eckert, Lee, Lew, Robinson, Wagner); *The World Economy Historical Statistics* (Angus Maddison); *The World Economy A Millennium Perspective* (Angus Maddison); *East Asia: From Chinese Predominance to the Rise of the Pacific Rim* (Arthur Cotterel); *The Escape from Hunger and Premature Death 1700–2100 Europe, America and the Third World* (Robert Fogel).

The figures for the first half of the nineteenth century were taken from *The World Economy Historical Statistics* (Angus Maddison); *The World Economy A Millennium Perspective* (Angus Maddison); *Korea's Place in the Sun: A Modern History* (Bruce Cumings); *A Korean Confucian Encounter with the Modern World* (Chai-sik Chung); *Korea Old and New: A History* (Eckert, Lee, Lew, Robinson, Wagner); *A Handbook of Korea: The Escape from Hunger and Premature Death 1700–2100 Europe, America and the Third World* (Robert Fogel).

The figures for the second half of the nineteenth century were taken from *The World Economy Historical Statistics* (Angus Maddison); *The World Economy A Millennium Perspective* (Angus Maddison); *Korea's Place in the Sun: A Modern History* (Bruce Cumings); *A Korean Confucian Encounter with the Modern World* (Chai-sik Chung); *Korea Old and New: A History* (Eckert, Lee, Lew, Robinson, Wagner); *A Handbook of Korea: The Escape from Hunger and Premature Death 1700–2100 Europe, America and the Third World* (Robert Fogel); *Monitoring the World Economy 1820–1992* (Angus Maddison).

The figures for the first half of the twentieth century were taken from *Korea's Place in the Sun: A Modern History* (Bruce Cumings); *A Korean Confucian Encounter with the Modern World* (Chai-sik Chung); *Korea Old and New: A History* (Eckert, Lee, Lew, Robinson, Wagner); *The World Economy Historical Statistics* (Angus Maddison); *The World Economy A Millennium Perspective* (Angus Maddison); *East Asia: From Chinese Predominance to the Rise of the Pacific Rim* (Arthur Cotterel); *Monitoring the World Economy 1820–1992* (Angus Maddison).

The figures for the second half of the twentieth century were taken from the *World Development Report 1981, 1991 & 2001* (The World Bank); *Trade Policy Review Republic of Korea 1992* (GATT); *Monitoring the World Economy 1820–1992* (Angus Maddison); *A Case of Successful Adjustment: Korea's Experience During 1980–84* (International Monetary Fund).

The figures from 1700 to 1949 are for the whole Korean peninsula (from then on, for South Korea alone).

TABLE 8. TAIWAN

	Man	GDP	Agri	Serv	Pop	Inf	Ex	Unem
18th Century	0.2	0.1	0.1		3.5			
19th Century	0.3	0.2	0.2		3.0			
20th Century	6.8	4.9	2.9		1.6			
1800-49	0.2	0.1	0.1		3.6			
1850-99	0.4	0.3	0.2		2.4			
190049	1.9	1.4	1.0		0.9			
195099	11.7	8.4	4.8	10.5	2.3	8.2	16.4	
1900s	1.0	0.7	0.5					
1910s	2.6	1.8	1.4					
1920s	3.3	2.3	2.0					
1930s	4.4	3.4	2.2					
1940s	-1.8	-1.0	-0.9					
1950s	12.2	7.8	5.0	10.1	3.5	20.3	6.1	
1960s	14.0	10.1	6.1	13.0	3.0	2.4	25.3	
1970s	13.2	9.6	5.2	12.3	2.1	10.2	30.2	
1980s	11.1	8.1	4.6	9.2	1.6	5.1	13.4	
1990s	7.8	6.3	3.3	7.7	1.1	3.2	7.1	2.6

The figures for the eighteenth century were taken from *Taiwan A New History* (Murray Rubinstein); *Ostasien: China, Japan, Korea* (Albert Kolb); *Chinese Economic Performance in the Long Run* (Angus Maddison); *The World Economy Historical Statistics* (Angus Maddison); *The World Economy A Millennium Perspective* (Angus Maddison); *East Asia: From Chinese Predominance to the Rise of the Pacific Rim* (Arthur Cotterel); *The Escape from Hunger and Premature Death 1700–2100 Europe, America and the Third World* (Robert Fogel).

The figures for the first half of the nineteenth century were taken from *Chinese Economic Performance in the Long Run* (Angus Maddison); *Taiwan A New History* (Murray Rubinstein); *Ostasien: China, Japan, Korea* (Albert Kolb); *East Asia: From Chinese Predominance to the Rise of the Pacific Rim* (Arthur Cotterel); *The Escape from Hunger and Premature Death 1700–2100 Europe, America and the Third World* (Robert Fogel).

The figures for the second half of the nineteenth century were taken from *Taiwan A New History* (Murray Rubinstein); *Chinese Economic Performance in the Long Run* (Angus Maddison); *Ostasien: China, Japan, Korea* (Albert Kolb); *East Asia: From Chinese Predominance to the Rise of the Pacific Rim* (Arthur Cotterel); *The Escape from Hunger and Premature Death 1700–2100 Europe, America and the Third World* (Robert Fogel).

The figures for the first half of the twentieth century were taken from *Governing the Market* (Robert Wade); *World Economic Growth* (Arnold Harberger); *Taiwan A New History* (Murray Rubinstein); *Chinese Economic Performance in the Long Run* (Angus Maddison); *Ostasien: China, Japan, Korea* (Albert Kolb); *East Asia: From Chinese Predominance to the Rise of the Pacific Rim* (Arthur Cotterel); *The Escape from Hunger and Premature Death 1700–2100 Europe, America and the Third World* (Robert Fogel).

The figures for the second half of the twentieth century were taken from *The Role of the State in Taiwan's Development* (Joel Aberbach, David Dollar & Kenneth Sokoloff); *Governing the Market* (Robert Wade); *World Economic Growth* (Arnold Harberger); *The Escape from Hunger and Premature Death 1700–2100 Europe, America and the Third World* (Robert Fogel).

TABLE 9. HONG KONG

	Man	GDP	Agri	Serv	Pop	Inf	Ex	Unem
18th Century	0.0	0.0						
19th Century	0.5	0.4						
20th Century	7.4	6.0						
1800-49	0.0	0.0						
1850-99	1.0	0.8						
1900-49	4.0	3.3						
1950-99	10.7	8.7		10.5	2.2	5.6	13.3	
1900s	2.4	2.0						
1910s	4.0	3.2						
1920s	3.3	2.8						
1930s	4.7	4.0						
1940s	5.5	4.5						
1950s	15.8	12.3		14.2	2.8	4.0	14.0	
1960s	14.4	10.2		13.8	2.5	2.4	12.7	
1970s	10.6	9.4	-11.0	11.0	2.6	7.9	8.3	
1980s	8.1	7.4		8.4	1.2	7.1	16.1	2.7
1990s	4.8	4.1		5.0	2.1	6.4	15.0	3.1

The figures for the eighteenth century were taken from *Chinese Economic Performance in the Long Run* (Angus Maddison); *Chinese Society in the Eighteenth Century* (Susan Nanquin & Evelyn Rawski); *China A New History* (John Fairbank); *The World Economy Historical Statistics* (Angus Maddison); *The World Economy A Millennium Perspective* (Angus Maddison); *East Asia: From Chinese Predominance to the Rise of the Pacific Rim*

(Arthur Cotterel); *The Escape from Hunger and Premature Death 1700–2100 Europe, America and the Third World* (Robert Fogel).

The figures for the first half of the nineteenth century were taken from *L'Asie Orientale du milieu du XIXe siècle a nos jours* (Nora Wang); *Chinese Economic Performance in the Long Run* (Angus Maddison); *Chinese Society in the Eighteenth Century* (Susan Nanquin & Evelyn Rawski); *China A New History* (John Fairbank); *The World Economy Historical Statistics* (Angus Maddison); *The World Economy A Millennium Perspective* (Angus Maddison); *East Asia: From Chinese Predominance to the Rise of the Pacific Rim* (Arthur Cotterel); *The Escape from Hunger and Premature Death 1700–2100 Europe, America and the Third World* (Robert Fogel).

The figures for the second of the nineteenth century were taken from *Chinese Economic Performance in the Long Run* (Angus Maddison); *China A New History* (John Fairbank); *The World Economy Historical Statistics* (Angus Maddison); *The World Economy A Millennium Perspective* (Angus Maddison); *East Asia: From Chinese Predominance to the Rise of the Pacific Rim* (Arthur Cotterel); *The Escape from Hunger and Premature Death 1700–2100 Europe, America and the Third World* (Robert Fogel).

The figures for the first half of the twentieth century were taken from *Trade Policy Review Hong Kong 1994* (GATT); *The Future of Hong Kong* (Hungdah-chiu Jao & Yuan-li Wu); *Hong Kong The Industrial Colony* (Keith Hopkins); *Hong Kong Capitalist Paradise* (Jon Woronoff); *Chinese Economic Performance in the Long Run* (Angus Maddison); *China A New History* (John Fairbank); *Monitoring the World Economy 1820–1992* (Angus Maddison).

The figures for the second half of the twentieth century were taken from the *World Development Report 1981, 1991 & 2001* (The World Bank); *Hong Kong The Industrial Colony* (Keith Hopkins); *Trade Policy Review Hong Kong 1992* (GATT); *Trade Policy Review Hong Kong 1994* (GATT); *The Future of Hong Kong* (Hungdah-chiu Jao & Yuan-li Wu); *Hong Kong Capitalist Paradise* (Jon Woronoff).

TABLE 10. SINGAPORE

	Man	GDP	Agri	Serv	Pop	Inf	Ex	Unem
18th Century	0.0	0.0	0.0					
19th Century	1.8	1.4	0.7					
20th Century	7.0	5.7	1.3	6.8			6.2	
1800-49	0.7	0.5	0.3					
1850-99	2.8	2.3	1.1					
1900-49	4.4	3.5	1.9	4.5			3.1	
1950-99	9.5	7.8	0.7	9.1	2.3	2.4	9.2	7.7
1900s	4.3	3.6	2.3	4.3				
1910s	5.0	3.8	2.0	5.0				
1920s	5.1	4.0	2.2	5.0				
1930s	3.4	2.6	1.4	3.7				
1940s	4.4	3.6	1.6	4.5				
1950s	6.3	5.4	2.5	6.0	4.0		3.1	16.2
1960s	12.0	9.3	5.0	12.2	2.4	1.1	4.2	10.1
1970s	11.8	9.4	1.7	11.0	1.4	5.7	11.0	5.8
1980s	8.4	7.0	-6.2	8.1	1.7	1.7	11.9	4.0
1990s	8.8	7.8	0.4	8.0	1.9	1.9	16.0	2.2

The figures for the eighteenth century were taken from *South and Southeast Asia since 1800* (Victor Purcell); *L'Asie Orientale du milieu du XIXe siècle a nos jours* (Nora Wang); *The World Economy Historical Statistics* (Angus Maddison); *The World Economy A Millennium Perspective* (Angus Maddison); *East Asia: From Chinese Predominance to the Rise of the Pacific Rim* (Arthur Cotterel); *The Escape from Hunger and Premature Death 1700–2100 Europe, America and the Third World* (Robert Fogel).

The figures for the first half of the nineteenth century were taken from *South East Asia* (Brian Harrison); *South and Southeast Asia since 1800* (Victor Purcell); *L'Asie Orientale du milieu du XIXe siècle a nos jours* (Nora Wang); *The World Economy Historical Statistics* (Angus Maddison); *The World Economy A Millennium Perspective* (Angus Maddison); *East Asia: From Chinese Predominance to the Rise of the Pacific Rim* (Arthur Cotterel); *The Escape from Hunger and Premature Death 1700–2100 Europe, America and the Third World* (Robert Fogel).

The figures for the second half of the nineteenth century were taken from *The Economic Growth of Singapore* (W. G. Huff); *South East Asia* (Brian Harrison); *South and Southeast Asia since 1800* (Victor Purcell); *L'Asie Orientale du milieu du XIXe siècle a nos jours* (Nora Wang); *The World Economy Historical Statistics* (Angus Maddison); *The World Economy A Millennium Perspective* (Angus Maddison); *East Asia: From Chinese Predominance to the Rise of the Pacific Rim* (Arthur Cotterel); *The Escape from Hunger and Premature Death 1700–2100 Europe, America and the Third World* (Robert Fogel).

The figures for the first half of the twentieth century were taken from *Trade Policy Review Singapore 1990* (GATT); *The Economic Growth of Singapore* (W. G. Huff); *South East Asia* (Brian Harrison); *South and Southeast Asia since 1800* (Victor Purcell); *L'Asie Orientale du milieu du XIXe siècle a nos jours* (Nora Wang); *Monitoring the World Economy 1820–1992* (Angus Maddison).

The figures for the second half of the twentieth century were taken from *World Development Report 1981, 1991 & 2001* (The World Bank); *Trade Policy Review Singapore 1990* (GATT); *The Economic Growth of Singapore* (W. G. Huff); *Economic Development of Singapore 1960–91* (Singapore Economic Development Board); *Singapore Facts and Pictures 1987–99* (Singapore Ministry of Communications and Information); *Singapore in Brief 1991–99* (Singapore Ministry of Trade and Industry); *Yearbook of Statistics Singapore 1991–99* (Singapore Department of Statistics).

References

Books

Abel, Christopher & Lewis, Colin (ed): *Latin America, Economic Imperialism and the State,* The Athlone Press, London, 1985.

Abreu, Marcelo & Verner, Dorte: *Long-Term Brazilian Economic Growth 1930-94,* OECD, Paris, 1997.

A Case of Successful Adjustment-Korea's Experience During 1980-84, International Monetary Fund, Washington D.C., August 1985.

A Handbook of Korea, Korean Overseas Information Service, Seoul, 1993.

Aberbach, Joel, Dollar, David & Sokoloff, Kenneth (ed): *The Role of the State in Taiwan's Development,* M.E. Sharpe, Armonk-London, 1994.

Adams, D.: *America in the 20th Century,* Cambridge University Press, London, 1967.

Adshead, S. A.: *China in World History,* St. Martin's Press, New York, 1995.

Africa South of the Sahara 2001, Europa Publications, London, 2001.

Africa South of the Sahara 2002, Europa Publications, London, 2002.

Ahmad, Sultan: *Regression Estimates of Per Capita GDP Based on Purchasing Power Parities, World Bank,* Washington D.C., 1992.

Albert, Bill: *South America and the World Economy from Independence to 1930,* The Macmillan Press Ltd., London, 1983.

Alexander, Robert: *An Introduction to Argentina,* Pall Mall Press, London, 1969.

Alford, B.: *British Economic Performance 1945-1975,* Cambridge University Press, Cambridge, 1995.

Aldcroft, D. & Fearron, P.(ed): *British Fluctuations 1790-1939,* Macmillan St. Martin Press, London, 1972.

Aldcroft, Derek & Richardson, Harry. *The British Economy 1870-1939,* Macmillan & Co. Ltd., London, 1969.

Aldcroft, Derek: *The British Economy Vol. I,* Wheatsheaf Books Ltd., London, 1986.

Allen, G.: *The British Disease*, The Institute of Economic Affairs, London, 1979.

Allen, G. C.: *A Short Economic History of Modern Japan*, George Allen & Unwin Ltd., London, 1972.

Allen, J. & Massey, D.(ed): *The Economy in Question*, SAGE Publications Ltd., London, 1988.

Allen, N. J. (ed): *Oxford University Papers on India Part 2*, Oxford University Press, Oxford, 1987.

Almanach der Schweiz, Verlag Peter Lang AG, Schweiz, 1978.

Amaral, Samuel: *The Rise of Capitalism on the Pampas*, Cambridge University Press, Cambridge, 1998.

Ambrose, Stephen & Brinkley, Douglas: *Rise to Globalism*, Penguin Books, New York, 1997.

Ashworth, William: *An Economic History of England 1870-1939*, Methuen & Co. Ltd., London, 1965.

Aslund, Anders: *Gorbachev's Struggle for Economic Reform*, Pinter Publishers, London, 1991.

Axtell, James: *Beyond 1492-Encounters in Colonial North America*, Oxford University Press, Oxford, 1992.

Baer, Werner: *Industrialization and Economic Development in Brazil*, Richard Irwin Inc., Homewood-Illinois, 1965.

Bagwell, Philip & Mingay, G.: *Britain and America 1850-1939*, Routledge Kegan Paul Ltd., London, 1970.

Bayly, Susan: *Caste, Society and Politics in India from the Eighteenth Century to the Modern Age*, *The New Cambridge History of India*, Cambridge University Press, Cambridge, 1999.

Bhagwati, Jagdish: *India in Transition*, Oxford University Press, Oxford, 1993.

Bailyn, Bernard: *The Ideological Origins of the American Revolution*, Harvard University Press, Cambridge-MA, 1992.

Bairoch, Paul: *Economics and World History*, Harvester Wheatsheaf, London, 1993.

Barber, William: *From New Era to New Deal*, Cambridge University Press, Cambridge, 1988.

Barnes, Gina: *The Rise of Civilization in East Asia*, Thames and Hudson, London, 1999.

Barraclough, Geoffrey: *Mediaeval Germany Vol. I*, Basil Blackwell, Oxford, 1979.

Batta, Paul: *Le Grand Maghreb, Editions La Decouverte*, Paris, 1990.

Befu, Harumi (ed): *Cultural Nationalism in East Asia*, Institute of East Asian Studies-University of California, Berkeley-CA, 1993.

Behari, Madhuri: *Indian Economy since Independence*, D. K. Publications, Delhi, 1983.

Beinart, Williams: *Twentieth Century South Africa*, Oxford University Press, Oxford, 1994.

Bergere, M. Bianco, L. & Domes, J.: *La Chine au XXe Siecle*, Fayard, Paris, 1989.

Berghahn, V.: *Modern Germany*, Cambridge University Press, Cambridge, 1985.

Bergier, Jean: *Naissance et Croissance de la Suisse Industrielle*, Francke Editions, Suisse, 1974.

Berkowitz, Edward: *America's Welfare State*, The John Hopkins University Press, Baltimore, 1991.

Bermant, Chaim: *Israel*, Thames and Hudson, London, 1967.

Berosman, Joel : *Brazil-Industrialization and Trade Policies*, Oxford University Press, London, 1970.

Berry, Laverle (ed): *Ghana-A Country Study*, Library of Congress, Washington D. C., 1995.

Bethel, Leslie (ed): *Brazil-Empire and Republic 1822-1930*, Cambridge University Press, Cambridge, 1989.

Bethel, Leslie (ed): *Spanish America after Independence 1820-1870*, Cambridge University Press, Cambridge, 1987.

Bethel, Leslie (ed): *The Cambridge History of Latin America Vol. I*, Cambridge University Press, Cambridge, 1984.

Bethel, Leslie (ed): *The Cambridge History of Latin America Vol. II*, Cambridge University Press, Cambridge, 1984.

Bethel, Leslie (ed): *The Independence of Latin America*, Cambridge University Press, Cambridge, 1987.

Bettelheim, Charles: *L'Economie Allemande sous le Nazisme Vol. I & II*, François Maspero, Paris, 1971.

Bharier, Julian : *Economic Development in Iran 1900-1970*, Oxford University Press, London, 1971.

Bhattacharya, Sabya sachi (ed) : *Situating Indian History*, Oxford University Press, Oxford, 1986.

Birmingham, David & Martin, Phyllis (ed) : *History of Central Africa—The Contemporary Years since 1960*, Longman, London, 1998.

Bix, Herbert: *Peasant Protest in Japan 1590-1884*, Yale University Press, New Haven-USA, 1986.

Blackwell, William: *The Beginnings of Russian Industrialization*, Princeton University Press, Princeton, 1968.

Blackwell, William: *The Industrialization of Russia*, Thomas Crowell Co., New York,
1970.

Blazant, Jan: *A Concise History of Mexico from Hidalgo to Cardenas*, Cambridge University Press, Cambridge, 1977.

Bogart, Ernest & Kemmerer, Donald: *Economic History of the American People*, Longmans Green & Co., New York, 1947.

Bolton, J. L.: *The Medieval English Economy 1150-1500*, The Garden City Press Ltd., London, 1980.

Bonilla, Heraclio (ed): *El Sistema Colonial en la América Española*, Editorial Critica, Barcelona, 1991.

Boorstin, Daniel: *Histoire des Americaines-Naissance d'une nation*, Armand Collin, Paris, 1981.

Boulding, Kenneth: *The Structure of a Modern Economy*, Macmillan Press, London, 1993.

Boyle, John: *Persia—History and Heritage*, Henry Melland, London, 1978.

Bramsted, Ernest: *Germany*, Prentice-Hall Inc., New York, 1972.

Brass, Paul: *The Politics of India since Independence, The New Cambridge History of India*, Cambridge University Press, Cambridge, 1990.

Breach, R. & Hartwell, R. (ed): *British Economy and Society 1870-1970*, Oxford University Press, Oxford, 1972.

Bremond, J., Chalaye, C. & Loeb, M.: *L'Economie du Japon*, Hatier, Paris, 1987.

Brenner, Y.: *A Short History of Economic Progress*, Frank Cass & Co. Ltd., London, 1969.

Britain 1984, The Central Office of Information, London, 1984.

Brown, Judith: Modern India—*The origins of an Asian Democracy*, Oxford University Press, Oxford, 1985.

Brown Richard: *Society and Economy in Modern Britain 1700-1850*, Routledge, London, 1991.

Bruno, M. & Sachs, J.: *Economics of Worldwide Stagflation*, Harvard University Press, Cambridge, Mass., 1985.

Buckley, Patricia: *The Cambridge Illustrated History of China*, Cambridge University Press, Cambridge, 1996.

Bulmer, Victor: *The Economic History of Latin America since Independence*, Cambridge University Press, Cambridge, 1994.

Burnett, John: *Plenty and Want*, Routledge, London, 1989.

Burns, Arthur: *Production Trends in the United States since 1870*, National Bureau of Economic Research, USA, 1934.

Bushnell, David & Macaulay, Neill: *The Emergence of Latin America in the Nineteenth Century*, Oxford University Press, Oxford, 1988.

Byrnes, Rita (ed): *Uganda-A Country Study*, Library of Congress, Washington D. C., 1992.

Byrnes, Rita (ed): *South Africa-A Country Study*, Library of Congress, Washington D. C., 1997.

Cain, P. J.: *Economic Foundations of British Overseas Expansion 1815-1914*, The Macmillan Press Ltd., London, 1980.

Campbell, Robert: *Soviet Economic Power*, Macmillan & Co., London, 1967.

Carter, Gwendolen & O'Meara, Patrick (ed): *Southern Africa—The Continuing Crisis*, Indiana University Press, Bloomington-USA, 1982.

Chambers, J. D.: *The Workshop of the World*, Oxford University Press, Oxford, 1961.

Chandavarkar, Rajinarayan: *The Origins of Industrial Capitalism in India*, Cambridge University Press, Cambridge, 1994.

Chandler, Lester: *America's Greatest Depression*, Harper & Row, New York, 1970.

Chang, Chun-shu & Chang, Hsueh-lun: *Crisis and Transformation in Seventeenth Century China*, University of Michigan Press, Ann Arbor, 1992.

Chaplin, Helen (ed): *Nigeria-A Country Study*, Library of Congress, Washington D. C., 1992.

Chaplin, Helen (ed): *Turkey-A Country Study*, Library of Congress, Washington D. C., 1996.

Chatterji, Joya: *Bengal Divided*, Cambridge University Press, Cambridge, 1994.

Chaudhuri, K.: *Asia Before Europe*, Cambridge University Press, Cambridge, 1990.

Chevalier, François: *L'Amérique Latine*, Presses Universitaires de France, Paris, 1993.

China at the Threshold of a Market Economy, International Monetary Fund, Washington D.C., September 1993.

Chou, Chin-sheng: *An Economic History of China*, Western Washington State College, USA, 1974.

Chung, Chai-sik: *A Korean Confucian Encounter with the Modern World*, Institute of East Asian Studies-University of California, Berkeley-CA, 1995.

Cipolla, Carlo: *Before the Industrial Revolution*, Routledge, London, 1993.

Clapham, John: *A Concise Economic History of Britain*, Cambridge University Press, Cambridge, 1949.

Chambers, J. D.: *Population, Economy and Society in Pre-Industrial England*, Oxford University Press, Oxford, 1972.

Clark, George: *The Wealth of England from 1496 to 1760*, Oxford University Press, Oxford, 1946.

Clark, Peter & Slack, Paul: *English Towns in Transition 1500-1700*, Oxford University Press, Oxford, 1976.

Clarke, Roger: *Soviet Economic Facts 1917-70*, Macmillan, London, 1972.

Clarke, Roger & Matko, Dubravko: *Soviet Economic Facts 1917-81*, Macmillan, London, 1983.

Clarkson, Leslie: *Death, Disease and Famine in Pre-Industrial England*, Gill and Macmillan Ltd., London, 1975.

Cleere, Henry & Crossley, David: *The Iron Industry of the Weald*, Leicester University Press, London, 1985.

Clough, Shepard: *Histoire Economique des Etas Unis*, Presses Universitaires de France, Paris, 1953.

Clough, Shepard : *European Economic History—The Economic Development of Western Civilization*, McGraw-Hill, New York, 1968.

Clough, S. B.: *Grandeur et Décadence des Civilizations*, Payot, Paris, 1954.

Cohen, Paul: *Discovering History in China*, Columbia University Press, New York, 1984.

Cohen, Stephen; *Rethinking the Soviet Experience*, Oxford University Press, Oxford, 1985.

Coleman, D. C.: *The Economy of England 1415-1750*, Oxford University Press, Oxford, 1977.

Cook, Chris & Paxton, John: *European Political Facts 1848-1918*, Macmillan, London, 1978.

Cook, M. A.(ed): *Studies in the Economic History of the Middle East*, Oxford University Press, London, 1970.

Cooley, John: *Libyan Sandstorm*, Holt-Rhnehart and Winston, New York, 1982.

Cornell, Hamelin, Oullet, Trudel: *Canada—Unite et diversite*, Holt, Rinehart et Winston, Quebec, 1971.

Costa, Emilia: *The Brazilian Empire-Myths and Histories*, The University of Chicago Press, Chicago, 1985.

Cotler, Julio & Fagen, Richard (ed): *Latin America and the United States—The Changing Political Realities*, Stanford University Press, Stanford, 1974.

Cotterel, Arthur: *East Asia-From Chinese Predominance to the Rise of the Pacific Rim*, Oxford University Press, Oxford, 1993.

Cowan, C. D.(ed): *The Economic Development of China and Japan*, George Allen & Unwin Ltd., London, 1964.

Crisis in Governance-A Review of Bangladesh's Development 1997, The University Press Ltd., Dhaka, 1998.

Crowder, Michael (ed): *The Cambridge History of Africa Vol. 8*, Cambridge University Press, Cambridge, 1984.

Cullen, L. & Smout, T.(ed): *Comparative Aspects of Scottish and Irish Economic and Social History 1600-1900*, John Donald Publishers Ltd., Edinburgh, 1976.

Cumings, Bruce: *Korea's Place in the Sun-A Modern History*, W. W. Norton & Co., New York, 1997.

Daniel, Elton: *The History of Iran*, Greenwood Press, Westport-London, 2001.

Davies, Norman: *Europe—A History*, Oxford University Press, Oxford, 1996.

Davis, Eric: *Challenging Colonialism-Bank Misr and Egyptian Industrialization 1920-1941*, Princeton University Press, Princeton, 1983.

Davis, Lance, Easterlin, Richard & Parker William (ed): *American Economic Growth*, Harper & Row Publishers, New York, 1972.

Davis, Lance & Huttenback, Robert: *Mammom and the Pursuit of Empire*, Cambridge University Press, Cambridge, 1988.

Davis, L., Hughes, J. & McDougall, D.: *American Economic History*, Richard Irwin Inc., New York, 1969.

De Crespigny, Rafe: *China this Century*, Oxford University Press, Oxford, 1992.

Deane, Phyllis: *The First Industrial Revolution*, Cambridge University Press, Cambridge, 1979.

Deiss, Joseph: *Economie Politique et Politique Economique de la Suisse*, Editions Fragniere, Suisse, 1979.

Deuchler, Martina: *The Confucian Transformation of Korea*, Harvard University Press, Cambridge-MA, 1992.

Deutsche Bundesbank Annual Report 1992-95, Frankfurt.

Devin, J. & Dickson, D.(ed): *Ireland and Scotland 1600-1850*, John Donald Publishers Ltd., Edinburgh, 1983.

Dictionnaire Geopolitique des Etats, Flammarion, Paris, 1994.

Dobb, Maurice: *Soviet Economic Development since 1917*, Routledge, London, 1960.

Dolan, Roland (ed): *Philippines-A Country Study*, Library of Congress, Washington D. C., 1993.

Dore, R.: *Structural Adjustment in Japan 1970-82*, International Labor Organization, Geneva, 1986.

Dornbusch, Rudiger & Edwards, Sebastian (ed): *The Macroeconomics of Populism in Latin America*, The University of Chicago Press, Chicago, 1991.

Dower, John: *Japan in War and Peace*, Harper Collins, London, 1995.

Duchene, Gerard: *l'Economie de l'URSS*, Editions La Decouvert, Paris, 1987.

Dukes, Paul. *A History of Europe 1648-1948: The Arrival, The Rise, The Fall*, Macmillan, London, 1985.

Duroselle, Jean-Baptiste : *L'Europe—Histoire de ses peuples*, Perrin, 1990.

East Asian Miracle, *Economic Growth and Public Policy*, The World Bank, IBRD, 1993.

Eastern Europe and the Commonwealth of Independent States 1999, Europa Publications, London, 1999.

Eberhard Wolfram: *A History of China*, University of California Press, USA, 1977.

Eckert, Lee, Lew, Robinson, Wagner: *Korea-Old and New-A History*, Harvard University Press, Cambridge-MA, 1990.

Economic Development of Singapore 1960-91, Economic Development Board, Singapore, 1992.

Edelmayer, F., Hausberger, B. & Weinzierl, M. (Hrsg): *Die beiden Amerikas*, Brandes & Apsel, Frankfurt, 1996.

Eisenstadt, S. N.: *Japanese Civilization-A Comparative View*, University of Chicago Press, Chicago, 1995.

Ekundare, Olufem: *An Economic History of Nigeria 1860-1960*, Africana Publishing Co., New York, 1973.

Elbaum, Bernard & Lazonick William (ed): *The Decline of the British Economy*, Oxford University Press, Oxford-USA, 1986.

Encyclopaedia of Asian History Vol. I, Macmillan Publishing Co., New York, 1988.

Encyclopaedia Universalis Vol. 1, Encyclopaedia Universalis France S. A., Paris, 1985.

Encyclopaedia Universalis Vol. 17, Encyclopaedia Universalis France S. A., Paris, 1985.

Encyclopaedia Universalis Vol. 21, Encyclopaedia Universalis France S. A., Paris, 1985.

Engerman, Stanley & Gallman, Robert (ed): *The Cambridge Economic History of the United States Vol. 1*, Cambridge University Press, Cambridge, 1996.

Etudes Economiques de l'OCDE-1996-Royaume-Uni, OCDE, Paris, 1996.

European Historical Statistics 1750-1970, B. R. Mitchell, Mcmillan Press Ltd., 1975.

Europe du Nord-Europe Mediane, Geographie Universelle, Belin-Reclus, Paris, 1996.

Eurostat (Statistical Office of the European Communities)-various years, *Statistical Yearbook*, Luxembourg.

Fage, J. D.: *A History of Africa*, Unwin Hyman, London, 1988.

Fairbank, John: *China-A New History*, Harvard University Press, Cambridge-Mass., 1992.

Fairbank, John & Goldman, Merle: *China-A New History*, Harvard University Press, Cambridge-MA, 1998.

Farley, Rawle: *The Economics of Latin America*, Harper & Row, New York, 1972.

Faulkner, Harold: *Histoire Economique des Etas Unis d'Amérique vol. IV*, Presses Universitaires de France, Paris, 1958.

Faulkner, Harold: *Histoire Economique des Etas Unis d'Amérique Vol. I*, Presses Universitaires de France, Paris, 1958.

Ferns, H. S. : *Argentina*, Ernest Benn Ltd., London, 1969.

Finzsch, Norbert: *Die Goldgräber Kaliforniens*, Vandenhoeck & Ruprecht, Göttingen, 1982.

Fite, Gilbert & Reese, Jim: *An Economic History of the United States*, Houghton Mifflin Co., Boston, 1965.

Floud, Roderick & McCloskey, Donald (ed): *The Economic History of Britain since 1700 Vol. II*, Cambridge University Press, Cambridge, 1981.

Floud, Roderick & McCloskey, Donald (ed): *The Economic History of Britain since 1700 Vol. I*, Cambridge University Press, Cambridge, 1994.

Food and Agriculture Organization of the United Nations-various years, *Production Yearbook*, FAO Statistics Series, Rome.

Fraser, J. & Gerstle, G.: *The Rise and Fall of the New Deal Order*, Princeton University Press, Princeton, 1989.

Frederick, William (ed): *Indonesia-A Country Study*, Library of Congress, Washington D. C., 1992.

Freund, Bill: *The Making of Contemporary Africa*, Lynne Rienner Publishers, Boulder-Colorado, 1998.

Frieden, Jefffrey: *Debt, Development and Democracy*, Princeton University Press, Princeton, 1991.

Furtado, Celso: *La Formation Economique du Bresil*, Publisud, France, 1998.

Furtado, Celso : *Economic Development of Latin America*, Cambridge University Press, Cambridge, 1970.

Fututake, Tadashi: *The Japanese Social Structure*, University of Tokyo Press, Tokyo, 1981.

Gadgil, D. R.: *The Industrial Evolution of India in Recent Times 1860-1939*, Oxford University Press, London, 1972.

Gagliardo, John: *Germany under the Old Regime 1600-1790*, Longman, London, 1991.

Galland, Xavier: *Histoire de la Thailande*, Presses Universitaires de France, Paris, 1998.

Gamble, Andrew: *Britain in Decline*, Macmillan Education Ltd., London, 1985.

Ganguli, B. N. (ed) : *Readings in Indian Economic History*, Asian Publishing House, Bombay, 1964.

Garon, Sheldon: *Molding Japanese Minds*, Princeton University Press, Princeton-New Yersey, 1997.

Garon, Sheldon: *The State and Labor in Modern Japan*, University of California Press, Berkeley-CA, 1987.

Gatrell, Peter: *The Tsarist Economy 1850-1917*, B.T. Batsford Ltd., London, 1986.

Gaxotte, Pierre: *Histoire de l'Allemagne*, Flammarion, Paris, 1975.

George, Pierre: *l'Economie de l'URSS*, Presses Universitaires de France, Paris, 1965.

Germany-OECD-Economic Surveys, OECD, Paris, 1992.

Gernet, Jacques: *La Chine Ancienne*, Presses Universitaires de France, Paris, 1992.

Goodman, D. & Segal, G.: *China in the Nineties*, Oxford University Press, Oxford-USA, 1991.

Gordon, Andrew: *The Evolution of Labor Relations in Japan*, Harvard University Press, Cambridge-MA, 1985.

Grant, Alexander & Stringer, Keith (ed): *Uniting the Kingdom?*, Routledge, London, 1995.

Grassby, Richard: *The Business Community of Seventeenth Century England*, Cambridge University Press, Cambridge, 1995.

Gravereau, Jacques: *Le Japon-l'ere de Hirohito*, Imprimerie nationale, Paris, 1988.

Gray Jack: *Rebellions and Revolutions*, Oxford University Press, Oxford-USA, 1990.

Gray, J. & White, G.(ed): *China's New Development Strategy*, Academic Press Ltd., London, 1982.

Greene, Jack & Pole, J. R. (ed): *The Blackwell Encyclopedia of the American Revolution*, Basil Blackwell, Cambridge-MA, 1991.

Greenough, Paul: *Prosperity and Misery in Modern Bengal*, Oxford University Press, New York-Oxford, 1982.

Grossman, James (ed): *The Frontier in American Culture*, University of California Press, Berkeley-Los Angeles, 1994.

Guroff, Gregory & Cartensen, Fred (ed): *Entrepreneurship in Imperial Russia and the Soviet Union*, Princeton University Press, Princeton, 1983.

Haber, Stephen: *Industry and Underdevelopment—The Industrialization of Mexico 1890-1940*, Stanford University Press, Stanford, 1989.

Hacker, Louis: *Major Documents in American Economic History Vol. I*, D. Van Norstrand Co., USA, 1961.

Haggerty, Richard (ed): *Venezuela-A Country Study*, Library of Congress, Washington D. C., 1993.

Hansen, Bent: *Egypt and Turkey*, Oxford University Press, Oxford, 1991.

Hao, Yen-ping: *The Commercial Revolution in Nineteenth Century China*, University of California Press, Berkeley-CA, 1986.

Harberger, Arnold (ed): *World Economic Growth*, ICS Press, USA, 1984.

Hardach, Karl: *Wirtschafts Geschichte Deutschlands im 20 Jahrhundert*, Vandenhoeck und Ruprecht, Deutschland, 1979.

Harding, Harry: *China's Second Revolution*, The Brookings Institution, Washington D.C., 1987.

Harris, Richard (ed): *The Political Economy of Africa*, Schenkman Publishing Co., Cambridge-MA, 1975.

Harris, Seymour: *American Economic History*, McGraw Hill, New York, 1961.

Heisenberg, Wolfgang (ed): *German Unification in European Perspective*, Brassey's, Bruxelles, 1991.

Henretta, James: *The Evolution of American Society 1700-1815*, D. C. Heath & Co., Lexington-MA, 1973.

Herail, Francine: *Histoire du Japon, Publications Orientalistes de France*, Paris, 1986,

Hernandez, Alicia (ed) : *Las Inversiones Extranjeras en America Latina 1850-1930*, Fondo de Cultura Economica, Mexico, 1995.

Herring, Hubert : *A History of Latin America—From the Beginnings to the Present*, Alfred a. Knopf, New York, 1968.

Hill, C. P.: *British Economic and Social History*, Edward Arnold Ltd., London, 1977.

Hobday, Michael: *Innovations in East Asia*, Edwar Elgar Publishing Ltd., Cheltenham, UK, 1997.

Hobsbawn, E. J.: *Industry and Empire*, Weidenfeld and Nicolson, London, 1968.

Hodges, Donald: *Argentina 1943-1976*, University of New Mexico Press, Albuquerque-USA, 1976.

Hoffman, Mccusker & Menard, Albert (ed): *The Economy of Early America-The Revolutionary Period 1763-1790*, University Press of Virginia, Charlottesville, 1988.

Holborn, Hajo: *A History of Modern Germany Vol. I*, Alfred A Knopf, New York, 1967.

Holderness, B. A.: *Pre-Industrial England*, J.M. Dent & Sons Ltd., London, 1976.

Hopkins, Keith (ed): *Hong Kong-The Industrial Colony*, Oxford University Press, London, 1971.

Hou, Chi-ming: *Foreign Investment and Economic Development in China 1840-1937*, Harvard University Press, Cambridge, Mass., 1965.

Houghton, Hobart & Dagut, Jennifer: *Source Material on the South African Economy Vol. 3*, Oxford University Press, Cape Town, 1973.

Howe, Christopher: *China's Economy*, Granada Publishing, London, 1978.

Huang, Ray: *China-A Macro History*, M. E. Sharpe Inc., Armonk-New York, 1988.

Hudson, Rex (ed): *Brazil-A Country Study*, Library of Congress, Washington D. C., 1998.

Hudson, Rex (ed): *Chile-A Country Study*, Library of Congress, Washington D. C., 1994.

Huff, W. G.: *The Economic Growth of Singapore*, Cambridge University Press, Cambridge, 1994.

Hughes, Jonathan: *American Economic History*, Scott Foresman & Co., Glenview, Illinois, 1987.

Human Development Report, United Nations Development Program (UNDP), Oxford University Press, Oxford. 2000.

Hunt, Michael: *Ideology and U. S. Foreign Policy*, Yale University Press, New Haven-London, 1987.

International Financial Statistics-various volumes, International Monetary Fund, Washington D.C.

ILO (International Labour Organization)-various years, *Key Indicators of the Labour Market*, Geneva.

Israel, J. J.: *Race, Class and Politics in Colonial Mexico 1610-1670*, Oxford University Press, London, 1975.

Issawi, Charles (ed): *The Economic History of the Middle East 1800-1914*, University of Chicago Press, Chicago, 1966.

Jack, Sybil: *Trade and Industry in Tudor and Stuart England*, George Allen & Unwin Ltd., London, 1977.

Jaffrelot, Christophe (ed): *Le Pakistan-Carrefour de Tensions Regionales*, Editions Complexe, 1999.

Jain, Purushottam Chandra: *Socio-Economic Exploration of Mediaeval India*, B. R. Publishing Corp. New Delhi, 1976.

Jalal, Ayesha: *The State of Martial Rule*, Cambridge University Press, Cambridge, 1990.

Jalan, Bimal: *India's Economic Crisis*, Oxford University Press, Oxford, 1991.

Jansen, Marius (ed): *The Emergence of Meiji Japan*, Cambridge University Press, Cambridge, 1995.

Jansen, Marius (ed): *Warrior Rule in Japan*, Cambridge University Press, Cambridge, 1995.

Jansen, Marius & Rozman, Gilbert (ed): *Japan in Transition-From Tokugawa to Meiji*, Princeton University Press, Princeton-New Yersey, 1986.

Jao, Hungdah Chiu & Wu, Yuan-li (ed): *The Future of Hong Kong*, Quorum Books, New York, 1987.

Jarausch, Konrad: *The Rush to German Unity*, Oxford University Press, Oxford, 1994.

Japan's Economy and Japan-U.S. Trade, The Japan Times, Tokyo, 1982.

Johnson, John (ed): *Continuity and Change in Latin America*, Stanford University Press, Stanford, 1964.

Jones, Geoffrey (ed): *Banking and Empire in Iran Vol. I*, Cambridge University Press, Cambridge, 1986.

Jones, Maldwyn: *The Limits of Liberty-American History 1607-1980*, Oxford University Press, Oxford, 1989.

Jones, E. L. (ed): *Agriculture and Economic Growth in England 1650-1815*, Methuen & Co. Ltd., London, 1967.

July, Robert: *Precolonial Africa-An Economic and Social History*, Division Publishing Ltd., England, 1976.

Kahan, Arcadius: *The Plow, the Hammer and the Knout*, University of Chicago Press, Chicago, p. 1985.

Kahan, Arcadius: *Russian Economic History*, University of Chicago Press, Chicago, 1989.

Kaldor, Nicholas: *Causes of Growth and Stagnation in the World Economy*, Cambridge University Press, Cambridge, 1996.

Kasar, Michael: *Soviet Economics*, Weidenfeld & Nicolson, London, 1970

Kaufman, Susan (ed): *Mexico in Transition, Council on Foreign Relations*, New York, 1988.

Kedourie, Elie: *The Middle Eastern Economy*, Frank Cass & Co., London, 1977.

Keep, John: *Last of the Empires*, Oxford University Press, Oxford, 1995.

Kellenbenz, Herman: *The Rise of the European Economy*, Weidenfeld & Nicolson, London, 1976.

Kennedy, Charles: *Bureaucracy in Pakistan*, Oxford University Press, Oxford, 1987.

Kenwood, A & Lougheed, A.: *The Growth of the International Economy 1820-1990*, Routledge, London, 1992.

Kerblay, Basile: *Modern Soviet Society*, Methuen & Co., London, 1983.

Kicza, John: *Colonial Entrepreneurs*, University of New Mexico Press, Albuquerque-USA, 1983.

Kidron, Machel: *Foreign Investments in India*, Oxford University Press, London, 1965.

Kindermann, Gottfried: *Der Aufstieg Koreas in der Weltpolitik*, Olzog Verlag, München, 1994.

King, Frank: *Money and Monetary Policy in China*, Harvard University Press, Cambridge, Mass., 1965.

Kingston, Paul: *Britain and the Politics of Modernization in the Middle East 1945-1958*, Cambridge University Press, Cambridge, 1996.

Kirby, M. W.: *The Decline of British Economic Power since 1870*, George Allen & Unwin Ltd., London, 1981.

Kirchner, Walter: *History of Russia*, Barnes & Noble, New York, 1965.

Kitchen, Martin: *The Cambridge Illustrated History of Germany*, Cambridge University Press, Cambridge, 1997.

Kitchen, Martin: *The Cambridge Illustrated History of Germany*, Cambridge University Press, Cambridge, 1996.

Kitchen, Martin: *The Political Economy of Germany 1815-1914*, McGill-Queen's University Press, Montreal, 1978.

Kneschaurek, Francesco: *La Suisse Face a une Nouvelle Phase de son Developpement*, Centre de Recherches Europeenes, Suisse, 1975.

Kolb, Albert : *Ostasien—China, Japan, Korea*, Quelle & Meyer Verlag, Heidelberg, 1963.

Kolko, Gabriel: *Main Currents in Modern American History*, Harper & Row, New York, p. 1976.

Konczacki, Z. & Konczaki, J. (ed): *An Economic History of Tropical Africa Vol. I*, Frank Cass, London, 1977.

Kort, Michael: *The Soviet Colossus*, Unwin Hyman Inc., New York, 1990.

Krisch, Henry: *The German Democratic Republic*, Westview Press, USA, 1985.

Krout, John: *The United States to 1877*, Barnes & Noble, New York, 1966.

Krout, John: *The United States since 1865*, Barnes & Noble, New York, 1965.

Krugman, Paul: *The Age of Diminished Expectations*, The MIT Press, Boston, 1991.

Kulke, Hermann & Rothermund, Dietmar: *A History of India*, Croom Helm Ltd., Great Britain, 1986.

Kulick, Elliot & Wilson, Dick: *Thailand's Turn—Profile of a New Dragon*, Macmillan, London, 1992.

Kurian, George: *Encyclopaedia of the Third World*, Mansell Publishing Ltd., London, 1982.

Kuznets, Simon: *Modern Economic Growth*, Yale University Press, USA, 1966.

Lacoste, Ives: *Dictionnaire Geopolitique des Etas*, Flammarion, Paris, 1994.

La Grande Bretagne à la Fin du XXe Siècle, Notes e Etudes Documentaires, Decembre 1994.

Lage und Probleme der Schweizerischen Wirtschaft, Schweizerische National bank, Bern, 1977.

Lal, Deepak: *Aspects of Indian Labour*, Oxford University Press, New York, 1989.

Lal, Deepak: *Cultural Stability and Economic Stagnation Vol. I*, Oxford University Press, Oxford, 1988.

Landes, David: *The Wealth and Poverty of Nations*, W. W. Norton & Co., New York, 1998.

Larrabee, Stephen: *The Two German States and European Security*, Macmillan, London, 1989.

L'Afrique—Reforme et Croissance, OECD, Paris, 2000.

Le Japon d'Aujourd'hui, Ministère des Affaires Etrangères, Tokyo, 1971.

L'Economie Suisse 1946-1986, Union de Banque Suisses, Suisse, 1987.

L'etat du Monde—Annuaire Economique et Geopolitique, La Decouvert, Paris.

Lee, C. H.: *The British Economy since 1700-A Macroeconomic Perspective*, Cambridge University Press, Cambridge, 1986.

L'etat du Monde-Annuaire Economique et Geopolitique, La Decouvert, Paris, 2002.

Levine, Salomon & Kawada, Hisashi: *Human Resources in Japanese Industrial Development*, Princeton University Press, Princeton, 1980.

Lewis, John: *The United States and the End of the Cold War*, Oxford University Press, Oxford, 1992.

Lloyd, T. O.: *The British Empire 1558-1995*, Oxford University Press, Oxford, 1996.

Lockhart, James & Schwartz, Stuart: *Early Latin America-A History of Colonial Spanish America and Brazil*, Cambridge University Press, Cambridge, 1983.

Lodge, George: *Engines of Change*, Alfred A. Knopf, New York, 1970.

Lombard, Denys: *La Chine Imperiale*, Presses Universitaires de France, Paris, 1967.

Lopez, Robert : *Naissance de l'Europe*, Librairie Armand Collin, France, 1962.

Lowe, Peter: *The Origins of the Korean War*, Longman, London, 1997.

Luck, Murray (ed): *Modern Switzerland*, Sposs Inc., USA, 1978.

Mabro, Robert & Rodwan, Samir: *The Industrialization of Egypt 1939-1973-Policy and Performance*, Oxford University Press, Oxford, 1976.

Macpherson, W. J. (ed): *The Industrialization of Japan*, Blackwell Publishers, Oxford, 1994.

McGann, Thomas: Argentina—*The Divided Land*, D. Van Nostrand Co., Princeton-USA, 1966.

McGuire, James: *Peronism without Peron*, Stanford University Press, Stanford, 1997.

Madison, Angus: *Economic Growth in Japan and the USSR*, George Allen & Unwin Ltd., London, 1969.

Madison, Angus: *L'Economie Chinoise-Une perspective historique*, OECD, Paris, 1998.

Mafeje, Archie & Rodwan, Samir (ed) : *Economic and Demographic Change in Africa*, Oxford University Press, Oxford, 1995.

Main Economic Indicators, Organization for Economic Cooperation and Development, OECD, Paris.

Majd, Mohammad Ghuli: *Great Britain & Reza Shah*, University Press of Florida, Gainesville-USA, 2001.

Major, J. & Kane, A.: *China Briefing 1987*, Westview Press, USA, 1987.

Malik, Iftikhar: *State and Civil Society in Pakistan*, Macmillan Press Ltd., London, 1997.

Mann, Golo: *The History of Germany since 1789*, Chatto & Windus, London, 1968.

Marichal, Carlos: *A Century of Debt Crises in Latin America*, Princeton University Press, Princeton, 1989.

Martin, Janet: *Medieval Russia 980-1584*, Cambridge University Press, Cambridge, 1996.

Mason, R. H. & Caiger, J. G.: *A History of Japan*, Charles E. Tuttle Co., Australia, 1997.

Mass, Jeffrey & Hauser, William (ed): *The Bakufu in Japanese History*, Stanford University Press, Stanford-CA, 1985.

Mathias, Peter: *The First Industrial Nation*, Methuen & Co. Ltd., USA, 1983.

Mathis, Franz: *Die Deutsche Wirtschaft im 16. Jahrhundert*, R. Oldenbourg Verlag, München, 1992.

Mauro, Frederic: *La Preindustrialization du Bresil*, CNRC, Paris, 1984.

Mauro, Frederic (ed): *Transport et Commerce en Amerique Latine 1800-1970*, Editions L'Harmattan, Paris, 1990.

Mazrui, Ali (ed) : *Histoire Generale de l'Afrique Vol. VIII*, Editions Unesco, Paris, 1998.

Mehta, F. A.: *Second India Studies—Economy*, Macmillan of India Ltd., Delhi, 1976.

McAuley, Mary: *Soviet Politics 1917-1991*, Oxford University Press, Oxford, 1992.

McCloskey, Donald (ed): *Essays on a Mature Economy-Britain After 1840*, Methuen & Co. Ltd., London, 1971.

Meditz, Sandra (ed): *Zaire-A Country Study*, Library of Congress, Washington D. C., 1994.

Merrick, Thomas & Graham, Douglas: *Population and Economic Development in Brazil*, John Hopkins University Press, Baltimore-London, 1979.

Merrill, Tim & Miro, Ramon (ed): *Mexico-A Country Study*, Library of Congress, Washington D. C., 1997.

Metclaf, Thomas: *Land, Landlords and the British Raj*, University of California Press, Los Angeles, 1979.

Metz, Helen (ed): *Algeria-A Country Study*, Library of Congress, Washington D. C., 1994.

Mexico-The Strategy to Achieve Sustained Economic Growth, International Monetary Fund, Washington D.C., September 1992.

Millward, R. & Singleton, J. (ed): *The Political Economy of Nationalization in Britain 1920-1950*, Cambridge University Press, Cambridge, 1995.

Milward, A. & Saul, S. B.: *The Development of the Economies of Continental Europe 1850-1914*, George Allen & Unwin Ltd., London, 1977.

Min, Tu-ki: *National Polity and Local Power*, Harvard University Press, Cambridge-MA, 1989.

Mitchell, B. R.: *European Historical Statistics 1750-1970*, Macmillan Press Ltd., 1975.

Moore, R. J.: *The Crisis of Indian Unity 1917-1940*, Oxford University Press, London, 1974.

More, Charles: *The Industrial Age*, Longman Inc., New York, 1989.

Moreland, W. H.: *From Akbar to Aurangzeb—A Study in Indian Economic History*, AMS Press, New York, 1975.

Morishima, Michio: *Why Has Japan Succeeded?*, Cambridge University Press, Cambridge, 1982.

Mörner, Magnus: *Ensayos sobre Historia Latinoamericana*, Corporacion Editora Nacional, Quito-Ecuador, 1992.

Munro, Forbes: *Africa and the International Economy 1800-1960*, J. M. Dent & Sons Ltd., London, 1976.

Munting, Roger & Holderness, B.: *Crisis, Recovery and War*, St. Martin Press, USA, 1991.

Murphy, Brian: *A History of the British Economy 1086-1740*, Longman Group Ltd., London, 1973.

Musson, A. E.: *The Growth of British Industry*, B.T. Batsford Ltd., London, 1978.

Nafziger, Wayne: *Learning from the Japanese*, M.E. Sharpe Inc., New York, 1995.

Naquin, Susan & Rawski, Evelyn: *Chinese Society in the Eighteenth Century*, Yale University Press, New Haven-London, 1987.

Needham, Joseph: *Clerks and Craftsmen in China and the West*, Cambridge University Press, Cambridge, 1970.

Niemi, Albert: *U. S. Economic History*, Rand McNally College Publishing Co., USA, 1975.

Nish, Ian: *Japan's Struggle with Internationalism*, Kegan Paul International, London, 1993.

Noman, Omar: *The Political Economy of Pakistan 1947-85*, KPI Limited, London, 1988.

North, Douglas: *The Growth of the American Economy to 1860*, Harper & Row, New York, 1968.

Nove, Alec: *An Economic History of the USSR*, Penguin Press, London, 1969.

Nove, Alec: *Political Economy and Soviet Socialism*, George Allen & Unwin Ltd., London, 1979.

Nyrop, Richard, Benderly, Beryl, Cover, William, Englin, Darrel & Kirchner, Robert: *Area Handbook for Egypt*, US Government Printing Office, Washington D. C., 1976.

OECD Economic Outlook, OECD, Paris, 1990.

OECD Economic Surveys-Switzerland, OECD, Paris, 1992.

OECD Economic Surveys-Japan, OECD, Paris, 1992.

OECD, Main Economic Indicators-various years, Paris.

Ogilvie, Sheilagh (ed): *Germany-A New Social and Economic History Vol. 2*, Arnold, London, 1996.

Ooms, Herman: *Tokugawa Ideology*, Princeton University Press, Princeton-New Yersey, 1985.

Orlovsky, Daniel: *The Limits of Reform-The Ministry of Internal Affairs in Imperial Russia 1802-1881*, Harvard University Press, Cambridge-MA, 1981.

Ortmann, Frank: *Revolutionäre im Exil*, Franz Steiner Verlag, Stuttgart, 1994.

Ortrowski, Donald: *Muscovy and the Mongols*, Cambridge University Press, Cambridge, 1998.

Osborne, Milton: *Southeast Asia*, Allen & Unwin, Sydney-London, 1987.

Palmier, Jean-Michel: *Lenine-l'art et la revolution*, Payot, Paris, 1975.

Parker, Geoffrey (ed): *The General Crisis of the Seventeenth Century*, Routledge & Kegan Paul Ltd., London, 1978.

Parker, Richard: *North Africa-Regional Tensions and Strategic Concerns*, Praeger, 1984.

Parker, W. H.: *A Historical Geography of Russia*, University of London Press, London, 1968.

Pendle, George: *Argentina*, Oxford University Press, London, 1963.

Peres, Wilson: *L'investissement direct international et l'industrialization Mexicaine*, OECD, Paris, 1990.

Perez, Louis: *The History of Japan*, Greenwood Press, Westport-USA, 1998.

Perkins, Dwight (ed): *China's Modern Economy in Historical Perspective*, Stanford University Press, USA, 1975.

Phongpaichit, Pasuk & Baker, Chris: *Thailand-Economy and Politics*, Oxford University Press, Oxford, 1995.

Pinson, Roppel: *Modern Germany*, The Macmillan Co., New York, 1966.

Pollard, Sidney: *The Development of the British Economy*, Routledge, London, 1992.

Pope, Rex (ed): *Atlas of British Social and Economic History since 1700*, Routledge, London, 1989.

Porter, Glenn (ed): *Encyclopedia of American Economic History Vol. I*, Charles Scribner's Sons, New York, 1980.

Porter, Michel: *The Competitive Advantage of Nations*, Macmillan Press Ltd., London, 1990.

Pottash, Robert: *The Army & Politics in Argentina 1928-1945*, Stanford University Press, Stanford, 1969.

Powelson, John: *Latin America—Today's Economic and Social Revolution*, McGraw Hill, New York, 1964.

Prados, Leandro & Amaral, Samuel (ed): *La Independencia Americana-Consecuencias Economicas*, Alianza Editorial, Madrid, 1993.

Purcell, Victor: *South and East Asia since 1800*, Cambridge University Press, Cambridge, 1965.

Ramsey, Peter: *The Price Revolution in Sixteenth Century England*, Methuen & Co. Ltd., London, 1971.

Rapp, Francis: *Les Origines Medievales de L'Allemagne Moderne*, Aubier, France, 1989.

Rawski, Thomas: *Economic Growth and Employment in China*, Oxford University Press, Oxford-USA, 1979.

Rawski, Thomas: *Economic Growth in Pre-War China*, University of California Press, USA, 1989.

Rawski, Thomas & Li, Lillian (ed): *Chinese History in Economic Perspective*, University of California Press, Berkeley-Los Angeles, 1992.

Ray, Rajat Kanta (ed): *Entrepreneurship and Industry in India 1800-1947*, Oxford University Press, Oxford, 1992.

Realites d'Israel, Centre d'information d'Israel, Jerusalem, 1992.

Reischauer, Edwin: *Histoire du Japon et des Japonais Vol. 1*, Editions du Seuil, France, 1973.

Reischauer, Edwin & Craig, Albert: *Japan-Tradition and Transformation*, Allen & Unwin, Siydney, 1989.

Reynaud, Alain: *Une Geohistoire-La Chine de Printemps et des Automnes*, Reclus, France, 1992.

Riado, Pierre: *L'Amérique Latine*, Presses Universitaires de France, Paris, 1993.

Riado, Pierre : *L'Amerique Latine de 1945 a nos jours*, Masson, Paris, 1992.

Ridings, Eugene : *Business Interest Groups in Nineteenth Century Brazil*, Cambridge University Press, Cambridge, 1994.

Robock, Stefan: *Brazil-A Study in Development Progress*, D.C. Heath & Co., Lexington-Mass., 1976.

Rock, David: *Argentina 1516-1987*, University of California Press, Berkeley, 1987.

Rock, David: *Authoritarian Argentina*, University of California Press, Berkeley, 1993.

Rock, David (ed): *Latin America in the 1940s*, University of California Press, Berkeley, 1994.

Rose, Caroline: *Interpreting History in Sino-Japanese Relations*, Routledge, London, 1998.

Rose, Michael: *The Relief of Poverty 1834-1914*, Macmillan Press Ltd., London, 1972.

Rosenberg, Nathan: *Technology and American Economic Growth*, Harper & Row, New York, 1972.

Ross, John (ed): *International Encyclopaedia of Population*, The Free Press, New York, 1982.

Rossabi, Morris (ed): *China Among Equals*, University of California Press, USA, 1983.

Rostow, Walt: *The World Economy*, University of Texas Press, USA, 1978.

Roth, Regina: *Staat und Wirtschaft im Ersten Weltkrieg*, Duncker & Humblot, Berlin, 1997.

Rothermund, Dietmar: *An Economic History of India*, Croom Helm Ltd., Australia, 1988.

Roustang, Guy: *Développement Economique de l'Allemagne Orientale*, Société d'Edition d'Enseignement Superieor, Paris, 1963.

Rovan, Joseph : *Histoire de l'Allemagne*, Editions du Seuil, 1994.

Rozman, Gilbert (ed): *The East Asian Region*, Princeton University Press, Princeton-New Yersey, 1991.

Rubistein, Murray (ed): *Taiwan-A New History*, M. E. Sharpe Inc., Armonk-New York, 1999.

Rudolph, Susan & Rudolph, Lloyd: *Gandhi-The Traditional Roots of Charisma*, The University of Chicago Press, Chicago, 1983.

Russell, A. J.: *Society and Government in Colonial Brazil 1500-1822*, Variorum, Great Britain, 1992.

Sabillon, Carlos: *World Economic Historical Statistics*, Algora Publishing, New York, 2004.

Sabillon, Carlos: *Manufacturing, Technology and Economic Growth*, M.E. Sharpe, New York, 2000.

Sagrera, Martin: *Los Racismos en las Américas*, IEPALA, Madrid, 1998.

Saletore, R. N.: *Early Indian Economic History*, Curzon Press, London, 1975.

San Martino, Ma. Laura: *Argentina Contemporànea-de Peron a Menem*, Ediciones Ciudad Argentina, Buenos Aires, 1996.

Sànchez-Albornoz, N.: *La Poblacion de América Latina*, Alianza Editorial, Madrid, 1994.

Sansom, George: *Histoire du Japon-Des Origines aux debuts du Japon moderne*, Fayard, Paris, 1988.

Scholl, Lars: *Ingenieure in der Frühindustrialisierung*, Vandenhoeck & Ruprecht, Göttingen, 1978.

Schwartz, Stuart: *Slaves, Peasants and Rebels-Reconsidering Brazilian Slavery*, University of Illinois Press, Chicago, 1996.

Scobie, James. *Argentina—A City and a Nation*, Oxford University Press, New York, 1971.

Scott, James: *The Moral Economy of the Peasant*, Yale University Press, New Haven-London, 1976.

Scribner, Bob (ed): *Germany-A New Social and Economic History Vol. I*, Arnold, London, 1996.

Sen, Sunil Kumar: *Working Class Movements in India 1885-1975*, Oxford University Press, Oxford, 1994.

Sharma, Ram Sharan: *Light on Early Indian Society and Economy*, Manaktala & Sons, Bombay, 1966.

Shaw, Timothy (ed): *Alternatives Futures for Africa*, Westview Press, Boulder-Colorado,1982.

Shumway, Nicolas: *The Invention of Argentina*, University of California Press, Berkeley, 1991.

Silver, Morris: *Economic Structures of the Ancient Near East*, Croom Helm, Sydney, 1985.

Singhal, D. P.: *A History of the Indian People*, Methuen, London, 1983.

Singapore in Brief 1991, Ministry of Trade and Industry, Singapore, 1992.

Smith, R. & Christian, D.: *Bread and Salt*, Cambridge University Press, Cambridge, 1984.

Smith, Thomas: *Native Sources of Japanese Industrialization 1750-1920*, University of California Press, Berkeley-Los Angeles, 1988.

South America, Central America and the Caribbean 2001, Europa Publications, London, 2001.

South America, Central America and the Caribbean 2002, Europa Publications, London, 2002.

Speake, Graham: *Cultural Atlas of Africa*, Facts on File Inc., New York, 1981.

Spear, Percival: *A History of India Vol. II*, Penguin Books, London, 1970.

Spear, Percival: *The Oxford History of Modern India 1740-1975*, Oxford University Press, Oxford, 1989.

Statistics de Base de la Communaute, Eurostat, Bruxelles, 1992.

Stein, J. & Stein, Barbara : *L'heritage colonial de l'Amerique Latine*, François Maspero, Paris, 1974.

Stepan, Alfred: *The Military in Politics-Changing Patterns in Brazil*, Princeton University Press, Princeton, 1971.

Stern, Robert: *Changing India*, Cambridge University Press, Cambridge, 1993.

Stirton, Frederick: *Class, State and Industrial Structure*, Greenwood Press, Westport-London, 1980.

Stokes, Eric: *The Peasant and the Raj*, Cambridge University Press, Cambridge, 1980.

Stueck, William: *The Korean War*, Princeton University Press, Princeton-New Yersey, 1995.

Sub-Saharan Africa—From Crisis to Sustainable Growth, The World Bank, Washington D. C., 1989.

Supple, Barry (ed): *The Experience of Economic Growth*, Random House, New York, 1963.

Surveys of African Economies Vol. 6, International Monetary Fund, Washington D. C., 1975.

Suzuki, Tessa: *A History of Japanese Economic Thought*, Routledge, London, 1989.

Tabb, William: *The Postwar Japanese System*, Oxford University Press, Oxford-New York, 1995.

Tames, Richard: *Economy and Society in Nineteenth Century Britain*, George Allen & Unwin Ltd., London, 1972.

Tanaka, Heizo: *Contemporary Japanese Economy and Economic Policy*, The University of Michigan Press, USA, 1991.

Tanaka, Stefan: *Japan's Orient*, University of California Press, Berkeley-CA, 1993.

Tarling, Nicholas (ed): *The Cambridge History of Southeast Asia Vol. 11*, Cambridge University Press, Cambridge, 1994.

Taylor, Arthur: *Laissez-Faire and State Intervention in Nineteenth Century Britain*, The Macmillan Press Ltd., Hong Kong, 1972.

Taylor, Arthur (ed): *The Standard of Living in Britain in the Industrial Revolution*, Methuen & Co. Ltd., London, 1975.

Thailand-Adjusting for Success, International Monetary Fund, Washington D.C., August 1991.

Thane, Pat & Sutcliffe, Anthony (ed): *Essays in Social History*, Oxford University Press, Oxford-USA, 1986.

Thapar, Romila: *A History of India Vol. I*, Penguin Books, London, 1966.

The Cambridge Economic History of Europe Vol. I, Cambridge University Press, Cambridge, 1971.

The Cambridge Economic History of Europe Vol. II, Cambridge University Press, Cambridge, 1987.

The Cambridge Economic History of Europe Vol. VII, Cambridge University Press, London, 1978.

The Cambridge Economic History of India Vol. II, Cambridge University Press, Cambridge, 1983.

The Cambridge Encyclopaedia of China, Cambridge University Press, Cambridge, 1991.

The Cambridge Encyclopaedia of Japan, Cambridge University Press, Cambridge, 1993.

The Cambridge Encyclopaedia of India, Pakistan, Bangladesh, Sri Lanka, Nepal, Bhutan and the Maldives, Cambridge University Press, Cambridge, 1989.

The Cambridge History of China Vol. I, Cambridge University Press, Cambridge, 1986.

The Cambridge History of China Vol. III, Cambridge University Press, Cambridge, 1979.

The Cambridge History of China Vol. VII, Cambridge University Press, Cambridge, 1988.

The Cambridge History of Japan Vol. V, Cambridge University Press, Cambridge, 1989.

The Cambridge History of Japan Vol. VI, Cambridge University Press, Cambridge, 1988.

The CIA Fact Book-various years, Central Intelligence Agency, USA.

The Europa World Yearbook 1992 Vol. II, Europa Publications, London, 1992.

The Far East and Australasia 2001, Europa Publications, London, 2001.

The Far East and Australasia 2002, Europa Publications, London, 2002.

The Federal Republic of Germany, International Monetary Fund, Washington D.C., January 1991.

The Fontana Economic History of Europe-The Emergence of Industrial Societies, William Collins & Son Ltd., London, 1976.

The Fontana Economic History of Europe-Contemporary Economies, William Collins & Sons Ltd., London, 1976.

The Long Debate on Poverty, The Institute of Economic Affairs, London, 1972.

The Middle East and North Africa 2001, Europa Publications, London, 2001.

The Middle East and North Africa 2002, Europa Publications, London, 2002.

The New Encyclopaedia Britannica-Macropaedia Vol. 16, Encyclopaedia Britannica Inc., Chicago, 1988.

The New Encyclopaedia Britannica-Macropaedia Vol. 20, Encyclopaedia Britannica Inc., Chicago, 1988.

The New Encyclopaedia Britannica-Macropaedia Vol. 22, Encyclopaedia Britannica Inc., Chicago, 1988.

The New Encyclopaedia Britannica-Macropaedia Vol. 24, Encyclopaedia Britannica Inc., Chicago, 1988.

The New Encyclopaedia Britannica-Macropaedia Vol. 28, Encyclopaedia Britannica Inc., Chicago, 1988.

The New Encyclopaedia Britannica-Macropaedia Vol. 29, Encyclopaedia Britannica Inc., Chicago, 1988.

The New Encyclopaedia Britannica-Micropaedia Vol. 5, Encyclopaedia Britannica Inc., Chicago, 1988.

The New Encyclopaedia Britannica-Micropaedia Vol. 10, Encyclopaedia Britannica Inc., Chicago, 1988.

The USA and Canada 1994, Europa Publications, London, 1994.

Thompson, Carol, Anderberg, Mary & Antel, Joan (ed): *The Current History-Encyclopaedia of Developing Nations*, McGraw Hill Inc., New York, 1982.

Thompson, F. (ed): *Landowners, Capitalists and Entrepreneurs*, Oxford University Press, Oxford, 1994.

Tiedemann, Arthur (ed): *An Introduction to Japanese Civilization*, Columbia University Press, New York, 1974.

Tomlinson, B. R.: *The Economy of Modern India 1860-1970*, The New Cambridge History of India Vol. 3, Cambridge University Press, Cambridge, 1996.

Tomlinson, Jim: *Problems of British Economic Policy 1870-1945*, Methuen & Co. Ltd., London, 1981.

Trade Policy Review-Argentina, World Trade Organization, Geneva, 1999.

Trade Policy Review-Brazil Vol. I & II, GATT, Geneva, 1992.

Trade Policy Review-Brazil, World Trade Organization, Geneva, 1996.

Trade Policy Review-Egypt, World Trade Organization, Geneva, 1999.

Trade Policy Review-Nigeria, World Trade Organization, Geneva, 1998.

Trade Policy Review-South Africa, World Trade Organization, Geneva, 1999.

Trade Policy Review-Hong Kong, GATT, Geneva, 1990.

Trade Policy Review-Hong Kong, GATT, Geneva, 1994.

Trade Policy Review-Indonesia Vol. I & II, GATT, Geneva, 1991.

Trade Policy Review-Japan Vol. I & II, GATT, Geneva, 1992.

Trade Policy Review-Republic of Korea Vol. I & II, GATT, Geneva, 1992.

Trade Policy Review-Singapore, Vol. I & II, GATT, Geneva, 1992.

Trade Policy Review-Switzerland, Vol. I & II, GATT, Geneva, 1991.

Trevelyan, G. M.: *A Shortened History of England*, Longmans Green & Co. Inc., New York, 1959.

Tsuru, Shigeto: *Japan's Capitalism*, Cambridge University Press, Cambridge, 1993.

Turnock, David: *A Historical Geography of Railways in Great Britain and Ireland*, Ashgate, England, 1998.

Ungar, Sanford: Africa—*The People and Politics of an Emerging Continent*, Simon & Schuster Inc., 1986.

United Nations-various years, *World Population Prospects*, New York.

United Nations Conference on Trade and Development-various years, *Handbook of International Trade and Development Statistics*, Geneva.

United Nations Development Program-various years, *Human Development Report*, Oxford University Press, Oxford.

United Nations Industrial Development Organization-various years, *International Yearbook of Industrial Statistics*, Vienna.

Vie, Michael: *Le Japon Contemporain*, Presses Universitaires de France, Paris, 1971.

Vincent, Bernard (ed): *Histoire des Etas Unis*, Presses Universitaires de Nancy, France, 1994.

Vogel, Erza: *Japan as No. 1*, Harvard University Press, Cambridge, Mass., 1979.

Wade, Robert: *Governing the Market*, Princeton University Press, Princeton, 1990.

Waldron, Arthur: *From War to Nationalism*, Cambridge University Press, Cambridge, 1995.

Walter, Richard: *Politics and Urban Growth in Buenos Aires 1910-1942*, Cambridge University Press, Cambridge, 1993.

Watson, Francis: *A Concise History of India*, Thames & Hudson, Great Britain, 1979.

Wang, Nora: *L'Asie Orientale du milieu du XIXe siècle à nos jours*, Armand Colin, Paris, 1993.

Webster, Daniel : *The History of Ireland*, Greenwood Press, Westport-CT, 2001.

Wegel, Oskar: *China im Aufbruch*, Verlag C. H. Beck, München, 1997.

Wehler, Hans: *Deutsch Gesellschaftsgeschichte 1700-1815*, Verlag C. H. Beck, München, 1987.

Westwood, J.: *Endurance and Endeavor*, Oxford University Press, Oxford, 1993.

Wickins, Peter: *Africa 1880-1980—An Economic History*, Oxford University Press, Oxford, 1986.

Wilber, Donald: *Iran—Past and Present*, Princeton University Press, Princeton, 1976.

Wilkie, James: *The Mexican Revolution-Federal Expenditure and Social Change since 1910*, University of California Press, Berkeley, 1967.

Wirth, John: *The Politics of Brazilian Development 1930-1954*, Stanford University Press, Stanford, 1970.

Whitaker, Arthur: *Argentina*, Prentice-Hall Inc., Englewood Cliffs-USA, 1964.

White, Lynn: *Policies of Chaos*, Princeton University Press, Princeton-New Yersey, 1989.

Whitney Hall, John (ed): *The Cambridge History of Japan-Early Modern Japan*, Cambridge University Press, Cambridge, 1991.

Will, Pierre: *Bureaucratie et Famine en Chine au 18e Siecle*, Mouton Editeur, Paris, 1980.

Wolpert, Stanley : *Jinnah of Pakistan*, Oxford University Press, New York-Oxford, 1984.

Wolpert, Stanley : *A New History of India*, Oxford University Press, New York, 1982.

Wolpert, Stanley: *Zulfi Bhutto of Pakistan*, Oxford University Press, Oxford, 1993.

Woodward, C. Vann (ed): *The Comparative Approach to American History*, Oxford University Press, Oxford, 1997.

World Bank, *World Development Report*-various years, Washington.

World Trade Organization-various years, Annual Report, Geneva.

Woronoff, Jon: *Hong Kong-Capitalist Paradise*, Heinemann Educational Books Ltd., Hong Kong, 1980.

Wright, Chester: *Economic History of the United States*, McGraw Hill, New York, 1941.

Wrigley, E.: *Continuity, Chance and Change*, Cambridge University Press, Cambridge, 1988.

Yamamura, Kozo (ed): *The Cambridge History of Japan-Medieval Japan*, Cambridge University Press, Cambridge, 1990.

Yarnell, Allen (ed): *The American People-Creating a Nation and Society*, Harper & Row, New York, 1986.

Yapp, M. E.: *The Near East since the First World War-A History to 1995*, Longman, London, 1996.

Yearbook of Statistics Singapore 1991, Department of Statistics, Singapore, 1992.

Xiang, Lanxin: *Recasting the Imperial Far East*, M. E. Sharpe Inc., Armonk-New York, 1995.

Zorrilla, Rubén: *Estructura Social y Caudillismo 1810-1870*, Grupo Editorial Latinoamericano, Buenos Aires, 1994.

Zysman, John & Cohen, Stephen: *Manufacturing Matters*, Basic Books, New York, 1987.

Also numerous articles from:

Asiaweek, Hong Kong

Bilan, Switzerland

Businessweek, New York

Cambio, Madrid

Comercio Exterior, Mexico D.F.

Der Spiegel, Frankfurt

EU Magazin, Germany
Focus-WTO, Geneva
Fortune, New York
Harvard Business Review, Cambridge, MA
Jeune Afrique-L'intelligent, Paris
Le Monde Diplomatique, Paris
Le Nouvel Afrique-Asie, Paris
Le Nouvel Economist, Paris
L'Hebdo, Switzerland
National Geographic, Washington D.C.
Newsweek, New York
Scientific American, New York
Spektrum der Wissenschaft, Deutschland
The Economist, London
The Far Eastern Economic Review, Hong Kong
The Middle East, London
Time, New York

INDEX

A

Act of Union, 84
Ad valorem, 112, 121, 161
Adam Smith, 37, 90, 118
Africa, 104, 154, 156, 173, 175, 177, 181-182,
    219, 262, 265, 271, 309-313, 315-316,
    319-321, 323-327
African slaves, 70, 79, 97
Agricultural instruments, 21
Agricultural surpluses, 75-76
Agriculture, 7, 14, 18-23, 25-33, 38, 42,
    44-45, 48, 50-52, 54, 56-57, 60-62,
    64-67, 69-73, 75-77, 83-84, 87-89, 91-93,
    95-97, 99-100, 103, 105, 107-109, 114-116,
    118, 120-122, 125-126, 132, 144-145,
    149, 153-154, 163-166, 170, 174-175, 178,
    184-187, 189, 192-193, 197, 201, 204-206,
    211, 214-217, 226, 229-230, 232,
    237-242, 248, 254, 257, 259-260, 263,
    270, 280, 286, 293-296, 315, 318
Alexander Fleming, 268
Alexander Hamilton, 100
Alsace & Lorraine, 46, 150
America, 3-4, 12, 39, 60, 67-68, 70-71, 75, 77,
    81, 87, 97-99, 104, 110, 135, 143, 146-147,
    154, 163, 168, 173, 175, 177, 180-182,
    206, 251, 262, 271, 276-277, 296-302,
    304-316, 318-320, 322-324
Antibiotics, 254, 268

Aristocracy, 33, 59, 61, 93, 112, 118, 126, 149,
    170, 220
Armament-related goods, 54, 63, 228
Armaments, 5, 13, 16-17, 19-24, 26-27, 31,
    33-34, 38, 40-41, 43, 46-47, 49, 51,
    53-54, 58, 65-66, 81, 93, 106, 122, 125,
    132-133, 138, 150, 162, 188, 196, 201-202,
    207-209, 228-229, 231, 235, 244-246,
    253, 265, 273, 280-281, 284
Armed forces, 81, 150, 229, 246, 263-264,
    280
Arsenals, 66, 71, 89, 122, 124, 240, 245, 281
Artillery, 17, 40, 49, 66, 221, 239
Aspirin, 151
Association of manufacturers, 257
Atlantic trade, 78, 100
August the Strong, 86
Australia, 19-20, 101, 124, 146-147, 156-157,
    179, 181, 320, 323
Austria, 46, 86, 112, 149, 220-221, 224, 262
Autarchy, 12
Authoritarianism, 197
Automobile, 6, 151, 184, 200, 215, 232, 252,
    255, 267

B

Balance of payment concerns, 220
Balanced budget, 203
Balkans, 220

Baltic States, 49, 61, 88
Bank of England, 179, 282
Bankers, 30, 61, 150
Barter, 29, 34, 66, 95, 101, 227
Battle of the Marne, 221
Bavaria, 27, 42, 86, 113, 224
Beijing, 122, 126-127, 172, 185-186, 189-190, 192-193, 206-210, 213
Belgium, 25, 42, 80, 86, 114, 117, 220, 222-223
Berlin, 86, 150-151, 159-160, 220-222, 227, 231, 234, 256, 279, 284, 323
Boer War, 110
Bolsheviks, 239
Bosnia, 220
Britain, 6, 9, 19, 25, 38, 75-87, 89, 92, 97-101, 103-105, 107-117, 120, 122-124, 127-131, 133, 135-136, 146-148, 151, 153, 156-157, 160, 162, 164, 167, 173, 175-183, 186-187, 190-193, 215-217, 220-221, 225, 230-231, 233-234, 237-238, 242, 251-253, 255, 260-263, 268, 271-287, 295-296, 310-312, 315, 318-321, 323-324, 326
British Isles, 25-26, 44, 84, 136, 178
Bubonic Plague, 26, 29
Buddhism, 31
Bureaucracy, 178, 318
Byelorussia, 245, 248

C

California, 156, 179, 310, 312, 314-316, 320, 322-324, 327
Canada, 12, 82, 98, 101, 124, 146-147, 157, 178-179, 181, 313, 325
Capital, 8-9, 28, 30, 32, 44, 49-50, 57, 61-65, 71, 76, 78, 84, 87, 90, 93, 105, 108, 118, 126, 133-134, 139, 142-144, 151, 154, 158-160, 162, 164-165, 171, 174, 176, 181-182, 186, 199-200, 207, 209, 216, 223-225, 227-228, 232, 242, 247, 253, 260, 263, 266, 272, 278
Capitalism, 47-48, 187, 233, 239, 241-243, 291, 303, 310, 312, 326
Capitalists, 41-42, 47, 62, 86, 88-89, 191, 199, 202, 290, 296, 326
Carnegie, 145
Carolingian Empire, 24

Cartels, 14, 115, 140, 142, 152-153, 161-162, 171-172, 175, 201-202, 249, 257, 259-260, 266, 272, 290
Catherine the Great, 90
Catholics, 59, 61
Central Bank, 142-143, 171, 179-180, 203, 223, 227, 229
Central government, 28, 31-33, 51, 71, 81, 93, 99-100, 124, 178, 206, 208, 212
Charlemagne, 24, 27-28
Charles I, 46-47, 53, 299, 322
Chemical fertilizer, 153, 184
Chiang Kai-shek, 208
Child bondage, 108
China, 6-7, 18-23, 31-35, 39-40, 42, 50-52, 65-68, 71, 73, 91-92, 94-96, 101, 121-124, 126-128, 167, 172-173, 185-190, 192, 196, 198, 201, 206-214, 216-217, 237, 261, 294, 301, 303-304, 306-307, 309, 312-314, 316-323, 325-326
Chongjo, 95
Choson Dynasty, 94
Christian era, 19-20, 23, 30
Civil war, 31, 33, 53-54, 58-59, 131, 139, 144, 147, 216, 220, 223, 236, 239-240, 251, 260, 263
Civilian manufacturing, 13, 17-18, 20-21, 24, 31-34, 42, 45, 49, 51, 53-54, 56, 58, 65-66, 71, 85-86, 90, 92, 97-98, 111-113, 122, 124, 130, 139, 148, 151, 168, 177, 188, 196, 198, 201, 203, 205, 222, 232, 240, 247, 253, 262, 264-266, 274, 280-282
Cixi, 186
Coal, 9, 48, 88, 114, 116, 120, 163, 174, 184, 223, 248, 282
Colbert, 58
Collectivization, 231, 242
Colonial possessions, 45, 104, 151, 156, 181, 197, 276
Colonists, 68-70, 97-99
Commerce, 18, 23, 25, 30-31, 34, 39, 52, 57, 61, 63, 66, 72, 80, 83, 93-94, 121, 125, 140, 150, 153, 171, 175, 257, 320
Commercial banks, 84, 159, 162, 180, 200, 233, 259
Commercial unification, 113
Communication, 117, 131, 265
Communism, 241

Competition, 8-9, 12, 14, 54, 90, 94, 109, 115, 140, 142, 152, 161-162, 171-172, 181, 191, 215-216, 290
Competition-hindering practices, 116, 140, 201, 212, 263
Computers, 268
Confucian culture, 188
Congress of Berlin, 159-160
Congress of Vienna, 104, 121
Conservatives, 186, 282-283
Construction, 3, 5-6, 14, 17, 22, 30-32, 34-35, 45, 47-49, 52, 56-57, 61-62, 64, 66, 72, 83, 88, 91, 93, 95-96, 106-107, 111, 113-115, 125, 131, 136, 141, 143, 149, 155, 160, 164, 166, 174, 184-185, 201, 203-204, 211-212, 225, 228, 232, 235-236, 248, 252, 254, 256-257, 260-261, 270, 280, 283, 291, 293-294
Consumption, 18, 28, 53, 62, 69, 77, 96, 127, 165, 179, 183, 249, 262
Corn Laws, 54, 109
Corruption, 210, 224
Cortes, 67
Craftsmen, 31, 34, 42, 82, 96, 321
Crimean War, 110, 157, 161-162, 166, 176
Culture, 11, 19, 50, 60, 79-80, 87, 122, 145-146, 154-156, 173, 186, 188, 195, 207, 212, 316
Currencies, 259, 276
Czechoslovakia, 200, 232-233, 262

D

Daimyo, 51
Dams, 258, 260-261
Daoguang, 121-122, 127
Dawes Plan, 224
DDT, 284
Defense expenditures, 17, 57, 81, 110, 139, 157, 159, 196, 198, 228, 244, 247, 256, 262-263, 265, 281
Democracy, 230, 311, 315
Democrats, 259, 266
Deng, 211
Denmark, 149
Depression, 7-9, 197, 206, 209, 212-213, 223-226, 229-230, 244, 257-259, 263, 265, 277-278, 298, 312
Descartes, 56
Devaluation, 225, 253

Dictatorship, 230, 236, 243
Disease, 32, 254-255, 296, 310, 312
Distribution of Industry Act, 283
Dodge Plan, 200
Dublin, 109
Dutch, 43, 55, 70, 72, 81, 94, 96, 128

E

East Asia, 3-4, 7, 12-13, 21, 75, 104, 185, 188, 190, 195-197, 276, 289, 304-308, 310, 317, 322
Eastern Europe, 41, 45, 49, 81, 200, 231-233, 265, 301, 314
Economic development, 7, 12, 16, 18, 21, 25, 27, 63, 94, 96, 100, 103, 136, 174, 293, 299, 301, 304, 308, 310-311, 313-315, 317, 320
Economic growth, 1, 3-6, 10-14, 16-17, 19, 28, 30-31, 37-42, 45, 47-48, 50-53, 58, 60, 63-66, 70, 72-73, 75-80, 84-86, 88-92, 94-97, 100-101, 103-104, 107, 109-111, 116-117, 120, 122-123, 125, 127, 129-130, 133, 135-136, 138-140, 142, 145-149, 151-152, 154-156, 159, 162, 164, 167, 170, 172-176, 178, 180-184, 187-188, 190, 192, 195, 198, 200, 202-205, 209, 212-215, 217, 221, 223-224, 226-228, 230-233, 235-237, 240-246, 249, 252, 254-255, 258-263, 265, 269, 271-278, 280-283, 286, 289-291, 293, 296-299, 301, 303-304, 306, 308-309, 313-314, 316-324
Economic stagnation, 8, 58, 115, 129, 185, 224, 290-291, 319
Economists, 1, 3-4, 6-11, 19, 37, 42, 47, 70, 110, 113, 142, 156, 164, 174, 180, 183, 202, 204-205, 227, 229, 235, 241-242, 246, 266, 274, 280, 282
Edo, 71-73, 92, 124-125
Education, 7-8, 35-36, 47, 49, 66, 100, 125, 145-146, 154-155, 164-165, 174-175, 178, 182, 204-206, 211, 225, 228, 235, 243, 260, 263, 270, 315
Educational services, 49, 144, 174
Efficiency, 8-9, 12, 14, 95, 109, 115, 152, 162, 181, 231, 257, 272, 282
Electric bulb, 141
Electric trains, 183, 279, 284
Electricity, 144, 184, 213, 252-253, 255-256, 261, 267, 279, 282, 284

Elizabeth I, 40, 42

Enclosure, 45, 76, 80, 108

Endogenous, 11, 176, 199, 240, 289

Engineering, 18, 133, 141, 174, 205

England, 6, 22, 25-29, 37-49, 53-63, 66-70,
76, 79, 84, 87, 98, 109, 131, 178-179, 193,
282, 296, 310, 312-313, 316-318, 322, 326

Epidemics, 34, 59, 254, 268

Equipment, 6, 34-35, 64, 82, 115, 145,
148-149, 151, 155, 163-164, 168, 174, 184,
204, 210-211, 215-216, 228, 230-232,
234, 238-239, 242-243, 245, 248,
255-256, 261, 274-275, 282

Europe, 3-4, 7, 23-30, 34-35, 37-51, 53-60,
62-65, 68, 72, 78-81, 83, 85-87, 89, 92,
94, 97, 107, 110-112, 114-121, 128, 136-138,
143, 146, 148, 150-151, 154-156, 158,
161, 163-164, 168, 173, 175-177, 181-182,
191, 200, 210, 219-220, 224-225, 228,
231-233, 238, 245, 253, 255, 259,
262, 264-265, 267, 271-273, 276-277,
279-280, 282-284, 289, 294, 296-302,
304-308, 312-314, 319, 321, 324-325

Exogenous variables, 41, 60, 136

Export markets, 77, 82, 104, 122, 181, 197,
274-276, 278

Exports, 7, 9, 12, 42, 54, 59-61, 68, 77-78, 80,
82-83, 90, 96, 98, 104, 109-110, 114, 120,
127, 136, 143, 148, 153, 163, 165, 168-169,
173, 178, 181, 190-191, 196-198, 200, 205,
208, 215-216, 220, 225, 230, 235, 238,
242, 274, 276-280, 293-295

F

Factory, 3-6, 8-13, 20-23, 27, 29-32, 34-35,
38, 41-43, 45, 47-53, 56-61, 64, 66,
69-72, 77, 82, 84-90, 92, 94-97, 100-101,
103-108, 110-112, 114, 118-123, 125-133,
135, 137-151, 153-166, 168, 170-180,
183-185, 187-193, 195-205, 208-217,
219-242, 244-249, 251-253, 255-258,
260-263, 265-272, 274-281, 283-286,
290, 294

Factory goods, 6, 8-9, 11-12, 20, 27, 29-30,
32, 34-35, 42, 45, 47, 49, 52, 57, 59, 66,
70, 72, 77, 82, 86, 88, 95, 97, 112, 118,
122, 125-126, 128-129, 138, 141, 144-145,
148, 150-151, 153, 155, 158, 163-164, 168,
178, 184, 187, 189-191, 195, 197, 200, 204,

211, 215-216, 221, 224, 229, 237-239,
245, 248, 253, 255, 262, 265, 267-268,
279, 281, 286

Factory output, 4-5, 9-12, 22-23, 27, 30-31,
34, 41, 48-53, 56, 58-59, 61, 66, 72, 82,
84-85, 92, 97, 101, 103-104, 106, 110,
119-120, 122-123, 129-130, 132, 135, 138,
144, 146-149, 151, 153-157, 159-164,
168, 170-171, 173, 176-177, 179, 183,
185, 187, 192-193, 195, 197-202, 205,
208, 210-217, 219-220, 222-225, 228,
230, 232-236, 238, 244-249, 252-253,
256-258, 261-263, 265-267, 271-272,
275, 277-280, 283-285, 290

Famine, 16, 20, 35, 44, 64, 68, 92, 109, 114,
124, 166, 187, 207, 240, 248, 304, 312,
327

Federal Reserve Bank, 258

Feudalism, 24, 158, 164, 170, 174

Fighter planes, 201, 221, 255, 281

Financial incentives, 4, 14, 54, 81, 89, 105,
111, 121, 130-131, 136, 158-161, 170-172,
178, 191-192, 197, 199, 202-203, 214-215,
225, 249, 251-252, 256-257, 266, 272,
276, 278, 290

Financial speculation, 60-61, 224, 227, 257,
274

Financial system, 18, 29, 57, 179, 259-260

First Opium War, 122, 127, 190, 192

Fiscal incentives, 89, 111, 224, 229, 256, 276

Fiscal rectitude, 123, 142

Fishing, 7, 17, 22-23, 25, 29, 35, 48, 56, 62, 71,
96, 99-100, 125, 143, 147, 174, 187-188,
193, 204, 211, 214-215, 248, 293

Five-year plan, 246

Food processing, 191

Food supply, 15-17, 19, 21-22, 50, 68, 73, 91,
114, 149, 166, 170-171, 187, 204

Foreign direct investment, 41-42, 84, 143,
159, 165, 200, 209, 213, 215, 224, 240

Forestry, 7, 22, 29, 56, 62, 100, 174, 187, 204,
211, 214-215, 293

Forestry equipment, 204, 215

France, 10, 19, 24-29, 39-40, 46, 58-61, 67,
78, 81, 85-87, 98, 100, 104, 111-117, 124,
149-151, 156-157, 159, 164, 171, 173, 176,
184, 186, 190, 220-224, 228, 231, 238,
253, 262, 271, 275, 280, 291, 312-316,
319, 322, 326

Franklin D. Roosevelt, 259

Frederick List, 112
Frederick the Great, 85-86
Frederick William I, 85
Free trade, 23, 79, 109, 123-124, 140, 152-153,
    168, 173, 181, 192-193, 217, 273, 278
Friedrich Krupp, 155

G

GDP, 4, 11-13, 38, 45, 47-48, 53, 58, 60,
    66, 77-85, 91-92, 97, 99, 103-105, 107,
    109-111, 113-118, 120, 123-125, 129-133,
    135, 137-140, 142, 145-147, 150-152,
    154-159, 161-162, 164-165, 167-183, 185,
    187, 192-193, 195-200, 202-210, 212-216,
    219-220, 222-239, 241-247, 251-253,
    257-263, 265-266, 269-272, 274-284,
    286-287, 290-291, 294-295, 297-307,
    309
George III, 79
George Washington, 99
German states, 29, 46-47, 58-59, 85-87,
    112-113, 117, 123, 148-150, 319
German unification, 150, 176, 219, 300, 316
Germany, 6, 9, 24, 26-30, 45-48, 58-61, 80,
    85-87, 111-115, 120, 123-124, 129-130, 135,
    148-157, 159, 161-162, 164, 167, 171, 173,
    176, 178-179, 181, 183-184, 195, 200, 207,
    219-234, 236, 238-239, 242, 244-246,
    252, 255, 262, 271-277, 279-285, 287,
    291, 294, 298-300, 304, 310-311, 315,
    317-320, 322, 325, 328
Gold, 60, 62, 110, 156, 179, 231, 240, 259-260,
    276, 278, 286
Government expenditure, 11-12, 48, 81, 89,
    91-93, 96, 111, 132, 138, 140-141, 147,
    151-152, 159, 162, 175, 178-179, 186, 196,
    198, 212, 216, 221, 227, 235, 255, 258,
    260, 263
Government policy, 10-11, 13, 72, 94, 139,
    141-142, 161, 176, 201, 259, 289
Government support, 4-5, 22, 24-25, 32,
    62, 70, 86, 95-96, 119, 131, 144, 151, 156,
    160, 170, 211, 253, 255, 268, 271-272,
    289-290
Grants, 31-32, 41, 47, 55, 67, 72, 84, 86,
    88-89, 91, 98, 100, 118, 121, 131, 139, 148,
    151, 158, 161, 172, 191, 228, 256, 267, 276,
    278-279, 286
Great Depression, 257

Gunpowder, 29

H

Han Dynasty, 21
Handicrafts, 29, 34, 96
Hat Act, 98
Health, 32, 100, 144, 154-155, 178, 206, 211,
    228, 235, 282
Heavy manufacturing, 9, 18-19, 22-23, 86,
    88, 95, 113, 119, 138, 140-141, 161, 174,
    199-201, 209, 214-215, 231-233, 240, 281
Henry the VIII, 41
Hideyoshi, 52
Highways, 204, 258, 260
Hiroshima, 247
History, 1, 3-6, 11-13, 16, 18-20, 23, 27-29,
    32-35, 37, 40-44, 47, 50, 52, 56, 58,
    60-62, 66, 70, 75, 82, 89, 93, 96-97,
    103-105, 107, 111, 113, 116, 123, 126-127,
    133, 135, 140-142, 144, 150, 154, 156,
    158, 161, 164-166, 174, 177-178, 180,
    184-185, 198, 202-205, 208, 210-211, 213,
    215, 222, 224, 226-228, 235-237, 243,
    245, 247, 254, 256, 259-261, 263-264,
    267, 269, 272-273, 281, 283, 289-291,
    293-294, 296-307, 309-327
Hitler, 227-229, 233, 244, 279
Holland, 25, 37, 39-40, 42-43, 45-46, 57, 61,
    80-81, 117
Hong Kong, 127-129, 140, 190, 192-193,
    206, 210, 215-217, 230, 235, 266, 293,
    306-307, 318, 324, 327-328
Honshu, 30, 32, 71
Hoover administration, 258, 260
Housing, 93, 100, 154, 165, 178-179, 204, 206,
    228, 231-232, 235, 249, 260, 270, 280,
    282-283
Hundred Years' War, 26-27, 38-39
Hunger, 15, 64, 67-68, 95, 171, 224, 227, 232,
    296-302, 304-308
Hyperinflation, 138, 223-225, 240

I

IBM, 268
Ideology, 12, 161, 188, 317, 321
Ieshige, 93
Ieyasu, 71

IMF (International Monetary Fund), 233
Import-substitution, 6, 8-9, 112, 219
India, 60, 81, 101, 123, 127-128, 140, 192, 294,
    310-312, 315, 317-320, 322-327
Industry, 3-4, 6-10, 22, 46, 49, 92, 100, 106,
    108, 119-120, 143-144, 149-150, 173, 283,
    294, 296, 308, 313, 316-317, 321-322, 324
Inefficiency, 289
Infant mortality, 154, 165, 236
Inflation, 11, 60, 73, 138, 142-143, 203, 210,
    222-224, 227, 229-230, 232, 240,
    293-295
Influenza epidemic, 254
Infrastructure, 7-8, 11, 35-36, 45, 64-65, 78,
    83, 89, 93, 95, 100, 114, 117, 153, 155, 164,
    174-175, 180, 190, 193, 204, 212, 216,
    224-225, 228-229, 233, 235, 258, 260,
    263
Interest rates, 159, 180, 182, 225, 258-260,
    265
Internal Revenue Service, 137
International trade, 8-9, 55, 326
Interstate Commerce Commission, 140
Investment, 5, 7-8, 13, 21-27, 29, 32-34,
    41-42, 44, 50-51, 53, 55, 57, 59-62, 65,
    67, 76, 78-79, 83-84, 87-88, 90, 92-93,
    95-96, 104-107, 109, 113, 116, 118, 122,
    128, 130, 133, 143-144, 149, 153, 159-160,
    162, 165, 170, 172, 174-175, 177, 180, 182,
    186, 188, 190-191, 193, 200-202, 204,
    207-210, 212-215, 217, 224, 228, 232,
    235, 237, 240, 242, 244, 246-248, 255,
    259, 261-262, 265, 268-269, 271-273,
    279, 281, 289-290, 304, 317
Investment-intensive, 4, 57, 86, 113, 171
Invincible Armada, 43
Ireland, 25, 44, 67, 84, 109, 178, 296, 314, 326
Iron, 17-20, 22, 25, 27, 30, 35, 47, 51, 62, 69,
    79, 81, 83, 86-89, 93, 95, 98, 105-106,
    113-114, 116-117, 120-121, 132, 136, 138,
    148, 150, 160-161, 163, 169, 174, 184, 205,
    209, 228, 234, 237, 239, 248, 251, 271,
    276, 282, 313
Italy, 24, 28, 46, 112, 230, 232-233

J

James Watt, 82
Japan, 6, 19-20, 30-34, 50-52, 65, 71, 73,
    91-93, 95-96, 124-126, 146, 154, 160,
    167-177, 181-182, 185-186, 188-192,
    195-214, 216-217, 226, 230, 233, 237,
    242-243, 261, 271, 273, 277-278,
    284-285, 287, 291, 294, 301-304, 306,
    310-311, 313-322, 324-327
Japanese, 19-20, 30-34, 51, 65, 71-72, 93-94,
    96, 124-125, 167-168, 170-171, 173, 176,
    189-191, 195, 197-203, 206, 208-210,
    213-216, 237, 261, 263, 265, 276,
    302-303, 314-315, 319-321, 324, 326
Jean de Gron, 63
Jews, 86
Jiaquing, 121
Jones Act, 256

K

Kangxi, 66, 91
Keynesian, 6-9, 225, 265
Keynesianism, 228, 260
KMT, 209
Konjong, 189
Korea, 20-21, 31, 52, 65, 91, 94-95, 123,
    126-127, 188-189, 197-198, 200, 212-215,
    226, 304-306, 309, 313-314, 319, 326
Korean peninsula, 19, 196, 209, 305
Koryo, 94
Kowloon peninsula, 192
Kyoto, 32-34, 51, 72

L

Land concessions, 17, 34, 72, 86, 98, 100, 148,
    191, 206
Land tax, 32, 66, 72, 86, 100, 191
Large-scale war, 20, 24, 26, 33, 38, 40, 46,
    50-51, 55, 61, 81, 137, 176-177, 220, 236,
    279
Latin America, 68, 104, 154, 173, 175, 177,
    180-182, 206, 262, 271, 309, 311-316, 318,
    320, 322-323
Lenin, 239
Leningrad, 244
Liberal economic policies, 75
Liberalization, 78-79, 90, 109, 127, 140, 158,
    291
Life expectancy, 68, 154, 165, 179, 206, 236,
    254, 293

Light manufacturing, 18, 22, 86, 88, 161, 174, 199, 209, 214

Liquidity problem, 278

Literacy, 29, 100, 164, 243

Living conditions, 4, 16, 27, 30, 32, 34, 45, 60, 68, 70, 75, 91, 97, 107, 118, 135, 138, 142, 155, 164-166, 179, 183, 185, 206, 211-212, 214, 217, 235-237, 248, 251, 254, 270, 282, 287

Locomotives, 105-106, 113-114, 120, 131, 133, 136, 139, 148, 161, 169, 171, 177, 209, 244, 251, 271

London, 26, 49, 53, 55-56, 59, 67-71, 80, 82, 85-86, 97-99, 103-106, 108, 127-129, 162, 176-177, 179-180, 191, 215, 259, 262, 268, 271, 273-276, 278-279, 281, 283-285, 309-328

London Economic Conference, 259

Louis XIV, 58, 85

Louisiana Purchase, 131

Low Countries, 29, 46, 60, 87

Luddite riots, 106

Lutheranism, 47

M

Macao, 51, 124, 210

Machine tools, 9, 83, 88, 105, 113, 119-120, 133, 136, 196-198, 205, 209, 224, 228, 240, 247, 251, 262, 271, 273

Machinery, 43, 47, 86, 91, 114, 119-120, 133, 153, 158, 161, 166, 168-169, 204, 210, 216, 229-232, 234, 238-239, 242-243, 245, 247-248, 255-256, 273-275

Macroeconomic, 296, 319

Mainstream economics, 12, 73, 243-244

Malaysia, 191-192, 215

Malnutrition, 20, 32, 35, 44, 64, 68, 109, 199

Manchu Dynasty, 65-66

Manchuria, 65, 198, 206, 208-212, 214, 246, 261

Manchurian campaign, 198

Manhattan Project, 268

Manufacturing, 3-14, 16-36, 38-45, 47-62, 64-73, 77, 81-101, 103-105, 107-115, 118-180, 183-193, 195-217, 219-242, 244-249, 251-259, 261-287, 289-291, 293-295, 323, 327

Mao, 211

Mark, 163-164

Market forces, 10, 48, 104, 116, 162, 178, 212, 240, 242, 246, 249, 290, 304

Marshall Plan, 232-233

Mathematics, 174

Max Weber, 187

Medical instruments, 144, 153, 155

Medicines, 6, 141, 144, 153, 183, 197, 233, 239, 262

Mercantilism, 7, 54, 59, 86, 104, 192

Mercantilist system, 68, 191

Mesopotamia, 19

Metals, 6, 9, 16, 18-20, 30-31, 39-40, 43, 45, 49, 52, 56, 60, 62, 72, 86, 88, 91, 95, 108, 113-114, 119, 125, 139, 148-149, 196-198, 201, 209, 214, 223-224, 247, 254-255, 262, 279

Microwave ovens, 268

Middle Ages, 23-27, 29-30, 35, 37, 39, 43-45, 50, 86

Middle East, 13, 16-19, 104, 265, 313, 317-318, 325, 328

Military manufacturing, 17, 19, 22, 31, 39, 42, 49, 51, 53, 56, 58, 65, 85, 90, 92, 97, 108, 113, 122, 124, 130, 168, 177, 196, 198, 240, 245, 253, 262, 264, 280

Mines, 114, 221

Ming Dynasty, 34, 50, 65

Mining, 3, 6-7, 9, 22, 25, 29, 42, 48, 52, 56, 61-62, 90, 96, 100, 114-115, 120, 152, 163, 174, 178, 184, 187, 204, 211, 214-215, 236, 248, 280, 294

Mining machinery, 204, 248

Modernization, 50, 52, 76, 170-171, 186, 189, 207, 318

Modernization of agriculture, 50, 76

Mongol, 23, 33, 39, 49-51, 65-66, 91

Monopoly rights, 41, 47, 55, 86, 88, 95

Morgan, 145

Mortality, 35, 44, 72, 154, 165, 185, 236, 249, 270

Moscow, 49-50, 87-88, 118-120, 136, 157-159, 162, 164, 196, 236-241, 244, 247

Motor vehicles, 204, 279

Munitions, 221, 239, 253, 262

Mussolini, 233

N

Nagasaki, 124, 247

Namibia, 156, 220

Napoleonic Wars, 77-78, 104, 109-113, 117-119, 121, 128, 130, 176
National debt, 100, 104, 111, 137, 257, 263
National security, 12-13, 51, 70, 92, 96, 106, 113, 119, 122, 132, 135, 157, 169, 182, 189, 197, 200, 219, 252, 256, 262, 264, 268, 275, 279
National security concerns, 12-13, 92, 96, 106, 113, 132, 135, 157, 182, 189, 197, 219, 262, 264
National Socialists, 227
Nationalists, 210, 246
Nationalization, 239, 249, 282, 296, 321
Natural resources, 11, 15, 20, 68-69, 75, 78-80, 99, 116, 145-147, 181
Natural sciences, 174, 205
Navigation Acts, 54-55, 63, 70, 109, 131
Nazis, 224, 227-228, 231, 279
Negative interest rates, 260
Neolithic, 15, 19-20, 27, 68, 96
New crops, 38, 44, 67, 76, 80
New Economic Program, 240
New York Stock Exchange, 224, 253, 258
New Zealand, 19-20, 124, 146-147, 179, 181
Newton, 56
Nicholas I, 119
Nicholas II, 238
Nintoku, 31
Nobunaga, 51-52
Non-financial incentives, 4, 14, 54, 81, 89, 105, 111, 121, 130-131, 136, 158-161, 170-172, 178, 191-192, 197, 199, 202-203, 208, 214-215, 224, 249, 252, 266, 272, 290
Non-interventionism, 178
Non-tariff barriers, 130, 140, 152-153, 192, 202
Normans, 26
North America, 3-4, 12, 60, 67-68, 71, 75, 77, 81, 87, 98, 110, 147, 154, 163, 168, 173, 177, 180-182, 206, 276, 310
North Korea, 21
Nutrition, 32, 154-155, 165, 206
NYSE (New York Stock Exchange), 253

O

Oil, 72, 120, 199, 213, 215, 228, 230
Oleg, 25
Osaka, 30, 72

Ottawa, 147
Ottoman Empire, 61, 88, 157
Overproduction, 154, 226

P

Paris, 10, 72, 85-86, 99, 150-151, 244, 309-316, 319-324, 326-328
Parliament, 43, 53-55, 79, 98-99, 105-106, 178, 277
Patent system, 6, 41, 43, 100
Peasant Bank, 238
Pensions, 93, 154
Pentagon, 268
Persia, 119, 311
Peter the Great, 63-64, 88-89, 115
Pharmaceuticals, 6, 144, 149, 151, 155, 255, 268, 285
Physiocratic, 109, 118, 158, 170, 178, 197, 237
Pizarro, 67
Poland, 46, 61, 86, 88, 119, 280
Policy makers, 1, 4-5, 9, 12-13, 17-18, 20, 32, 34, 42, 55, 59, 67, 70-71, 73, 85, 92, 95-96, 99-100, 109, 113, 118, 126, 129, 136, 148, 156, 160, 164, 167-171, 178, 180-181, 185, 188, 190, 197, 202-205, 213-214, 220, 231, 233, 236, 240, 256, 261-262, 265-266, 271-272, 274-275, 277, 279-280, 282
Political organization, 277
Poor Law, 58
Population growth, 22, 37, 66, 75-77, 91, 97, 101, 123, 145-146, 155, 158, 164, 174, 205, 236, 270, 287
Porcelain, 22, 86, 88
Portugal, 40, 45, 55, 67, 79
Portuguese, 51, 72, 96, 128
Poverty, 1, 58, 60, 224, 237, 264, 296, 319, 323, 325
Precious metals, 6, 39-40, 43, 49, 52, 60, 254
Prices, 14, 17, 31, 41, 43, 57, 60, 73, 88, 93, 95, 107, 114, 142, 144, 153, 158, 165, 169, 171, 187, 203, 223-224, 226-228, 236, 255-256, 258-259, 263, 266, 268, 274, 279, 293-294
Primary goods, 8-9, 28, 34, 45, 48, 56, 69, 113, 159, 163, 187, 191, 204, 211, 215
Primary sector activities, 3, 5, 19, 45, 48, 56, 174, 185, 187, 248

Private sector, 5, 14, 17, 22, 31-32, 50, 57, 61-62, 65, 72, 83, 86, 88, 90, 93, 96, 113, 125, 131, 148, 152, 159, 162, 169, 171-172, 174, 182, 186, 200, 207, 229, 241, 262-263, 268, 272, 284-285, 289-290
Privatization, 33, 88, 95, 171-172, 203, 291
Productivity, 6-7, 13, 20-21, 29, 32, 34, 37, 42-44, 47, 56-57, 61-62, 64, 75, 82, 87-88, 91, 95, 101, 108, 115, 121, 140, 142, 144, 152, 154, 163, 166, 172, 182-183, 185, 196, 201, 211, 219, 234-235, 241, 248, 269, 285-286
Profit possibilities, 100, 125, 172
Protectionism, 79, 153, 173, 181, 273, 276
Protestant ethic, 188
Protestantism, 80
Protestants, 59
Prussia, 85-86, 111-112, 114, 148-150
Public borrowing, 103, 151, 171, 227
Public debt, 26, 62, 89, 103-104, 111, 138-139, 175, 178, 203, 227, 229, 256, 260, 266, 274
Public sector, 62, 103, 175, 178, 203, 227, 229, 266, 274
Public sector debt, 175, 178, 203, 227, 229, 266, 274
Public works, 45, 180, 228, 260, 278

Q

Quianlong, 91

R

Radar, 268, 284
Railroad, 105, 113-114, 131, 136, 139, 143, 147, 149, 157-160, 166, 172-173, 178-179, 190, 207, 209, 214, 227, 235-236, 247, 251, 267
Railroad-related manufacturing, 114, 131, 148
Rationalization, 116, 144, 230, 234
Raw materials, 55, 68-69, 82, 85, 104, 129, 138, 181, 190-191, 197, 212, 220, 222, 228, 231-232
Recession, 7-8, 58, 60, 114, 130, 139, 153, 197-198, 204, 210, 220-221, 239, 253, 255, 274, 279, 282

Reconstruction, 12, 93, 197, 199, 233, 244, 246
Reformation, 42
Religion, 11, 60, 72
Republicans, 257, 259, 262, 266
Robert Peel, 178
Rockefeller, 145
Romans, 25, 27
Rome, 17-19, 23, 27-28, 46, 233, 315
Royal Air Force, 280
Royal Society of Science, 56
Ruhr, 223
Rule of law, 206
Russia, 4, 6-7, 23-25, 35, 39, 42, 47-50, 61-64, 66, 68, 81, 87-91, 94, 115-120, 124, 129-130, 135-136, 140, 154, 156-157, 159-166, 173, 176-177, 179, 181, 196, 206, 208, 219-221, 231, 236-239, 242, 247-249, 262, 289, 294, 300-301, 304, 311, 316, 318, 320-322

S

Savings, 17, 49, 57, 105, 121, 154, 199, 223, 228, 231-232, 269, 275
Saxons, 26
Scandinavia, 49, 116
Schacht, 229
Schmalkaldic League, 47
Science, 11, 56, 66, 285
Scotland, 25, 44, 84, 178, 296, 314
Sea vessels, 169, 271
Secession, 131, 136, 251
Seclusion, 72-73, 124, 126, 167, 188
Second Opium War, 190, 192
Self sufficiency, 7
Seoul, 188-189, 309
Serfdom, 88, 115, 118, 158, 165, 243-244
Services, 3, 5, 14, 29-31, 33, 47-50, 52, 56-57, 61-62, 66, 91, 93, 95-96, 100, 106-107, 111, 125, 127-128, 140-141, 143-144, 166, 174, 184-185, 190, 201, 203-204, 211-212, 217, 229, 248, 254, 257, 260, 280, 282, 291, 293-294
Seven Years' War, 98
Shanghai, 206
Sherman Antitrust Act, 140
Shinto, 72
Shipbuilding, 21-23, 32, 40, 42-43, 55-57, 63, 70, 83, 98, 100, 106, 113, 122, 151, 172-173,

183, 196, 209, 213-215, 220, 228, 252, 255-256, 271, 273, 276, 284, 286

Shogun, 33-34, 71-72, 93, 124-125

Shotoku, 31

Siberia, 42, 160, 237

Singapore, 127-129, 140, 154, 167, 177, 190-193, 215, 217, 230, 249, 266, 307-308, 314, 317, 324, 327

Slavery, 67, 79, 97, 244, 323

Smallpox, 32

Social change, 47, 188, 327

Social welfare, 57-58, 153-154, 235, 254, 257, 264-265, 273, 277, 282, 291

Song Dynasty, 22, 32, 35

South Asia, 206, 307-308, 322

Sovereignty, 71, 96, 149-150, 193, 222, 231

Soviet figures, 241

Soviet Union, 7, 48, 140, 200, 210, 231, 240-247, 291, 301, 316

Soviets, 210, 231-233, 243-245, 247

Spain, 38-40, 43-46, 49, 55, 59-60, 67, 79, 81, 97, 131, 176, 233, 252

Spaniards, 67, 96

Speculation, 60-61, 224, 227, 257-258, 274

St. Petersburg, 89, 120, 157

Stalin, 233, 241-246

Standards of living, 61

State Commercial Bank, 121

State factories, 4, 17, 22, 30-31, 41, 47, 72, 81, 91, 93, 114, 119-120, 158-159, 168-170, 191, 207, 214, 249

Steam engine, 6, 82, 114, 119

Stimulation efforts, 179

Submarines, 222, 234, 255, 275, 281

Subsidies, 4, 9, 11-13, 17, 20, 22-23, 26, 28, 31-33, 35, 40-43, 47-48, 54, 56-57, 59-60, 62-66, 69-70, 72, 82-90, 92-96, 98-101, 103-107, 109, 111-114, 119-120, 122, 125-127, 129-132, 135-136, 139-140, 143-144, 146-151, 154, 156-161, 163-165, 168-174, 176-180, 186, 188-193, 196-198, 201, 206-211, 213-216, 220, 224-225, 227-228, 230, 233-237, 251-258, 262, 266-269, 271-272, 274-275, 277-278, 283-285, 293

Subsidization, 5, 21-22, 28-30, 35, 42-43, 47-48, 50, 53, 58-60, 84, 93, 95, 97, 104, 120-122, 124, 132, 137, 144, 146-147, 149, 151-152, 157, 159, 161-162, 165, 175, 178, 180, 185, 195-196, 199-201, 204-206,

208-209, 211, 213, 219, 223, 228, 230, 234-235, 247, 251-253, 255-257, 267, 269-271, 275-276, 282-283, 285, 287

Sui Dynasty, 21, 31

Support for manufacturing, 5, 7, 11-12, 17, 21-22, 24-26, 31-34, 39-40, 42, 48, 50-53, 62, 64, 67, 73, 85-86, 88-89, 92, 94, 96, 99-100, 105, 111-113, 118-119, 121, 123-124, 126, 129, 141, 147, 156, 161, 172-173, 175-179, 183, 186, 188-190, 197-198, 208-211, 214, 220, 222-224, 230, 232-233, 235-236, 242, 247-248, 253, 256, 266, 271, 282, 284-285, 287, 289-290

Sweden, 59, 61, 88, 119

Switzerland, 46, 86-87, 117, 156, 320, 327-328

Synthetic fertilizers, 108

Synthetic oil, 228

Synthetic rubber, 228

T

Taiwan, 91, 94, 96, 126-127, 172, 186, 188-190, 198, 212-215, 230, 235, 305-306, 309

Tang Dynasty, 21, 31

Tariff protection, 54, 257

Tariffs, 7, 60, 88, 100, 103, 112-113, 121, 129-131, 137-138, 140, 152-153, 158, 161, 173, 181, 192, 202, 257, 259, 273

Tax exemptions, 32, 47, 59, 67, 72, 86, 88-89, 95, 98, 100, 161, 191, 228, 279

Tax revenue, 33, 126, 225

Taxation, 17, 26, 41, 91-92, 98-99, 110-111, 137, 141, 158, 163, 168, 170, 175, 208, 227

Technical progress, 54, 150, 173, 200, 234, 247, 266-267, 283-284

Technological development, 12-13, 18, 21, 27-30, 32, 40, 43, 49, 61, 64, 68, 79, 88, 94-96, 100, 106, 120, 132-133, 138, 161, 182-183, 196, 200-201, 211, 234-235, 247, 267-268, 283, 285

Technological innovation, 17, 22, 40, 44, 126, 285

Technological pace, 13, 17-18, 40, 49, 53, 56, 63-64, 95, 132, 149, 182, 196, 211, 234, 283

Technological progress, 17, 34, 47, 50, 54, 63, 116, 138, 173, 184, 267, 284

Technological unemployment, 43

Technology, 4-7, 9-10, 12-13, 15-16, 19-20, 22-23, 25-27, 29-35, 42-43, 45-47, 49, 51, 55-56, 60-61, 63-64, 66, 72, 82-84, 87, 89, 92, 94-96, 100, 105-108, 110, 112, 114-116, 119-120, 122-123, 126, 132-133, 137-138, 141-142, 144, 148-149, 151, 153, 159, 161-163, 165-166, 173-175, 182-185, 187, 196, 198, 200-201, 211, 215, 219, 221, 228, 230, 234-235, 238, 243, 245-247, 254-255, 263, 266-269, 280-281, 283-285, 289-290, 298, 323

Telecommunications, 3, 248, 282

Telephone, 6, 141

Tennessee Valley Authority, 261

Terms of trade, 107, 187

Textiles, 6, 40, 42-43, 47, 54, 56, 59, 62, 66, 72, 79, 82, 85-86, 88, 93, 95, 98, 105-106, 112, 117, 125, 191, 196, 205, 207, 213, 216, 220

The Allies, 103, 210, 213, 222, 224, 231, 233, 239, 253, 265, 275-276

The West, 4, 7, 26-27, 45, 49, 66, 88-89, 91-92, 94-95, 98, 120-121, 123-124, 126, 157-160, 163-164, 167-170, 172-173, 176, 185-186, 192, 195-196, 200-201, 205, 208-210, 216, 221, 231-232, 234, 237-240, 243, 245, 247, 321

Theodore Roosevelt, 252

Thirteen Colonies, 98, 131

Thirty Years War, 58, 60-61

Thomas Raffles, 128

Tokugawa government, 71, 168

Tokyo, 20, 30, 71, 124, 174-175, 189-190, 195-198, 200-201, 206, 208-209, 213-214, 315, 318-319

Tokyo University, 174, 315

Tonghak revolt, 189

Tractors, 144, 204, 230, 244, 248, 256, 286

Trade, 6-10, 13, 17, 19, 22-26, 29-30, 34, 38-42, 45, 47, 50, 54-61, 63-64, 66, 70, 72-73, 75, 77-79, 82-84, 87-91, 95-97, 99-101, 104, 107, 109, 111-112, 115, 117, 121-125, 127-131, 136-138, 140, 142-144, 148, 150, 152-153, 158, 161-165, 167-168, 172-175, 181, 184, 187-190, 192-193, 197, 201-202, 204-205, 211, 217, 226-228, 235, 239, 242, 249, 257-260, 263, 272-274, 276-279, 290, 293, 296, 303, 305, 307-308, 310, 317-318, 324, 326-327

Trade barriers, 7-9, 13, 24, 60, 88, 100, 121, 124, 138, 140, 142-144, 152-153, 163, 181, 192, 197, 201-202, 226, 249, 257, 259-260, 273, 276-278

Trade blockade, 99

Trade deficit, 127

Trade protection, 7-10, 23, 41, 54, 73, 109, 112, 121, 124, 129-131, 162, 173, 193, 226, 259, 272, 290

Trade surplus, 123, 127

Trading partners, 87, 101, 181-182, 187, 273, 276-277

Trains, 6, 9, 105-106, 113, 136, 141, 143, 148-150, 153, 158, 160-162, 164-165, 174, 177, 179, 183, 186, 204, 207-208, 211, 223, 227, 234-235, 248, 251-253, 256-257, 267, 271, 279, 282, 284-285

Transport, 23, 34, 45-46, 78, 83, 105-106, 117, 128, 131, 143-144, 158, 160, 190-192, 197, 209, 211, 216, 223, 248, 282, 320

Treaty of Nanking, 128

Treaty of Shimonoseki, 186, 189

Treaty of Westphalia, 59

Treaty Ports, 122, 206, 208-210

Troop mobilization, 177, 221, 237

Truman administration, 265

Tsar, 63, 88, 118, 158, 237-239

Turkey, 88, 119, 316

U

U.S., 9, 297-298, 317, 321

Ukraine, 88, 245-246, 248

Underemployment, 10, 180-181, 221-222, 264

Unemployment, 1, 10, 13-14, 43, 106-107, 126, 142, 154, 180, 183, 220-223, 225, 227-229, 232, 239, 258-262, 264-265, 274-276, 279, 281-282, 286, 290, 293, 295

Unemployment benefit, 282

Uniforms, 33, 42, 47, 106, 108, 119, 157, 169, 197, 239, 262

Unionization, 155, 183

Urals, 88, 116, 196, 245

V

Vaccination, 185

Versailles Treaty, 222
Virginia, 68, 70, 317

W

Wages, 14, 29, 106-107, 110, 116, 125, 142, 154, 165-166, 183, 185, 203, 212, 225-226, 229-230, 239, 260, 266, 274, 290
Wanli, 65
War, 5, 7, 11-13, 15-18, 20, 22-24, 26-31, 33-34, 38-42, 45-47, 50-55, 58-62, 64-65, 68, 77-79, 81-83, 85-86, 88, 92, 94, 97-100, 103-104, 110-111, 117, 119, 122, 124, 127-128, 130-132, 136-140, 144, 147, 149-151, 153-154, 157-158, 161-162, 166, 168-169, 172, 176-177, 182, 189-190, 192, 195-199, 203, 206-208, 210-211, 216, 219-223, 225-226, 228-241, 244-246, 248, 251-256, 260, 262-266, 268, 271-276, 278-284, 286, 299, 303-304, 314, 319-321, 324, 326
War of Independence, 77
War of Spanish Succession, 79
War reparations, 150, 189, 199, 207, 222-223, 246, 255, 274-276
War ships, 17, 20
Warship technology, 196, 221
Washington, 99, 101, 130-132, 136-137, 139-140, 147, 178, 180, 200, 202, 225, 232-233, 252-266, 268-269, 277, 309-310, 312, 314-317, 320-321, 324-325, 327-328
Wealth creation, 4, 14, 17, 40, 57, 92, 121, 129, 140, 154-155, 183, 206, 242, 254, 256, 269, 274, 283, 289
Weapons, 13, 15-21, 23-25, 27-31, 33, 40, 46-47, 49, 51-52, 54, 56, 58-59, 61-62, 64-66, 68-69, 71-72, 81, 83, 87-89, 91-92, 94, 98, 104, 108, 111-113, 122, 125-127, 130-133, 137-139, 141, 148-152, 156-158, 160-162, 165, 168-169, 172-177, 186, 188-190, 195-204, 207-209, 214, 219-222, 227-229, 231, 233, 235-240, 244-247, 253, 256, 262-264, 266, 271, 273-275, 279-282, 285
Weimar, 223, 225, 276
Western Europe, 7, 24, 37, 39, 41, 45, 47-51, 53, 60, 62-63, 65, 78-81, 86, 89, 92, 110, 115-121, 161, 164, 168, 175, 232-233, 238, 265, 276, 282, 289

Westinghouse, 145
Wheel, 6, 16, 20, 56
White Lotus Rebellion, 122-123
William II, 151
Wilson administration, 254
Women, 165, 206, 221, 228-229, 243, 249, 264, 281
Working conditions, 108, 142, 165-166, 185, 206, 236, 249, 270
World Bank, 233, 293-294, 296, 298, 300-301, 303-305, 307-309, 314, 324, 327
World War I, 197, 208, 216, 220, 225-226, 234-235, 239-240, 244, 253-255, 263, 272, 274-275, 279, 284, 286
World War II, 104, 154, 182, 203, 210, 216, 231, 234, 244-245, 262-264, 266, 268, 278, 281, 284, 286

X

Xinjiang, 91

Y

Yamato, 30-31
Yongjo, 95
Yongzheng, 91
Yoshimune, 93